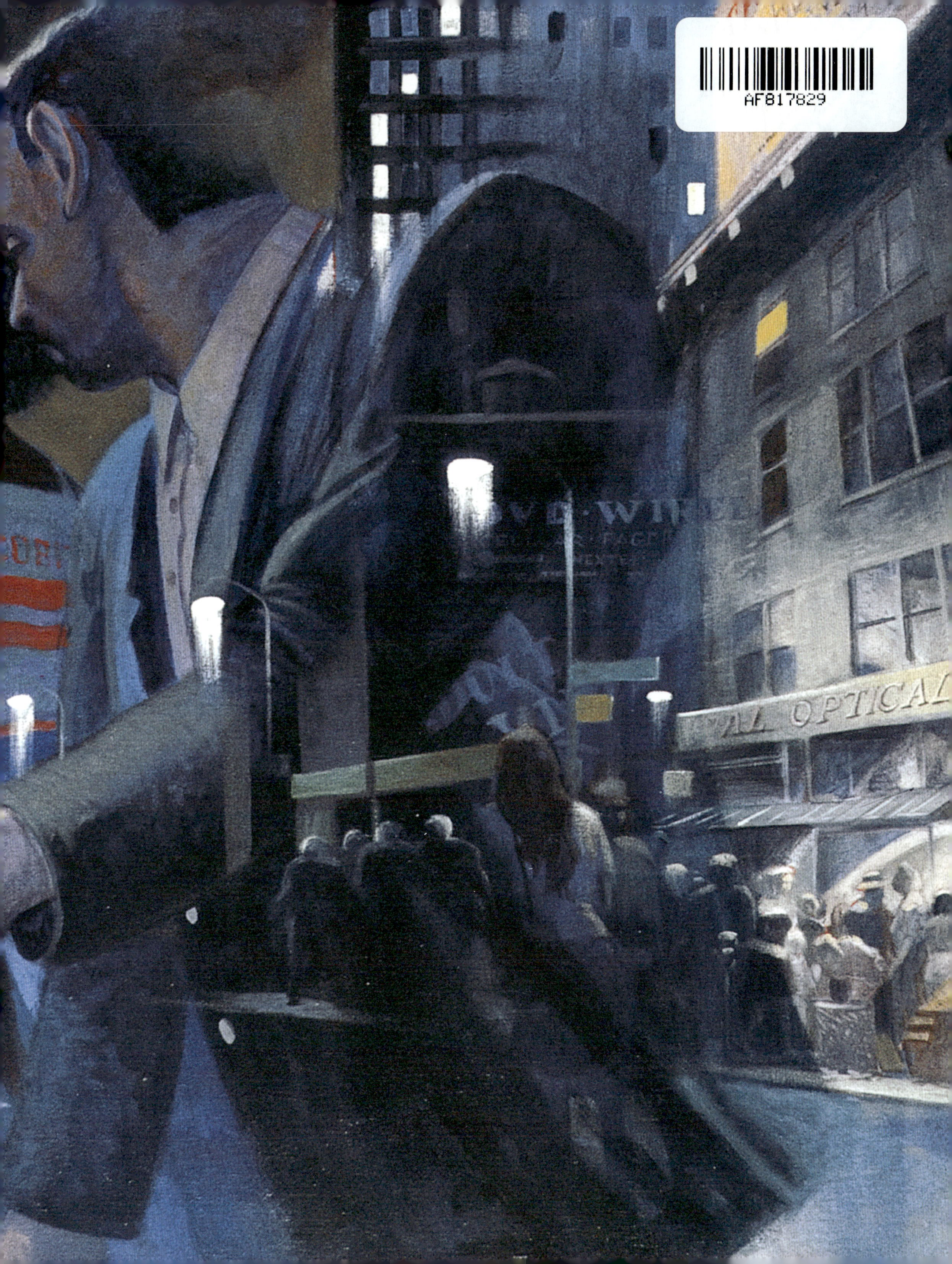
OPTICAL

Cynthia Maris Dantzic

100 New York Painters

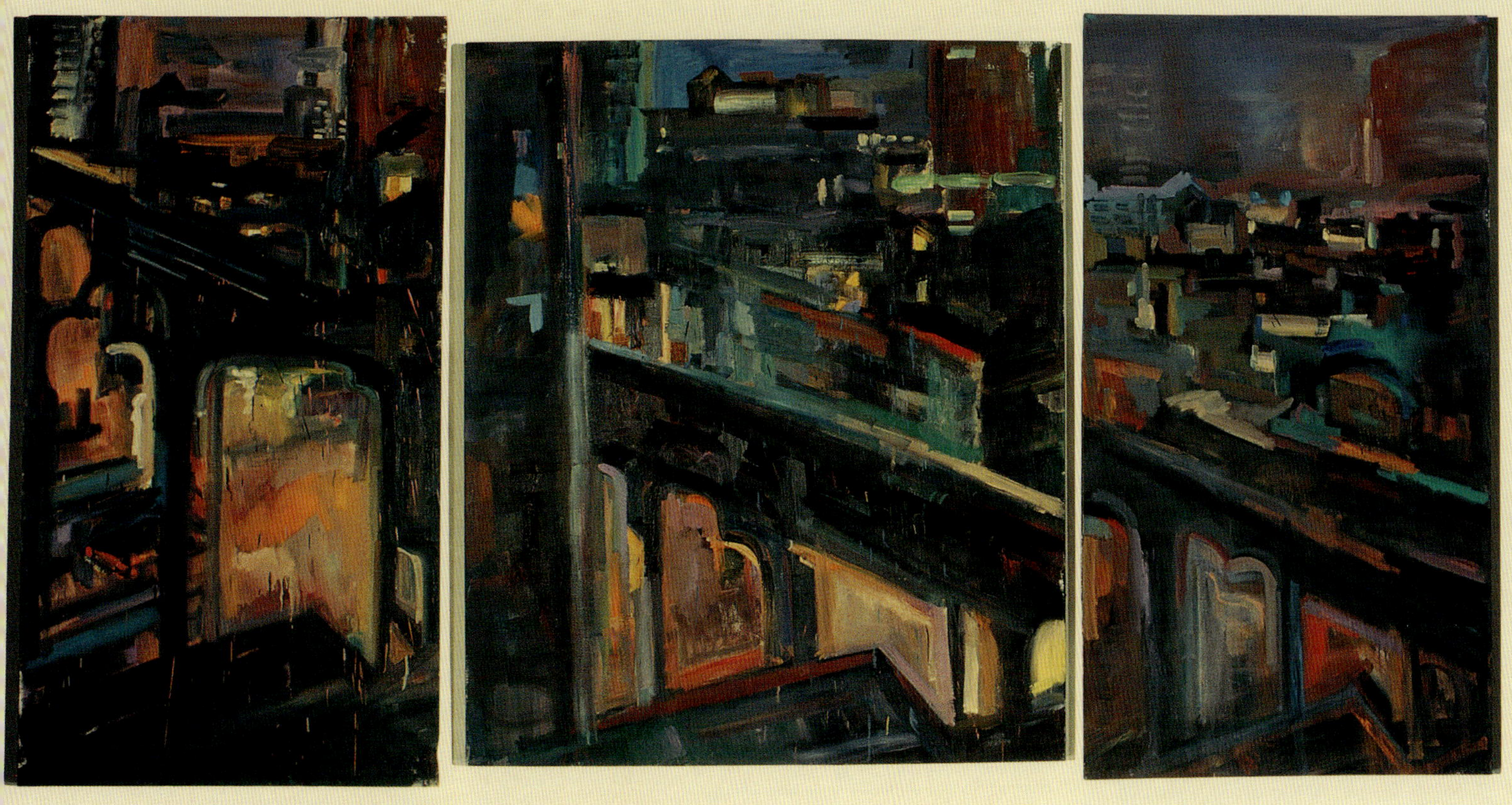

Schiffer Publishing Ltd

4880 Lower Valley Road, Atglen, PA 19310 USA

My dedication,
for all that you are, and do:
To you, Gray, with love.

Other Schiffer Books by Cynthia Maris Dantzic
Antique Pocket Mirrors: Pictorial and Advertising Miniatures

Other Schiffer Books on Related Subjects
100 Artists of the Southwest, by Douglas Bullis
100 Artists of the West Coast, by Douglas Bullis

Library of Congress Cataloging-in-Publication Data

Dantzic, Cynthia Maris.
100 New York painters / Cynthia Maris Dantzic.
p. cm.
Includes bibliographical references and index.
ISBN 0-7643-2543-4 (hardcover)
1. Painting, American—New York (State)—New York—20th century—Catalogs. 2. Painters—New York (State)—New York—Biography. I. Title. II. Title: One hundred New York painters.

ND235.N45D36 2006
759.147—dc22

2006019615

Designed by "Sue"
Type set in Zapf Humanist Demi BT/Adobe Jenson Pro

ISBN: 0-7643-2543-4
Printed in China

Front cover images: (left to right, first row) Rachel Dinnerstein, see page 82; Mary Beth McKenzie, see page 156; Dik Liu, see page 142; (second row) Lennart Anderson, see page 24; Ella Yang, see page 214; Richard Mayhew, see page 154; Jack Beal, see page 38; (third row): Sue Ferguson Gussow, see page 118; Yvonne Jacquette, see page 126; Chuck Close, see page 66; (fourth row) Faith Ringgold, see page 178.

Back cover images: (left to right, first row) Emma Amos, *Yo Man Ray Yo*, see page 21; Wolf Kahn, *Large Tree Line*, see page 133; (second row) Arthur Coppedge, *RKO Bushwick*, see page 71; Vincent Longo, *Through the Lattice*, see page 145; Simon Dinnerstein, *Calling Card*, see page 84; (third row) Leigh Behnke, *Annie View*, see page 43; Nicolas Carone, *Untitled*, see page 56; Emily Mason, *Juice*, see page 153; George Tooker, *The Subway*, see page 207.

Spine image: Vivian Tsao, see page 208; endsheet image (detail), Robert Birmelin, see page 46; title page image, Judy Cuttler, see page 73.

Published by Schiffer Publishing Ltd.
4880 Lower Valley Road
Atglen, PA 19310
Phone: (610) 593-1777; Fax: (610) 593-2002
E-mail: Info@schifferbooks.com

In Europe, Schiffer books are distributed by
Bushwood Books
6 Marksbury Ave.
Kew Gardens
Surrey TW9 4JF England
Phone: 44 (0) 20 8392-8585; Fax: 44 (0) 20 8392-9876
E-mail: info@bushwoodbooks.co.uk
Website: www.bushwoodbooks.co.uk
Free postage in the U.K., Europe; air mail at cost.

Acknowledgments

Certainly, my first words of gratitude and acknowledgment must go to Peter Schiffer, who enthusiastically urged, then convinced me to undertake this sensitive, challenging, and ultimately, most rewarding assignment. Despite the many reasons one might wish to avoid the charge to select one hundred New York painters and develop a book worthy of that designation, it has been a learning experience I have come to appreciate and savor. Many thanks for your confidence in my abilities to produce this book. Also at Schiffer Publishing, I am thankful for the very courteous, patient, and dedicated assistance of Karen Choppa, Donna Baker, and Doug Congden-Martin.

In addition to the many painters known to me personally over the years, as classmates, colleagues, neighbors, fellow artists, and students, I have had the delight of getting to meet and often work with many others, their studio assistants and gallery personnel, whom I wish to acknowledge here.

But before I enjoy the satisfaction of sharing the names of this legion of supportive and unselfish individuals with the reader, I must applaud one outstanding person in a special way. I send a symbolic bouquet to Jeanne A. Butler, typist, word-processor, obsessive perfectionist, and friend; this book could never have taken shape and achieved word-perfect form without your precisionist skills and sensibilities. Thanks also to Jeanne's niece, Julia Porter, for editorial niceties.

At Long Island University, my professional second home for these forty and some years, generous assistance has been provided in many ways by administrators, colleagues, technical staff and their associates. I extend my thanks particularly to Provost Gale Stevens-Haynes, Dean David Cohen, Visual Arts Department Chair Bob Barry, Faculty Media Resource Center Director Devabrata Mondal and staff members Alisa Yalan-Murphy, Kan Fang, and Srikanth Penumalla, Student Media Resource Center Director Farhad Farhadi and assistants Zena Kennedy and Lucia Cañarte. And special thanks go to Mary LiVoti and Daphne Horton of the secretarial staff.

I am deeply indebted to the many individuals at New York art galleries who patiently searched for and delivered information and images needed for these pages.

Specific gallery staff members whose invaluable contributions merit my expression of gratitude include: at the Forum Gallery: Robert and Cheryl Fishko, Heather Parks, Nicola Lorenz, Michele Lesstein, and Bonnie Meyers; at the Betty Cuningham Gallery: Philip Ennik; at the Tibor de Nagy Gallery: Rachel Kozinn and Rebecca Moed; at the Robert Miller Gallery: Amy Young; at the Ettinger Gallery: Fran Bradford; at Jim Kempner Fine Art: Laura Fried; at the Women's Studio Center: Melissa Wolf; at David Findlay Jr. Fine Arts: Louis Newman, Lisa Dubins, Katie Leonard, and Janay Wong; at the McKee Gallery: Karen Behnke; at the PaceWildenstein: Jennifer Joy, Jon Mason, Ken Fernandez, and Charlie Manzo; at the Kenkeleba Gallery: Corinne Jennings; at the June Kelly Gallery: June Kelly; at the Flomenhaft Gallery: Eleanor Flomenhaft; at the Babcock Gallery: Lilly Gray and Lisa S. Koonce; at the Alexandre Gallery: Phil Alexandre, Ellen Robinson, and Marie Evans; at the Aljira Center: Victor Davson; at the Marlborough Gallery: Julie Tambussi; at the Phoenix Gallery: Linda Handler; at the Mary Boone Gallery: Ron Warren; at the D C Moore Gallery: Bridget Moore, Sandra Paci, and Ed de Luca; at the Salander O'Reilly Gallery: Caitlin Fitzgerald, Sarah Arnett, Steven Harvey, Catherine Bernstein, and Suzanne Obuck; at the Anita Shapolsky Gallery, Petra Valentova; at Meredith Ward Fine Art, Kirk Montague; at the Fischbach Gallery: Lawrence di Carlo; at the Noho Gallery: Leon Yost; at the Cheim & Read: John Cheim and Chris Burnside; at the Prince Street Gallery: Nancy Grilikhes; at the Blue Mountain Gallery: Marcia Clark; at the von Lintel Gallery: Natasha Ogilvie and John Tevis; at the ACA Gallery: Lauren Rice and Dorian Bergen; at the Ameringer & Yohe Fine Art: James Yohe and Mary Joan Waid; at the Bowery Gallery: Barbara Grossman; at the Greenberg van Doren Gallery: Kristen Lorello and Dorsey Waxter; at Gallery Henoch: George Henoch Schechtman; at the Viridian Gallery: Vernita Nemec; at the Denise Bibro Gallery: Denise Bibro; at the Knoedler & Company: Melissa de Medeiros and Christina Viera; at the Lohin-Geduld Gallery: Ro Lohin and Emily Sessions. Museum and other institutional staff members who have been particularly helpful include: at the Whitney Museum, Anita Duquette and Joan Harrah; at the New Britain Museum of American Art, Jennifer Waldon; at the University of Rochester's Memorial Art Gallery, Grant Holcomb; and at the Pennsylvania Academy of the Fine Arts, Barbara Katus.

Studio managers and artists' assistants whose efforts are applauded include Susanna Singer, Grace Matthews, Maureen St. Onge, Janie Samuels, Juan Gomez, Eileen Hanavan, Lily Cohen, Darren Bader, Diana Urbanska, and Michael Volonakis.

Thanks also to Lisa Bush Hankin for sending images of paintings in her collection, to Sherry Christhilf for help in locating a Frankenthaler painting, to Margaret Kerr for assistance with the work of her husband, Robert Richenburg, and to Robert W. Speier, who knows why!

I express my thanks to Bruno Palmer-Poroner, for many years of professional encouragement, countless hours of enriching historic conversation, useful suggestions for this book, and for presenting my first solo exhibition of Modular Paintings years ago, at his West 56th Street East Hampton Gallery. Also, my thanks to Bruno and to Diana Gisolfi, Evelyn Yce, Benny Andrews, and Rick Mayhew, for recommending painters whose works I had not known, some of whom are included here.

Artists to whom I am indebted for their contributions although their works, regrettably, were not able to find a place in this book, include Nancy Azara, Cecily Barth Firestein, Kimberly M. Bylo, and many graduate student painters at Hunter College.

For personal kindnesses and other often-intangible contributions, I salute the friendship of Nancy Gleason. And, of course, I always appreciate the many forms of encouragement offered by my son, Grayson.

For their daily assistance and care of my husband, the photographer Jerry Dantzic, without which I could not have devoted my time and energies to this project, my thanks and a hug to Irma Robertson and Elsy Jean-Jacques.

Finally, I'd like to acknowledge the very important contribution of many reviewers, critics, and catalogue essayists, whose often insightful, perceptive, and carefully phrased descriptions and analyses of the works of many of these 100 painters provided me with understanding and appreciation of exhibitions I was not privileged to attend and of works I was not able to see. In some instances, I have included very brief phrases or descriptions from these writings in my short biographic essays. These writers include: Phyllis Lader, Gerda Barber, Ed McCormack, Sally Davis, William Zimmer, Ronny Cohen, Irving Sandler, David Cohen, Tara Scully, Dore Ashton, Stanley I. Grand, Raymond J. Steiner, Dominique Nahas, Michael Kimmelman, Joan T. Washburn, Hilton Kramer, Vivien Raynor, David Shirey, Heli Haapasalo, Andrew Forge, Laurence Campbell, Martica Sawin, Louis Finklestein, and Robert Kushner. I cannot list them all. For more expanded writings by these and others, you are encouraged to find additional information at the library or on the Internet.

Of course, my most important acknowledgment must be to the 100 New York painters themselves, who have created works that show the unspeakable richness of human experience and the ineffable beauty we human beings are capable of achieving, through art.

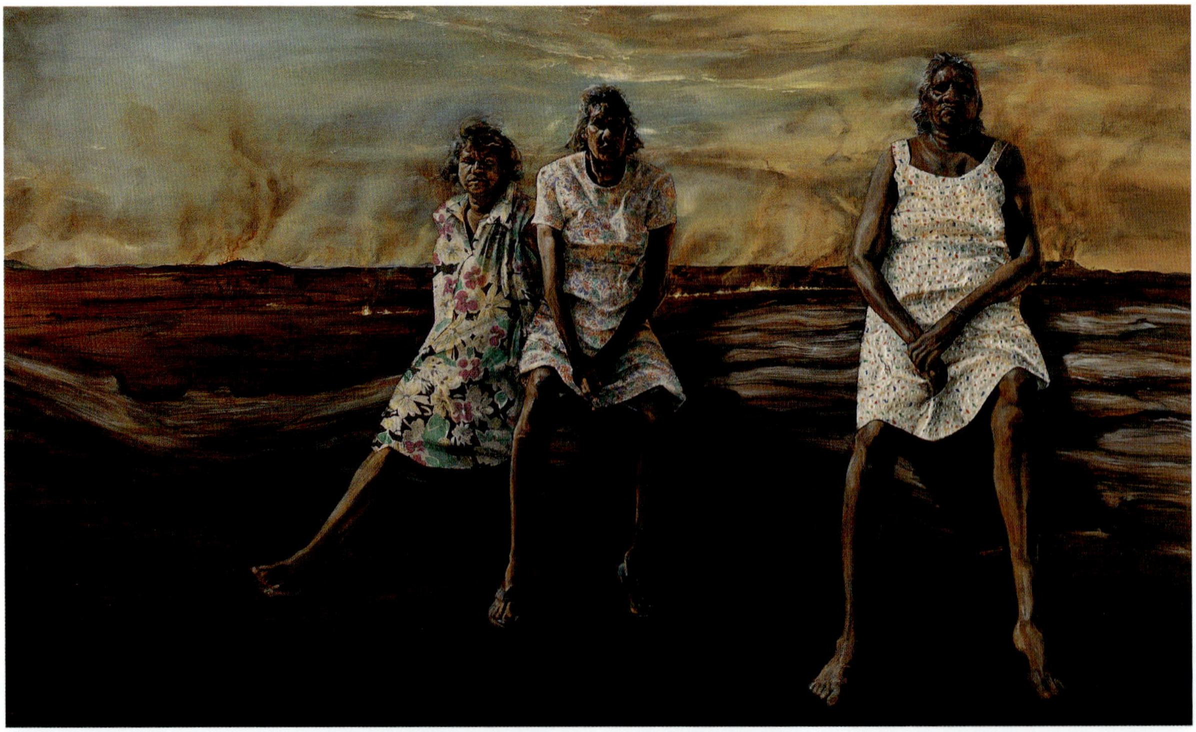

Kelynn Zatarain Alder

Contents

Acknowledgments ... 3
Introduction ... 7

The Painters ... 18
Kelynn Zatarain Alder ... 18
Emma Amos ... 20
Arthur Anderson ... 22
Lennart Anderson ... 24
Benny Andrews ... 26
Richard Anuszkiewicz ... 28
Steven Assael ... 30
Donald Baechler ... 32
Richard Baker ... 34
Will Barnet ... 36
Jack Beal ... 38
Miriam Beerman ... 40
Leigh Behnke ... 42
Siri Berg ... 44
Robert Birmelin ... 46
Jane Bolmeier ... 48
Richmond Burton ... 50
Charles Cajori ... 52
Virginia Hoyt Cantarella ... 54
Nicolas Carone ... 56
Bernard Chaet ... 58
Ellen Cibula ... 60
Ed Clark ... 62
Marcia Clark ... 64
Chuck Close ... 66
Lisa Collado ... 68
Arthur Coppedge ... 70
Judy Cuttler ... 72
Lisa Corinne Davis ... 74
Francks Francois Deceus ... 76
Dorothy Deon ... 78
Harvey Dinnerstein ... 80
Rachel Dinnerstein ... 82
Simon Dinnerstein ... 84
Marylyn Dintenfass ... 86
Lois Dodd ... 88
Martha Mayer Erlebacher ... 90
Richard Estes ... 92
Paul F. Fabozzi ... 94
David Ferrando ... 96
Eric Fischl ... 98
Janet Fish ... 100
Louise Fishman ... 102
Audrey Flack ... 104
Helen Frankenthaler ... 106
Sondra Freckelton ... 108
Jane Freilicher ... 110
Sonia Gechtoff ... 112
Bob Goodnough ... 114
Cheryl Gross ... 116
Sue Ferguson Gussow ... 118
Mary Hambleton ... 120
Glen Hansen ... 122
Esther Hyneman ... 124
Yvonne Jacquette ... 126
Valerie Jaudon ... 128
Cecily Kahn ... 130
Wolf Kahn ... 132
Alex Katz ... 134
Barbara Kulicke ... 136
Marion Lerner-Levine ... 138
Jack Levine ... 140
Dik Liu ... 142
Vincent Longo ... 144
Robert Mangold ... 146
Helene K. Manzo ... 148
Anthony Martino ... 150
Emily Mason ... 152
Richard Mayhew ... 154
Mary Beth McKenzie ... 156
Lee Anne Miller ... 158
Don Nice ... 160
Doug Ohlson ... 162
Philip Pearlstein ... 164
Tracy Phillips ... 166
Howardena Pindell ... 168
Stephanie Rauschenbusch ... 170
Catherine Redmond ... 172
Paul Resika ... 174
Robert Richenburg ... 176

Faith Ringgold 178
Marie Roberts 180
Dorothea Rockburne 182
Shunji Sakuyama 184
William Scharf 186
Laura Schiavina 188
Johan Sellenraad 190
Kendall Shaw 192
Susan Sills 194
Pat Steir 196
Posoon Park Sung 198
Robert Swain 200
Barbara Takenaga 202
Bob Tomlinson 204
George Tooker 206
Vivian Tsao 208
Audrey Ushenko 210
Gian Berto Vanni 212
Ella Yang 214
Darryl Zudeck 216

Notes 218
Suggested Reading 222
Index 223

Introduction

New York, as the oft-acknowledged Art Capital of the contemporary world, the current Paris, the center of an energetic, diverse, even divergent outpouring of the visual and performing arts, is looked to for clarification, inspiration, and understanding, as well as for delight and esthetic nourishment. It is a touchstone for exemplars of the norm and its extremes, the exceptions and unexpected intimations of what is to come, and a treasury of icons from the past.

In this book, you will find a broad, representative sampling of many kinds of paintings that have been made and are continuing to be produced by 100 extremely individual New York painters. In this post-millennium period, with so many visual artists introducing and combining new and non-traditional mediums and methods of creating and presenting their work—incorporating or working solely with electronic, digital, and other technologies—and others freely taking from previously separable mediums or combining them in inventive ways in New York, and surely throughout the United States, it seems a good time to take a look at an overview of works that can still be called paintings.

For readers in New York, this book may provide a structure to bring into focus the great range of painting styles, subjects, mediums, even philosophies of art you may encounter in New York galleries, museums, and studios.

For readers away from New York, it should help to provide a sense of the broad range of painters whose works, taken as a whole, define the art life of this vibrant, eclectic global hub.

A mosaic of very different identities comes together here to form the very personification of "unity in diversity," as well as its complement, "diversity in unity." Look for the works of a number of painting families in these pages. You will find siblings, couples, and occasionally their children, often revealing quite separate styles and approaches to their art. These include Beal/Freckleton, Cibula/Sellenraad, Martino/Cuttler, Kahn/Kahn/Mason, and all three Dinnersteins.

It has been a privilege to correspond, speak with, and often meet almost all of these 100 painters, to visit some of their studios, and to have been presented with a generous number of works from which to choose those you will see here. Perhaps the most striking studio is that of Ed Clark, several blocks south of the Empire State Building, with a twelfth floor, close-up view of the majestic tower changing colors with the latening of the day and becoming a graphic silhouette against the darkened sky. The epitome of New York! What a splendid perch for this long-time New York painter!

Selection of Painters

This selection of New York painters is, of necessity, an arbitrary, personal choice. Given the many hundreds of accomplished women and men whose works might have been included, I have tried to portray a representative grouping of artists and of the many kinds of paintings they create. Admittedly, many, even many of the best, will not be found in these pages. I must (and do) acknowledge the large number of those who might as well have been included. And, although you may recognize the names and works of a large number, this company of 100 painters should serve to introduce you to many whose names and works are less celebrated, though no less deserving of attention.

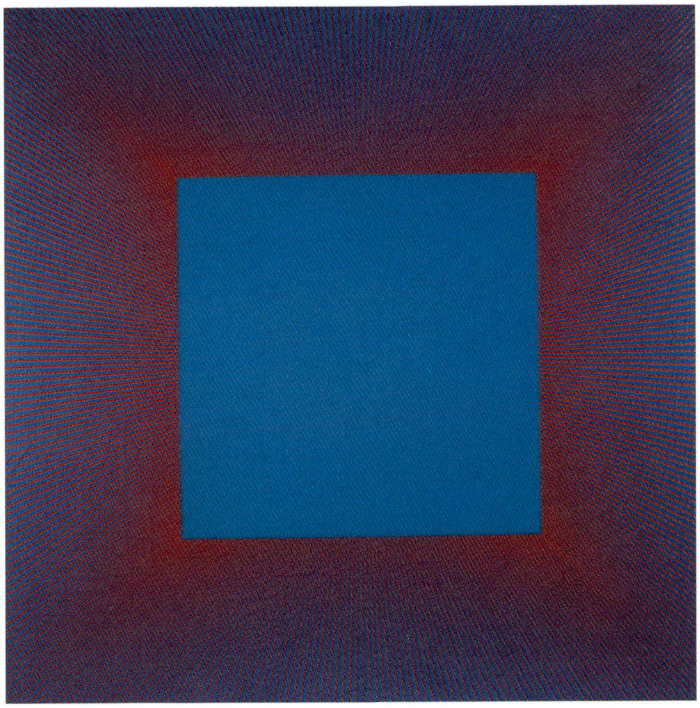

Richard Anuszkiewicz (pp. 28-29)

You will encounter a number of household names and iconic museum-owned works known far beyond the confines of New York. These will be supplemented by less familiar, even relatively unknown names, yet not, to my mind, of lesser merit. It has been necessary for me to define certain criteria, which I will try to convey, perhaps more clearly than they may have been applied, to each painter and each painting presented. After all, the visual experience must be seen; mere words can never fully do the job.

To ascribe the designation, "New York Painter," these considerations were applied, but not with equal weight:

- Birthplace in New York (several over ninety years ago!).
- Schooling or art training in New York.
- Residence in New York, now or for any extended period.

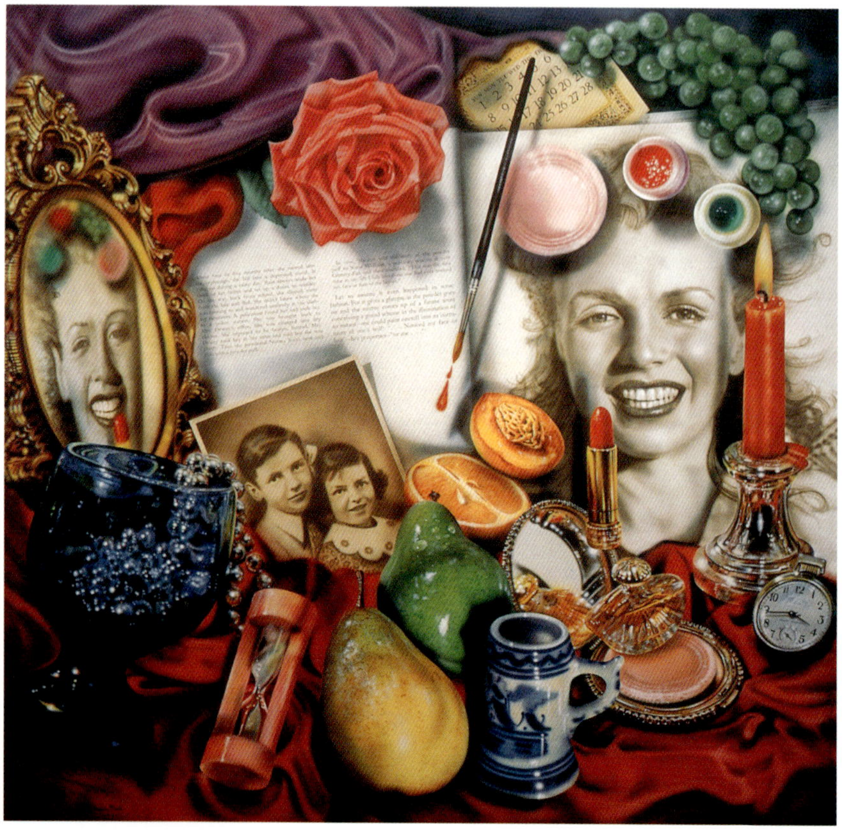

Audrey Flack (pp. 104-105)

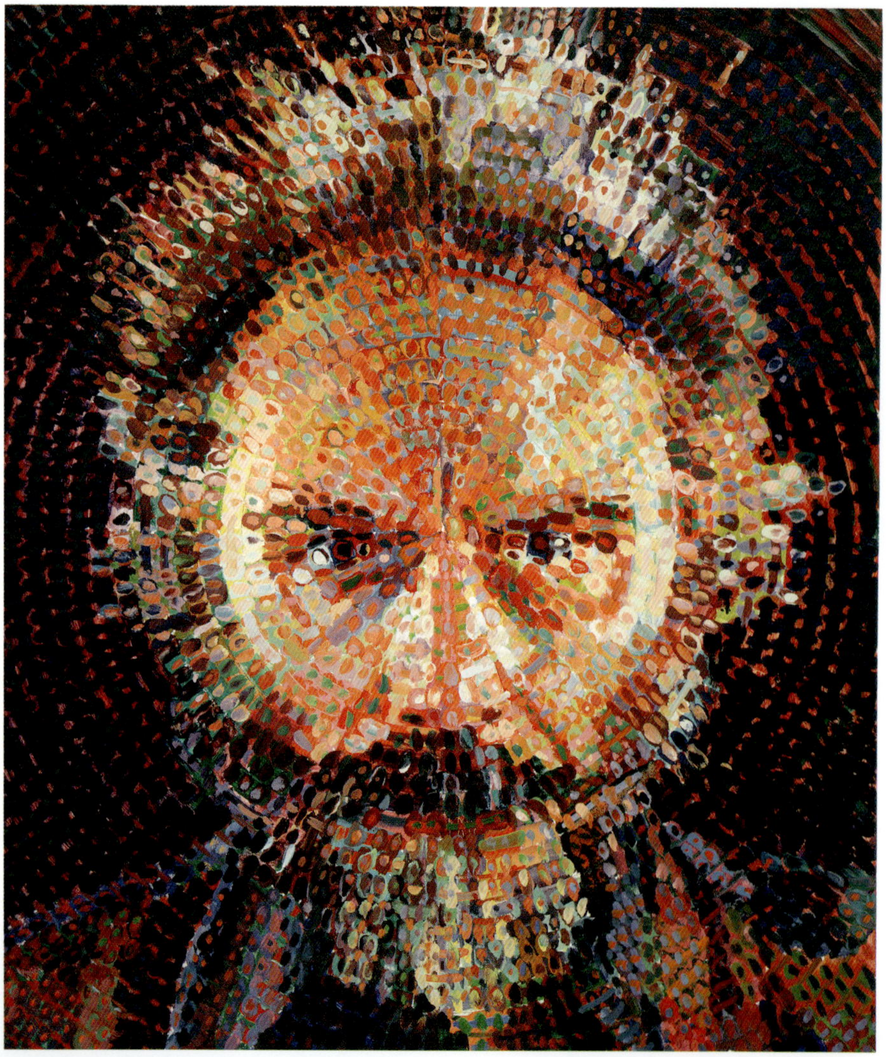

Chuck Close (pp. 66-67)

- Studio in New York.
- Gallery affiliation in New York.
- Teaching at a New York or neighboring location—art school, college or university art department.

Schools whose faculty members and alumnae/i will be found here include:

- The Art Students League
- The National Academy of Design
- The Cooper Union
- Hunter College
- Brooklyn College
- Long Island University's Brooklyn Campus
- Pratt Institute
- The New York Studio School
- The Brooklyn Museum Art School

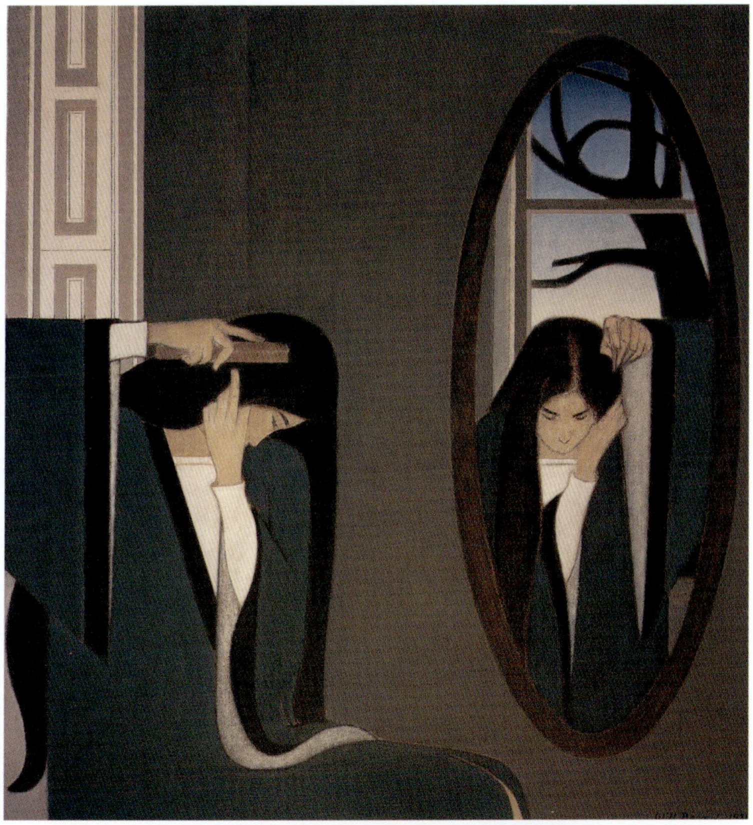

Will Barnet (pp. 36-37)

Although birthplace was noted, many New York painters were born elsewhere, some as far away as Japan, Germany, or ... California! Some painters, having spent many years in New York, now reside elsewhere. "Don't my sixty-two years in New York count?" asked one of my personal favorites. Of course they do!

Many of these painters exhibit regularly in New York galleries, among them a number of the most distinguished 57th Street commercial galleries (particularly in the renowned Fuller Building at 11 East 57th Street, or nearby), such as D C Moore, David Findlay, the Forum, PaceWildenstein, and the Alexandre. Some are affiliated with commercial galleries in the more recently developed Chelsea area west of 9th Avenue, from 19th to 27th Street, or in Soho. Still others exhibit at artist-run galleries largely in the Chelsea area or at the historic Westbeth, a Greenwich Village complex where artists reside, maintain studios, and exhibit in the Westbeth Gallery.

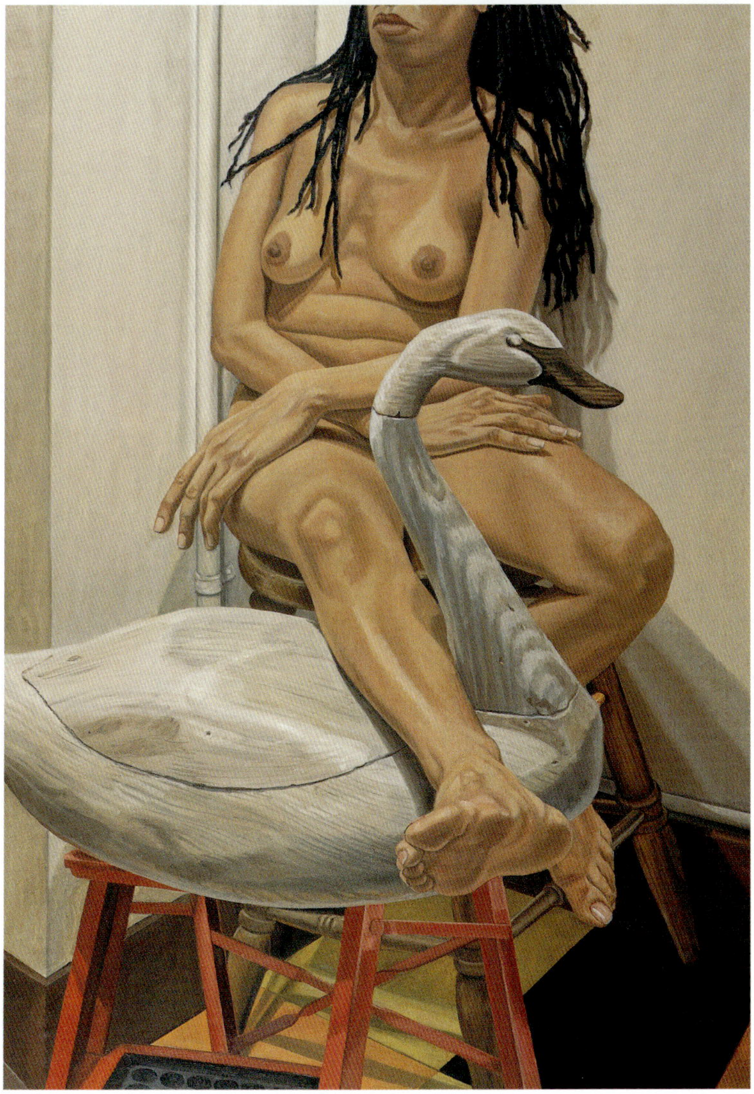

Philip Pearlstein (pp. 164-165)

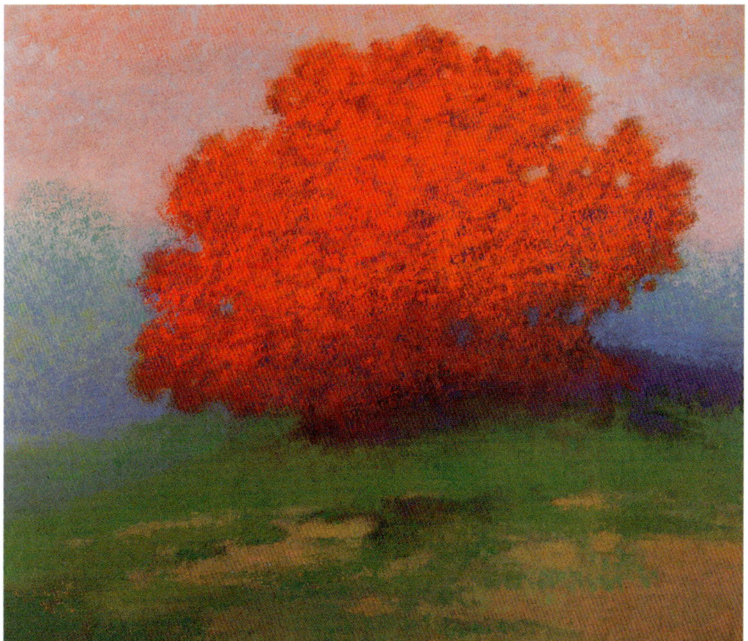

Richard Mayhew (pp. 154-155)

Some painters do not yet have (or no longer have) a gallery affiliation, but exhibit from time to time at invitational shows, or regularly with a community or neighborhood art group, many in Brooklyn.

Many of these painters were known to me through general reputation or personally, as teaching colleagues, members of professional art organizations such as the CAA, classmates (at Yale, Pratt, BMAS...), neighbors (in Park Slope, Brooklyn), long-time friends, or students. Several were strongly recommended by artists invited to participate or by their galleries' staff members. It was a privilege to be introduced in this way to a number of painters whose works had previously been unfamiliar to me. A major decision was made to include only painters living at this time, though daily the ranks of long-time New York painters are, alas, reduced.

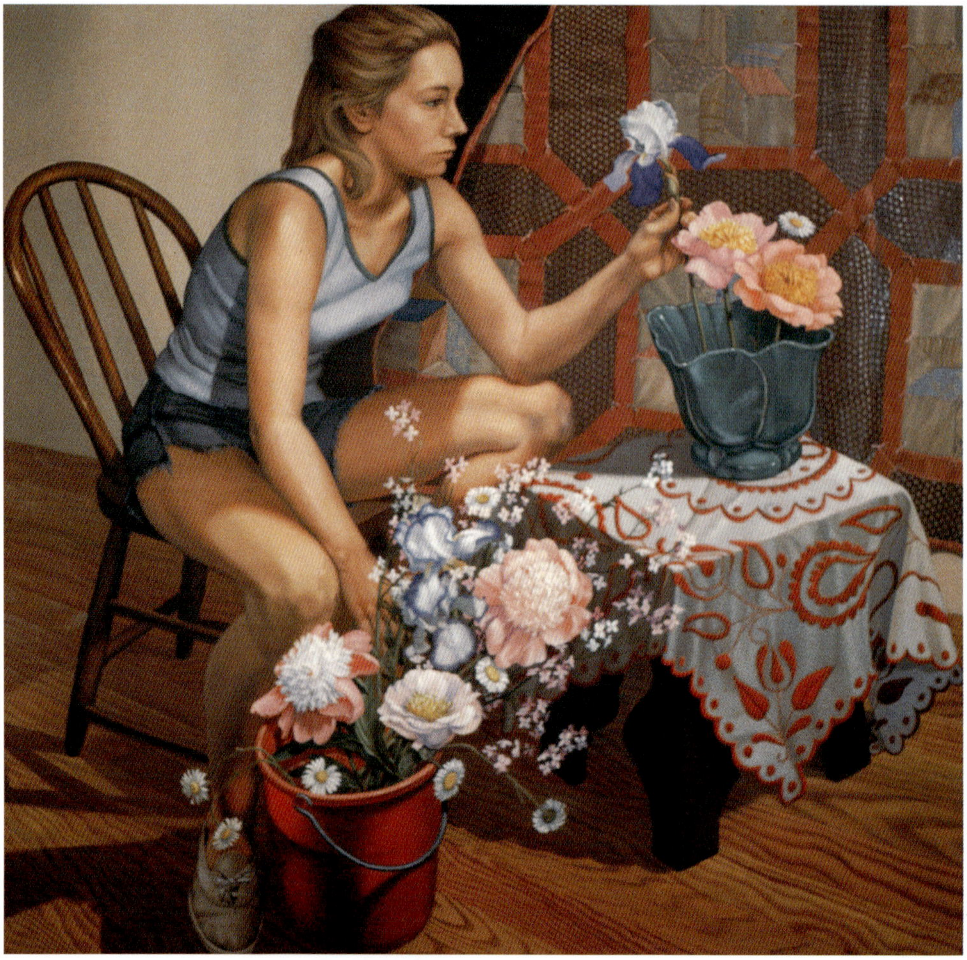

Sondra Freckelton (pp. 108-109)

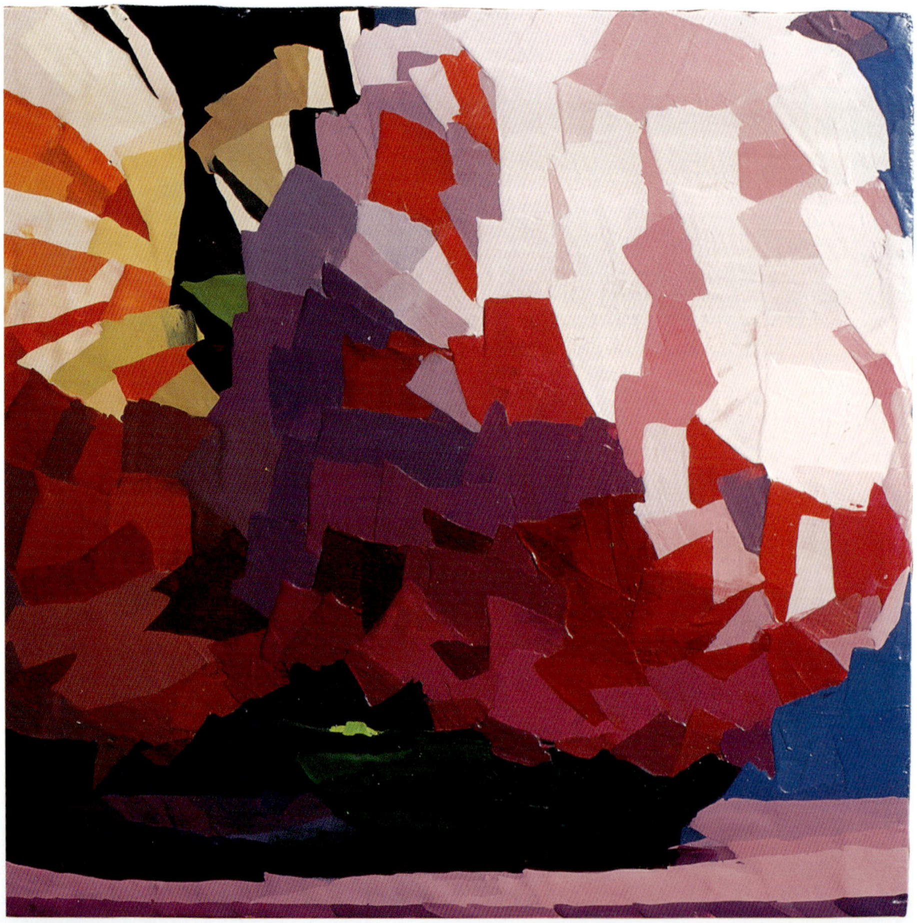

In the necessarily brief biographic sketches, I have endeavored to present each painter in a way that will give a sense of the artist's uniqueness—not simply listing degrees and other professional credentials, but selecting information that will help support, reinforce, or clarify specific works shown. Note that over one-third of the painters are elected members of the select National Academy of Design, entitled to list NA after their name, and quite a few have taught there or received NA awards as well. Often a statement specifically provided for this book, comments taken from the artist's previous writings and interviews, or excerpts from the critical appreciation of others will accompany the abbreviated introduction to each painter's works.

Dik Liu (pp. 142-143)

Criteria For Works Included

A difficult decision had to be made, in order to assure a representative range of New York painters, to present a truly rich diversity of artistic styles, genres, materials and subjects, without completely altering the very definition of painting itself. Some would stretch this definition to include works in pastels or crayon, watercolors, and various printmaking mediums. Although a compelling case could be made (and was) for these, in order to include works that would clearly be eligible for exhibition and award criteria as "paintings," I have endeavored to apply this guideline: *Is the work primarily a planar, more or less flat, two-dimensional composition, using some areas of actual viscous spreadable paint on its surface, whether or not additional elements or materials have been added or incorporated into the work?*

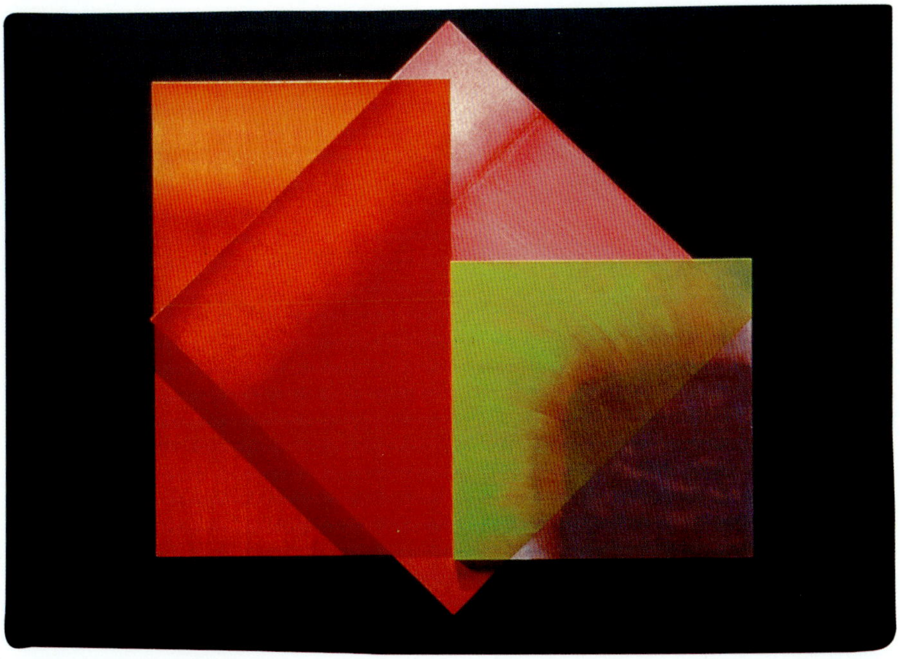

Dorothea Rockburne (pp. 182-183)

If a work listed three measurements, including depth or thickness, I did not include it, with the rare exception of works combining several canvases or panels. If the work was done originally in pastel, watercolor, or a printmaking technique, even if areas of paint and other materials have been added, it was not included as primarily a painting. Works that would be eligible for exhibitions in the category of "aqueous media" were also not included. What of oils, or acrylics, but on paper? What of egg tempera? Casein? Gouache? "Mixed media?" Hard choices had to be made, and I tried not to shrink from making them, arbitrary as some may indeed appear! However, I have tried to note if a painter also works in these or other mediums, even though examples of such works are not shown.

Adding to the challenge was the need to limit the number of final images to the publisher's requirements. This was a difficult task as well, and I am sure there are those who will disagree with some of the choices! Mea culpa and all that, yet this book will be able to claim that it does present a broad spectrum of paintings by 100 New York painters, all alive and well and painting away, as we go to press!

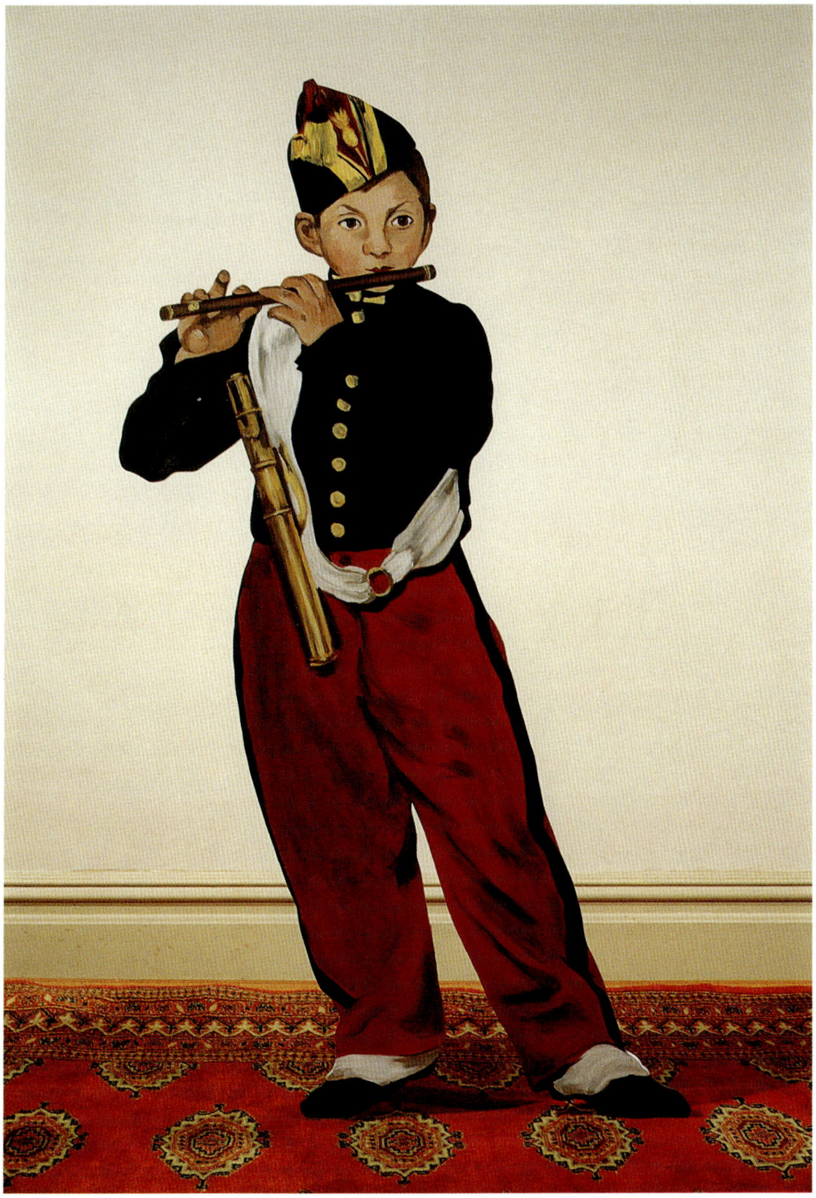

Susan Sills (pp. 194-195)

Painting, in All Its Variety

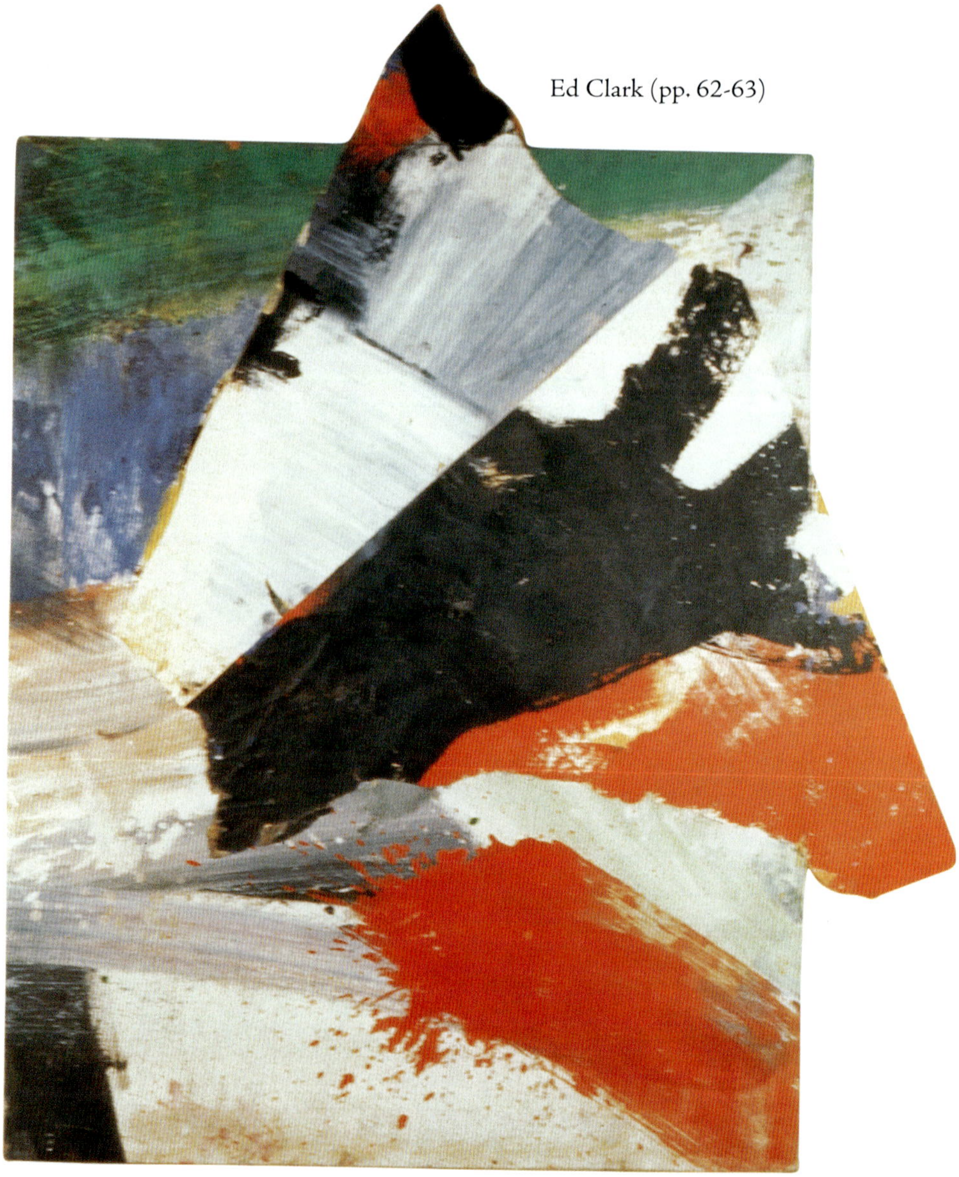
Ed Clark (pp. 62-63)

Now that I have defined in a general way the guidelines used in identifying 100 New York painters and the materials or mediums in which they work, a word must be said about the very works—the paintings—themselves. On the following pages, you will find works that more than span the gamut of painterly concerns, from super-exact photographic realism in re-producing or re-presenting literal subject matter as seen by the painter, to non-subjective, non-objective works of sheer color interaction—the latter achieving eye-delighting visual effects with no apparent relationship to the perceived world or subject matter, other than color, the subject that matters to these painters most of all. Some invoke the power and mystery of perceived color alone, the activity of color's interaction with color, the electricity or melt, the transparency experienced where color meets color, at the very edge, or along bands of color. Of course, paintings in which color alone is the subject do not necessarily rely on a geometric or even a "hard edge" structure. The Hans Hofmann legacy informs as many contemporary painters as that of Josef Albers. Indeed, the two "schools" may appear to work together seamlessly in some of the works you will see. (Keep in mind that the designation "non-objective" doesn't imply lack of purpose or objective to these works, but rather that they don't intend to re-present actual objects as their subject matter.)

In addition to, or perhaps in between, these extremities, are countless ideas, schools, styles, or other categories into which the vast array of painterly concerns may be placed. Of course, not every painting or every painter may be located within such often arbitrary, overlapping, or even generally accepted groupings.

The very form of a painting may be the subject of lively discussion. Since every canvas or panel has some periphery or shape, what kinds of shapes may be called "shaped" canvases? The traditional rectangle, square (or tilted as a diamond), and tondo (or circular format), raise no critical eyebrow, yet other less clearly geometric, even irregular and free-form shapes cause some to challenge their "bona fides" as paintings. One of our 100, Ed Clark, is often credited with the introduction (in 1946!) of an irregularly "shaped canvas," opening a new door for the avant-garde of the day. Several of our 100 have carried this idea to various extremes, and yet the concept that a planar surface has (indeed, *must* have) some shape, and not necessarily a predetermined geometric outline, continues to invite discussion, even concern.

Among painters who choose to depict or suggest the human form, there are myriad alternatives to precise, camera-sharp rendition. Every degree of softness, of simplification, of abstraction (or reduction to basic elements), can be found. Every kind of personal expression of the painter's relationship, attitude, or feeling toward the real, imagined, remembered, or suggested figure, or the general movement or gesture of a figure, may be seen. The very action of the painter's arm or hand moving over the surface of the canvas to capture or suggest the merest allusion to a human existence—these can all be discovered in differing ways, as each painter is indeed a unique, inimitably human, being.

We may marvel at the human mind, its inventive capacity and the ability of some to control detail to its utmost minute subdivision, its almost uncanny ability to re-create on canvas what was seen, the level of precision attained by those who have pursued this skill to depict the object of perception "to its innermost parts." But it is equally marvelous to appreciate, to take delight in the widely divergent ways specific subject matter can be presented, sometimes barely identifiable as it is merely suggested by a hint of movement or gesture, sometimes more involved with the movement than the inspiring figure, place or event—even at times with the unfilled spaces between and around them. (There is no "negative" space!)

With regard to the identity of human personages shown or implied in a painting, among many choices are:

- The likeness or sense of the painter as seen or imagined, that is, the self-portrait.
- The appearance of a professional model, or a client, posing for the artist.
- One's family members or friends, seen, remembered, imagined ...

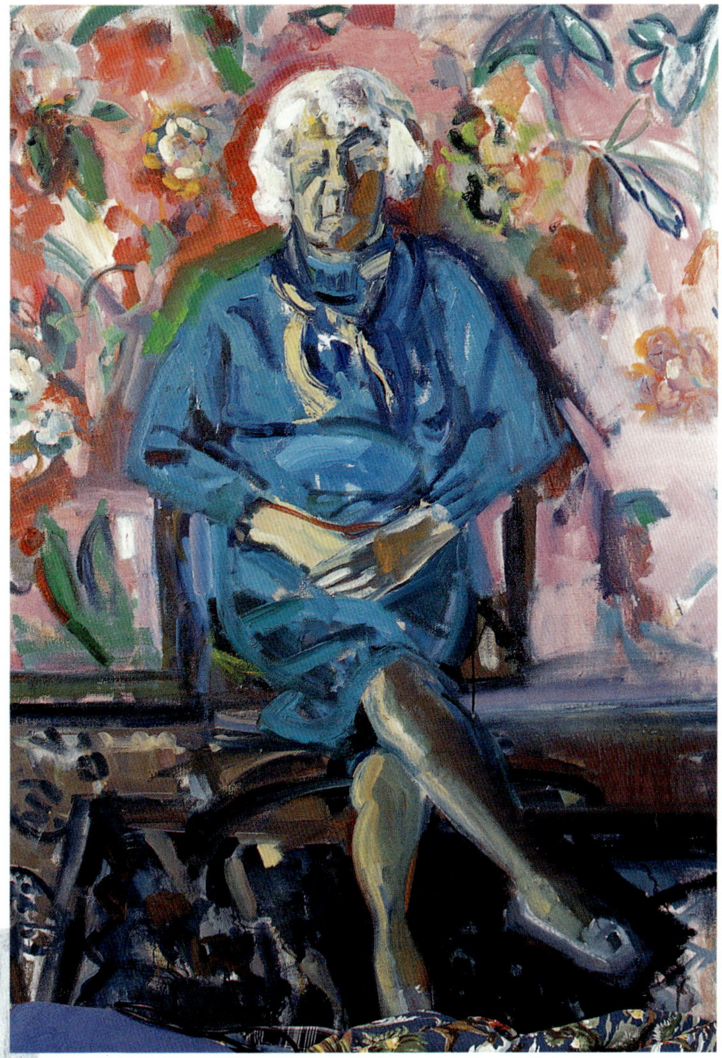

Judy Cuttler (pp. 72-73)

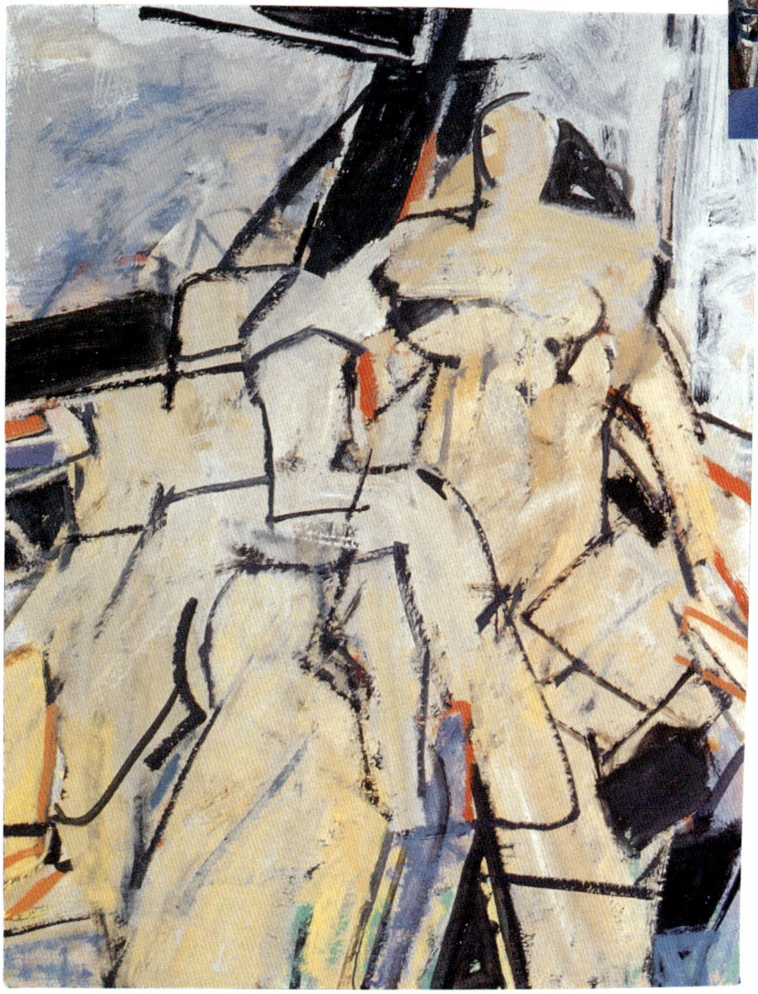

- A face or figure from memory or a sensed "group memory."
- An archetype or general personage, often intended to show the sufferings, indignities, or other experiences of various religious, national, cultural, or ethnic population groups.
- Mythological figures.
- Allegorical tableaus re-created.
- Figures from history, literature or religious sources.
- or ...

Beyond the representation of perceived or imagined human beings, painters are often inspired to depict or devise living forms of other creatures, or of plants and flowers. The city pigeon and country turkey, the potted plant, and flowering garden or field, will be seen.

Charles Cajori (pp. 52-53)

Other observed subjects include: the still life, arranged or discovered groupings of objects, generally in an indoor setting, the interior or exterior of architectural structures in their environments, the city-scape, the natural land- sea- or sky-scape. You will find many clearly New York locations presented in a number of the city scenes, with various degrees of literal allegiance to their subject, whether outdoor, architectural, or subterranean, in underground subway train imagery. In many paintings you will find an aspect or feature of New York as seen through the eyes, memory, or imagination of the artist. Some "plein air," outdoor works were created at the actual site, some re-created from studies or sketches, later, in the studio.

Of course, New York painters travel, even reside, abroad, and so you will see images of Italy and New England, Australian and Mexican individuals and locations. Fantasy, dreams, and the surreal inspire many painters, as well as figures of mythology and religious or historic personages and events. Political persuasion motivates many a painter's brush.

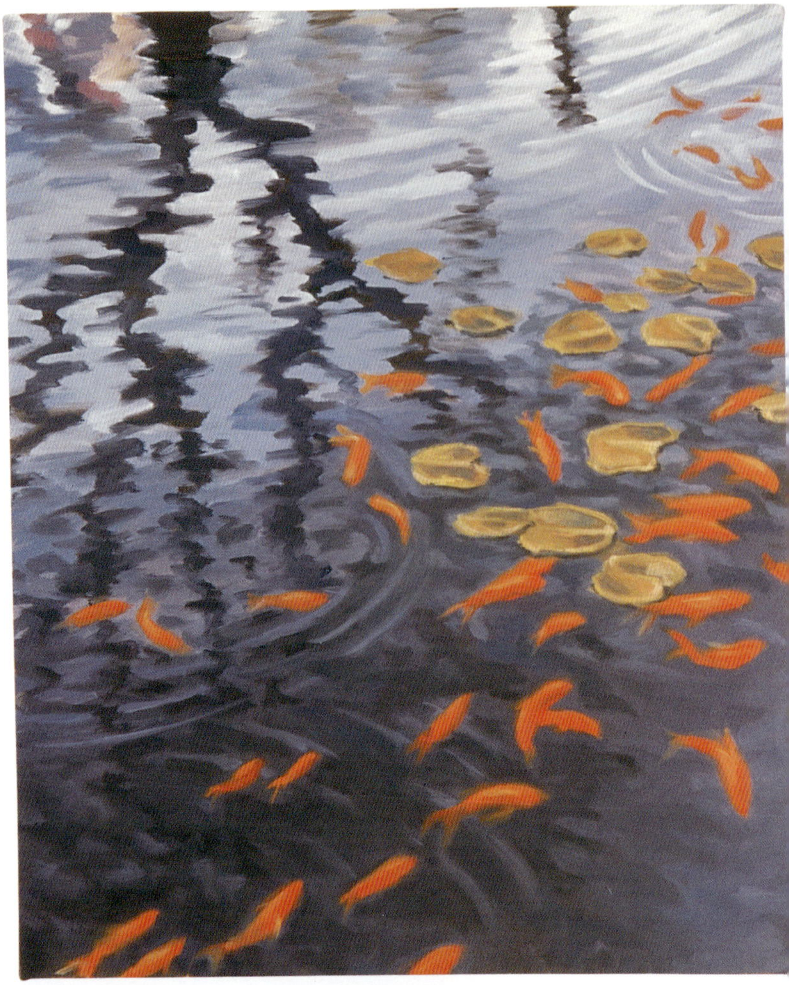

Ella Yang (pp. 214-215)

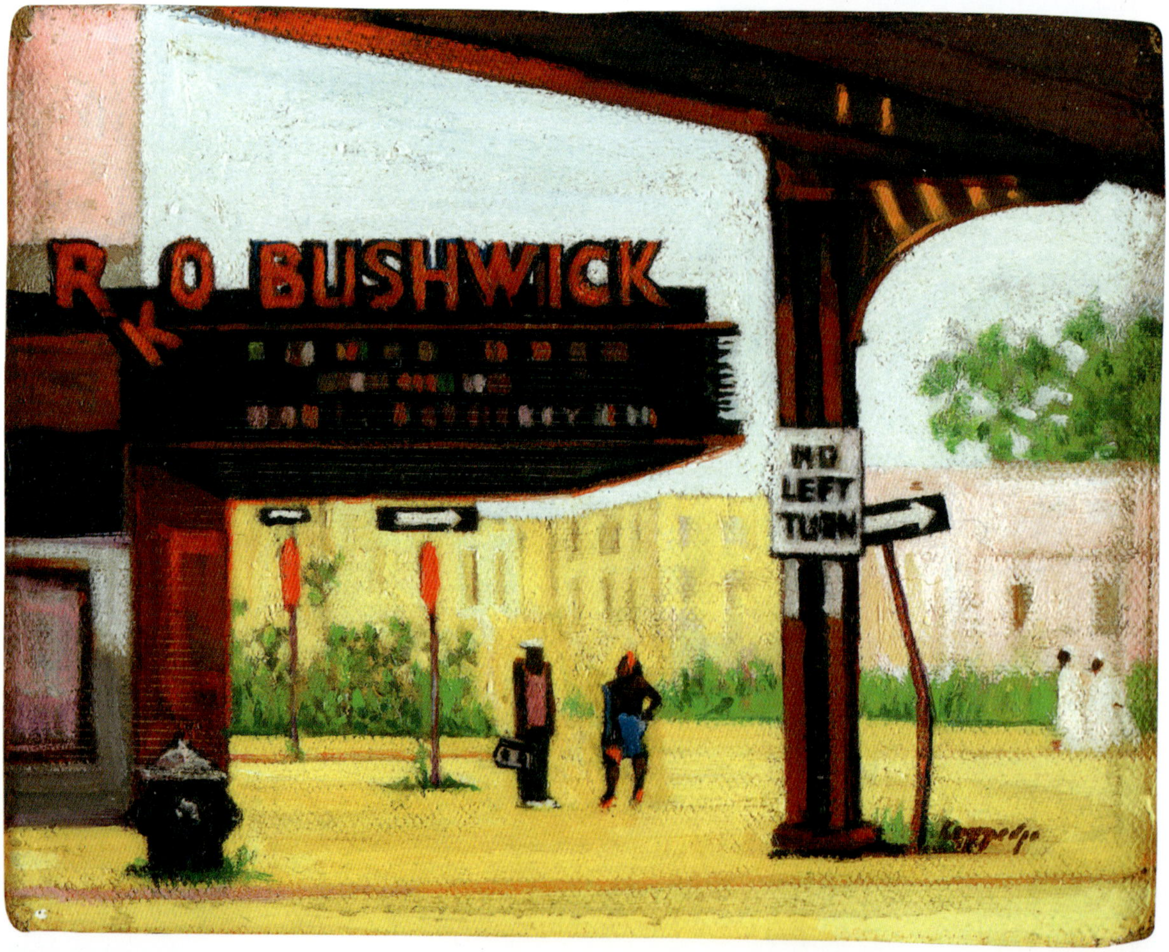

Arthur Coppedge (pp. 70-71)

In all these pictorial areas we may see the abstracting or reduction to basic elements, often with the loosening of brush-stroke and intermingling of "figure" and "ground," even to the point of melding "contained" and "containing" spaces to create a single unified planar experience, with either the achievement of overall flatness (as in cubism) or the look of depth and space (as in some abstract expressionist works, or "action paintings"); or, to use the term introduced by Palmer-Poroner, "lyrical expressionism," which suggests a greater emphasis on color and a sense of orchestrated movement over the surface of the canvas, beyond that characterized by the term "action painting." Allusion or reference to an originating subject may be reduced to the merest suggestion, or excluded altogether. In works relying on geometric relationships, you may find specific homage to the Golden Mean with its associated Equiangular Spiral, as well as variously arranged grids, patterns, stripes, and repeated units of design, sometimes reduced in size so that a pattern's individual units appear to merge into an overall surface texture. Symmetry, particularly bilateral, inkblot symmetry, is seen in a number of pattern paintings, in which identical but mirrored elements are disposed on either side of an often implied central vertical axis. Radial symmetry, whose elements move out in rays from a central point, may be discovered often in works called optical, retinal, or color field.

Uncover for yourself the delights of each visual epiphany! There is such a richness and diversity of subject, style, technique, philosophy ("esthetic," if you will), even of the very nature of painting that it would be more than presumptuous to assign a clear category to these 100 painters or their works; indeed, over time, such categories often evolve and change so that the works of any individual may be placed in several arbitrary categories. For the most part, I shall leave such filing to the reader.

Valerie Jaudon (pp. 128-129)

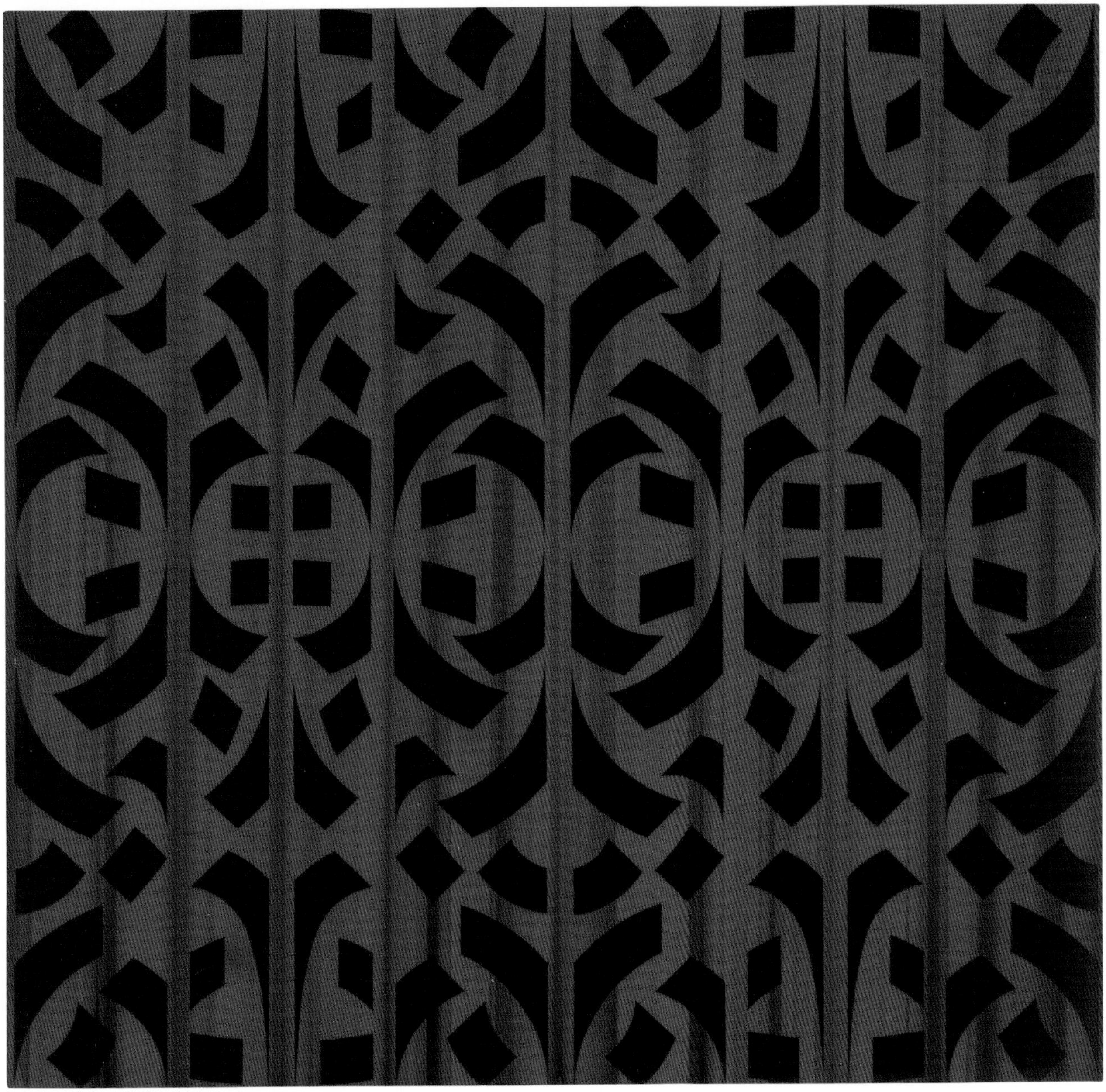

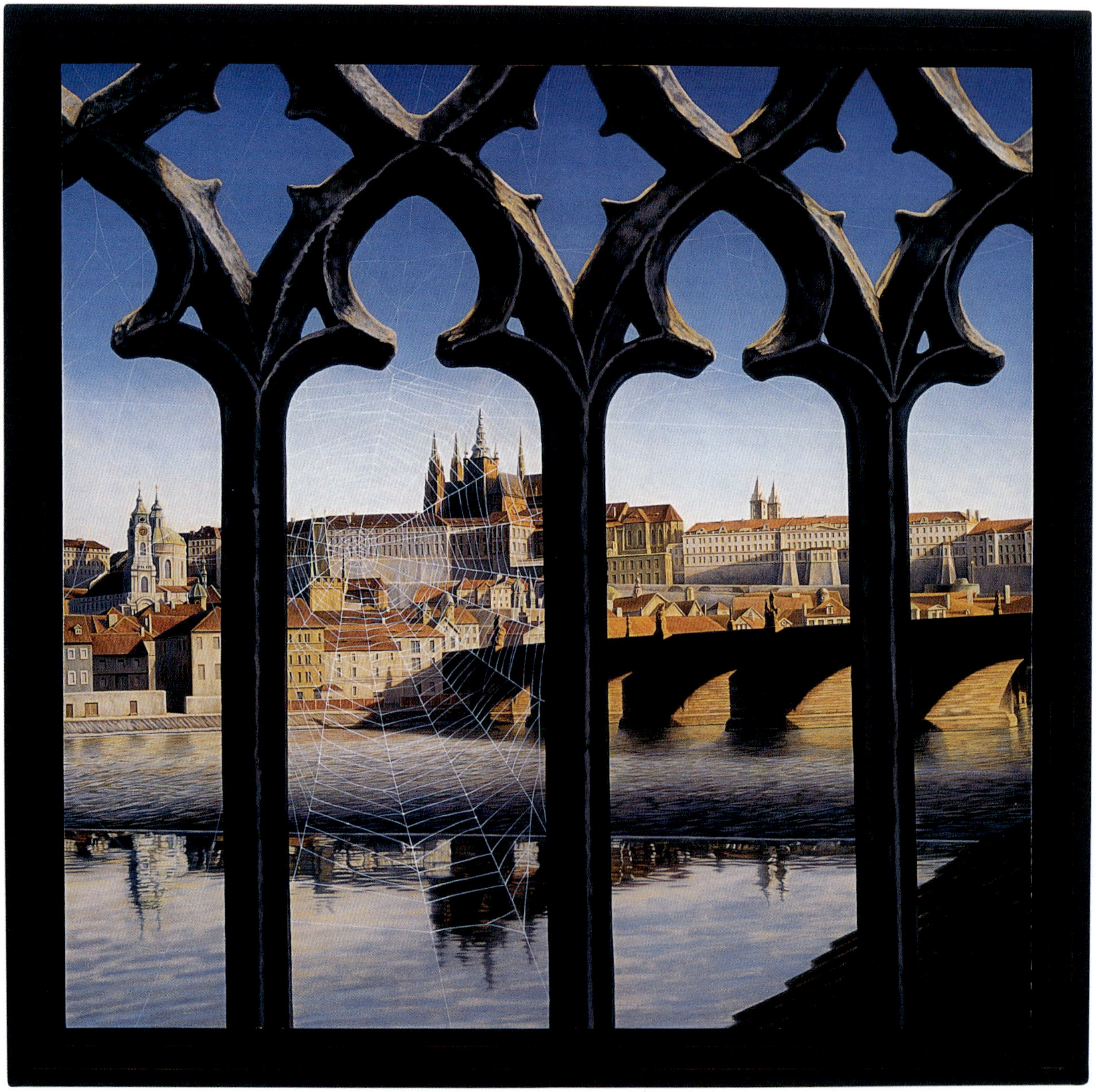

Glen Hansen (pp. 122-123)

Expect to find recent works, as well as paintings from an earlier period of an artist's oeuvre—as near as Kelynn Alder's "Coney Island," painted specifically for this book, and as distant as George Tooker's iconic allegory, "Subway," painted in 1950.

Just as these 100 painters are not to be construed as the 100 "best" or "most worthy," even those included are not necessarily represented by what each might consider his or her best works; the limitations of publication sometimes require omission of works that might not translate well, reduced in size to the printed page. Certain detail-laden or close-value works simply would be lost in translation to the page. The artist's own preference has been respected where possible.

Certainly, there will be disagreement over the choice to include, or exclude, a particular painter. As I have said earlier, of the many hundreds that might have been selected, this is clearly an arbitrary choice. In the end, though, I hope you will find a nicely balanced overview, showing the grand variety and richness of the painters' art, produced by this very broad company of 100 New York painters. It is to be hoped that this glimpse of the vast array of works by New York painters will whet each reader's interest in and appreciation of so wide, so divergent, and so excellent a collection of serious, accomplished, and dedicated painters. In addition to the old friends you may recognize with delight, I hope there will be at least an equal number introducing their works to you for the first time, to be added to your personal treasury, your own collection of New York painters. From Alder to Zudeck, enjoy the journey!

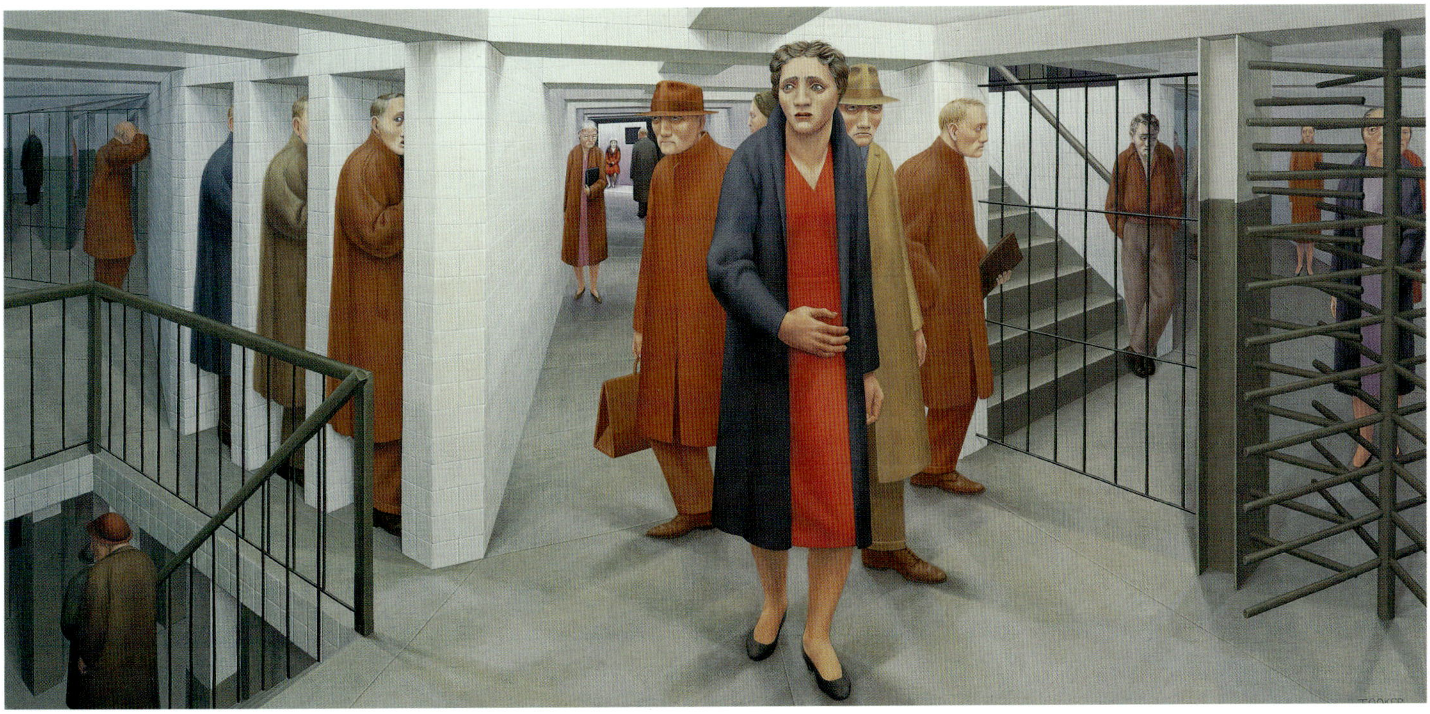

George Tooker (pp. 206-207)

Kelynn Zatarain Alder

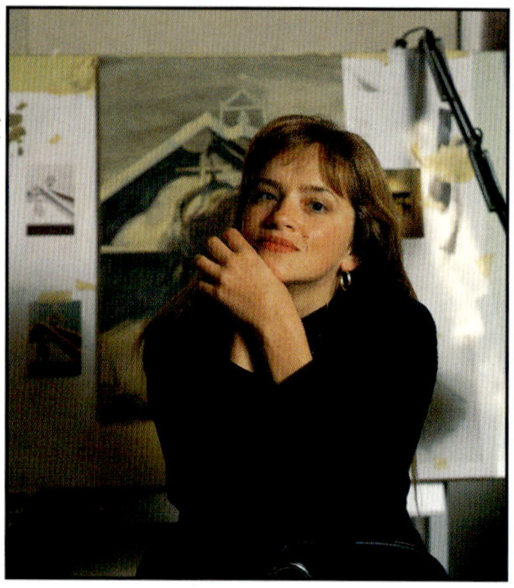

Courtesy of the artist.

Kelynn Zatarain Alder, a self-defined "visual essayist with a wanderlust,"[1] pursues many enthusiasms, which extend from celebrating her heritage (half Mexican-Irish Catholic, half Russian-Jewish/Cherokee) by painting the Lacandon Maya (and establishing a Children's Art Workshop in Mexico), to swimming the Long Island Sound to raise funds for a hurricane rescue effort! Alder also honors her family by taking her Mexican grandmother's surname as her middle name.

A graduate of Parsons School of Design and the School of Visual Arts, she has an extensive career as an illustrator and teacher and is an instructor at the School of Visual Arts. Alder has lived in and traveled to many countries, documenting indigenous people and their cultural artifacts. In Australia, she created "personified landscapes"[2] of individuals such as aboriginal Gagudju elder Bill Neidjie and his sons, and the "Three Graces." "Coney Island," part of an international series of Outdoor Vendors, was completed for this book.

She acknowledges her instructor, David Pasalaqua, "who taught me to see with my own vision and to draw with both hands," and Marshall Arisman, "who taught me to paint with my heart ..."[3]

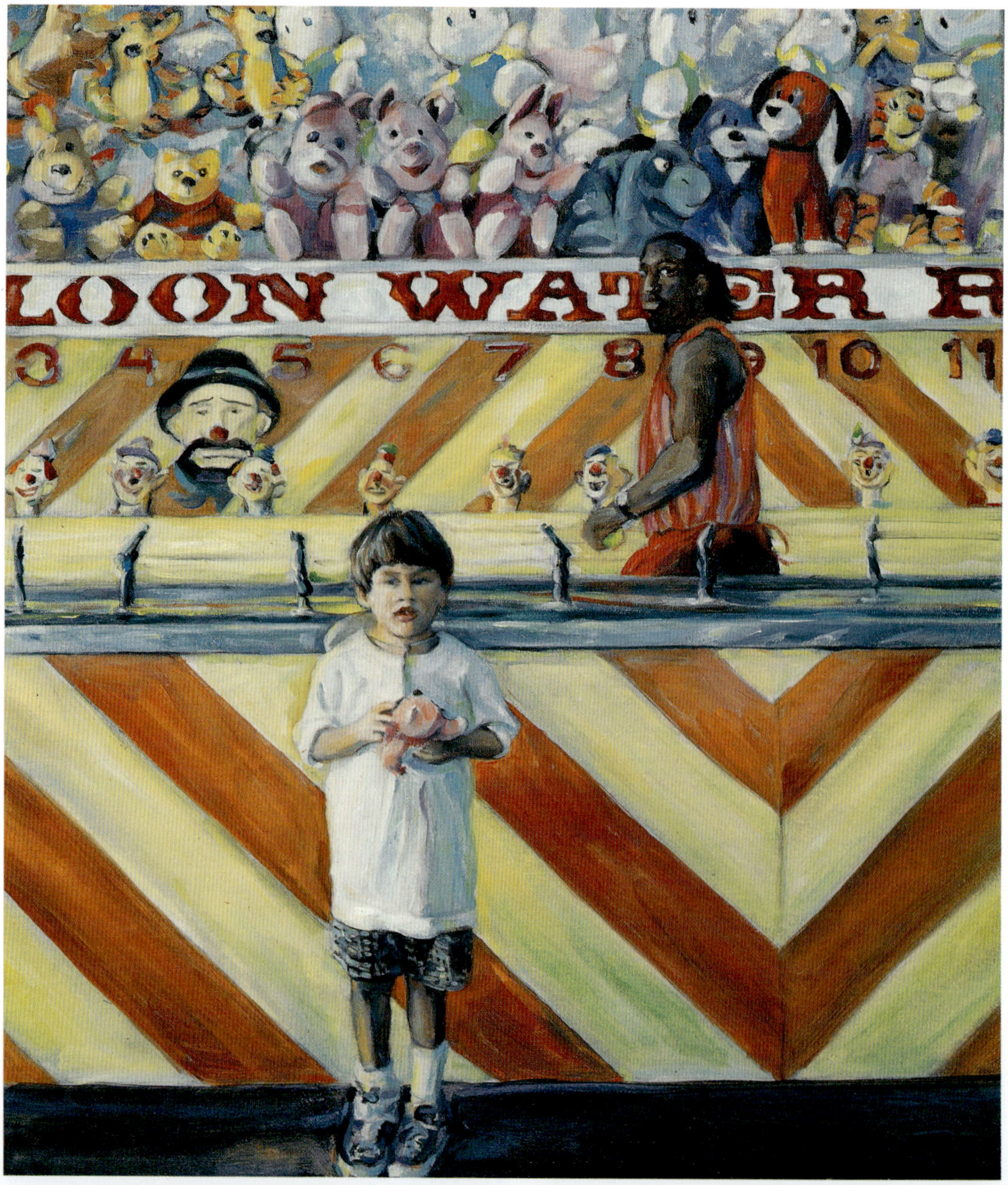

Coney Island Head Shots, oil on linen, 14" x 11", 2005.

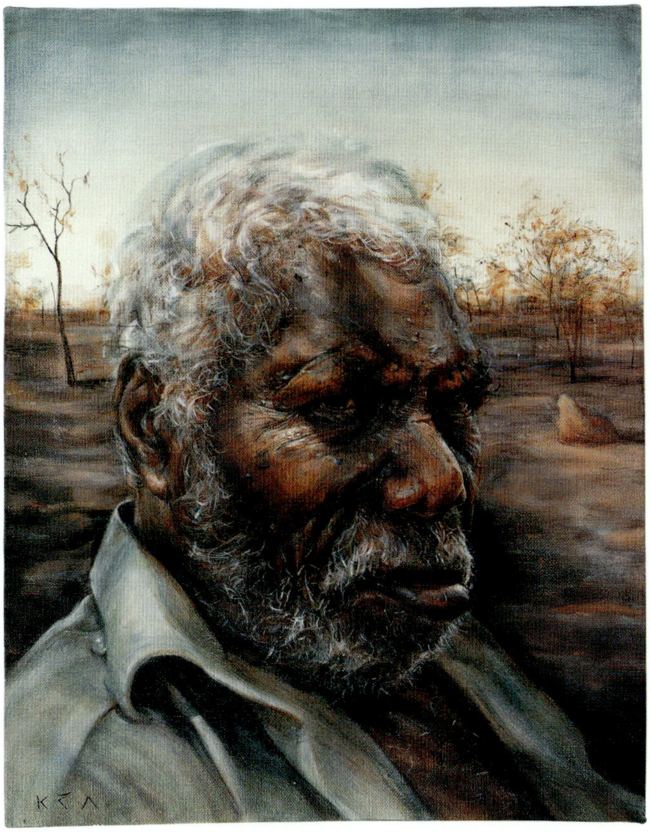

Bill Neidjie, oil on canvas, 18" x 14", 1991.

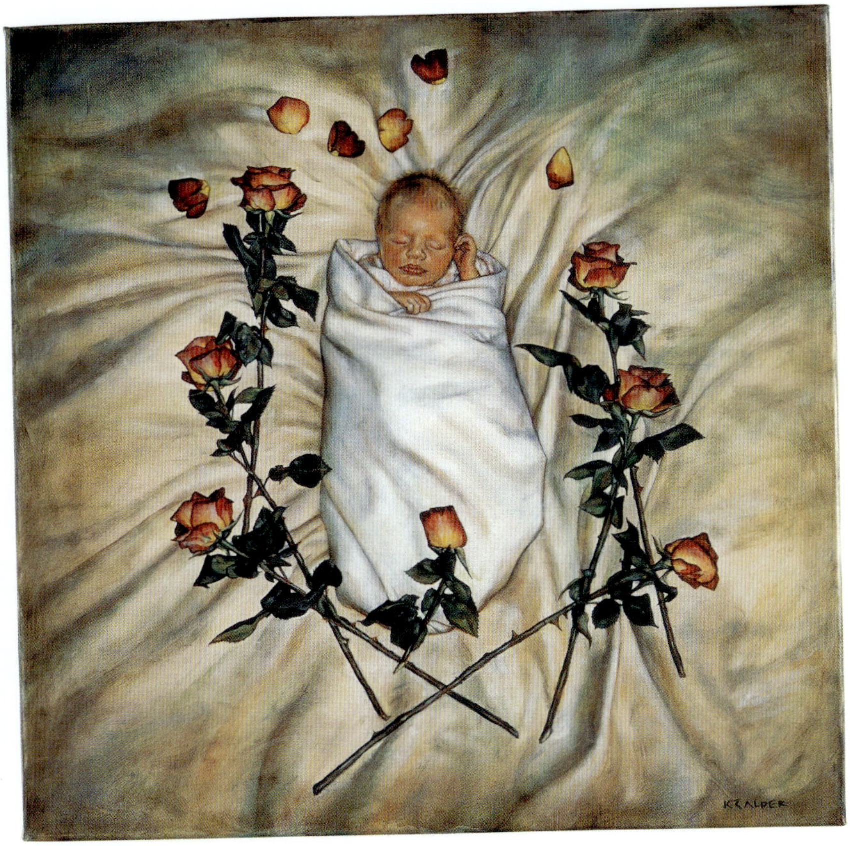

Maya Chole with Roses, oil on linen, 18" x 18", 1998.

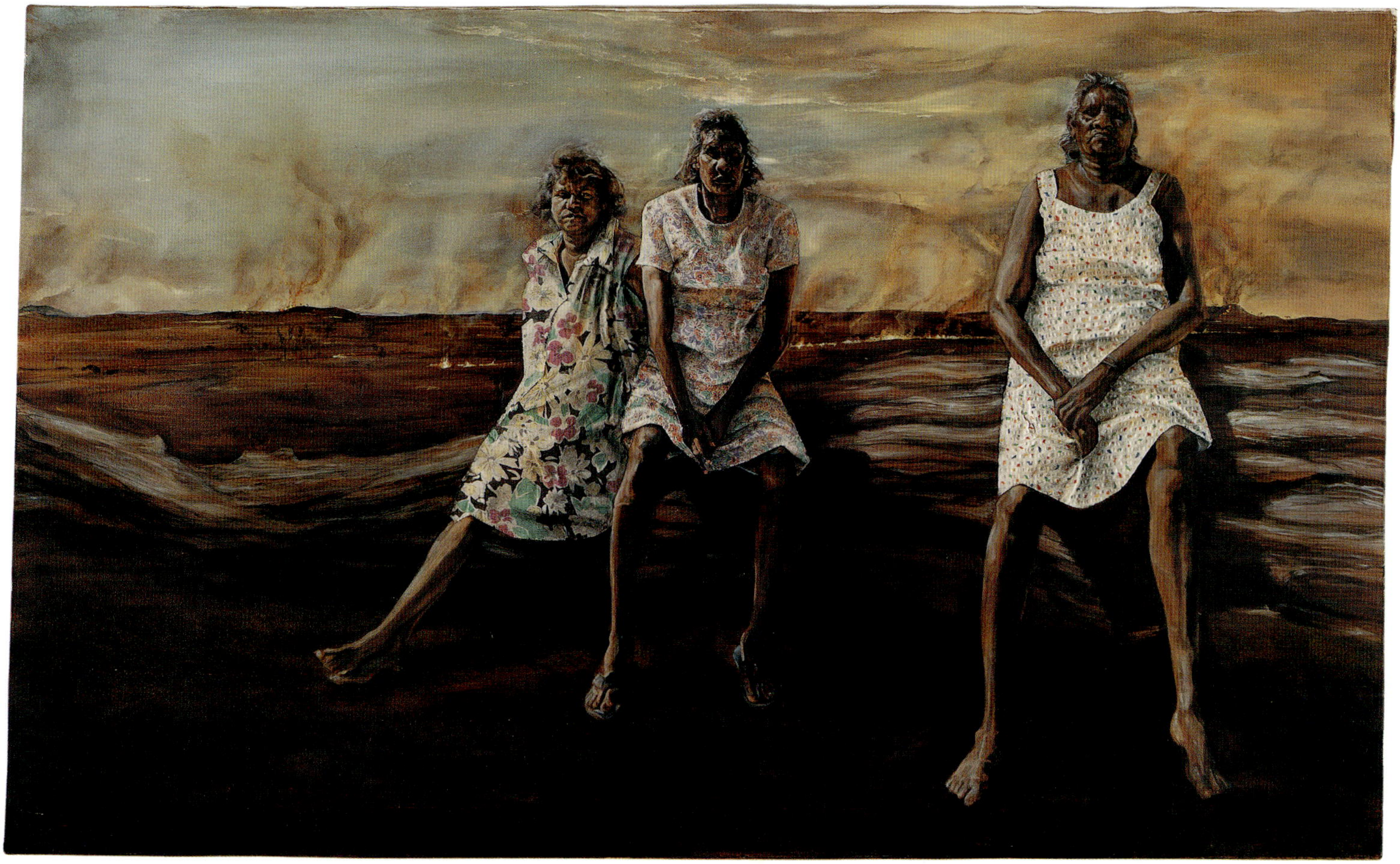

The Three Graces, oil on canvas, 31" x 49", 1991.

Emma Amos, chair of the Visual Arts Department at the Mason Gross School of the Arts at Rutgers University, often refers to her family's rich history in Atlanta, Georgia, where she started on the path to her lifelong pursuit of art. At New York University she was mentored by Hale Woodruff and invited to become the only woman member of the historic Spiral group including Romare Bearden, Richard Mayhew, Charles Alston, and other distinguished black New York artists.

Amos's use and combining of many techniques, mediums, and materials reflect her eight years as a designer/weaver for Dorothy Tiebes, and much time printmaking at Robert Blackburn's workshop.

She has sought to heighten awareness in the viewer of questions relating to gender, color, and other issues of identity, often by juxtaposing apparently incongruous elements. Combining traditional western materials with African textiles, she creates banner-like canvases as well as a series of historic portraits, numerous satiric portraits, and ironic, playful, or otherwise didactic paintings and prints.

Winner of many awards and honors, Amos's works are found in major museums and collections, including New York's Museum of Modern Art. She is represented by Chelsea's Flomenhaft Gallery.

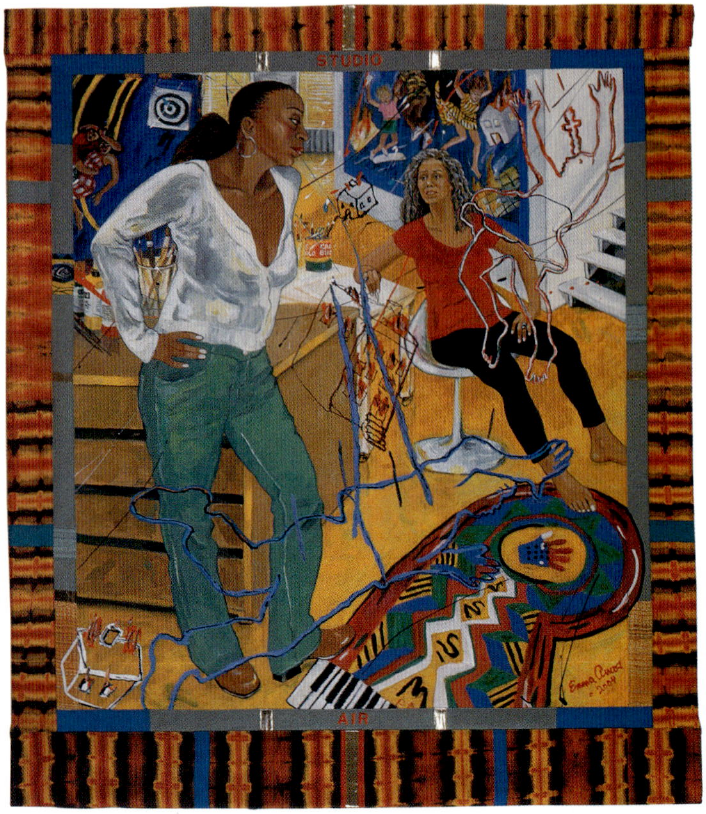

Studio Air, acrylic on linen canvas, African fabric borders, 72" x 61", 2004. *All art © Emma Amos/Licensed by VAGA, New York, NY.*

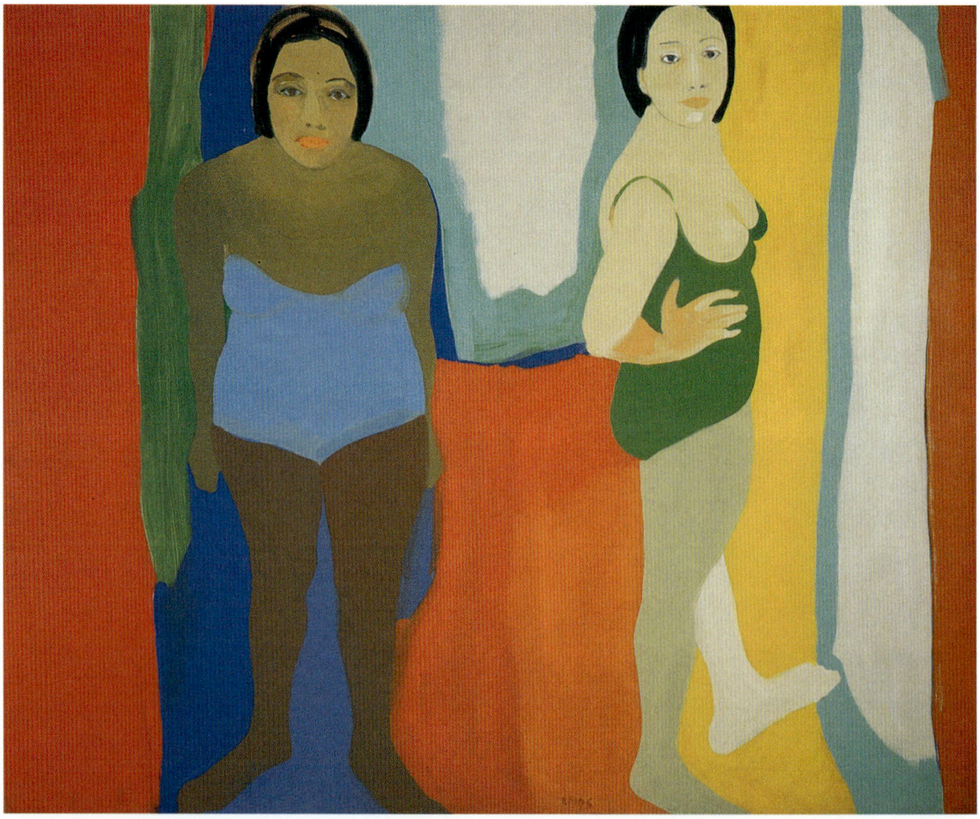

Two Standing Women, oil on linen, 50" x 60", 1966.

Emma Amos

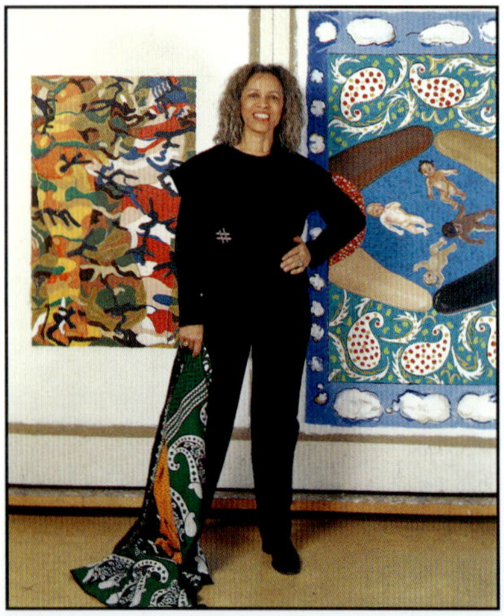

Photograph by Becket Logan.

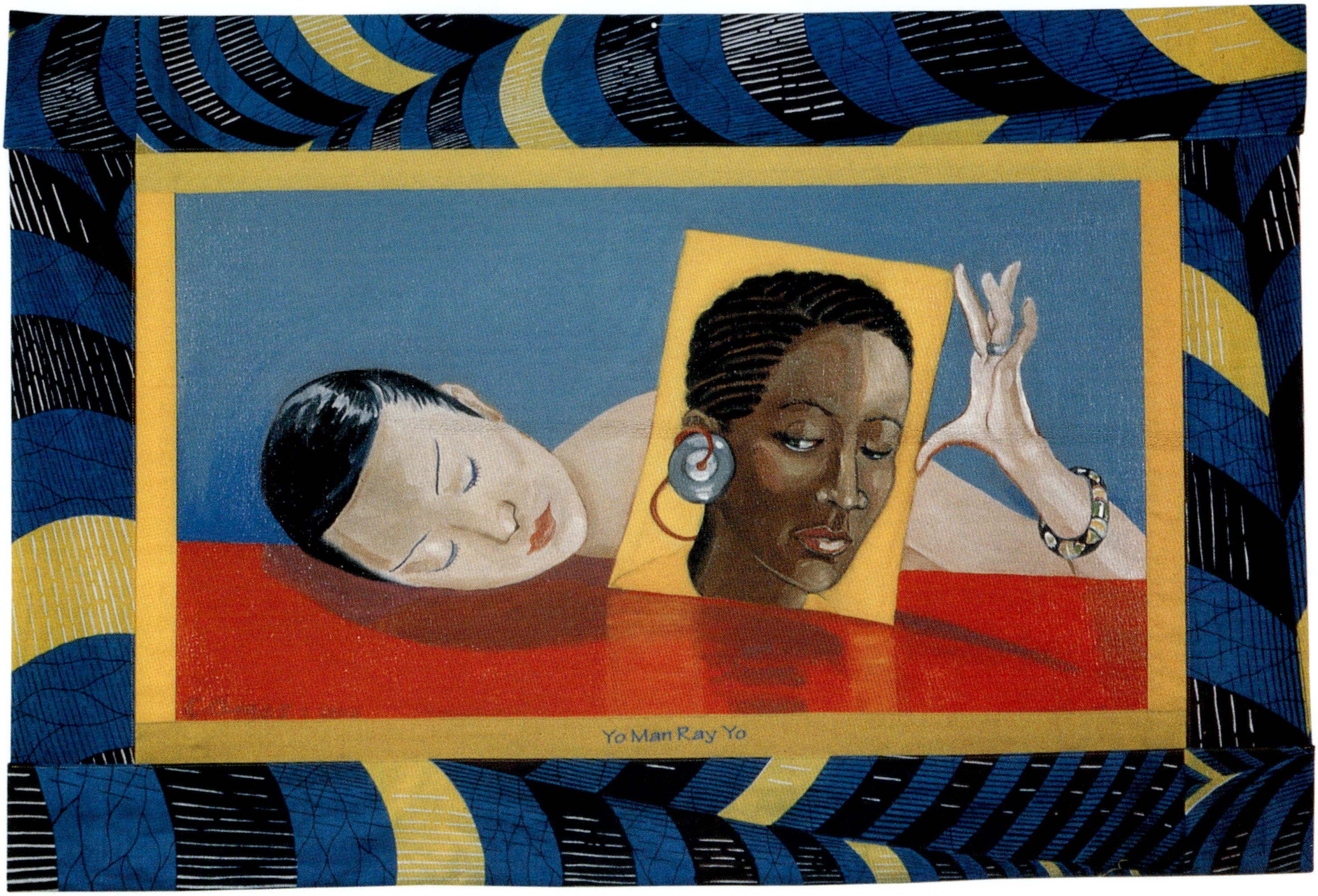

Yo Man Ray Yo, oil on African fabrics, 31.5" x 47", 2000.

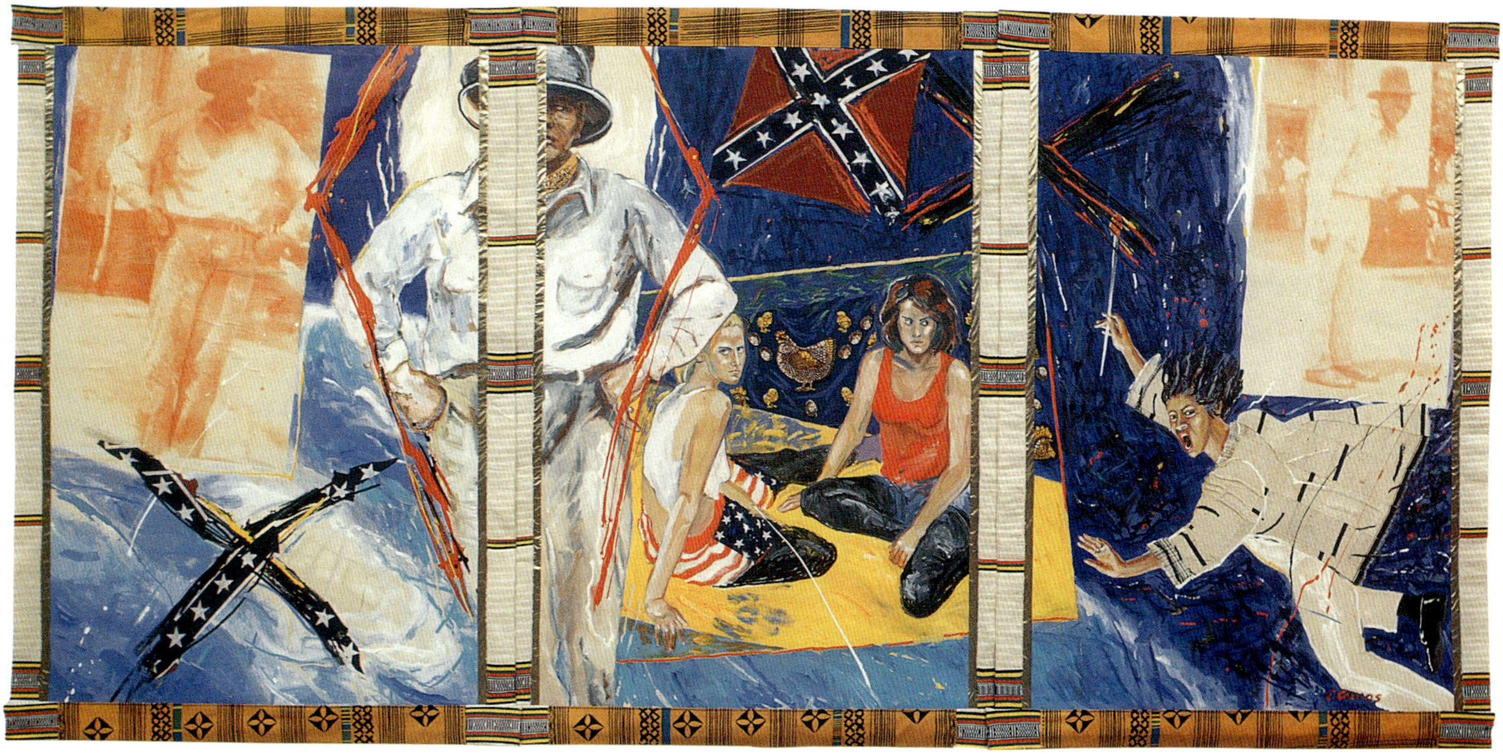

The Overseer, acrylic/linen canvas, with African fabric and borders, 84" x 168" triptych, 1992.

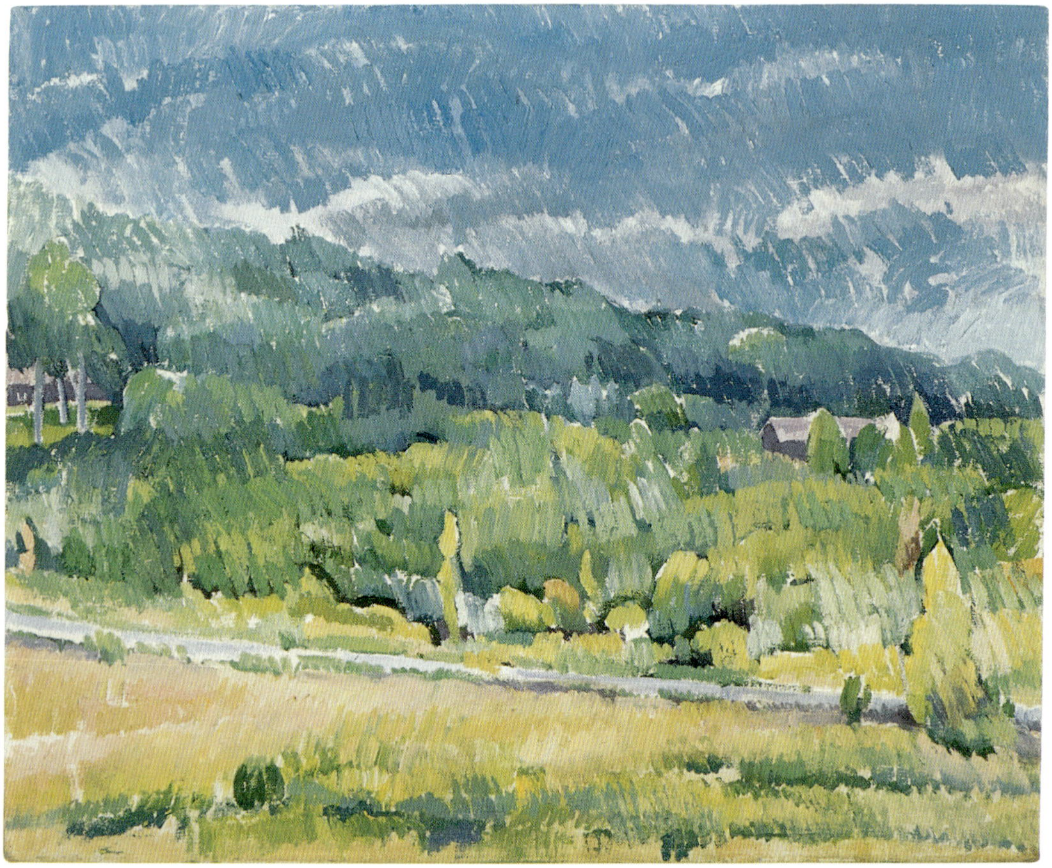

Putney Road 2, oil on canvas, 22" x 24", 1987.

Arthur Anderson

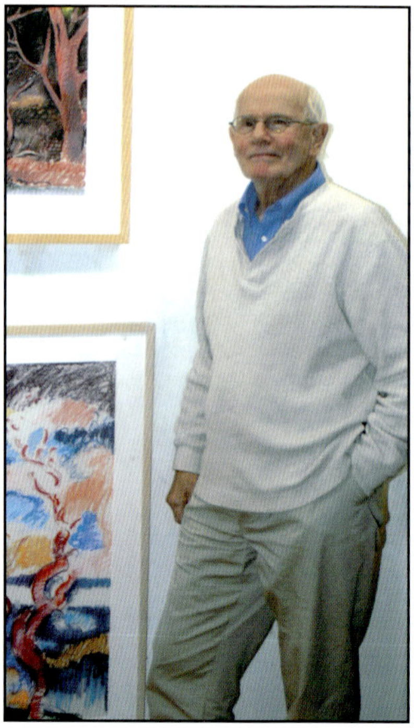

Courtesy of the artist.

Arthur Anderson, whose lengthy academic career began with a Yale teaching fellowship, was Chairman of Fine and Performing Arts at York College of the City University of New York.

In recent years, his work has moved almost seamlessly from oils to pastels, which he considers equally to be paintings. Anderson's most recent of many exhibitions was held at the Atlantic Gallery in the Soho area of New York.

Anderson says, "a special interest in color grew out of my early years of study with Josef Albers. As assistant ... in his color and drawing classes, I was encouraged to find decisive color qualities in whatever I, myself, drew. It was the start of a lengthy pursuit. Discrete tree structures ultimately captured my interest ... making up images ... that had a lively interplay of stems and intervals ... I resorted mostly to short 'alla prima' strokes with ... white ground showing ... This maintained an important sense of energy and freshness."[4]

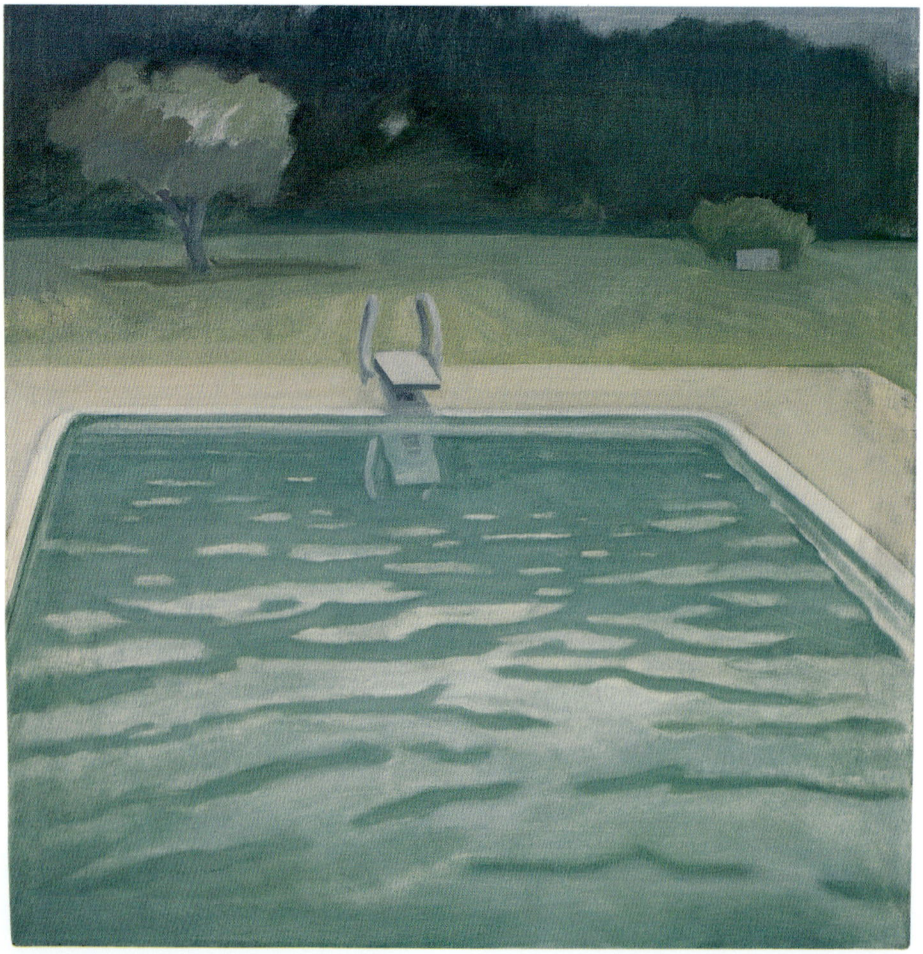

Yaddo Pool, oil on canvas, 30" x 27", 1978.

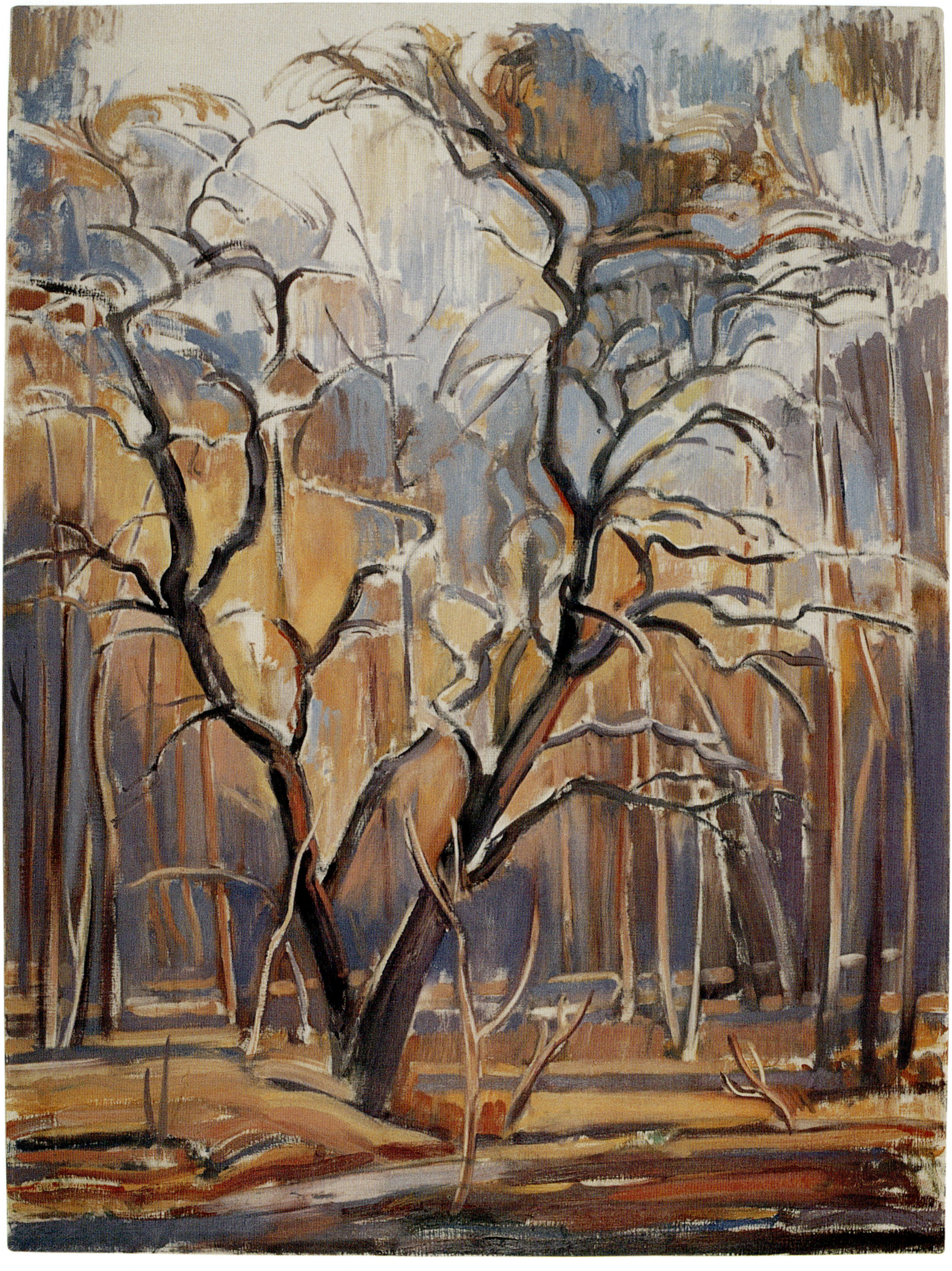

Oscawanna Tree, oil on canvas, 54" x 40", 1989.

Lennart Anderson

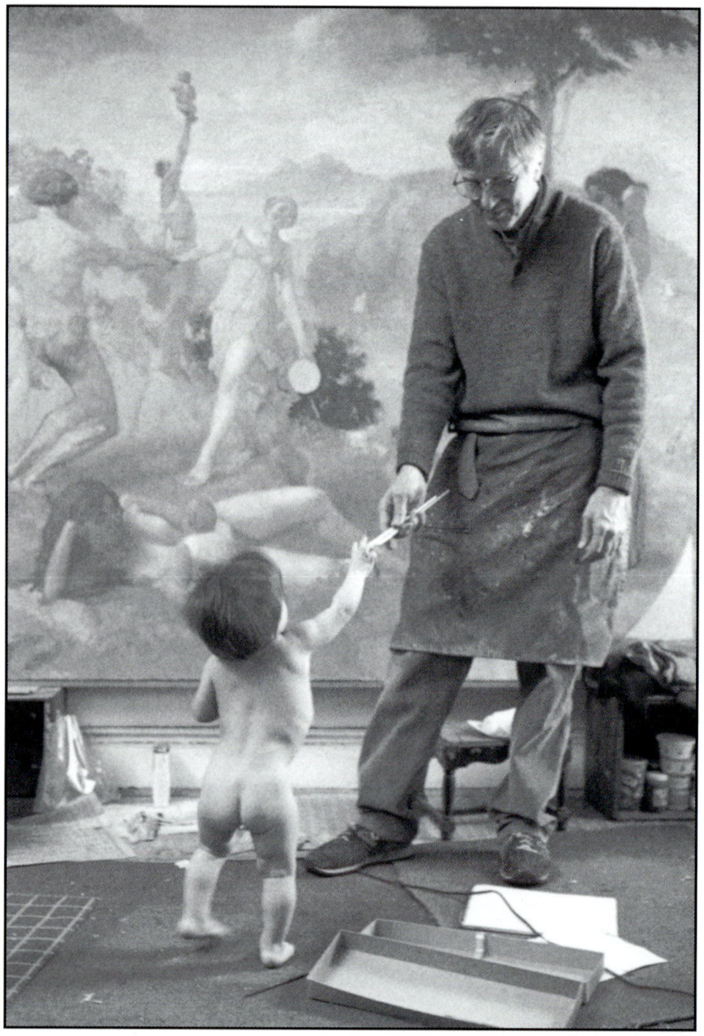

The artist with daughter, Jeanette. *Photograph by Barbara Anderson.*

Lennart Anderson, who studied at the Art Students League with Edwin Dickinson, has been represented by the Salander-O'Reilly Galleries for over ten years, and has a lengthy teaching history as well.

An elected member of the distinguished National Academy of Design, his works are in many collections, including the Brooklyn Museum and the Whitney Museum of American Art, and he has received awards and grants from the National Endowment for the Arts and the John Simon Guggenheim Memorial Foundation.

Anderson's classic paintings often evoke superlatives in reviews of his exhibitions: "Rarely does an artist justify the view that the act of painting is serious and grave ... The gift of art is given to few. It has been given to (him) in full measure ... the very fabric of the paint itself is elegiac ... Anderson remains a still life painter of extraordinary power ... his generation ... has produced none finer ... We are moved by the numinous quality of quotidian things ..." (Maureen Mullarkey).[5]

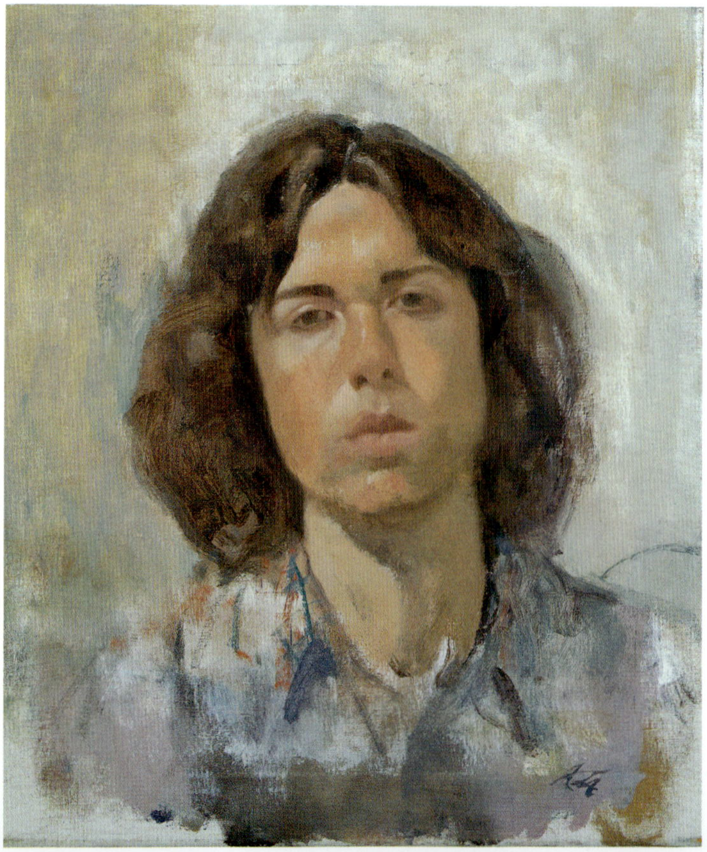

Head of Anne Devaney, oil on canvas, 18" x 15", 1981. *Courtesy of Salander-O'Reilly Galleries.*

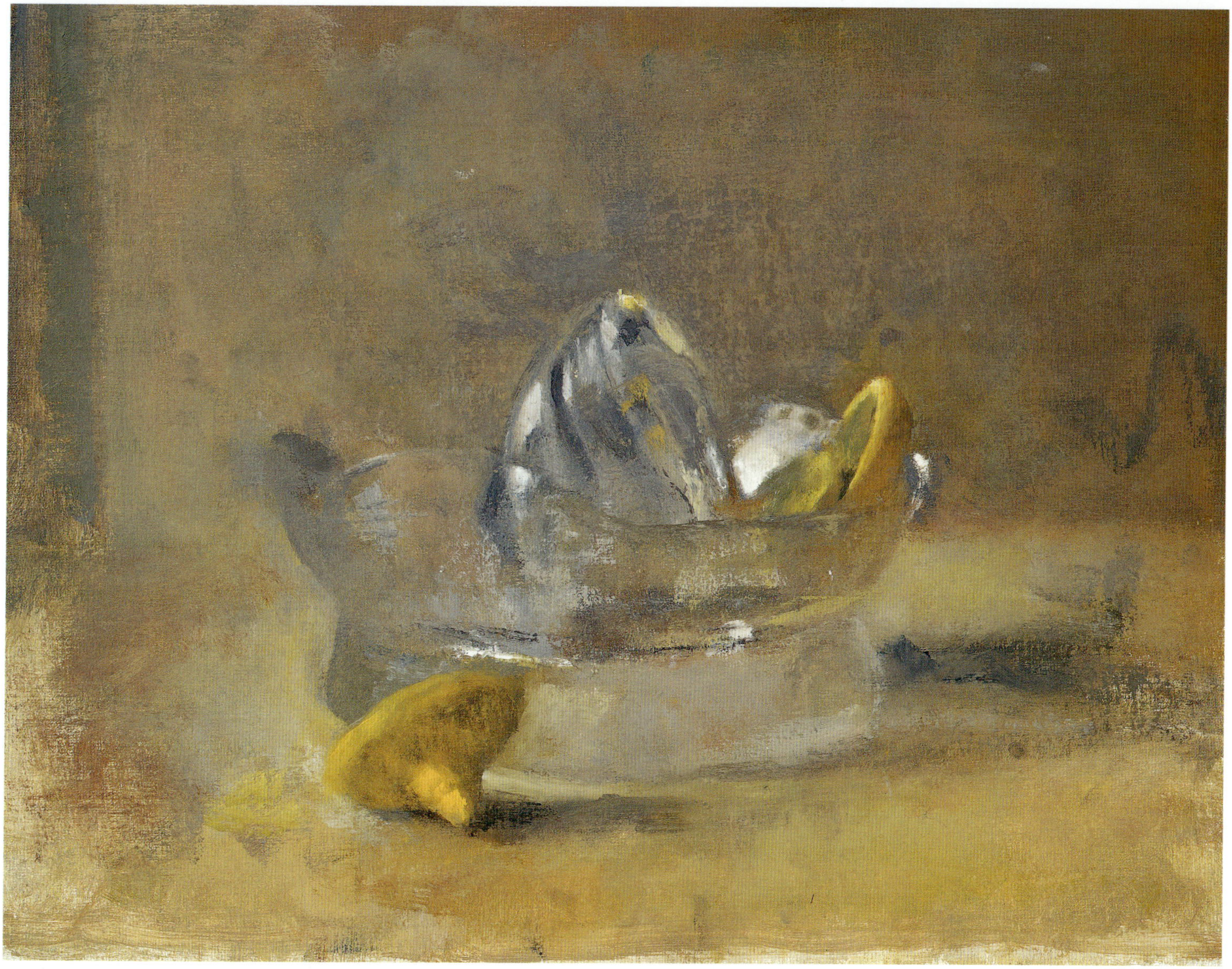

Untitled (Lemons and Juicer), oil on canvas mounted on panel, 12" x 15". *Courtesy of Salander-O'Reilly Galleries.*

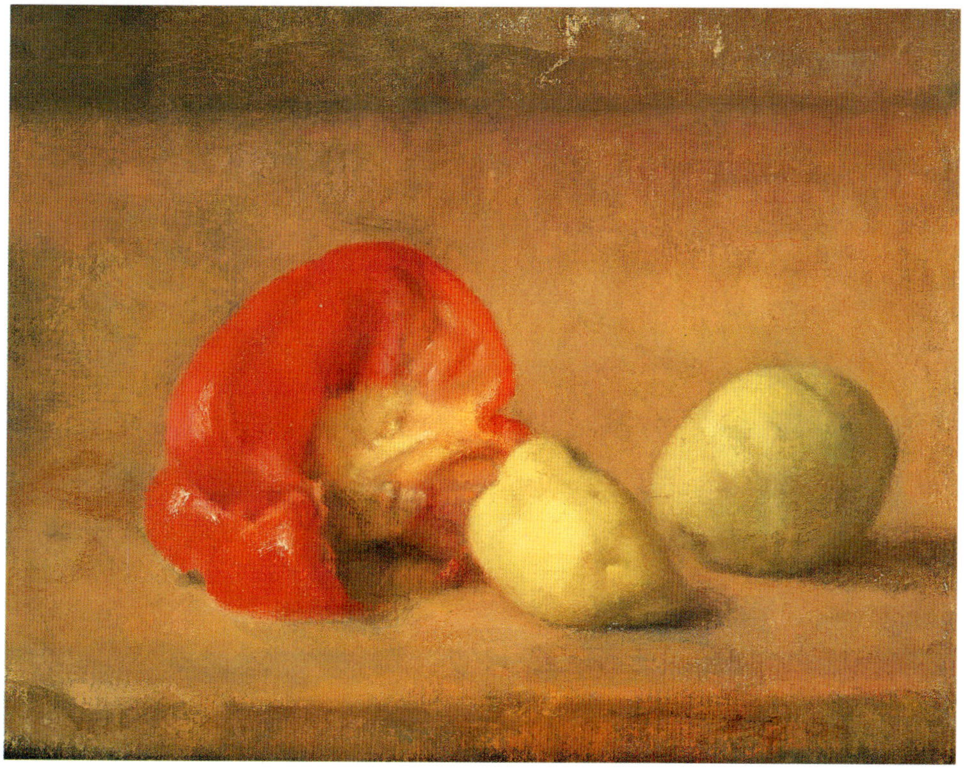

Pepper and Potatoes, oil on board, 9" x 11", 2000. *Courtesy of Salander-O'Reilly Galleries.*

Benny Andrews

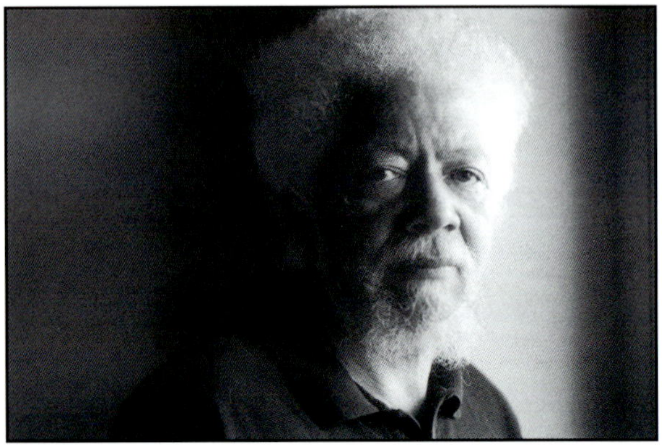

Photograph by Jerry Siegel.

Benny Andrews, whose strong figurative works often combine paint with burlap cloth and other collaged materials, has been called a quintessential American artist, taking as his subjects individuals from every part of the American fabric and history. One time Director of the Visual Arts Program at the National Endowment for the Arts, and long-time Professor of Art at New York's Queens College, Andrews remains always connected to his rural Southern roots. He exhibited works in 1991 with his folk-artist father, George.

A social activist, he has worked with many organizations and has taught art in prison programs. Rejecting efforts to categorize his work or identity, Andrews says, "I grew up in a contentious, narrow world of racism, sexism and poverty. My struggle has been to expand my horizon beyond that and not let it consume me."[6] Yet, he champions the concept of a uniquely black aesthetic, as one of many equally American components. Long affiliated with the ACA Gallery, he has works in over thirty museum collections and has received many awards and honors.

Portrait of Viola Andrews, oil and collage on canvas, 68" x 48", 1986.

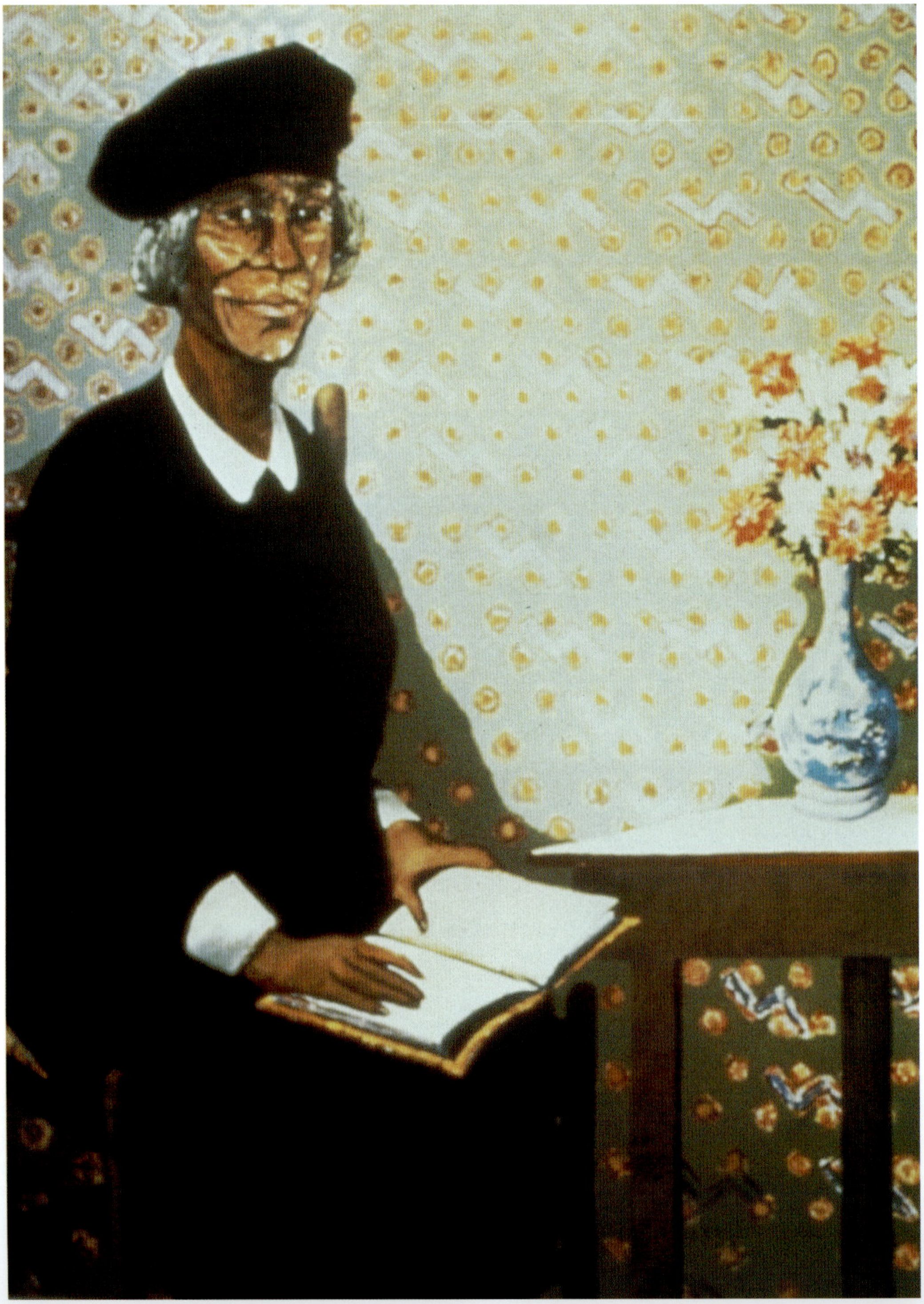

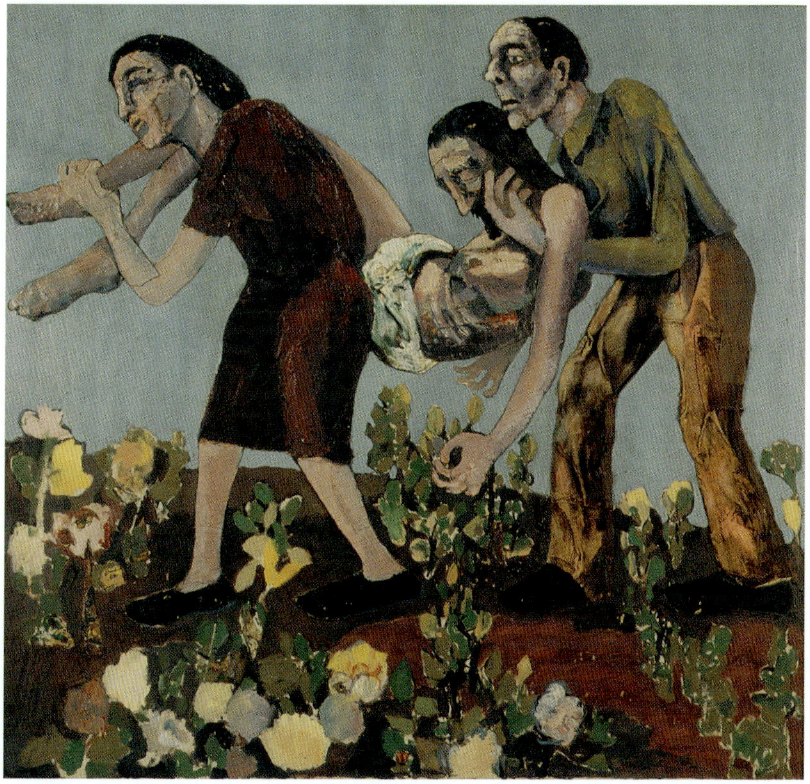

Burden, oil and collage on canvas, 50.5" x 51", 1963.

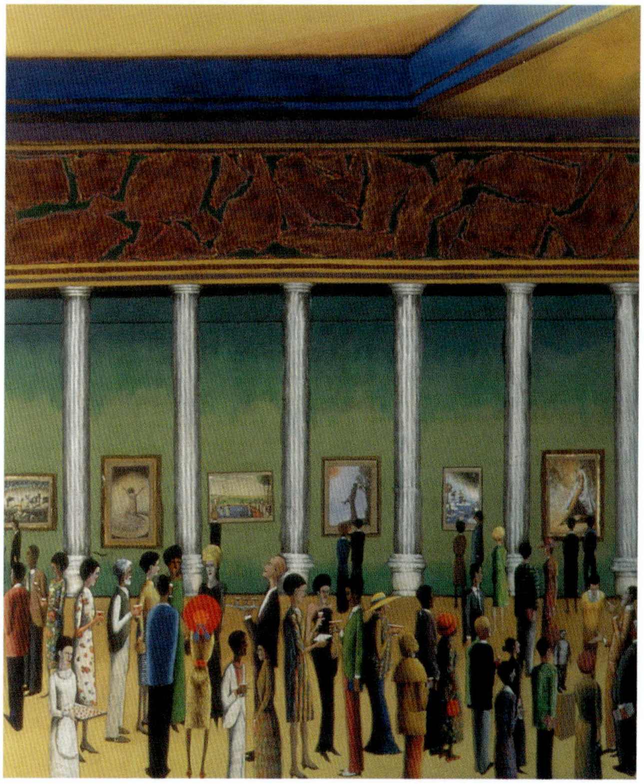

Reception (Interior Series), oil and collage on canvas, 86" x 72", 2002.

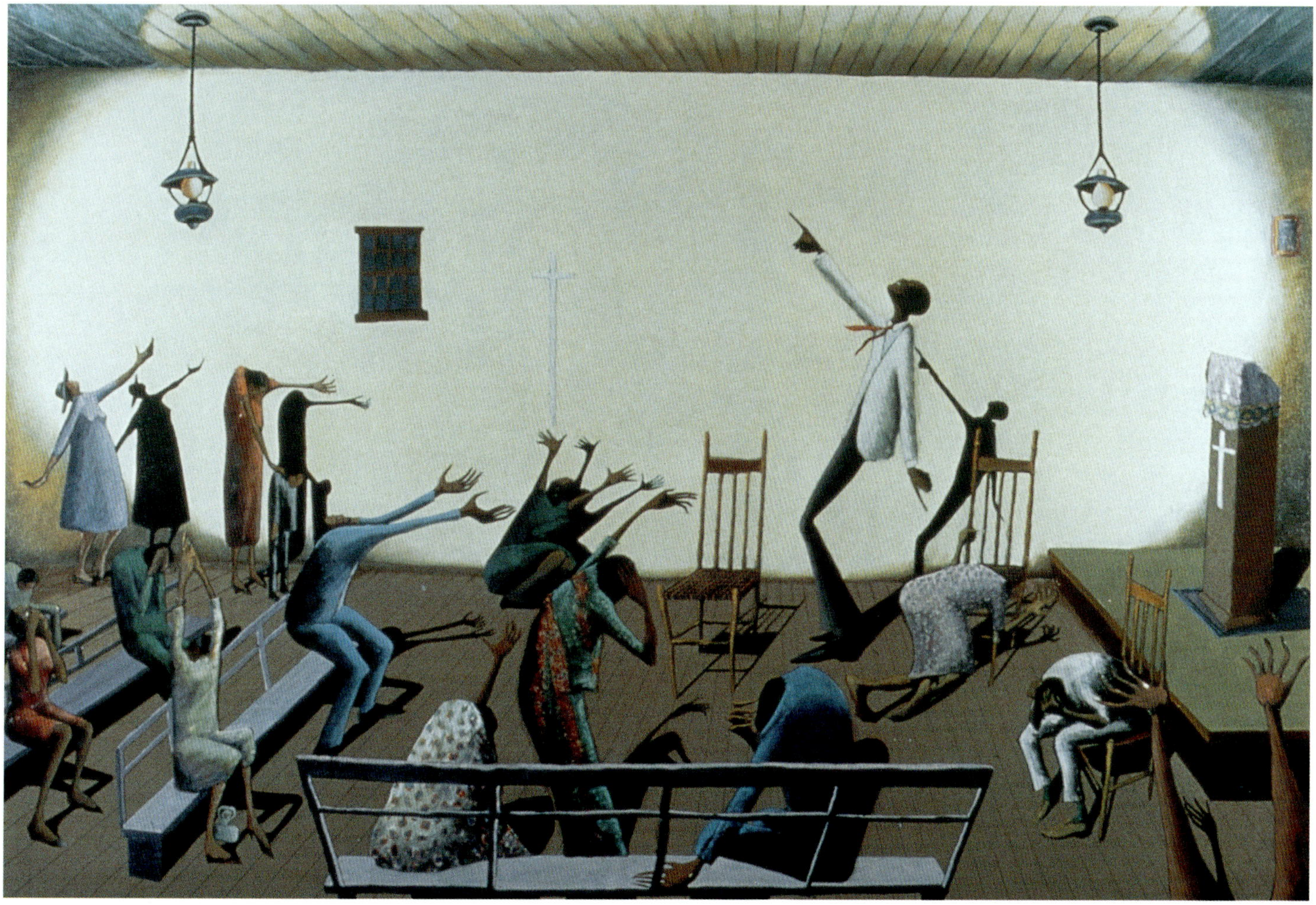

Revival Meeting (Revival Series), oil and collage on canvas, 50" x 72", 1994.

Richard Anuszkiewicz

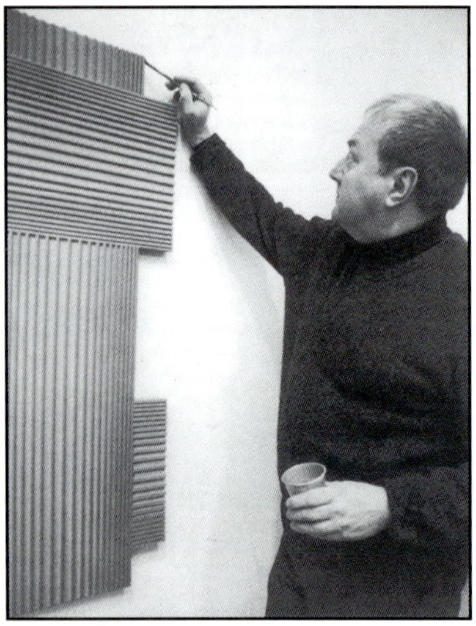

Photograph by Stephanie Anuszkiewicz.

Richard Anuszkiewicz, an elected National Academician, is often called a pioneer of color-driven, perceptual "Op" Art, having been included in the seminal 1965 Museum of Modern Art exhibition, "The Responsive Eye."

A favorite student of Josef Albers at Yale, Anuszkiewicz always keeps the lessons of the master's now historic course in color interaction in mind, although by now his personal vision and inventive creativity have moved his work far beyond presentation of classic optical effects. In scintillating lines and bands of close-valued complementary colors, Anuszkiewicz achieves a shimmer of electric vibrations, often creating the appearance of colors seen but not in actuality present on the canvas.

Over the years, Anuszkiewicz has moved from the flatness of the canvas to often three-dimensional linear and planar constructions in which unfilled spaces help to define form. His works appear in countless museums and collections, and he is represented in New York by David Findlay Jr Fine Art.

Temple of Mondrian, acrylic on canvas, 84" x 72", 1983.

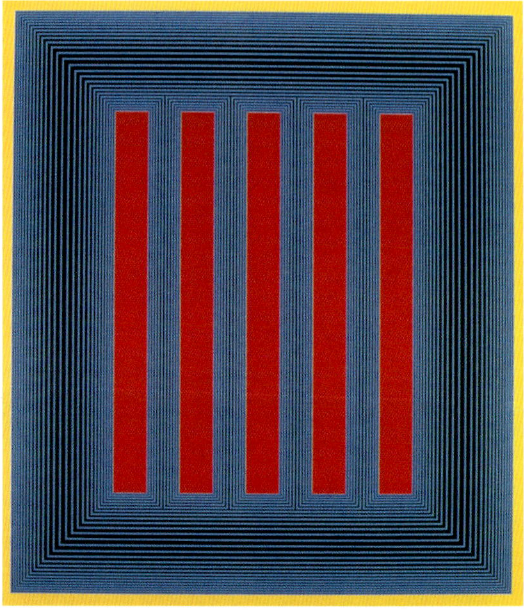

All Things Do Live in the Three, acrylic on masonite, 22" x 36", 1963. *Collection of Neil K. Rector, Columbus, Ohio. All art © Richard Anuszkiewicz/Licensed by VAGA, New York, NY.*

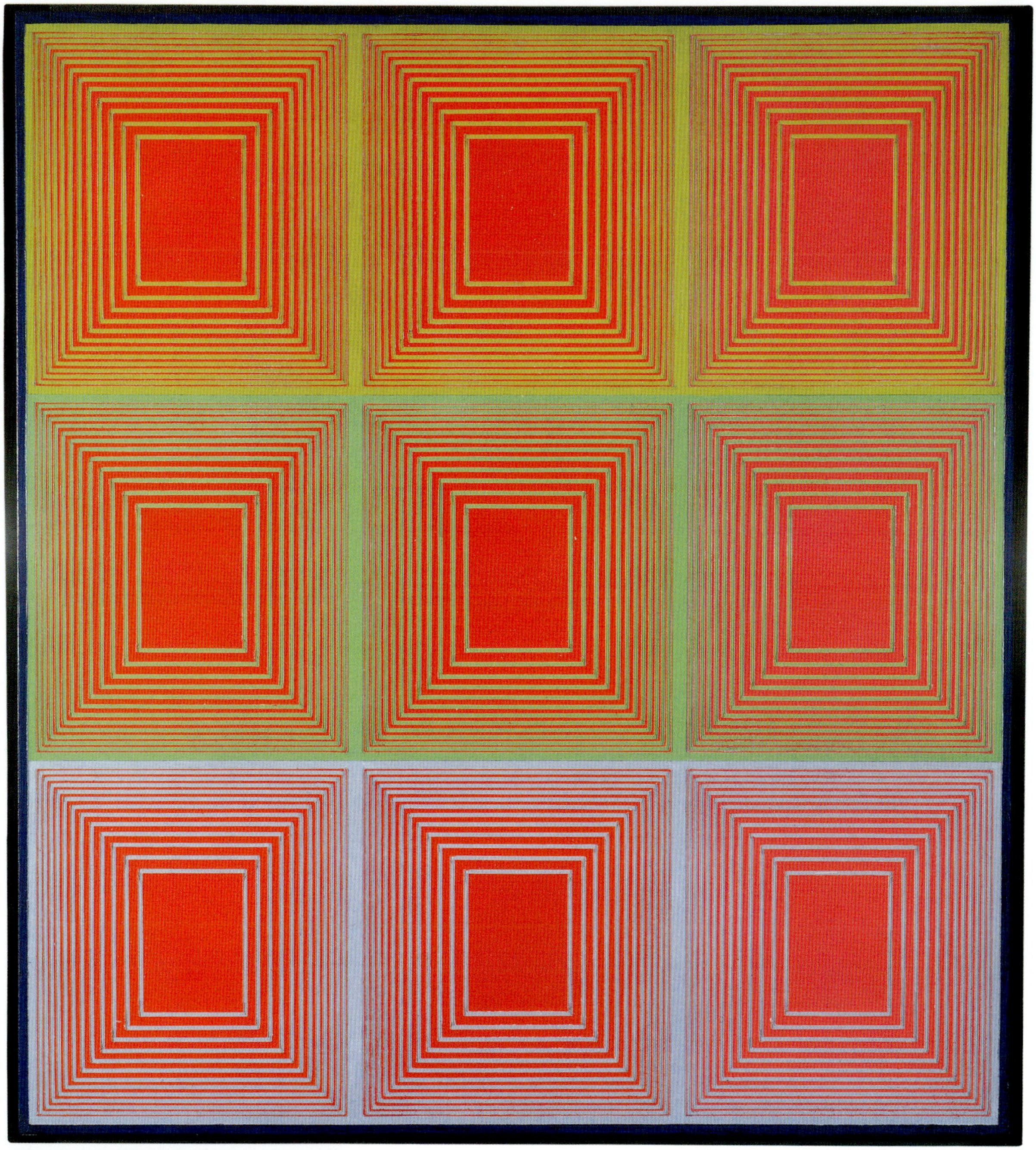

Neon Squares, acrylic on board, 17.5" x 15.5", 1969. *Collection of Steven M. and Lisa Bush Hankin, New York, NY.*

Blue Green Square, acrylic on panel, 48" x 48", 1978.

Steven Assael

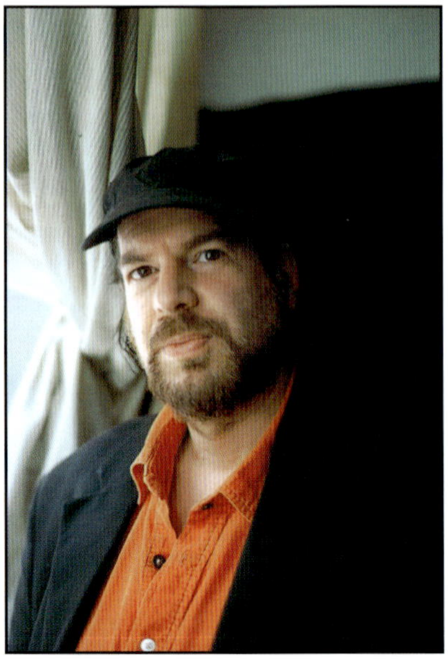

Photograph © Cynthia Dantzic.

"D", oil on linen, 62.5" x 98.25", 1998. *Collection of Seven Bridges Foundation.*

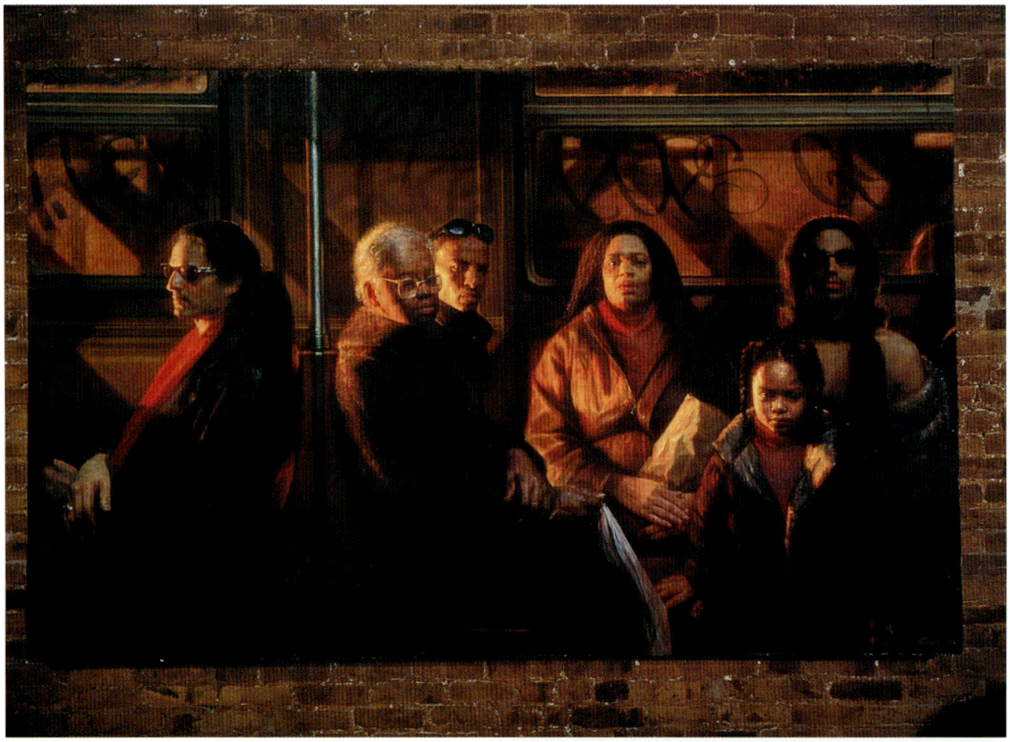

Steven Assael, who has taught for many years at New York's School of Visual Arts and New York Academy's graduate school, is a graduate of Pratt Institute. Honesty and meticulous observation characterize his studies of the figure, always painted from life, and crafted with an extraordinary draftsmanship.

Often creating mysterious suggested narratives around his intensely depicted figures, Assael says he achieves form inspired by an initial emotive response to his subject, remaining flexible through the sequential accumulation of subtle events made evident in the work.

Represented by the Forum Gallery in New York, he has a long record of exhibitions, grants, and awards, with paintings in numerous collections, including the Metropolitan Museum of Art.

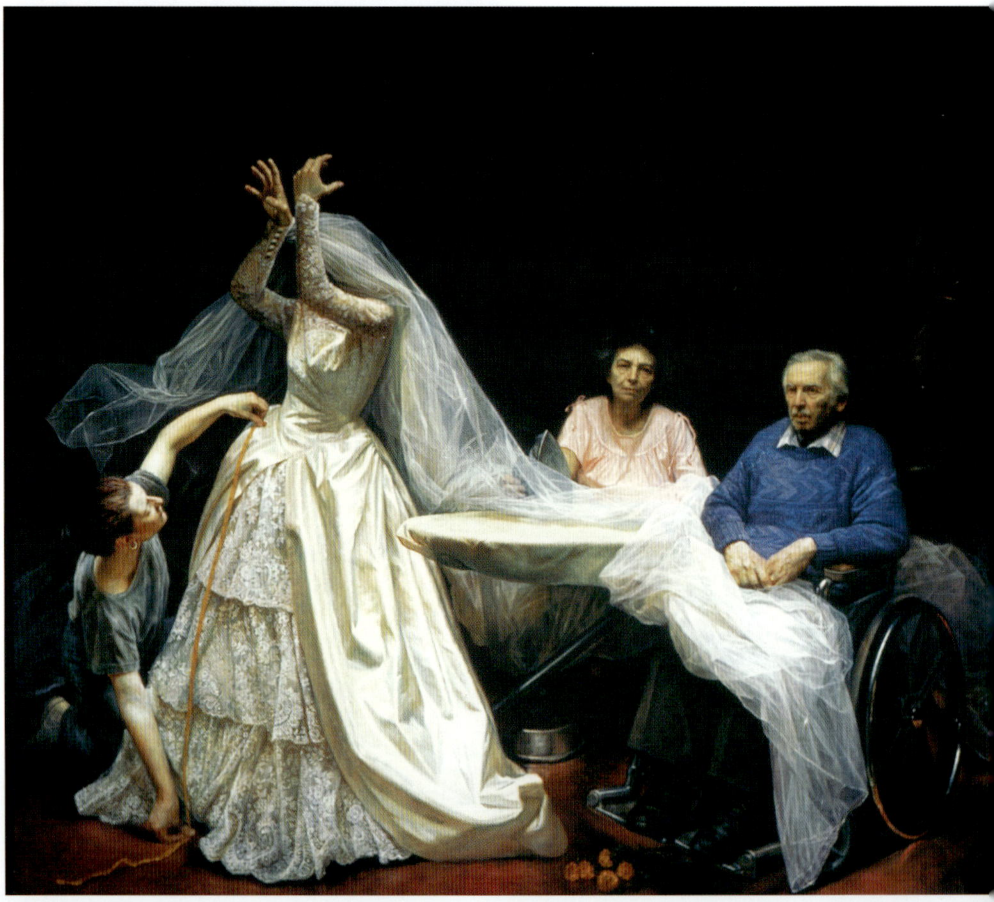

Preparation of the Bride, oil on linen, 96" x 108", 1994. *Collection of Seven Bridges Foundation.*

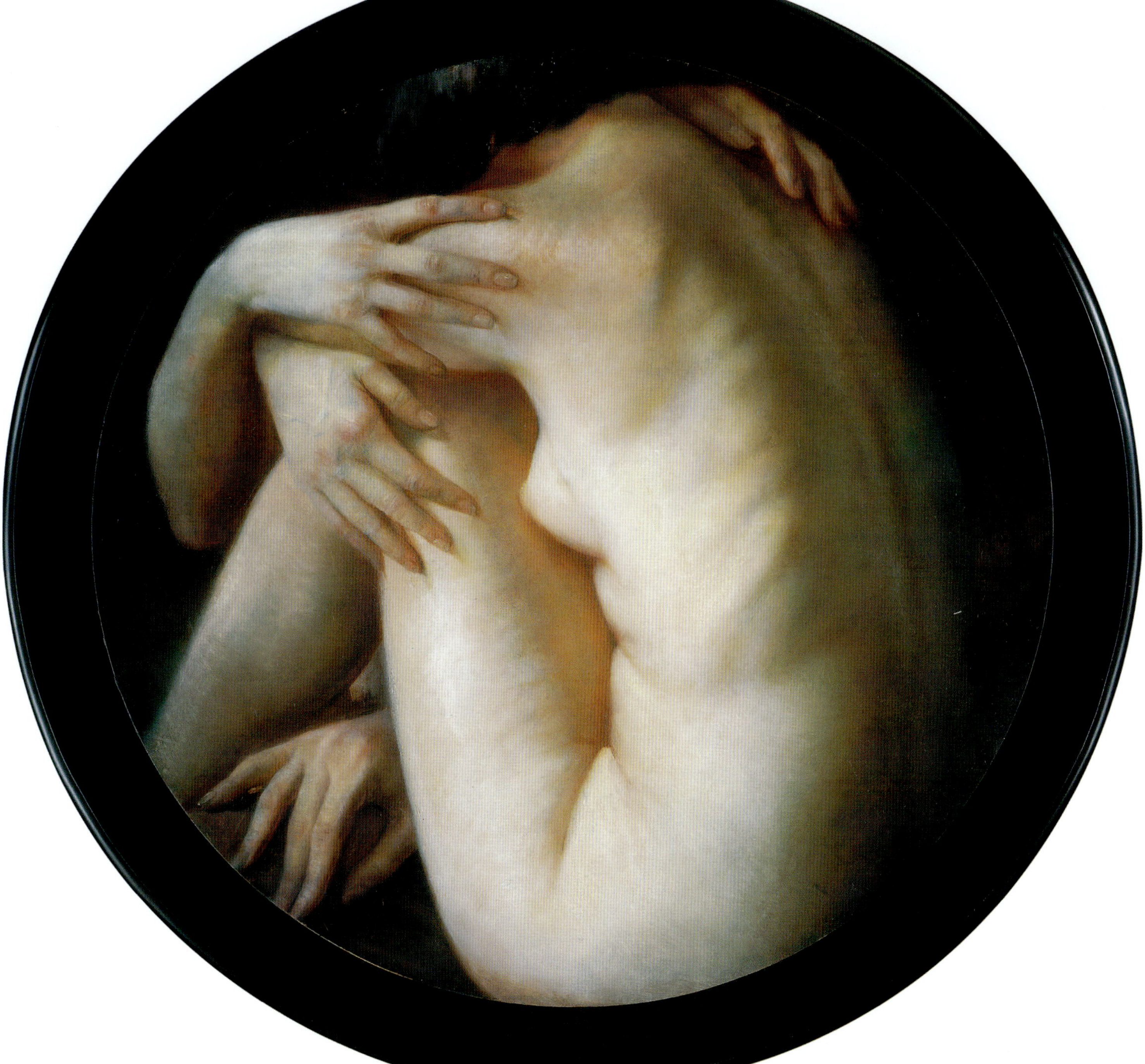

Figure 2, oil on panel, 30" diameter, 2003. *Courtesy of Forum Gallery.*

Donald Baechler

Donald Baechler, whose purposefully cartoon-like imagery and collaged surface paintings are in a class all their own, has achieved a wide international following. He maintains a New York studio and exhibits regularly at the Cheim & Read Gallery. Baechler often incorporates so-called naïve sources such as children's drawings and various folk-art traditions in his paintings.

He attended Cooper Union and the Maryland Institute College of Art, also studied in Germany, and has had works included in numerous New York and European exhibitions and collections.

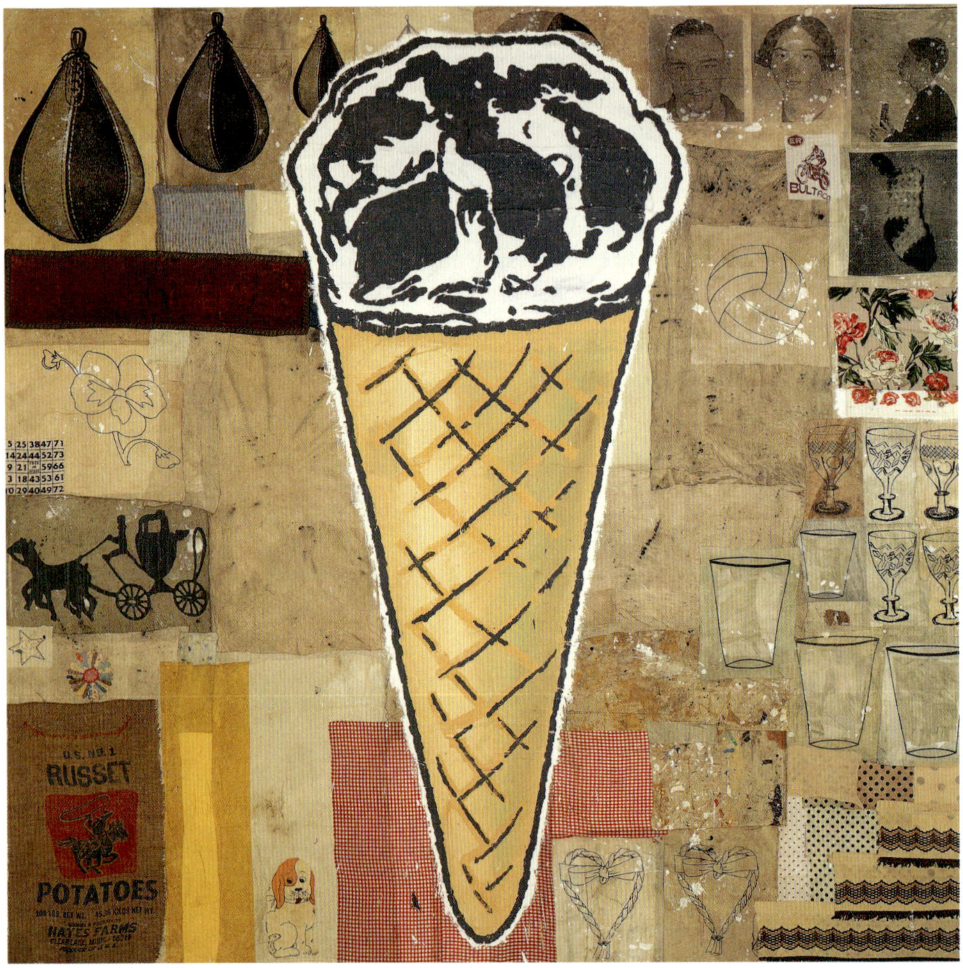

Bultaco, acrylic and fabric collage on canvas, 144" x 144", 1998. *Courtesy of Cheim & Read.*

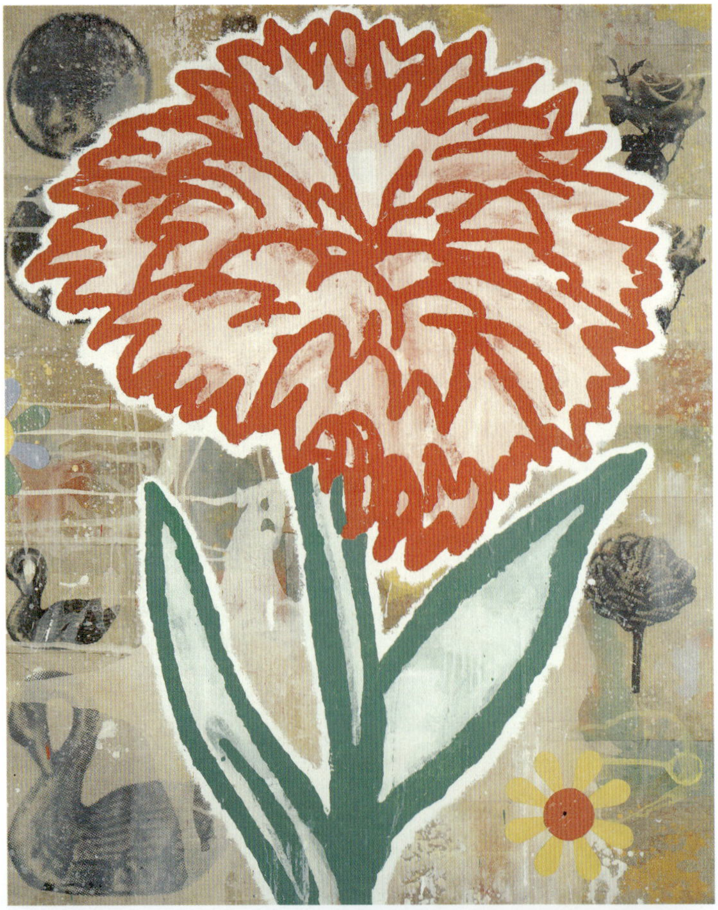

Pale Truths, acrylic and fabric collage on canvas, 100" x 80", 2004. *All art © ARS, New York. Courtesy of Cheim & Read.*

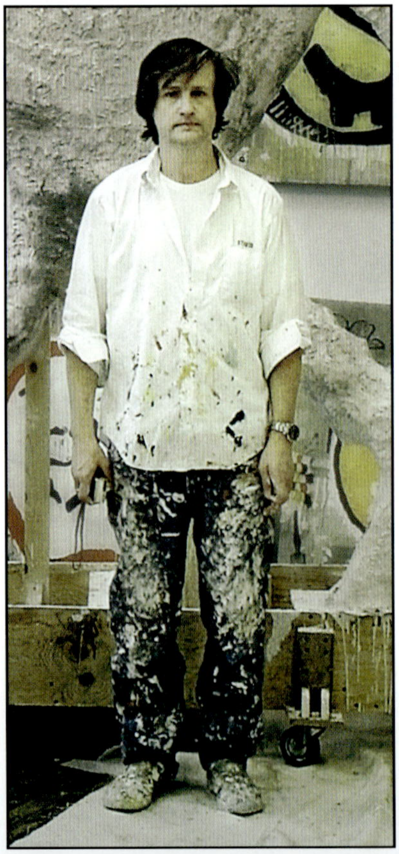

Courtesy of the artist.

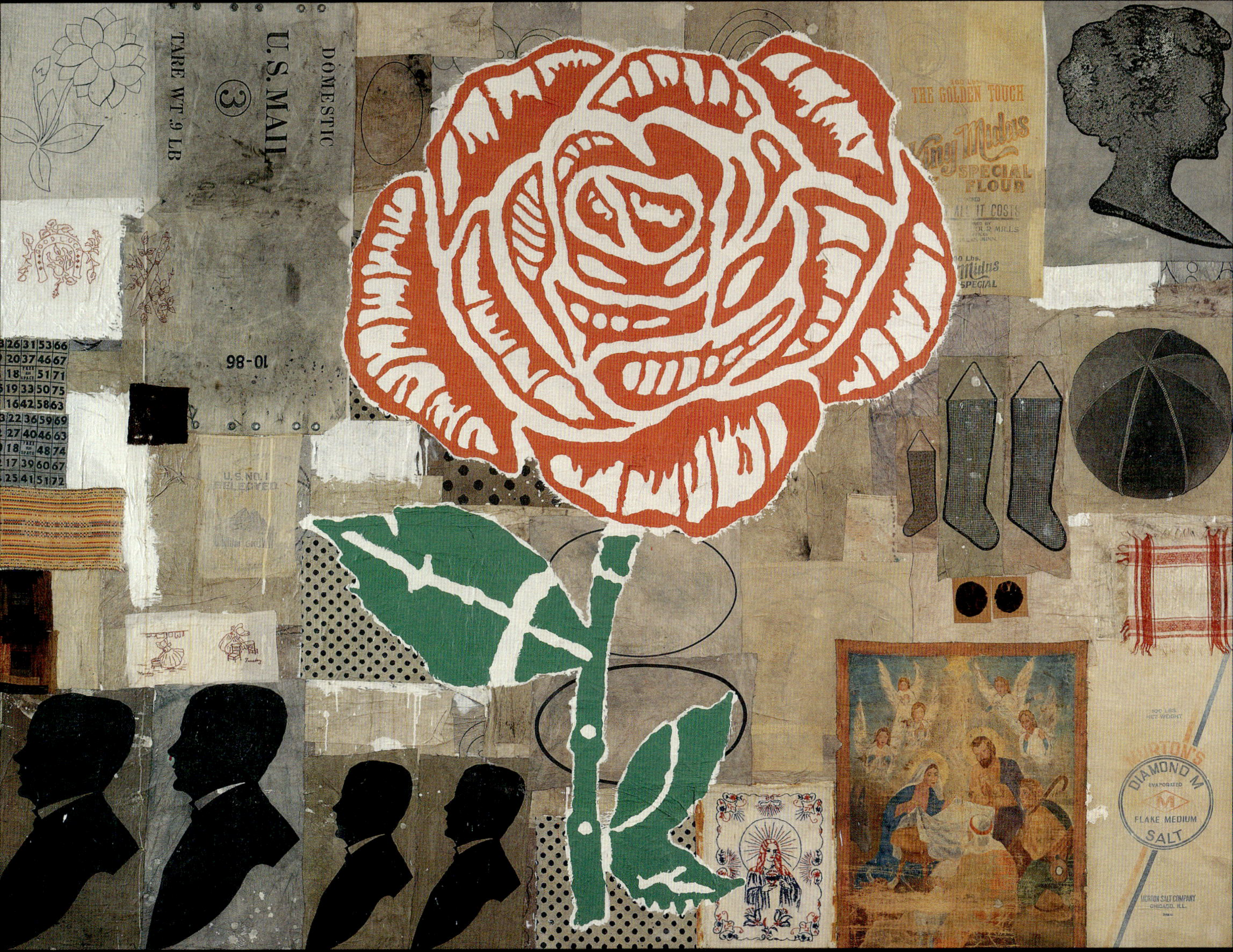

Golden Touch (The Rose of Santa Cruz), acrylic, rhoplex and collage on canvas, 111" x 144", 1995. *Courtesy of Cheim & Read.*

Richard Baker's precisely rendered paintings of unexpectedly juxtaposed foreground objects and distant landscape elements have often been called Surrealist. Indeed, noted critic for the New York Observer, Hilton Kramer, says, "At his best, he's as good as Magritte, and his wit is a lot subtler ..." Kramer calls Baker "a first rate realist."[7]

His surprising groupings of quotidian subjects have included beetles, bottles, flowers in vases, glasses of water, paper ephemera, books by modern writers, crustaceans, and the oddly balanced chunk of watermelon. His often-precarious compositions are packed into the intimate space of unusually small canvases.

Baker studied at the School of the Museum of Fine Arts in Boston and the Maryland Institute College of Art in Baltimore. A Brooklyn resident, he is represented by the Tibor de Nagy Gallery on Fifth Avenue in New York, and has had many group and solo exhibitions.

Richard Baker

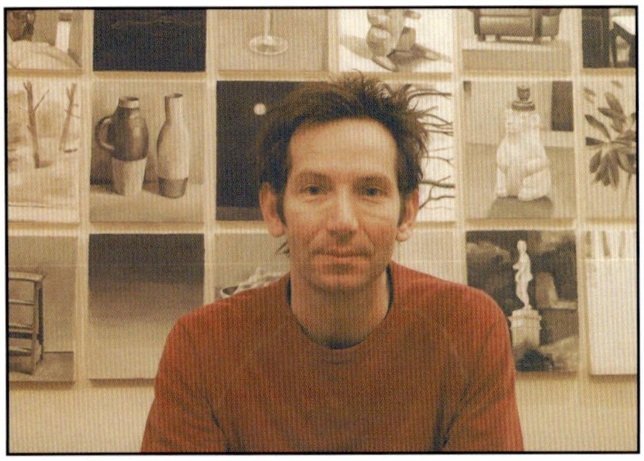

Courtesy of Tibor de Nagy Gallery.

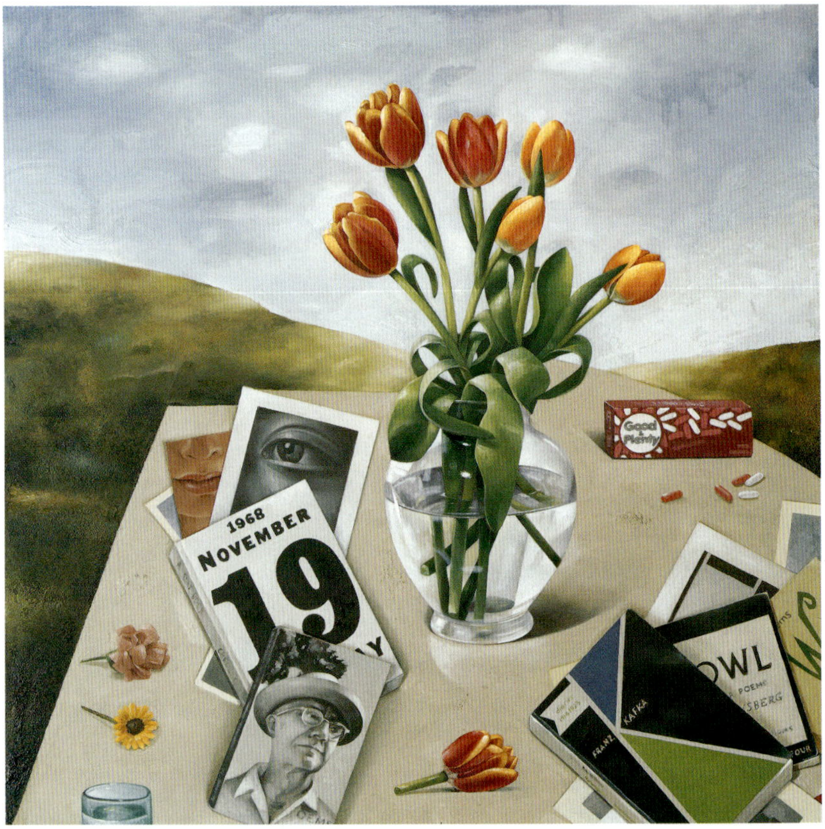

Plenty Good Scatter, oil on linen, 32" x 30", 2004. *Courtesy of Tibor de Nagy Gallery.*

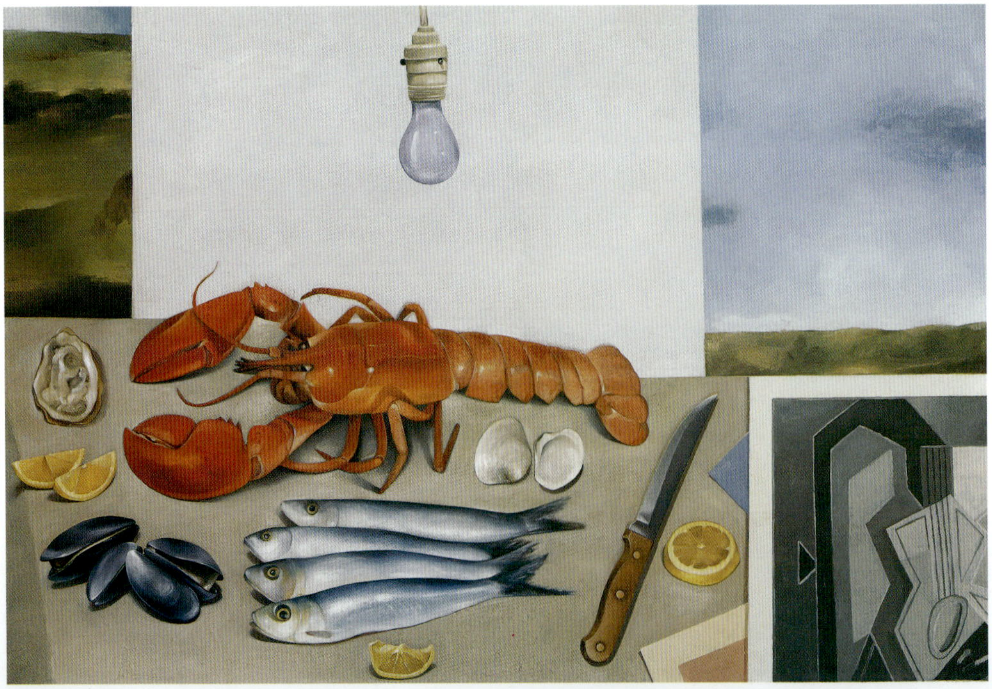

Agreeable View, oil on linen, 24.5" x 35.25", 2005. *Courtesy of Tibor de Nagy Gallery.*

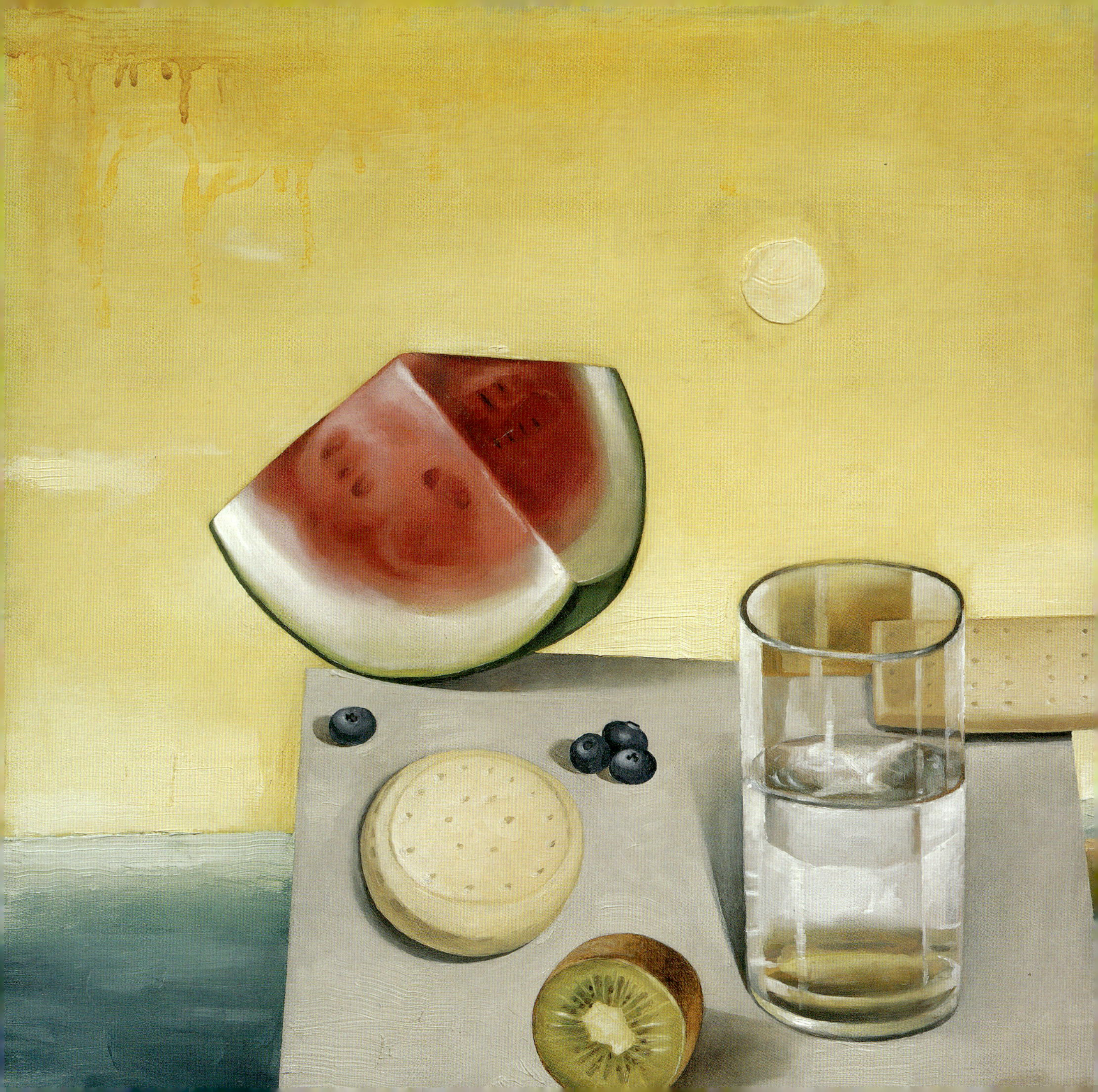

Will Barnet

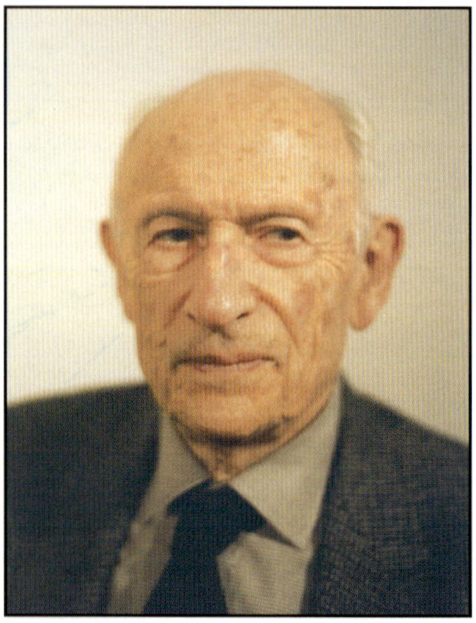

Photograph © Cynthia Dantzic.

Will Barnet, whose career extends to his work in the 1930s with the WPA's New York Region Graphic Arts Projects, taught first at the New School for Social Research, then for over thirty years as Professor of Painting at the Cooper Union and at the Art Students League.

Winning numerous awards for painting, drawing, woodcuts, and other prints, Barnet has also taught and lectured far and wide, from Saskatchewan, Canada to the Vatican Museum in Rome. His works are in virtually every major museum and collection. Elected to the National Academy of Design, the American Academy, and the Institute of Arts and Letters, he has resided at the National Arts Club in Gramercy Park for many years.

Barnet's early studies at the School of the Museum of Fine Arts in Boston with Philip Hale and at the Art Students League with Stuart Davis made a lasting impression. He says, "I still believe very strongly in training. There is an interesting book a friend of mine is writing on Picasso and his training when he was twelve. You think you could have had Picasso without his severe training—forget it."[8]

Barnet, too, shows a lengthy journey through many styles and ideas, from abstraction to a lyrical, curvilinear figurative simplicity, often incorporating family members and the ever-present feline companion.

His work is shown at the Babcock Galleries.

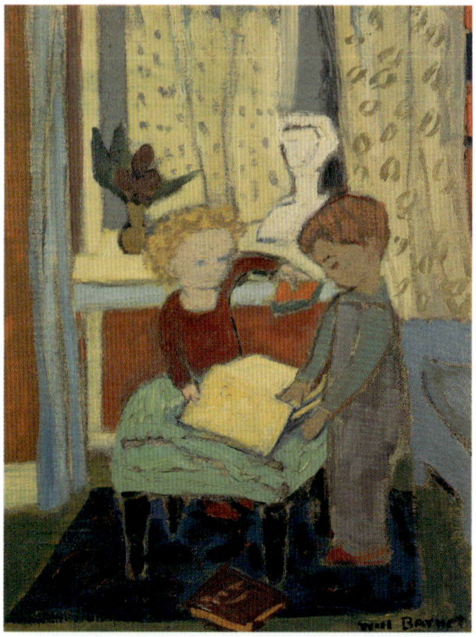

The Scrap Book, oil on canvas, 24" x 18", c.1947. *Courtesy of Babcock Galleries.*

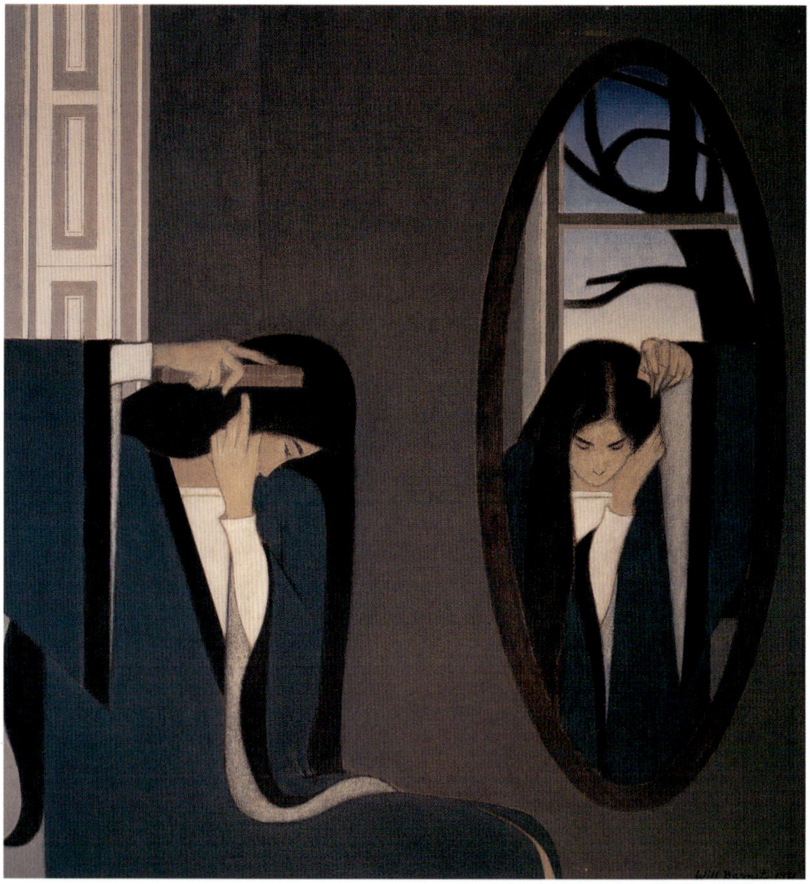

Combing, oil on canvas, 46" x 35.5", 1981. *Courtesy of Babcock Galleries.*

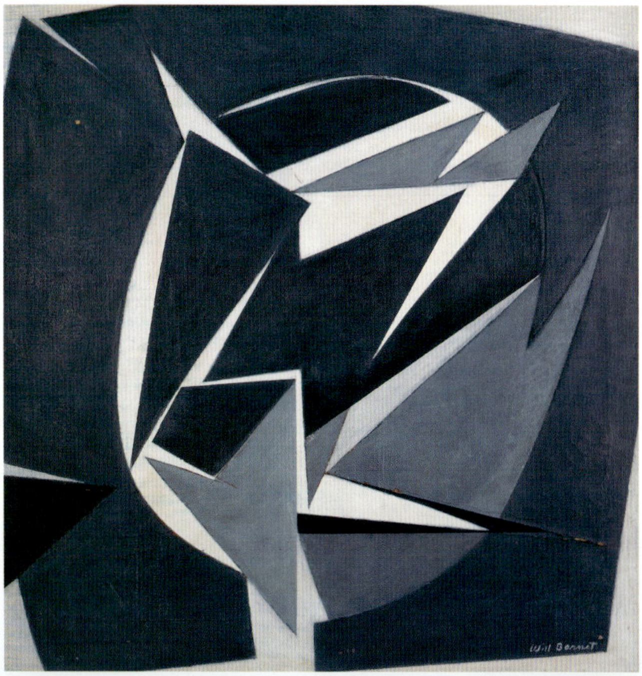

Air Traffic (Grey Geometric), oil on canvas, 27" x 26", 1958. *Courtesy of Babcock Galleries.*

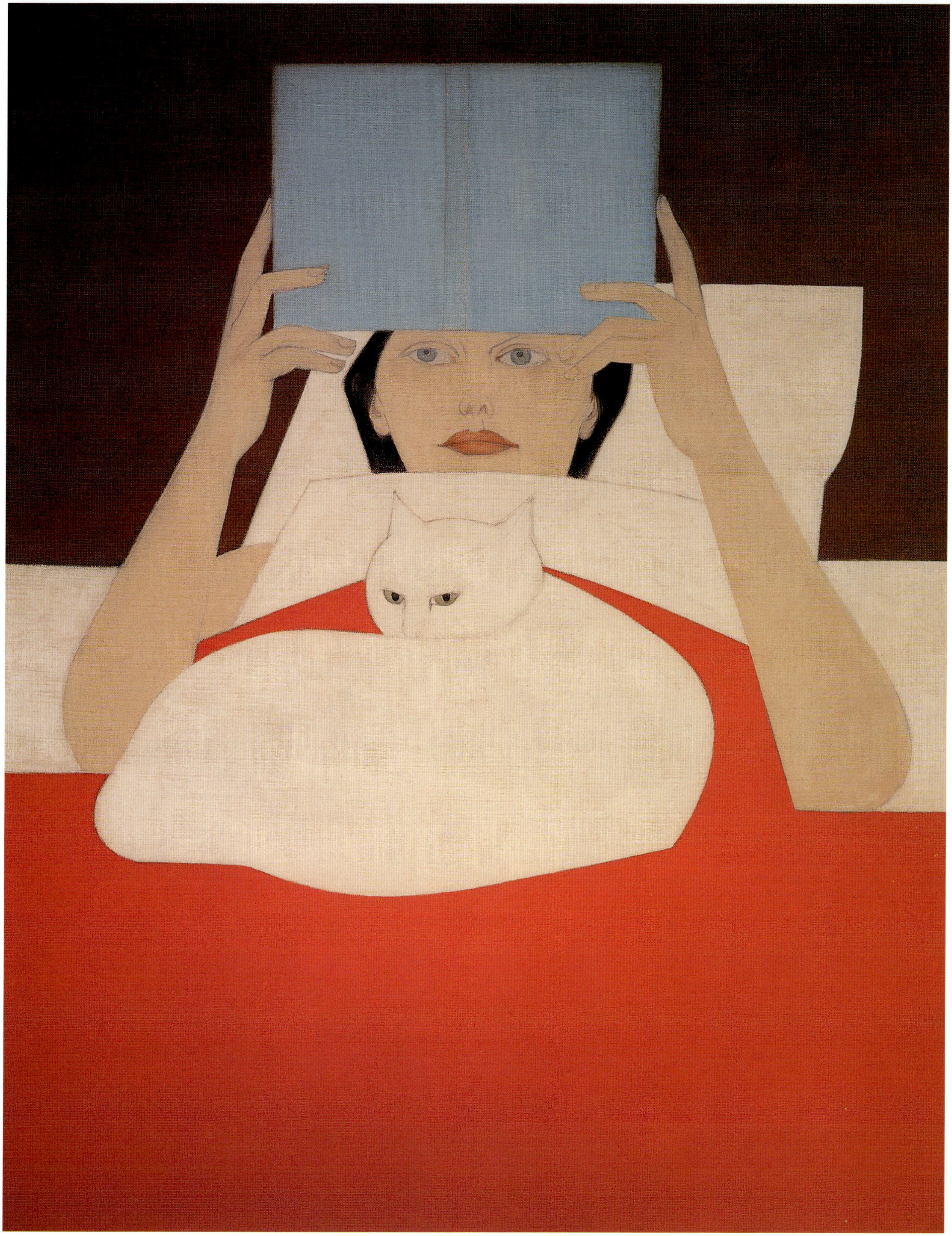

Woman Reading, oil on canvas, 45" x 35", 1965. *Courtesy of Babcock Galleries. All art © Will Barnet/Licensed by VAGA, New York, NY.*

Jack Beal

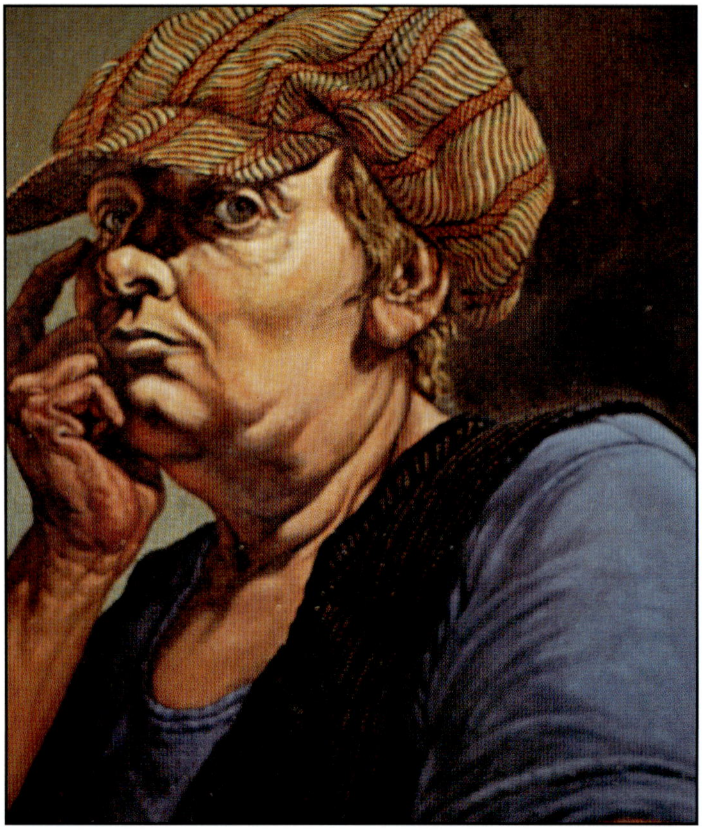

Envy (self portrait), oil on canvas, 26" x 22", 1977. *Courtesy of the artist.*

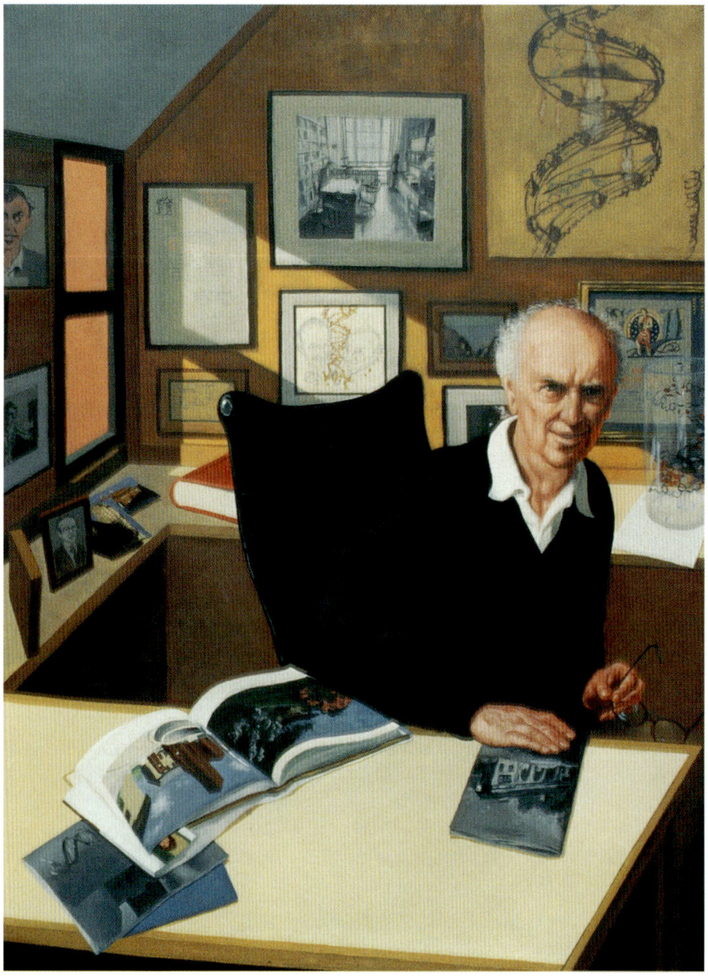

James Dewey Watson PhD, oil on canvas, 66" x 48", c.1994-95. *Collection of National Portrait Gallery, Washington, D.C.*

Jack Beal's work elicits poetic and admiring praise. He has been called a social realist, a hyper-realist, a muralist who celebrated the history of labor, a reviver of the figurative tradition, and a painter "whose brushes catch the beauty of life ... honor the commonplace, and celebrate the moral vision in (a) mannered style."[9] Beal himself says:

> Enough! The major tragedy of art in the 20th century was that artists made it flat. Under the misguided notion called *The Integrity of the Picture Plane* almost everything vital to the making and understanding of art was forbidden, and the practice of art became the act of playing with some of the simplest aspects of picture-making. The illusions of space and volume were outlawed, and all the important subjects of eternal art were considered unfashionable, passé and antique. Now, in the 21st century, artists have the freedom to overthrow this most destructive of all restrictions ... Instead of looking at the picture surface as a flat plane, it can be seen as a window looking into the picture space. This understanding ... encourages artists to work in every aspect of Art: from realism to total abstraction; from deliberate flatness to pictorial illusion ...[10]

Beal studied at the College of William and Mary, the School of the Art Institute of Chicago, and the University of Chicago, citing the teachings of Isobel MacKinnon and Kathleen Blackshear as particularly inspiring. He has lectured at over one hundred colleges and art schools and is an elected member of the National Academy of Design. He is represented in New York by the George Adams Gallery.

Beal and his wife, the painter Sondra Freckleton, share an upstate residence in New York.

Danäe II, oil on canvas, 68" x 68", 1972. Collection of the Whitney Museum of American Art.

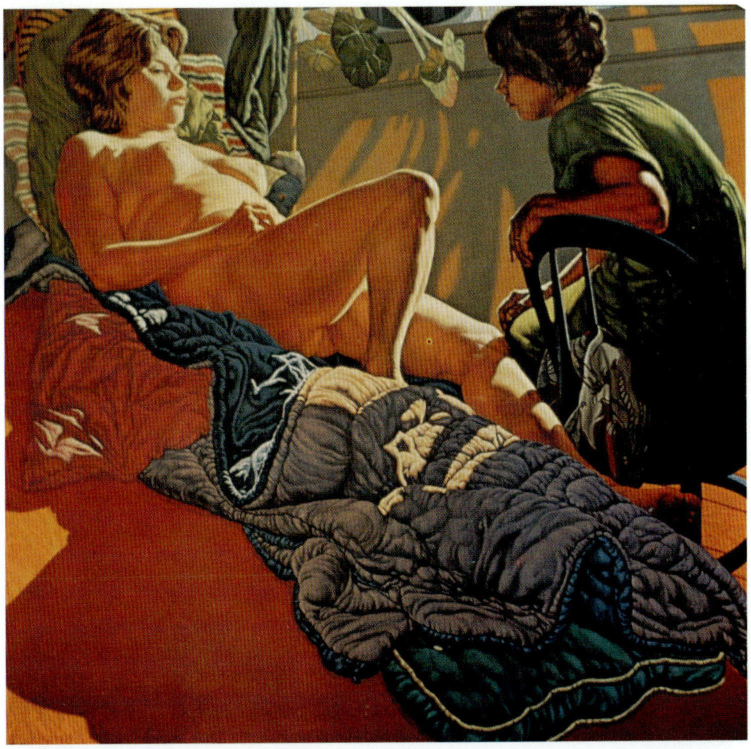

The History of Labor in America 20th C.-Technology, oil on canvas, 146" x 150", c.1974-77. Collection of United States Department of Labor, Washington, D.C.

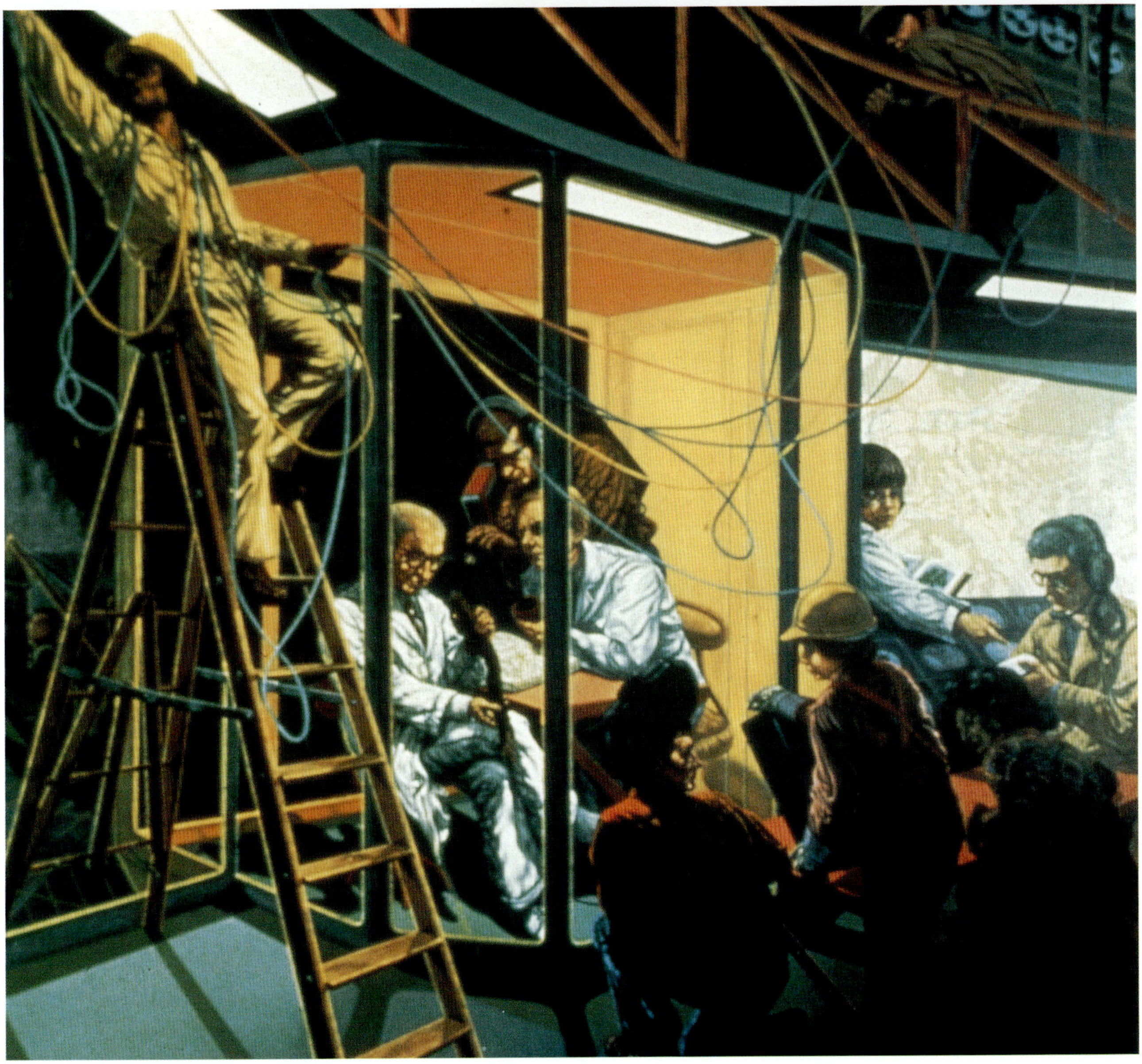

Miriam Beerman

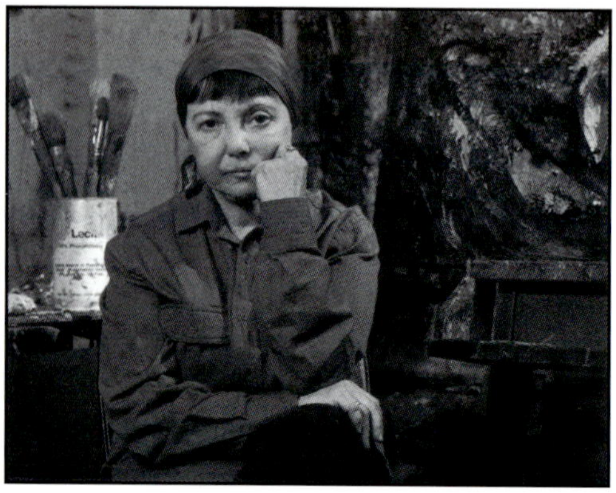

Photograph by W. Randolph Schaffer.

Miriam Beerman says she has spent most of her life "creating images that are responses to the brutality of our time ... seek[ing] the beauty and vigor of paint and the poetry that inspires the act of painting. Human and animal forms are usually somewhere in my work ... the angels and demons of an inner perception. ... Seven of the ten biblical plagues ... were painted with tremendous urgency ... seeing these archaic themes as part of the present ... the Holocaust, Hiroshima and the threat of nuclear disaster ..."[11]

Early years as an abstract expressionist are still imprinted in later work. "The physicality of the medium helps create ideas. Forms emerge out of the thickness of the paint ... Automatic gestures lead to ... emotional intensity ... and ... strange[ly], suggestions of comic relief ... the tragic and comic go hand-in-hand."[12]

Though Beerman has been called a painter of evil and pain, she believes in "the redemption, metamorphosis and resurrection of the human spirit."[13]

A graduate of the Rhode Island School of Design, she studied with Yasuo Kuniyoshi at the Art Students League, then at the New School for Social Research.

Beerman was given the first solo show for a woman at the Brooklyn Museum in 1971, and has exhibited widely since. Her works are in numerous collections—those of the Brooklyn Museum, the Whitney Museum of American Art, the Jewish Museum in New York, and the Israel Museum in Jerusalem among them—and she has devoted many years to teaching.

Turkey, oil on canvas, 72" x 69", 1971.

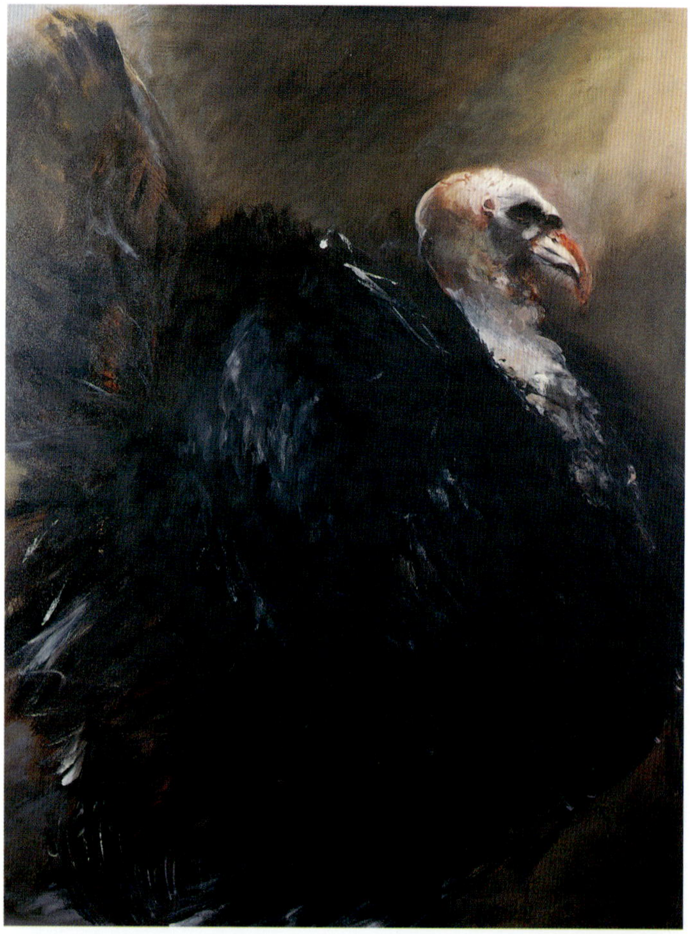

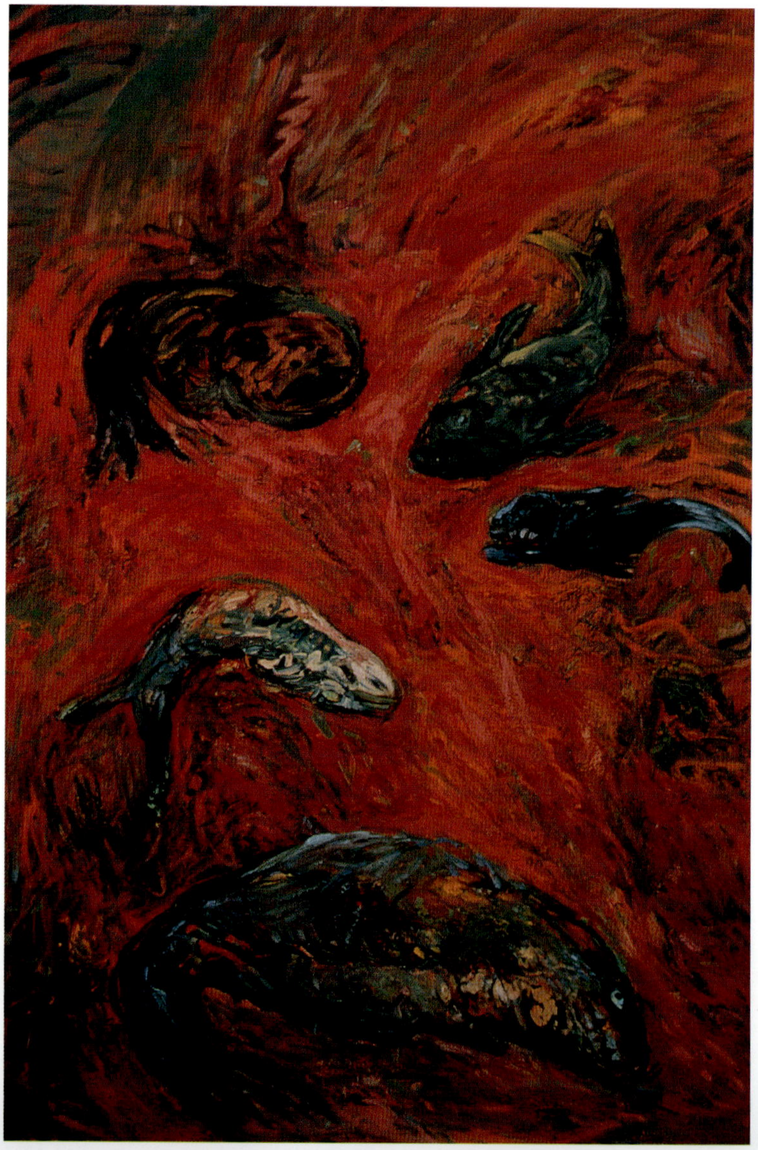

The Plagues (Rivers of Blood), oil on canvas, 98" x 64", 1986.

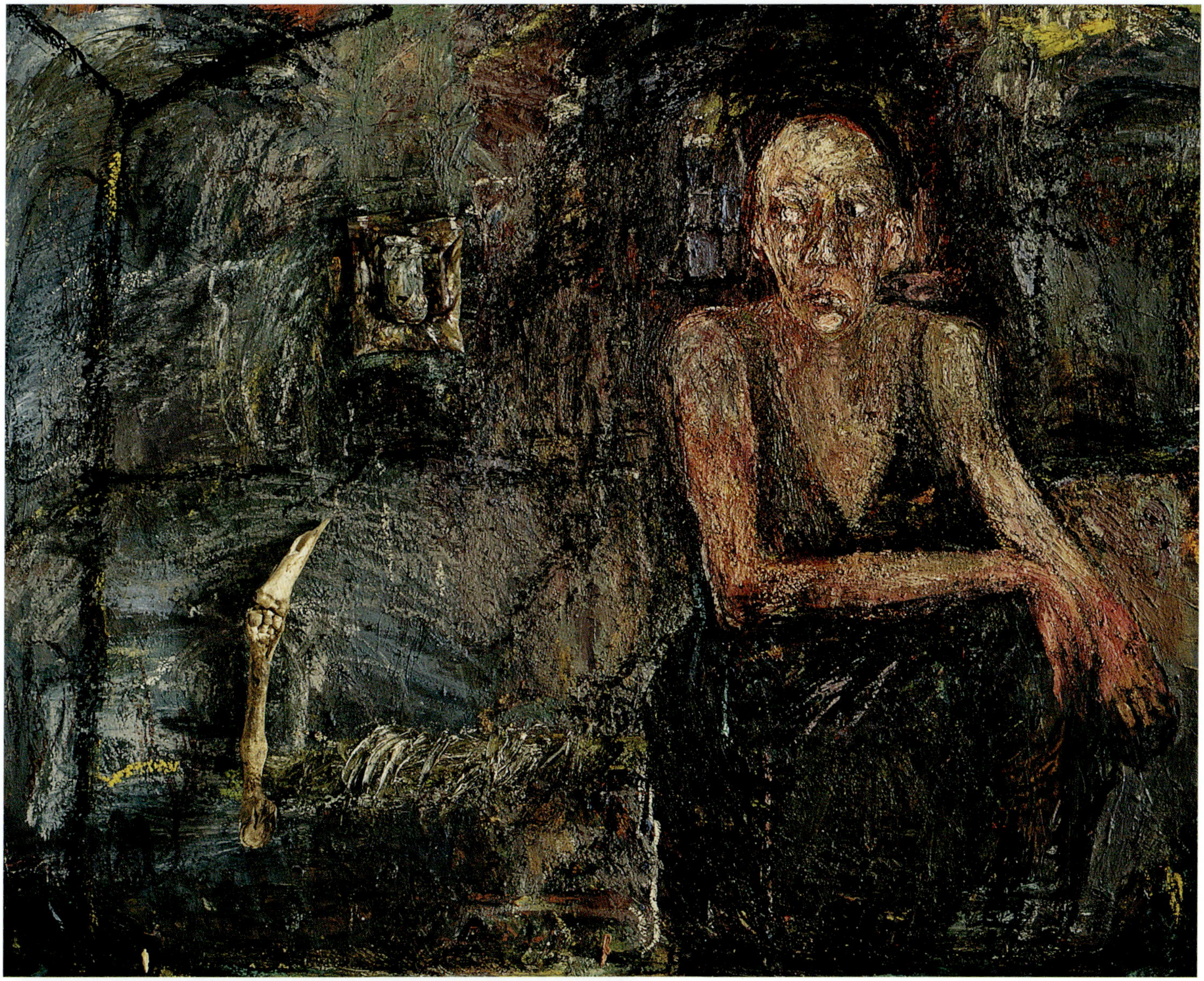

Outside Finches Singing, oil on linen, 62" x 75", 1997.

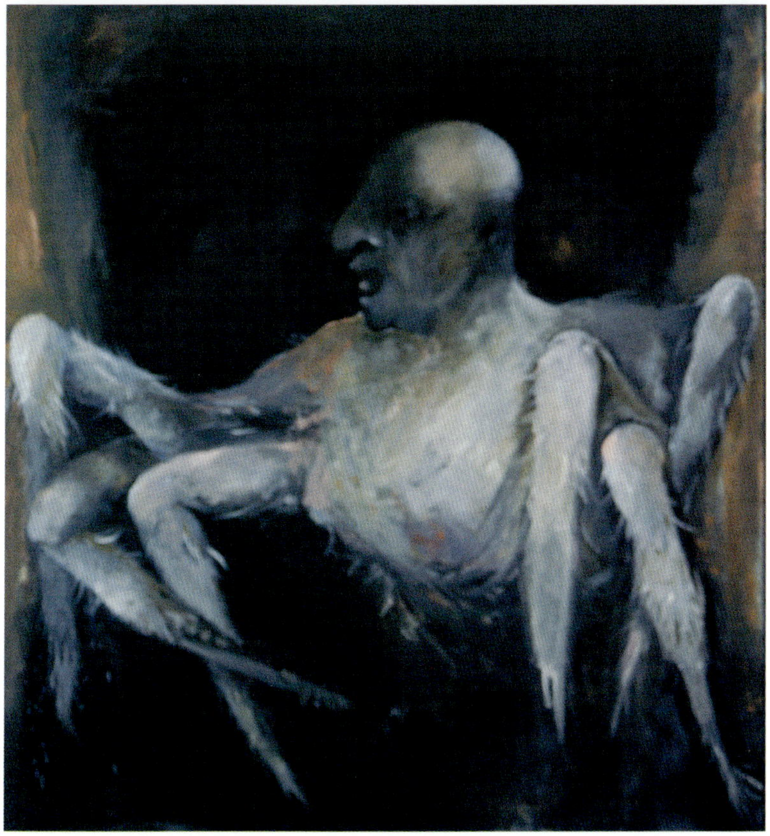

Ritual of My Legs (after Neruda), oil on canvas, 52" x 58", 1974.

Leigh Behnke's love of New York informs most of her work, in which she often juxtaposes on a single canvas one large architectural view with a band of smaller related images below, giving the viewer a sense of greater familiarity with differing aspects of the subject and a feeling of moving through space over a duration of time.

In some works, a section of sky may reveal distant galaxies or be seen through blossom-laden branches on one side of an open, lace-covered window, while leafy branches veil the water lily-covered surface of a lake on the other side of a main panel.

Behnke's precisionist work has been called cinematic, or modular, with its surprising vantage points, seeming to tilt and tip pictorial space. In addition to her unique compositional devices, color and light also intrigue this painter. "I'm interested in how these disparate images dialogue with each other," she says.[14]

A graduate of Pratt and New York University, she has taught for over twenty-five years at the School of Visual Arts, exhibits widely throughout the United States, and is represented by the Fischbach Gallery in New York.

Leigh Behnke

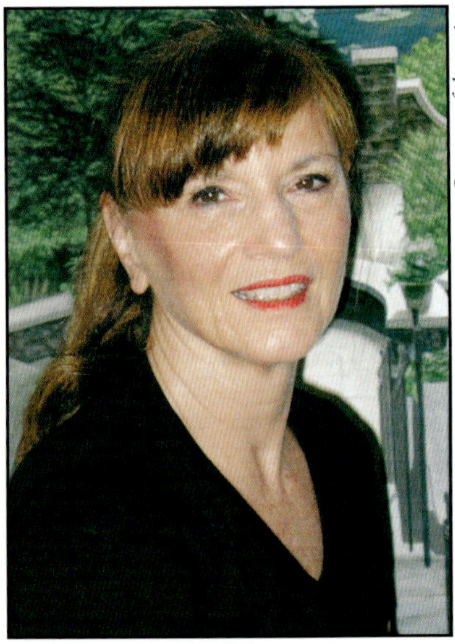

Courtesy of the artist.

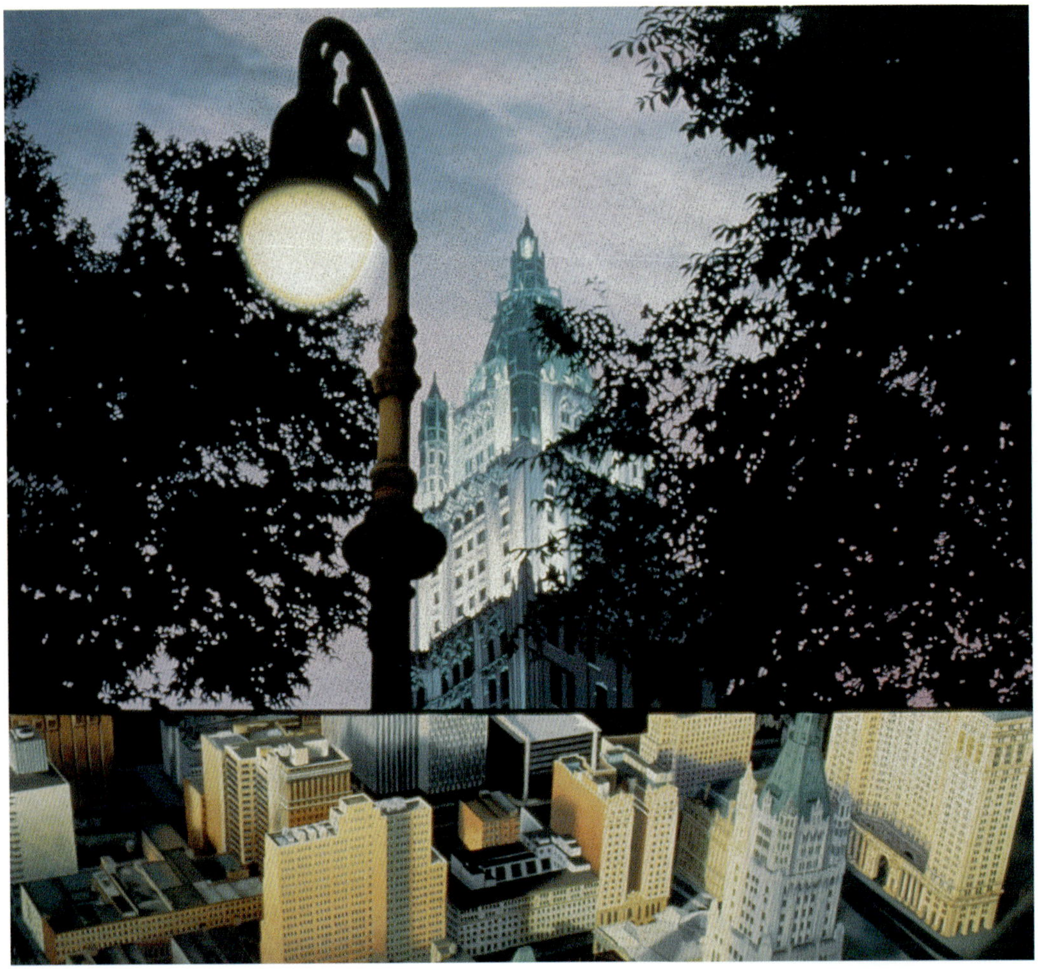

Downtown: Evening Light, oil on canvas, 44" x 48", 1989. *Courtesy of the Fischbach Gallery.*

Veiled Landscape, oil on panel, 16" x 41", 2001. *Courtesy of the Fischbach Gallery.*

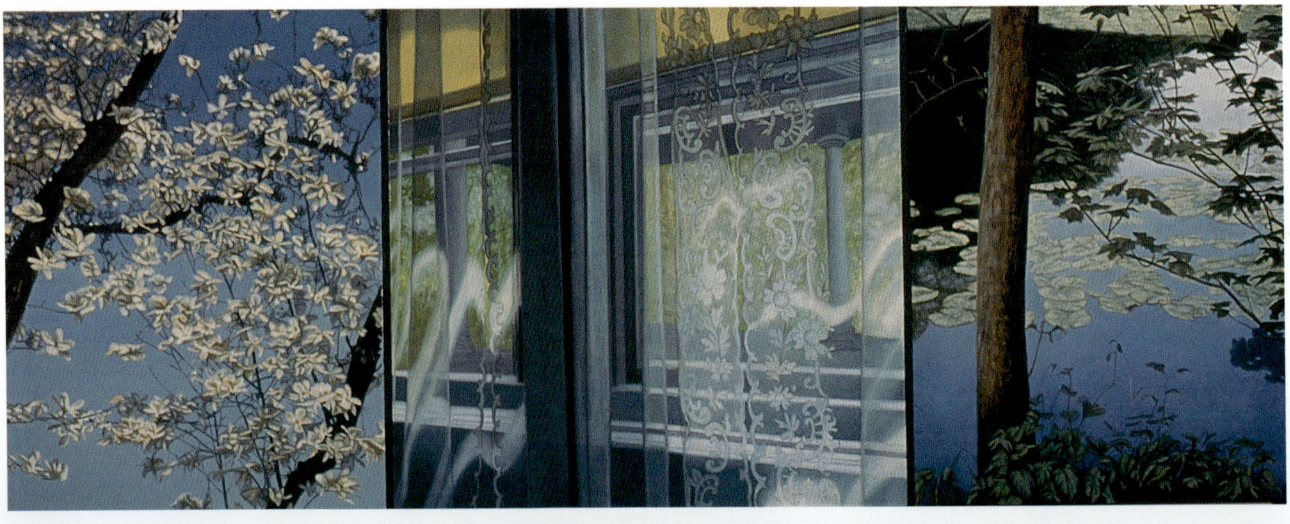

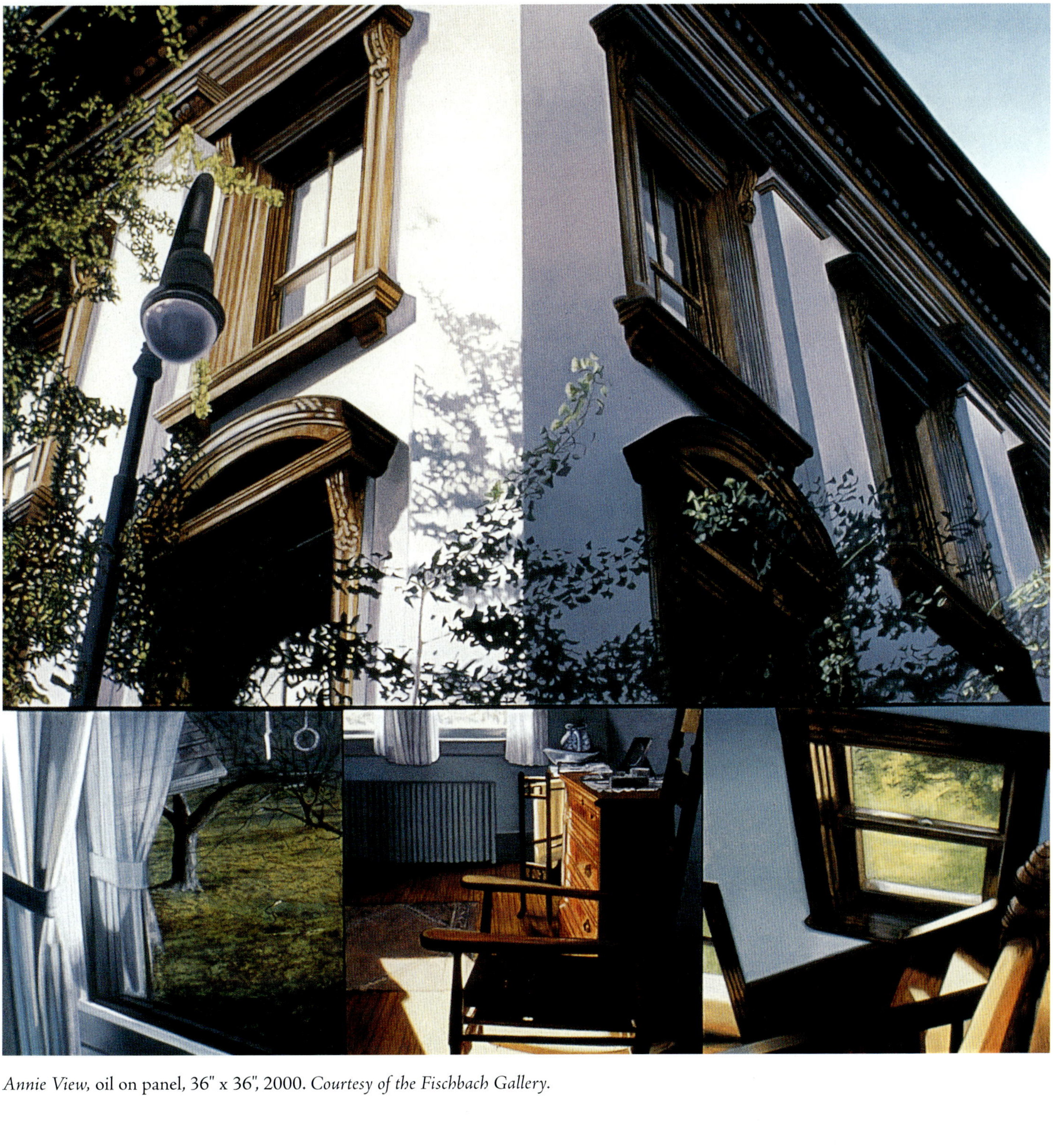

Annie View, oil on panel, 36" x 36", 2000. *Courtesy of the Fischbach Gallery.*

Siri Berg

Siri Berg's fascination with geometry is evident in her many paintings of luminous, overlaid bands of color. Unexpected textural effects in her often-systemic series of paintings and collages result from a rich experimentation with intarsia (inlays) and overlays, laminations, and various uses of wet and dry paint layerings on the planar surface. Drawn to opposites, patterns, and multiple meanings, Berg has written about the connection between her work and "the Kabala, the study of mysticism in the Jewish religion."[15]

Born in Sweden, she has been a New Yorker for most of her life, exhibiting in both countries as well as in Israel, China, Australia, and Germany.

A member of the American Abstract Artists, Berg has taught color and design at New York University's Parsons School of Design since 1977. She is represented in New York by the Broadway Gallerie.

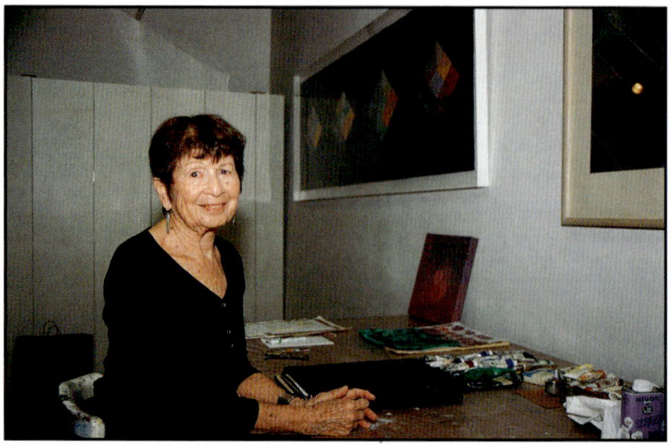

Photograph by Catarina Aström.

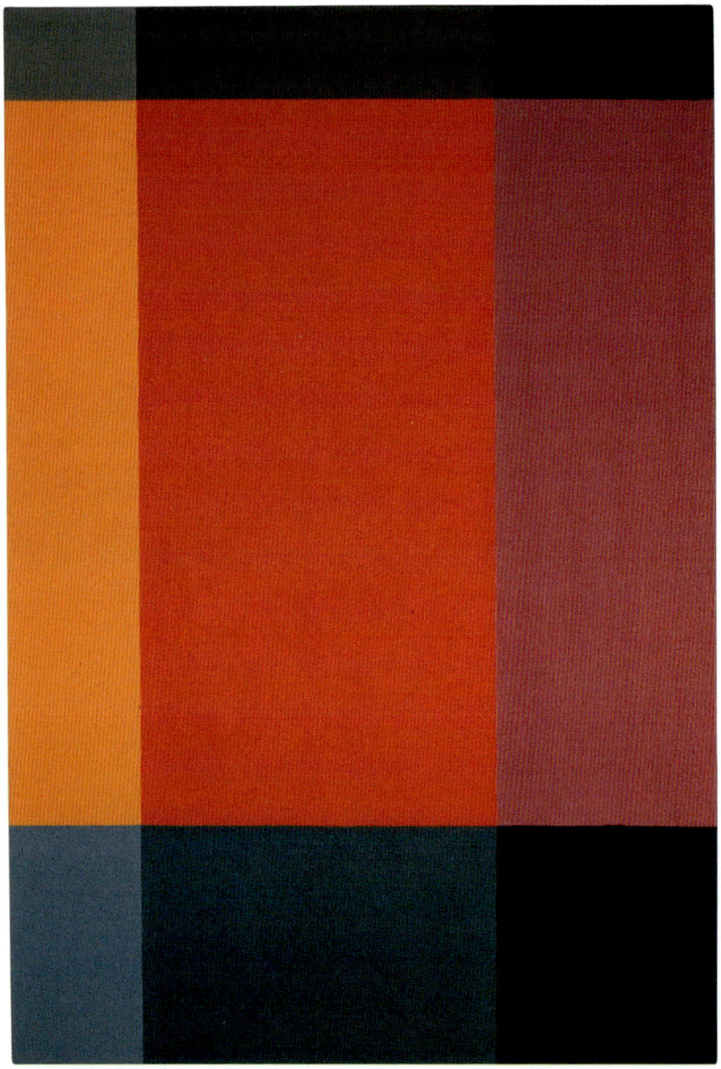

Bars, oil on linen, 30" x 20", c.1999. *All art © Siri Berg/Licensed by VAGA, New York, NY.*

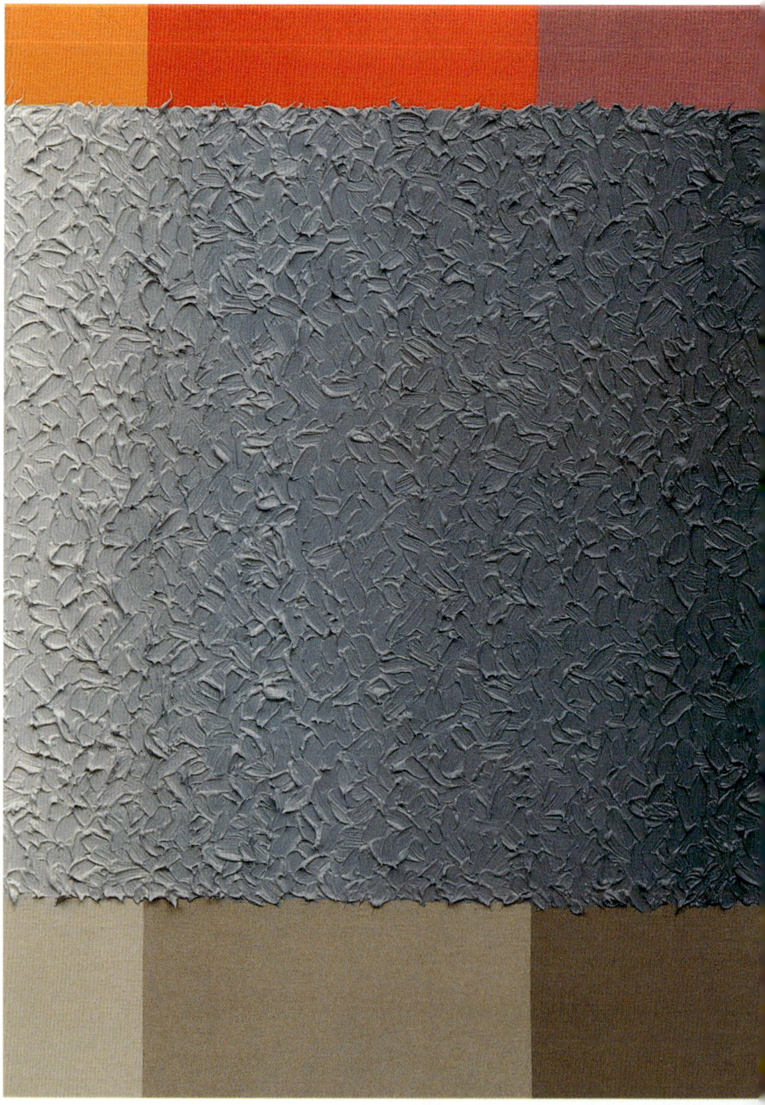

Bars, oil on linen, 30" x 20", c.1999.

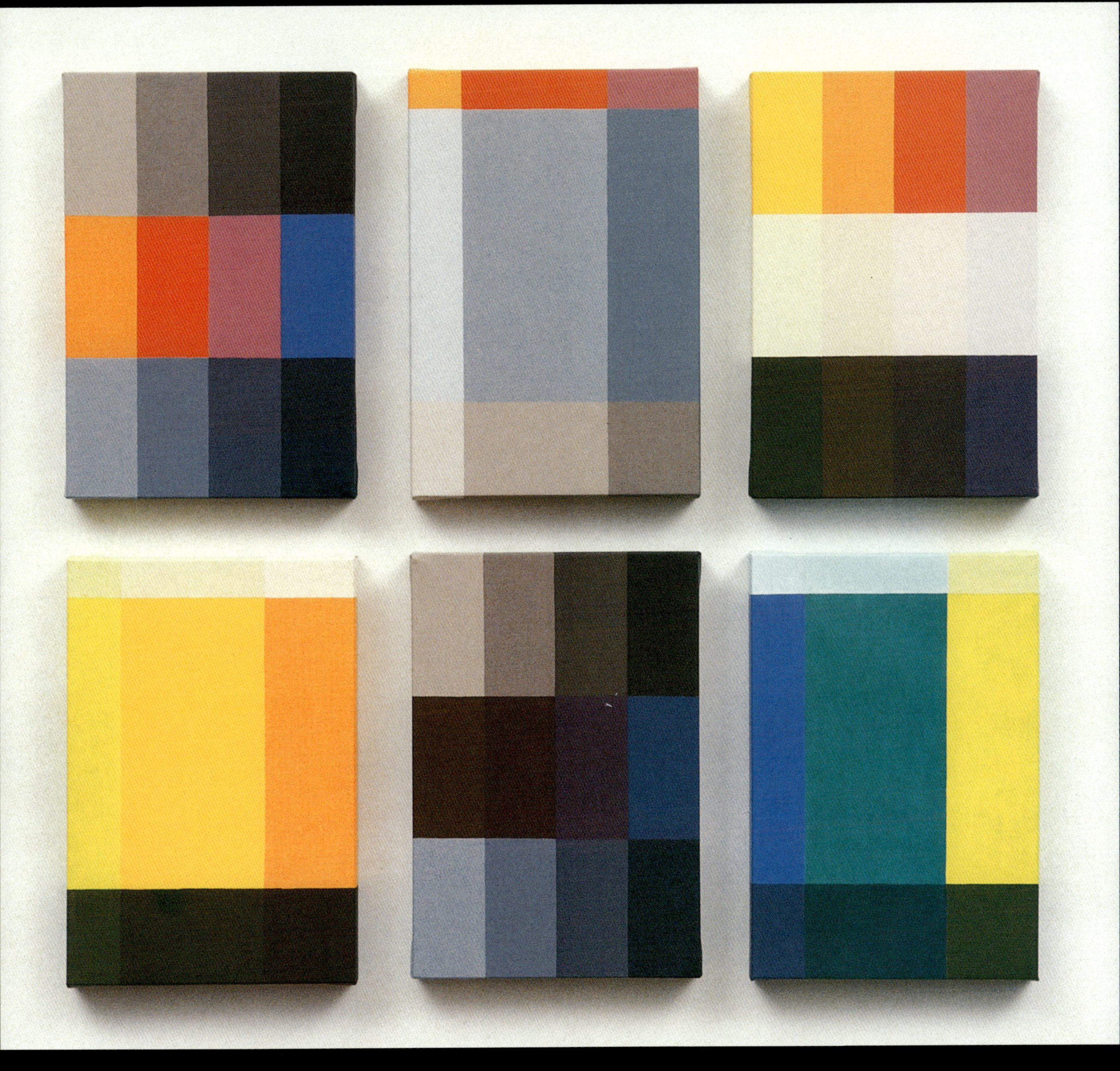

Bars and *Straight Line*, oil on linen, each painting 15" x 10", c.1999.

Robert Birmelin

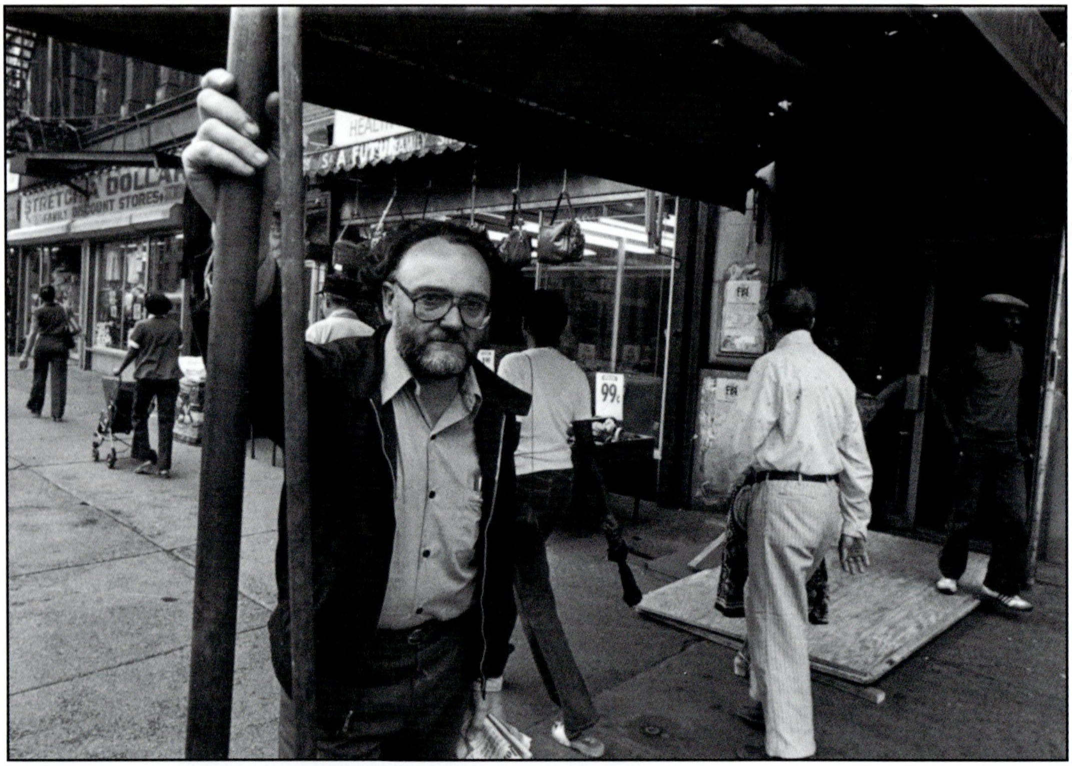

Photograph © Michel Saskine.

Robert Birmelin, whose work is "rooted in direct observation and a practiced exercise of visual memory," calls art "finally, a social act, a transaction between persons, real and depicted ... With the city paintings, I am among others in the intimate anonymity of public spaces. The viewer and I are participants in the energy of the urban street ... attempting to navigate through [its] visual overload, [as] ... the scanning eye seeks its path. ... Other paintings are meditations on the intimate relationships between people in their domestic environment ... playing with vagaries of memory. ..."[16]

Birmelin does not use photographs, but begins with gestural images and from an inner image. His task is "to create a world both I, the artist, and others can believe in and enter into."[17]

A graduate of Yale's School of Art, with previous study at New York's Cooper Union, Birmelin also studied at London's Slade School of Art. Winner of numerous grants and awards, he is an elected member of the National Academy, has taught as a Professor at Queens College of the City University of New York since 1974, and has lectured throughout the United States. He is represented by the Peter Findlay Gallery in New York's historic Fuller Building.

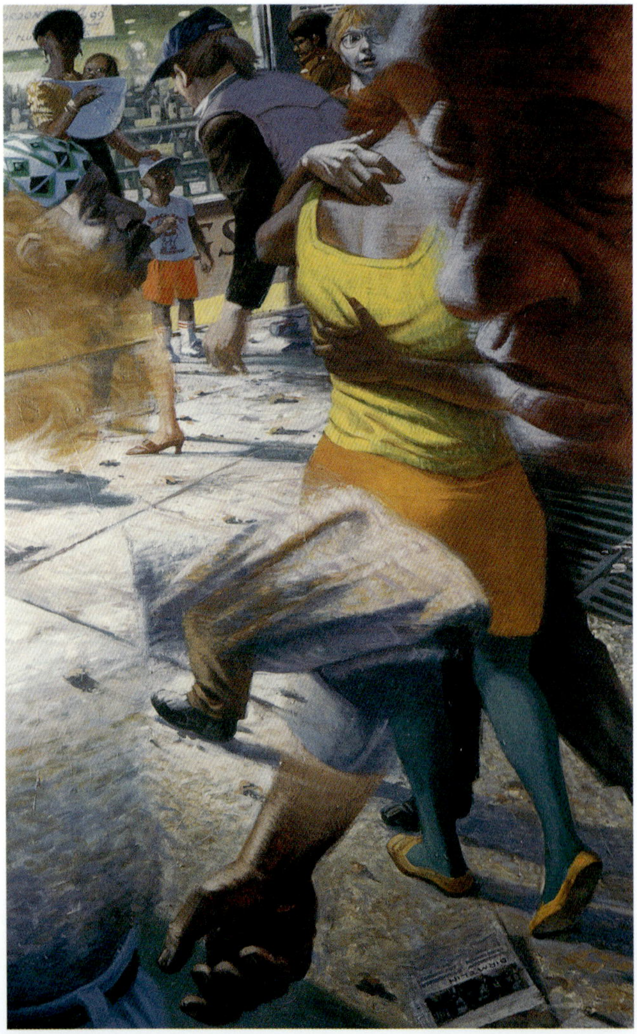

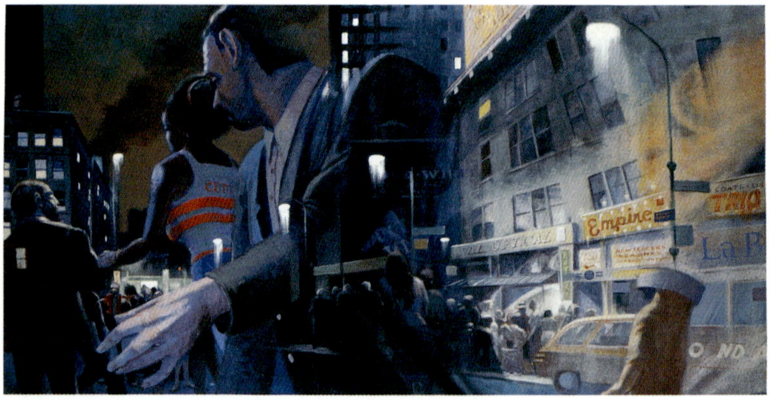

Night, acrylic on canvas, 48" x 78", 2002.

Other Lives–An Embrace (Yellow), acrylic on canvas, 78" x 48", 1990. *Private collection.*

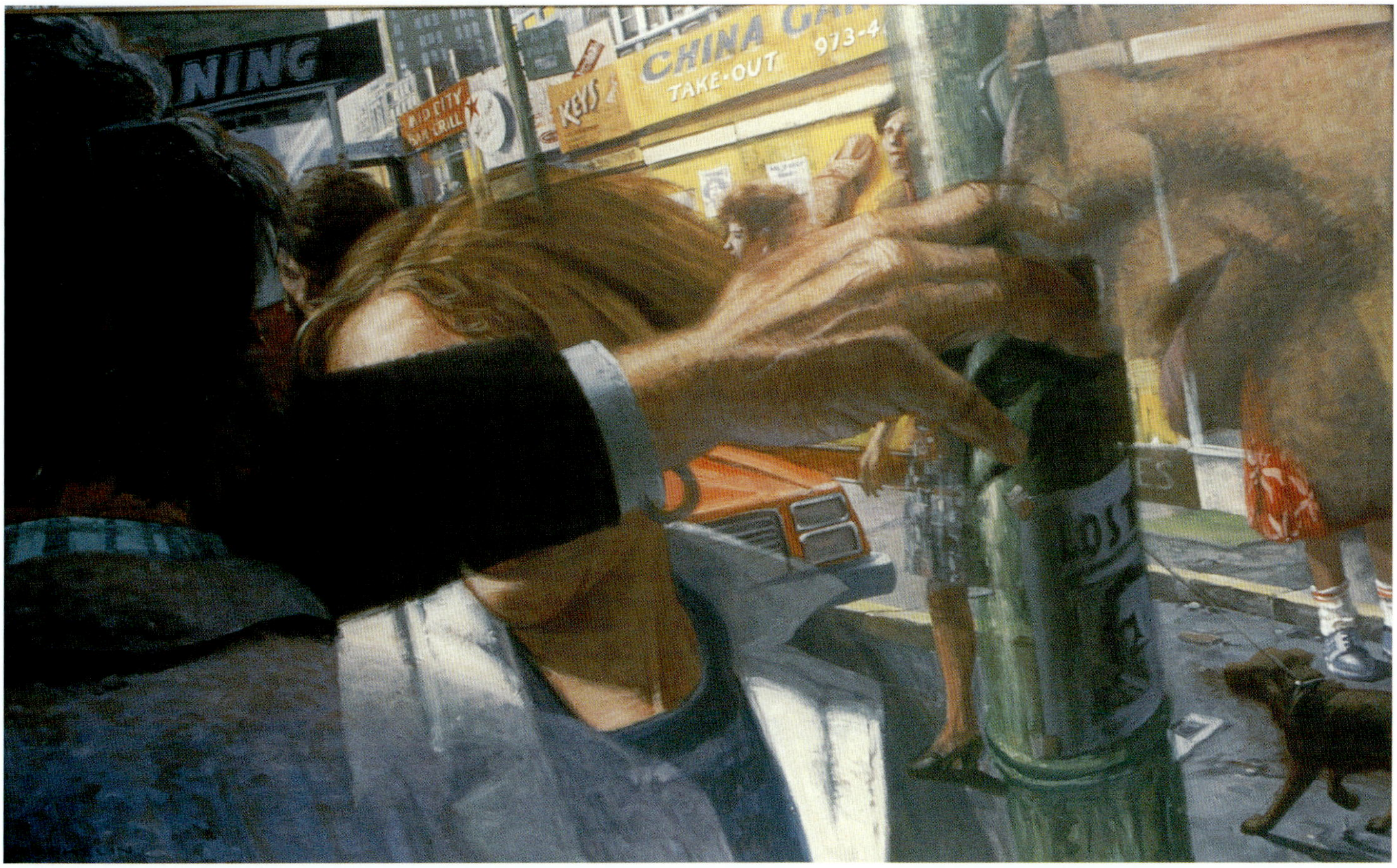

China Garden, acrylic on canvas, 48" x 78", 1985. *Private collection.*

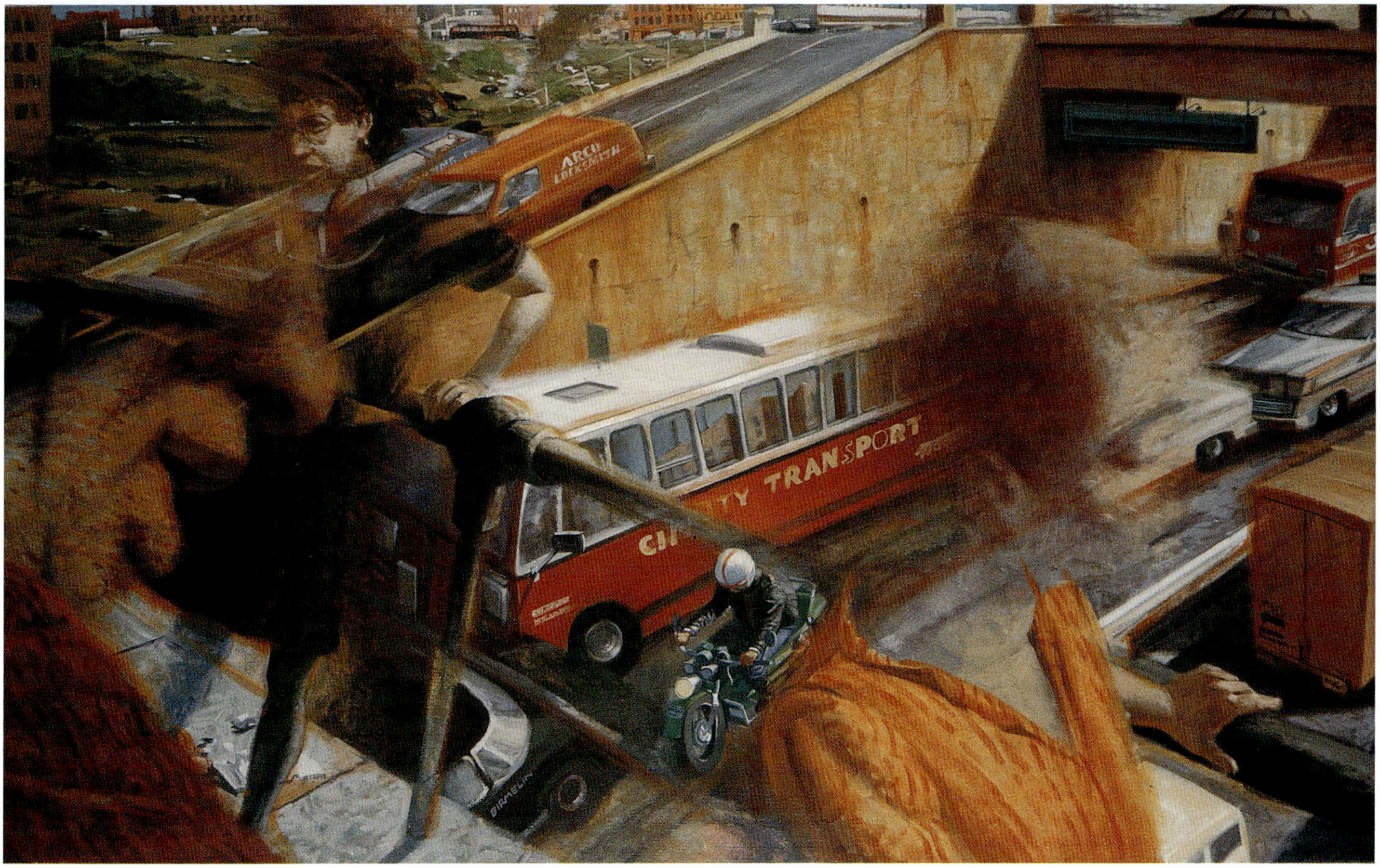

The Overpass (Red Bus), acrylic on canvas, 48" x 78", 1993. *Collection of the National Academy of Design.*

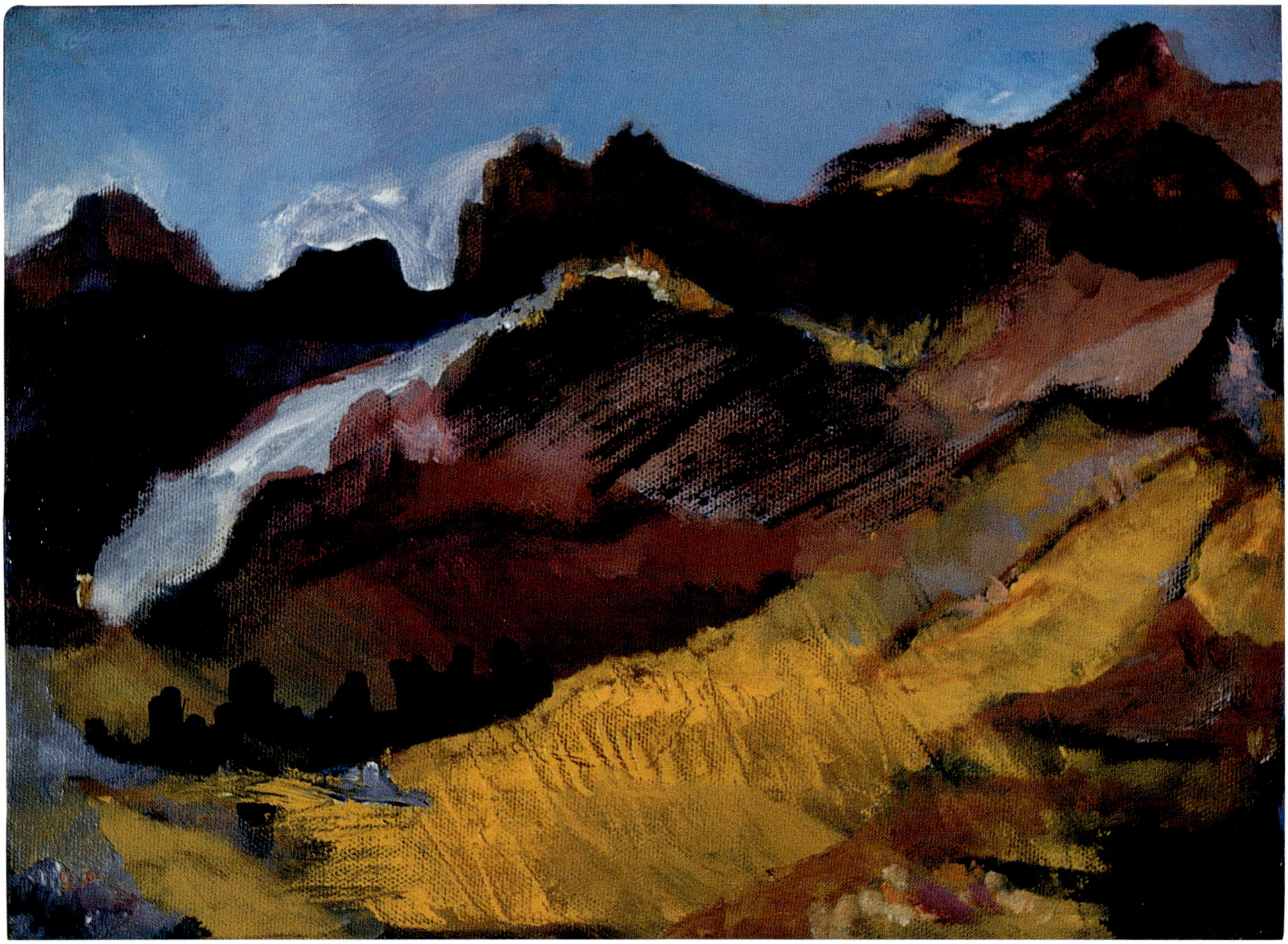

Maroon Bells, Colorado, acrylic on canvas, 9" x 12", 2001.

Jane Bolmeier

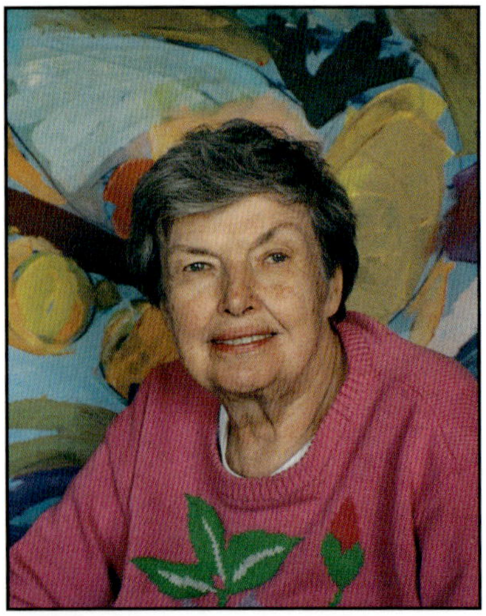

Photograph by Arlene Gottfried.

Jane Bolmeier is a long-time resident of New York's historic Westbeth, a residential and studio complex in the far western section of Greenwich Village, and exhibits regularly at Westbeth's gallery.

She received a doctorate in Art Criticism at Chapel Hill and studied for several summers with Hans Hofmann, who was "an inspirational, supportive teacher."[18]

Bolmeier, a member of New York Artists Equity, was moved to paint "the changing colors and moods of Provincetown," when she left her studio after 9/11 because of the "rancid smell of decay, the smoke, the confusion, the shock, and the devastation."[19] Since then, she has continued to enjoy painting in Provincetown on the beach, relishing "the purity of the air and its sparkle."[20]

For Bolmeier, early large abstract New York paintings have been followed by many series of still life, floral, landscape, and beachscape scenes, becoming perhaps freer and more abstract over time. She cherishes her Westbeth studio, which she notes, "faces the Hudson River!"[21]

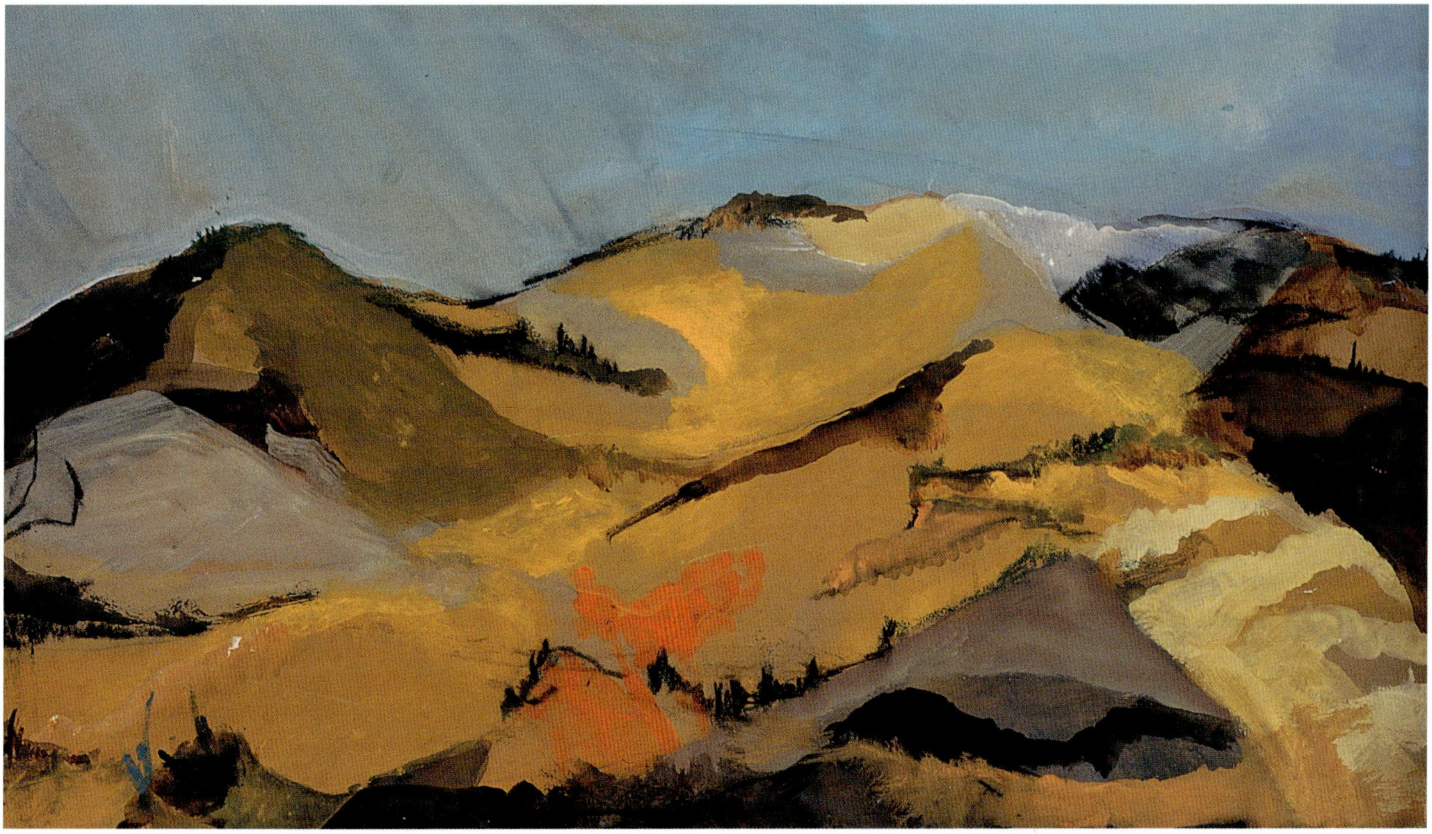

Snowmass, Colorado, acrylic on board, 10" x 16", 2000.

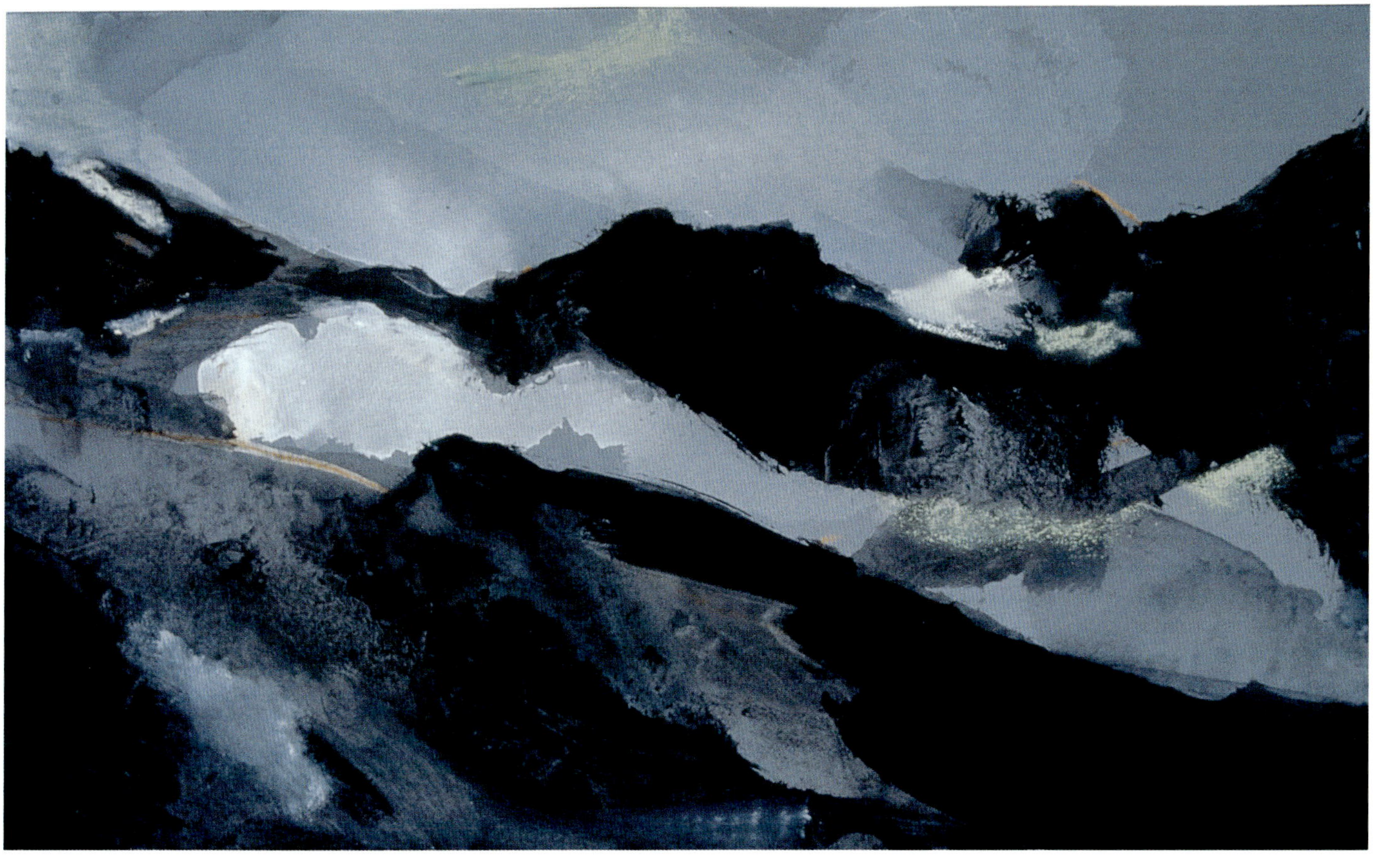

Hovering Clouds, acrylic on board, 10" x 16", 2000.

Richmond Burton has been called a "decorative abstractionist ... who paints in a kind of mosaic fashion, his ... fluid, episodic grids and arabesques exhibit an exuberance of color and sensuality."[22] Although an early grid matrix has often disappeared in Burton's latest works, his paintings continue to suggest a strong sensual layering, a texture of erotic mark and movement. Burton writes of his "I AM (Androgynous)" paintings, "they express my fascination with sexuality and my conviction that the next revolution will be a sexual one ... blurring (all) distinctions."[23]

Burton's works may be seen in many museum collections. He has exhibited in Europe and throughout the United States, and is a graduate of Rice University in Houston, Texas. He is represented by Cheim & Read in New York.

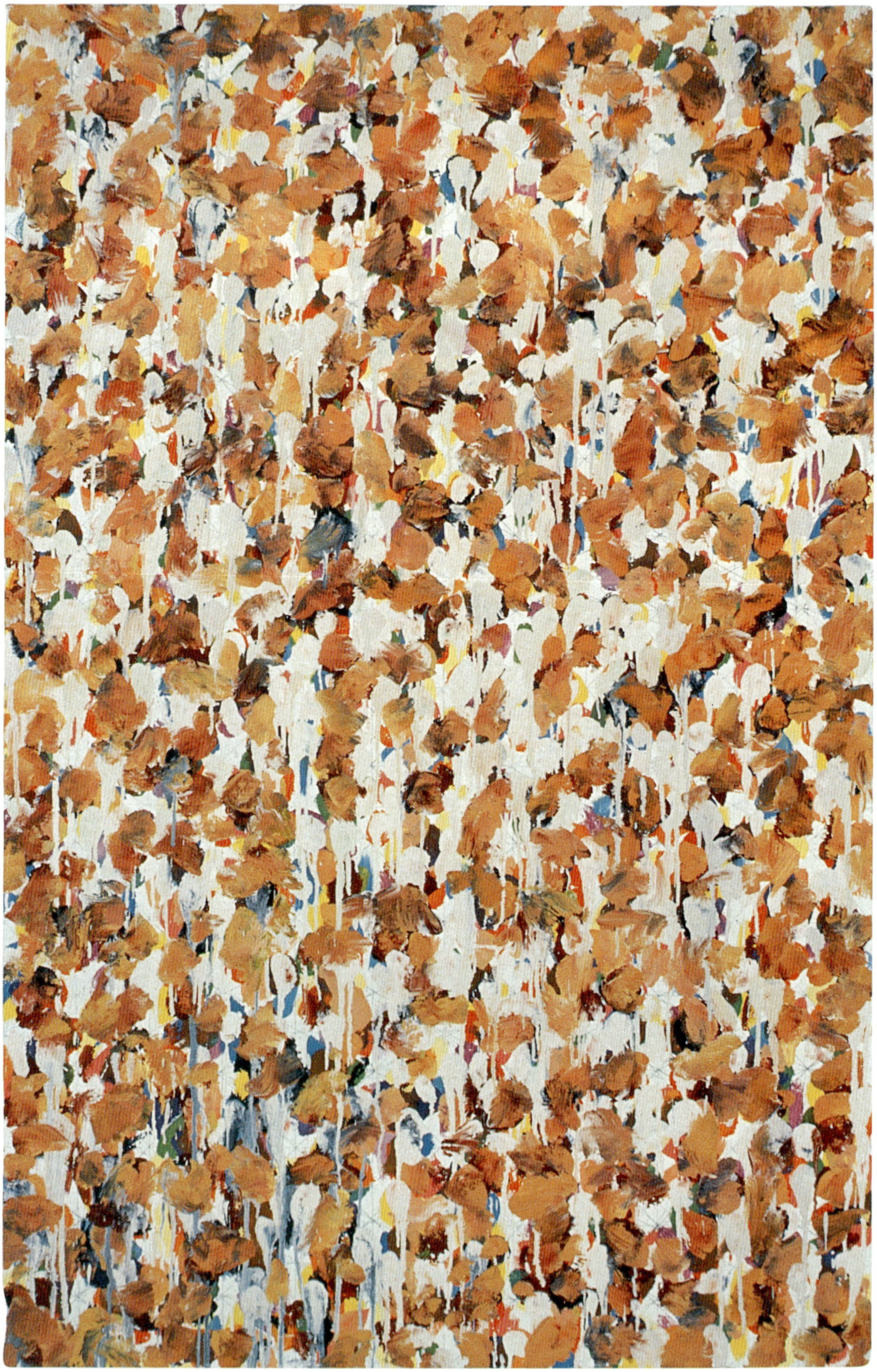

Mary in the Kelp, oil on linen, 63" x 40", 1994.

Richmond Burton

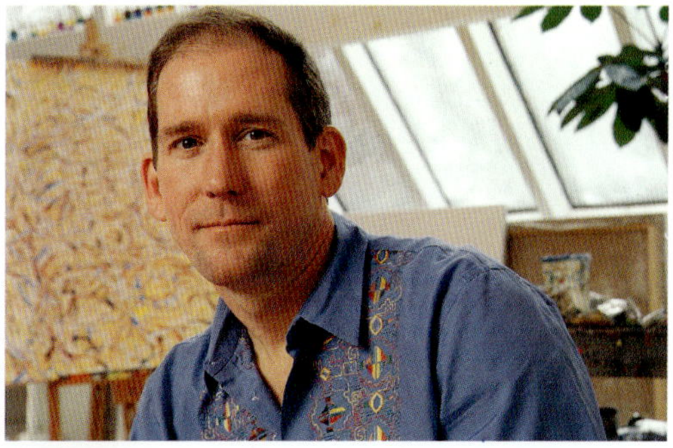

Photograph © Will Ryan.

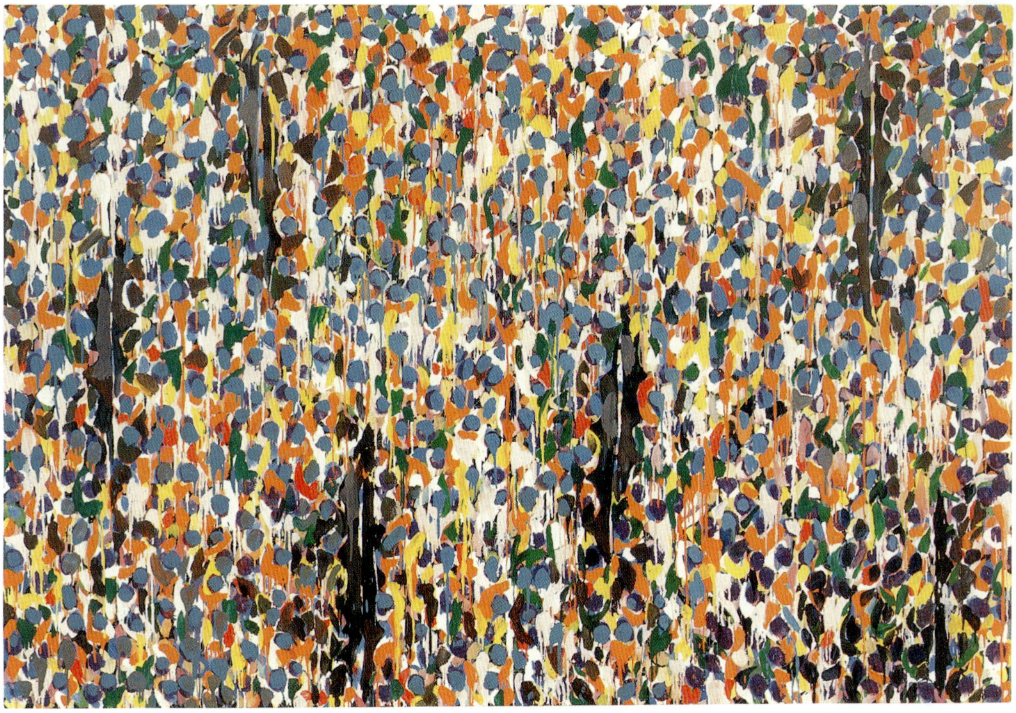

Zone, oil on canvas, 84" x 120", 1995.

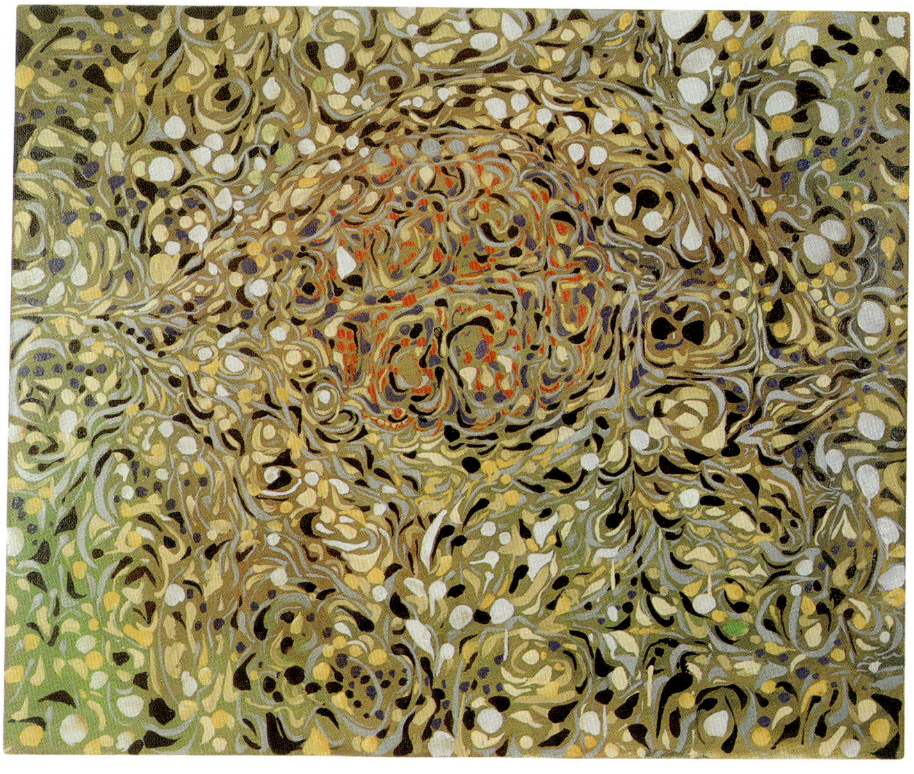

I AM (Holographic 3), oil on linen, 42" x 50", 2001.

Charles Cajori, whose figurative-expressionist abstractions have earned him many awards and honors, including a John Simon Guggenheim Memorial Fellowship and elected membership in the National Academy of Design, continues to "confront an issue which also occupied Cézanne and deKooning ... how to paint the fleshy female figure, the central subject of western art, in a fluid space."[24] Irving Sandler adds, "Cajori's ambition is to reconcile a swift continuum of space ... with single and multiple figures, as, he says, a new space ... created by Pollock ... the space (that was) to our time what perspectival space was to the Renaissance."[25]

As gleaned from many statements and interviews, Cajori says his concerns include "both the closed form (the sign of the human presence) and ambiguity ... the mystery ... for me the erotic is the vehicle for getting at the credibility of the figure."[26]

Andrew Forge calls Cajori's "preoccupation with space ... a romance ... (and) a mystery. The key to his experience is the movement of the eye ... the threshold between the mind's (search) to consolidate the shifting data of perception and established ... material for measurement. ... He continues to explore ... his imagined world, (in) an argument that will not stop: space/form; flatness/depth; closed/open; particular/general; endless pairs ... that once resolved, turn ... to renew the argument from an unfamiliar angle ... always. ... "[27]

Cajori, called a second-generation member of the New York school (his first solo show was at the Tanager Gallery in 1956), studied at Colorado College, the Cleveland Art School, and Columbia University. His works are in many major museums and collections. He is represented by David Findlay Jr Fine Art and the Lohin-Geduld Gallery in New York.

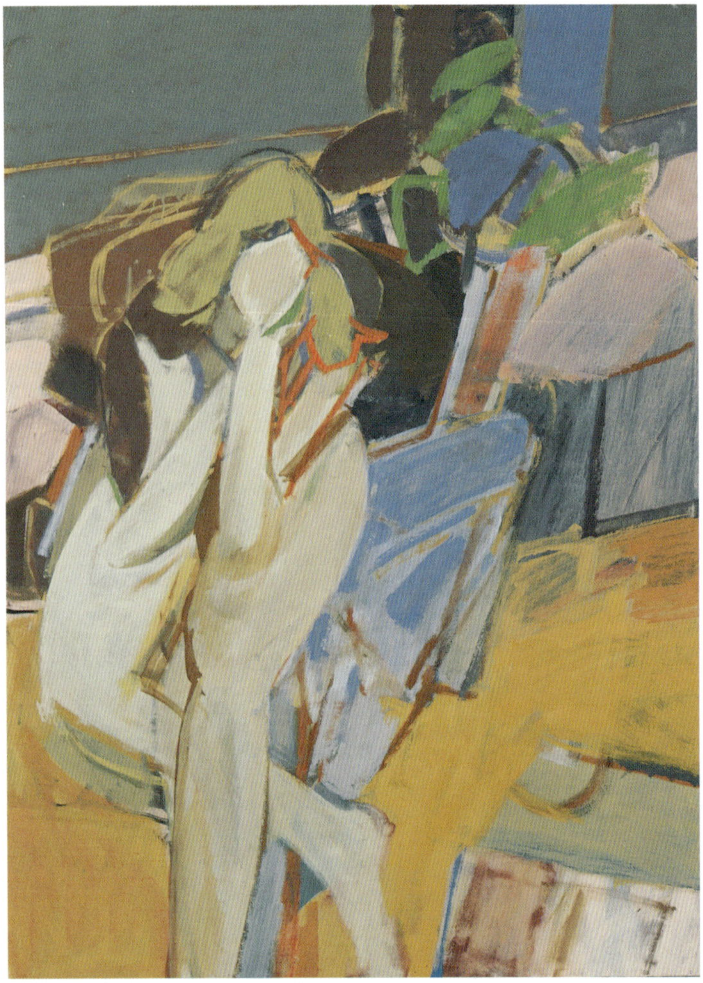

Untitled-84x-014, oil on linen, 50" x 36", 1984. *Private collection.*

Charles Cajori

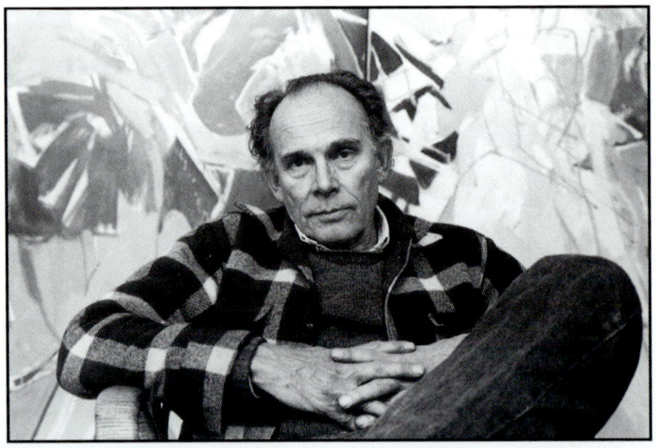

Photograph by Nancy Tutko.

Untitled-00x-004, oil on linen, 42" x 32", 2000. *Private collection.*

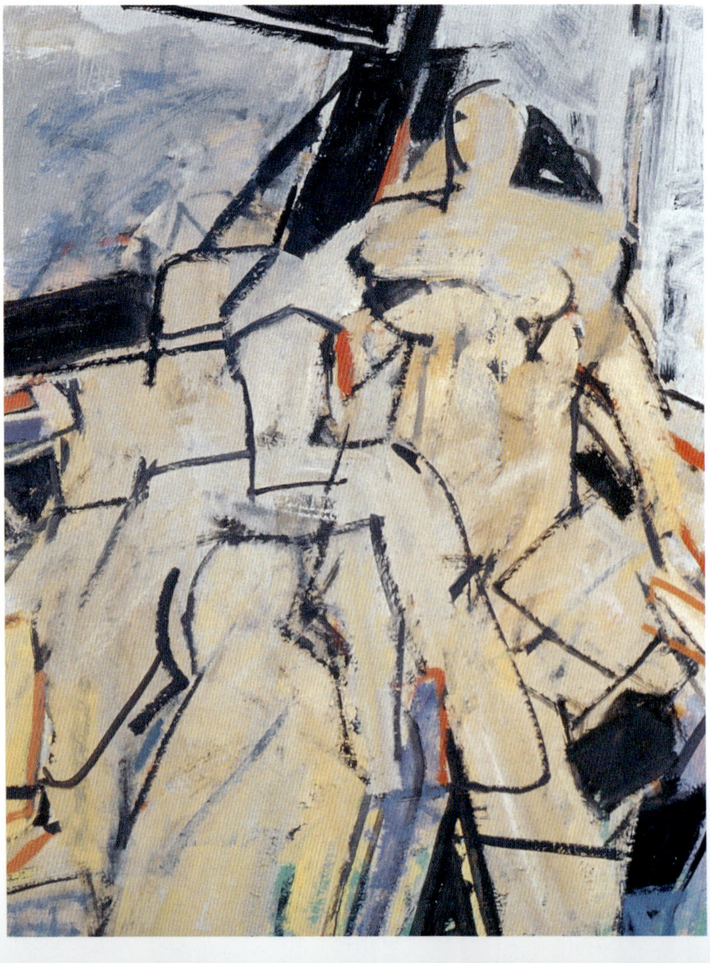

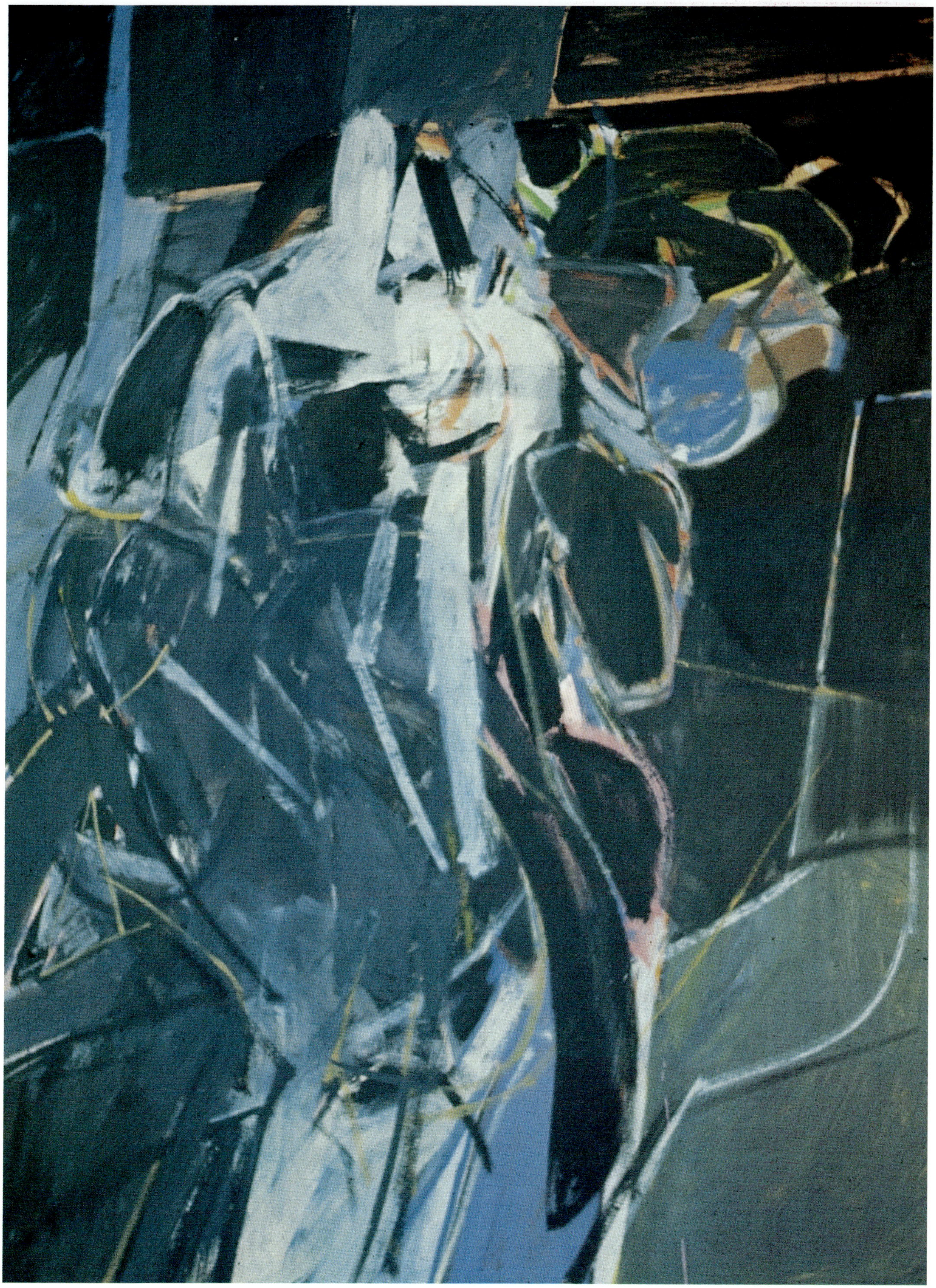

Untitled-83x-070, oil on linen, 66" x 48", 1983. *Collection of The Hirshhorn Museum, Washington, D.C.*

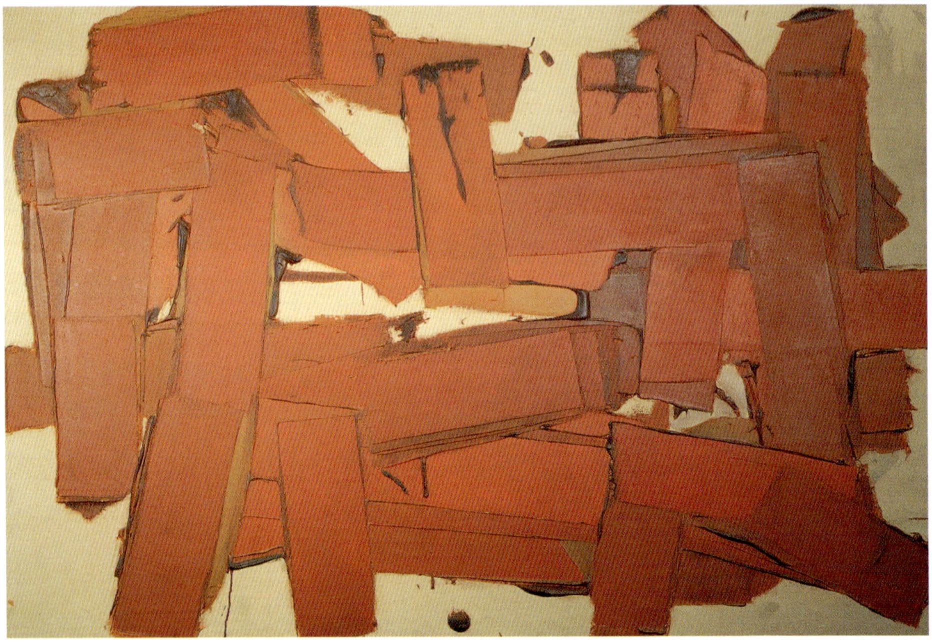

Big Red, acrylic over acrylic plaster and marble dust on canvas, 56" x 72", 1974.

Virginia Hoyt Cantarella

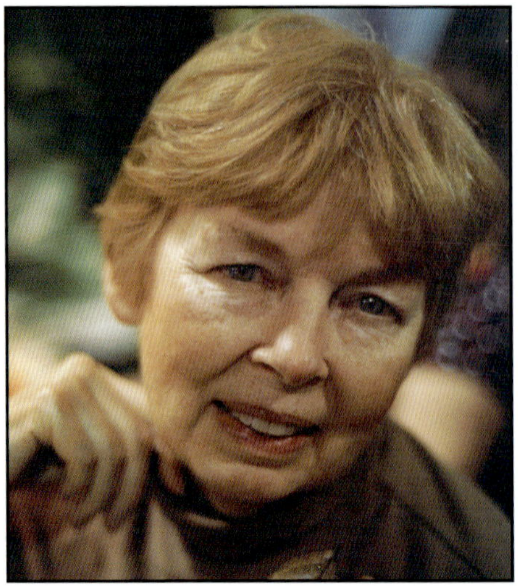

Photograph © Cynthia Dantzic.

Virginia Hoyt Cantarella, whose painting career was interrupted for many years while she achieved distinction as a medical illustrator specializing in ophthalmic surgery for twenty medical textbooks, studied at the Boston Museum School. Here, she learned fresco techniques and "became interested in working with plaster. I developed an acrylic-based plaster with marble dust, used as a ground for paintings with subject matter, and have spattered and scraped—in my abstract, without subject matter, paintings."[28]

Cantarella has taught medical illustration at Long Island University, was a governor of the Brooklyn Museum, and a trustee of the Brooklyn Institute of Arts and Sciences. Her works have won prizes at the Silvermine and Cooperstown annual exhibitions, and she was honored to be chosen for the Multiple Sclerosis Society's exhibition, "The Creative Will," which toured the United States for two years.

Cantarella's anatomical drawings are featured in the author's textbook, *Drawing Dimensions, A Comprehensive Introduction*.

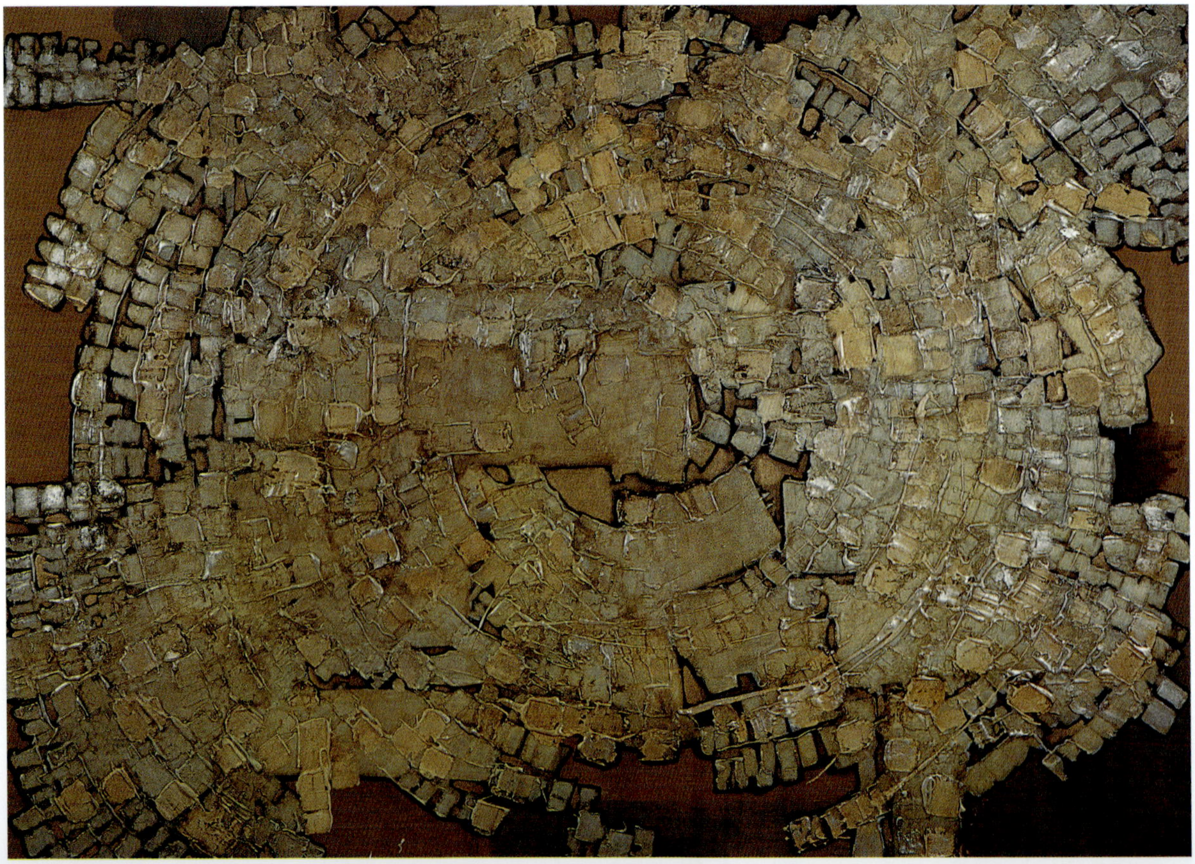

Archaeology, acrylic over acrylic plaster and marble dust on canvas, 44" x 60", 1982.

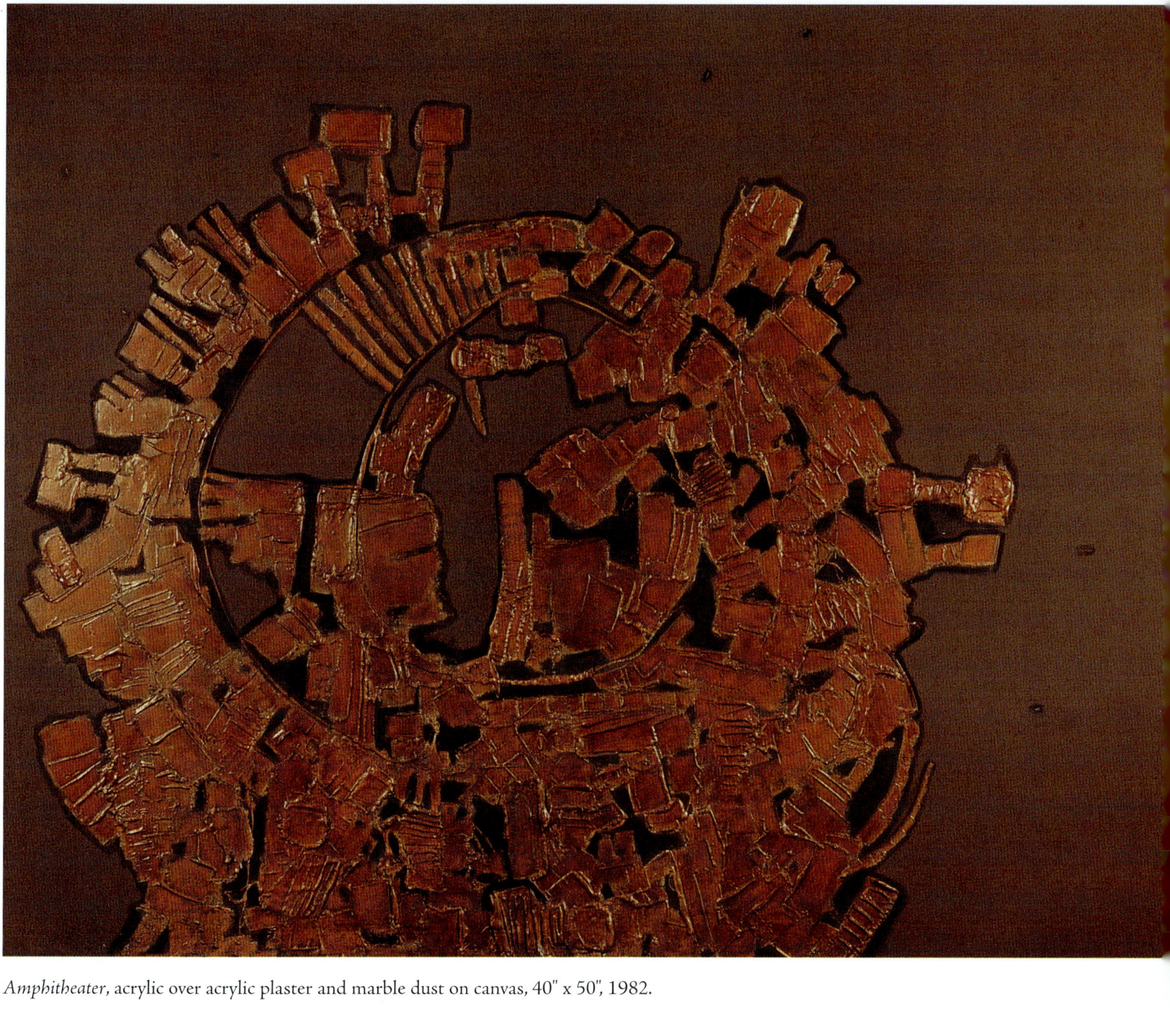

Amphitheater, acrylic over acrylic plaster and marble dust on canvas, 40" x 50", 1982.

Nicolas Carone

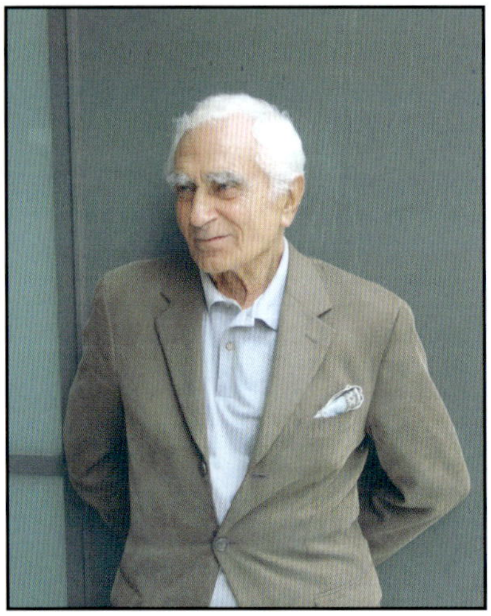

Courtesy of Lohin-Geduld Gallery.

Nicolas Carone, a founding faculty member of the New York Studio School, where he taught for more than twenty years, was represented in the historic Ninth Street Show of 1951 with other seminal Abstract Expressionists. He has continued to work in innovative ways, from automatism and free association to classical figuration, cubist planar construction, and other approaches, and to build unique "surreal scenarios where dreams and reality intermingle."[29]

His figurative drawing skills provide "the weight of true human drama. … Carone plumbs the depths of our collective psychological and emotional states … using free association with accidental spills and unconscious marks. …"[30]

Carone's time as studio assistant to Leon Kroll, as well as his friendships with Hans Hofmann, Jackson Pollock, and others, were early influences on his work, closely associated with the development of Modernism in New York.

He studied at the National Academy of Design (of which he is now an elected member), the Art Students League, and the Hans Hofmann School of Fine Arts. Carone has won many prizes, including a Fulbright Fellowship. He has had numerous solo exhibitions, and his works are in many leading Museum collections. He has taught at universities including Yale, Columbia, Brandeis, and The Cooper Union. His work is represented by David Findlay Jr Fine Art and the Lohin-Geduld Gallery in New York.

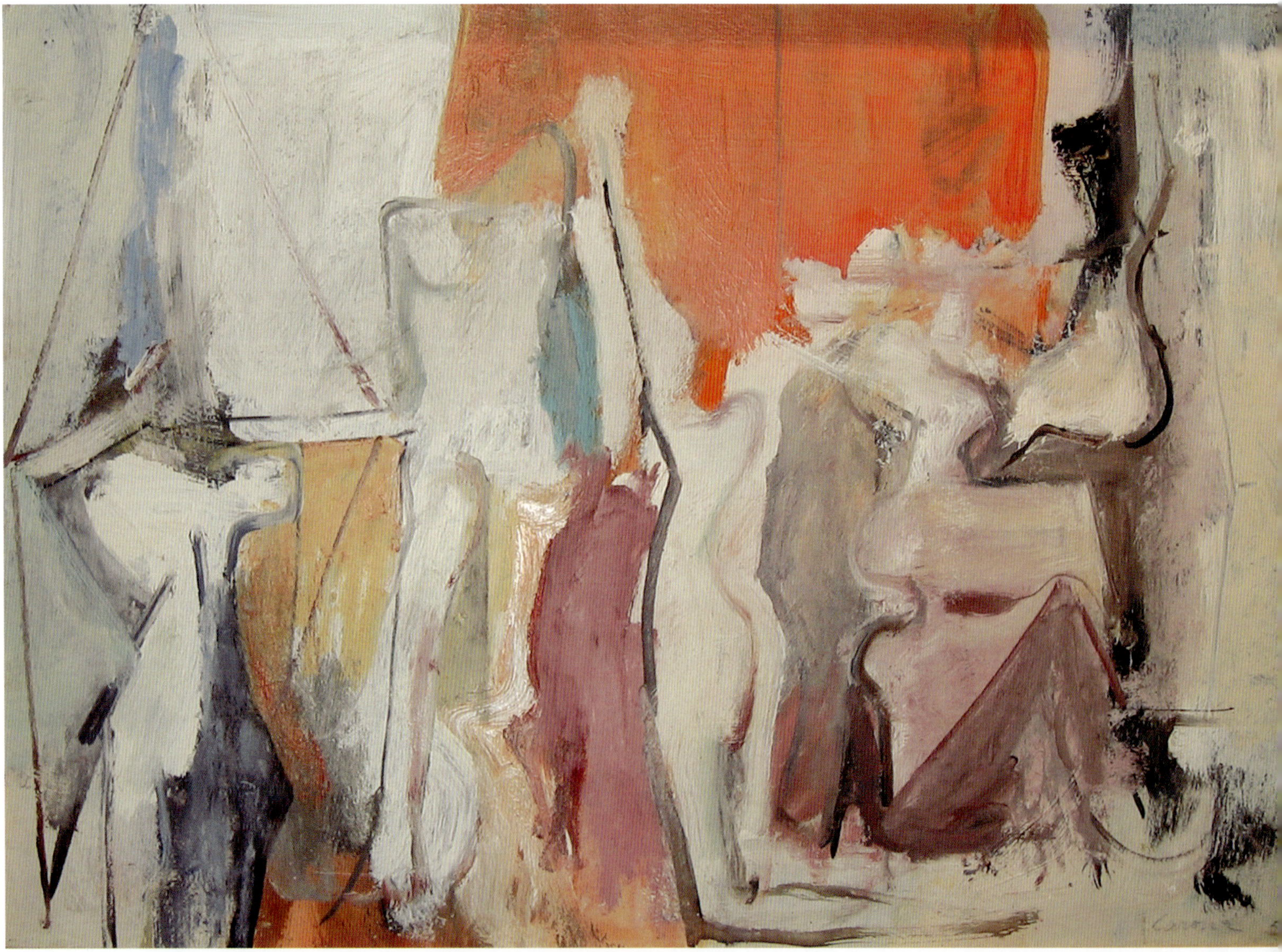

Untitled, oil on paper, 25" x 31", 1956. *Courtesy of Anita Shapolsky Gallery.*

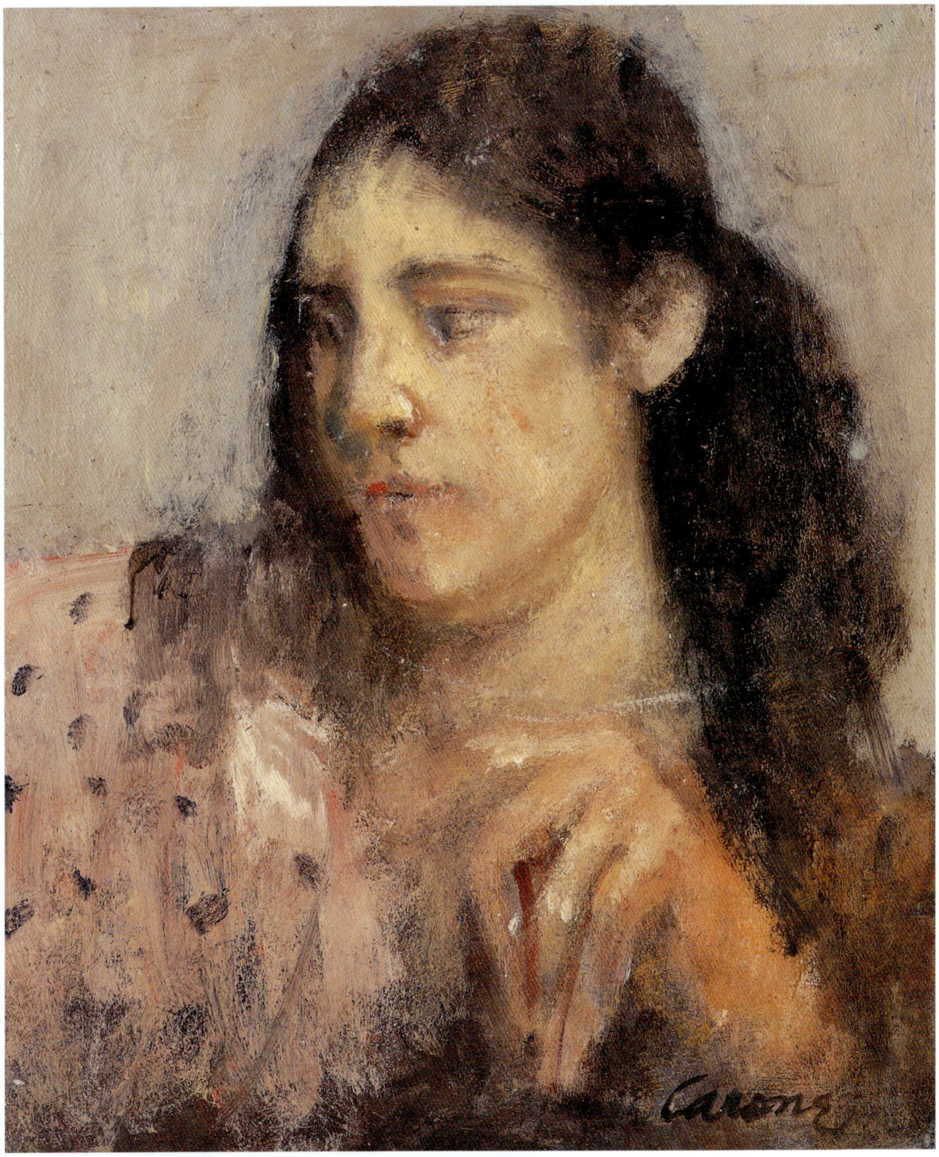

Calabane, oil on panel, 16.5" x 20.5", c.1985-2003. *Courtesy of David Findlay Jr Fine Art.*

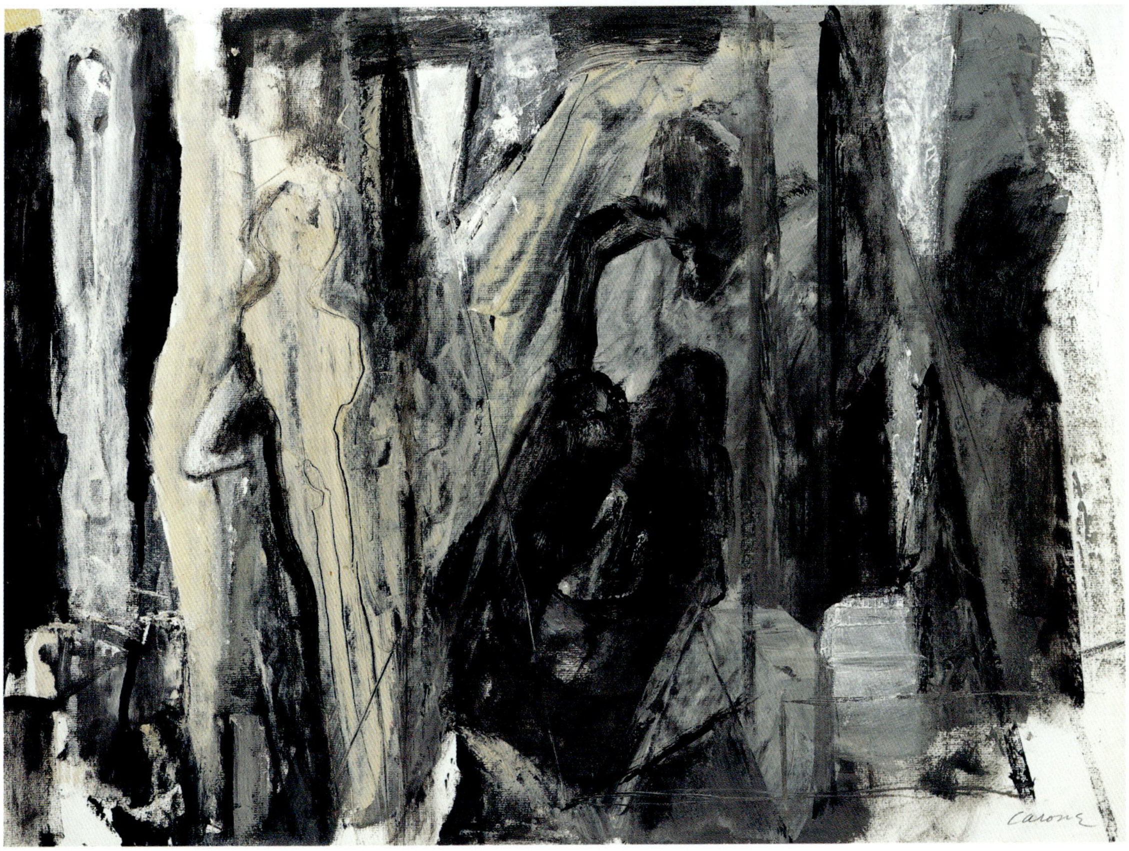

Untitled, mixed media on paper, 19" x 25", 2000. *Courtesy of Lohin-Geduld Gallery.*

Bernard Chaet

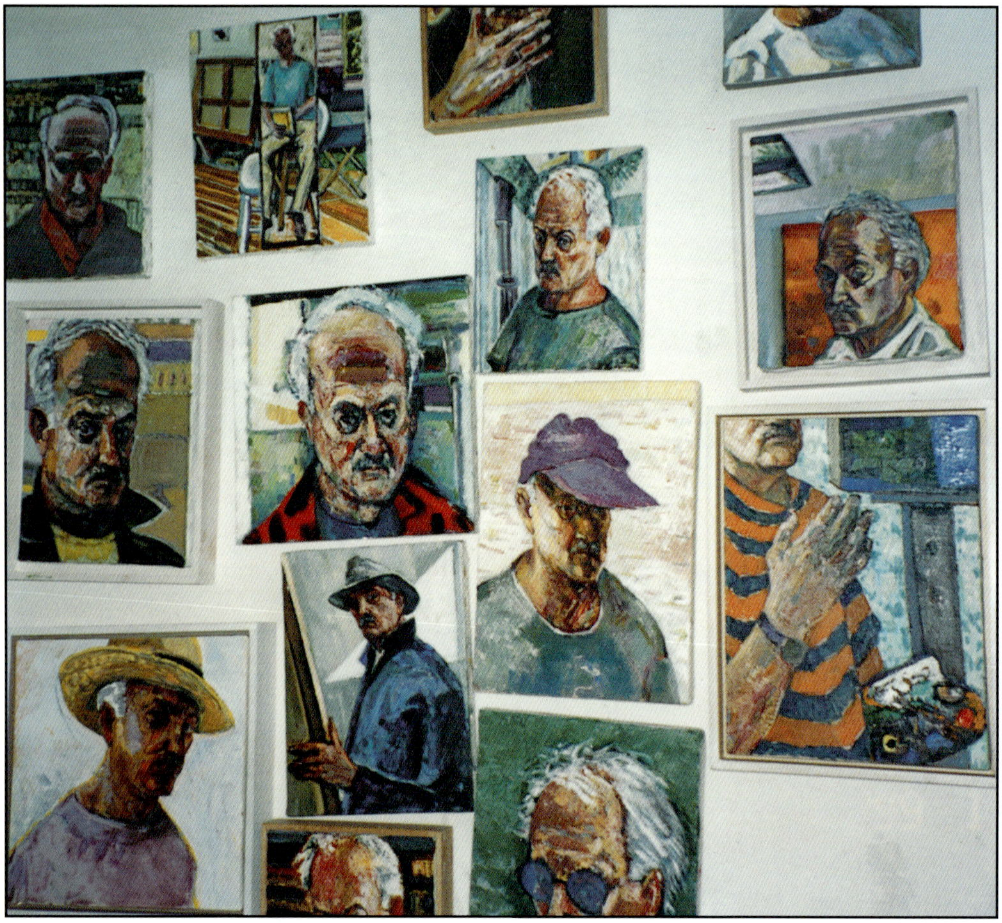

Grouping of self portraits, oil on canvas. *Courtesy of David Findlay Jr Fine Art.*

Bernard Chaet, a Professor of Painting at Yale for over twenty-five years, studied at the School of the Boston Museum of Fine Arts and at Tufts University. An elected member of the National Academy of Design, he is the author of several now-classic texts, including *The Art of Drawing* and *An Artist's Notebook*. Chaet's summer studio at Cape Ann, Massachusetts provides the setting for many of his energetic, color-filled paintings of the rocky coast and shoreline.

Chaet's special interest in the self-portrait has brought forth a large body of probing, honest, and freshly-seen studies. When questioned, he says, "Vanity? Yes, but ... a vanity to communicate with the ... masters who inspire. ..."[31]

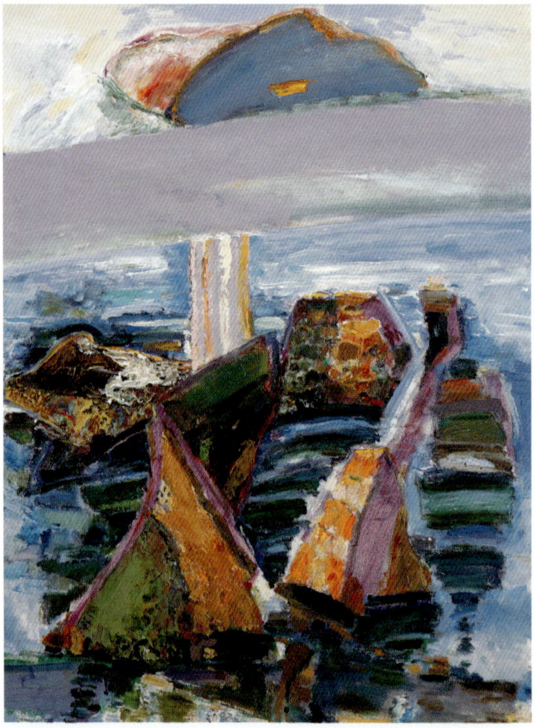

Morning Song, oil on canvas, 40" x 30", 2004. *Private collection. Courtesy of David Findlay Jr Fine Art.*

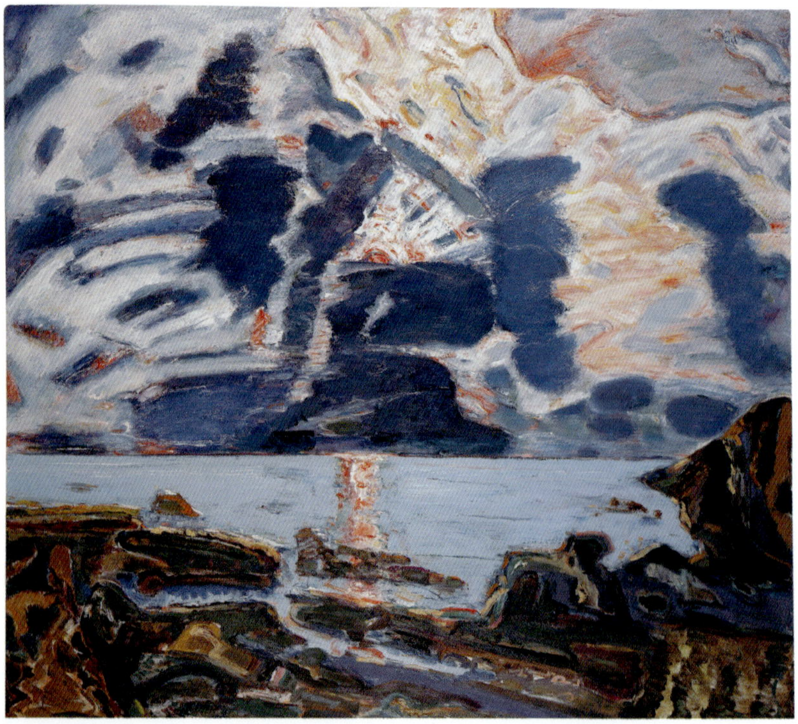

A.M., oil on canvas, 46" x 50", 2000. *Henry Ward Ranger Purchase Prize, National Academy of Design, 2003. Courtesy of David Findlay Jr Fine Art.*

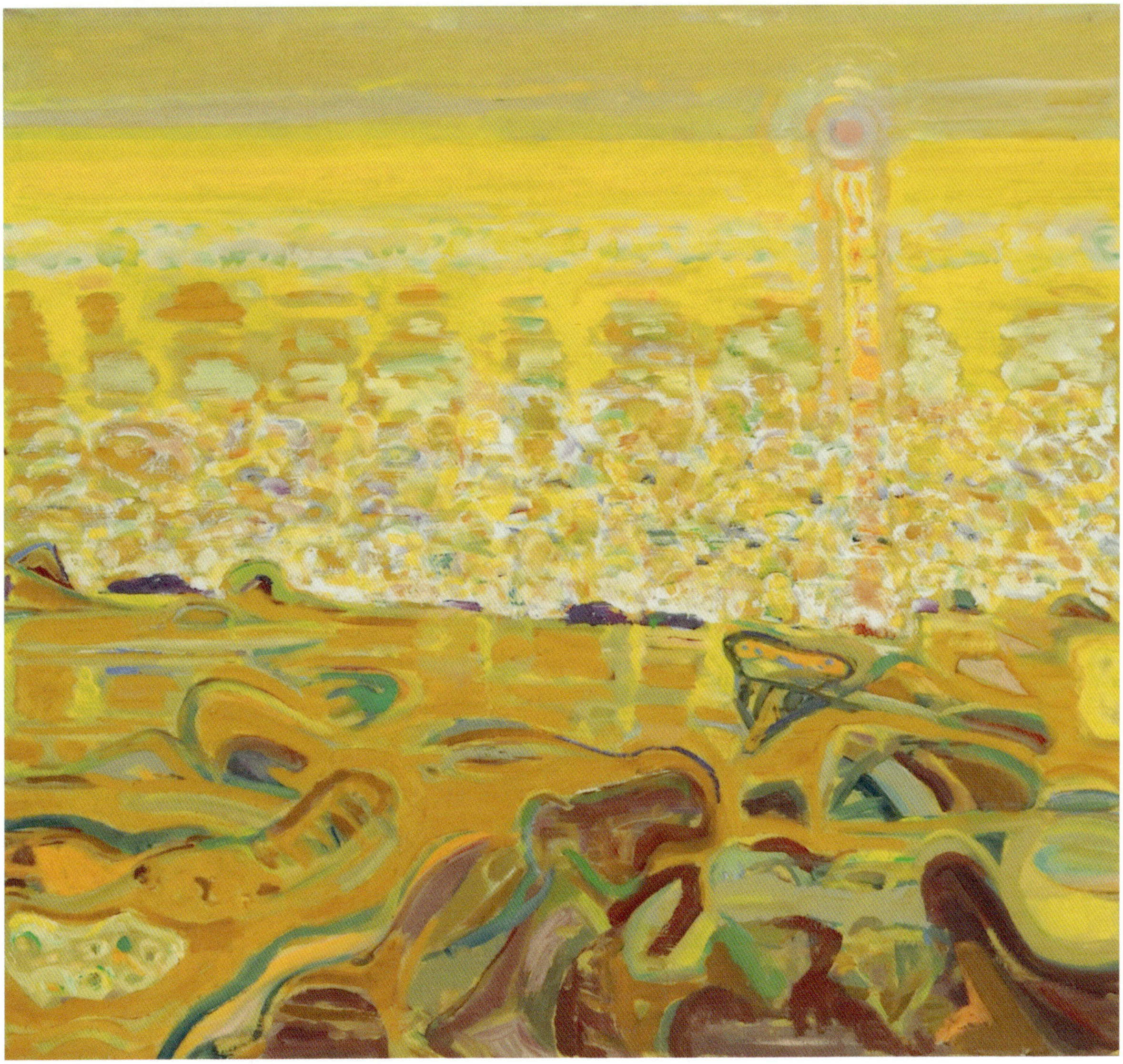

Ochre Morning, oil on canvas, 36" x 36", c.1993-2003. *Courtesy of David Findlay Jr Fine Art.*

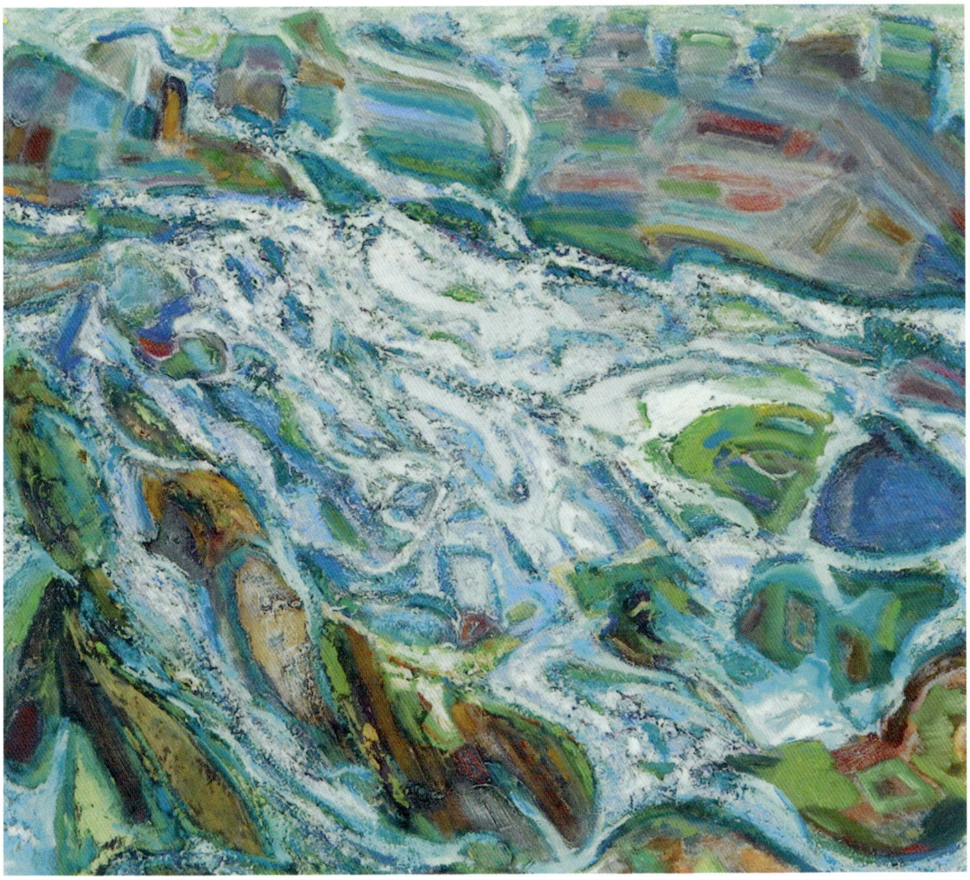

His paintings and drawings have been exhibited throughout the United States and appear in many museum collections, notably the Metropolitan Museum of Art and the Brooklyn Museum, where he was included in its 1955, "Golden Years of American Drawing." He was also shown at the 1956 Artists Annual at the historic Stable Gallery in New York. Chaet is currently represented by David Findlay Jr Fine Art in New York's famed gallery center, the Fuller Building, on 57th Street and Madison Avenue.

Eddy, oil on canvas, 24" x 26", c.1998-2002. *Courtesy of David Findlay Jr Fine Art.*

Ellen Cibula

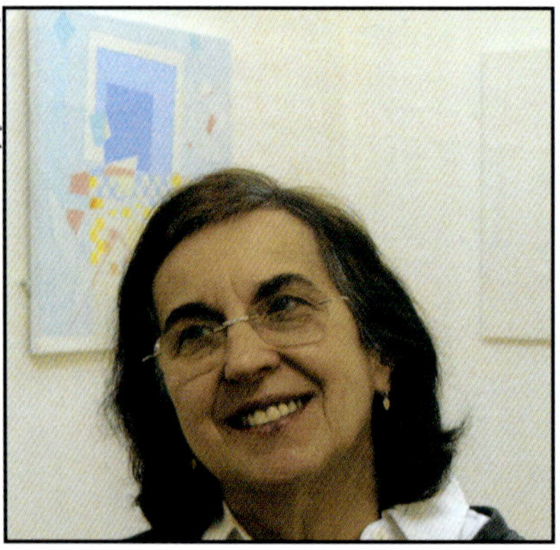

Courtesy of the artist.

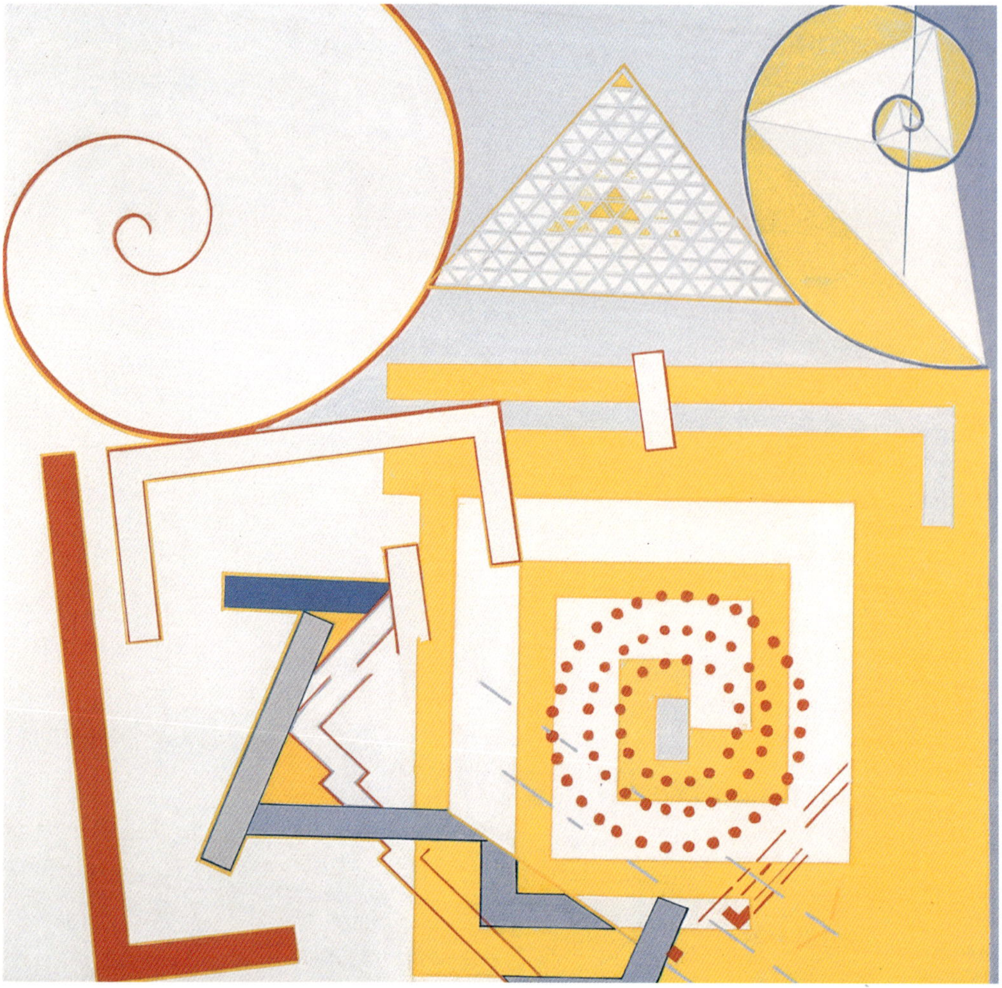

Universe (AHA), acrylic on canvas, 20" x 20", 2002.

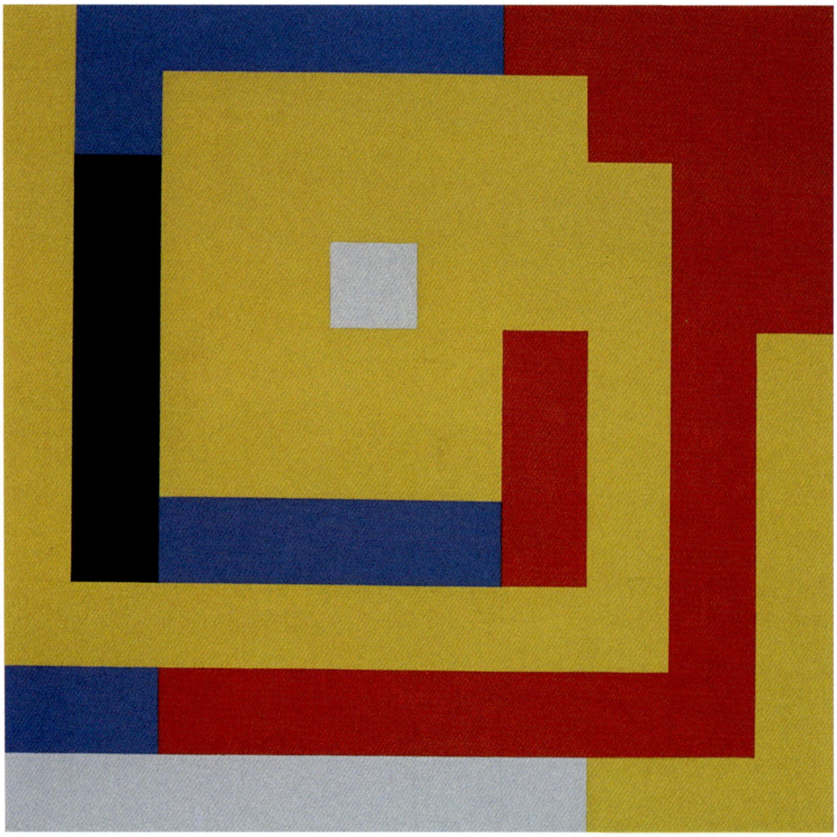

Untitled, acrylic on canvas, 20" x 20", 1991.

Ellen Cibula, whose earlier geometric works were often based on the grid, numerical progressions, spiral structures, and primary colors, more recently has chosen to "explore chaos; ... my essential concerns are space, movement, velocity, light and the play of it all.... Instead of calculating perfection, I take a random leap into the void of the canvas. ..."[32]

Cibula, who studied at Mundelein College and the School of the Art Institute of Chicago, has taught color at the Parsons School of Design. Cibula's work has been shown widely in New York, as well as Chicago, Dallas, and Philadelphia.

She and her husband, the painter Johan Sellenraad, have worked at their Soho studio in New York since 1972.

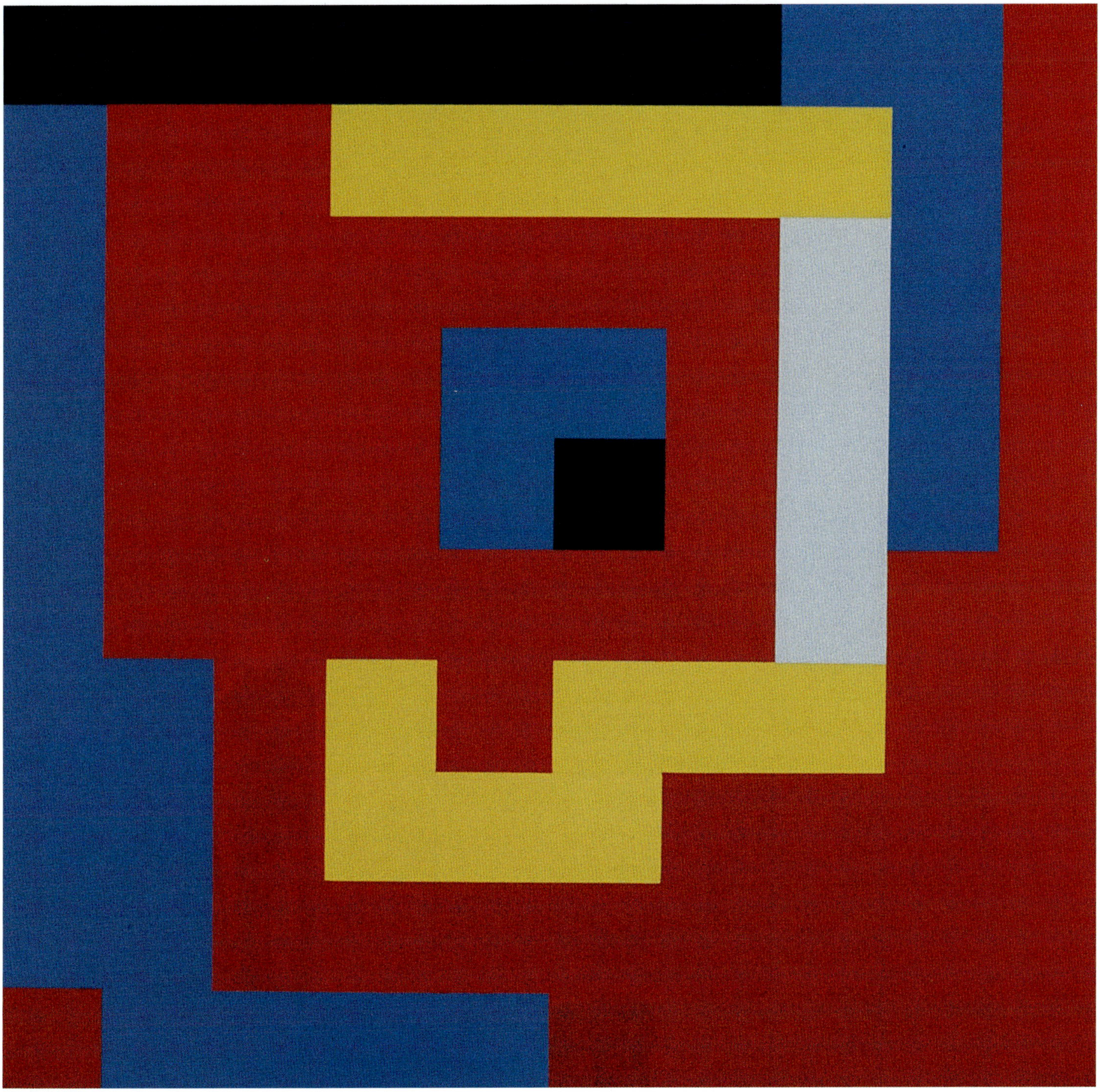

Untitled, acrylic on canvas, 30" x 30", 1991.

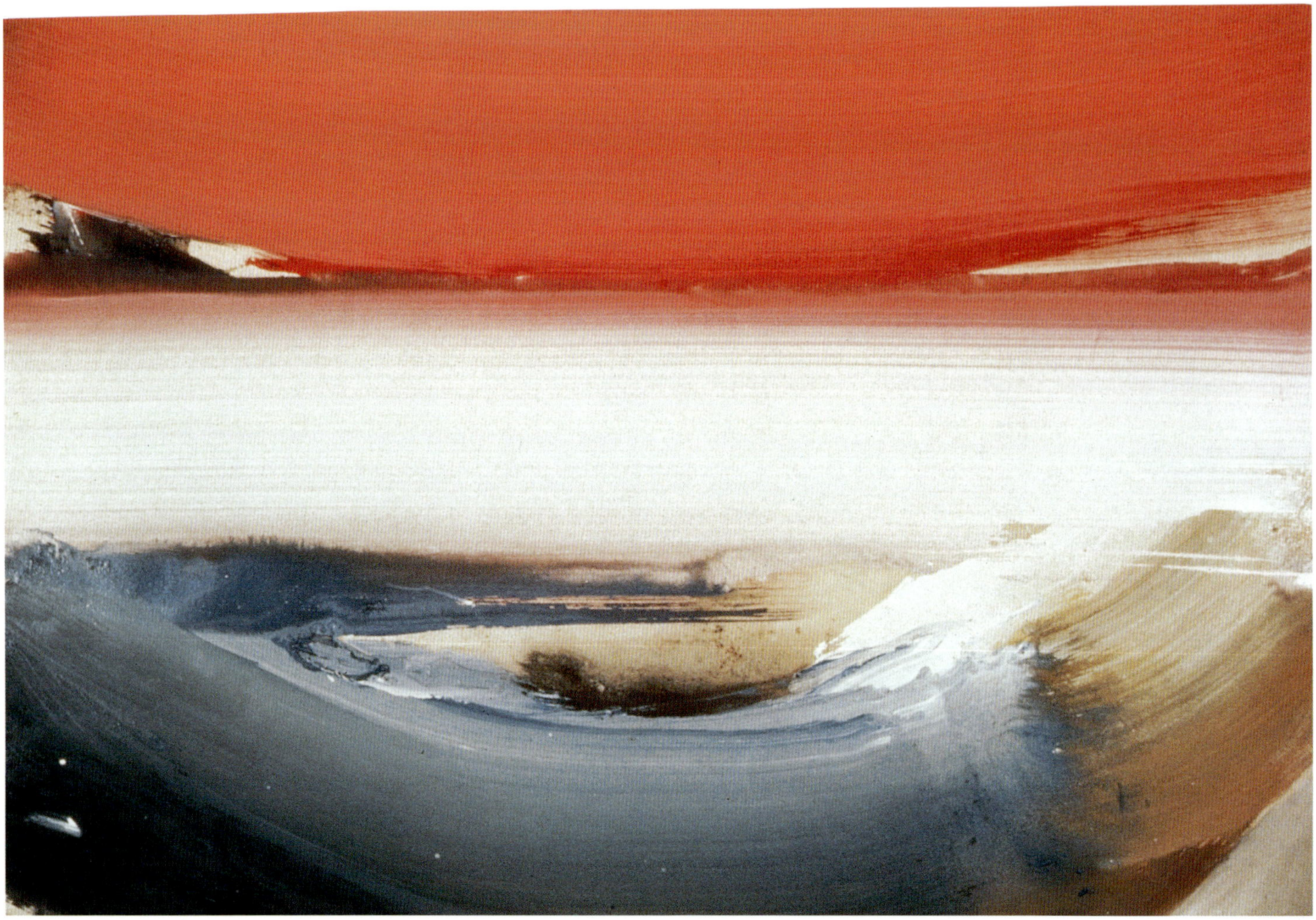

Untitled, acrylic on canvas, 50" x 66", 1987. *Courtesy of the artist.*

Ed Clark

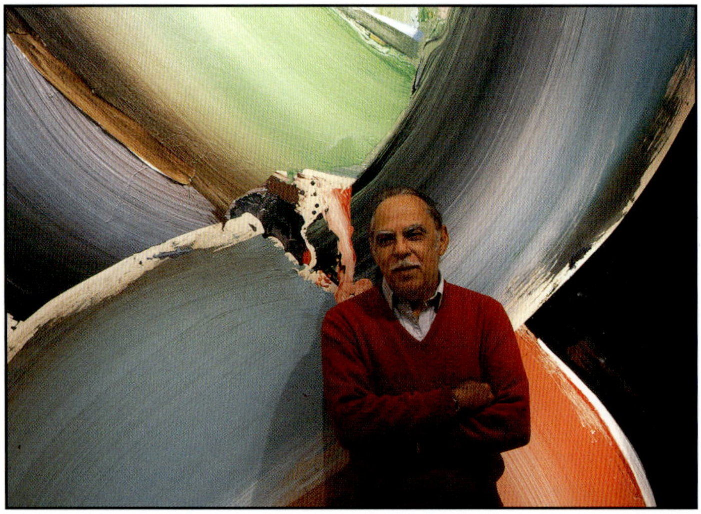

Courtesy of the artist.

Edward Clark, credited with the first shaped-canvas painting, shown at the Brata Gallery in 1957 where he was a charter member, is also known as the innovator of the push-broom technique, which enables him to move paint in bold swaths across large, floor-positioned canvases in all directions.

Born in the Storyville section of New Orleans, Clark studied at the Art Institute of Chicago and later in Paris, where he lived and painted for five years before settling in New York; his midtown Manhattan twelfth floor studio looks out directly at the Empire State Building.

An abstract painter whose works are often conceived on a grand scale, Clark has employed oval formats and explored many geometric, linear, and striped motifs. He has always been an innovator, resisting categories. As far back as 1968 he proclaimed, "Art is not subject to political games; its importance elevates it above any racial difference. All men of talent, of noble spirit, can make it."[33]

A winner of numerous prizes and awards, Clark's many nationwide and European exhibits reflect his travels around the globe, "from Sicily to Egypt: for the sake of the search,"[34] as a 1997 exhibition neatly announced. He is represented by the G.R. N'Namdi Gallery in New York and Chicago.

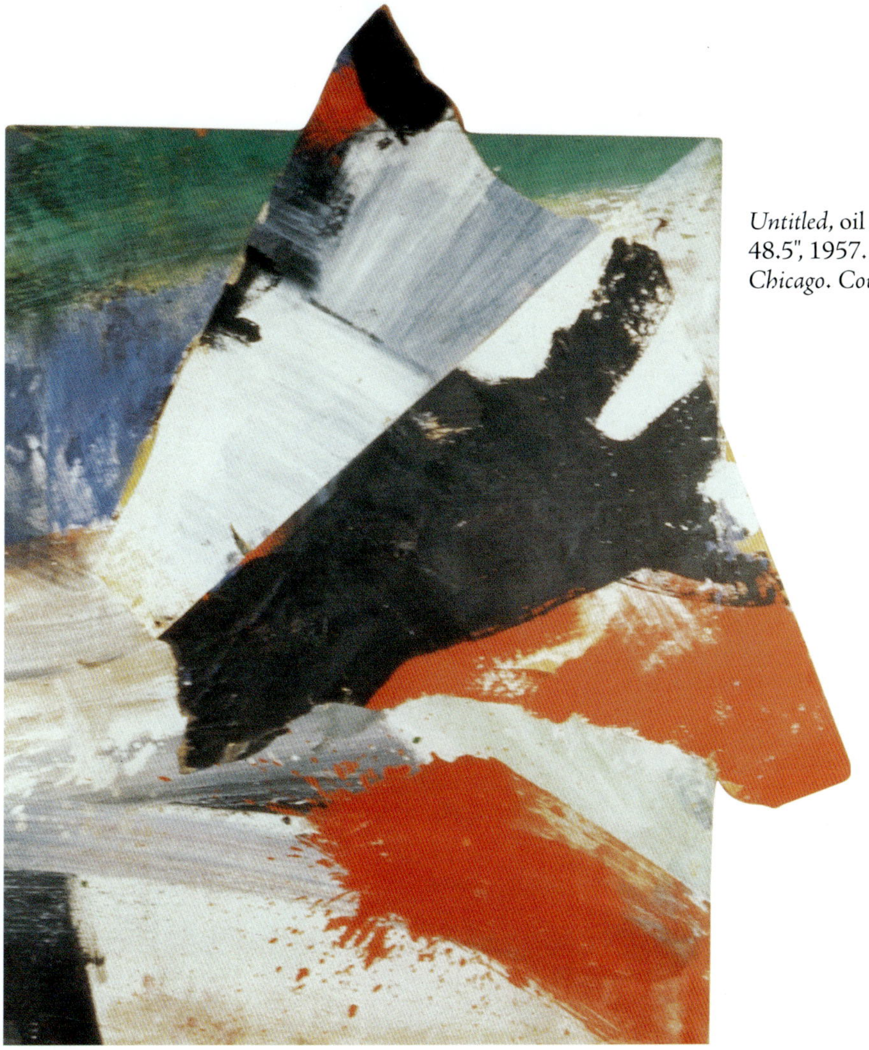

Untitled, oil and paper on masonite, 72" x 48.5", 1957. *Collection of Art Institute of Chicago. Courtesy of the artist.*

Untitled, acrylic on canvas, 55.5" x 69", 1989. *Courtesy of the artist.*

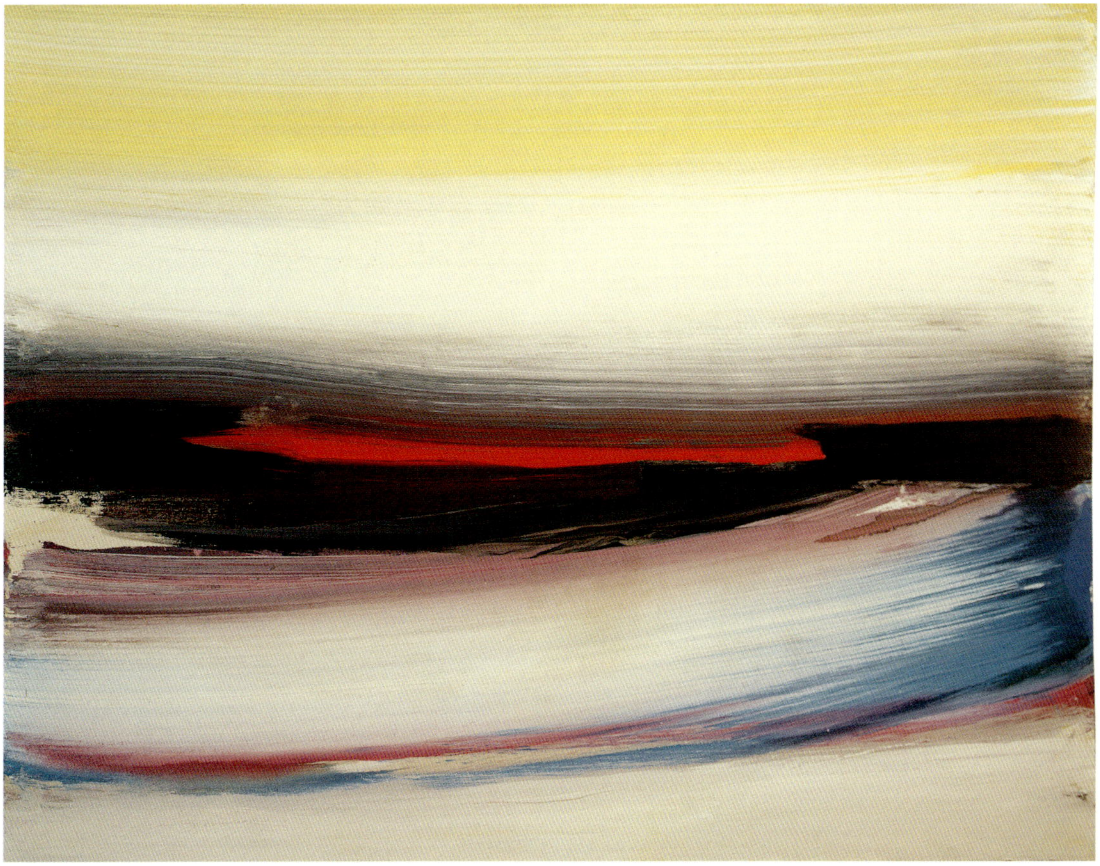

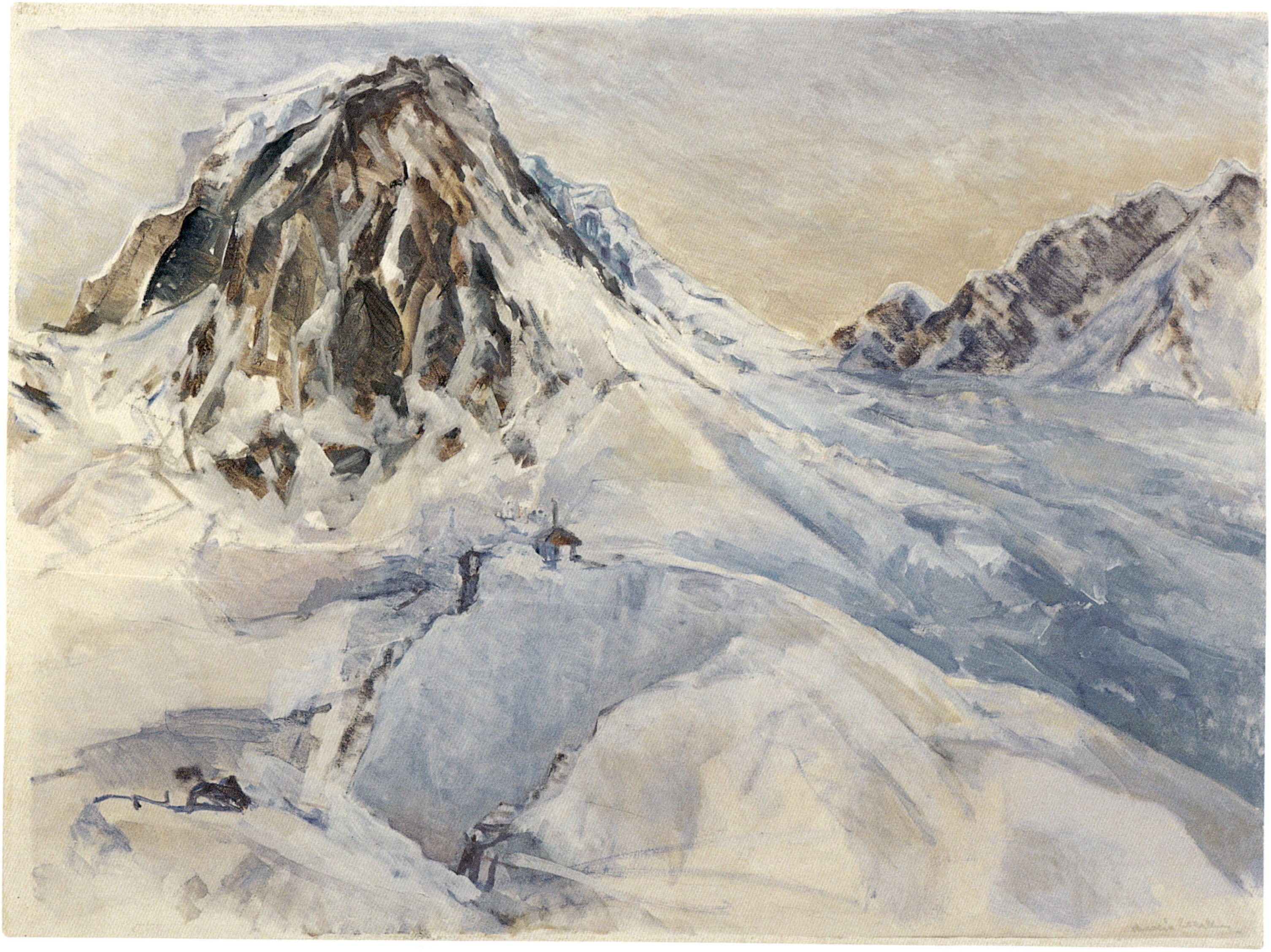

Don Sheldon's Cabin, Alaska, oil on canvas panel, 37" x 48", 2004.

Marcia Clark

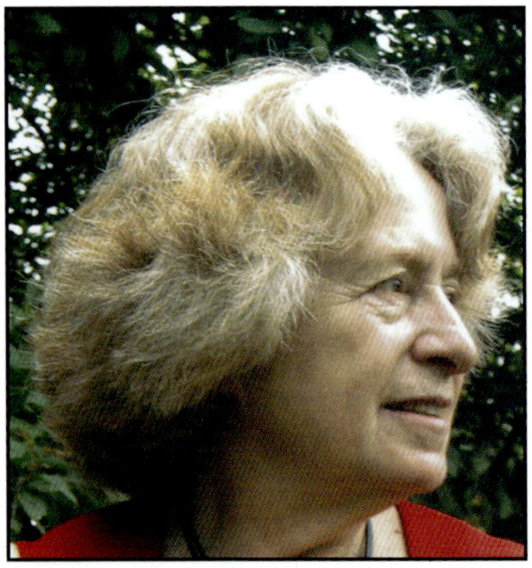

Courtesy of the artist.

Marcia Clark, who directs the Blue Mountain Gallery in New York's Chelsea district, attended the Yale University School of Art, where she studied with Josef Albers, Neil Welliver, Bernard Chaet, and Alex Katz. Later she studied at The State University of New York's New Paltz campus, where she did independent research on the 19th century painter, Thomas Cole, "retracing his travels. ... Discovering [Cole] ... inspired me to return home from my long indenture to Cézanne and European tradition."[35]

In painting her expansive views of nature, she has often been moved to make spatial extensions, adding side panels to her canvases and watercolors. Clark has experimented with extreme viewpoints, aerial bird's eye perspectives, incorporating peripheral vision and spatial concepts derived from abstract expressionism.

"Most of my projects begin in the field and are completed on location," says Clark. "The larger pieces are done in the studio."[36]

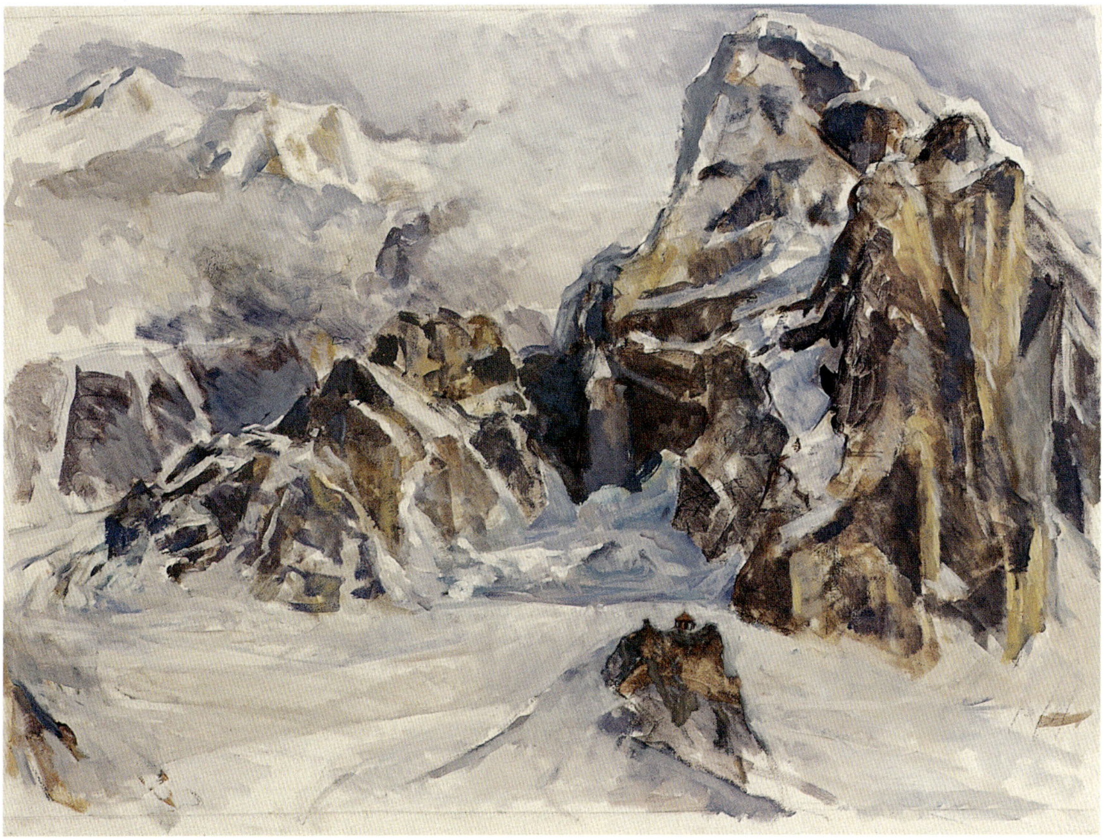

Cabin Site, oil on canvas, 30" x 40", 2002.

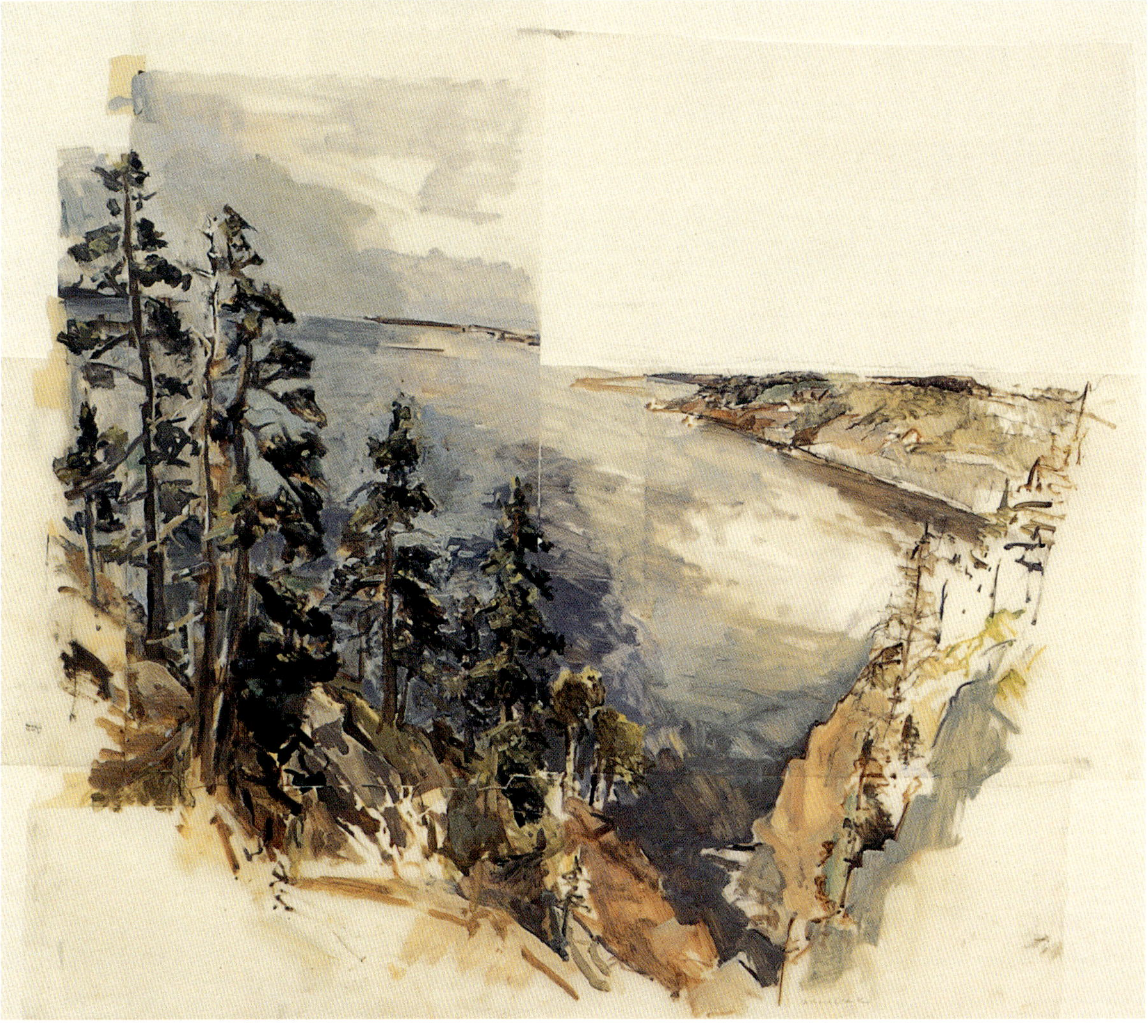

Overlook, MDI, oil on mylar, 36" x 40", 2004.

Chuck Close

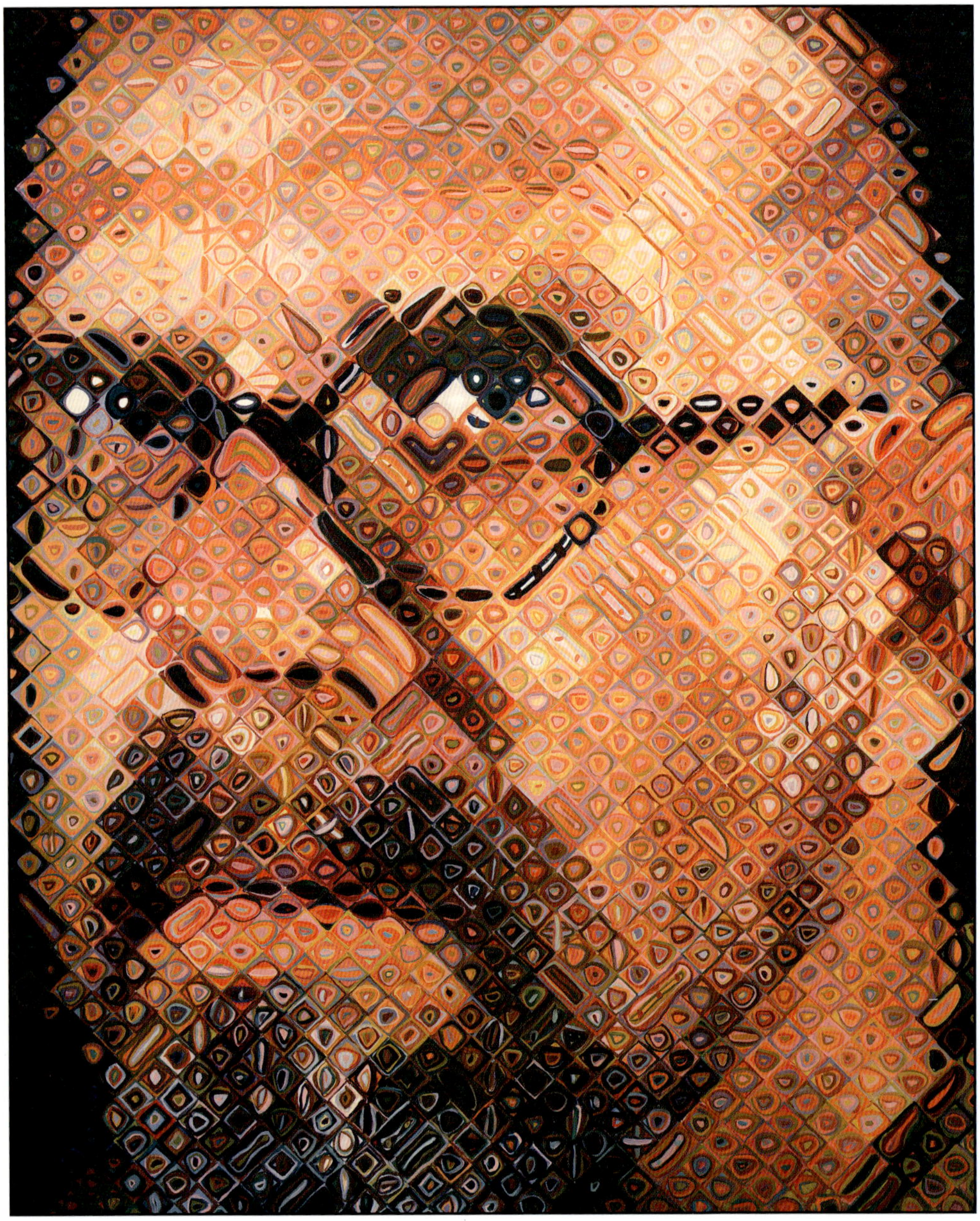

Self Portrait, oil on canvas, 102" x 84", 1997. *Photograph by Ellen Page Wilson. © Chuck Close. Courtesy of PaceWildenstein, New York. Collection of the Museum of Modern Art, Gift of Agnes Gund, Jo Carde and Ronald S. Lauder, Donald L. Bryant, Jr., Leon Black, Michael and Judy Ovitz, Anna Maria and Robert F. Shapiro, Leila and Melville Straus, Doris and Donald Fisher, and purchase.*

Chuck Close, whose frontal, gridded, large, compelling paintings are often of fellow artists, family members, or his own likeness, has redefined the genre of portraiture in our time.

Constantly re-inventing the specifics of description, Close has worked for nearly forty years from sub-divided photographs, with an amazing variety of materials and concepts, from finger-printed markings through a staggering range of tesserated yet unified sub-divisions, "constantly exploring and discovering new ways to activate, even burst, the bounds of each cell, the miniature looping compositions which somehow orchestrate to complete (each) work."[37]

Surmounting overwhelming physical challenges, Close uses sophisticated hydraulic equipment that permits him to continue to paint as freely as before his 1988 catastrophe. Close has expressed his disdain for technology and does not use computers in his work, indeed questions their very identity as labor-saving devices.

An MFA graduate of Yale's School of Art, he received a Fulbright grant to study in Europe, then taught at the University of Massachusetts. The 1967 Whitney Biennial included work by Close, and the Museum of Modern Art first showed his paintings in 1973. His monumental portraits, photographs, and prints are in virtually every major museum and collection, and he continues to exhibit unexpectedly new and inventive canvases. Close is represented by PaceWildenstein in New York.

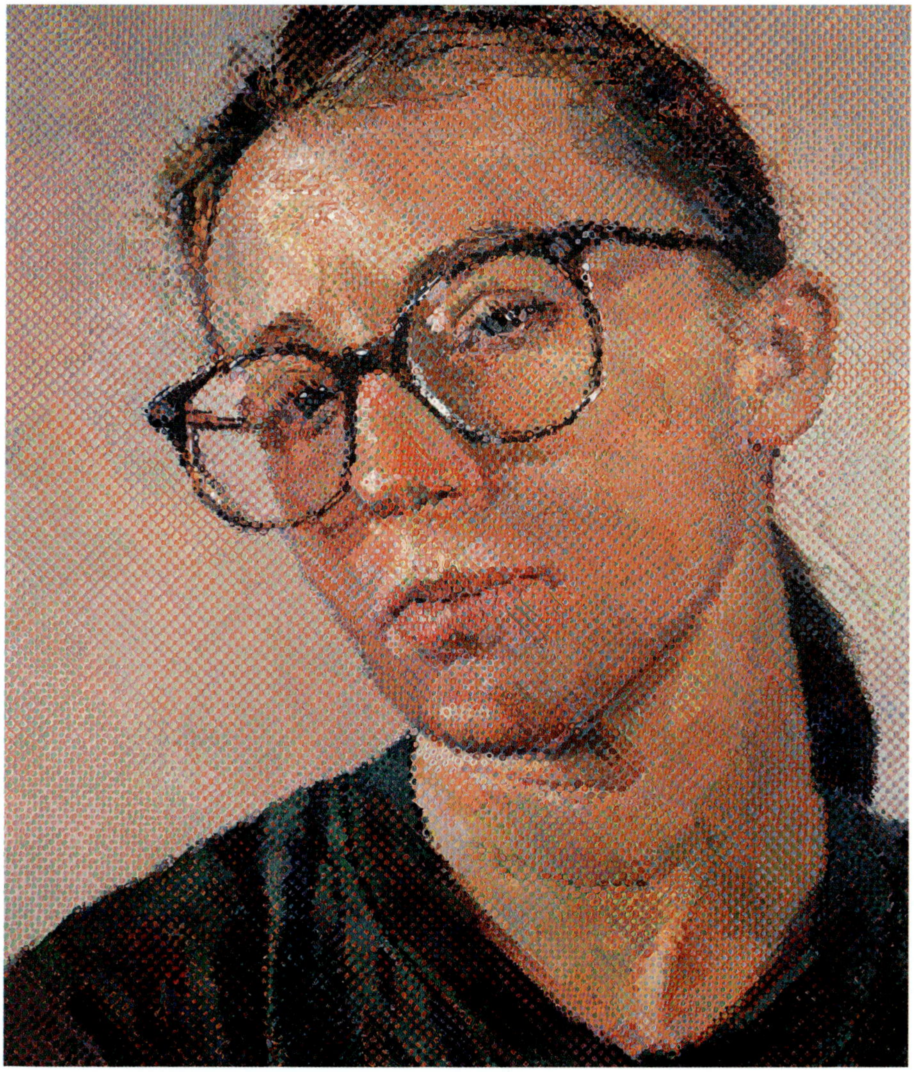

Cindy, oil on canvas, 102" x 84", 1988. *Photographed by Bill Jacobson Studio. Private collection © Chuck Close. Courtesy of PaceWildenstein, New York.*

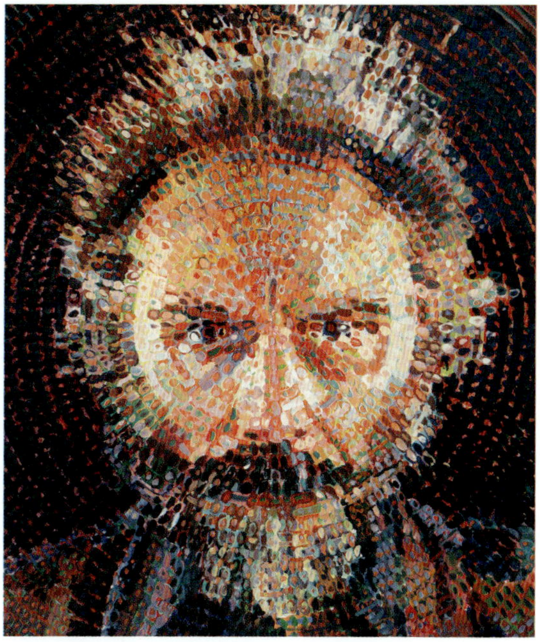

Lucas II, oil on canvas, 36" x 30", 1987. *Photographed by Bill Jacobson Studio. Private collection © Chuck Close. Courtesy of PaceWildenstein, New York.*

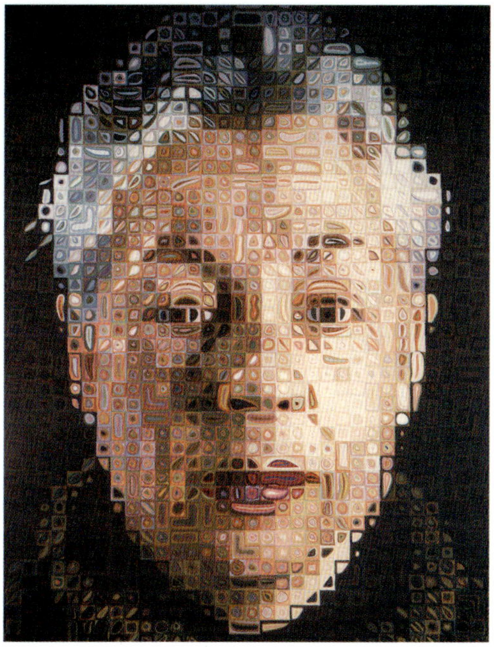

Lynda, oil on canvas, 108.5" x 84", 2004. *Photograph by Kerry Ryan McFate. © Chuck Close. Courtesy of PaceWildenstein, New York.*

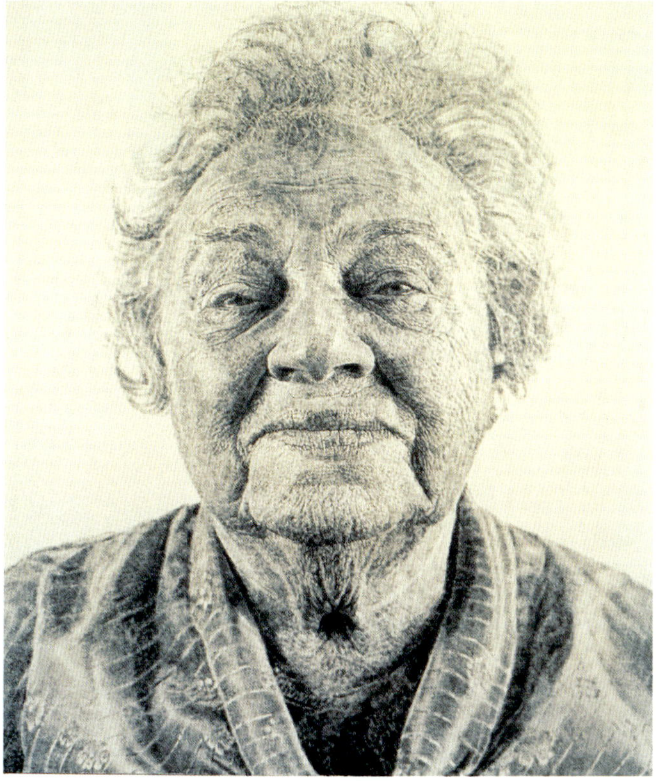

Fanny/Fingerpainting, oil on canvas, 102" x 84", 1985. *Collection of The National Gallery of Art, Washington, D.C., Lila Acheson Wallace Fund. © Chuck Close. Courtesy of PaceWildenstein, New York.*

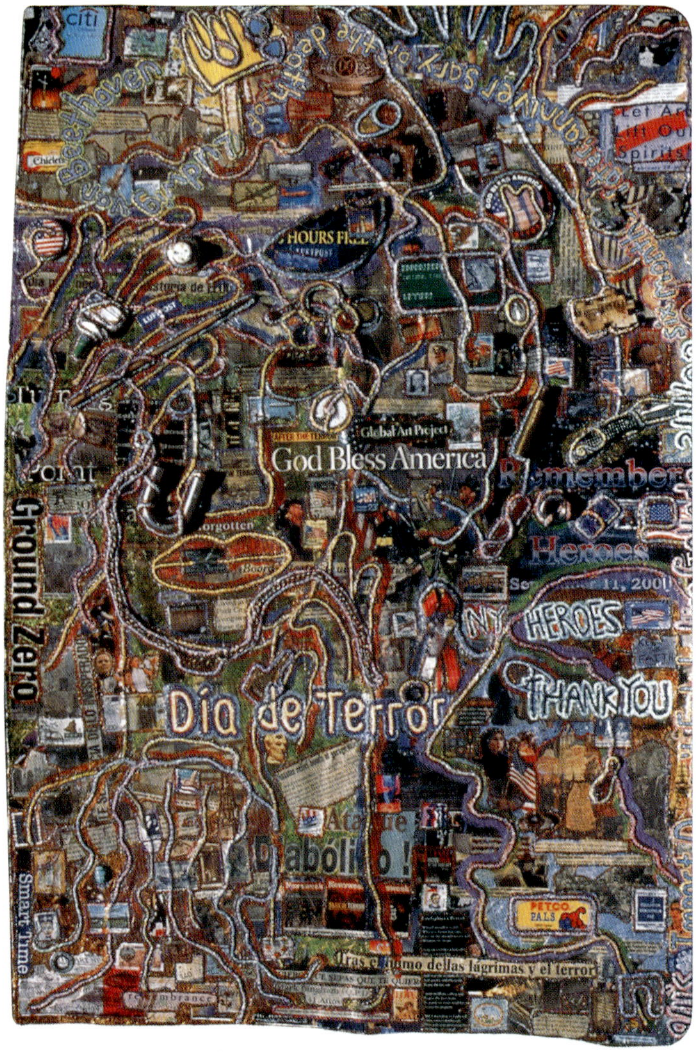

9/11's Impact Doesn't Fade, acrylic, collage, found objects on canvas, 38" x 25", 2002.

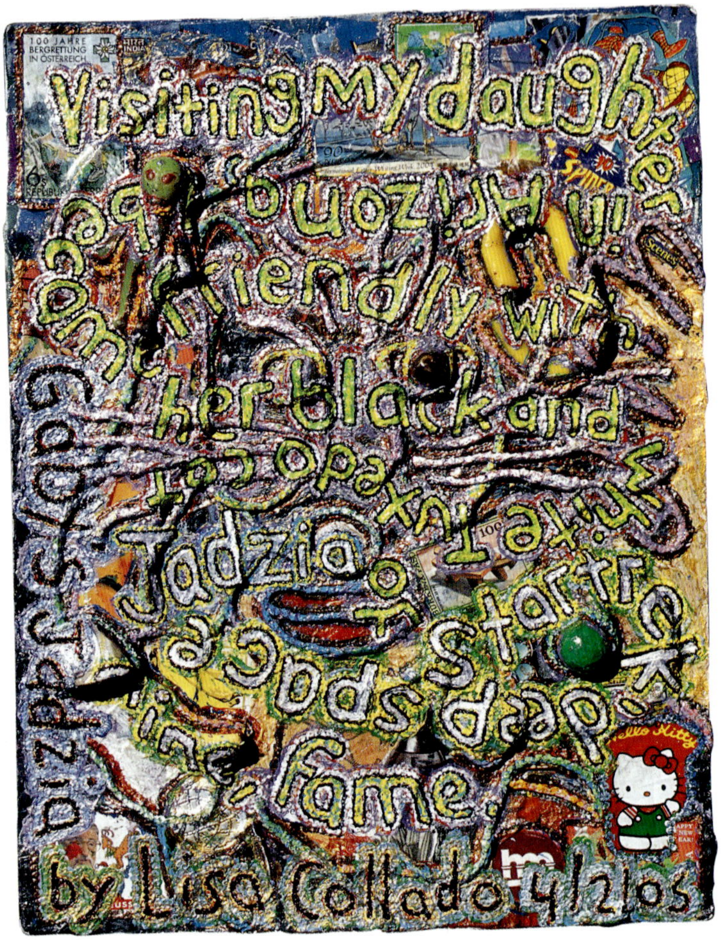

Gaby's Jadzia, acrylic, collage, found objects on cardboard, 12.75" x 10.25", 2005.

Lisa Collado

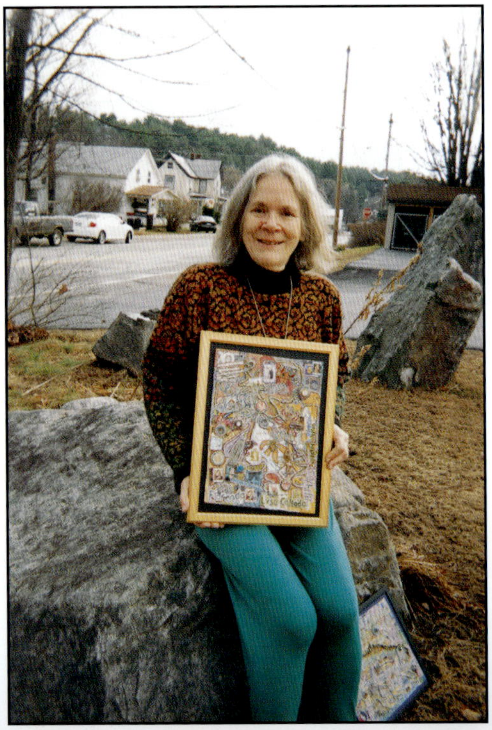
Courtesy of the artist.

Lisa Collado, former president of the National Association of Women Artists (NAWA), long a champion of women's rights in the arts, was asked to write six biographies for the St. James Press's *Encyclopedia of Women Artists*.

Receiving a BA from SUNY's Empire State College and an MA from New York University, Collado has won Pollock-Krasner and Adolph and Esther Gottlieb Grants. She names Van Gogh, Munch, Kahlo, and Schapiro as major influences on her art and philosophy.

Collado has developed a uniquely complex, multi-layered collage-painting style, in which she tries to "integrate different materials to form a painting ... with specific areas of text and found objects that treat whatever I'm preoccupied with at the time."[38] Political, feminist, and multi-cultural concerns are often those "preoccupations" for Collado.

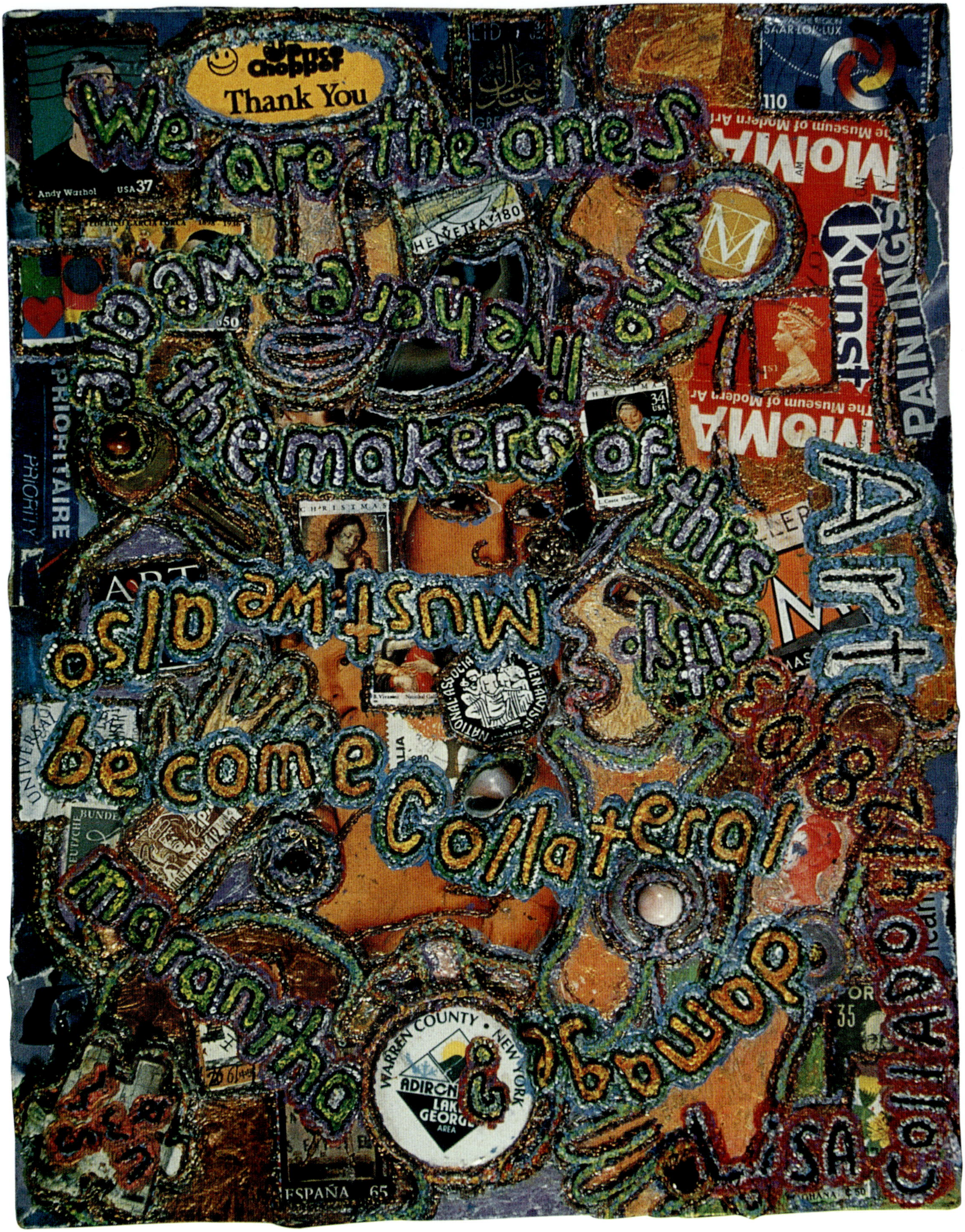

Collateral Damage, acrylic, collage, found objects on paper, 11" x 8.5", 2003. *Collection of Maria Salud Agassiz, Geneva.*

Arthur Coppedge

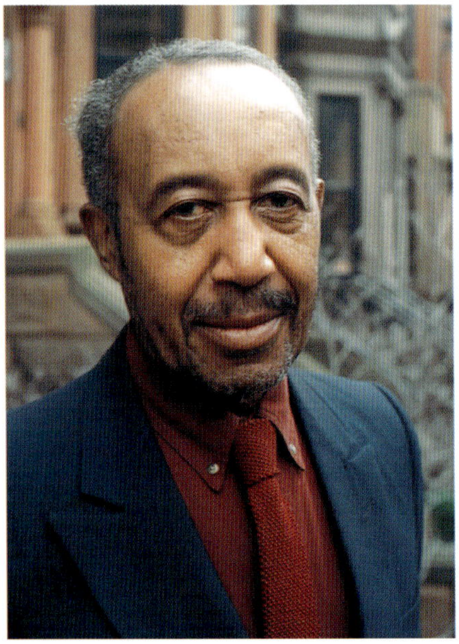

Photograph © Cynthia Dantzic.

Arthur Coppedge, who identifies as a painter first and a product of Brooklyn, says, "I paint my world. ... Much of my work is of the people and things of Brooklyn. That's where I'm from!"[39] Tracing his own heritage to Scottish, Cherokee, Blackfoot, and Ashanti ancestors in Ghana, he considers himself Southern American.

Born in Brooklyn, Coppedge attended Brooklyn College, and studied at the Brooklyn Museum Art School with Isaac Soyer, David Levine, Reuben Tam, and Louis Grebenak. He worked with its Director, Augustus Peck, and later taught at the school. He also taught at the National Academy of Design, the School of Ethical Culture, and the Walden School. He was named Artist-in-Residence at the Brooklyn Campus of Long Island University.

Awarded a prize in painting by the National Academy of Design, he was one of fifty artists selected by the U.S. Department of the Interior to represent each state in the Bicentennial exhibition at the Corcoran Gallery in Washington, D.C.

Coppedge's paintings have been shown also at the Fogg Museum in Cambridge, Massachusetts, the Brooklyn Museum, the Studio Museum in Harlem, and the High Museum in Atlanta, Georgia, among many others.

Public and corporate collections that have acquired his works include the Chase Manhattan Bank, the University of Wisconsin, Brooklyn Union Gas, and Black Enterprise Magazine.

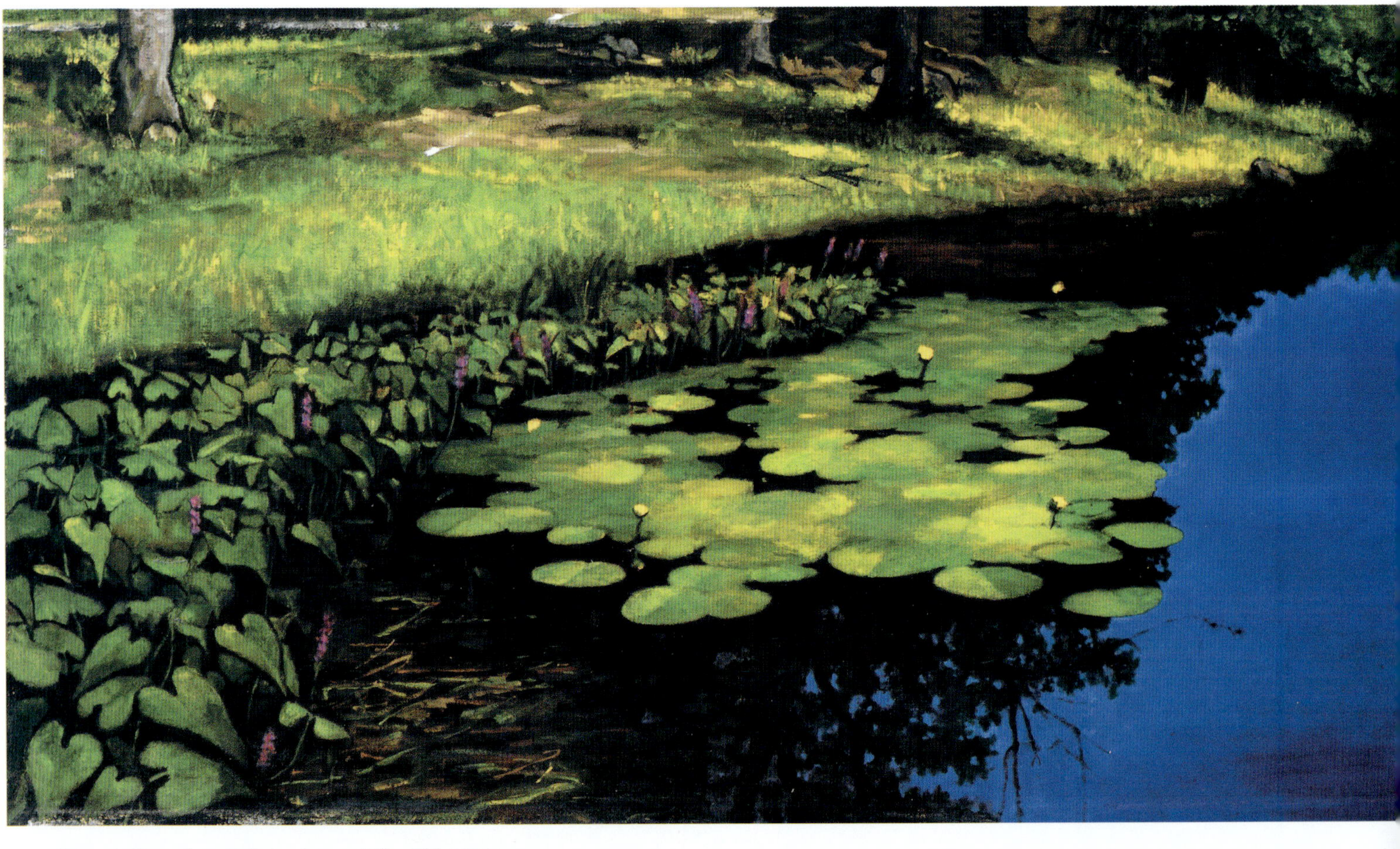

Water Lilies, oil on Belgian linen, 24" x 30", 1978.

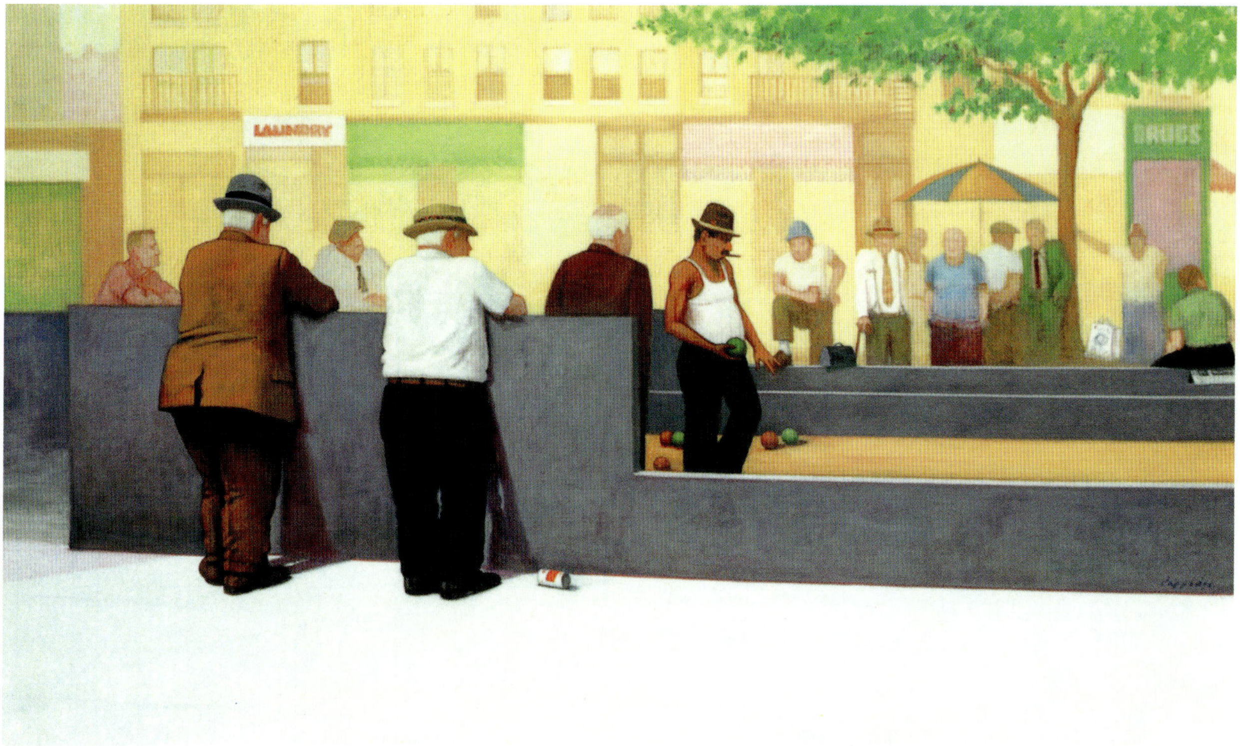

The Game (Bocci Players), oil on linen, 4' x 6', 1969.

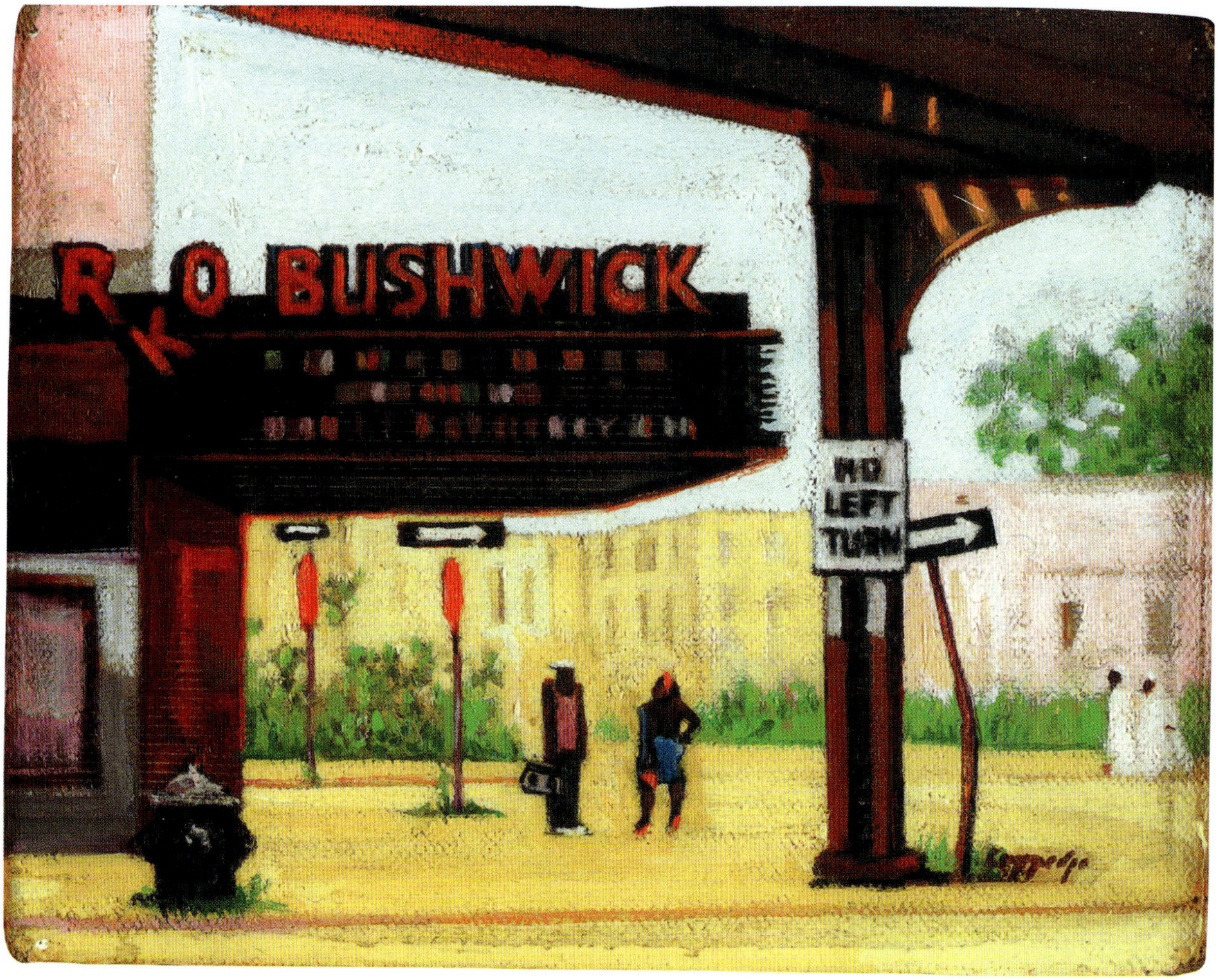

RKO Bushwick, oil on panel, 11" x 12", 1977.

Judy Cuttler

Judy Cuttler, who, from the age of seven, audited classes with her father, a Professor of Art History at the University of Iowa, has a long history of study and association with such distinguished artists as Leland Bell, Nell Blaine, and Robert deNiro at The Cooper Union, and the New York Studio School.

She also achieved early distinction as a classical pianist and has always been "drawn to modern painters who felt an affinity between color and music, such as Klee, Matisse, and Kandinsky. My background in music has helped me think of painting in terms of rhythms, visual harmonies, and counterpoint ... my goals are to combine the two visions, abstract and figurative, via color."[40]

Of Cuttler, Nell Blaine says she has "a bold sense of essence and a fresh, structural use of color. ... There is a breath and scale ... she is accomplished in portraits as well as still life and landscape. [Cuttler's] paintings have immediacy and depth of feeling combined with an honest approach."[41] Her "loaded brushstrokes"[42] have been called reminiscent of deKooning, exuding painting energy. DeNiro calls her, "the best colorist, and ... most accomplished compositionist, working today."[43]

Cuttler, who was artist-in-residence at the Cadet Fine Arts Forum, West Point, is represented by the Bowery Gallery and also exhibits regularly as a member of the Westbeth Gallery.

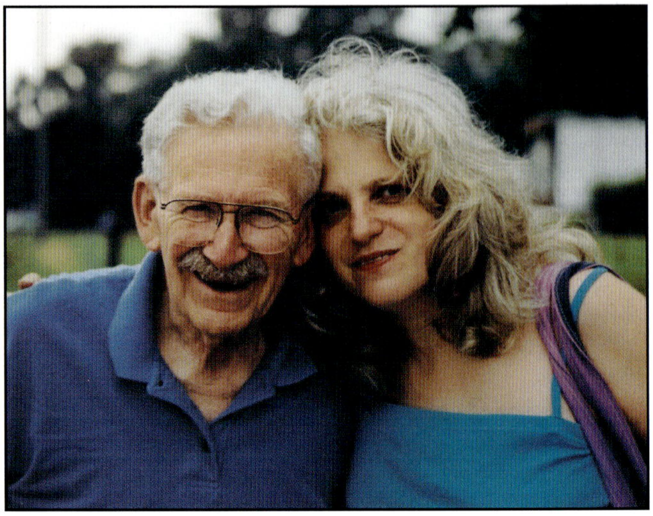

The artist with her father, Charles Cuttler.

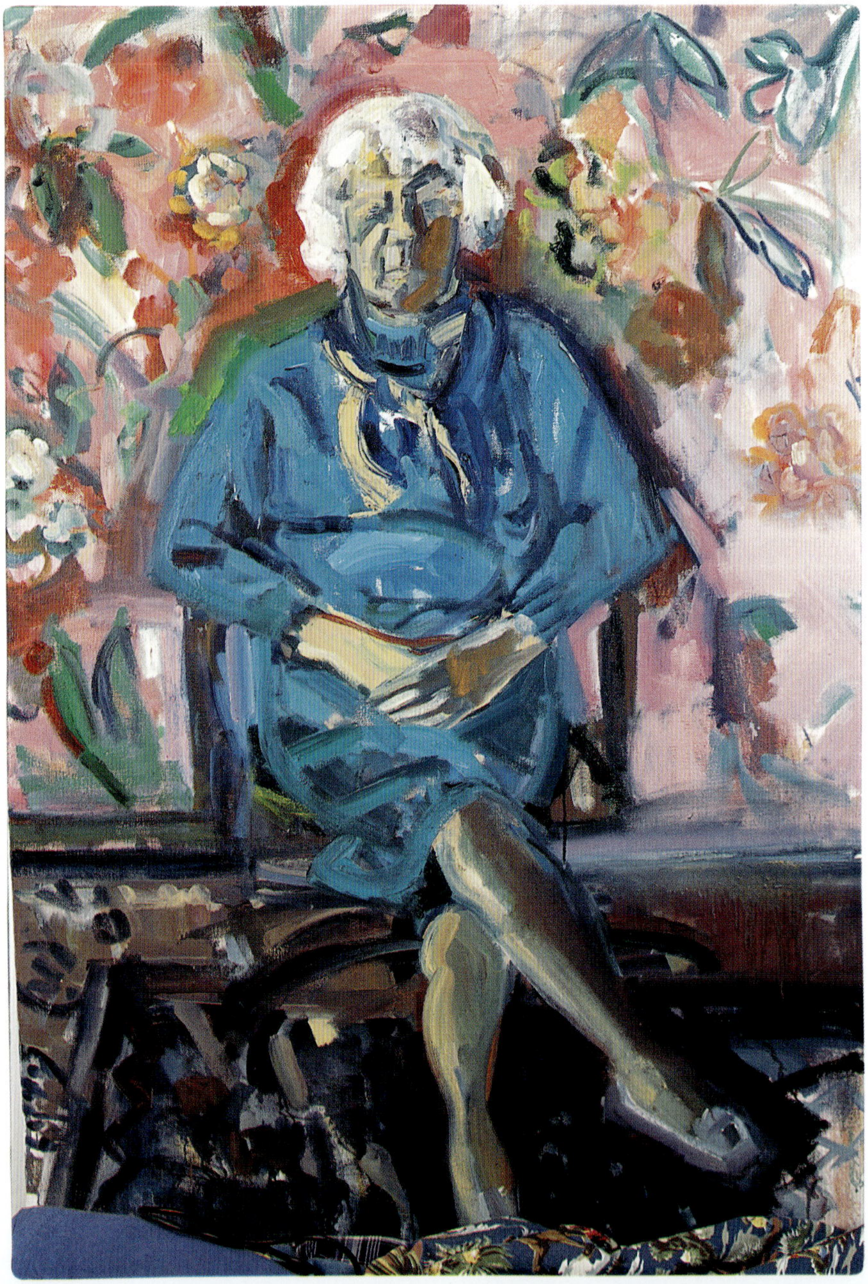

Portrait of My Mother, oil on canvas, 4' x 6', 1997. *Photograph by C. Carone.*

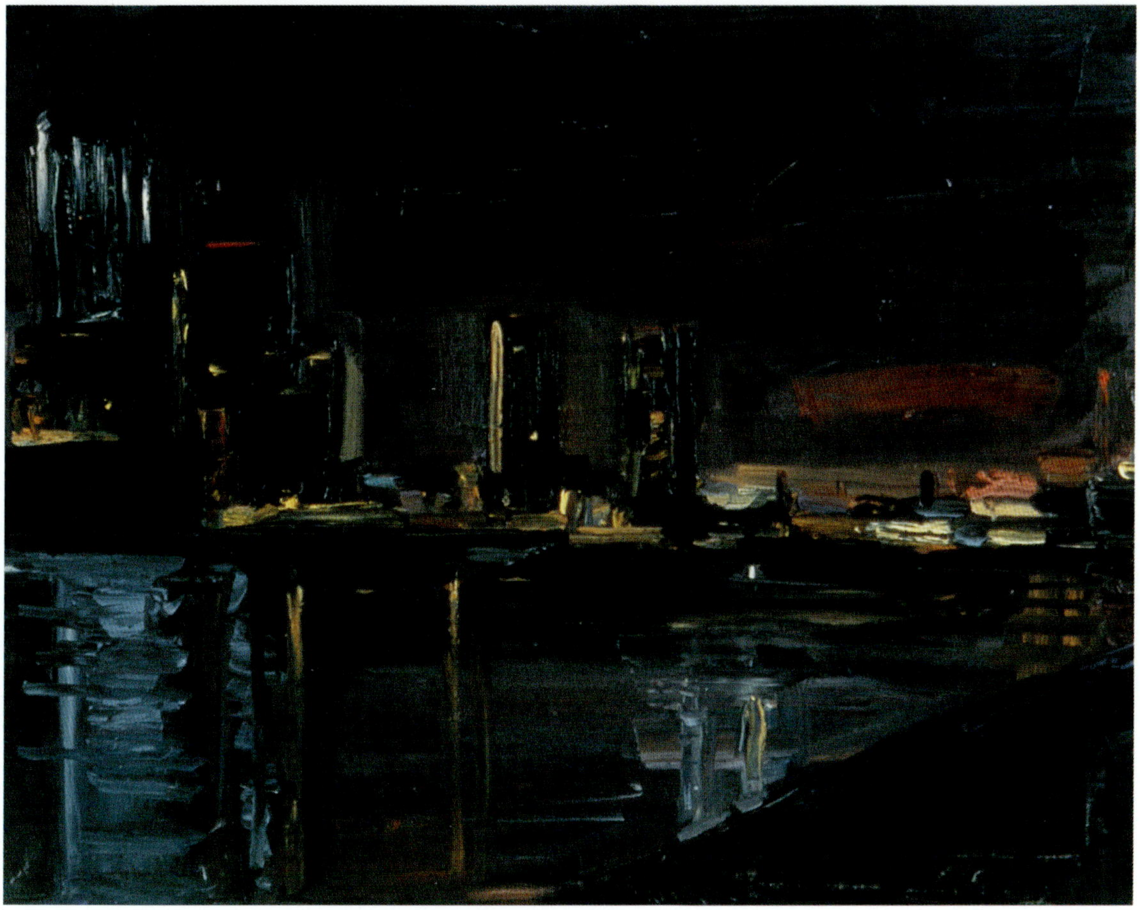

Hudson River Waterfront, night, oil on canvas, 24" x 30", 1991.

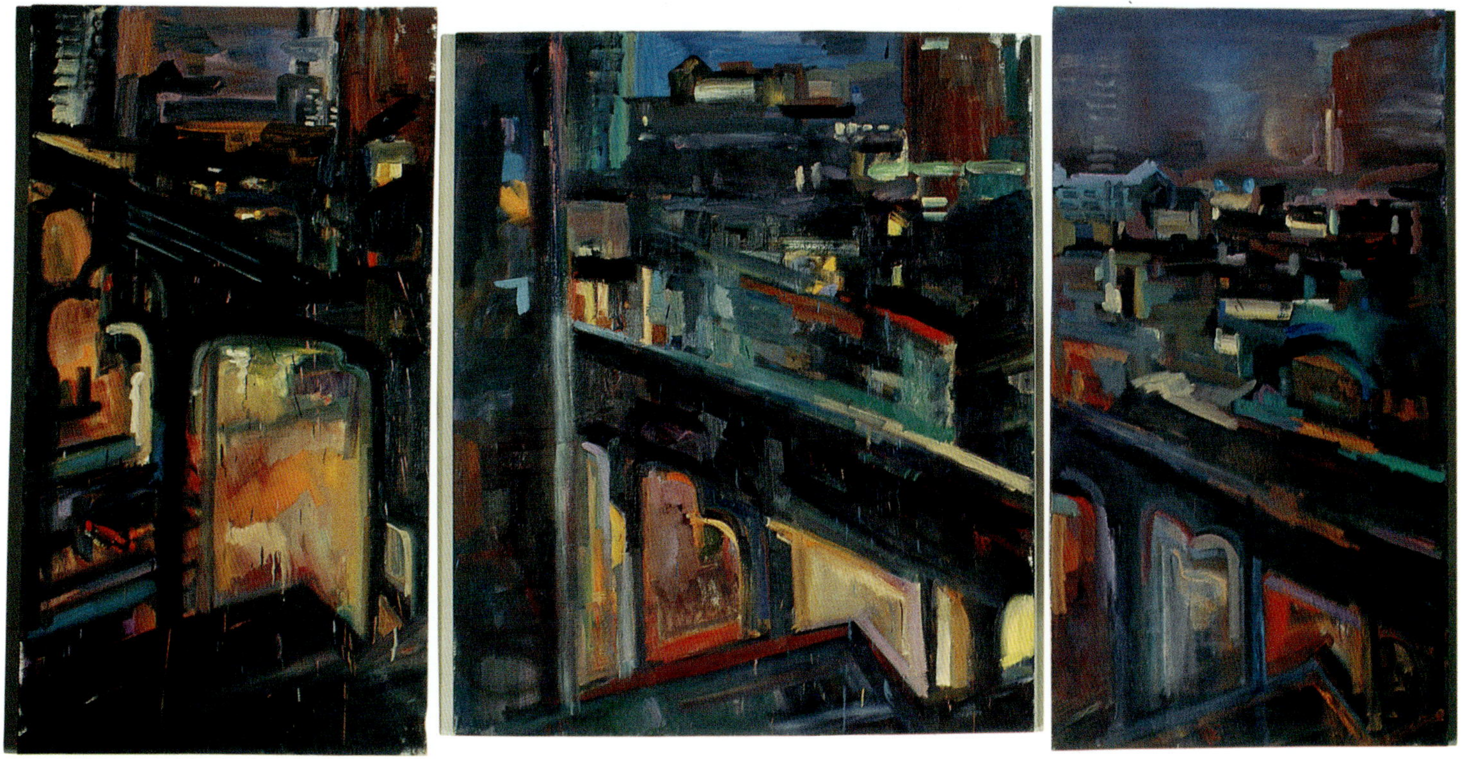

Hi-line Triptych, oil on canvas, left and right panels 96" x 52", center panel 90" x 74", 1991.

Lisa Corinne Davis

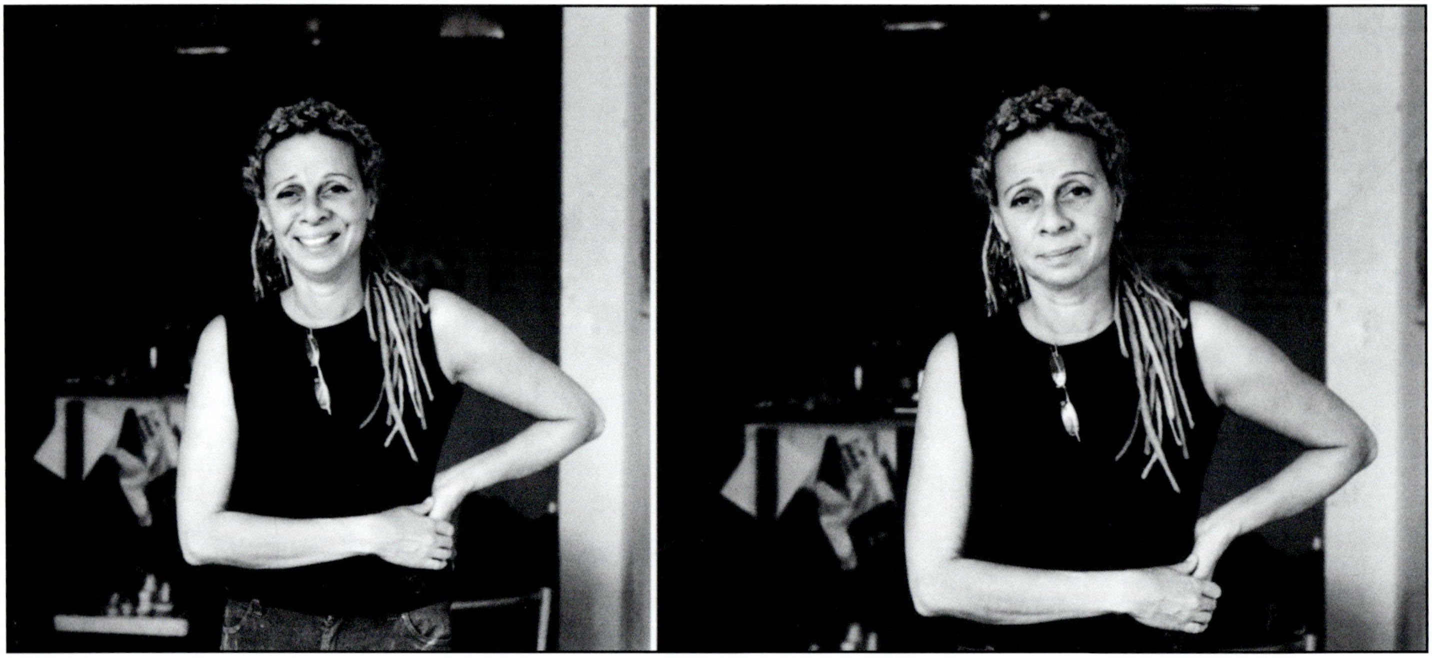

Two-part Portrait, 2006. *Photograph © Reiner Leist.*

Lisa Corinne Davis, whose academic career includes faculty appointments at Hunter College of the City University of New York, Yale University, the Parsons School of Design, and the Maryland Institute College of Art, is an MFA graduate of Hunter, and a BFA graduate of Brooklyn's Pratt Institute. She has served as an apprentice to such painters as Jennifer Bartlett, Jack Tworkov, and Elizabeth Murray.

Davis's minutely checkered collage paintings, often overlaid with linear, bulging, curvilinear elements, suggest the texture created by the multiplicity of individuals in our culture. This complex body of work is presented in response to "the seemingly definitive categories of racial and ethnic groups and society's need to label and categorize them."[44] Davis is represented by the June Kelly Gallery in New York's Soho area.

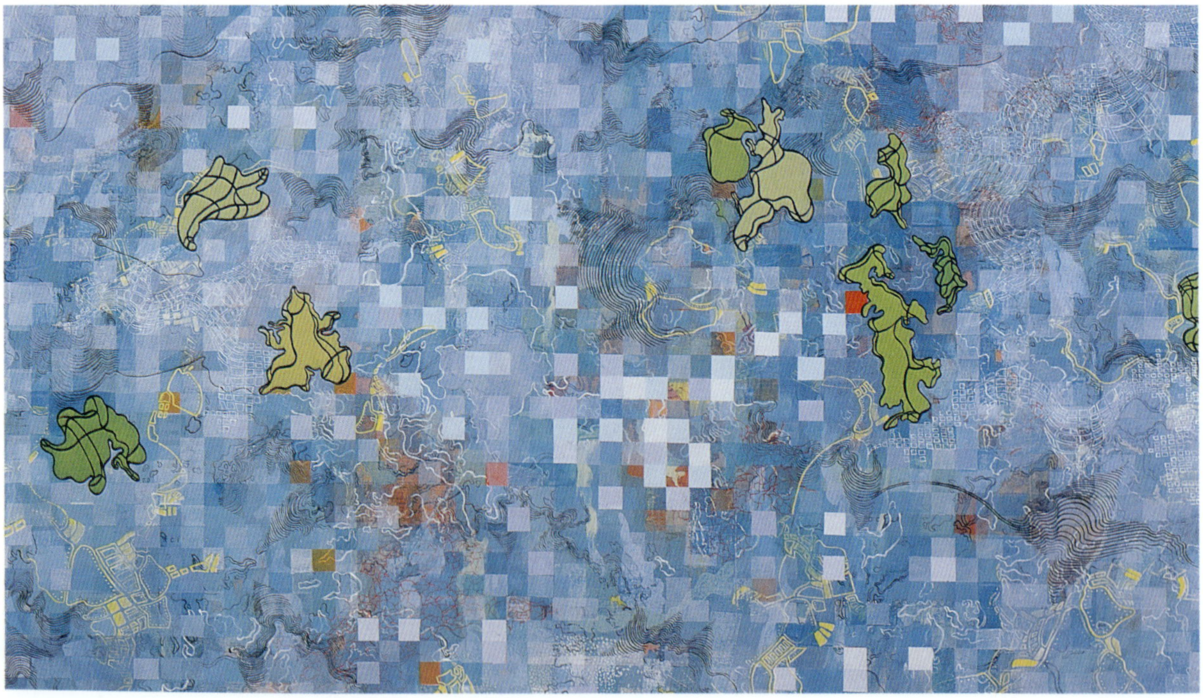

What, Where, How?, oil and collage on wood panel, 32" x 55", 2005.

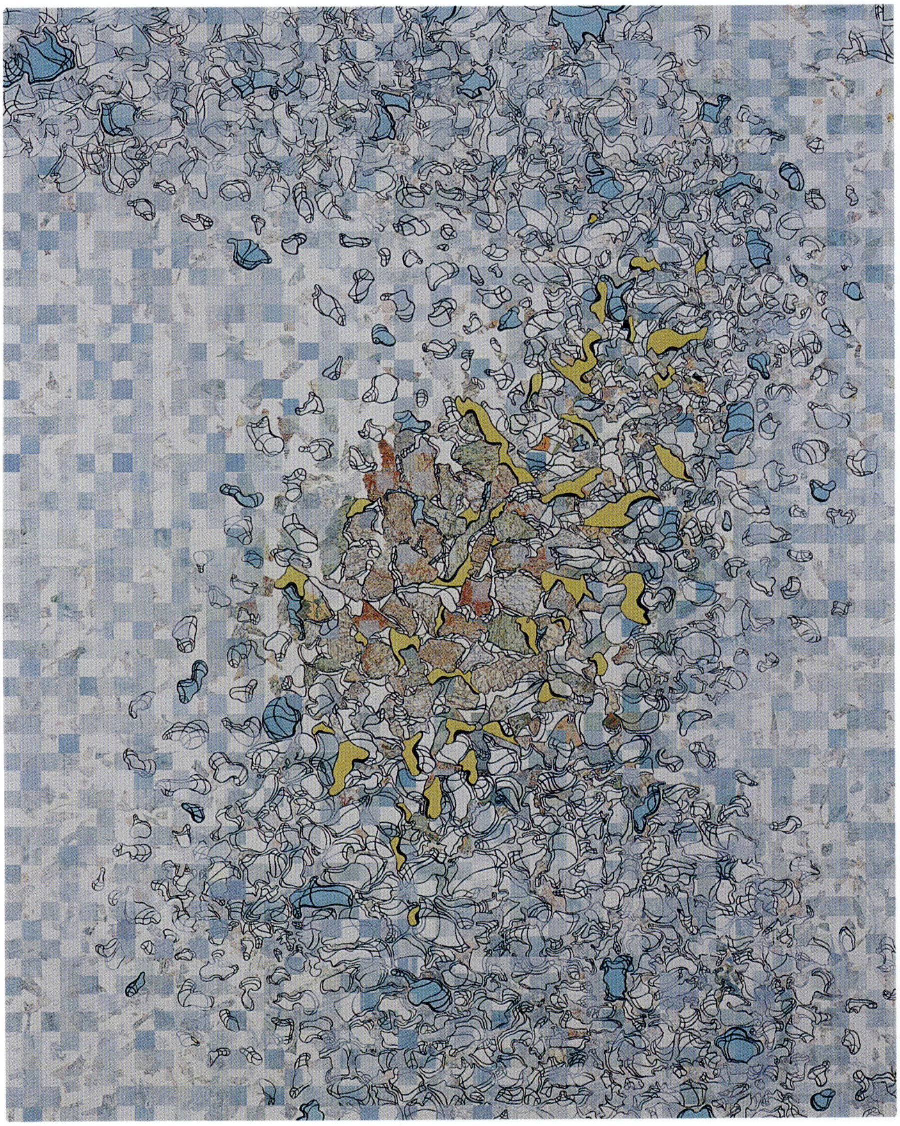

Got It, oil and collage on wood panel, 60" x 47.5", 2005.

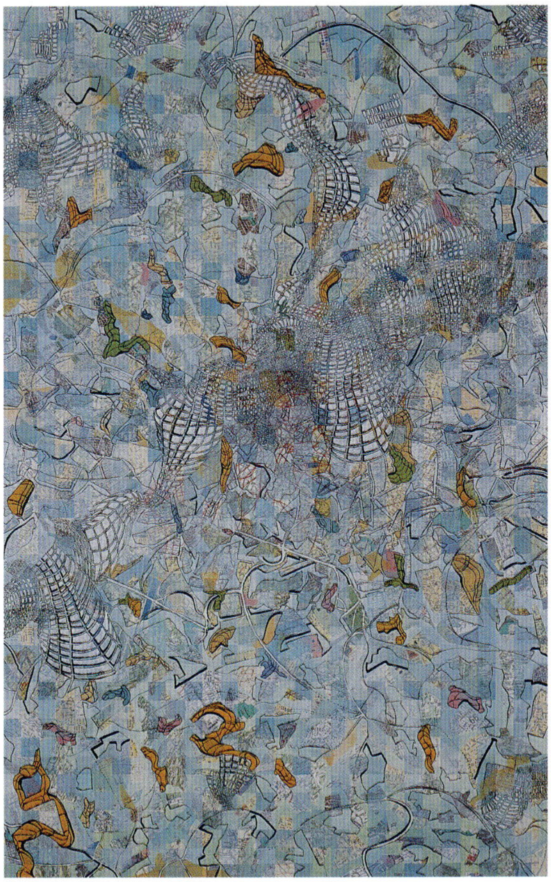

Location, Location, oil and collage on wood panel, 48" x 36", 2005.

Francks Francois Deceus, who has studied at Bob Blackburn's printmaking studio and is a graduate of Long Island University, continues to search for aspects of his Haitian origin and identity through his strongly personal work in painting and printmaking. Commissioned by the Brooklyn Academy of Music to produce original art for Dance Africa, Deceus has paintings in the collections of the Schomburg Center for Cultural Research and Medgar Evers College.

His works have been seen in numerous solo exhibitions including several at the UFA Gallery, the Brooklyn Campus of Long Island University's Salena Gallery, the Kenkeleba Gallery, and the Brooklyn Museum, all in New York; at additional galleries in California and Tennessee; and in group exhibitions at the National Civil Rights Museum in Memphis, Tennessee, among others. Deceus's work has been featured in the International Review of African-American Art.

Francks Francois Deceus

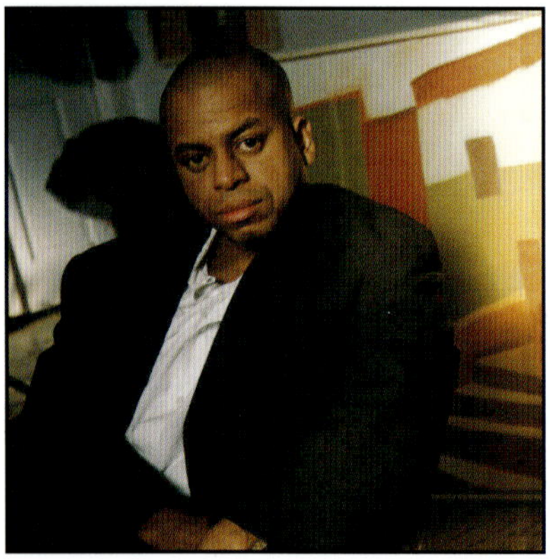

Photograph by Suné Woods.

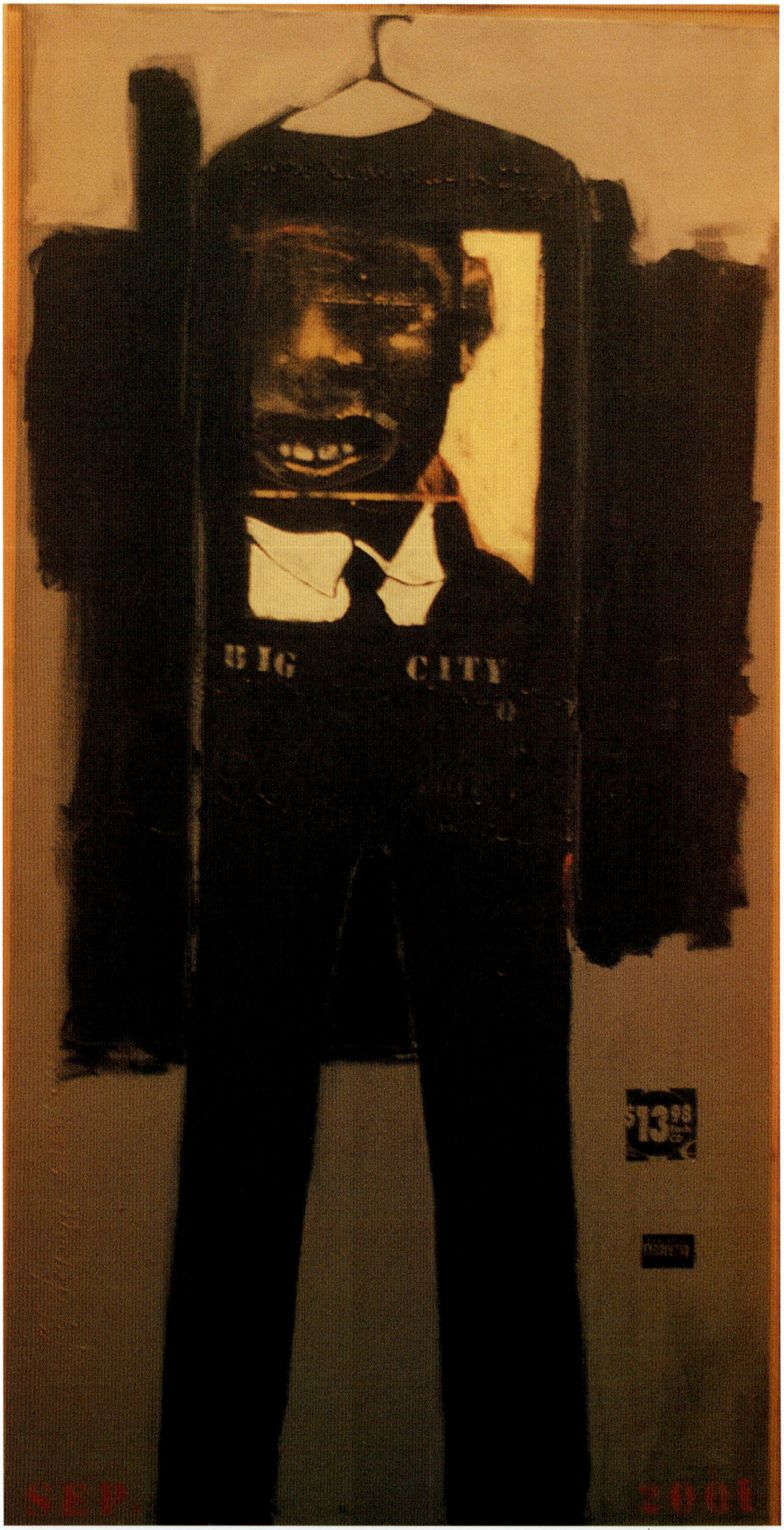

Big City, mixed media, acrylic, silkscreen, collage on canvas, 48" x 24", 2001.

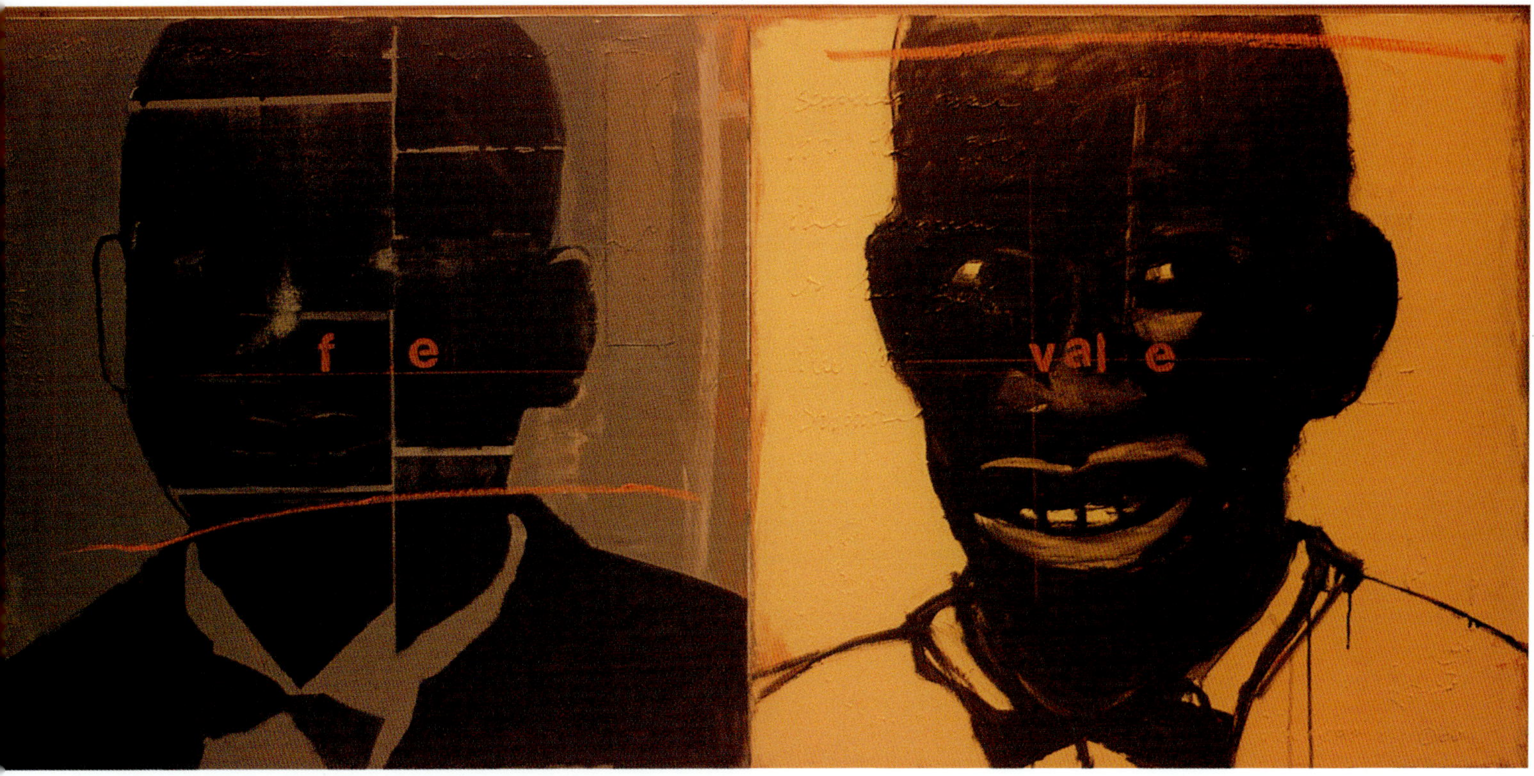

Face Value, mixed media on canvas, 30" x 60", c.2001-2002

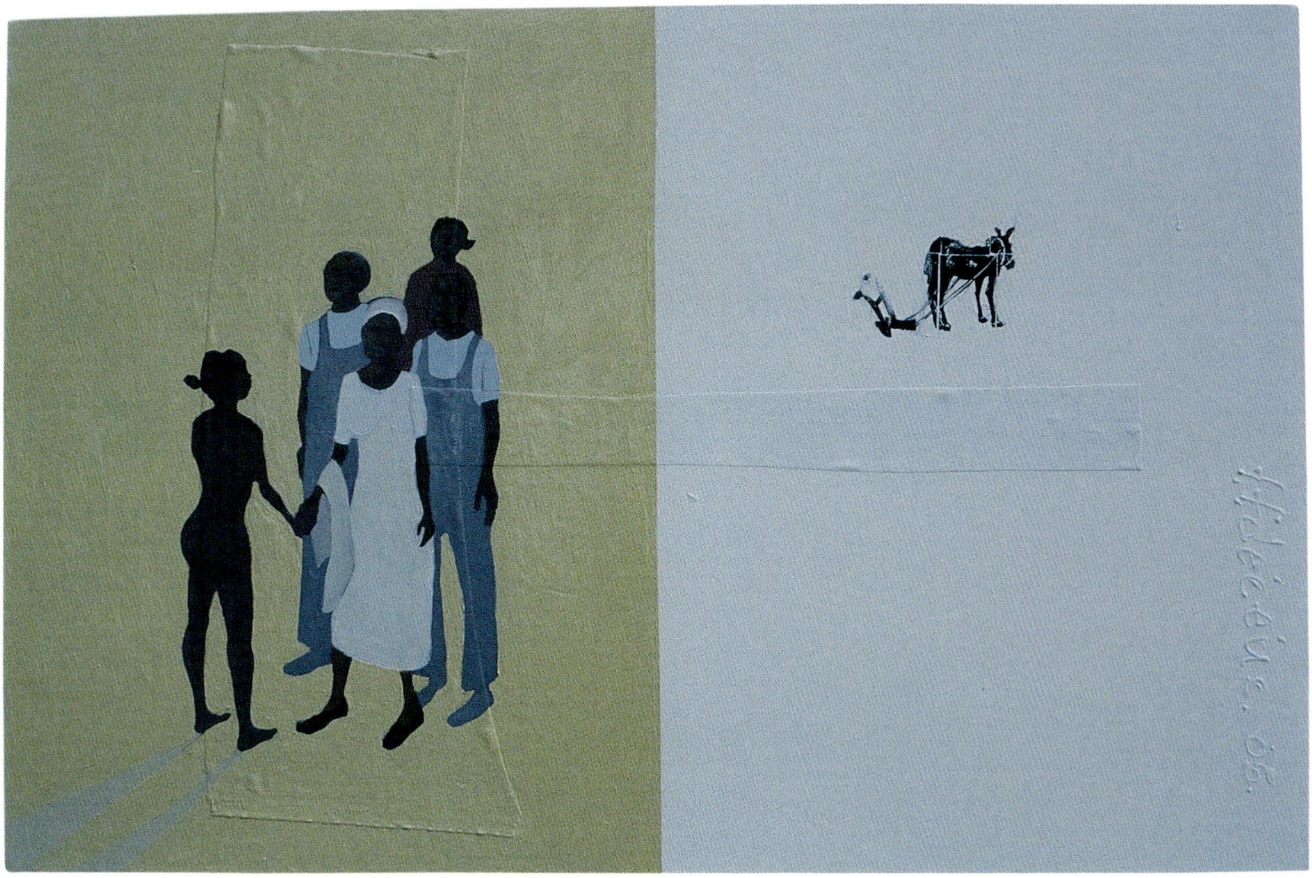

Helping Hand, mixed media on canvas, 24" x 36", 2005.

Dorothy Deon

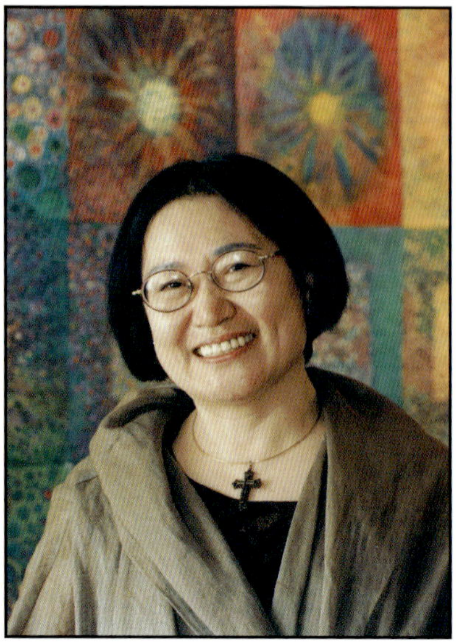
Courtesy of the artist.

Dorothy Deon, whose ultimate theme is expressed as "oneness with God,"[45] shows this driving impulse through paintings filled with luminous cells of light and color. Often resembling microscopic concentric configurations, her pulsating, shimmering canvases have been said to help the viewer experience "cells of light in states of luminous eruption."[46]

Deon, who holds a degree in Fine Arts from Ewha Women's University in her native Korea, also studied at the Art Students League and the Fashion Institute of Technology in New York.

She has had many solo and group exhibitions at the Phoenix Gallery and others in New York, Germany, France, and Korea. Deon is also the winner of several awards, including the Grand Prix de France International and Special Recognition of the Korean Government in Seoul.

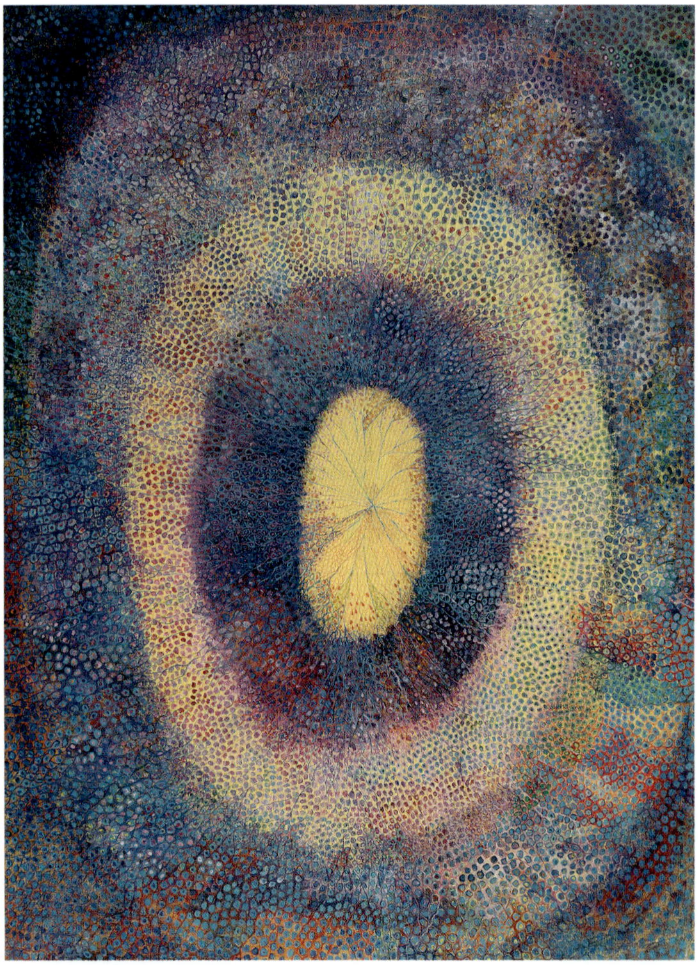

Cell of Love, oil on canvas, 48" x 36", 1983.

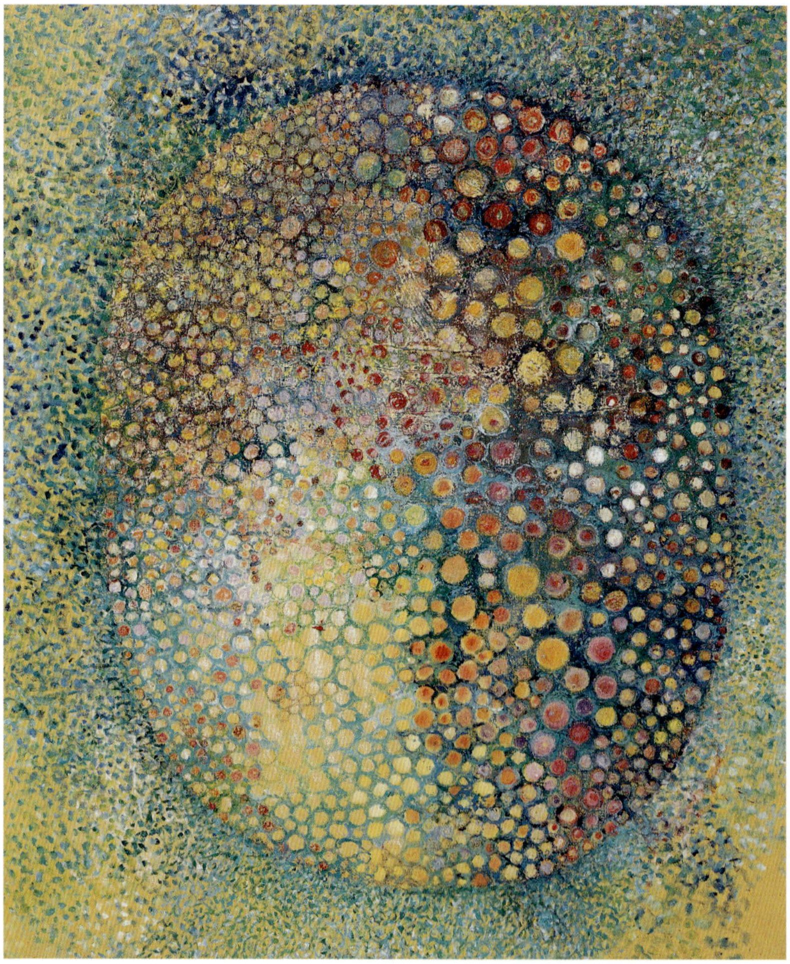

Oneness, oil on canvas, 161" x 130", 2003.

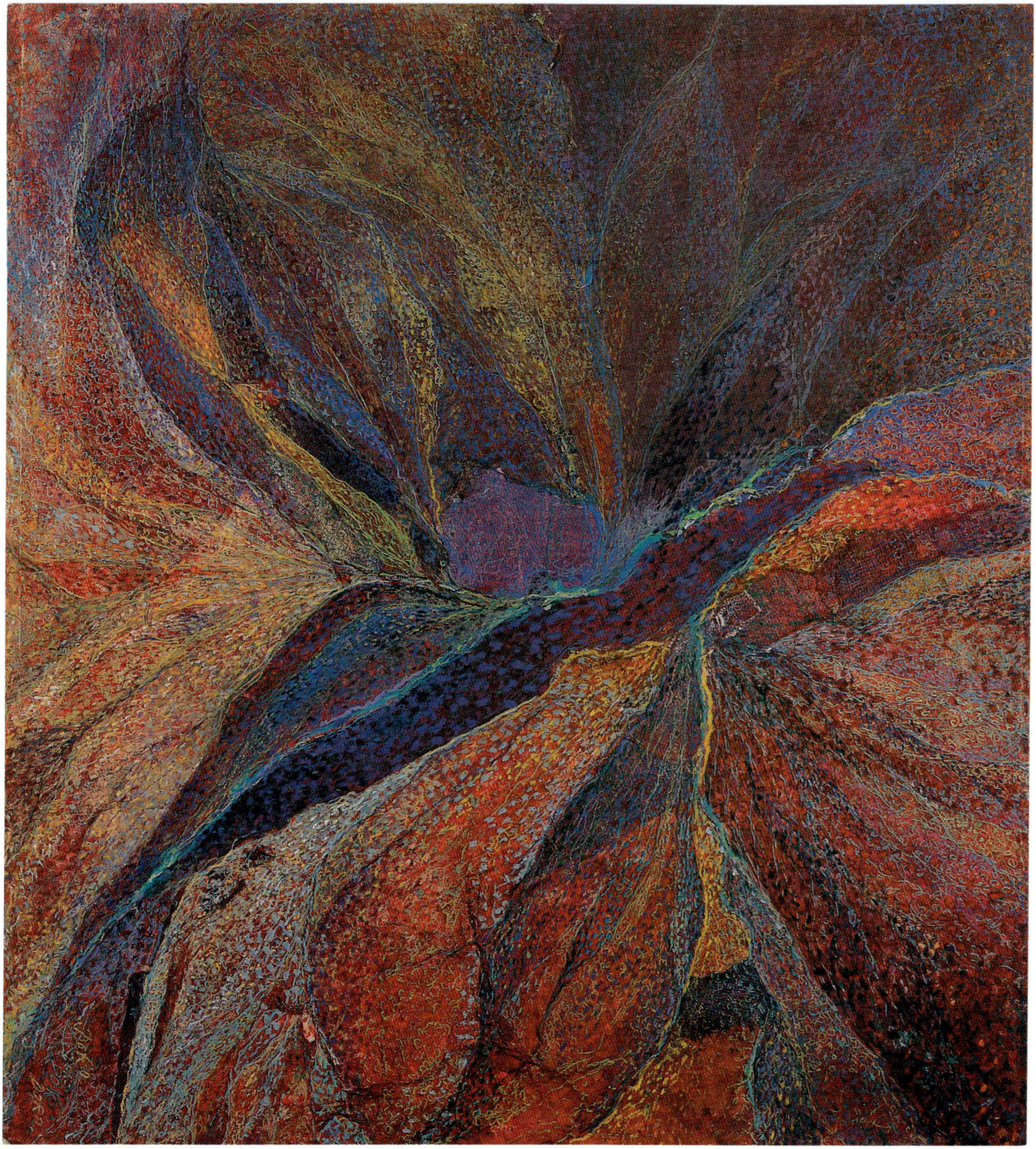

Golgotha, oil on rice paper, 50" x 48", 1991.

Harvey Dinnerstein, whose "lifelong subject has been the human condition,"[47] often includes himself in figurative compositions, to "convey [his] sense of the artist as witness and to emphasize the personal quality of the work."[48] To this artist, whose social consciousness pervades his oeuvre, every aspect of his meticulously crafted paintings is imbued with meaning.

From his early days in the then Jewish section of Brownsville in Brooklyn, when he studied with Moses Soyer, and at the Art Students League with Yasuo Kuniyoshi and Julian Levy, Dinnerstein has continued to draw constantly in a small sketchbook. He organizes these studies to form "a comprehensive unity of form and content, ever mindful of the great figurative artists of the past, but expressing a personal vision that relates to our time."[49] Studying the works of historical painters such as Rembrandt, Titian, and Degas in museums provided his most important training. He also admires the more recent Thomas Eakins and Käthe Kollwitz.

Dinnerstein's teaching career includes many years at the School of Visual Arts and the National Academy of Design, and over twenty-five years at the Art Students League. His drawings during the mid-20th century civil rights movement, and his many publications, stand with numerous gallery and museum exhibitions as a vast compendium of achievement, along with awards granted by many fine arts and labor groups. An elected member of the National Academy of Design, Dinnerstein has works in many major collections, including New York's Metropolitan Museum of Art and the Whitney Museum of American Art. He is represented in San Francisco by the Frey-Norris Gallery.

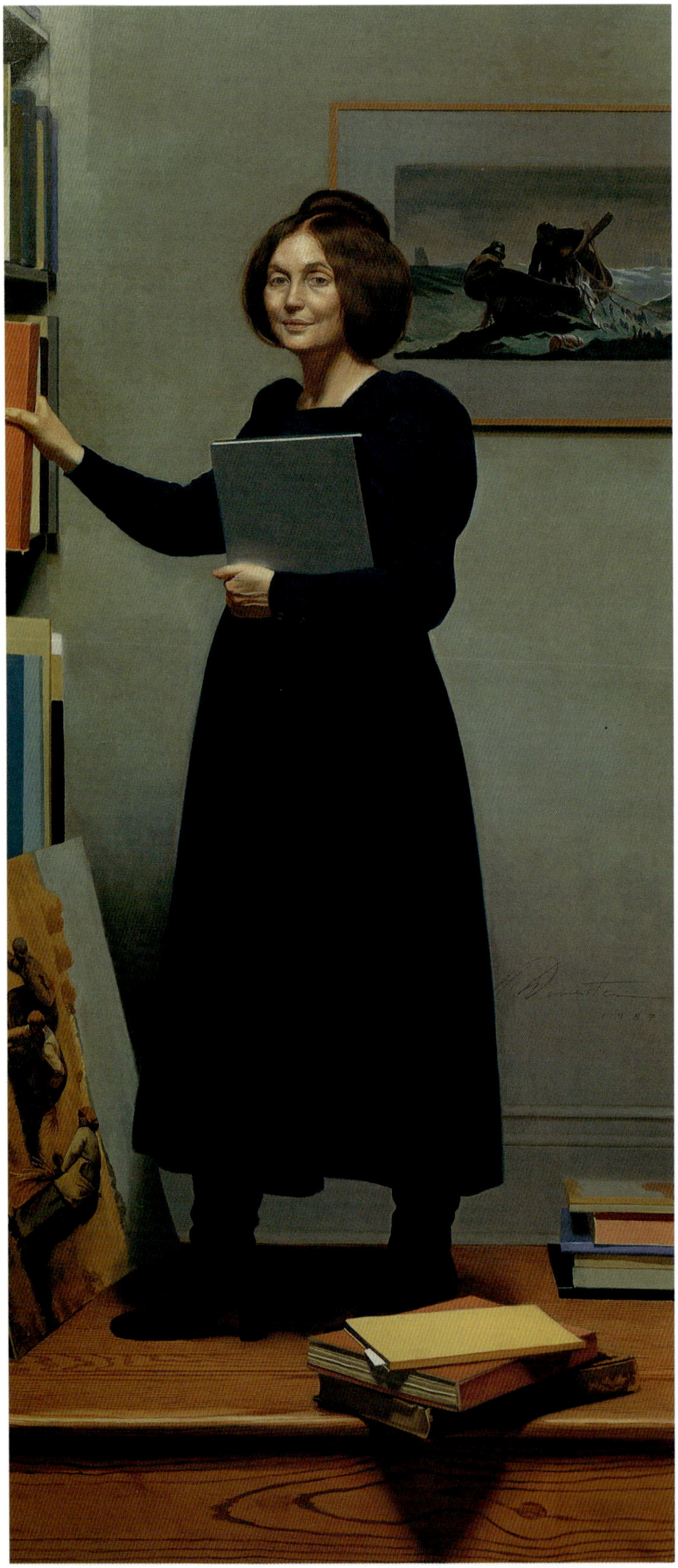

The Art Historian (Lois Dinnerstein), oil on canvas, 83.25" x 36.75", 1987. *Collection of Mr. And Mrs. Jerome Sowalsky.*

Harvey Dinnerstein

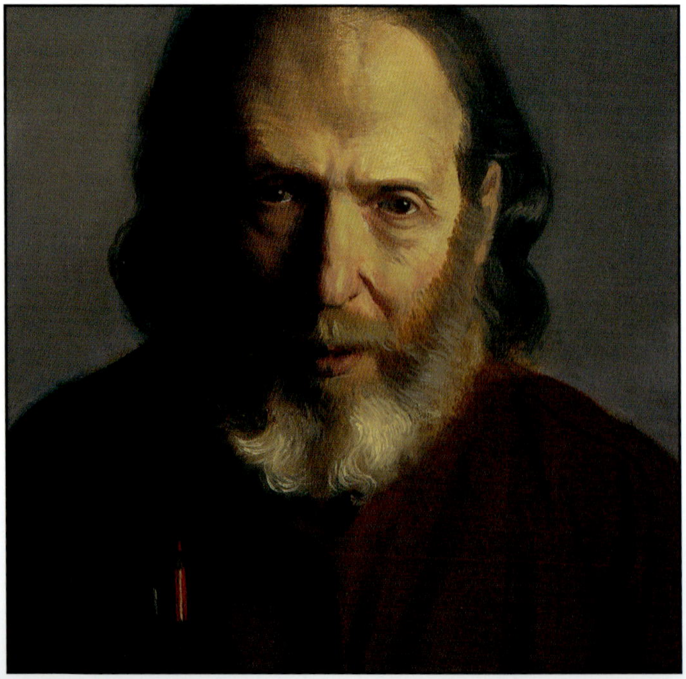

Self Portrait, oil on canvas, 9" x 9", 1999.

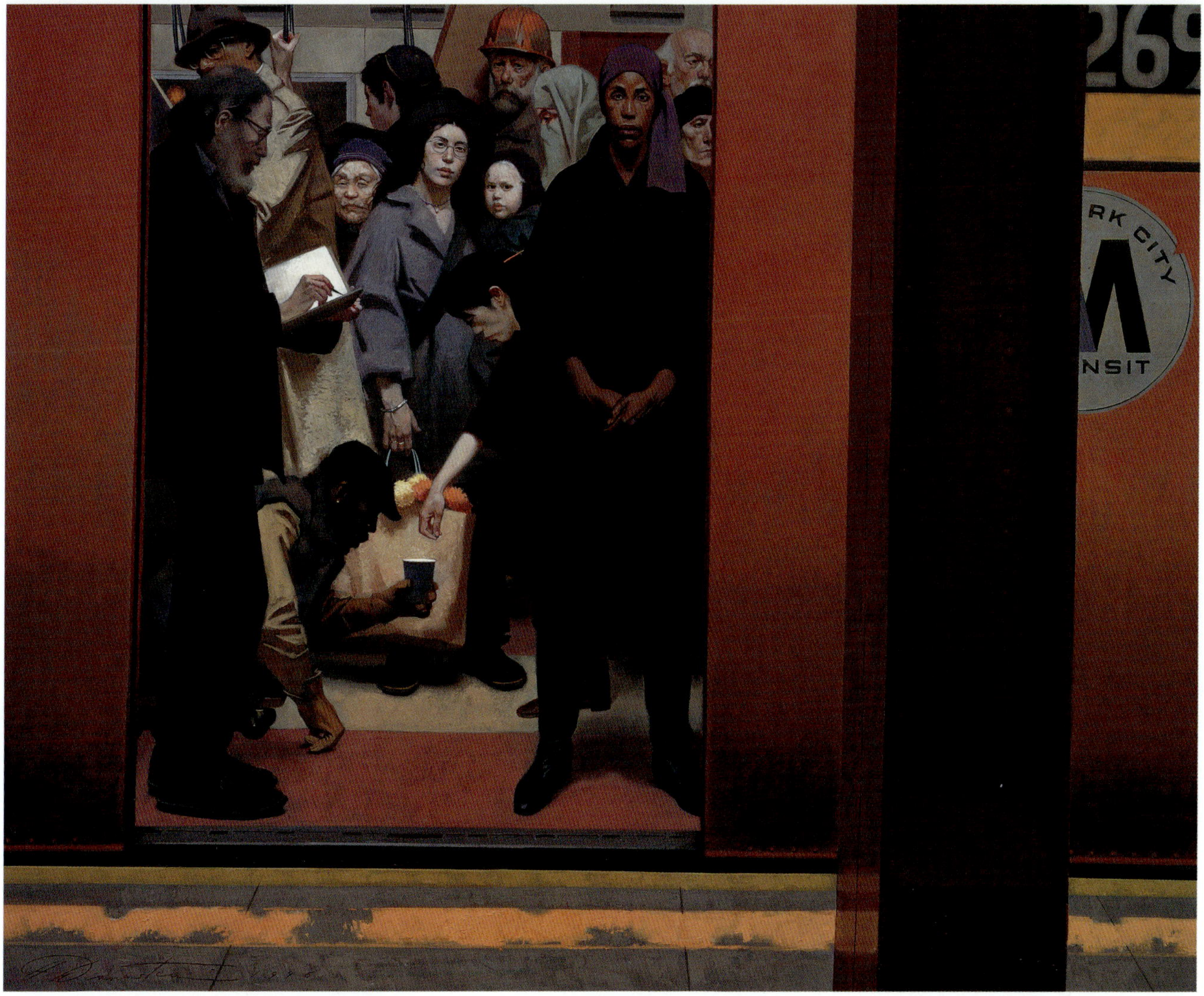

Underground Together, oil on canvas, 90" x 107.25", 1996. *Collection of Terry Basolo.*

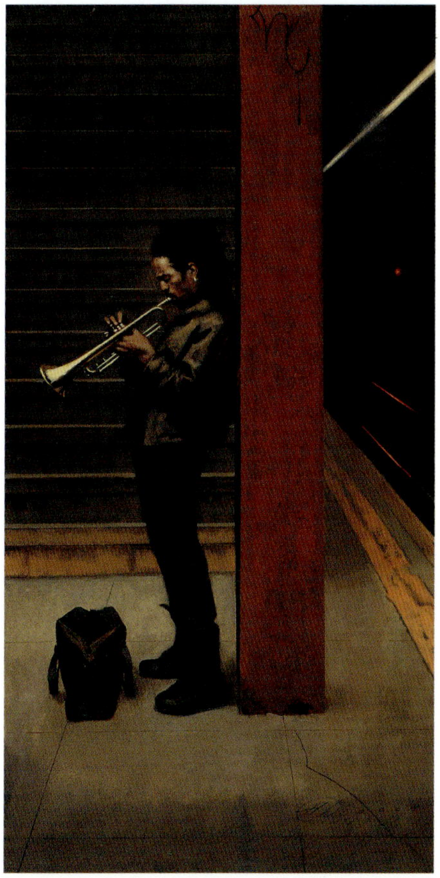

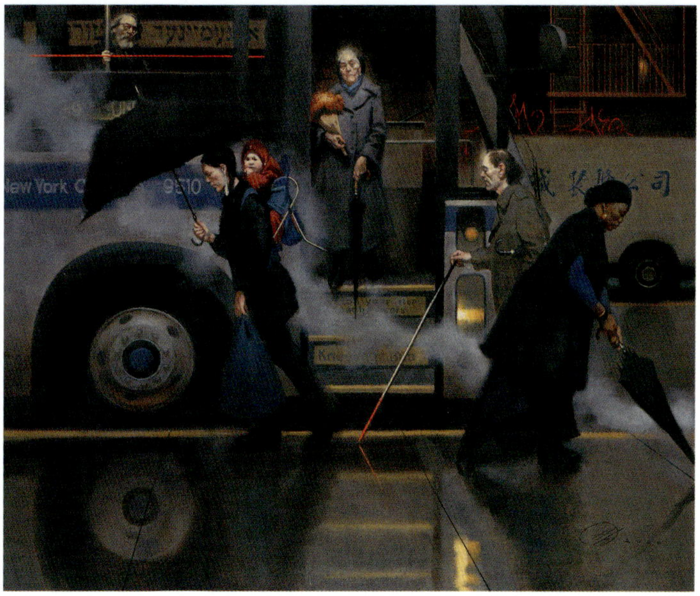

Rainy Evening, Lower East Side, oil on canvas, 35" x 41", 2000. *Collection of Jenny and Jack Rootman.*

Subway Musician, oil on canvas, 32" x 16", 2004. *Collection of Peggy and Yogen Dalal.*

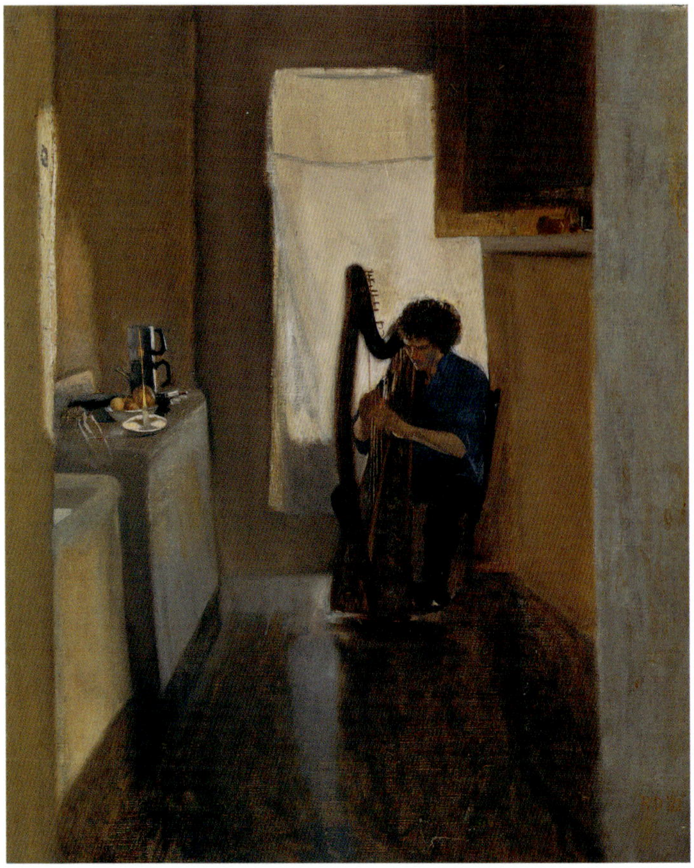

Dennis, oil on canvas, 10" x 16", 1982. *Collection of Ira Robbins.*

Rachel Dinnerstein, a second generation painter who acknowledges her father, Harvey Dinnerstein, as her first inspiration, names Bruce North's teaching and Bruce Kurland's work as other profound influences. A graduate of the High School of Music and Art and a student at the Art Students League, the National Academy of Design, and the New York Studio School, she has received a Portrait Award from the National Academy.

Dinnerstein holds classes in her Borough Park, Brooklyn studio. Her work has been included in group exhibitions at the Brooklyn Ethical Culture Society and the Brooklyn Museum.

Rachel Dinnerstein

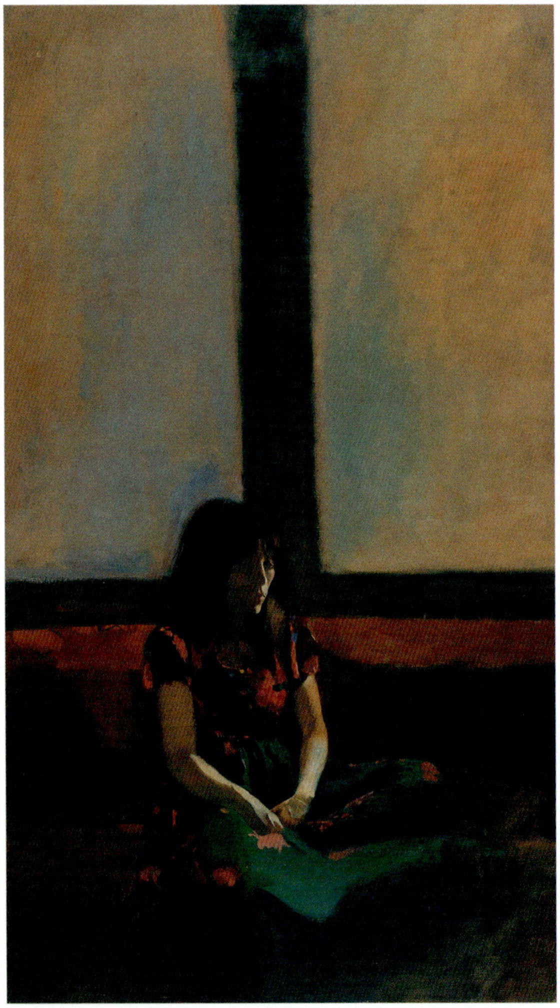

Susan, oil on canvas, 31.5" x 17.75", 1994. *The Thomas B. Clarke Prize, National Academy of Design.*

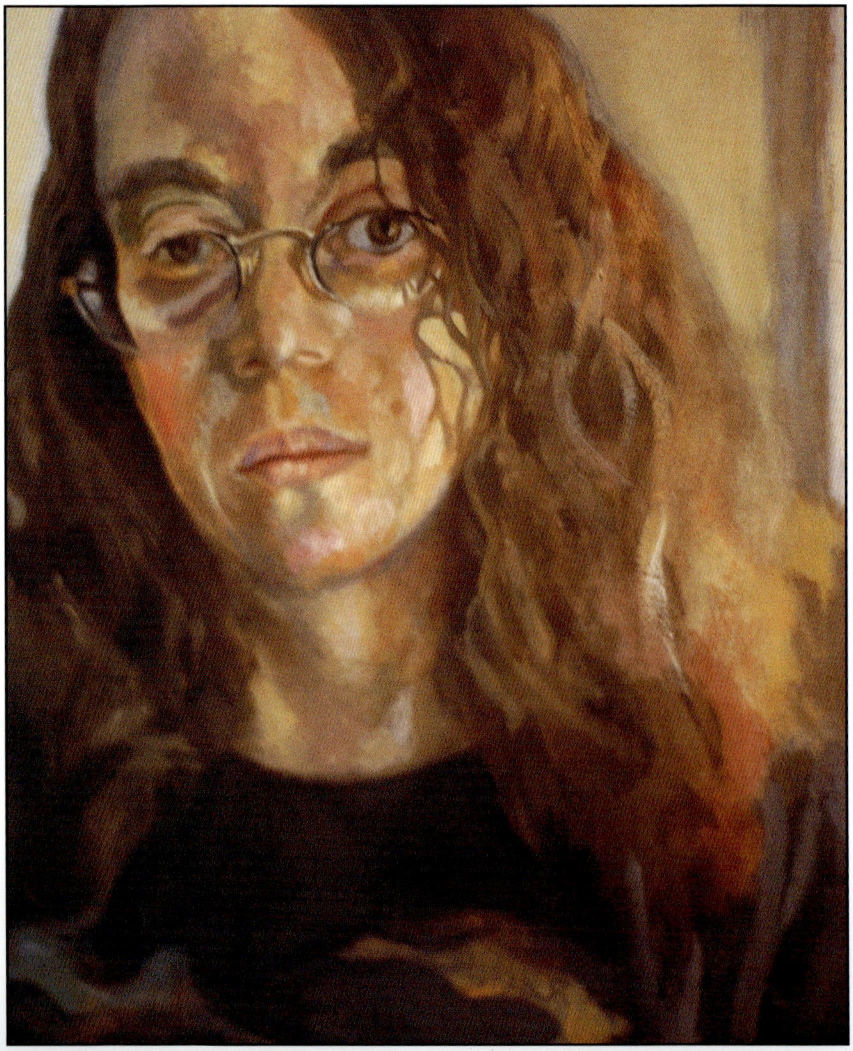

Self Portrait, oil on masonite, 8.5" x 11", 2001.

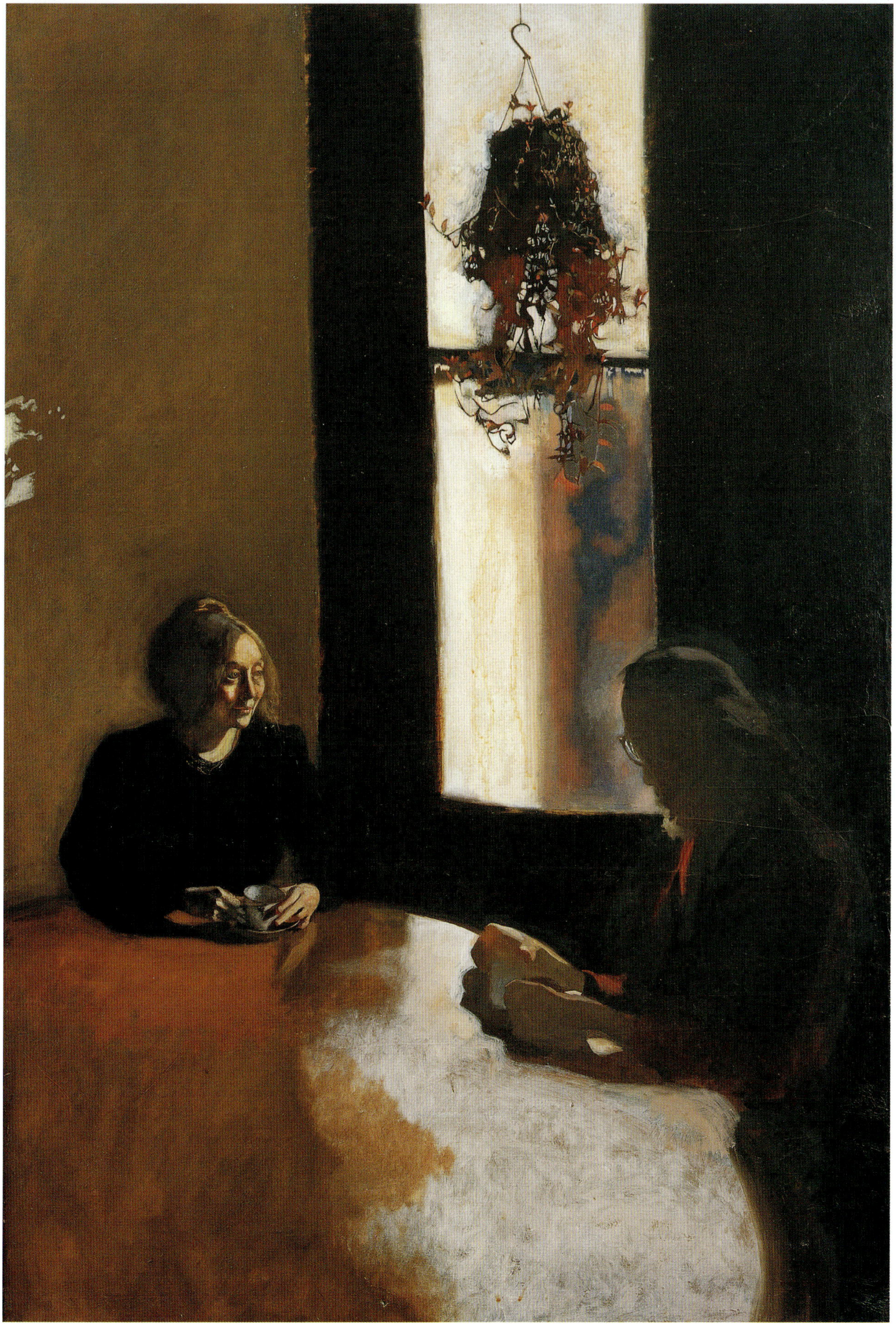

Portrait of my Mother and Father, oil on canvas, 36" x 24", 1987.

Simon Dinnerstein, whose early family portrait 3-panel "Fulbright Triptych" extends across fourteen feet, often paints the figure in unexpected juxtaposition with landscape or interior elements. (The infant daughter, Simone, pictured on his wife's lap, is now a concert pianist.) His "psychologically complicated and visually demanding"[50] images often contain much specific information, presented in great detail, which cannot be extracted from any page-sized reproduction.

The winner of numerous awards, Fulbright and Louis Comfort Tiffany Grants, The Rome, Ralph Fabri and Canon Prizes, the Childe Hassam, American Academy of Arts and Letters awards and others, he has had seventeen solo exhibitions and is affiliated with the ACA Gallery in New York. He is a graduate of the City College of New York and studied at the Brooklyn Museum Art School with Louis Grebenak, David Levine, and Richard Mayhew.

An elected member of the American Academy of Design, Dinnerstein, speaking of his influences, says "what interests me is the ability of ... Degas, Balthus, Lucien Freud and Antonio López García ... to deal with the figure ... to create art ... rich in scale, yet abstract, adventurous, experimental ... deeply human ... a combination of modernism and tradition ... of skill, medium and ... a fresh, personal response to the human form in art. ... Hopefully, my work speaks to these issues."[51]

Dinnerstein has taught for many years at The New School for Social Research, Parsons School of Design, and New York City Technical College.

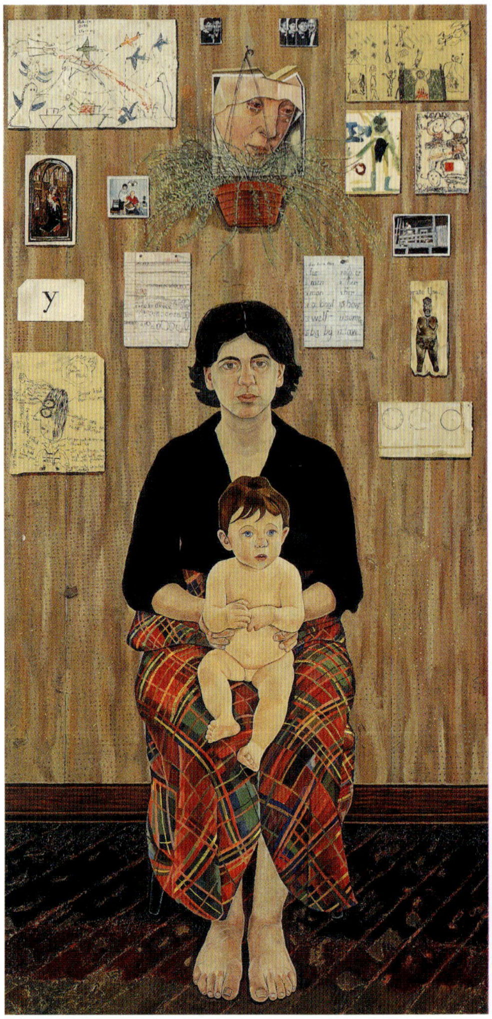

The Fulbright Triptych, oil on wood panels (79.5" x 156"), c.1971-74. Left panel, 79.5" x 38.25"; middle panel, 79.5" x 79.5"; right panel, 79.5" x 38.25". *Collection of Palmer Museum of Art, Pennsylvania State University, Gift of Friends of the Palmer Museum of Art.*

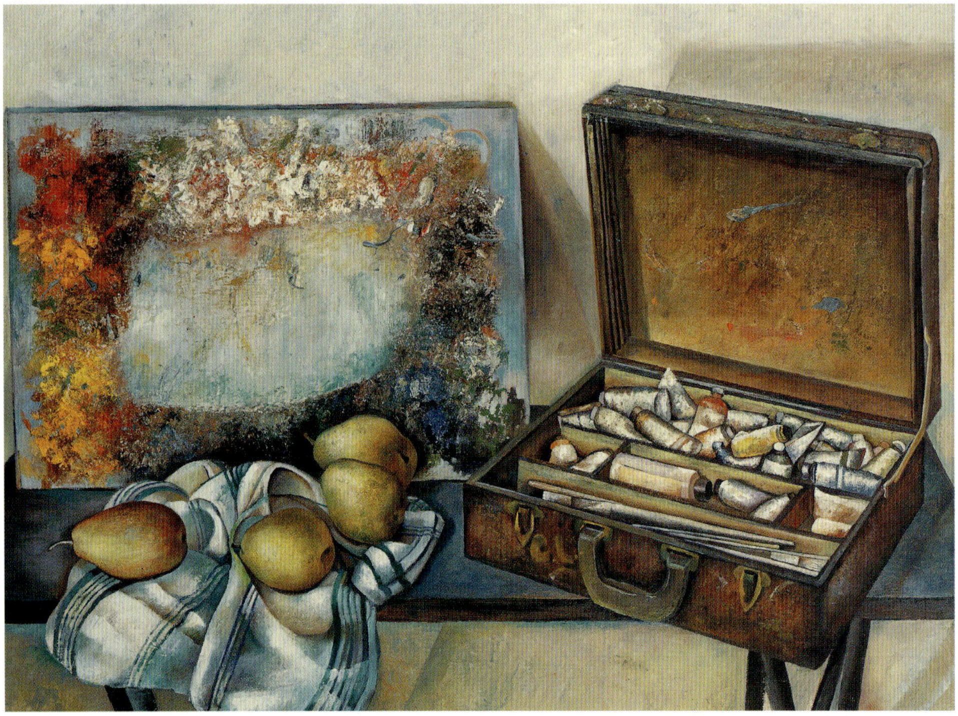

Calling Card, oil on wood panel, 25.5" x 33", 1980. *Collection of Lorraine and Harry Shatz. Courtesy of the artist and ACA Gallery.*

Simon Dinnerstein

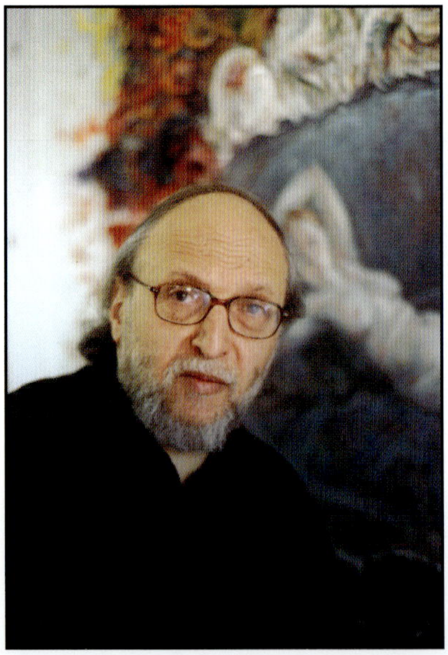

Photograph © Cynthia Dantzic.

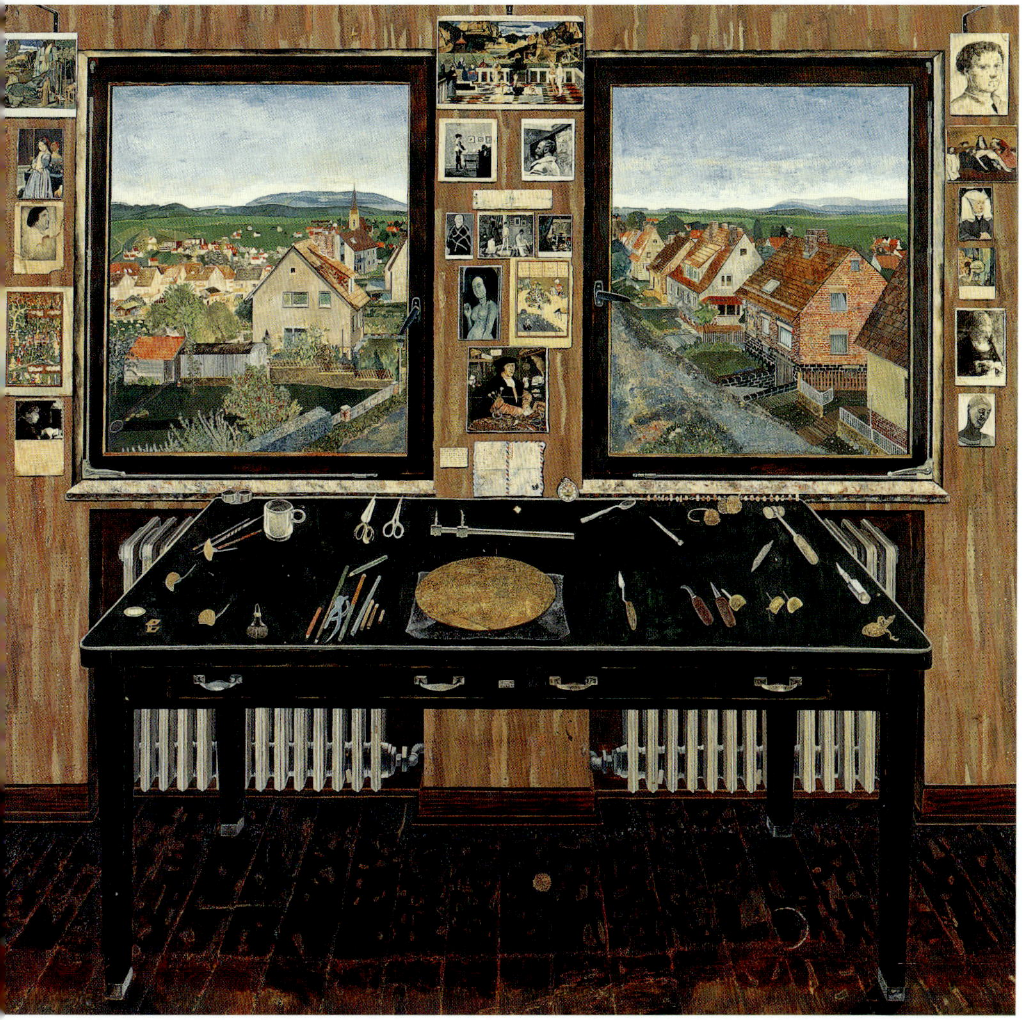

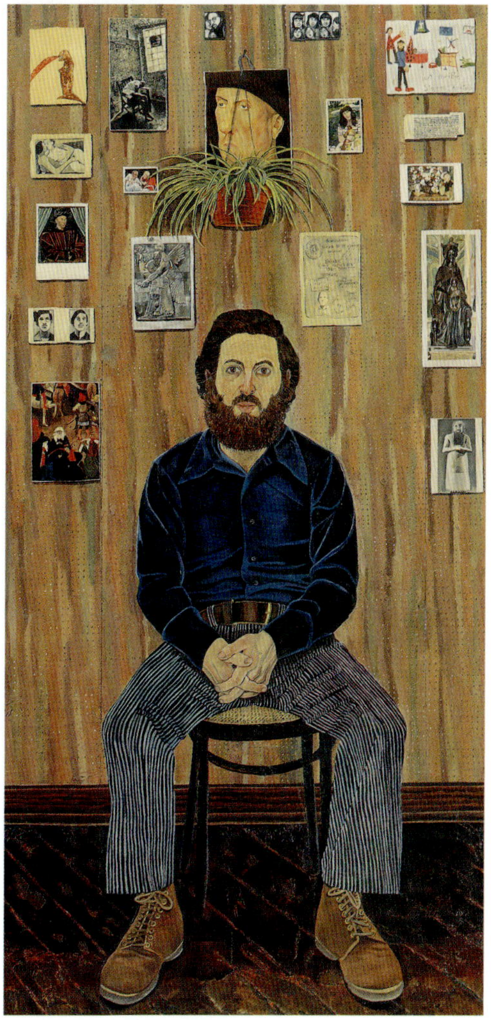

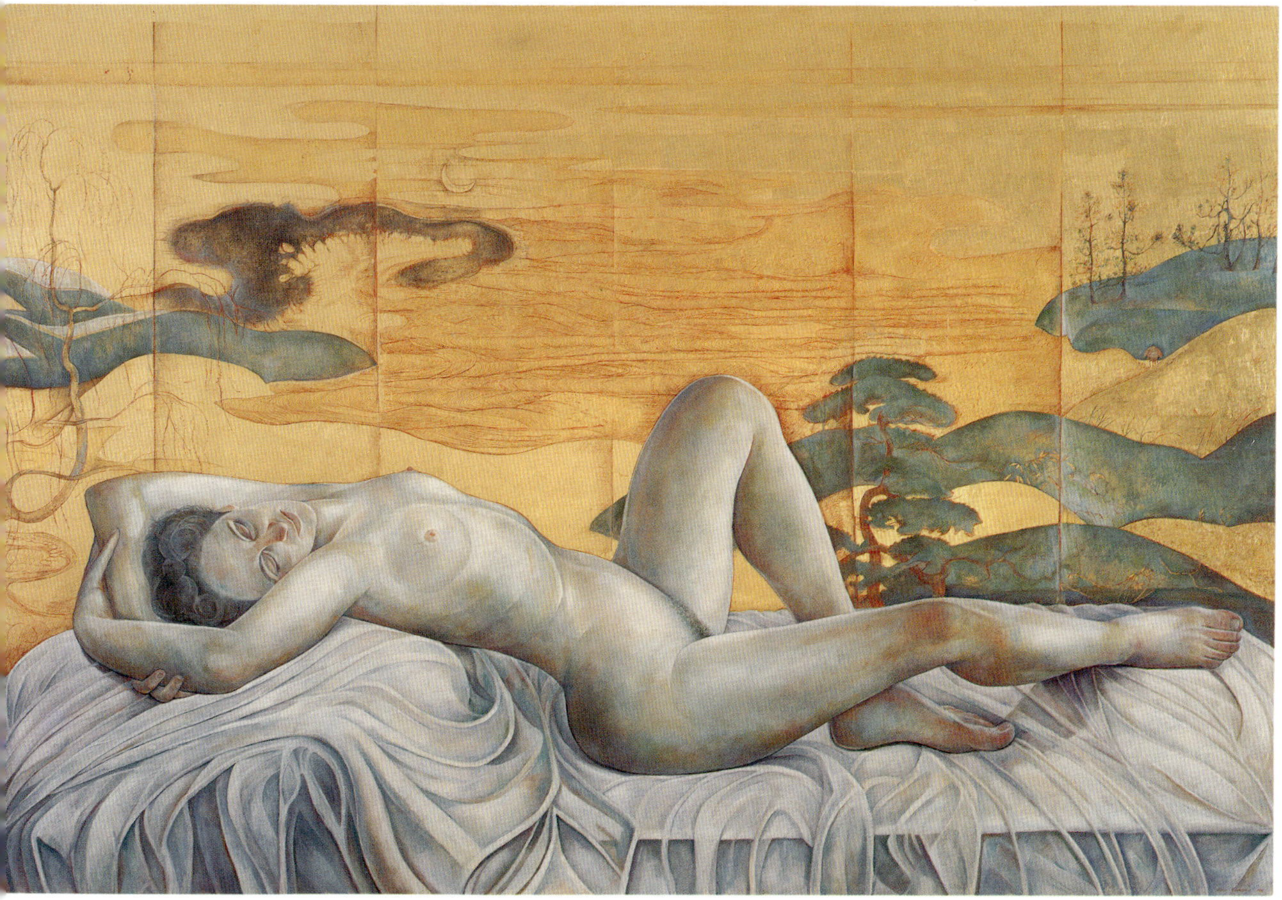

Passage of the Moon, oil and gold leaf on wood panel, 47.5" x 67.5", 1998. *Courtesy of the artist and ACA Gallery.*

Marylyn Dintenfass

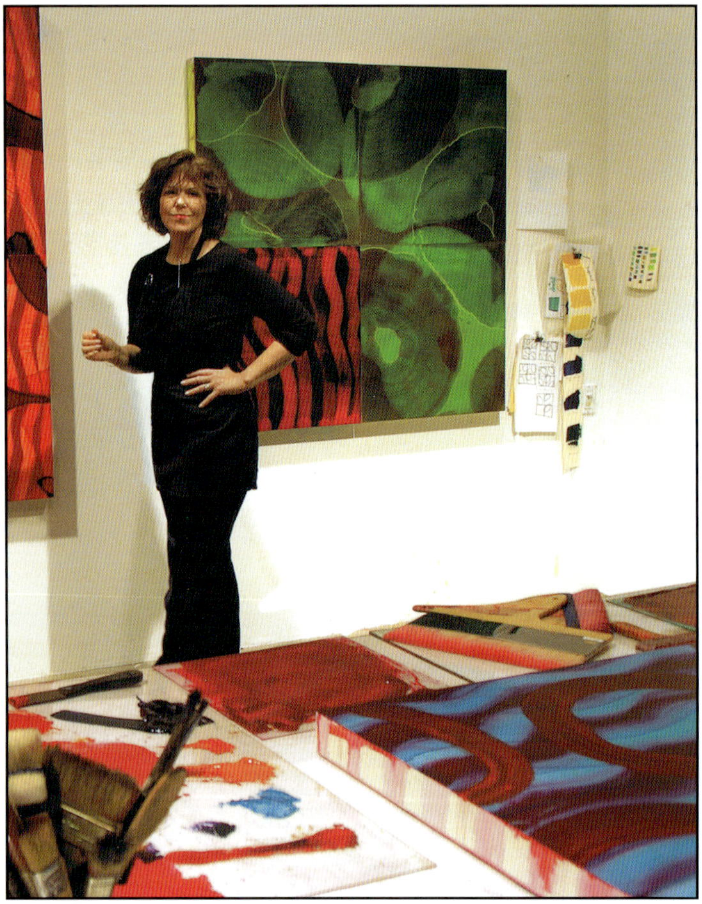

The artist in her studio, Chelsea, New York, 2005.

Marylyn Dintenfass, whose works are to be found in over forty public and corporate collections, among them the Metropolitan Museum of Art, has shown her paintings in many solo exhibitions throughout Europe, Israel, Japan, Canada, and the United States. She has been a MacDowell Fellow twice, has received grants from the New York Foundation for the Arts and the National Endowment for the Arts, and has held several teaching positions in Norway, Jerusalem, Toronto, and, in New York, at the Parsons School of Design.

A graduate of Queens College in New York, she studied with John Ferren, Barse Miller, Elias Friedensohn, "rock solid teachers who provided powerful foundation. ... Barbara Rose, a visionary offering a leap into the next generation, and Larry Poons and Andy Warhol (who) visited and inspired ('incited') the challenge to the status quo."[52]

Dintenfass, whose paintings "are about biographical connections and narrative associations ... [using] luminous transparent color, gestural line and the gestalt of components ..."[53] says she looks to channel Agnes Martin's spareness, Mark Rothko's dense, saturated color fields, and Cy Twombly's fluid gestures.

She is represented by Franklin Riehlman Fine Art.

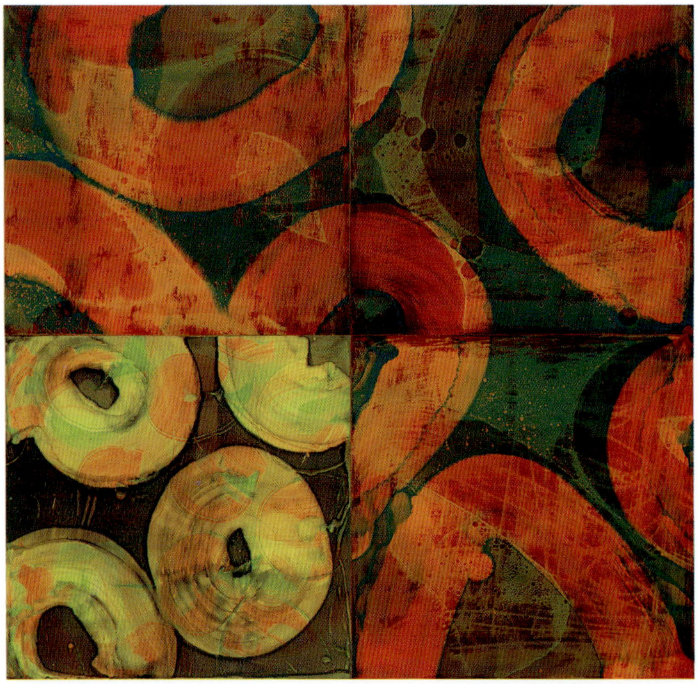

Amber Sky and Tangerine Moon, oil on panel, 48" x 48", 2004.
Courtesy of Franklin Riehlman Fine Art.

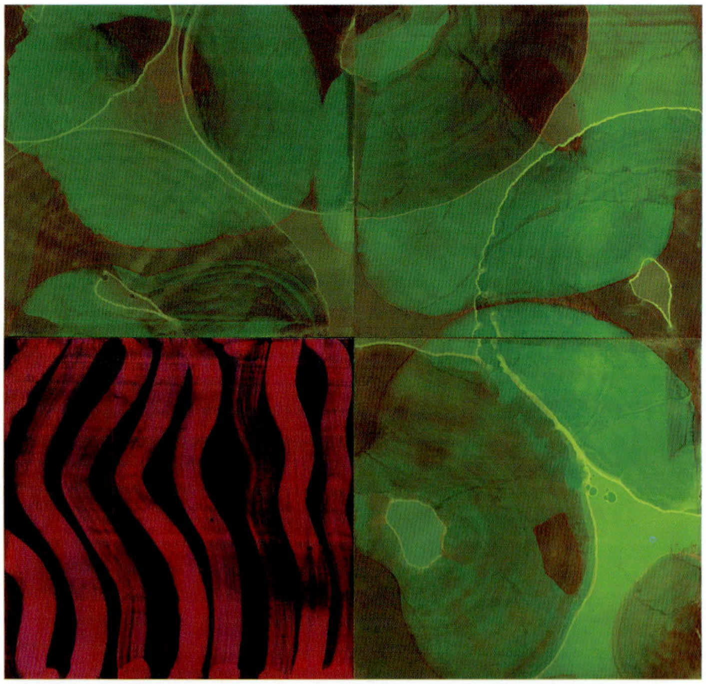

Supreme Greens and Rhubarb Ties, oil on panel, 48" x 48", 2005.
Courtesy of Franklin Riehlman Fine Art.

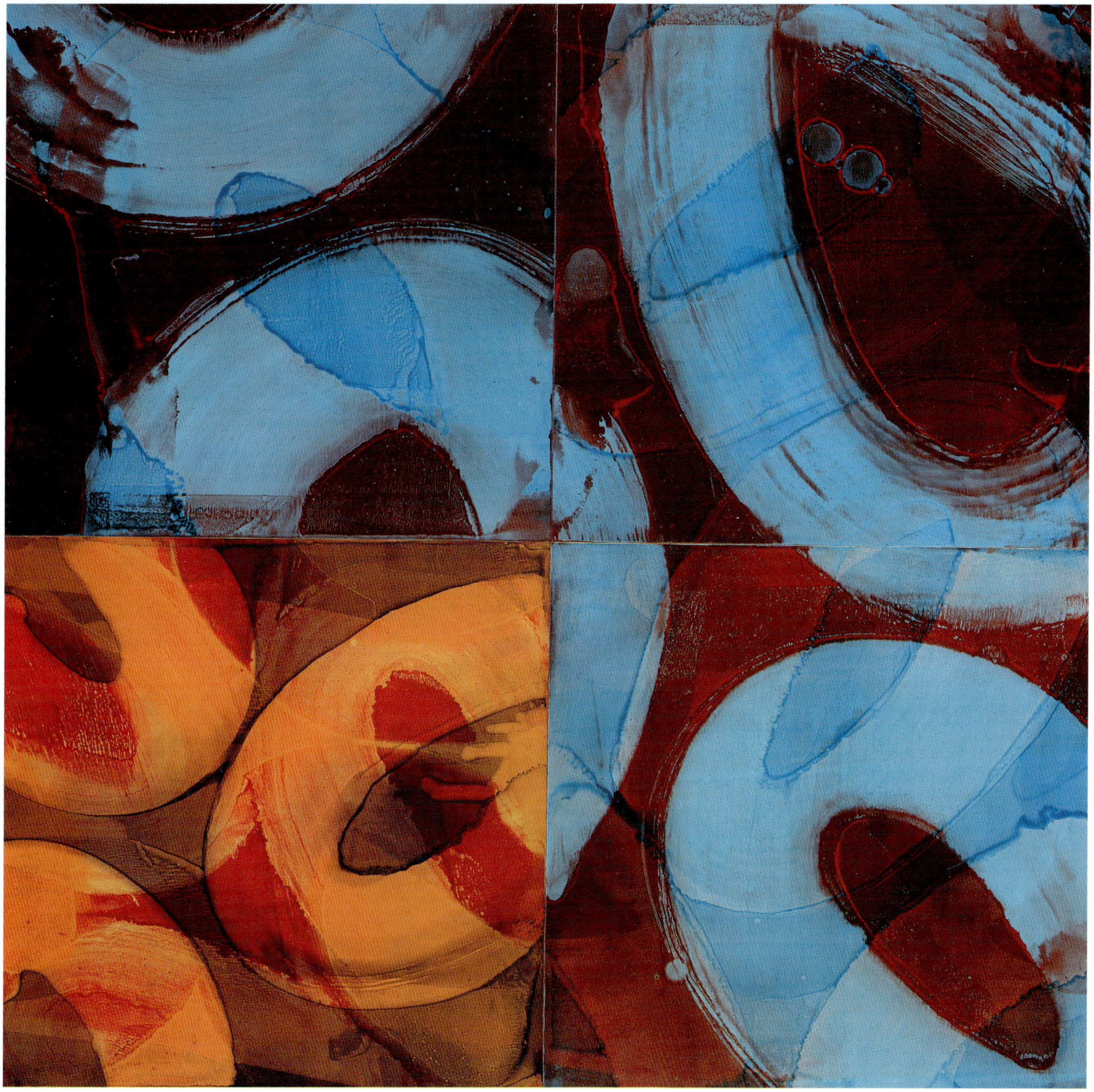

Unspoken Reflection, oil on panel, 48" x 48", 2004. *Courtesy of Franklin Riehlman Fine Art.*

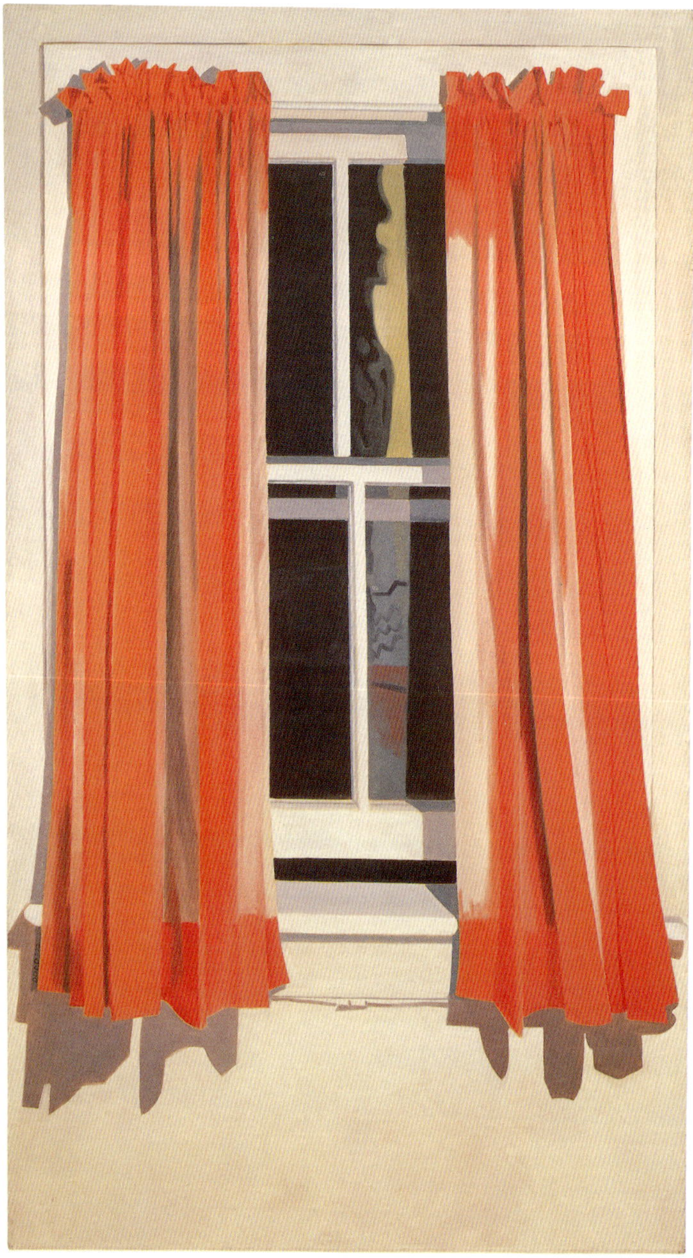

Night Window–Red, oil on linen, 66" x 36", 1972. *Courtesy of Alexandre Gallery. All art © Lois Dodd/Licensed by VAGA, New York, NY.*

Lois Dodd

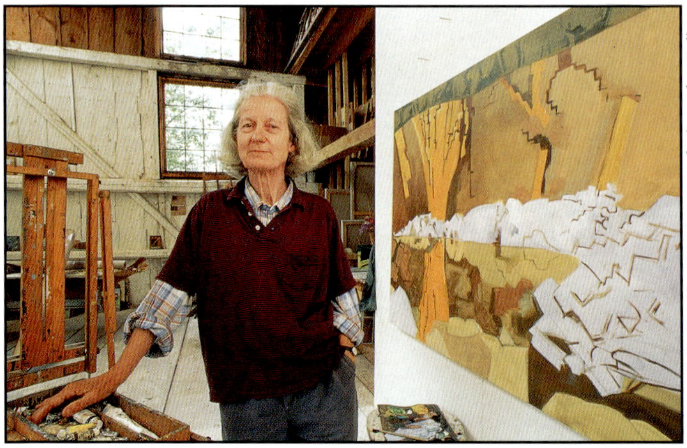

Photograph by Bob Brooks. Courtesy of Alexandre Gallery.

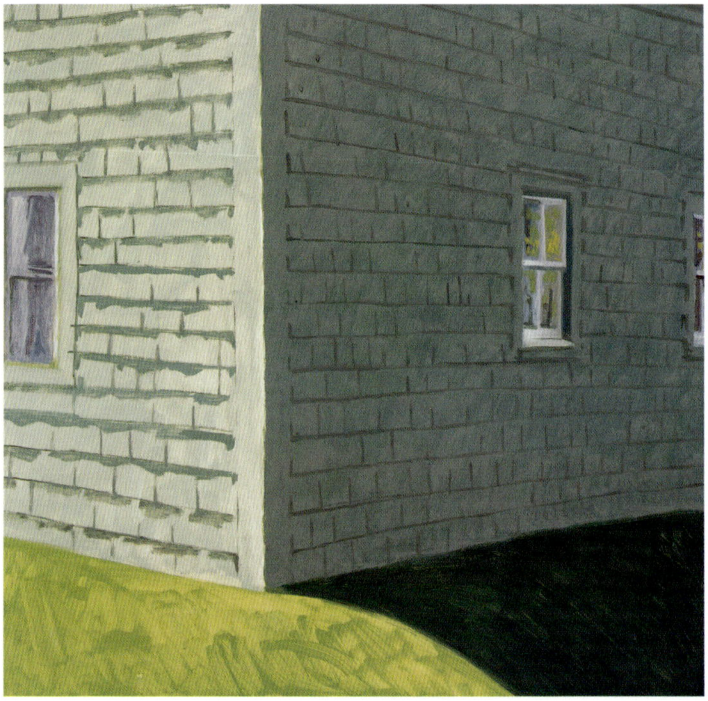

Morning Corner, oil on masonite, 20" x 20", 1983. *Courtesy of Alexandre Gallery.*

Lois Dodd creates small, quickly painted panels that "record the act of translating place into paint"[54] and are all "fundamentally landscapes ... close to home"[55]—whether that home is in Maine, New Jersey, or New York. Sometimes these serve as the spur to larger paintings or works in other media, such as monoprints. Painting "totally in the present ... she [looks for] the confluence of form and color ... not catching the fleeting moment ... but ... what remains still, what is essential."[56] (Deborah Weisgall).

Dodd has won awards from the American Academy and Institute of Arts and Letters, the National Academy of Design, The Cooper Union, the Italian government, and others.

She has taught at Brooklyn College, at colleges and art schools in Louisiana, Maine, Vermont, and Pennsylvania, and in Nova Scotia, and has works in many public and corporate collections.

An elected National Academician, Dodd studied at The Cooper Union and has been represented in many solo and group exhibitions throughout the United States. She was an early founder of the historic Tanager Gallery, and is represented by the Alexandre Gallery in New York's Fuller Building.

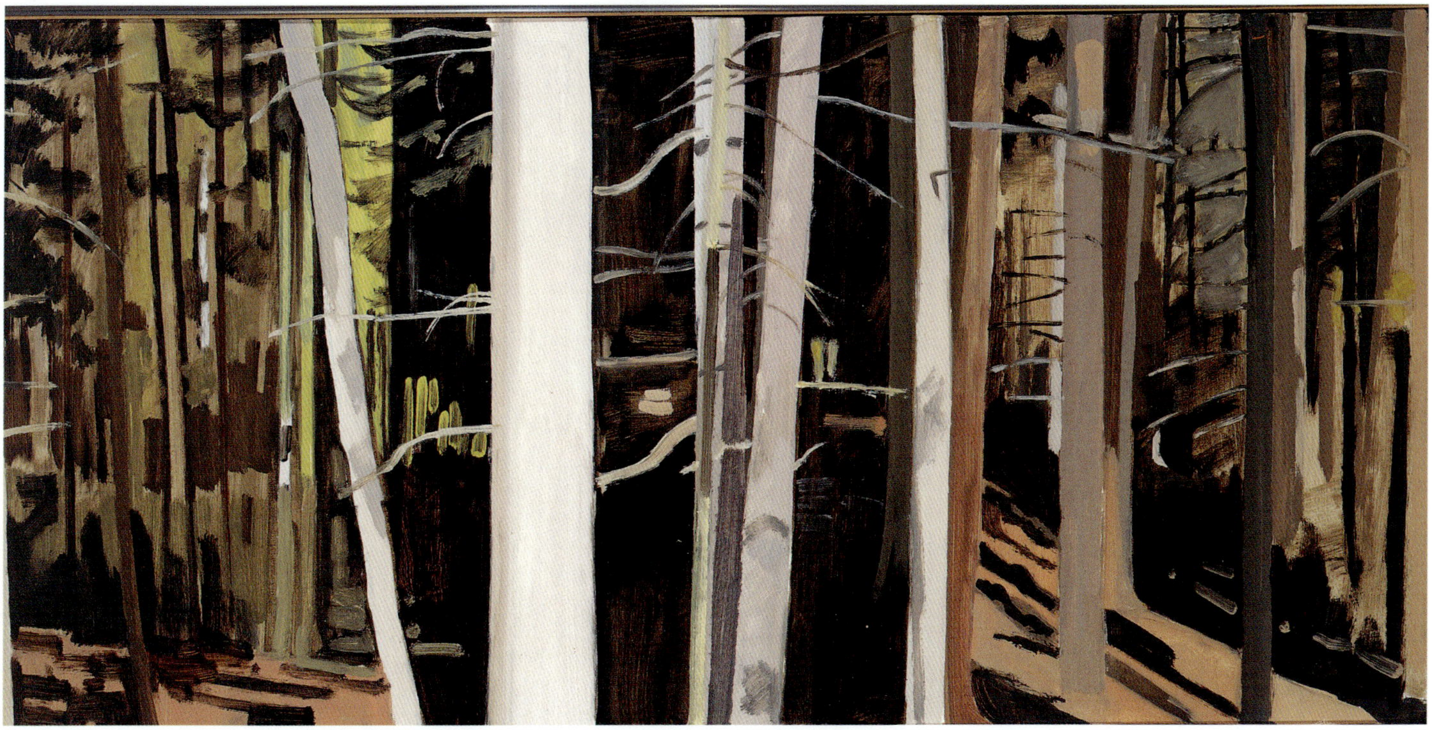

Horizontal Woods, oil on masonite, 12" x 24.5", c.1975-6. *Courtesy of Alexandre Gallery.*

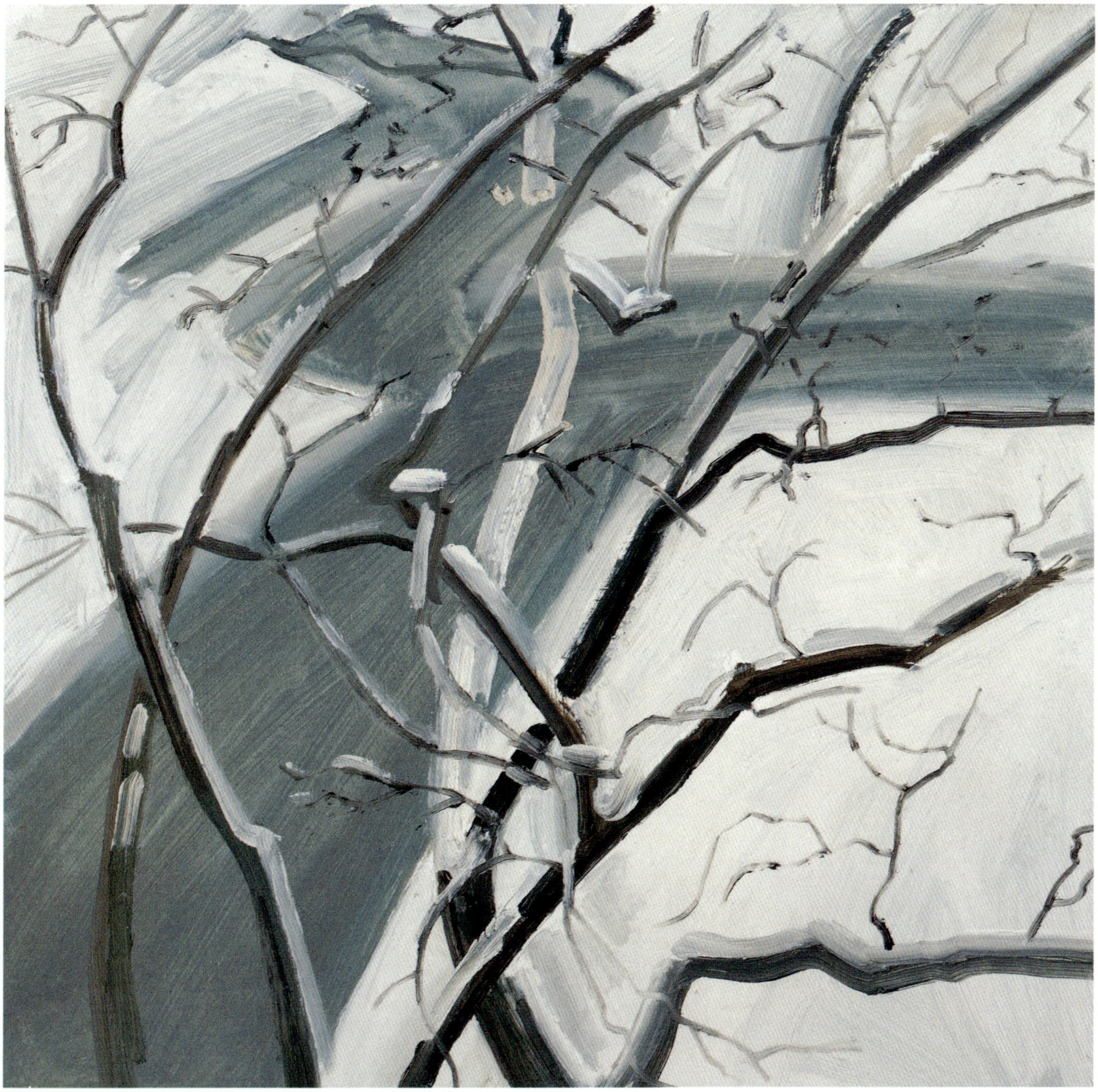

View Over High Street, oil on masonite, 11.75" x 11.75", c.2001-02. *Courtesy of Alexandre Gallery.*

Martha Mayer Erlebacher

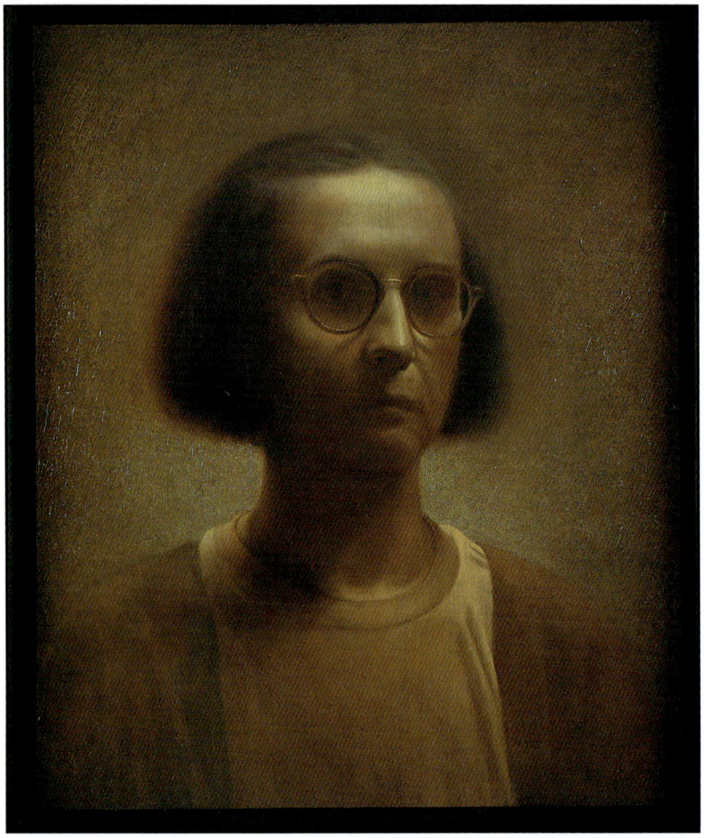

Self Portrait, oil on canvas, 17" x 14", 1992. © *Martha Mayer Erlebacher, Courtesy of Forum Gallery, New York.*

Martha Mayer Erlebacher, who holds two degrees from Brooklyn's Pratt Institute, has taught at the Graduate School of Figurative Art of the New York Academy of Art for over ten years and has been Chairman of its MFA programs. In addition, she has served for many years on the faculty of the Philadelphia College of Art.

Affiliated in New York with the Forum Gallery, Erlebacher has won many awards, including the Pratt Dean's Medal for Highest Scholastic Achievement, a Yaddo Fellowship, and a Senior Fellowship from the National Endowment for the Arts.

A participant in an extensive list of nationwide group and one-person exhibitions, Erlebacher began as "an abstractionist ... became disenchanted ... and wanted to draw and paint the figure ... as a volumetric entity ... to create paintings which forcefully recreate the human form [to] speak in a convincing way about human life ... to transcend the particular moment ... the visual metaphor [is] the vehicle to bridge [the gap between] the phenomenological world and the interior world of ideas and emotions, in The Cycle of Life, through the ancient symbols air, fire, earth and water. ... Art must reorder reality and create works ... outside of time to invite contemplation of the great spiritual questions."[57]

"Erlebacher distills the essentials of existence in luminous still-life and powerful figurative paintings,"[58] says her gallery director, Robert Fishko.

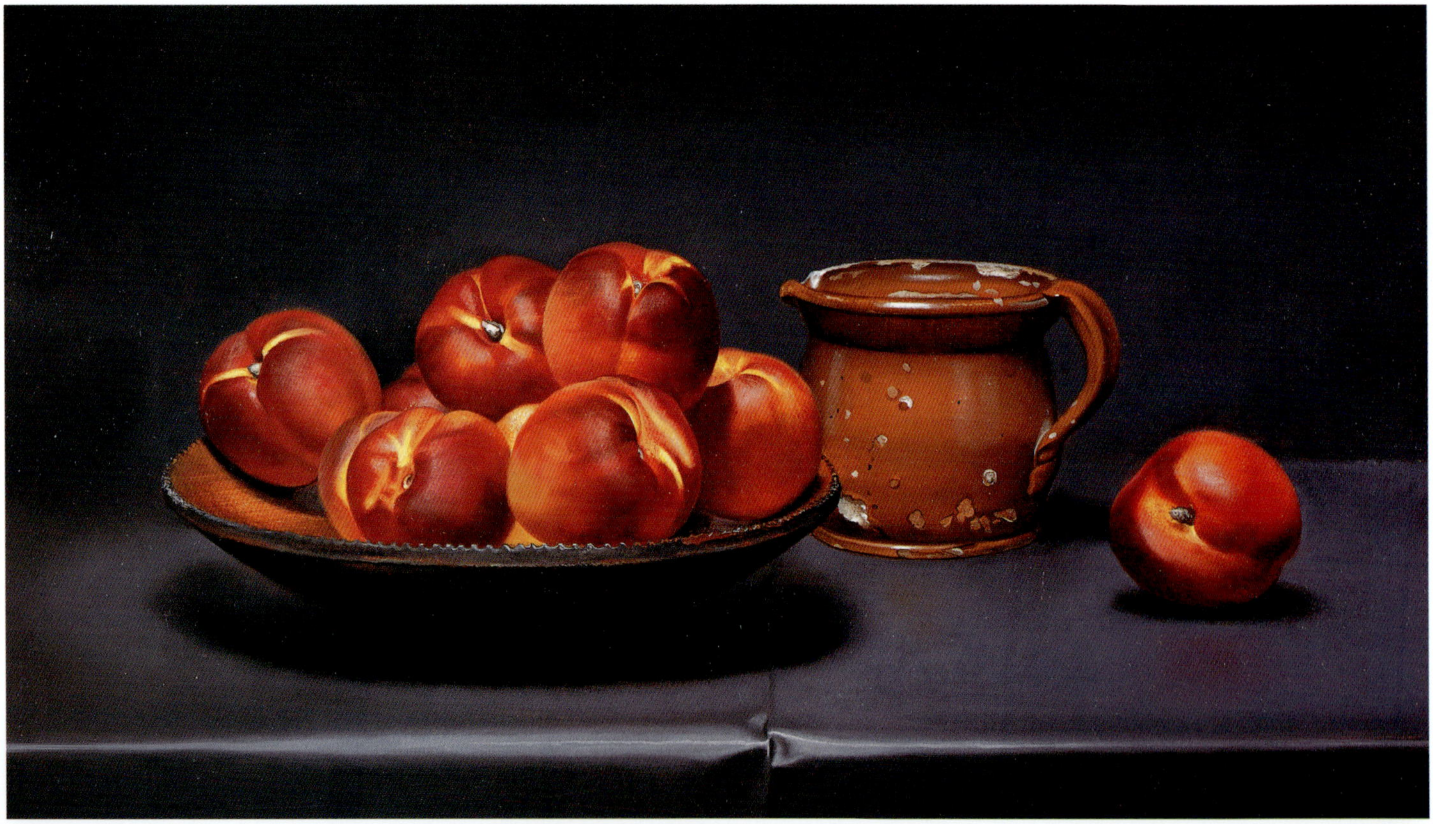

Nectarines and Redware, oil on canvas, 13" x 22", 2003. © *Martha Mayer Erlebacher, Courtesy of Forum Gallery, New York.*

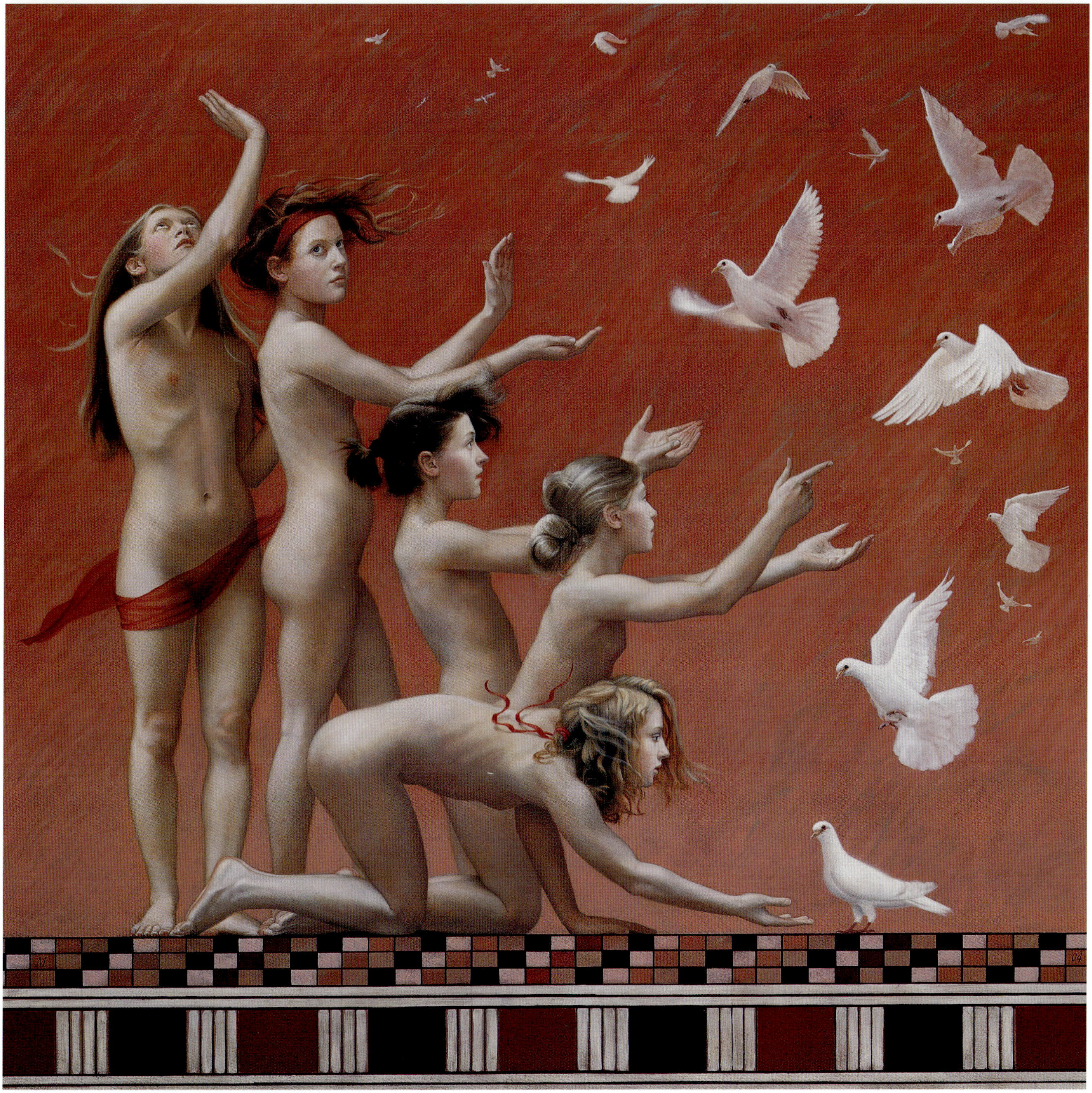

The Cycle of Life, Air: Childhood, oil on canvas, 64" x 64", 2004. © *Martha Mayer Erlebacher, Courtesy of Forum Gallery, New York.*

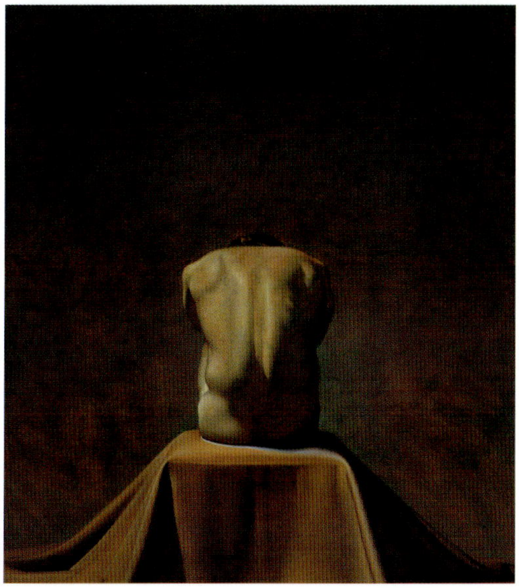

Back III (Joshua), oil on canvas, 44" x 38", 2002. © *Martha Mayer Erlebacher, Courtesy of Forum Gallery, New York.*

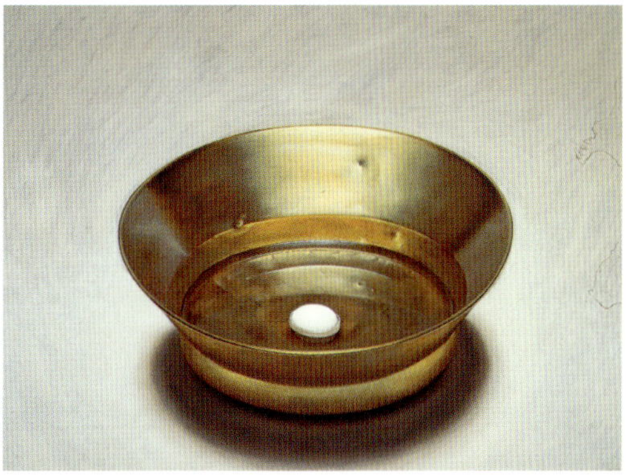

Cosmogonic Egg, oil on canvas, 24" x 30", 1998. © *Martha Mayer Erlebacher, Courtesy of Forum Gallery, New York.*

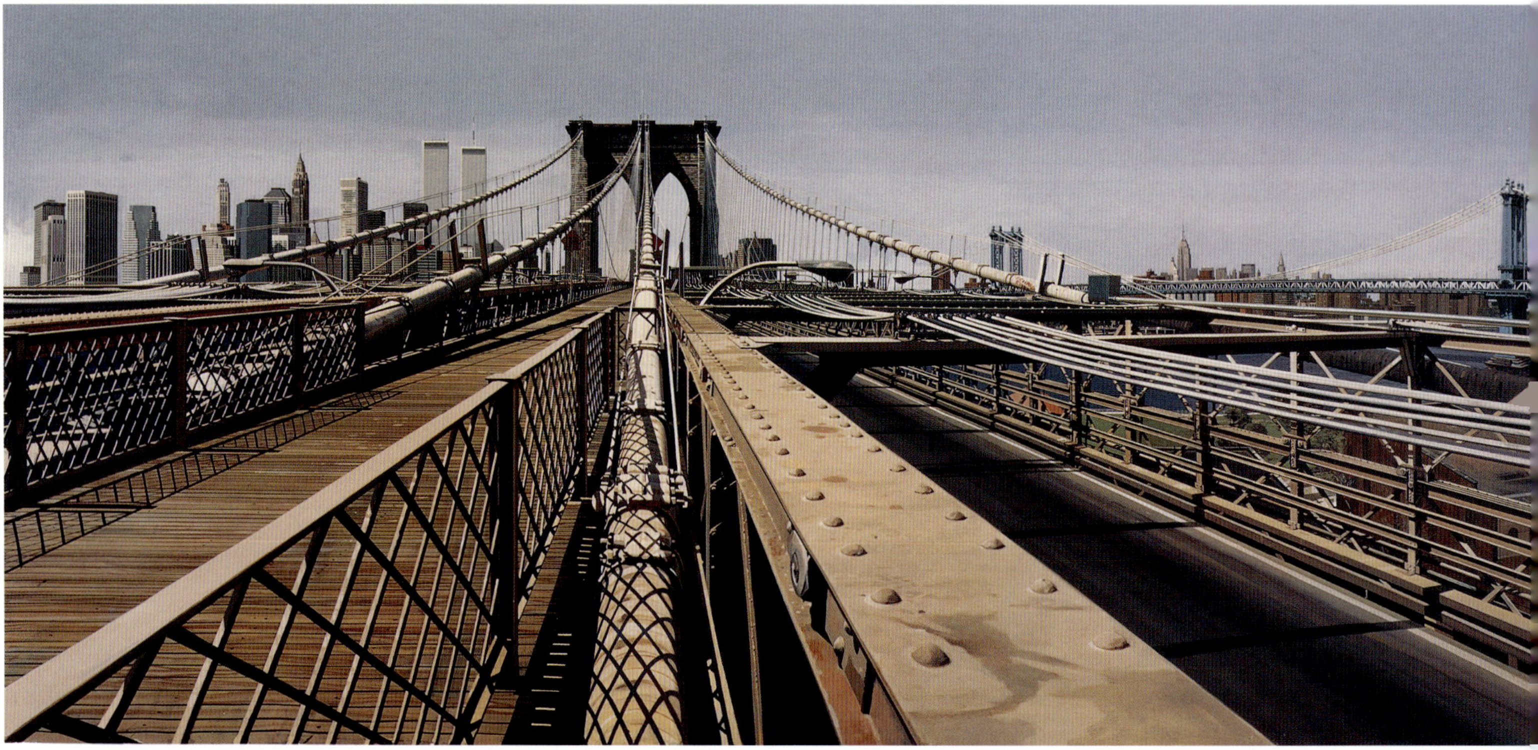

Brooklyn Bridge, oil on canvas, 39" x 78", 1993. *Courtesy of Marlborough Gallery.*

Richard Estes

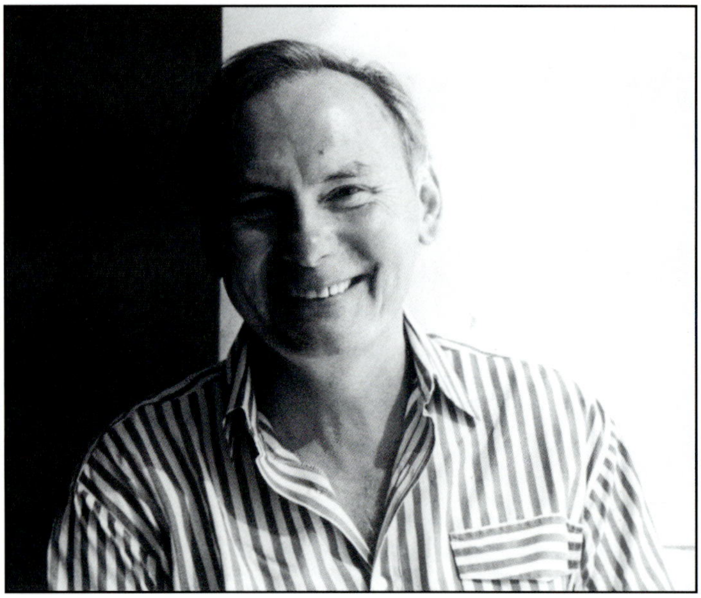

Photograph by John Gruen, Courtesy of Marlborough Gallery.

Richard Estes, one of the founders of photo-realism, creates paintings that have been called "at once traditional, contemporary and timeless. ... His utterly precise muted portraits of Manhattan ... hint at the haughtiness ... that typifies the metropolis ..."[59]

After studying at the Chicago Art Institute, Estes worked for ten years as an illustrator, until he met Allan Stone and Ivan Karp of the Castelli Gallery, who gave him his first shows in New York. He has been represented by the Marlborough Gallery for many years, and is an elected member of the National Academy of Design. Estes admires the realist works of Canaletto and Bellotto, and more recently, of Eakins, who also used photographic sources as a basis for much of his work. Estes makes his own color photographs, then paints freehand, creating composites of several views, often incorporating the distorted reflection of architectural subjects seen in storefront windows.

His paintings have been exhibited and collected around the world and may be seen at such locations as the Museum of Modern Art, the Solomon R. Guggenheim Museum, and the Whitney Museum of American Art in New York.

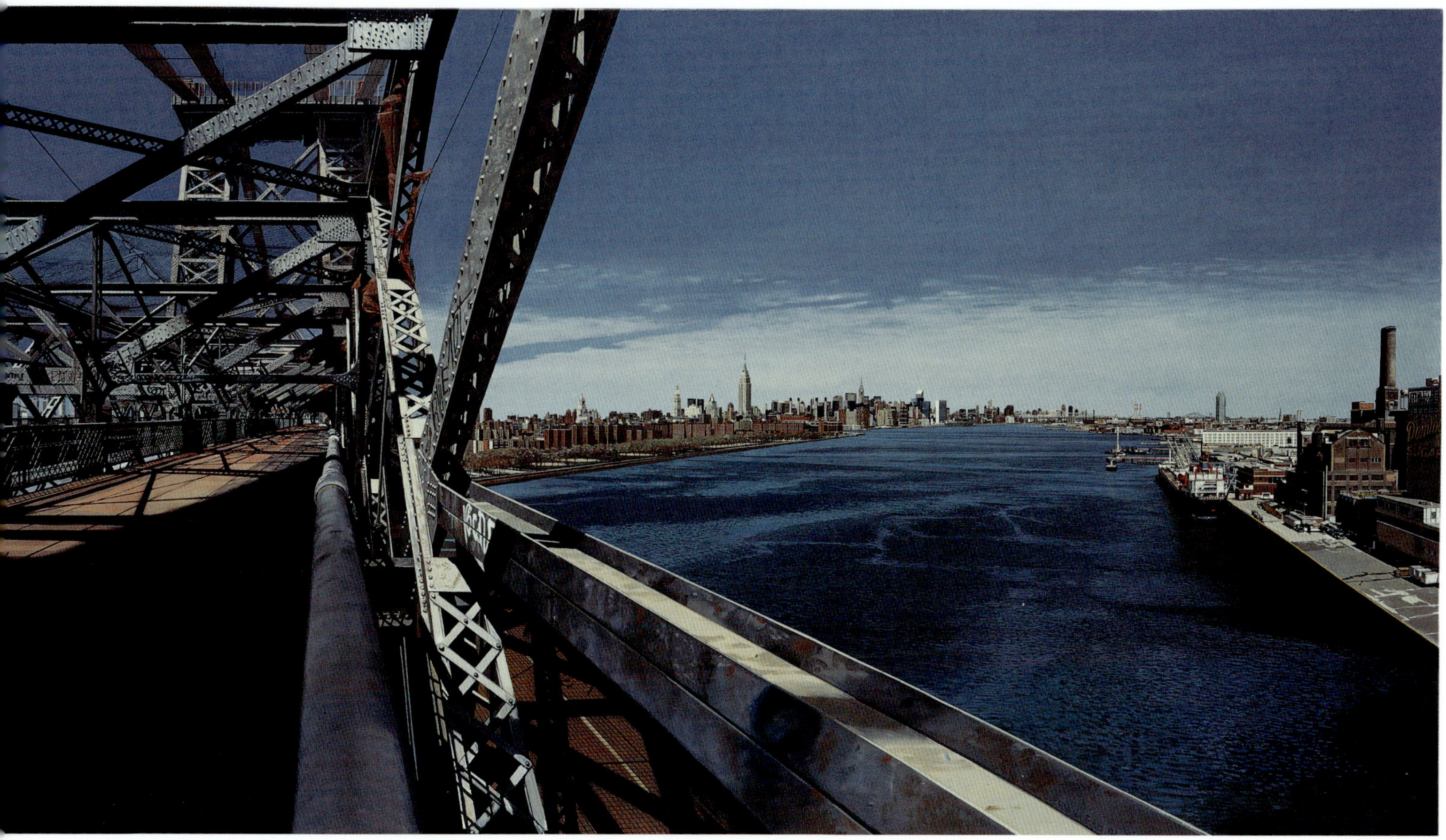

East River, oil on canvas, 43" x 74", 1994. *Courtesy of Marlborough Gallery.*

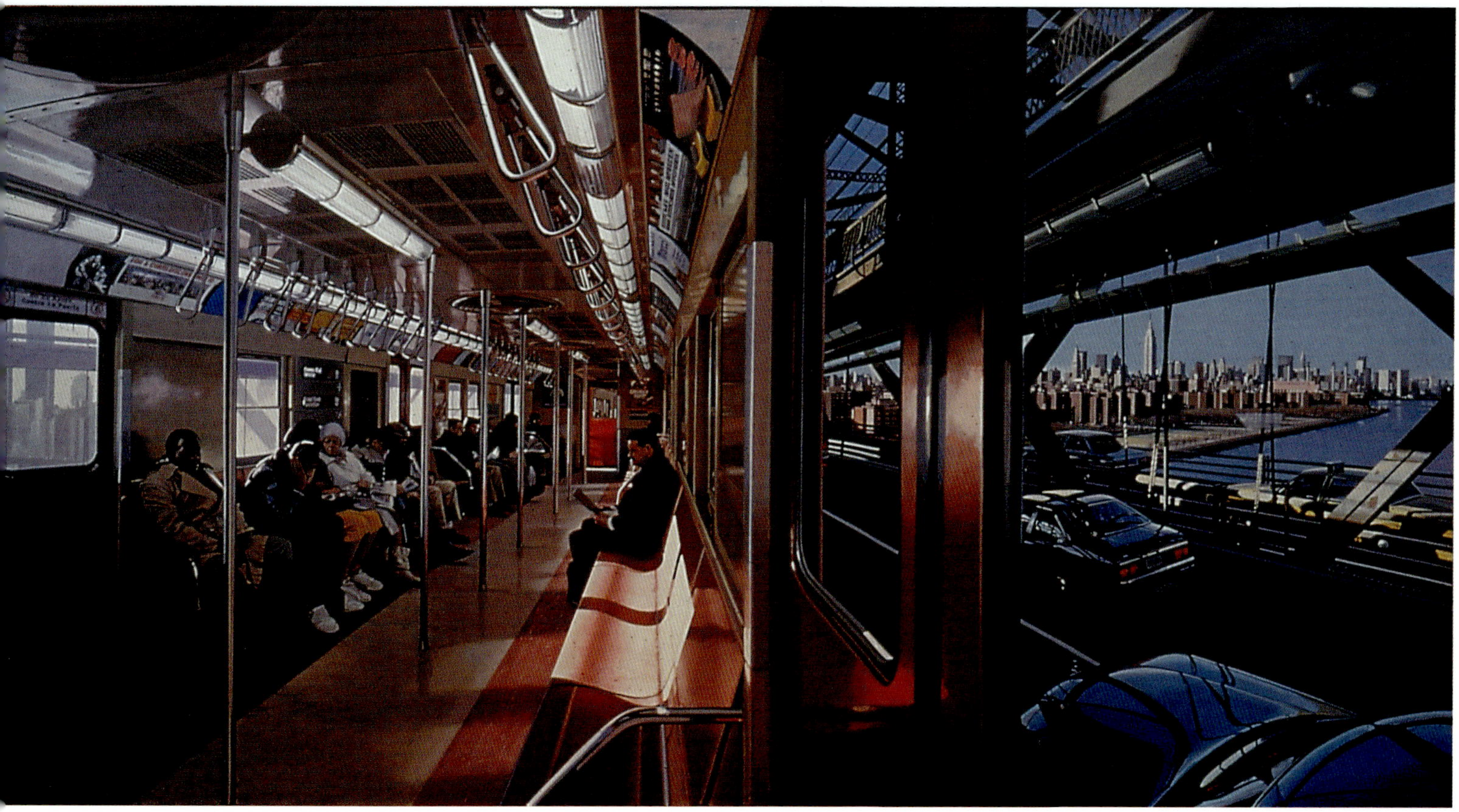

Williamsburg Bridge, oil on canvas, 36" x 66", 1987. Courtesy *of Marlborough Gallery.*

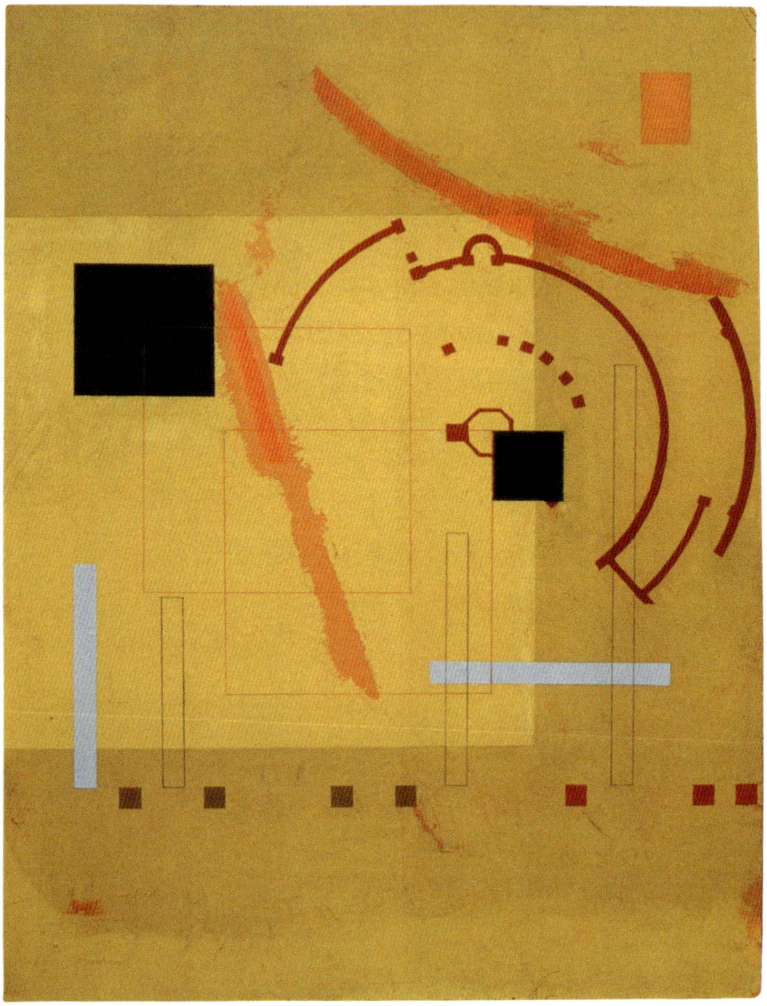

Santo Stefano #1, oil on canvas, 48" x 36", 2000.

Paul F. Fabozzi

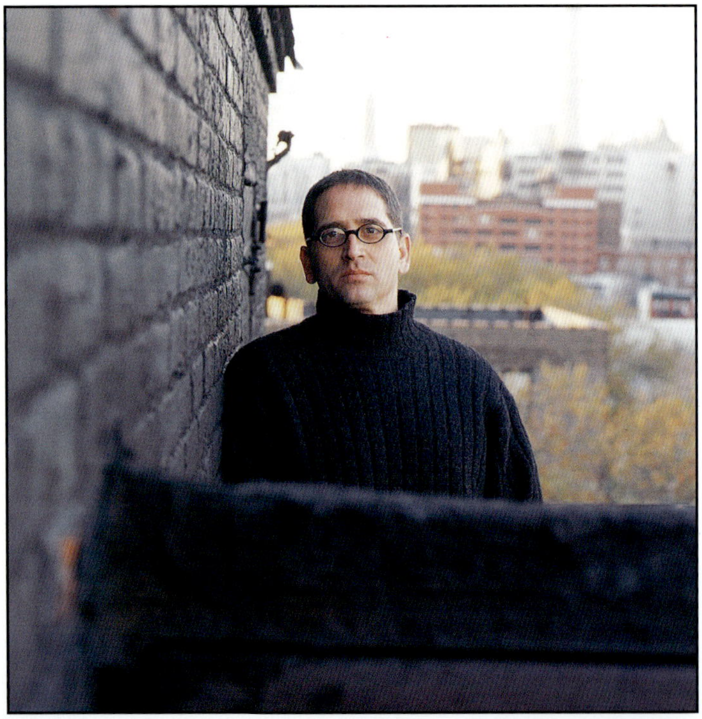

The artist, on studio roof in Long Island City. *Photograph by Michael Marfione.*

Paul F. Fabozzi, who collects shapes culled from still photos and even numbers counted by the pedometer as the raw material of his paintings, "celebrates the simple act of breathing,"[60] as he moves through space—the cornerstone of being, for him. He superimposes upon the physical place the topographical, and finally the ordered, controlled geometric—and then the element of color to add a new dimension, the color of memory reflected by thought. He "employs personal mapping methodologies, diagrams of experience, to connect the phenomenological and epistemological interpretation of place; that is, the received knowledge of a place and the firsthand experience of it."[61]

After receiving a BFA in painting at Alfred University, Fabozzi went on to earn an MFA at the University of Pennsylvania and then studied in Italy. A recipient of several academic, research and travel grants, he has been teaching for many years at St. John's University in New York, where he is currently Chairperson of the Department of Fine Arts. Fabozzi's works have appeared in exhibitions around the United States and in Italy.

He is represented by the G. W. Einstein Gallery.

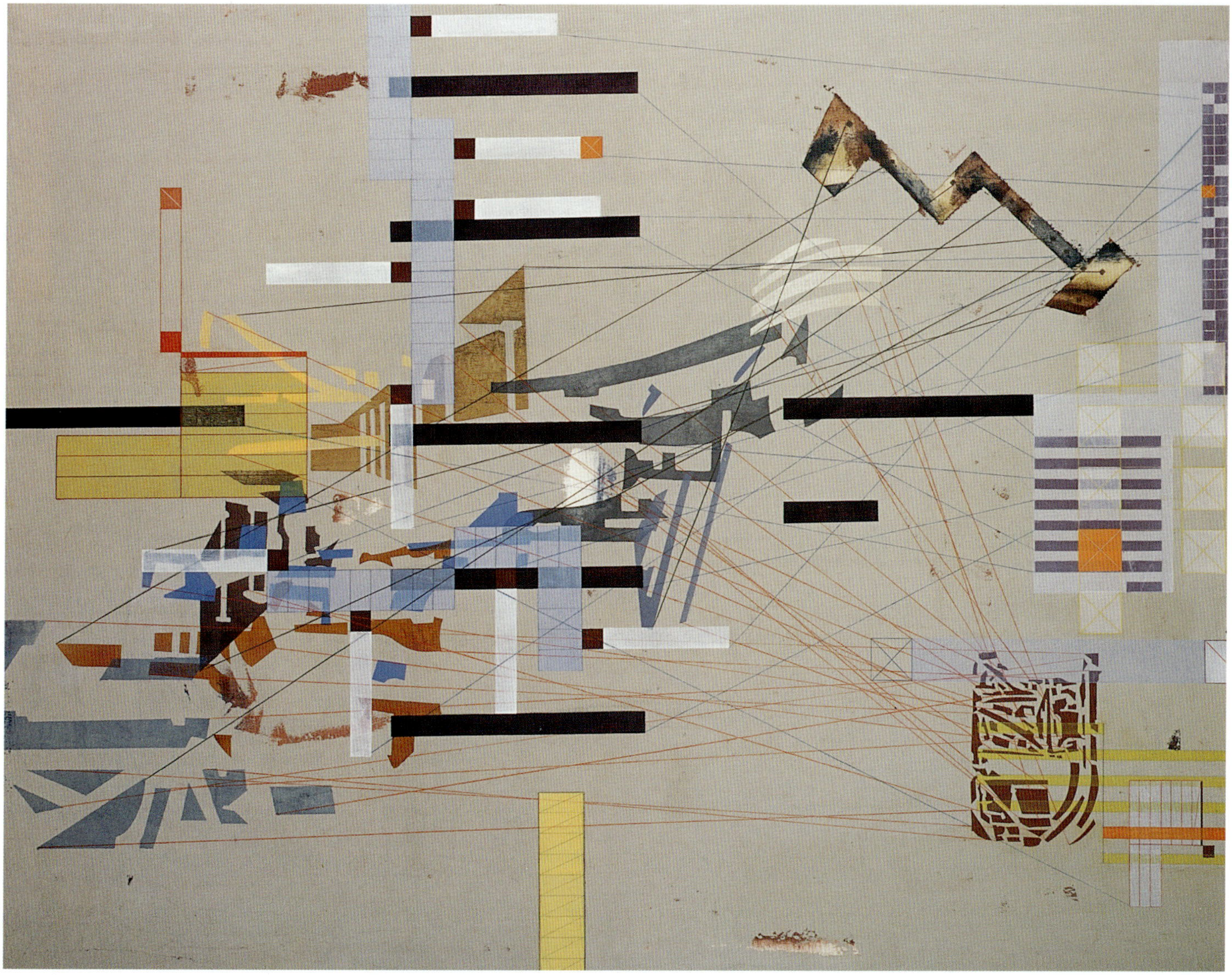

Midtown #2 (From Hell's Kitchen to Times Square), oil on canvas, 48" x 60", 2005.

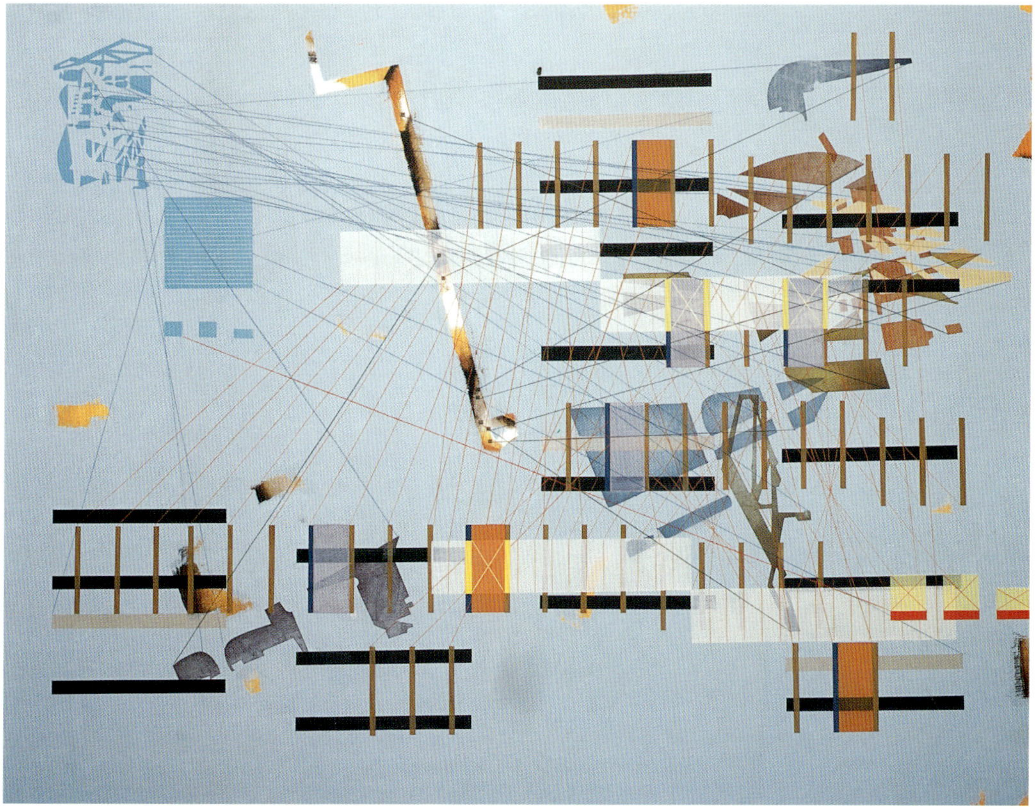

Astoria #3, oil on canvas, 48" x 60", 2005.

David Ferrando

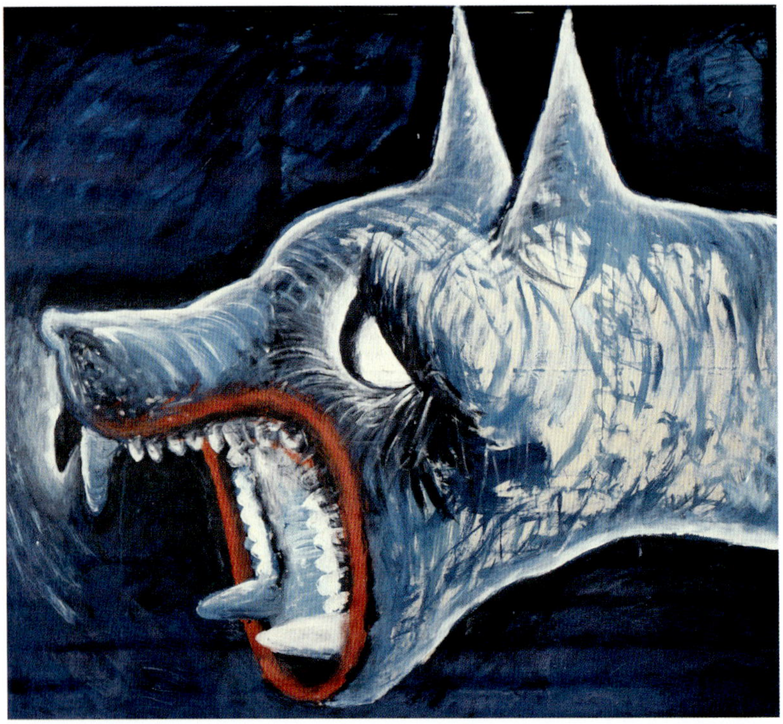

Mesopotamia, acrylic on canvas, 68" x 70", 1985.

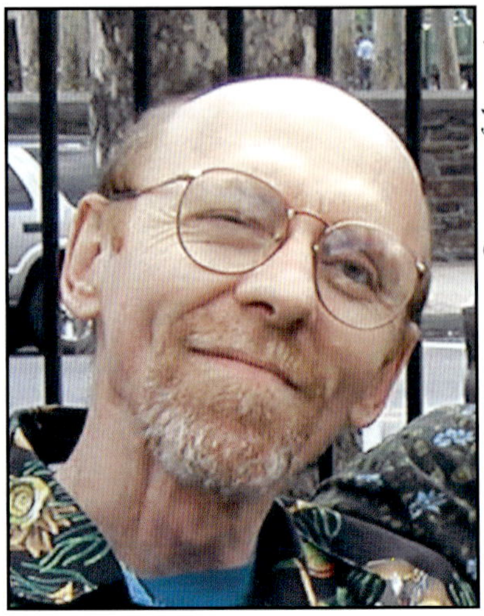

Courtesy of the artist.

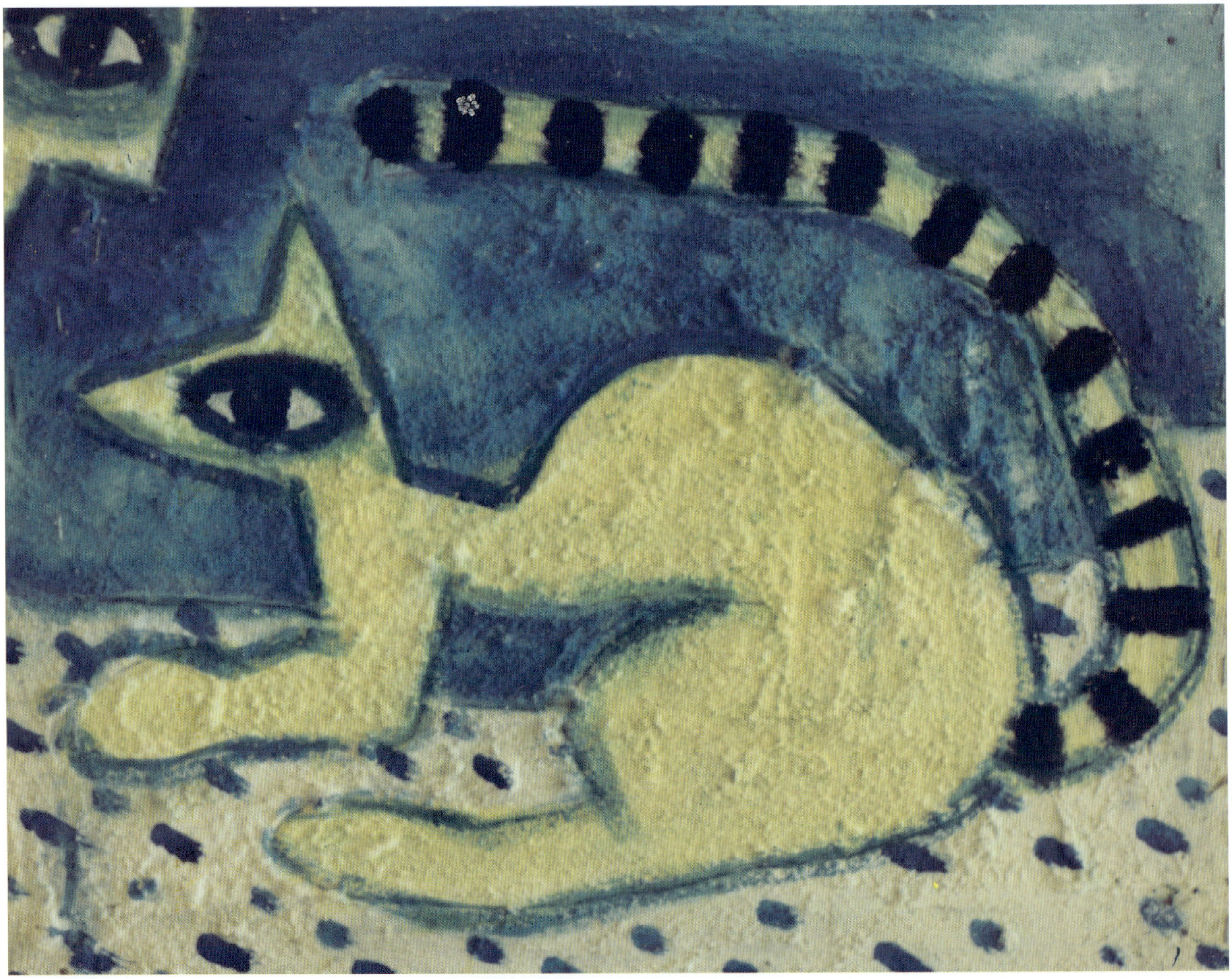

Blue Egypt, acrylic and mixed media on canvas, 28" x 34", 1998. *Collection of J. Nickerson.*

David Ferrando, who earned the German equivalent of an MFA after receiving the Dayton Art Institute's BFA degree, has had his works exhibited internationally, in Iceland and Germany, while living in Europe for ten years. He strongly believes "in the process of the creative act of art making. Rarely do I have a preconceived idea of a finished work, but during the act of painting ... the work is channeled through me, from the universe."[62]

In addition to painting, Ferrando writes and performs poetry and short stories in New York. He was represented in several Metropolitan Museum of Art Invitational exhibitions, often participates in open studios and lectures throughout the city, and has taught art to children. He has been Ulster County's Artist in Residence.

Ferrando believes that the making of art is a kind of map for the journey of life, and says, "God is dreaming through me ... the art-making process heals me. When others see it, it heals them. ... "[63]

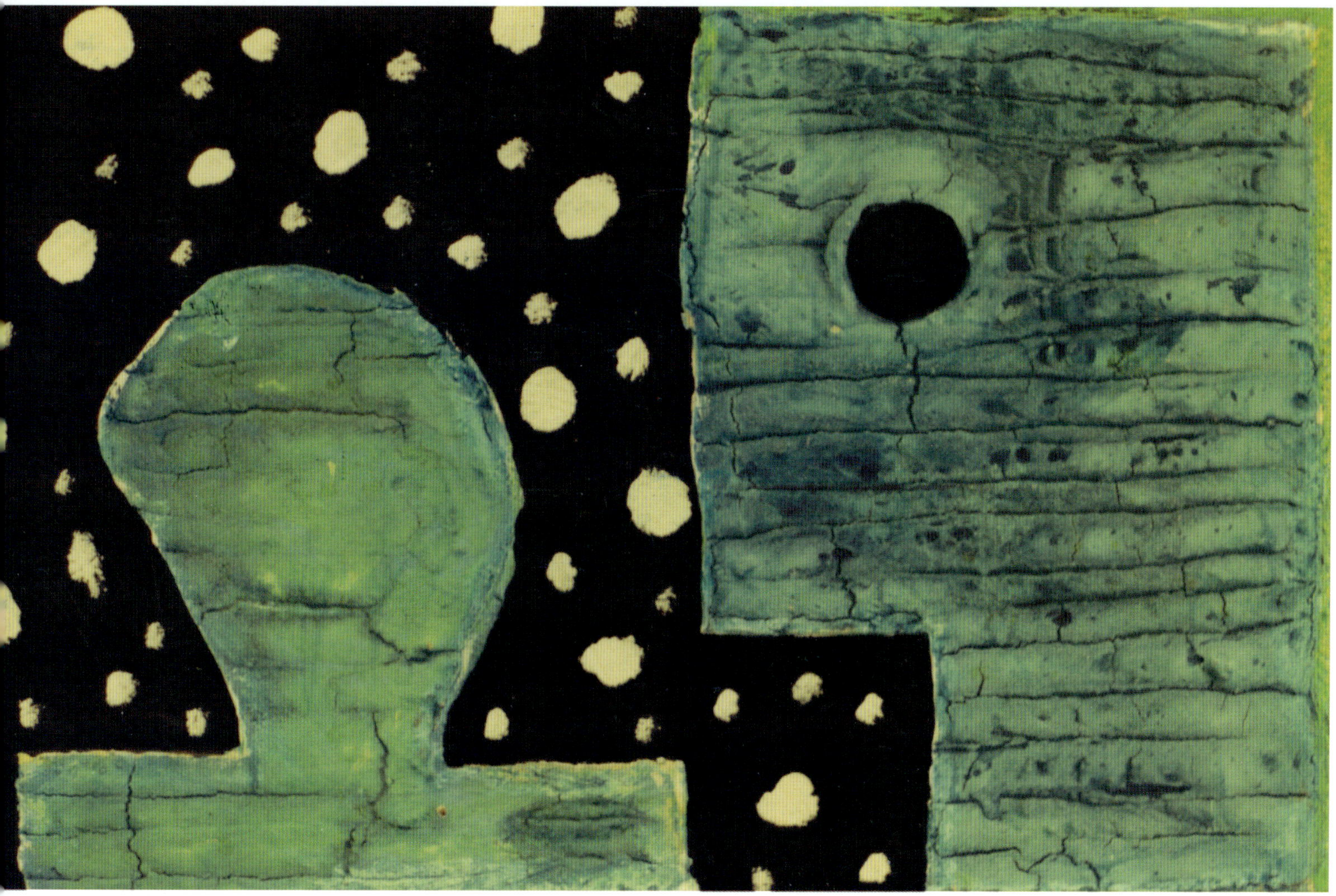

Two Heads, acrylic and mixed media on canvas, 24" x 36", 1998. *Collection of J. Nickerson.*

Eric Fischl

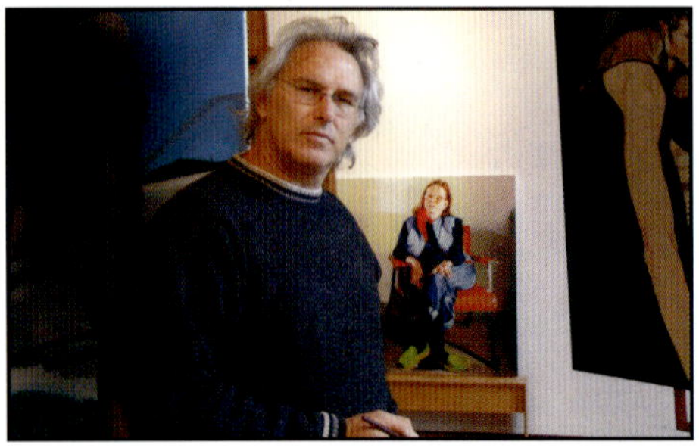

Courtesy of the artist.

Eric Fischl, an elected National Academician, spent many years studying, then teaching, in Arizona, California, Chicago, and Nova Scotia, before moving back to New York, his birthplace. He has received an honorary doctorate from the Nova Scotia College of Art and Design, the Society of Arts Academy Honours for distinction in art, and has been a visiting artist at the New York Academy of Art.

Fischl's works, now in many public and private collections, have been included in exhibitions at the Museum of Modern Art, the Venice Biennale, the Whitney Museum of American Art, and the Smithsonian, among many others. His narrative paintings, based on the figure, often describe intimate and sexually charged subjects and situations. Called "a true American realist," he is said to "work at a pitch of psychological truth not known in American narrative art. … "[64] Fischl has been called the "painter laureate of American anxiety, who desires to turn the viewer into a voyeur, a reluctant … [even] embarrassed witness … to … psycho-sexual suburban dramas … and disturbing images of dysfunctional family life."[65]

Fischl is represented by the Mary Boone Gallery in New York.

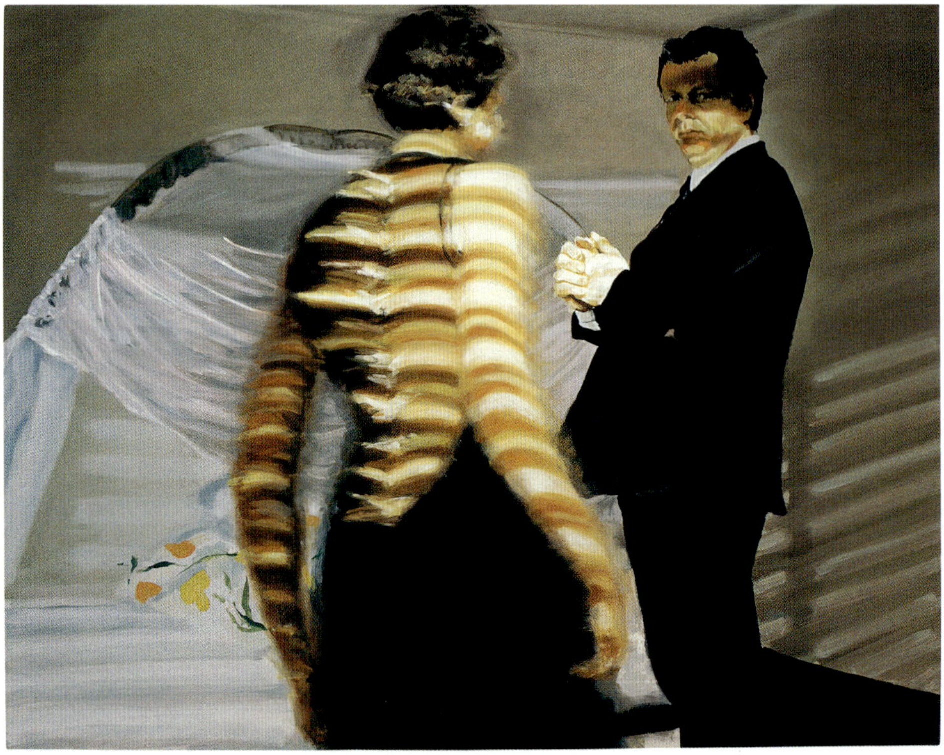

Bedroom Scene #6 (Surviving the Fall Meant Using You for Handholds), oil on linen, 72" x 90", 2004. *Collection of Paul Allen, Microsoft. Courtesy of Mary Boone Gallery.*

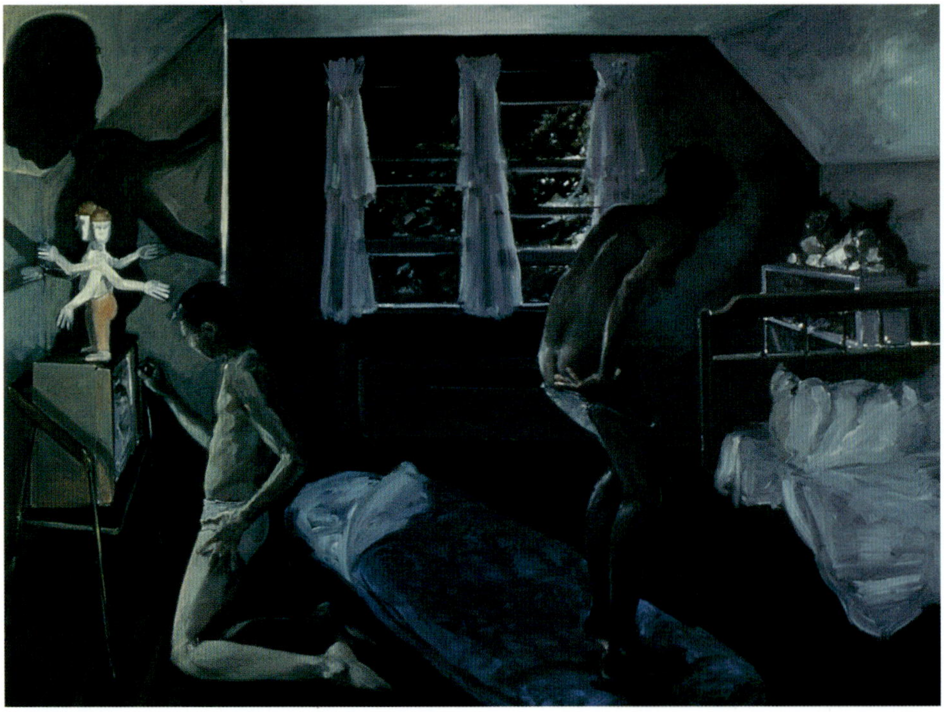

Slumber Party, oil on canvas, 84" x 108", 1983. *Collection of Doris Ammann. Courtesy of Mary Boone Gallery.*

Opposite:
Untitled – What Stands Between the Artist and his Model, oil on linen, 72" x 54", 1994. *Collection of Tom Gaynor, National Museum of American Art. Courtesy of Mary Boone Gallery.*

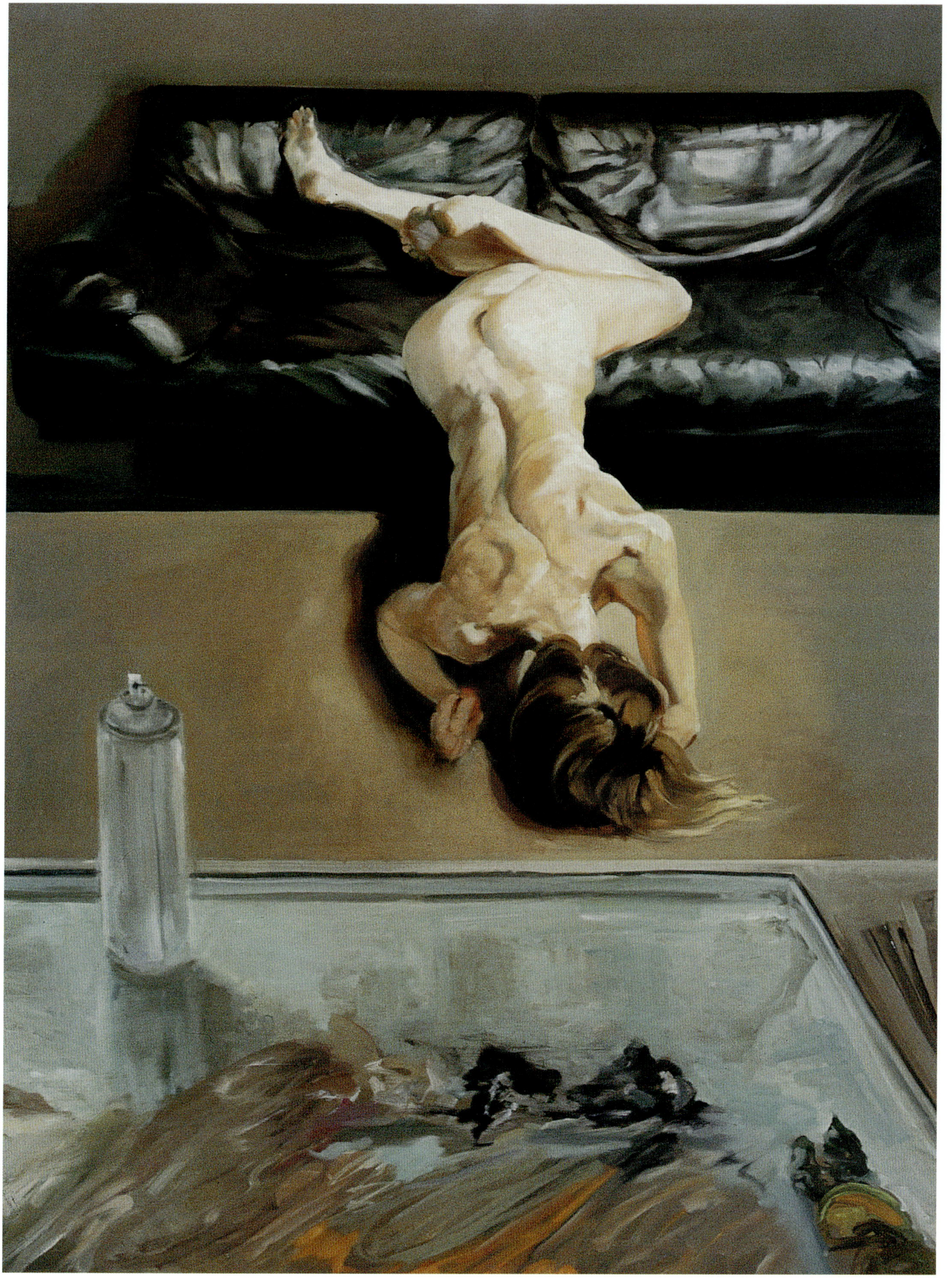

Janet Fish

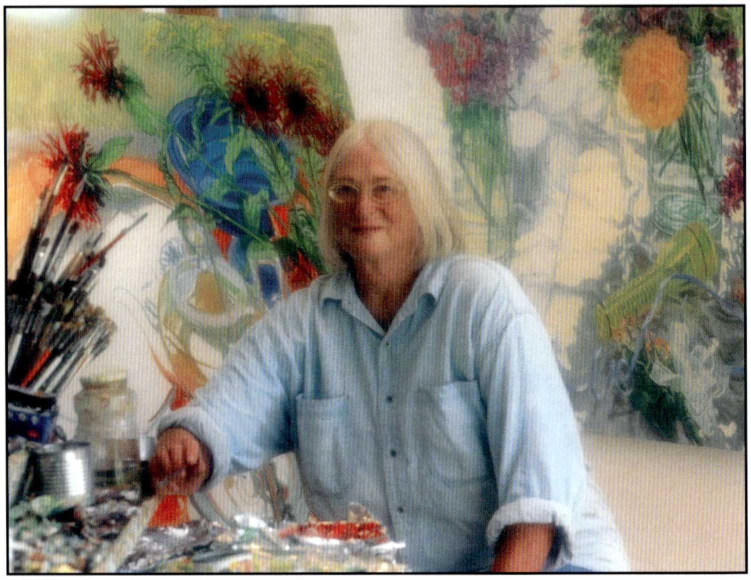

Courtesy of D C Moore Gallery.

Janet Fish credits Josef Albers at Yale with "making you very aware of the interactions of color ... see better is what it made you do,"[66] although she says, "the course was not really where I am with color."[67] She also studied with Leonard Baskin, Alex Katz, Neil Welliver, and Philip Pearlstein, each influencing her work in very differing ways. Fish is an elected National Academician and winner of numerous awards. "What you see affects how you see,"[68] she says; in her early still lifes she began to see that the light over the volume (of plastic-wrapped produce) became the subject of the painting. This led to studies of transparency in bottles and glass.

"Now," she says, "I put things together, composing, based on echoes and repetitions, things that relate in visual ways."[69] Of the "palpable energy" seen in her work, Fish says, "Light is energy ... color is light ... light is color and energy ... forming the painting and the energy of the paint."[70]

"Objects ... aren't the subject at all," says Fish, "the object is one of the tools like the paint and brush. The real subject is the light, movement and color, and echoes of the objects in one's mind."[71]

Her large-scale paintings press their subjects up close to the picture plane, emphasizing their dramatic proportions. They may be seen in most major public and corporate collections, including the Metropolitan Museum of Art and the Whitney Museum of American Art in New York. She is represented by the D C Moore Gallery.

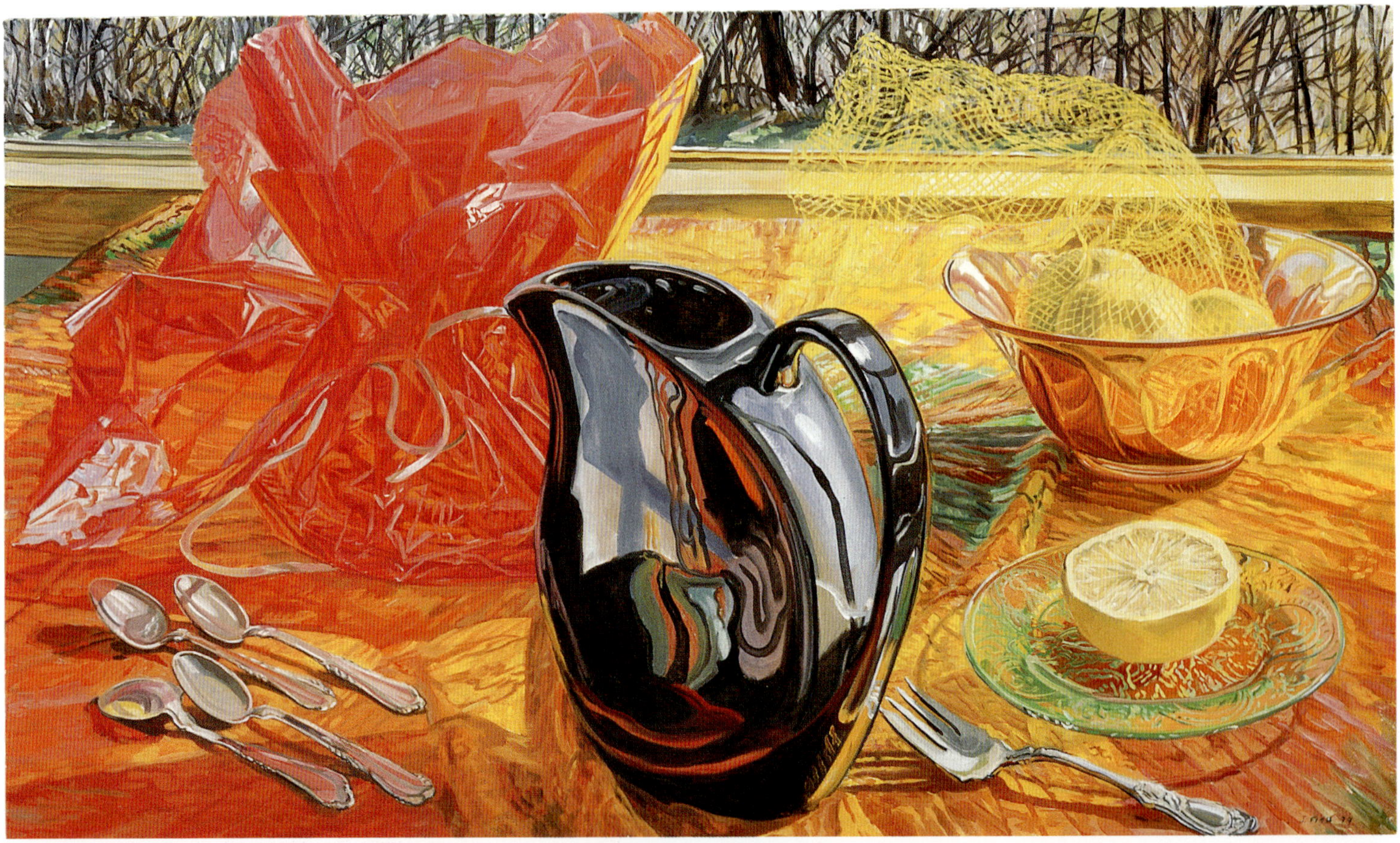

From Alexis, oil on canvas, 42" x 70", 1999. *Photograph © Beth Phillips. Courtesy of D C Moore Gallery. All art © Janet Fish/Licensed by VAGA, New York, NY.*

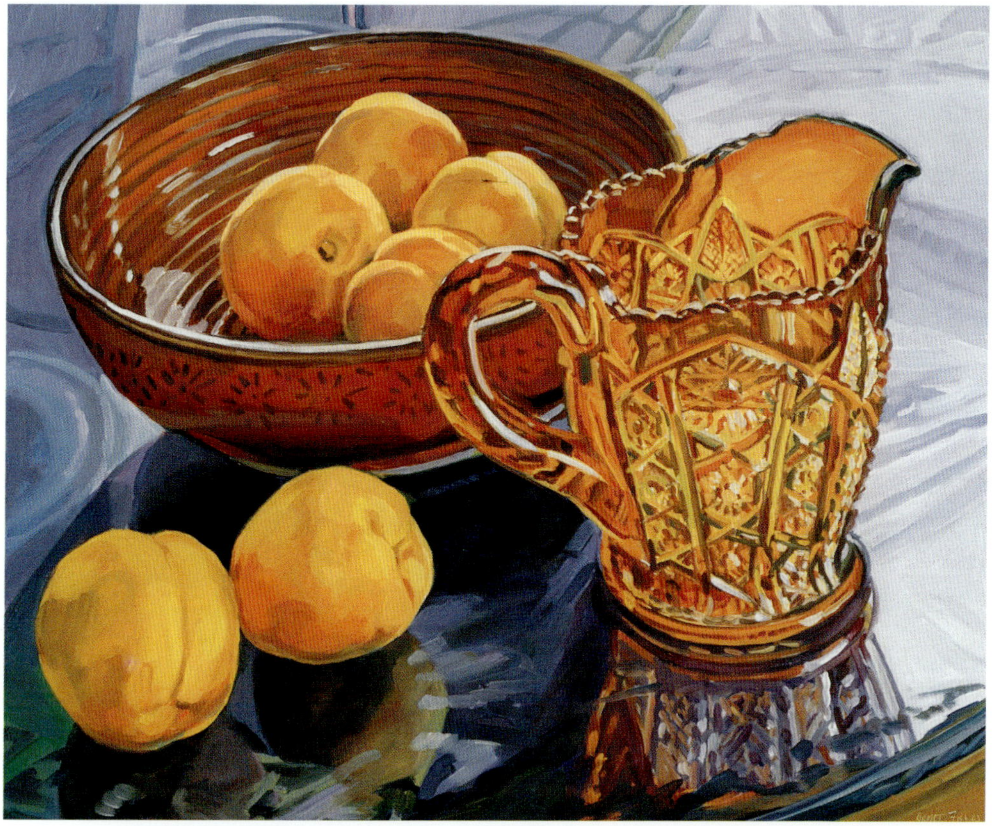

Nectarines, Orange Pitcher, oil on canvas, 22" x 26", 2003. *Photograph © Beth Phillips. Courtesy of D C Moore Gallery.*

Ingrid's Clementine with Tulips, oil on canvas, 50" x 70", 1999. *Photograph © Beth Phillips. Courtesy of D C Moore Gallery.*

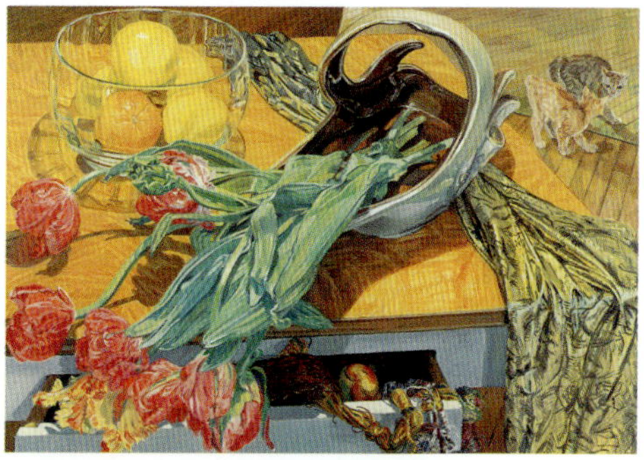

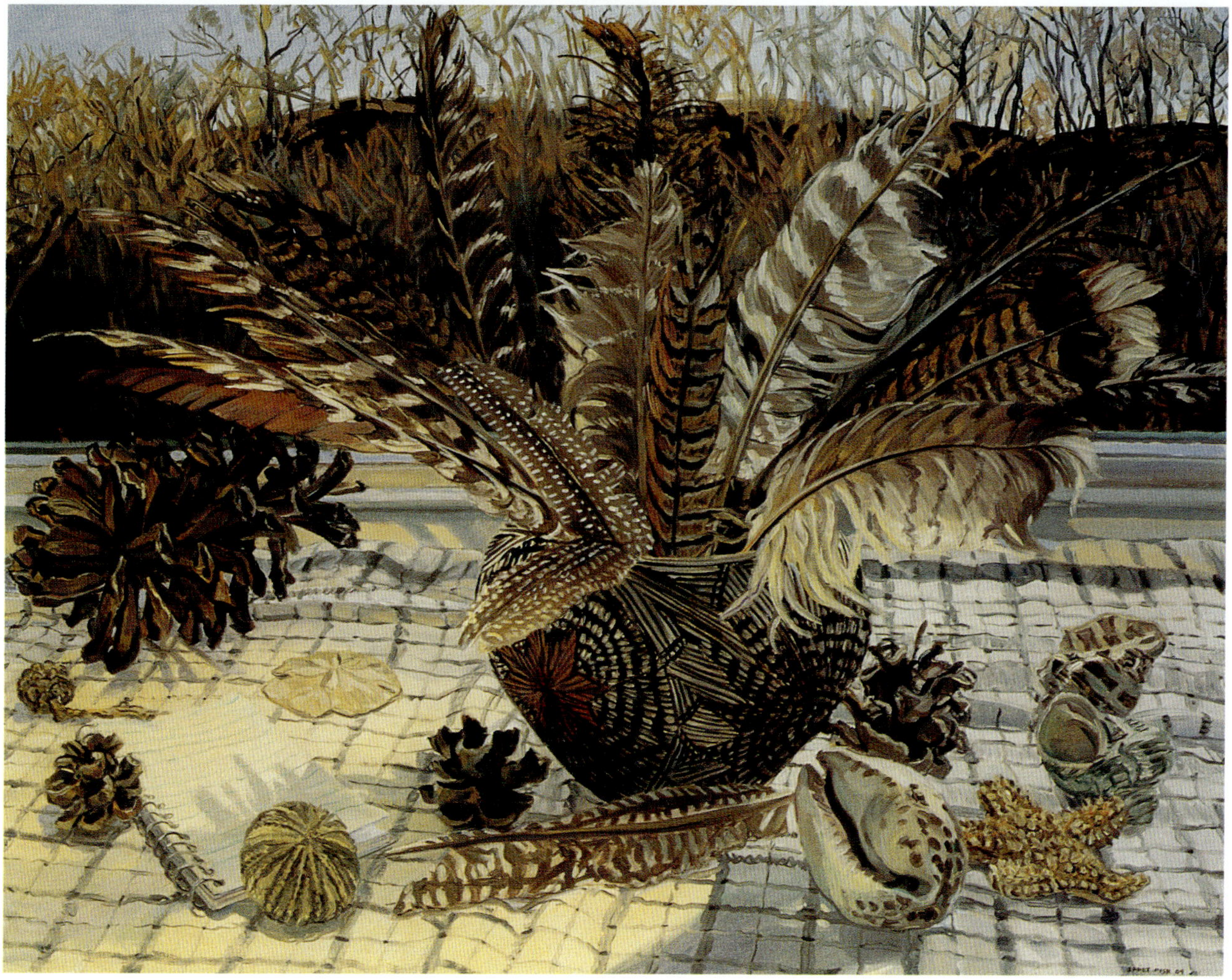

Feathers, oil on canvas, 40" x 50", 2004. *Photograph © Beth Phillips. Courtesy of D C Moore Gallery.*

Louise Fishman

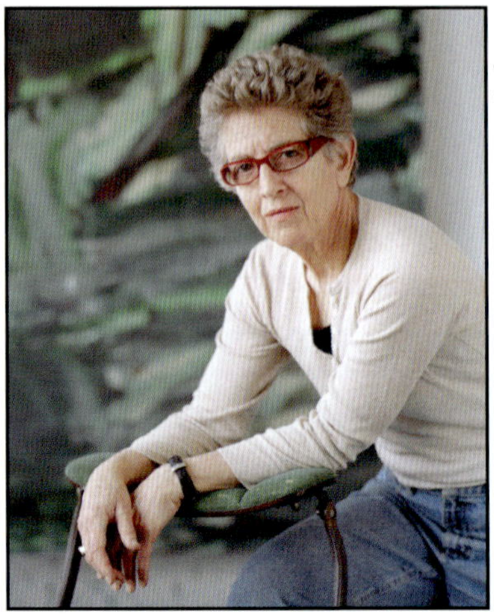
Photograph © Nina Subin. Courtesy of Cheim & Read.

Louise Fishman, winner of a Guggenheim Fellowship among several major awards, has long painted large-scale works generally called "second generation abstract expressionist."[72] Her overlaid softly geometric or broadly linear canvases reveal "subtle calibration of color and light, gesture that creates, with flat, careful layered mark, open oscillating space ... to suggest ... unspecified interior psychological [or] exterior, urban ... areas. ..."[73]

With degrees in art from the Tyler School of Fine Arts in Pennsylvania, and the University of Illinois in Champaign, she moved to New York in the mid-sixties. Her education included travels to Eastern Europe, where she visited Auschwitz, Terezin, and other World War II sites. Fishman has participated in numerous exhibitions with social and societal themes. Her many group exhibitions include several at the National Academy of Design, the Lesbian and Gay Community Services Center, and the Jewish Museum in New York, as well as "Drawing the Line Against AIDS" at the Peggy Guggenheim Collection in Venice, and "Artists for Pride" at the Nexus Gallery in Philadelphia.

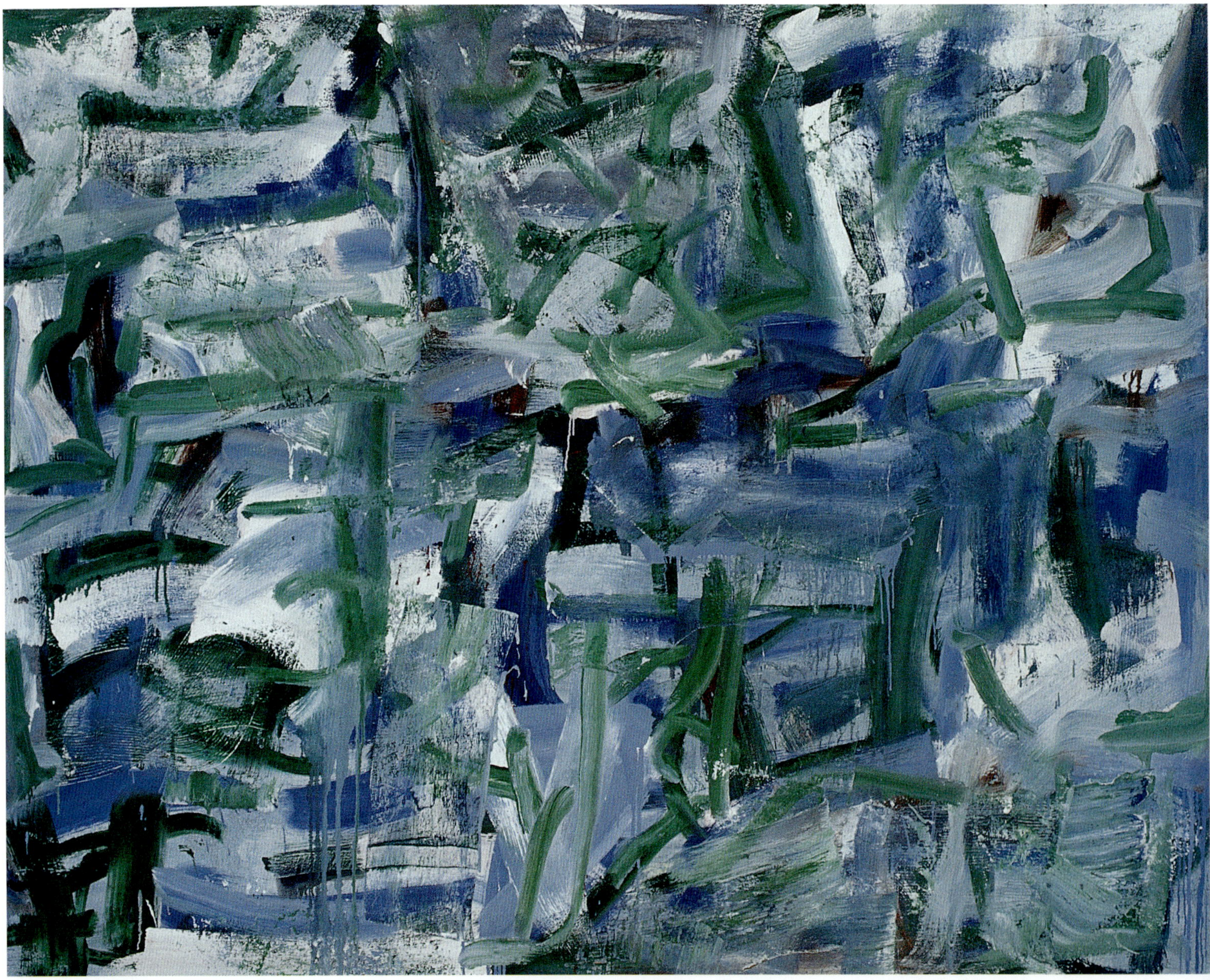

A Few Things for Themselves, oil on linen, 70" x 87.75", 2005. *Courtesy of Cheim & Read. All art © Louise Fishman/Licensed by VAGA, New York, NY.*

Casa Cenote, oil on linen, 57" x 76", 2000. *Courtesy of Cheim & Read.*

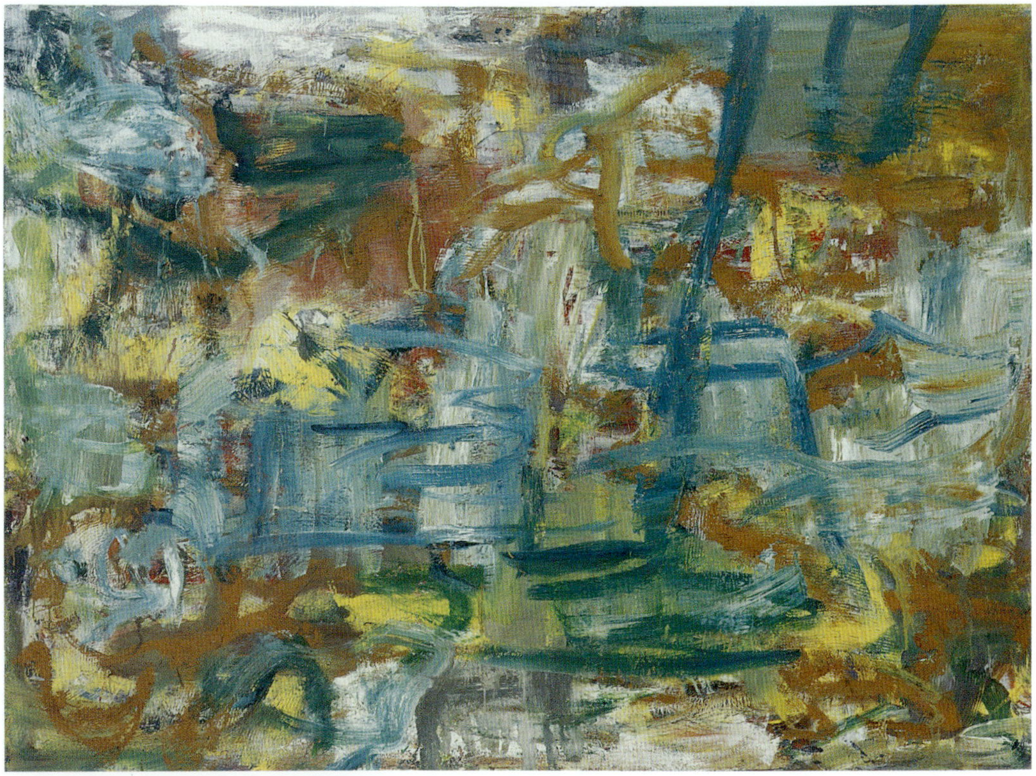

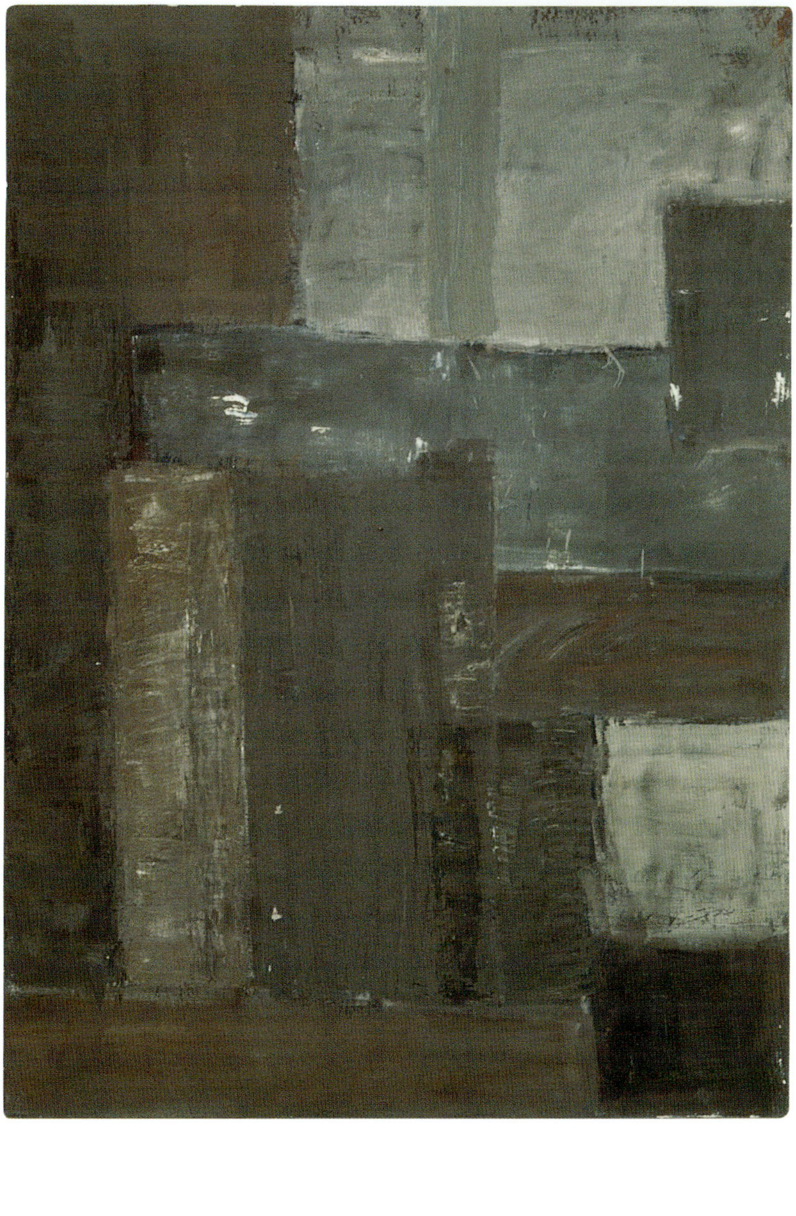

Her works may be found in public collections such as the Metropolitan and Jewish Museums in New York, The National Museum of Women in the Arts, in Washington and the Art Institute of Chicago.

Fishman's academic career includes teaching at Parsons School of Design, The Cooper Union, Howard and Columbia Universities, Pratt Institute, and the Chicago Art Institute.

DORTN, oil on linen, 77" x 54", c.1987-88. *Courtesy of Cheim & Read.*

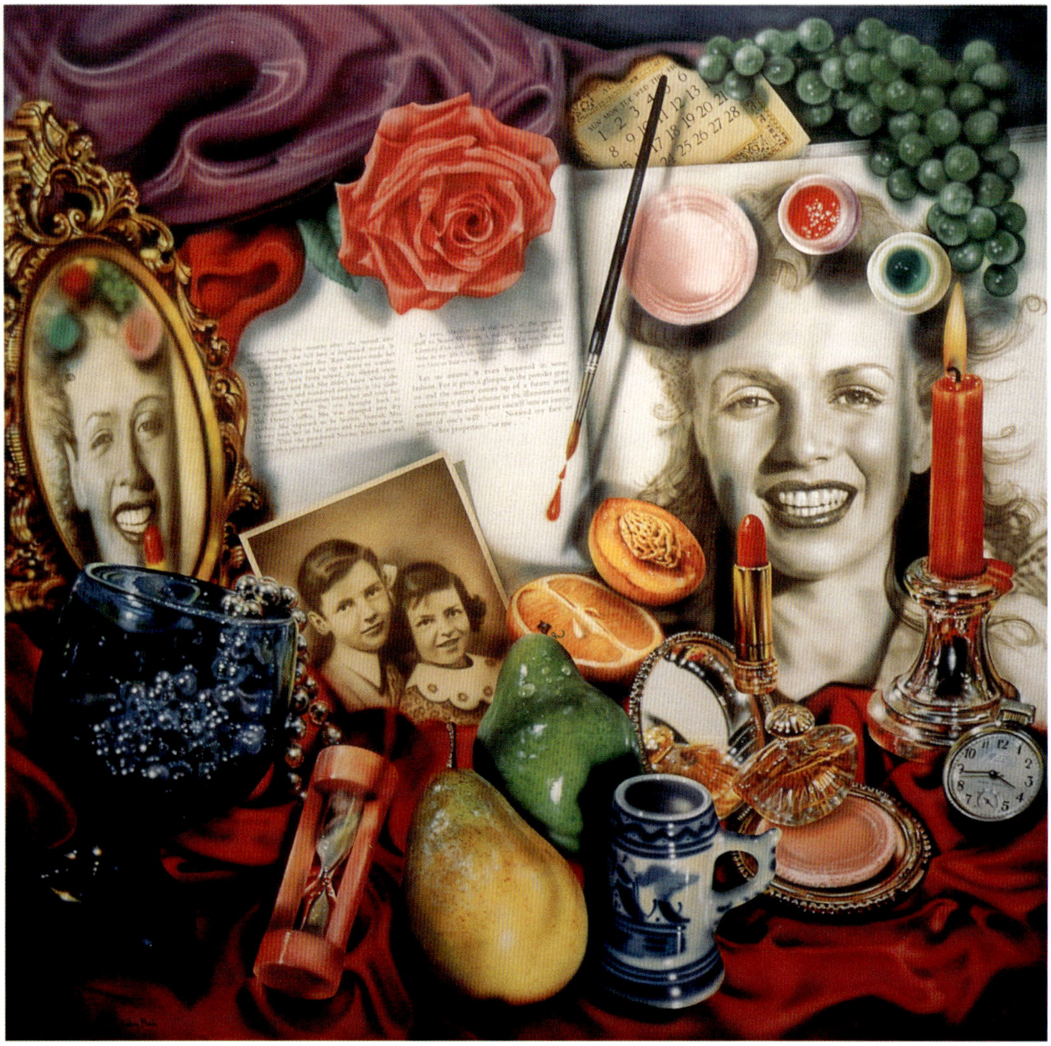

Marilyn (Vanitas), oil over acrylic on canvas, 96" x 96", 1977. *Collection of the University of Arizona Museum of Art, Museum purchase with funds provided by the Edward J. Gallagher, Jr. Memorial Fund.*

Audrey Flack

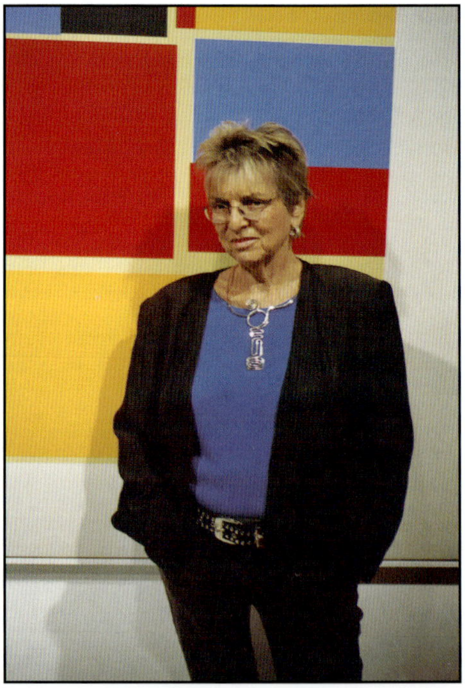

The artist at The Cooper Union memorial for Bob Slutzky, 2005. *Photograph © Cynthia Dantzic.*

Audrey Flack studied at The Cooper Union, then at Yale "on scholarship under Josef Albers,"[74] and has an honorary doctorate from George Washington University. She delivered a commencement address at the Pennsylvania Academy of Fine Arts, where she said, in part:

> I believe in art.
> I do not believe in the 'art world' as it is today.
> I do not believe in art as a commodity.
> Great art is in exquisite balance. It is restorative.
> I believe in the energy of art,
> and through the use of that energy,
> the artist's ability to transform his or her life
> and, by example, the lives of others ...[75]

In her large, photo-realist canvases, Flack reveals a concern for feminist issues through subjects included in her "luminous spatial maze(s) of intricately ordered objects."[76]

Her works, widely exhibited, can be seen in many private and public collections, such as the Metropolitan Museum of Art and the National Museum of Women in the Arts, the latter in Washington, D.C.

Flack's teaching career includes numerous national and international lectureships; she has taught at New York University, Pratt Institute, and the University of Pennsylvania. After Mary Cassatt, she was the first woman included in Janson's revised *History of Art*. She is represented by the Louis K. Meisel Gallery.

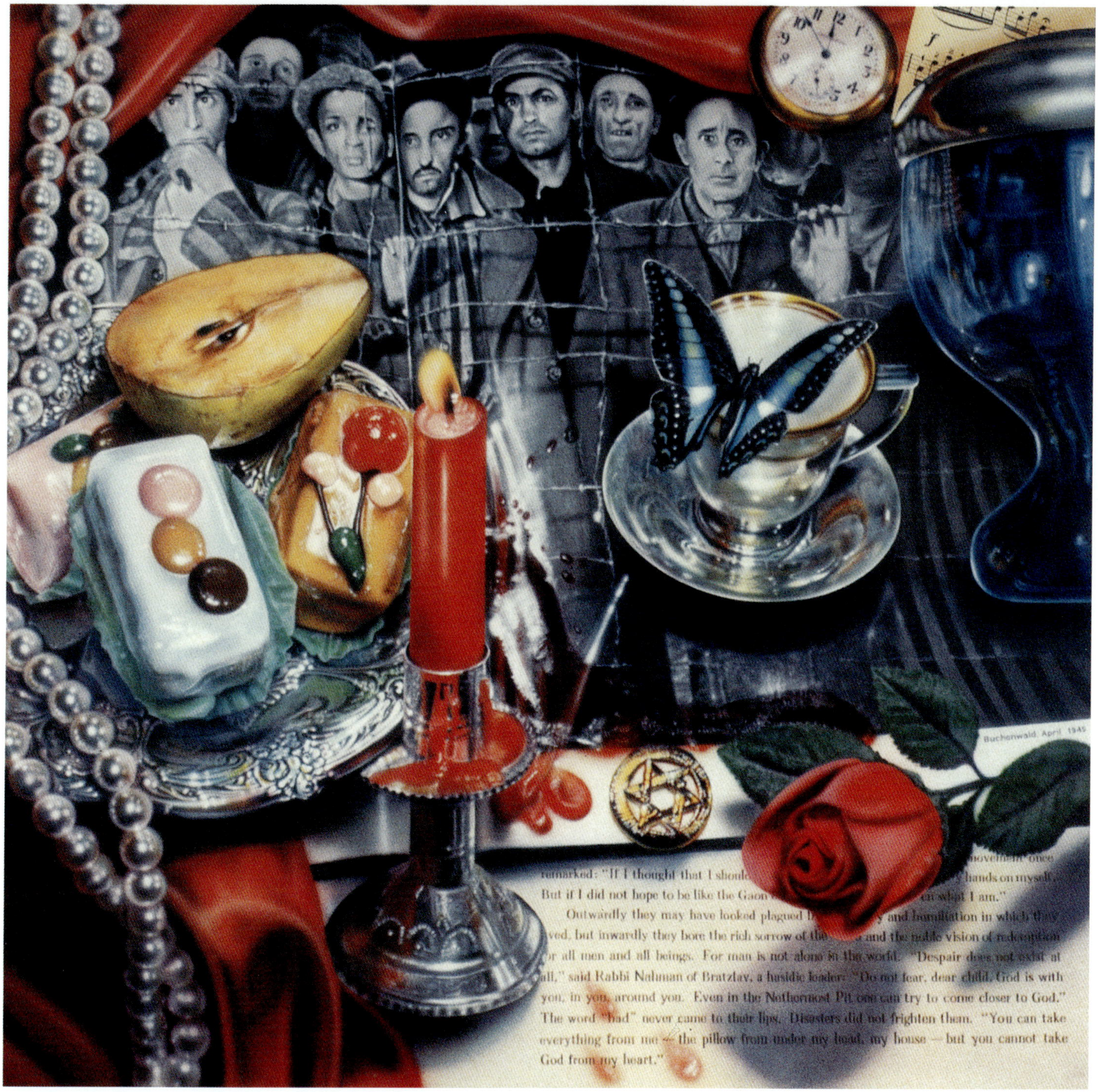

World War II (Vanitas), acrylic on canvas, 8' x 8', 1977. *Incorporating a portion of the photograph, "Buchenwald, April, 1945," by Margaret Bourke-White, © Time, Inc., Private collection of David Pincus.*

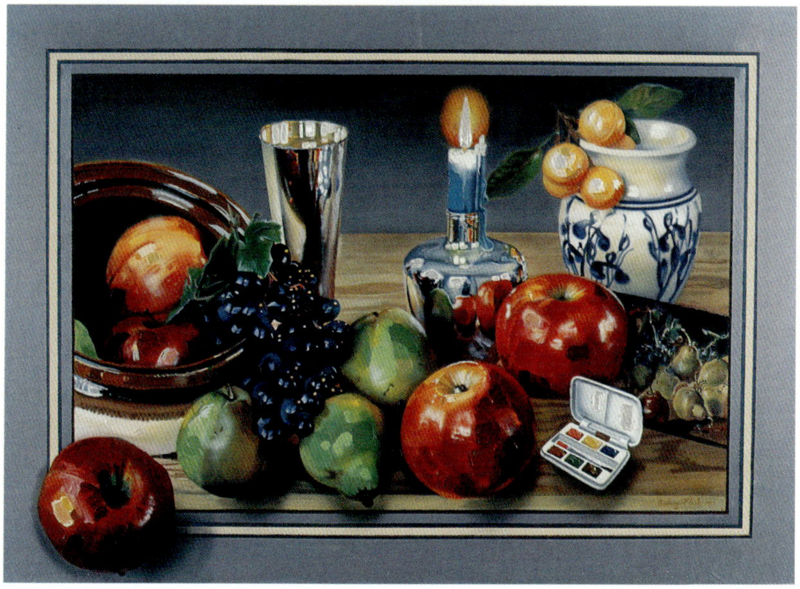

Roman Beauties, oil over acrylic on canvas, 54" x 74", 1983. *Collection of Sidney Bestoff, Courtesy of Louis K. Meisel Gallery.*

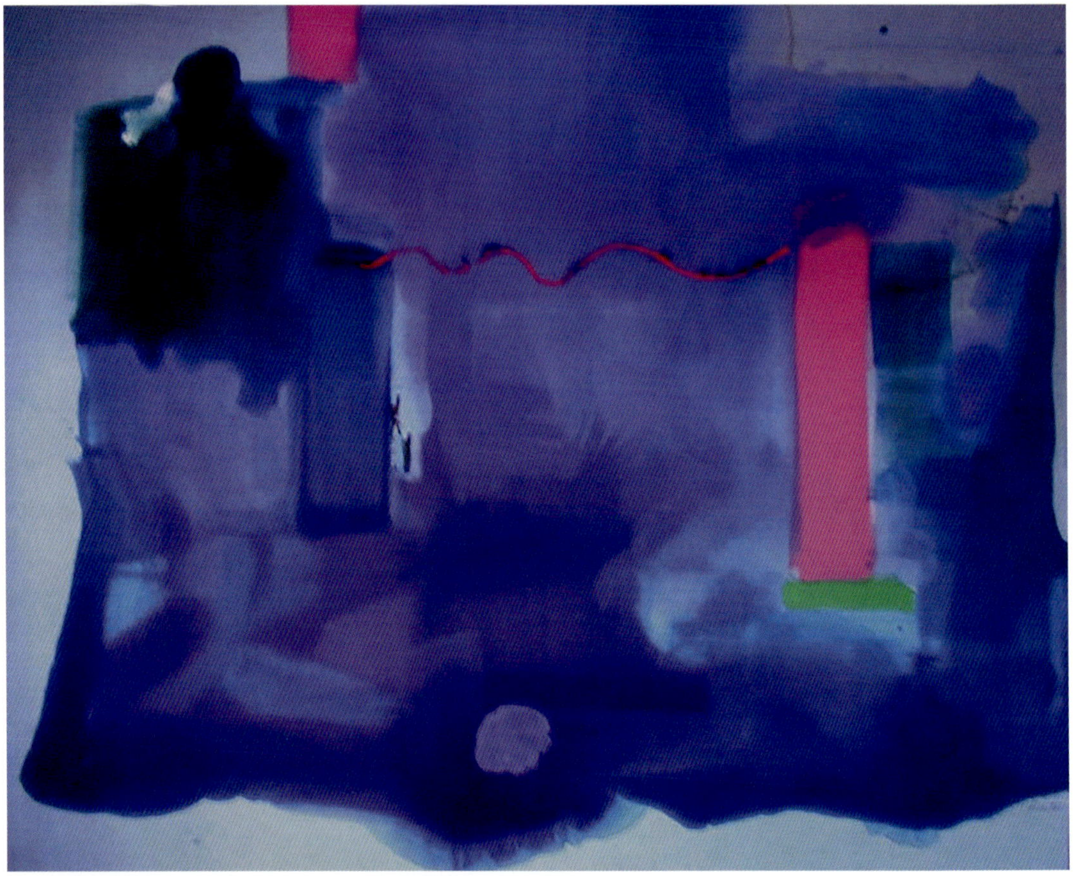

Sugar Blues, acrylic on canvas, 90.5" x 107", 1988. *Collection of Mr. and Mrs. Stuart M. Christhilf.*

Helen Frankenthaler

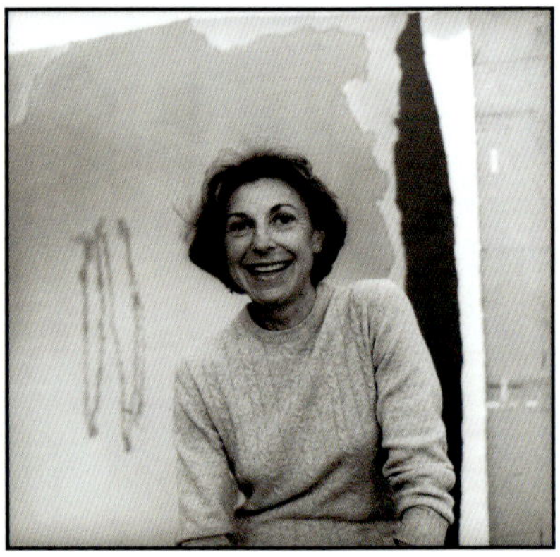

Helen Frankenthaler at Tyler Graphics, Ltd., 1993. *Photograph © Marabeth Cohen-Tyler.*

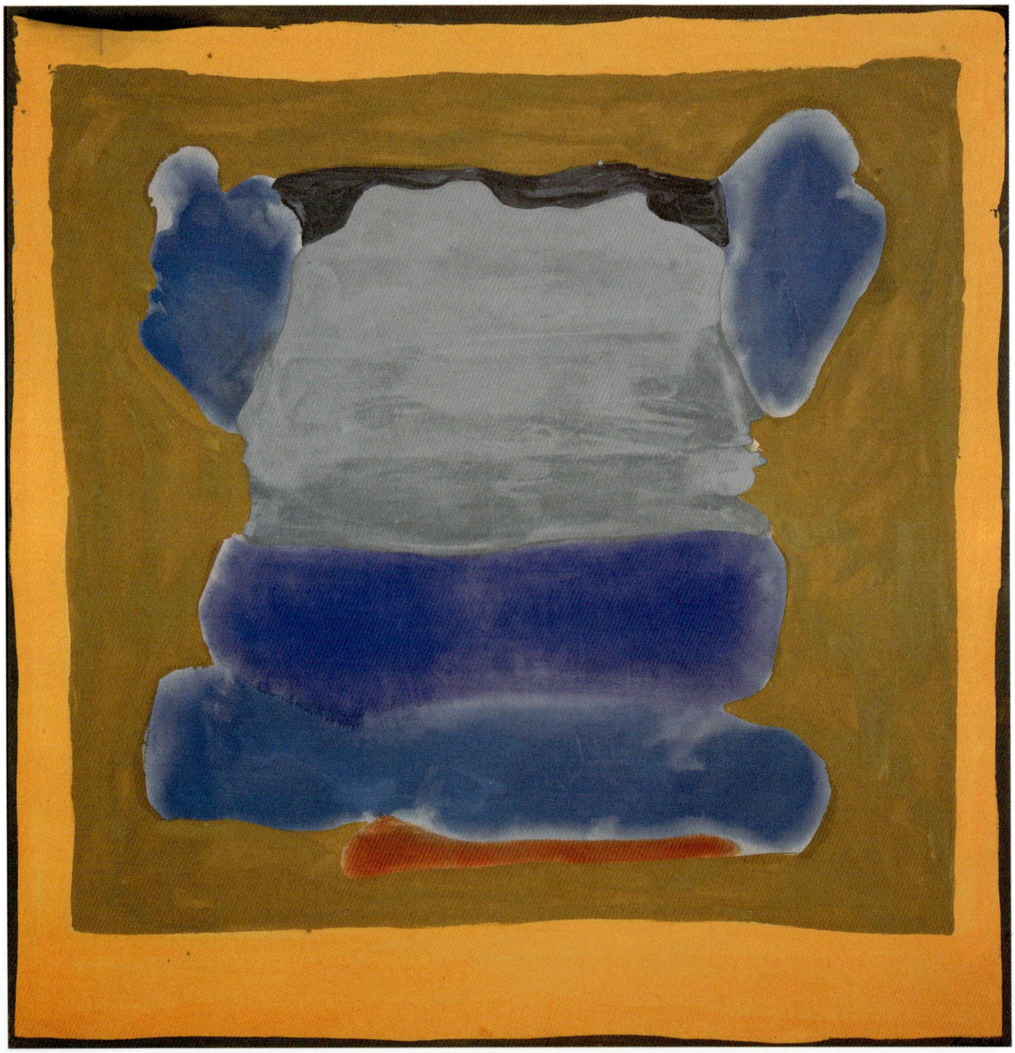

Buddha's Court, acrylic on canvas, 98" x 94", 1964. *Courtesy of Ameringer & Yohe Fine Art.*

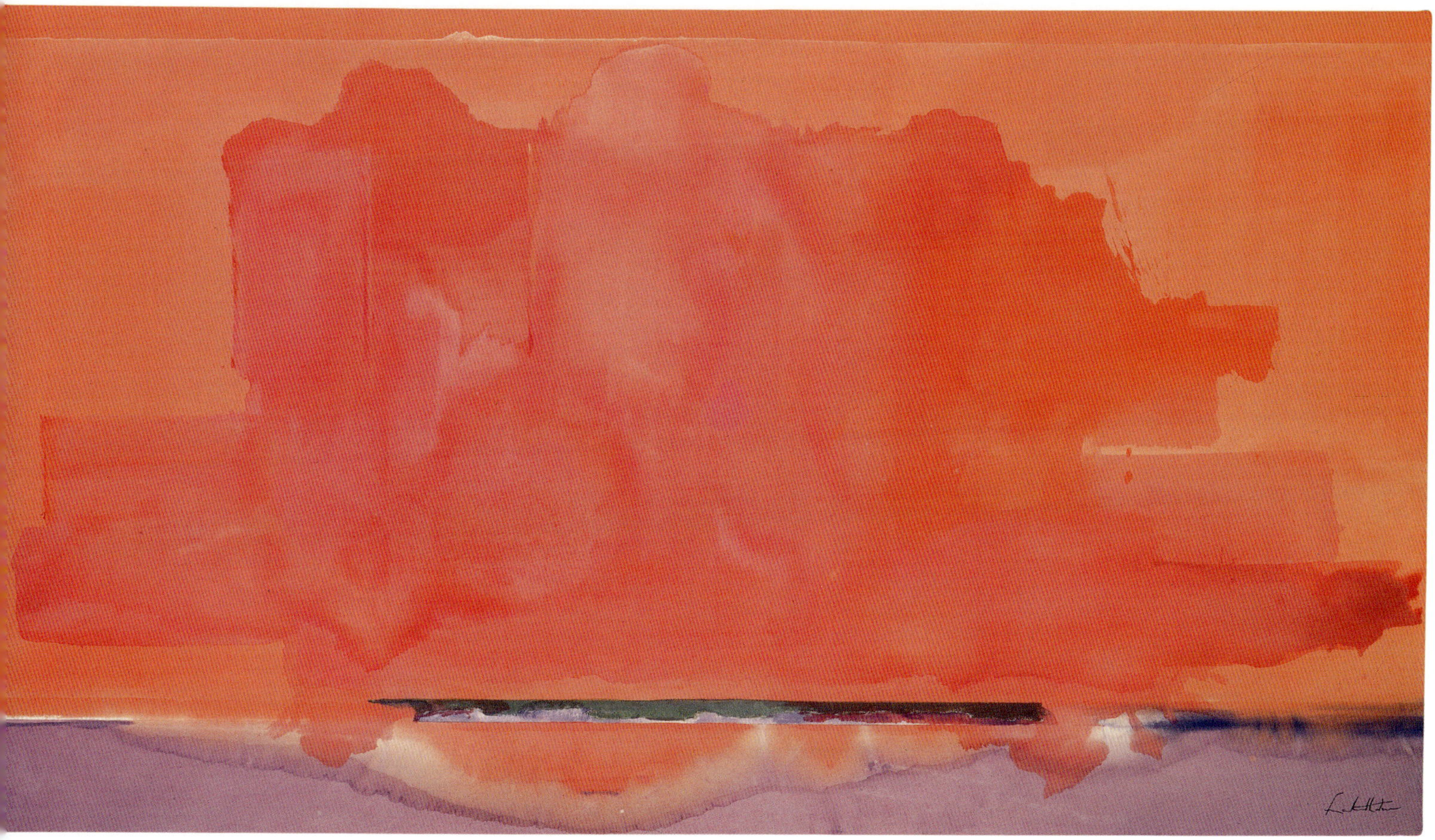

Castle, acrylic on canvas, 6' 3.5" x 10' 10", 1989. *Courtesy of Ameringer & Yohe Fine Art.*

Helen Frankenthaler, a native New York Abstract Expressionist who studied with Rufino Tamayo, Paul Feeney, and Hans Hofmann, is an elected member of the National Academy of Design. She developed the technique of soak-stain paintings—large-scale landscape-inspired abstractions with thin, poured washes of pigment over unprimed canvas—that have influenced a generation of color-field and minimalist painters. Discussing the "seemingly contradictory impulses of abstraction and representation in Frankenthaler's stain paintings," Robert Godfrey says we can sense "the traditional easel-painter's control and the expressionist's gestural freedom. ... The viewer can experience the arabesque of (her) markmaking ... the space moves in and out: it breathes ... emitting a transcendental light akin to the 19th century luminists. ... What comes through ... is essence over matter."[77]

In addition to her groundbreaking Color Field paintings, Frankenthaler has a long history of work in sculpture, ceramics, printmaking, costume and set design, and book illustration. Her recent paintings have moved from canvas to the innovative use of oversize sheets of paper. She has taught at such institutions as Yale, Harvard, Princeton, and New York University, is the recipient of numerous awards, and has exhibited widely throughout the world. Her works may be found in most important museums and other public collections.

Among her major exhibitions have been two retrospectives, at the Whitney Museum of American Art and at the Museum of Modern Art. Frankenthaler's work may be seen at the Knoedler & Company, Ameringer & Yohe, Greenberg Van Doren, Jim Kempner, and other top New York galleries. She is represented by Knoedler & Company.

Sondra Freckelton

Courtesy of the artist.

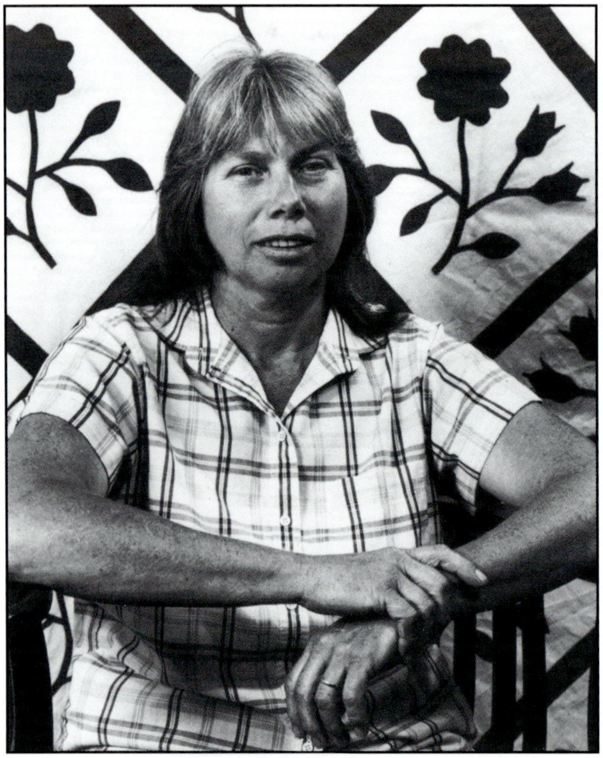

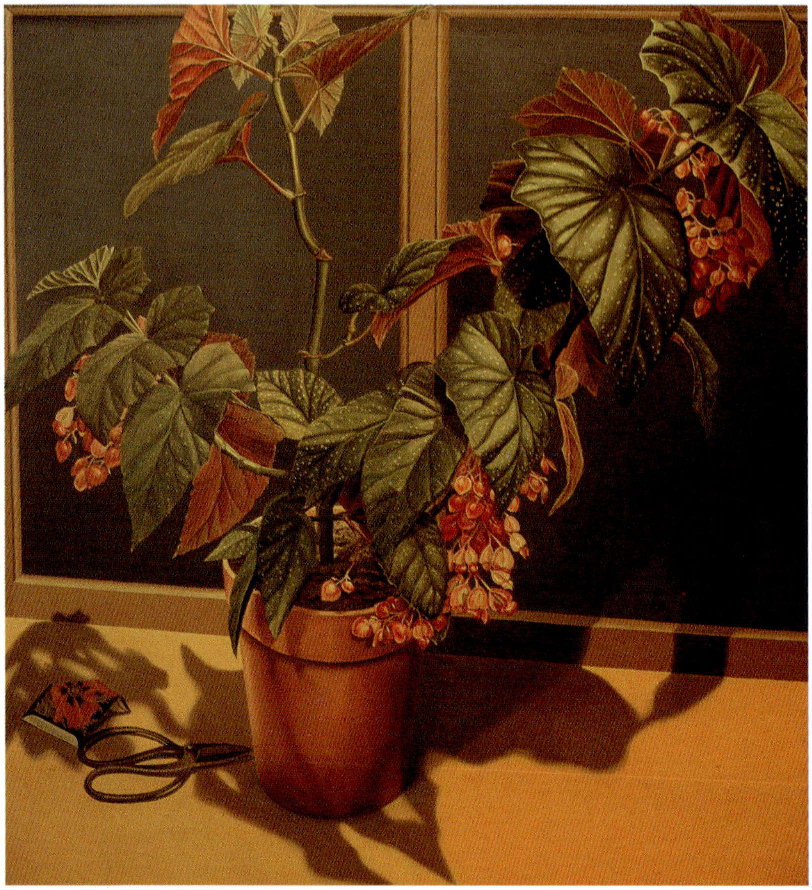

Angelwing, oil on canvas, 40" x 36", 1974.

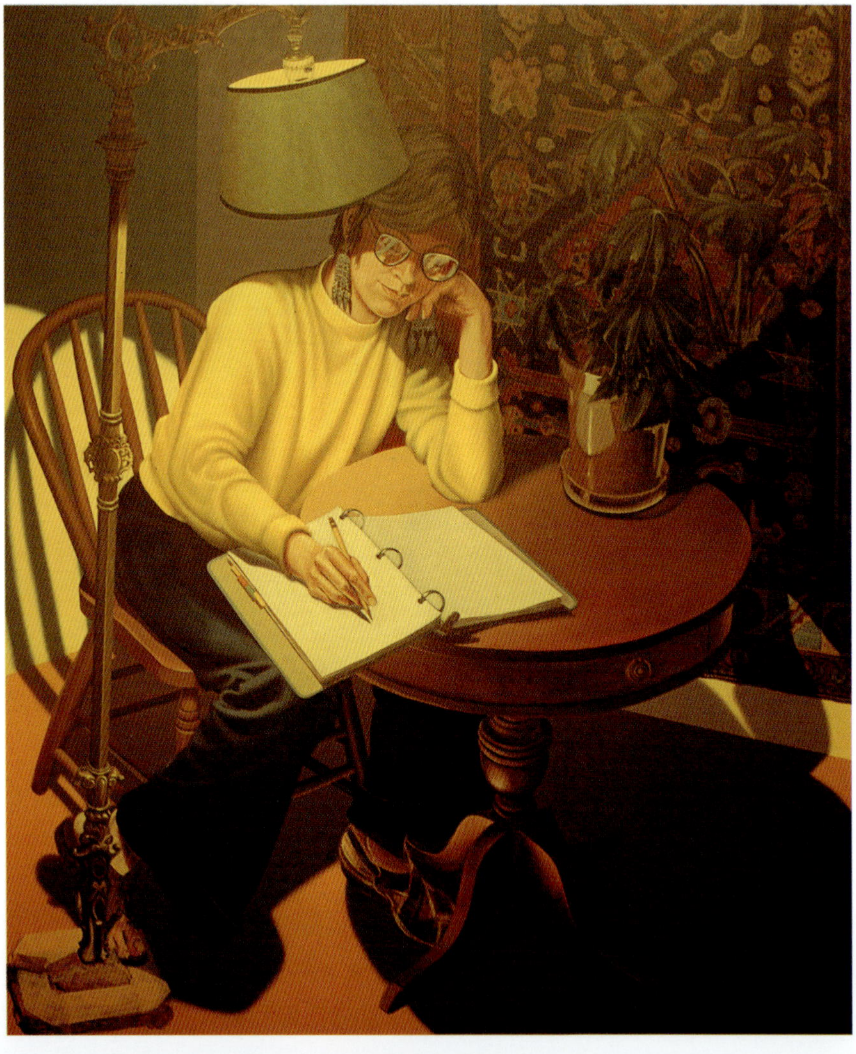

Sondra Freckelton, widely known for large-scale, light-struck interior water color compositions, has worked as intensely in wood and plastic sculpture and oils as well, turning from early abstraction to an abiding devotion to meticulous realism. Domestic household and garden subjects are elevated by Freckelton, who "brings them into direct confrontation with the viewer. ..."[78] Her works, often called modern history paintings, "speak not about wars and kings, but about life ... the things we do now, have done before, and will be doing forever. ..."[79]

Mary Writing, oil on canvas, 60" x 50", 1973.

Freckelton studied at the School of the Art Institute of Chicago, and has taught at The Cooper Union, the Downtown Community School, and at her country home in upstate New York.

Affiliated formerly with the Robert Schoelkopf Gallery in New York, she has exhibited widely and has works in the collections of the Bank of New York, The Readers Digest Association, and Amerada Hess Corporation in New York, among others.

Her many honors and awards include an honorary Doctorate of Letters from Hollins College, Virginia, and elected membership in the National Academy of Design in New York.

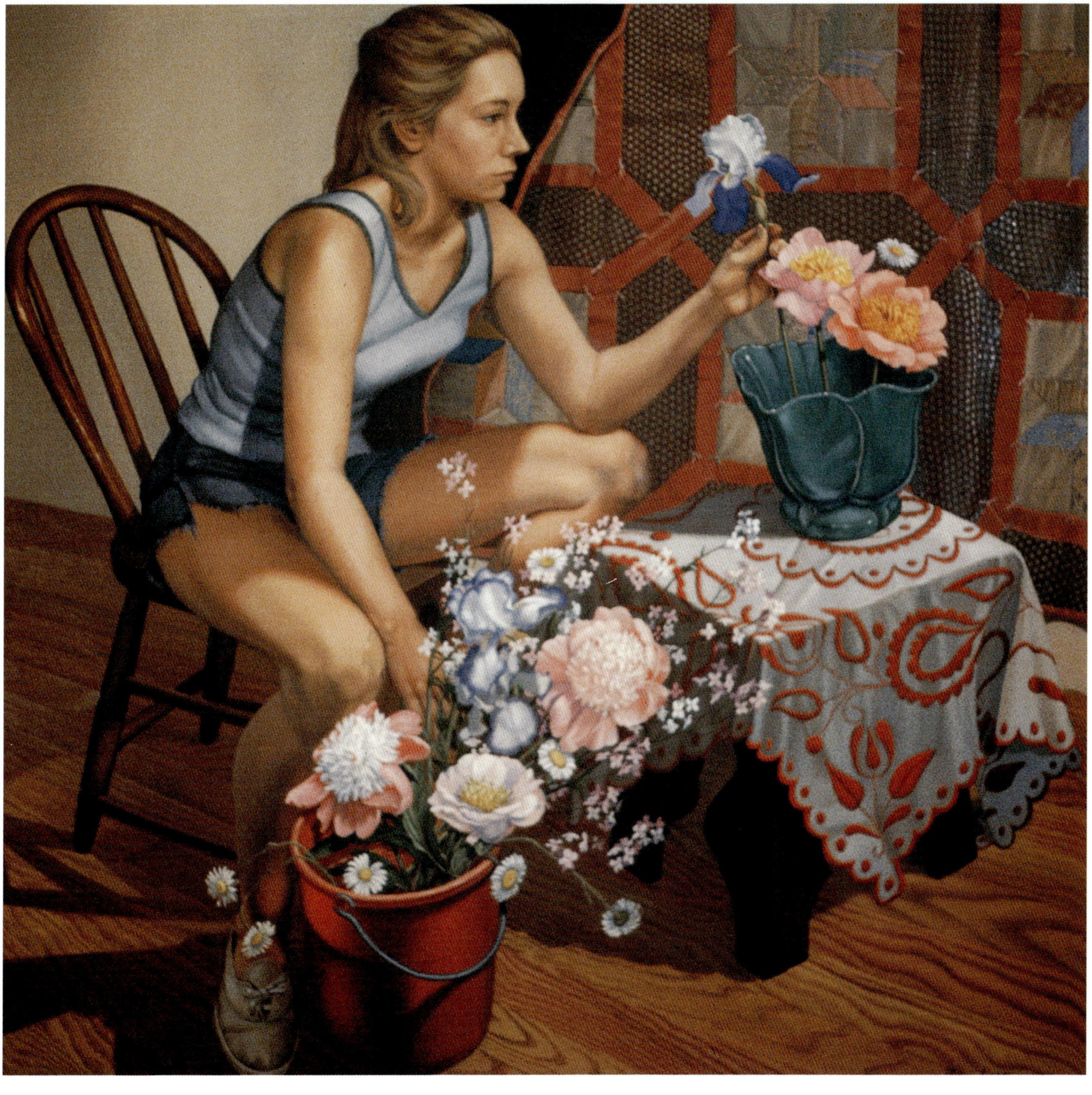

Anne Arranging Flowers, oil on canvas, 48" x 48", 1985. *Collection of Vinson & Elkins.*

Jane Freilicher

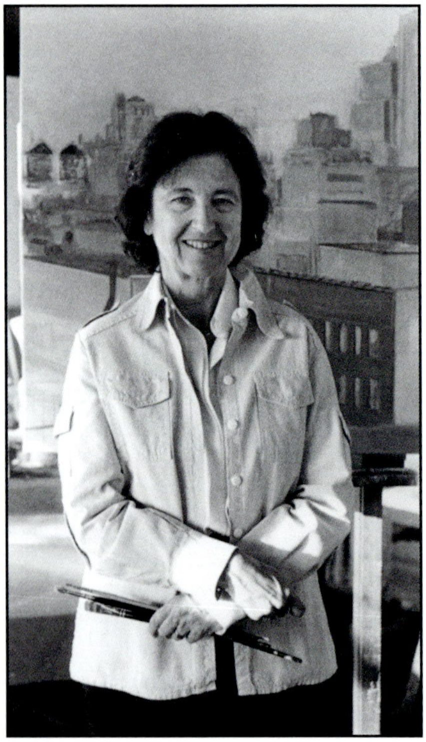

Photograph © Nancy Crampton. Courtesy of Tibor de Nagy Gallery, New York.

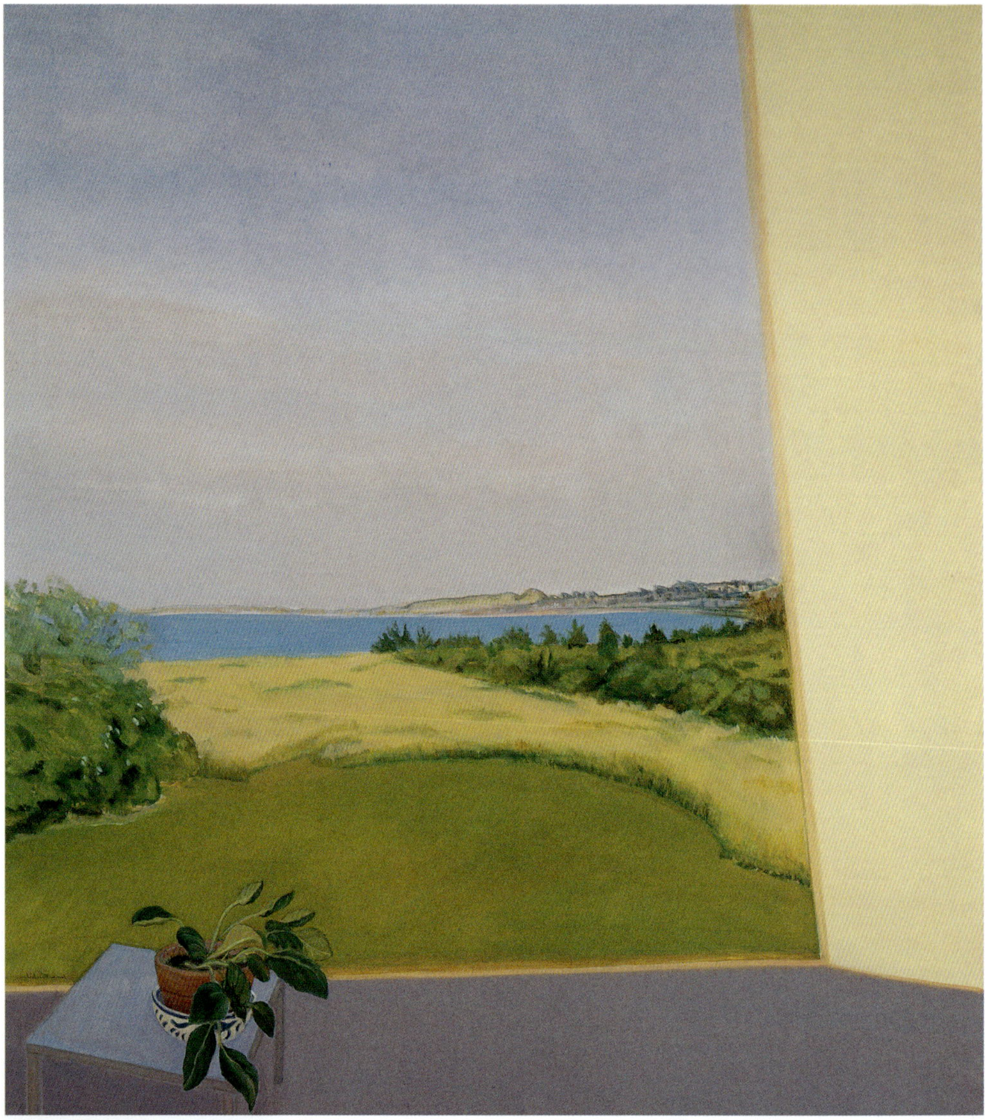

View over Mecox (Yellow Wall), oil on linen, 80" x 70", c.1991-93. *Collection of Memorial Art Gallery of the University of Rochester: Gift of Lynne Lovejoy in memory of her husband, Dr. Frank Lovejoy, Jr. Photograph by James Via.*

Nasturtiums Before a Red Cloth, oil on linen, 20" x 20", 2003. *Courtesy of Tibor de Nagy Gallery.*

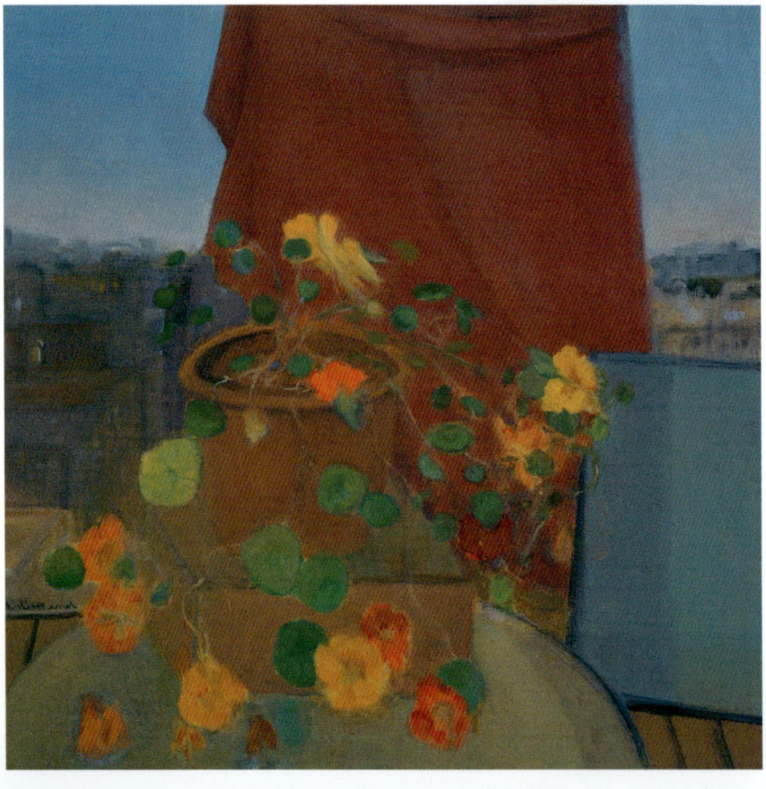

Jane Freilicher, who studied with Hans Hofmann, has had a long, distinguished career, moving through early abstract expressionist works to painterly landscapes and cityscapes, finding a focus on interior window scenes with floral arrangements that are often informed by the early bursts of abstract expressionist color.

Represented by the Tibor de Nagy Gallery, where she has had numerous one-artist exhibitions for more than fifty years, Freilicher has been included in countless groundbreaking group and individual showings with such titles as, "American Views: Memory, Nostalgia and the Idea of Place,"[80] "Surroundings: Responses to the American Landscape,"[81] "Abstraction/Realism: The

Great Debate,"[82] "Women's Work: A Century of Achievement in American Art,"[83] "New Approaches to the Still Life,"[84] "Color as a Subject,"[85] "The Painterly Landscape,"[86] "American Women Artists in Pioneers,"[87] and "Students of Hans Hofmann,"[88] (at the Museum of Modern Art).

Freilicher has earned degrees from Columbia University and Brooklyn College. Her works have been shown and collected by nearly every major art museum, including The Corcoran Gallery of Art in Washington, D.C., the Brooklyn, Whitney, and Metropolitan Museums, the Museum of Modern Art, and the National Academy of Design in New York.

Freilicher has been Vice President of Art on the Board of Directors for the American Academy of Arts and Letters, is an elected member of the National Academy of Design, and the recipient of many awards and honors.

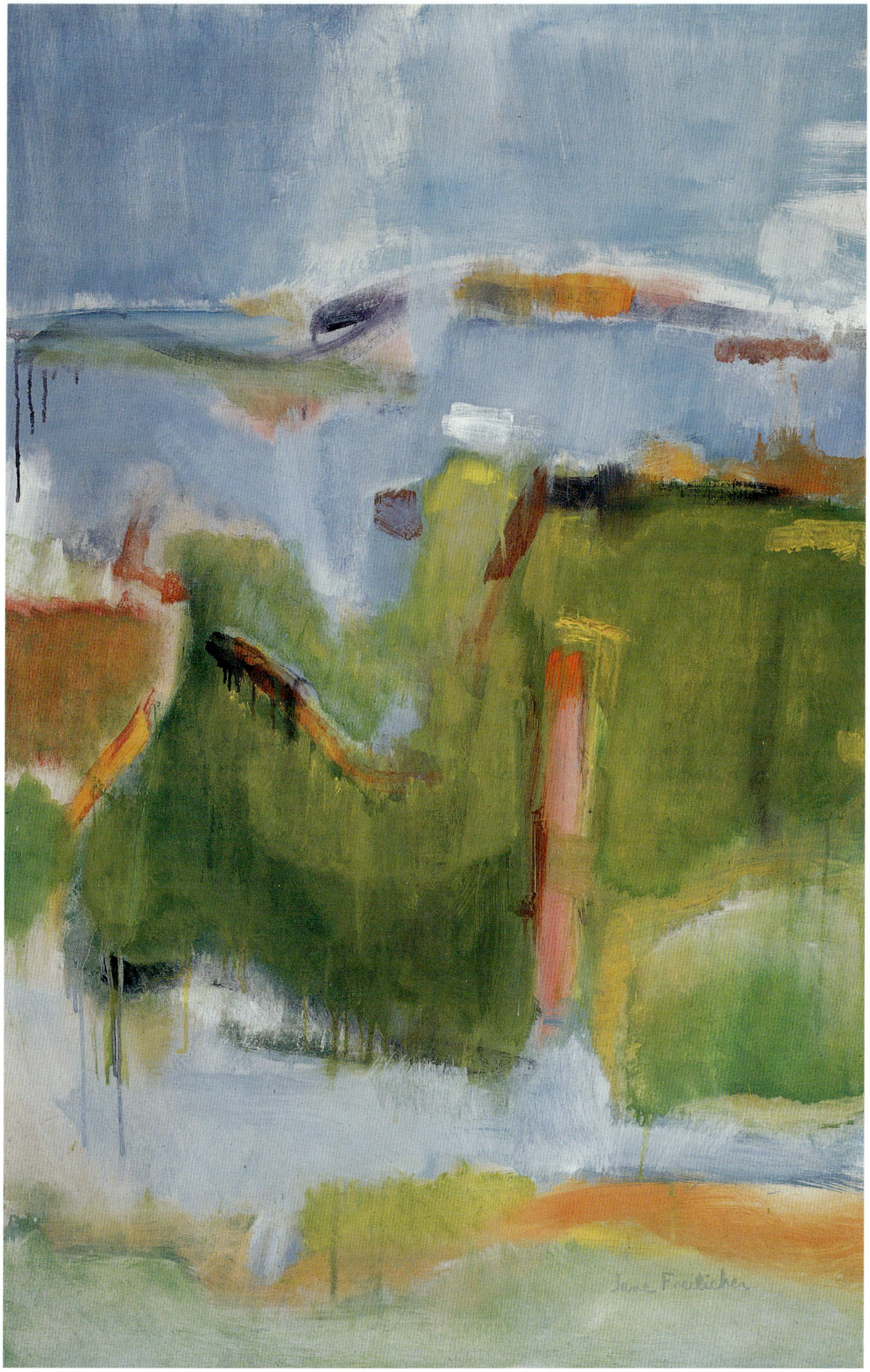

Blue and Green Abstraction, oil on linen, 45" x 29", 1960. *Courtesy of Tibor de Nagy Gallery, New York.*

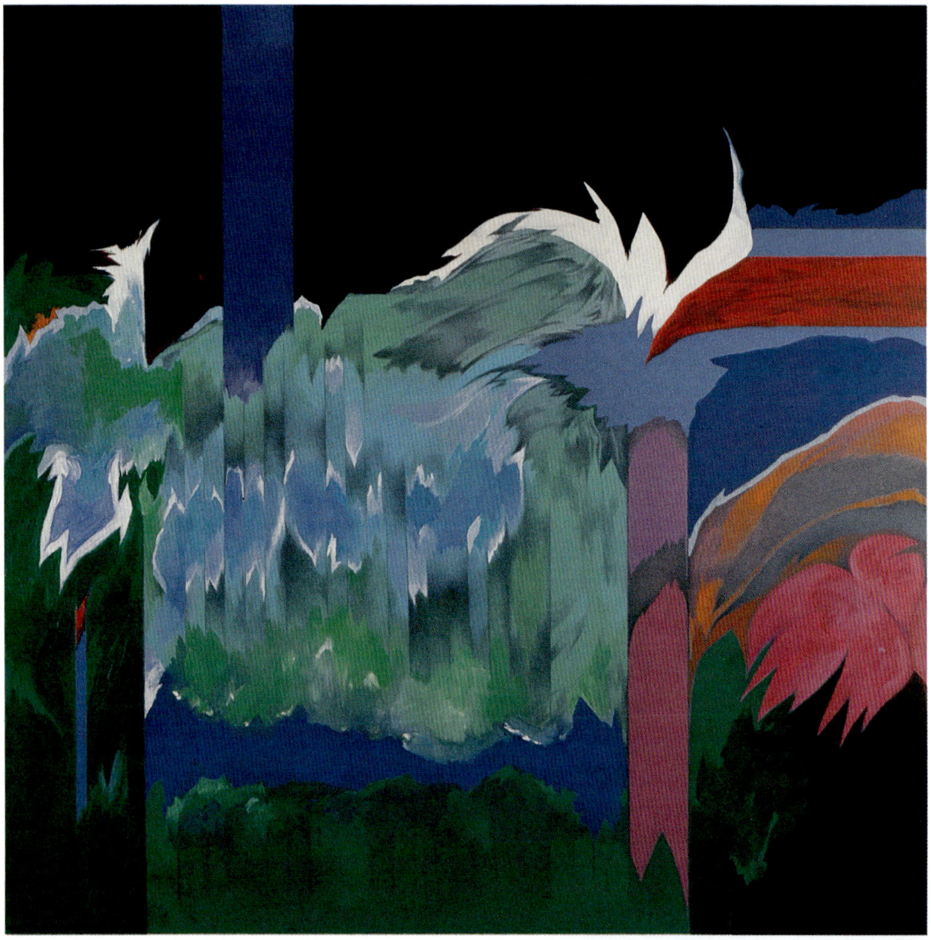

Waterfall & Garden, acrylic and graphite on canvas, 60" x 60", c.1991-95.

Sonia Gechtoff

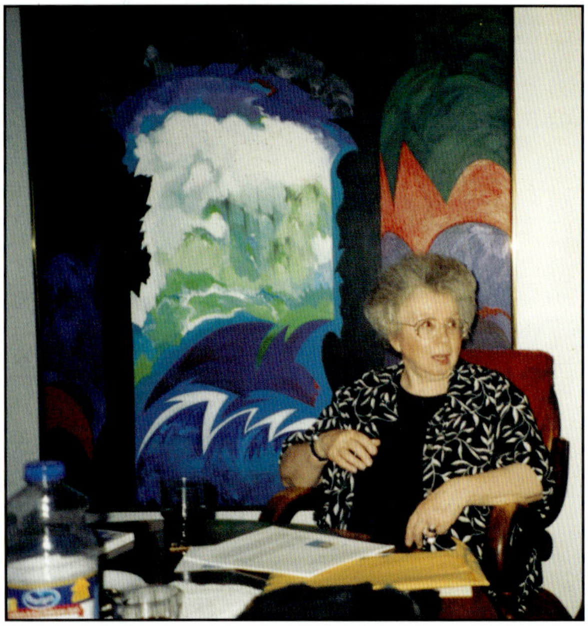

The artist with *Guardian of the Green*, c.1991-2000. *Photograph by Nancy Steen.*

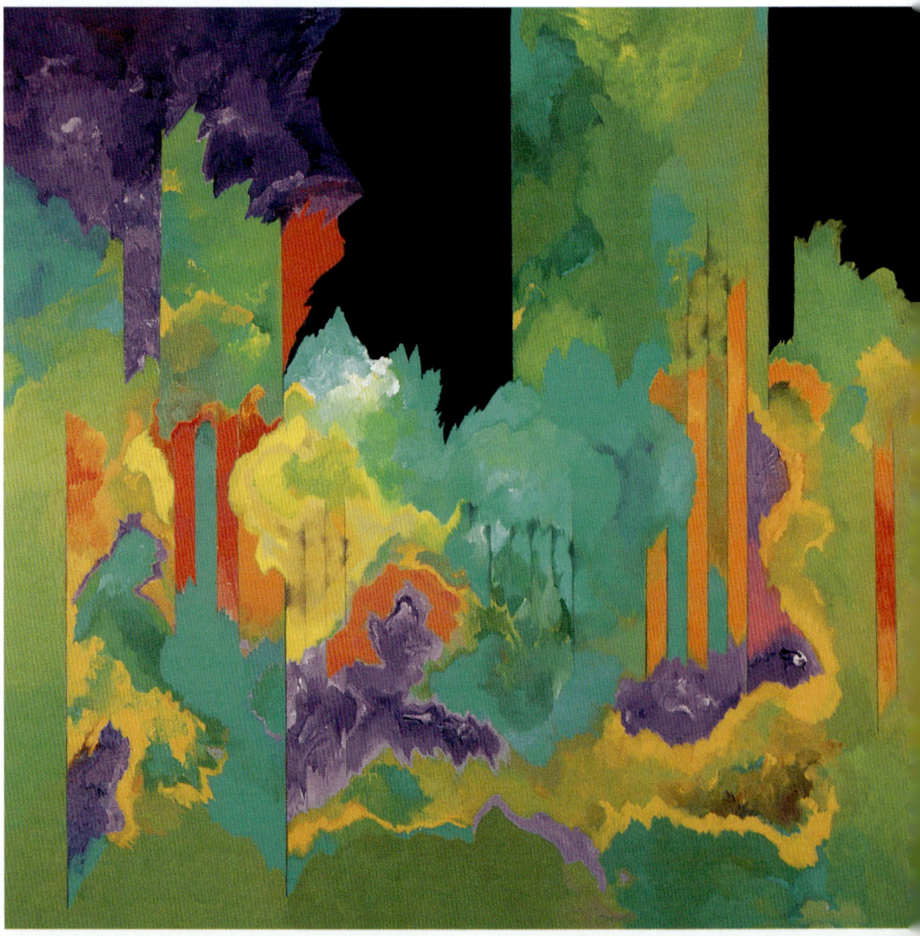

Siena, acrylic and graphite on canvas, 60" x 60", c.1991-95.

Sonia Gechtoff, an elected member of the National Academy of Design, has taught at the Academy, as well as at New York University, Queens College, the University of New Mexico, and the Chicago Art Institute. She has also been a visiting artist at schools throughout the United States.

Gechtoff acknowledges her father, Russian-born painter of Impressionist landscapes, Leonid Gechtoff, as her first teacher, and later received a BFA at the Philadelphia Museum School of Art.

Her own works have been characterized as abstract-expressionist "... about energy, movement, vitality and natural forces suggested through pure painting. ..."[89]

Earning early success in New York during the 1950s, Gechtoff's works have been exhibited widely and she is the recipient of Pollock-Krasner and Gottlieb Grants, among others. Gechtoff's New York solo exhibitions include the Kraushaar, Poindexter, and Gruenebaum Galleries, and she has been included in numerous group exhibitions across the United States. Her paintings may be found in the permanent collections of many corporate and museum collections, among them those of the Chase Manhattan Bank, 3M and Menil Corporations, the Whitney, Metropolitan and Guggenheim Museums, as well as the Museum of Modern Art in New York.

Gechtoff resides and maintains a studio in the West Village's historic Westbeth.

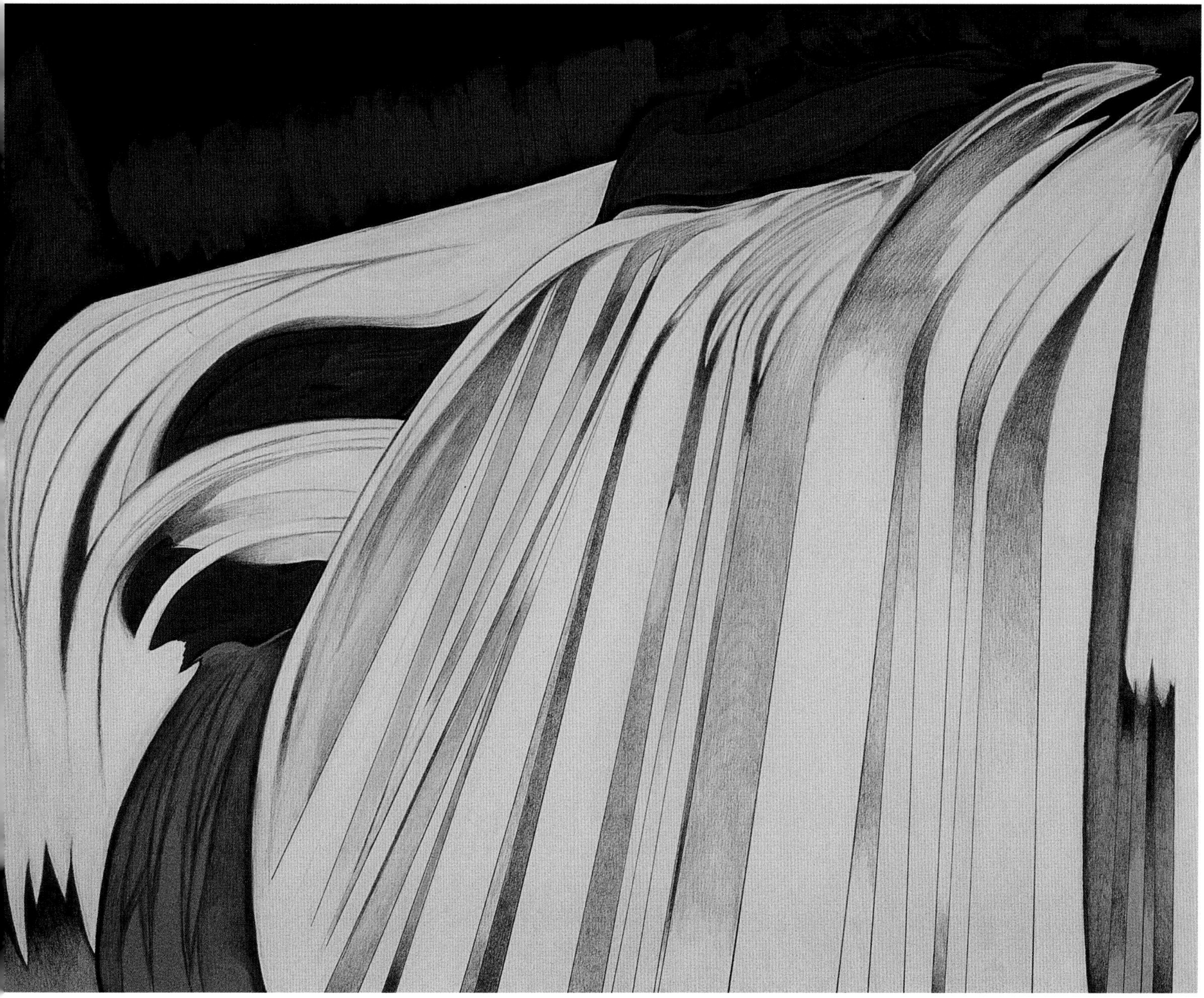

Red Rock Waterfall, acrylic with graphite on Arches cover, 33" x 40", 1987.

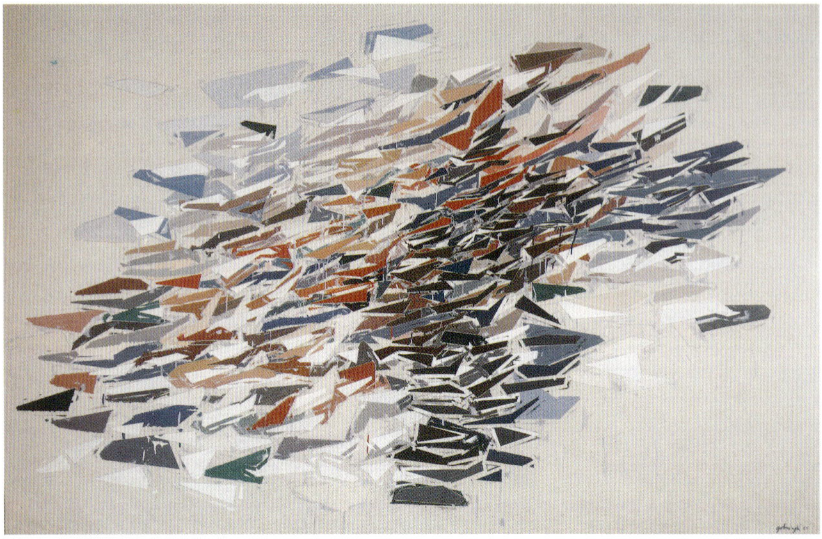

Angular Lift, oil and acrylic on canvas, 68" x 104", 1985. *Courtesy of Katharina Rich Perlow Gallery.*

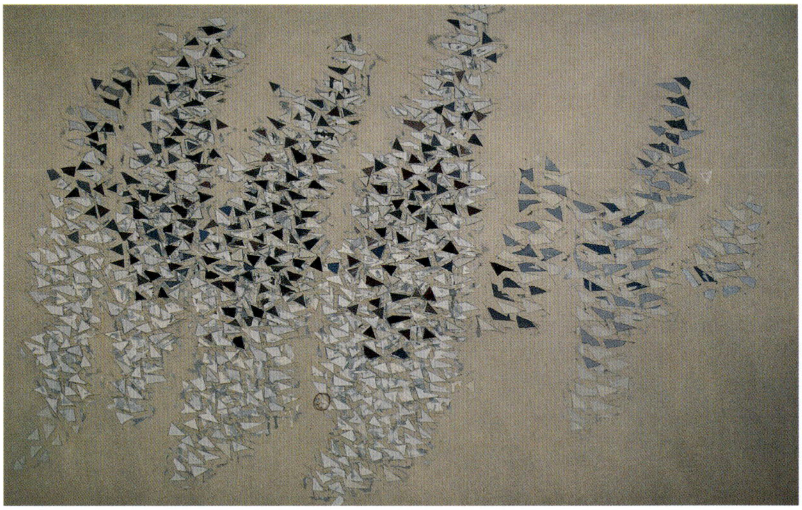

R-8, oil and acrylic on canvas, 42" x 66", 1985. *Courtesy of Katharina Rich Perlow Gallery.*

Bob Goodnough

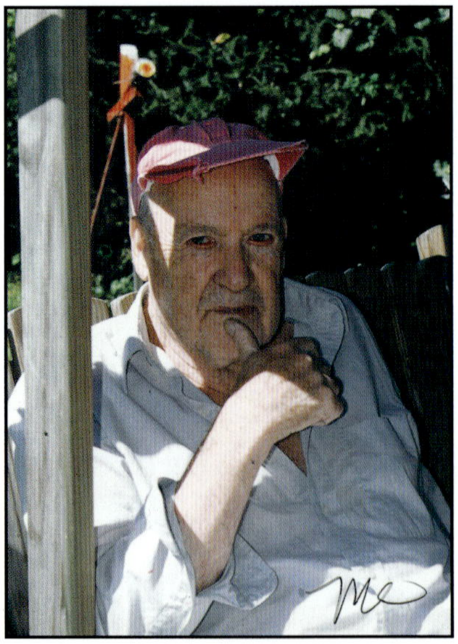

Courtesy of the artist.

Bob Goodnough, equally known for his monumental paintings, wall installations, and sculptures, came to New York after graduating from Syracuse University. He studied at New York University with Tony Smith, met Hale Woodruff and Jackson Pollock, and wrote a series of reviews of major artists of the day for *Art News*.

Among the many honors accorded Goodnough are a one-person exhibition at the Whitney Museum of American Art, inclusion in the U.S. Pavilion at a Venice Biennale, and the awarding of a John Simon Guggenheim Memorial Fellowship.

Although Goodnough refers specifically to his installation of "Floating Panels" at the New Castle County Courthouse when he says, "My intention here is to uplift the spirit of those who see it," he may as well be speaking of his lifelong oeuvre. His softly geometric, triangulated constellations have often been seen as organic, associative. "It is natural ... to see shapes and figures ... [Even in the most abstract art] people ... search for something ... they can name."[90]

Clement Greenberg has called Goodnough, "... one of the better painters of the time ... which comes to saying he's one of the best. ... The *very* best new painting has been abstract for decades now ... it's in the new context of the abundance of abstract painting that is good, that is strict, that has level—in this context, Goodnough's art stands out."[91]

Naming Hans Hofmann, Jackson Pollock, and Michelangelo as major influences, Goodnough continues to work with what his wife, Miko, calls "endless creative energy;"[92] this was acknowledged by the National Academy of Design (of which he is an elected member) when it awarded Goodnough's "Breakthrough" its Edwin P. Palmer Memorial Prize for painting. He is represented by the Perlow Gallery in New York.

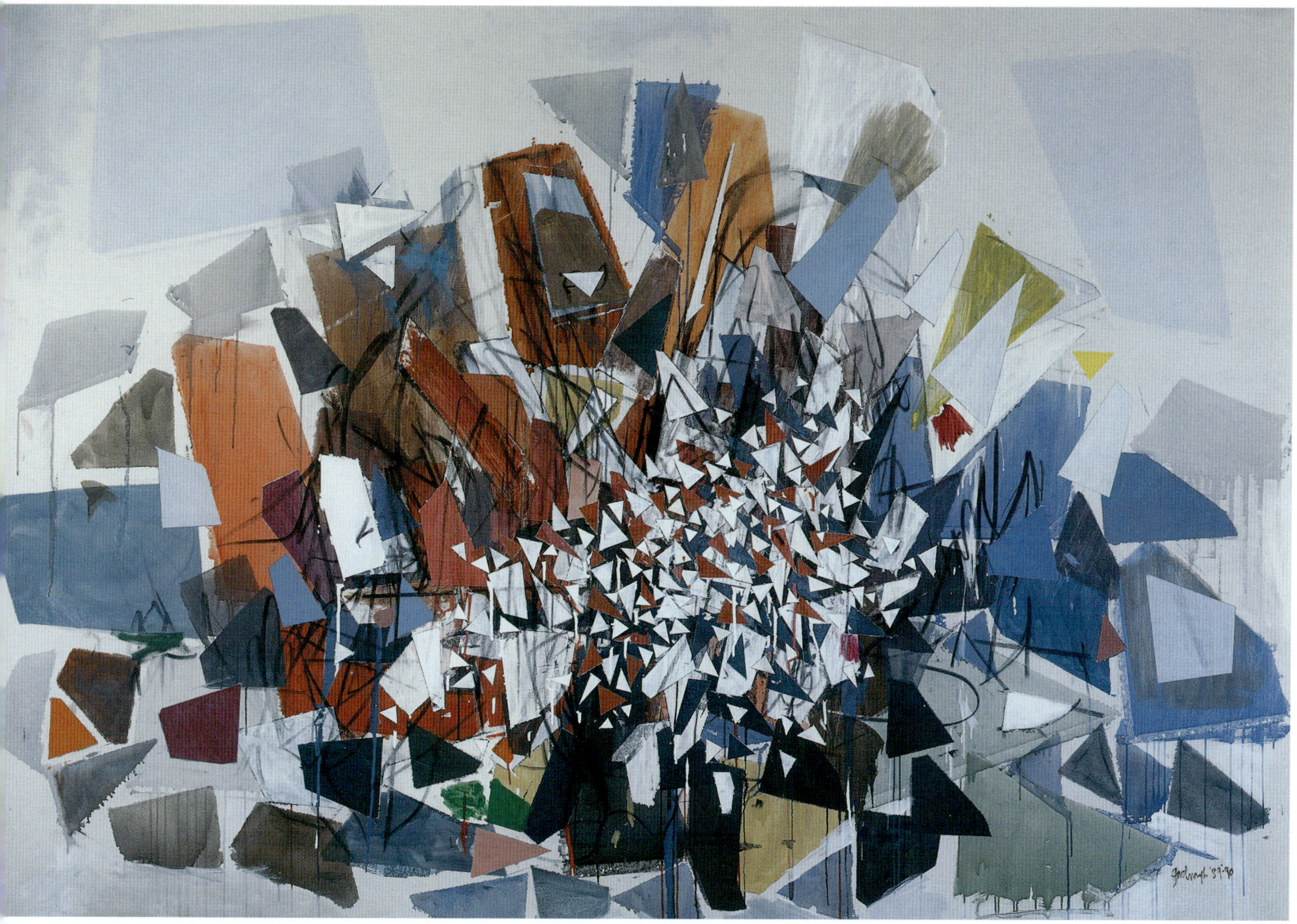

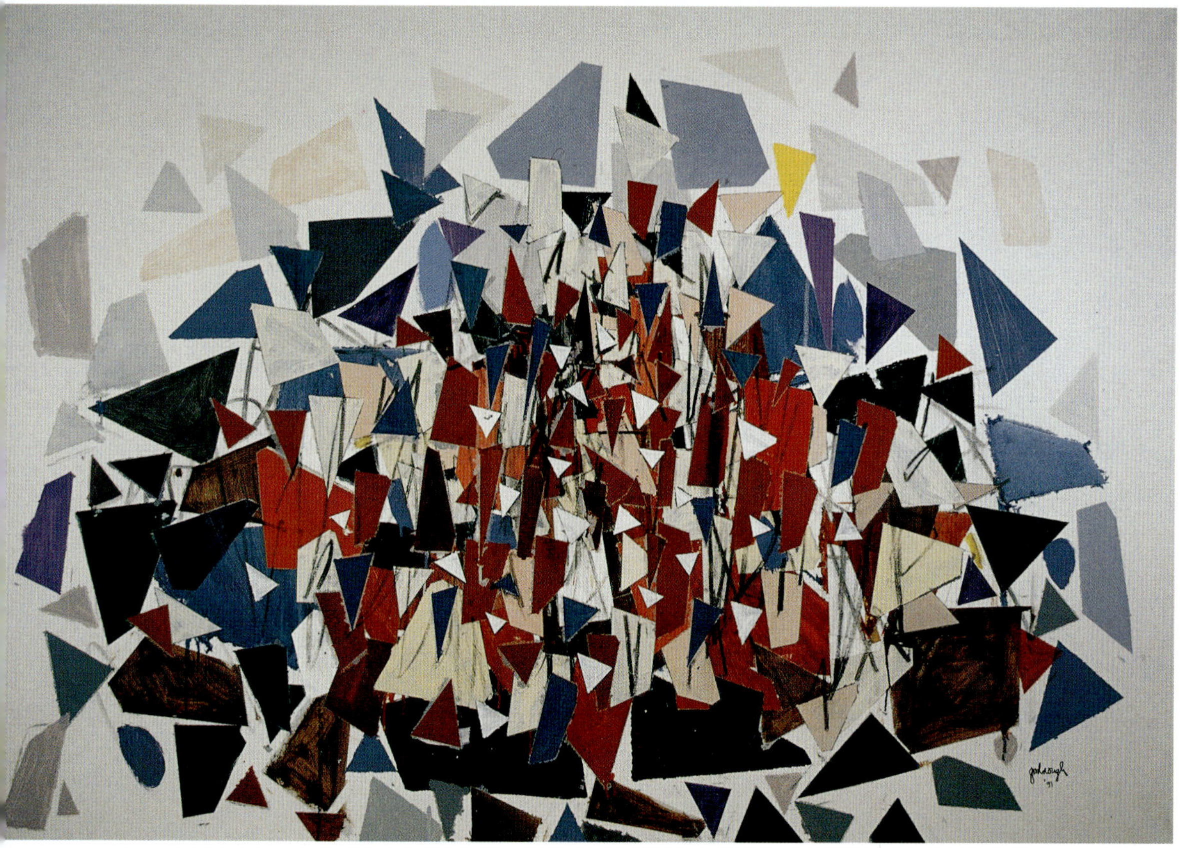

KRA, acrylic and oil on canvas, 62" x 88", c.1989-90. *Collection of Lisa and Steven M. Hankin, New York.*

N-4, oil and acrylic on canvas, 48" x 68", 1991. *Courtesy of Katharina Rich Perlow Gallery.*

Cheryl Gross, who teaches at Brooklyn's Pratt Institute where she earned her BFA, received its "Highest Honors Circle Award for Outstanding Academic Achievement." She also studied at Hunter College, the Art Students League, and the School of Visual Arts. Her works have been exhibited at the Brooklyn Museum, the Museum of the City of New York, the Brooklyn Arts and Cultural Association, and many galleries and museums in the United States, Russia, and Japan.

Gross, who developed and has taught programs in digital illustration and photography, incorporates these mediums with painting in her layered works, often to tell a story or make a political or social statement. Gross says she equates her work with creating an environment by transforming her inner thoughts into reality, much as an architect's reality becomes the foundation of the work.

She admires Edward Hopper's sense of emotional seclusion, Lucian Freud's observation of people, Cy Twombly's simplicity, Antonio Tapies' and Anselm Kiefer's texture, and Luis Gonzalez Palma's combining of photography and paint.

Gross feels her Brooklyn-born urban influence has added an edge to her work, and though now residing in the rural countryside of New Jersey, she still maintains a studio in New York.

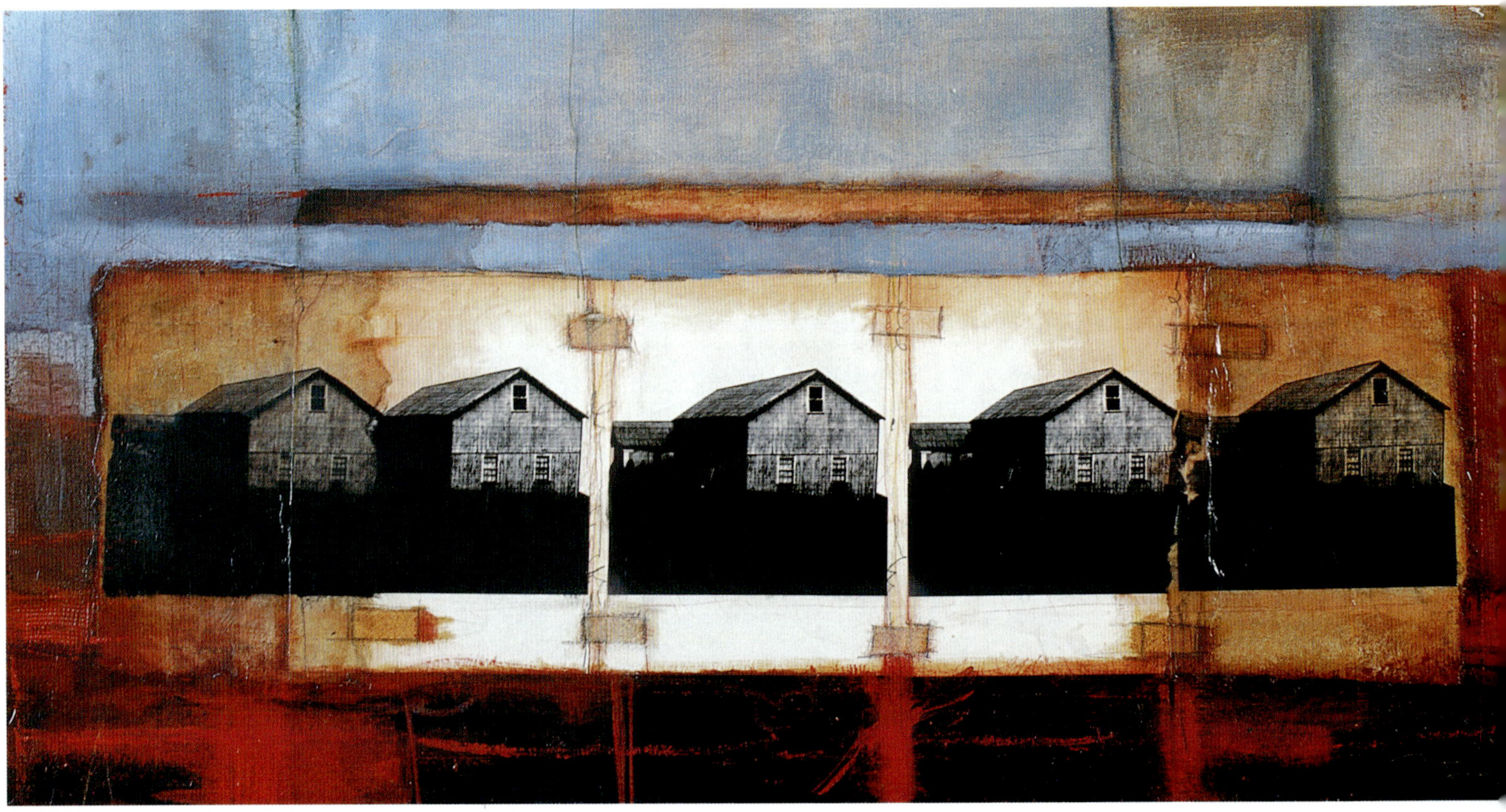

4 Houses, acrylic and mixed media (self-generated digital photography, pencil, paper, crayons, oil pastels) on canvas, 24" x 36", 2005.

Cheryl Gross

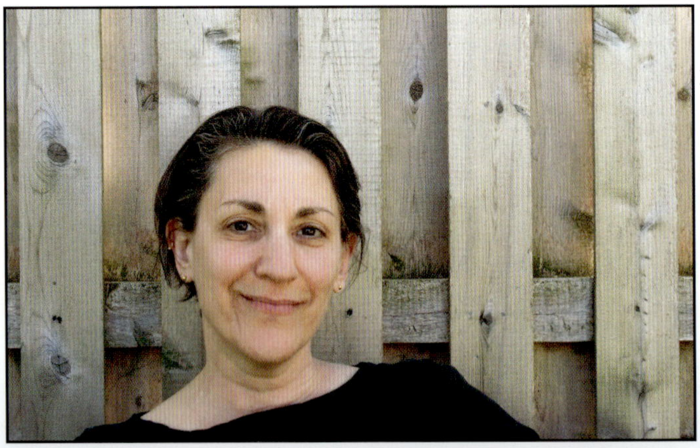

Courtesy of the artist.

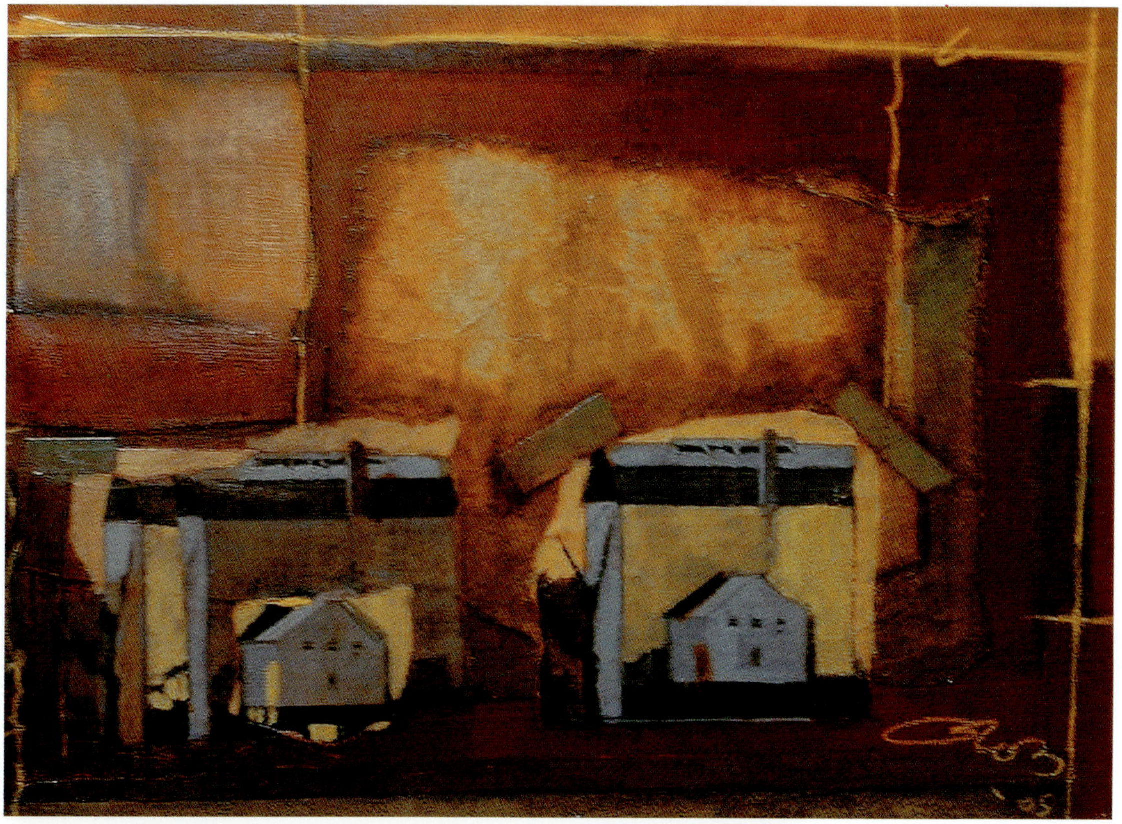

Houses Along the Delaware, acrylic and mixed media on canvas, 24" x 36", 2005.

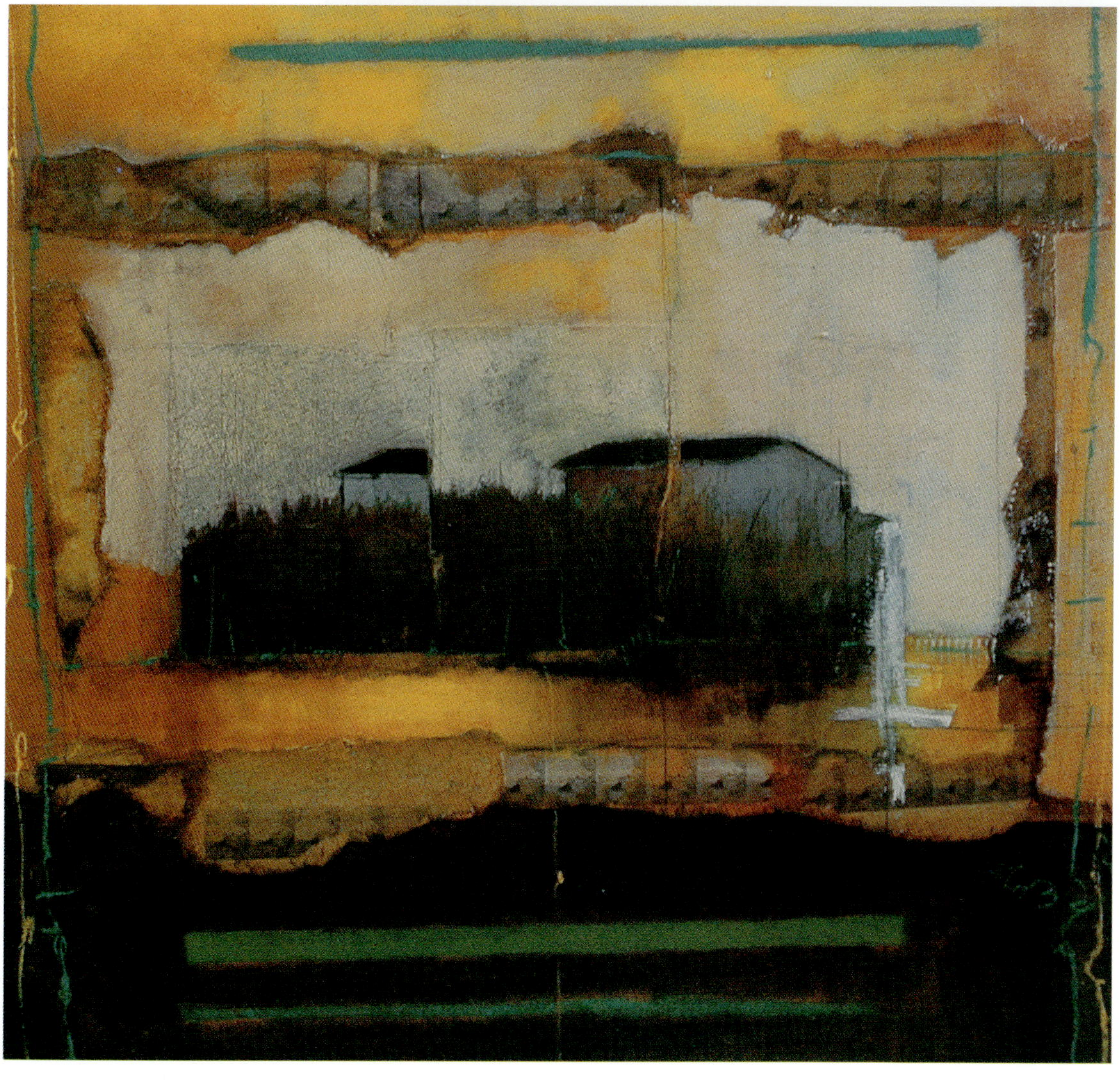

Country School, acrylic and mixed media on canvas, 36" x 36", 2005.

Sue Ferguson Gussow

Sue Ferguson Gussow, Professor Emerita at The Cooper Union, taught in both its Schools of Art and Architecture for twenty of her thirty-five years there. A Cooper graduate, she also received degrees from Columbia and Tulane Universities, and has taught at New York's Frick Collection, New York University, Columbia University, Manhattanville College, Parsons School of Design, and Alfred University.

Her works are included in numerous museum and private collections, notably The Cooper-Hewitt Museum of Design of the Smithsonian Institution, the Museum of Modern Art's Members' Lending Collection, and the collections of Dore Ashton, George and Mary Campbell, Jr., and Francois de Menil, among many others.

Gussow's paintings and drawings have been seen in many solo exhibitions, including a forty-year Retrospective at The Cooper Union, the Palace of Journalists, St. Petersburg, Russia, and Tulane University, New Orleans.

Her group exhibitions include locations in Germany, Japan, Russia, and many of the United States. Impeccably skillful drawings are a strong focus for Gussow, who credits the teachings of Stefano Cusumano and the friendship of Al Blaustein as special influences and inspirations.

Gussow often paints family, friends, and students in her vivid, freely brushed signature style. She maintains a studio in the Tribeca area of New York and spends much time at her second home in Amagansett, New York.

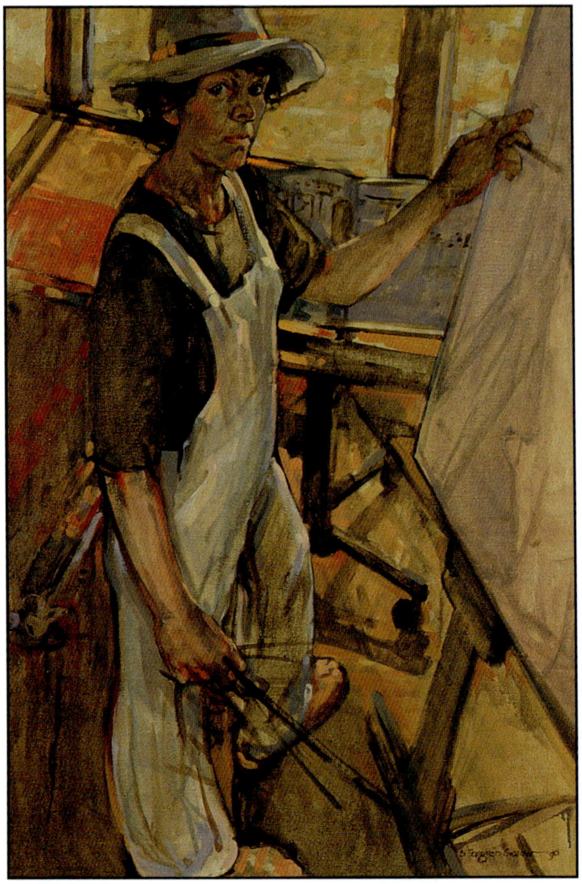

Self Portrait, oil on canvas, 37" x 24", 1997. *Courtesy of the artist.*

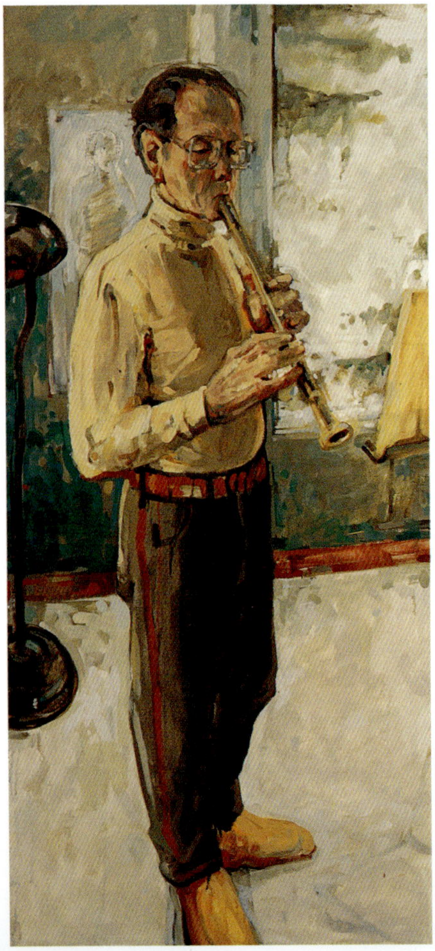

Donald on Alto Recorder, oil on canvas, 48" x 22", 1996. *Courtesy of the artist.*

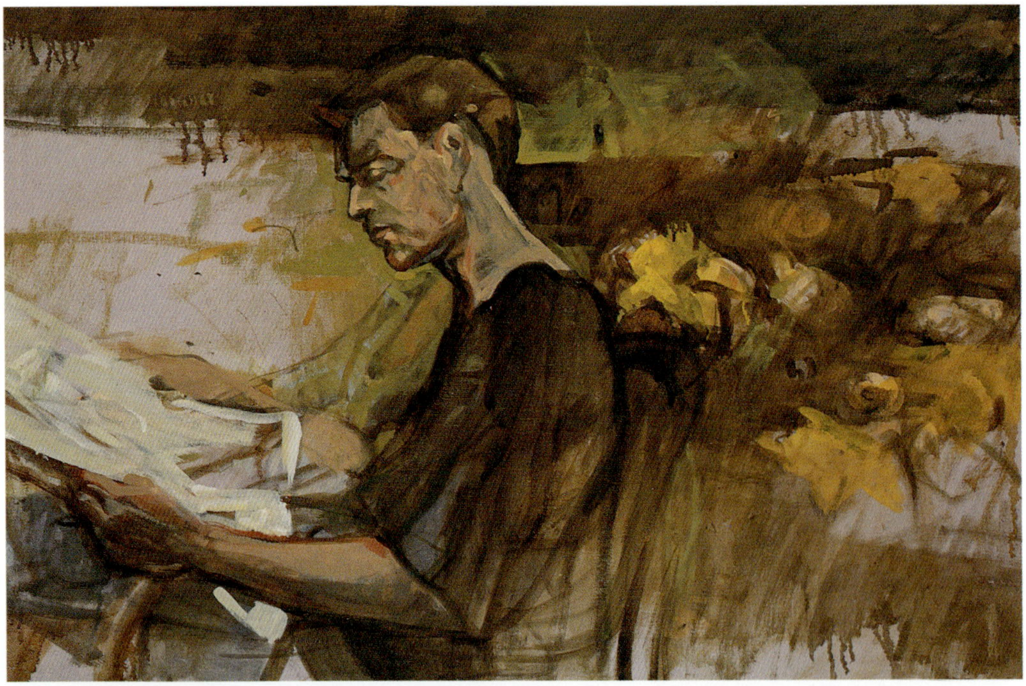

Christopher, oil on canvas, 24" x 36", 1995. *Courtesy of the artist.*

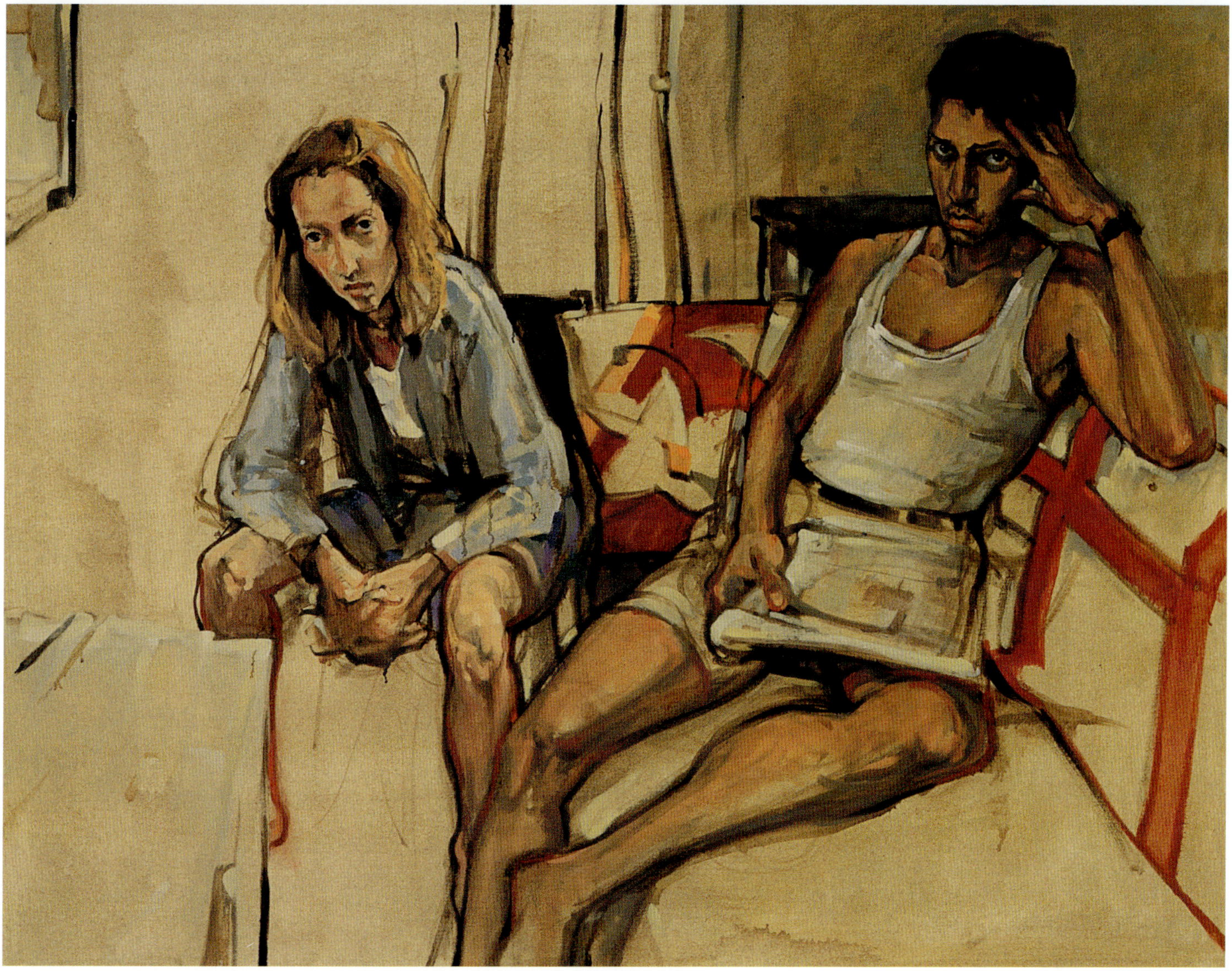

Olga & Toni, oil on canvas, 40" x 50", 1997. *Courtesy of the artist.*

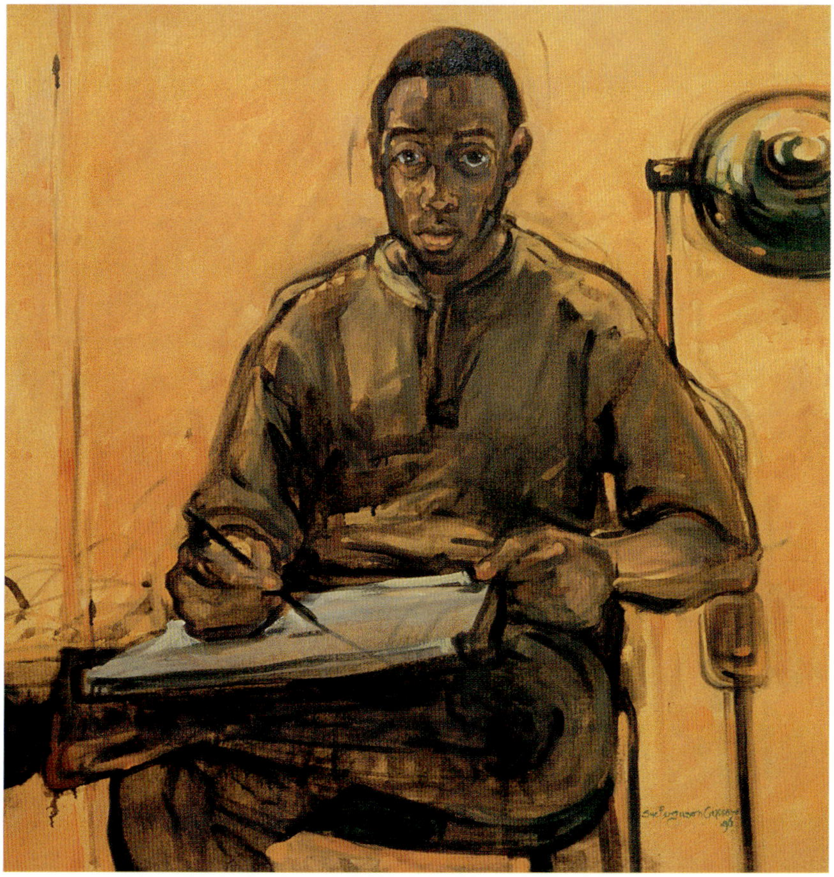

Anthony, oil on canvas, 33" x 30", 1996. *Courtesy of the artist.*

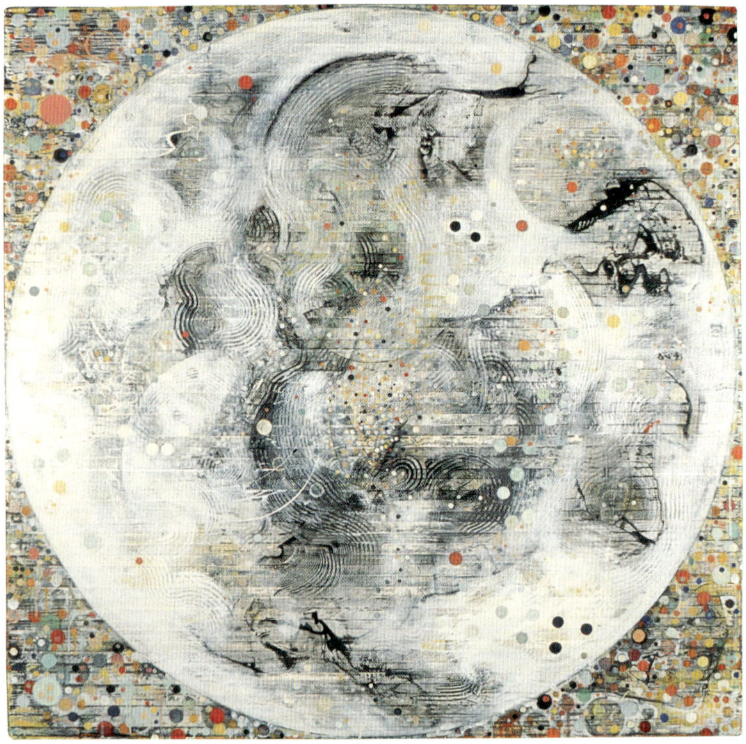

Dot Calm, alkyd, oil on canvas on panel, 52" x 52", 2004.

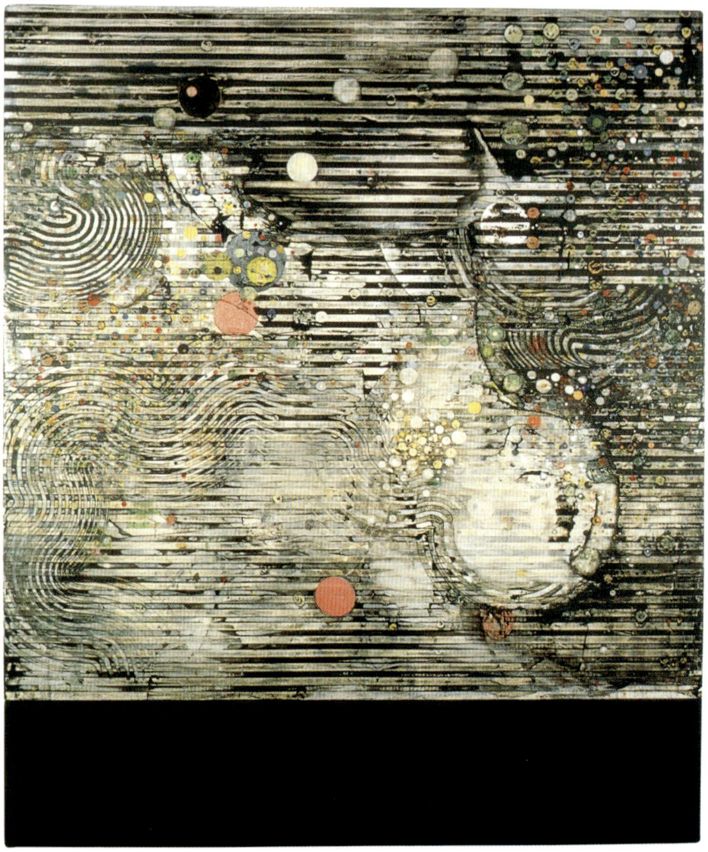

Query, oil and alkyd on panel, 64" x 52", 2004.

Mary Hambleton

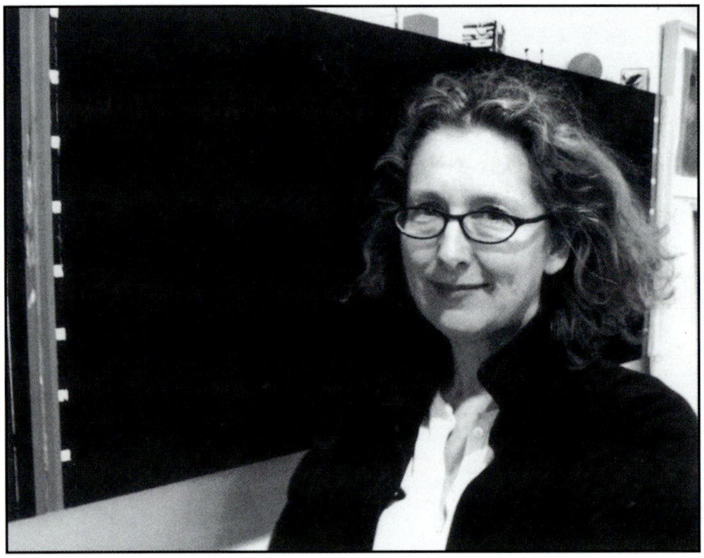

Photograph by Nene Humphrey.

Mary Hambleton, "a painter's painter,"[93] in the words of Benny Andrews, is concerned with light, structure, and a frequent reference to botanical forms. She "cannot give up the geometric or the organic,"[94] though she says she has tried. Alternating fields of stripes, and variously sized circles, coils, or swirls often appear in her abstract yet mystical canvases, giving her work "an edge," corresponding to "something about the world right now. . . ."[95] She explores "the symbolic possibilities of abstraction, incorporating an appreciation of transience,"[96] perhaps as a response to her continuing struggles with cancer, permanently altering her awareness. "Painting for me ... allows all these ... things to exist at one time."[97]

A faculty member of Parsons School of Design, Hambleton has also taught at the Rhode Island School of Design and is a graduate of the San Francisco Art Institute. She has additionally studied at Bennington College in Vermont, and in Italy.

Her works in drawing, painting, and panels with sculptural forms are in many American and European collections, and have been seen in group and solo exhibitions here and abroad. She is represented by the Pamela Auchincloss Gallery in New York.

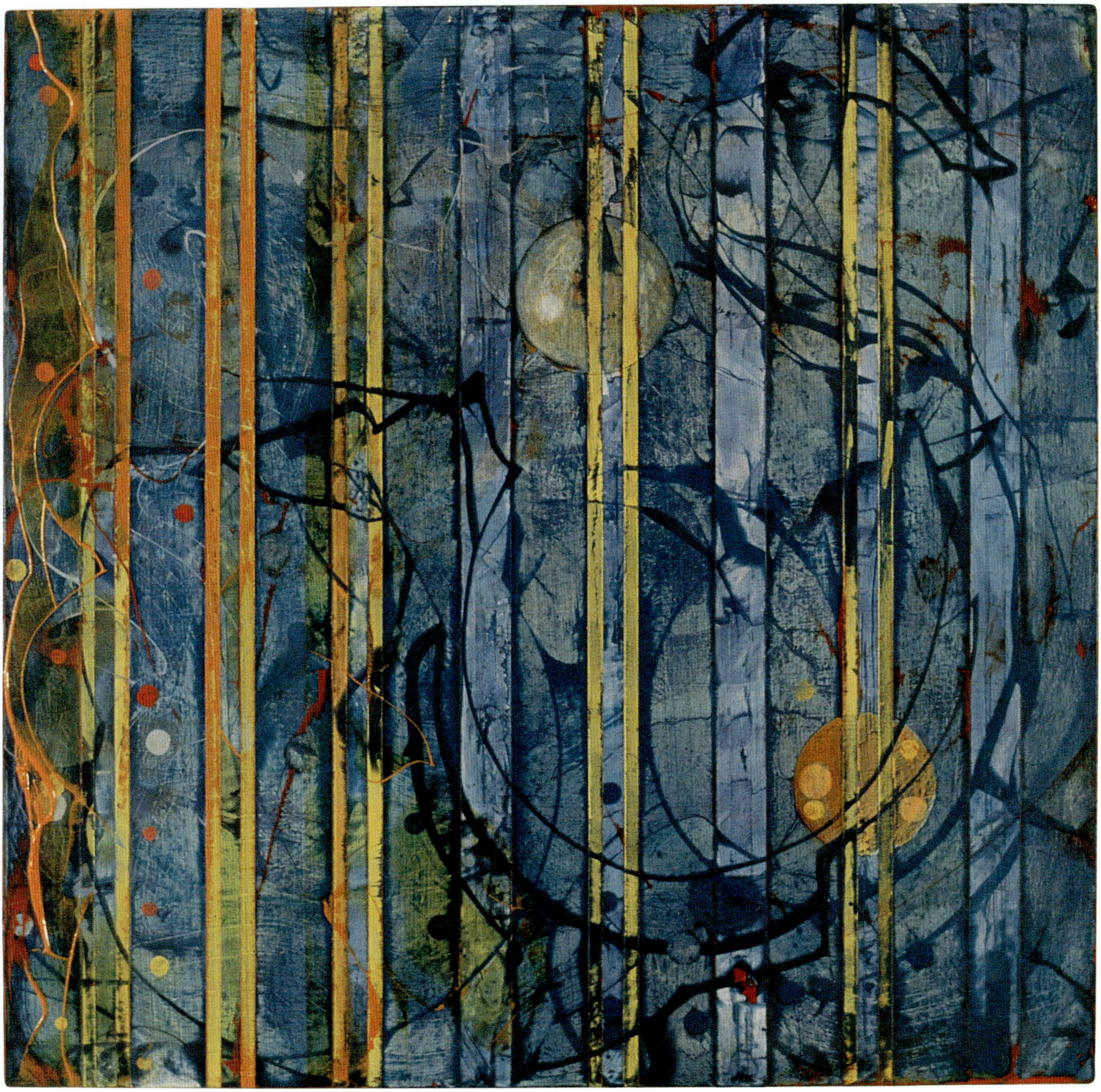

Quench, oil and alkyd on wood panel, 20" x 20", 2004.

Glen Hansen

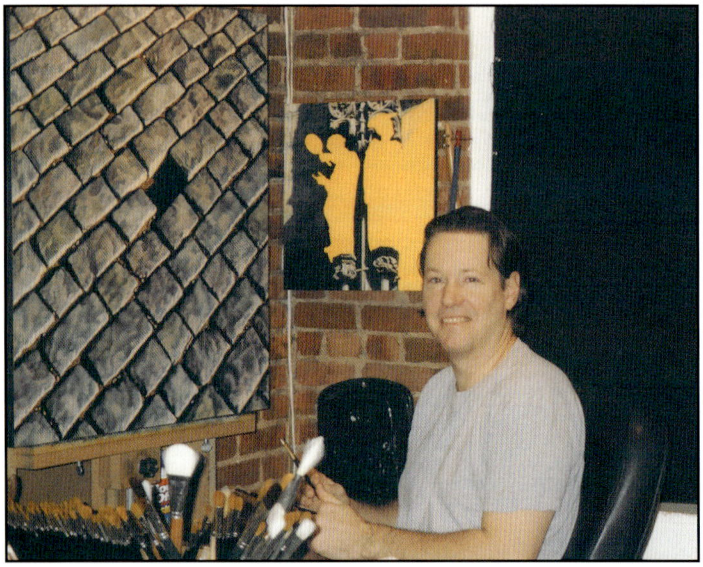

The artist at easel with painting from *Praha*.

Glen Hansen travels to many cities for architectural subjects that will, through his paintings, "relate to the viewer the excitement of discovering a structure for the first time."[98] His work, "somewhere between the Precisionists and the Photo-realists,"[99] deals with control and organization.

Hansen carefully relates his compositions to the scale and shape of the canvas, such as the formal, enclosed, box-like square, or the tense parameters of the circular tondo. He starts with on-site pencil and oil studies, then incorporates his own photographs into the final works.

Hansen is an instructor at the School of Visual Arts, where he earned his BFA, and is represented by the Fischbach Gallery in New York.

Hansen has had solo exhibitions in New York and Pennsylvania, and his works have been included in many group exhibitions. Among the many collections in which his works appear are the Metropolitan Museum of Art, General Electric, and Grey Advertising in New York, and those of dozens of private individuals.

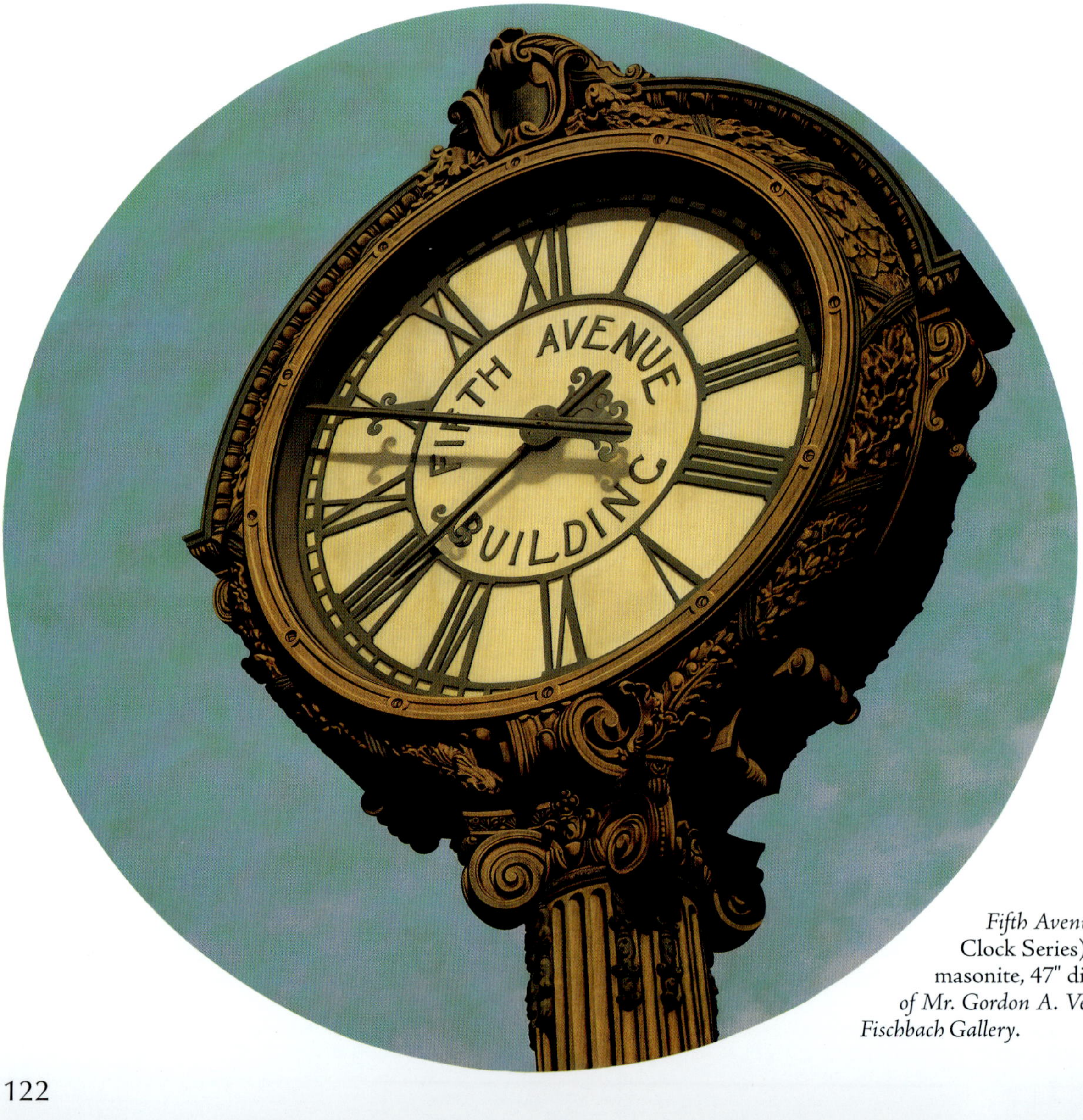

Fifth Avenue Building (Street Clock Series), oil on canvas on masonite, 47" diameter, 1991. *Collection of Mr. Gordon A. Vehling. Courtesy of Fischbach Gallery.*

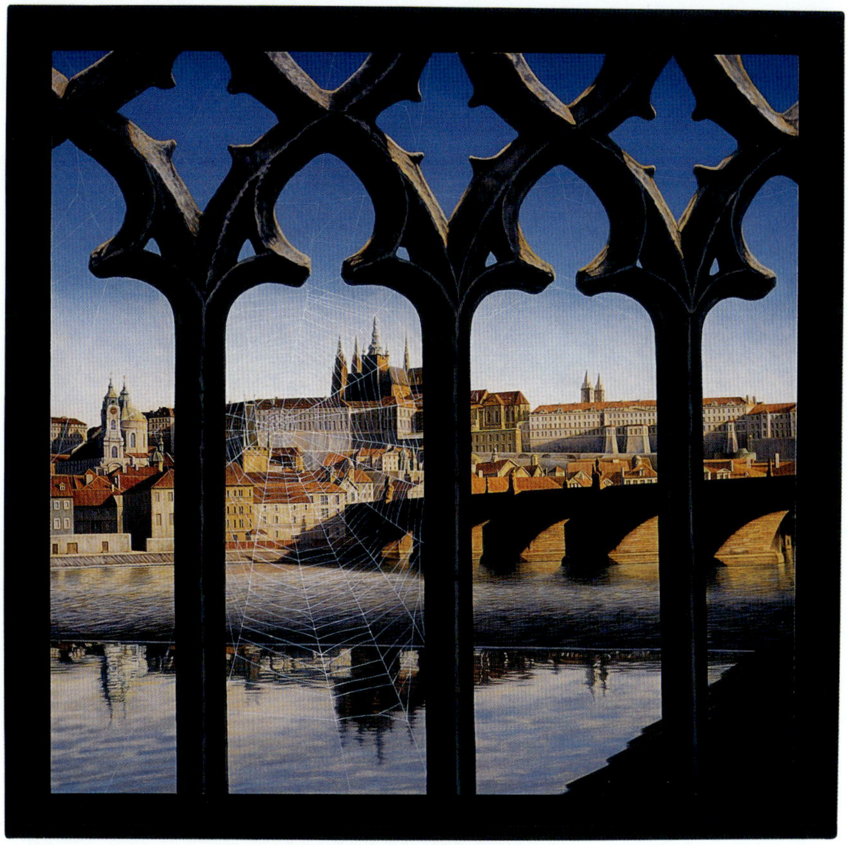

Praha-Virgo, oil on panel, 24" x 24", 2004. *Private collection. Courtesy of Fischbach Gallery.*

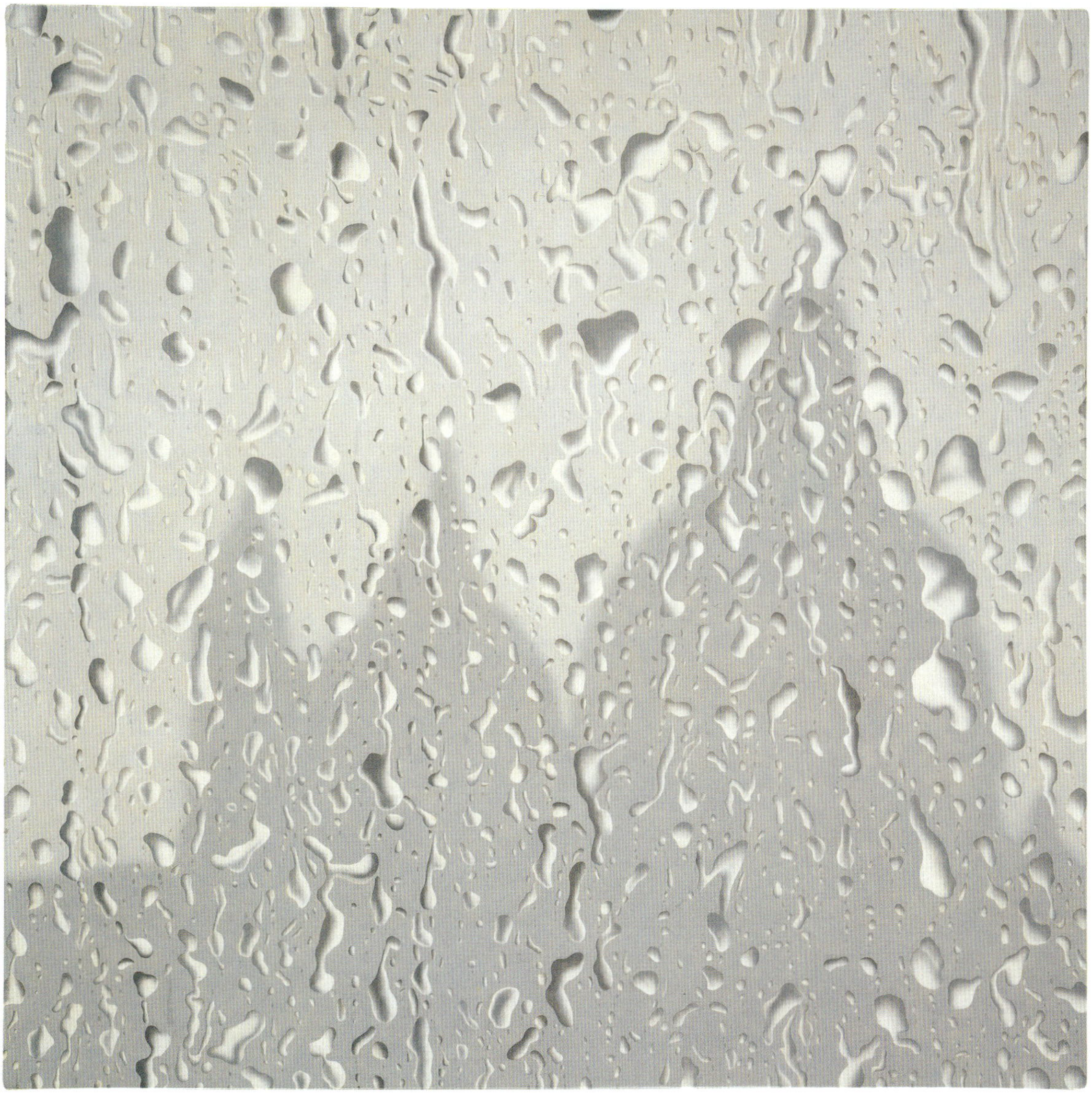

Salute (Paintings of Venice), oil on canvas, 24" x 24", 1999. *Courtesy of Commerce Bancshares, Inc., Missouri.*

Esther Hyneman

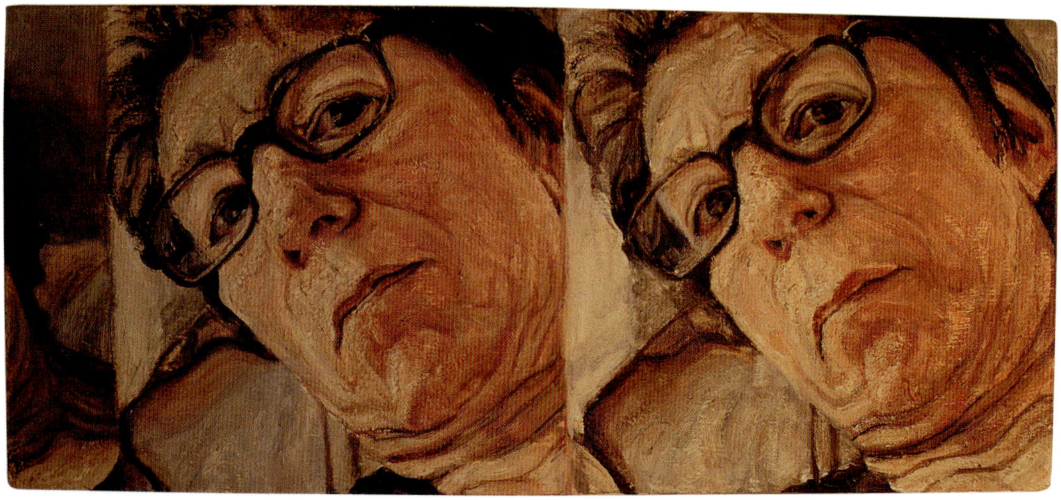

Self Portrait, oil on linen, 12" x 26", 1999. *Courtesy of the artist.*

NYC Bus, oil on canvas, 22.5" x 24.5". *Collection of Long Island University.*

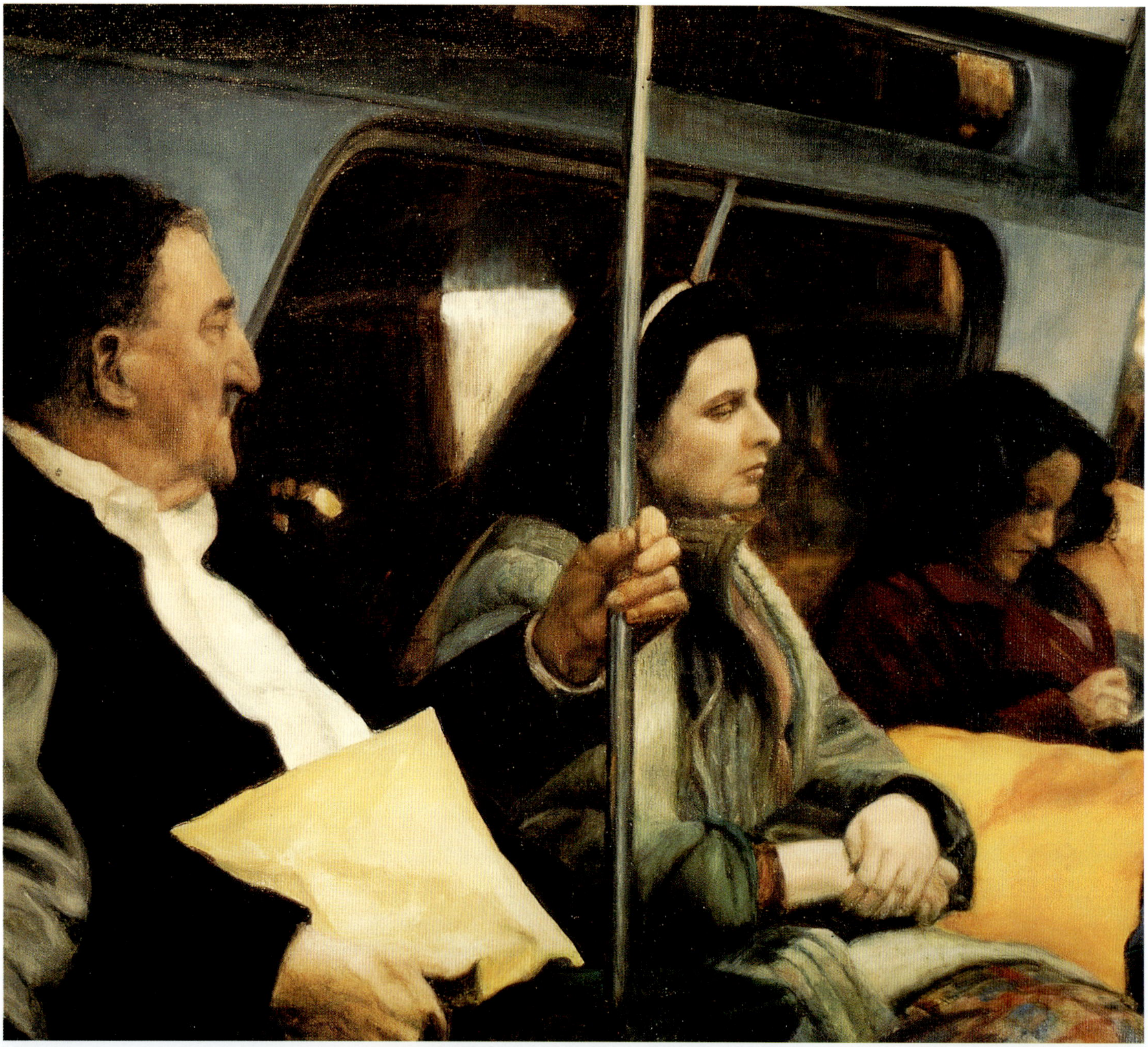

Esther Hyneman, a retired Professor of English at the Brooklyn Campus of Long Island University, taught portrait painting there as well. In addition to receiving her BA from Goucher College and MA/PhD degrees from Columbia University, she studied at the Brooklyn Museum Art School, the Art Students League, and the New York Academy of Art, and enjoyed an art residency at the MacDowell Colony for the Arts. She was awarded First Prize in Painting by the National Association of Women Artists, and has won several other awards.

Hyneman's work is inspired by a long list of "Realists: Rembrandt, Velazquez, Goya, Beckmann, Freud ... all driven to paint the human face."[100] Her work has appeared on the cover of *Feminist Studies*, in the opening show of the Lesbian Herstory Archives, Brooklyn, New York, and the Women's Caucus for Art Exhibition at Lincoln Center, New York.

Hyneman's struggles with various experiences of sexism and identity have led her to trust her instincts and have assured her "that painting, even Realist painting, can still be a viable means of making sense of our time and ourselves.... The desire to bring the figure to life is the essence of representation ... I owe to feminism my reinvention of myself as a painter." Hyneman, who considers her work visually provocative, adds, "the emotional connection, the personal attraction ... precedes any ideas ... for me, painting is rooted in my gut rather than my head."[101]

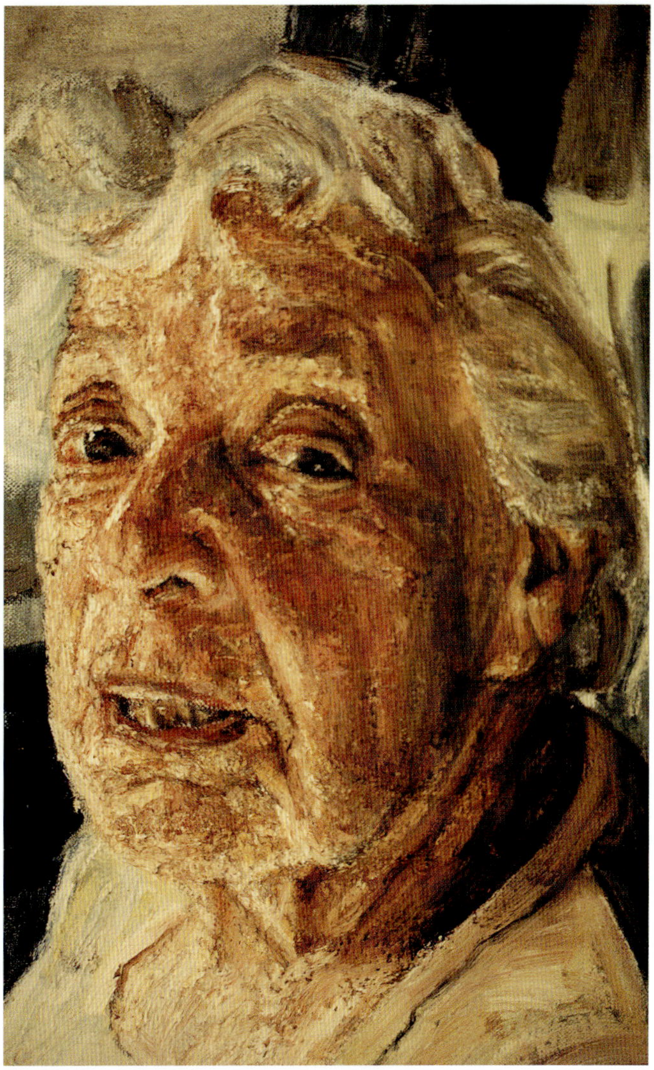

Marcey Jacobson in 1995, 14" x 8", 1995. *Courtesy of the artist.*

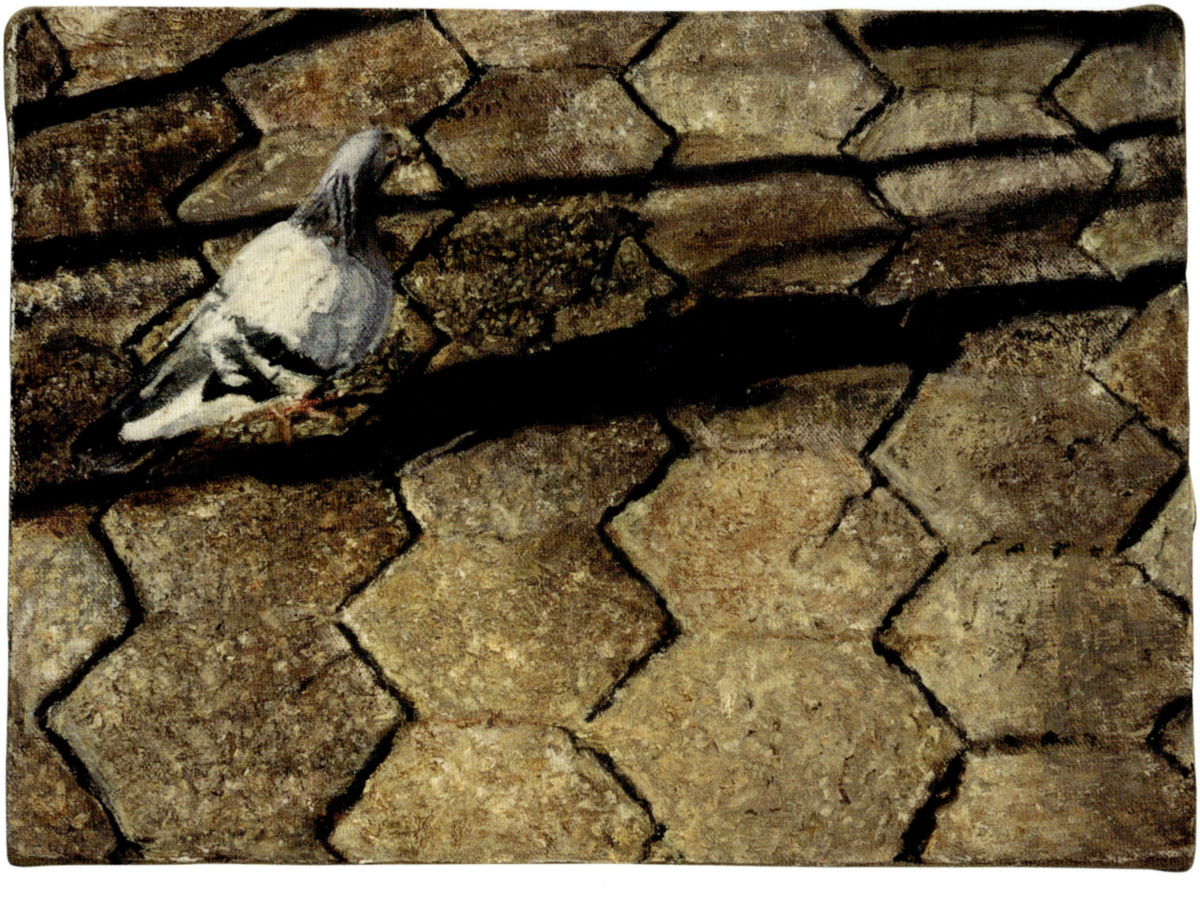

Urban Bird: 2, oil on linen, 13" x 18", 2003. *Collection of Seymour Kleinberg, New York City.*

Yvonne Jacquette

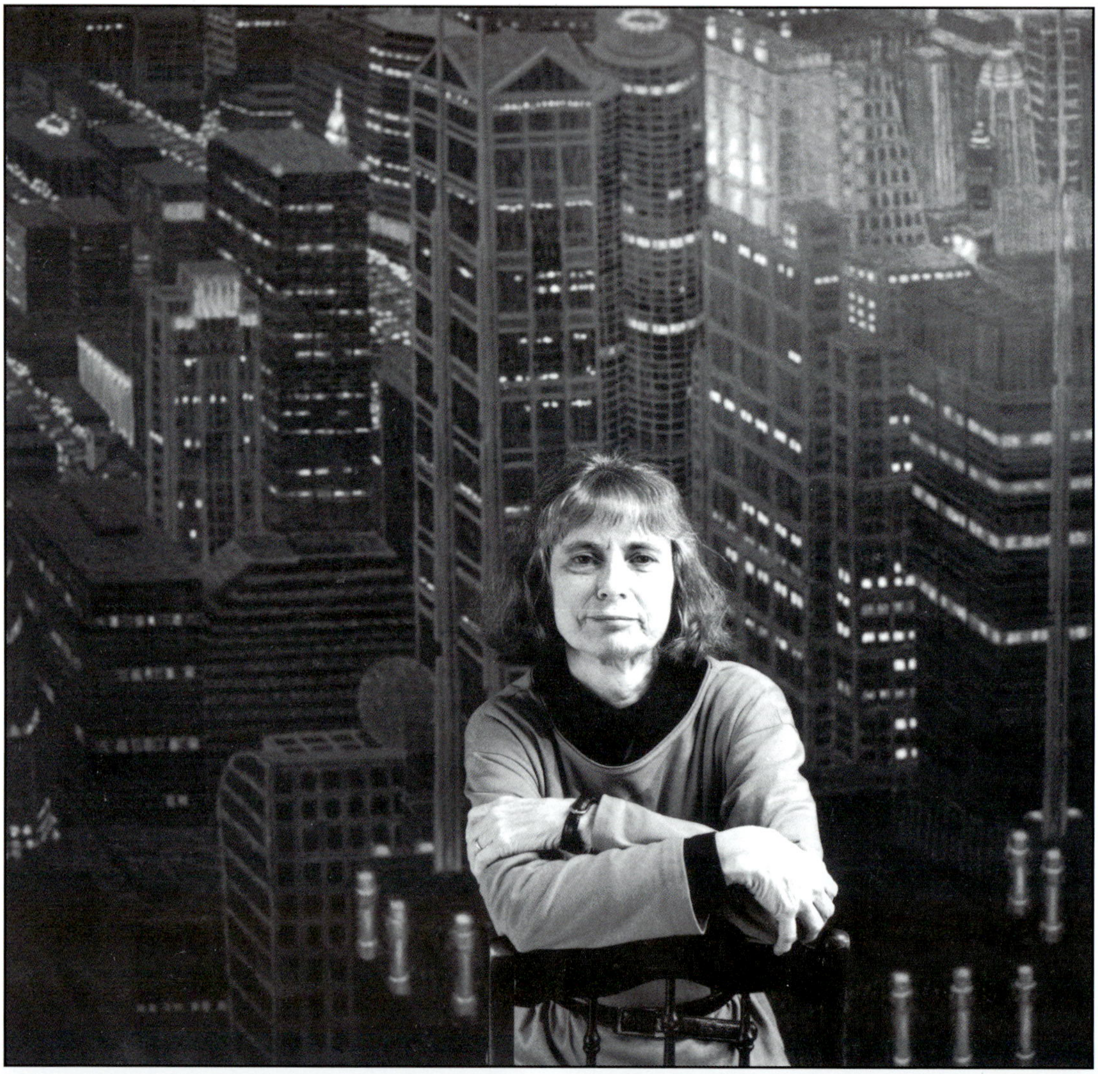

Courtesy of D C Moore Gallery.

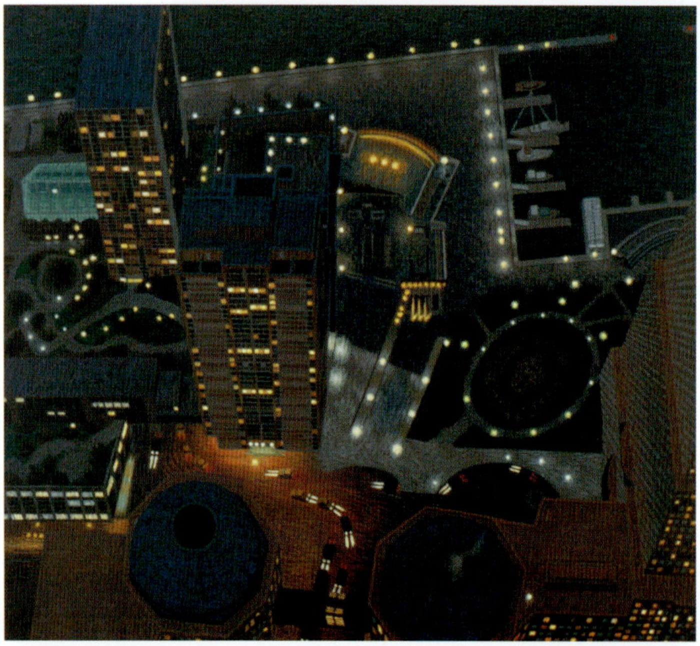

Vertiginous World Financial Area, oil on canvas, 72.25" x 78.25", 1999. *Private collection. Courtesy of D C Moore Gallery, New York.*

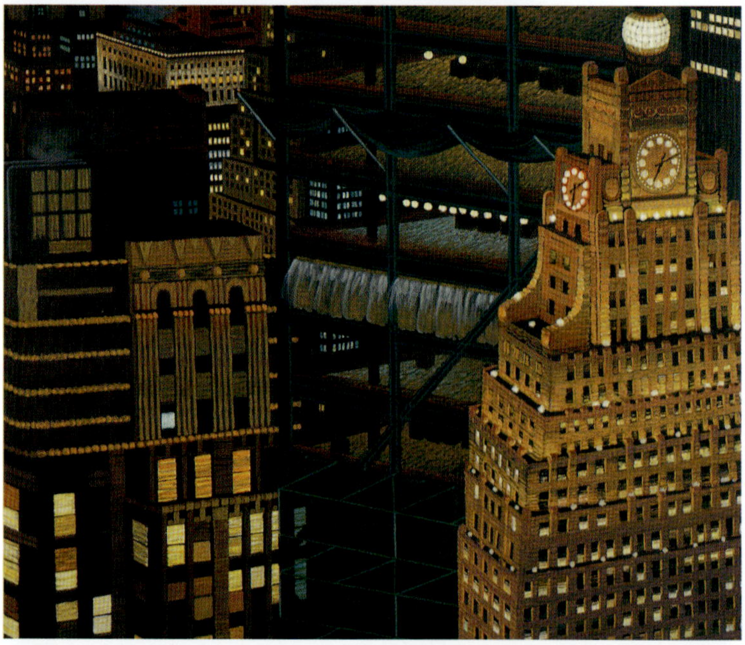

Above Times Square, oil on canvas, 63" x 72.5", 2003. *Courtesy of D C Moore Gallery, New York.*

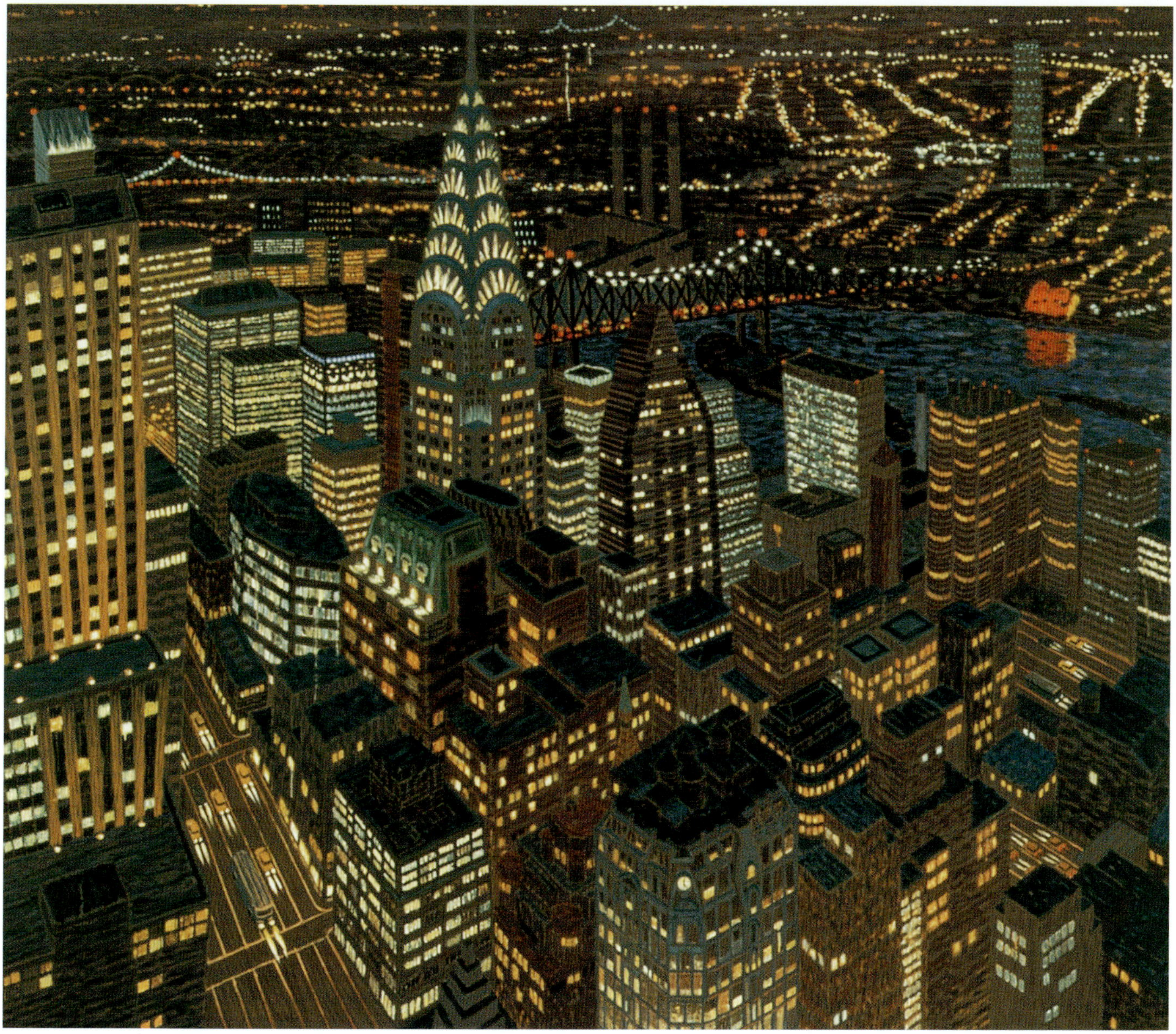

Chrysler Building Composite at Dusk, oil on linen, 75.5" x 86", 1997.
Private collection. Courtesy of D C Moore Gallery, New York.

Yvonne Jacquette, "aerial muse"[102] of land- and city-scape painting—as the national retrospective of her works proclaimed—has made the overhead vantage point her own. Across America as well as in several Asian locations, she has looked out upon cities, farmlands, and natural sites to find particular topographies and patterns that "examine the relationship between the man-made and the natural. ..."[103] Perspective and viewpoint are often skewed or re-pictured in her dazzling interpretations, using dots and dashes of light and color, always appearing magically believable and convincing.

A graduate of the Rhode Island School of Design and recipient of a John Simon Guggenheim Memorial Foundation Fellowship Award, she is a member of the American Academy of Arts and Letters, and an elected National Academician. Jacquette, who is represented by New York's D C Moore Gallery, has been the subject of many solo exhibitions and publications, with titles such as "Vantage on High,"[104] "Eye in the Sky,"[105] and "A Cocktail of Perception and Invention: The Vast, Dark and Dramatic Paintings of Yvonne Jacquette."[106]

Her works are in many major public and corporate collections, notably the Brooklyn Museum, the Metropolitan Museum of Art, and the Museum of Modern Art, New York, as well as the Cantor Arts Center and Cowles Charitable Trust.

Jacquette has taught at Moore College of Art in Philadelphia, Parsons School of Design in New York, and the University of Pennsylvania, among others, and has received the Painters Award from the American Academy of Arts and Letters.

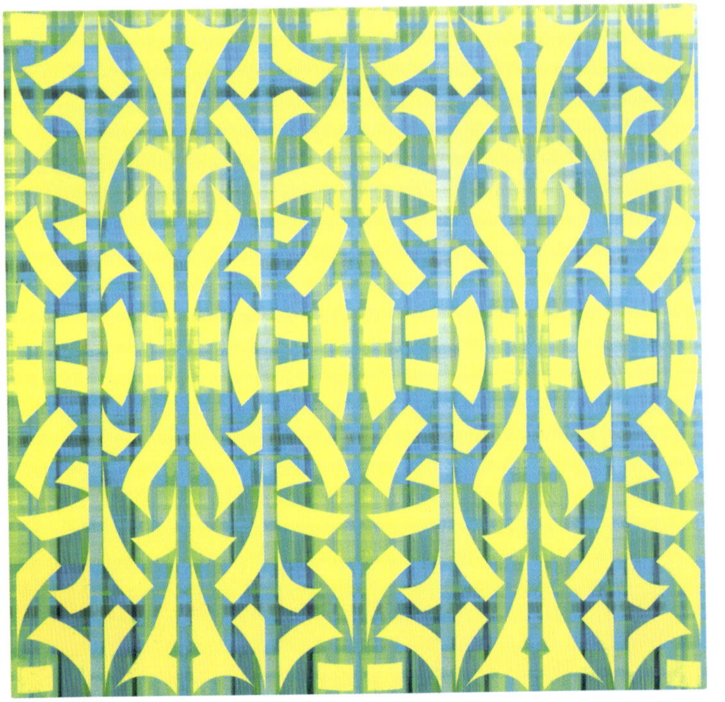

Now and Forever, oil and alkyd on canvas on board, 72" x 72", 2003. *Courtesy of Von Lintel Gallery.*

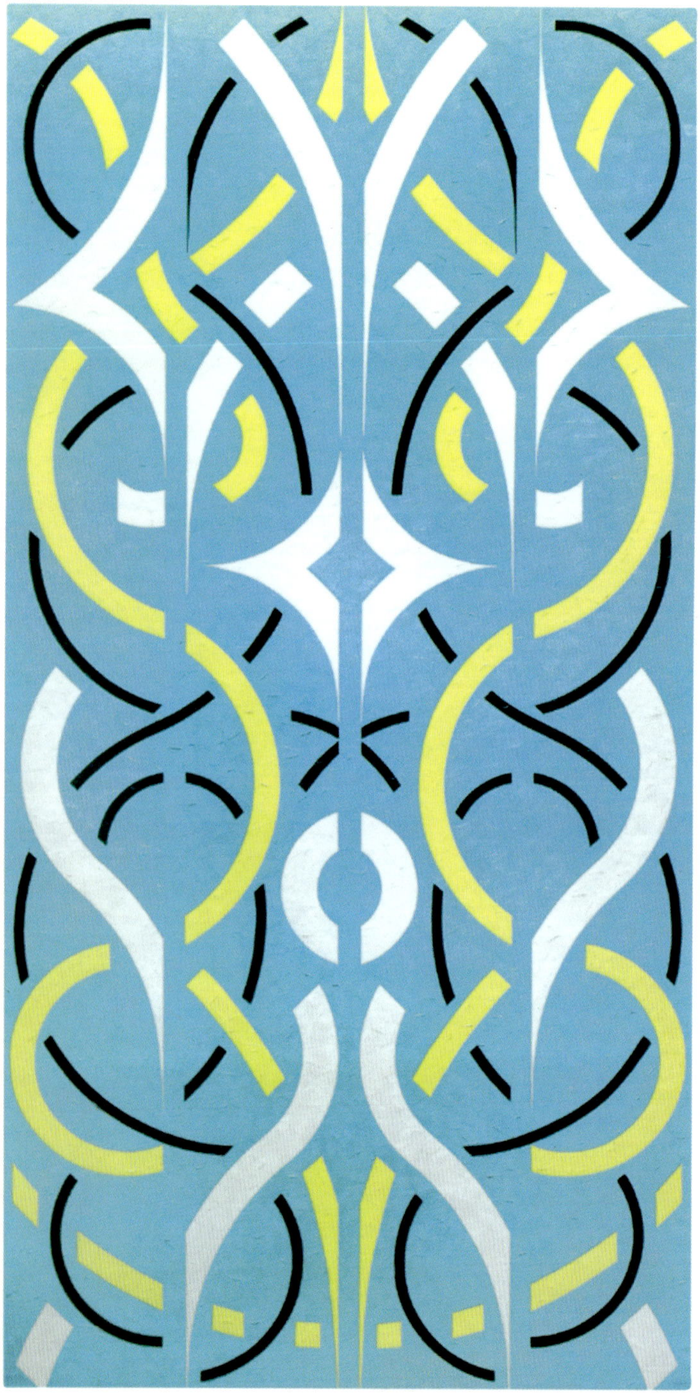

True to Life, oil on canvas, 96" x 48", 2005. *Courtesy of Von Lintel Gallery.*

Valerie Jaudon

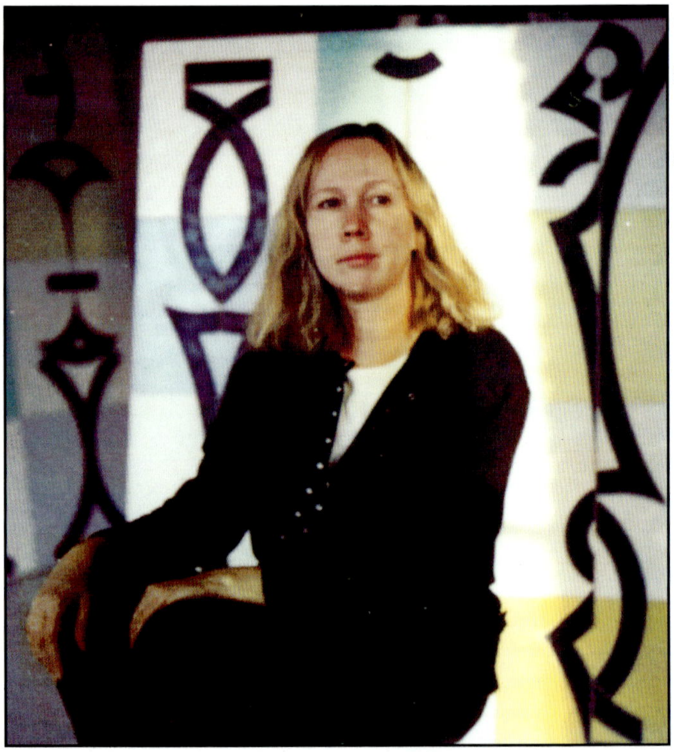

Courtesy of the artist.

Valerie Jaudon, long associated with the geometric, symmetry-driven, richly colorful decorative genre known as "Pattern Painting," is strongly committed to the beauty, universality, and lasting significance of ornament in art.

Previously represented for many years by the historic Sidney Janis Gallery and the Holly Solomon Gallery in New York, she is now affiliated with the Von Lintel Gallery. Her work has appeared in solo and group exhibitions around the United States and worldwide, with such titles as, "The

Legacy of Pattern and Decoration,"[107] "Pattern: Between Object and Arabesque,"[108] "Geometric Abstraction,"[109] and "Five Contemporary Masters."[110]

Jaudon, born in Mississippi, studied at Mississippi University for Women, the Memphis Academy of Art, Tennessee, the University of the Americas in Mexico City, and St. Martins School of Art, London. A faculty member at Hunter College, she has also lectured widely—in New York at The New School and the School of Visual Arts, the Institute of Fine Arts at New York University, in New Haven at Yale University's School of Art, in California at the Santa Monica Museum of Art, and also in Chicago, Philadelphia, Baltimore, and in Denmark.

Jaudon is a recipient of numerous awards, including a CAPS grant, an Art Award from the Mississippi Institute of Arts and Letters, and the Honored Artist Award of the Mississippi Committee of the National Museum of Women in the Arts.

She has also created many public and architectural projects, including site-specific garden elements in Alabama, wall murals in Georgia and New York, and an entrance hall floor in Frankfurt, Germany.

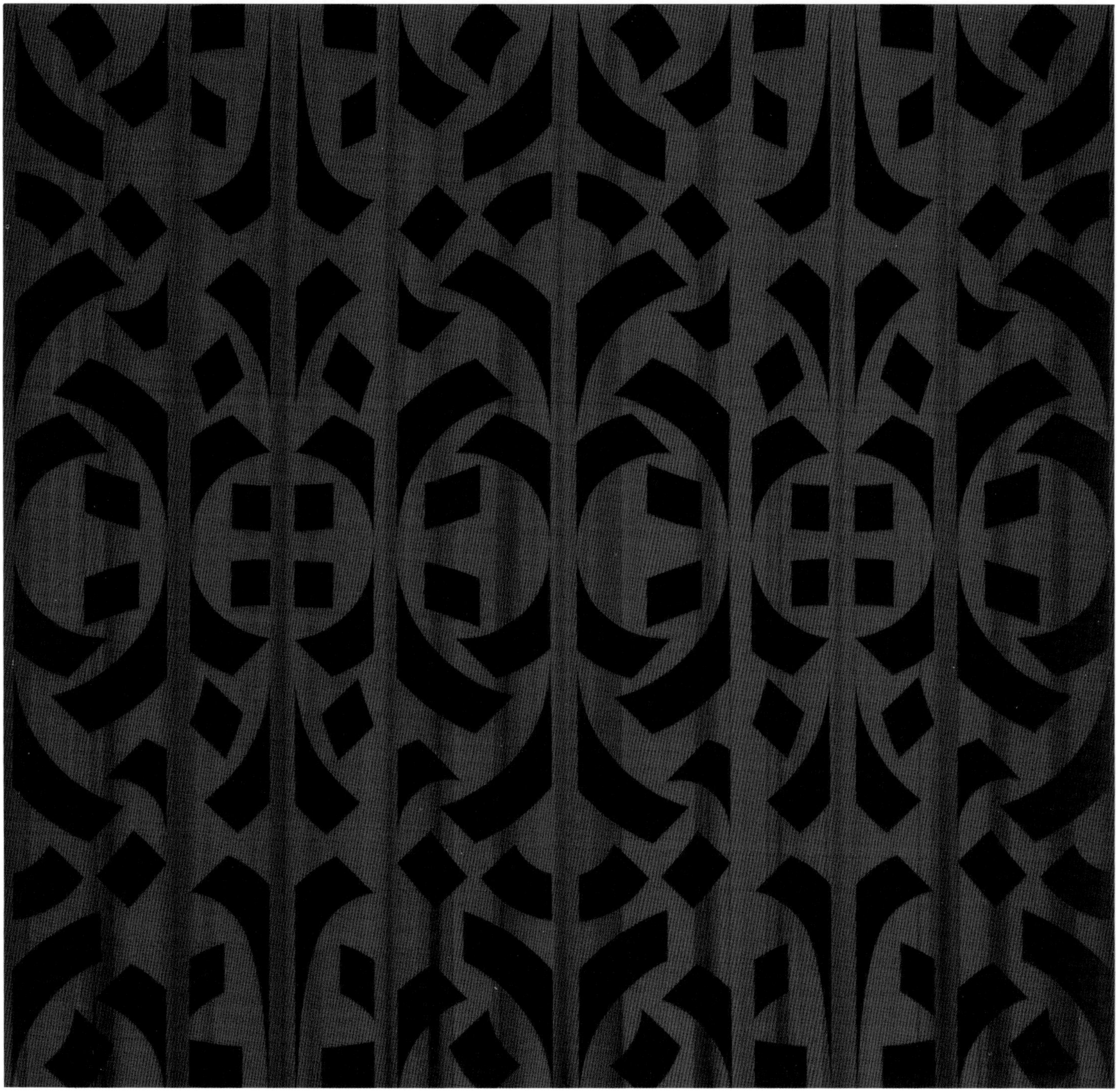

True Confession, oil and alkyd on canvas, 60" x 60", 2000. *Courtesy of Von Lintel Gallery. All art © Valerie Jaudon/Licensed by VAGA, New York, NY.*

Cecily Kahn

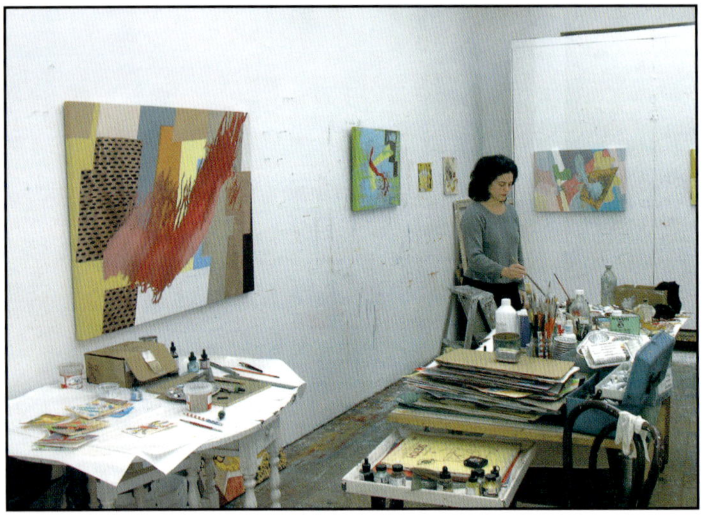

Photograph by Abbie Zuidema.

Cecily Kahn, a third-generation abstract painter, has had her works exhibited at Hunter College's Leubsdorf Art Gallery along with those of her mother, Emily Mason, and her grandmother, Alice Trumbull Mason. In addition, she is the daughter of the painter, Wolf Kahn.

A graduate of the Rhode Island School of Design, Kahn has studied at the International School of Graphics in Venice, Italy, and at the Calografia Nazionale, in Rome.

Her works in painting and printmaking have appeared in many group exhibitions in New York, Pennsylvania, Maine, and Connecticut, as well as Barcelona in Spain, Dublin in Ireland, and Venice and Rome in Italy.

Kahn is represented by the Lohin-Geduld Gallery in New York and is Chair of the Board of The Painting Center, an artist-run gallery. She is a member of the American Abstract Artists group.

Of her work, Kahn says "it involves the process of integrating different elements to co-exist peacefully and easily within a composition. ... Paint surfaces are explored by [using] various mediums ... poured or thickly applied. Color and form are used ... organically and ... in consciously formal decisions, [in] an attempt to marry process painting with constructivist plasticity. ..."[111]

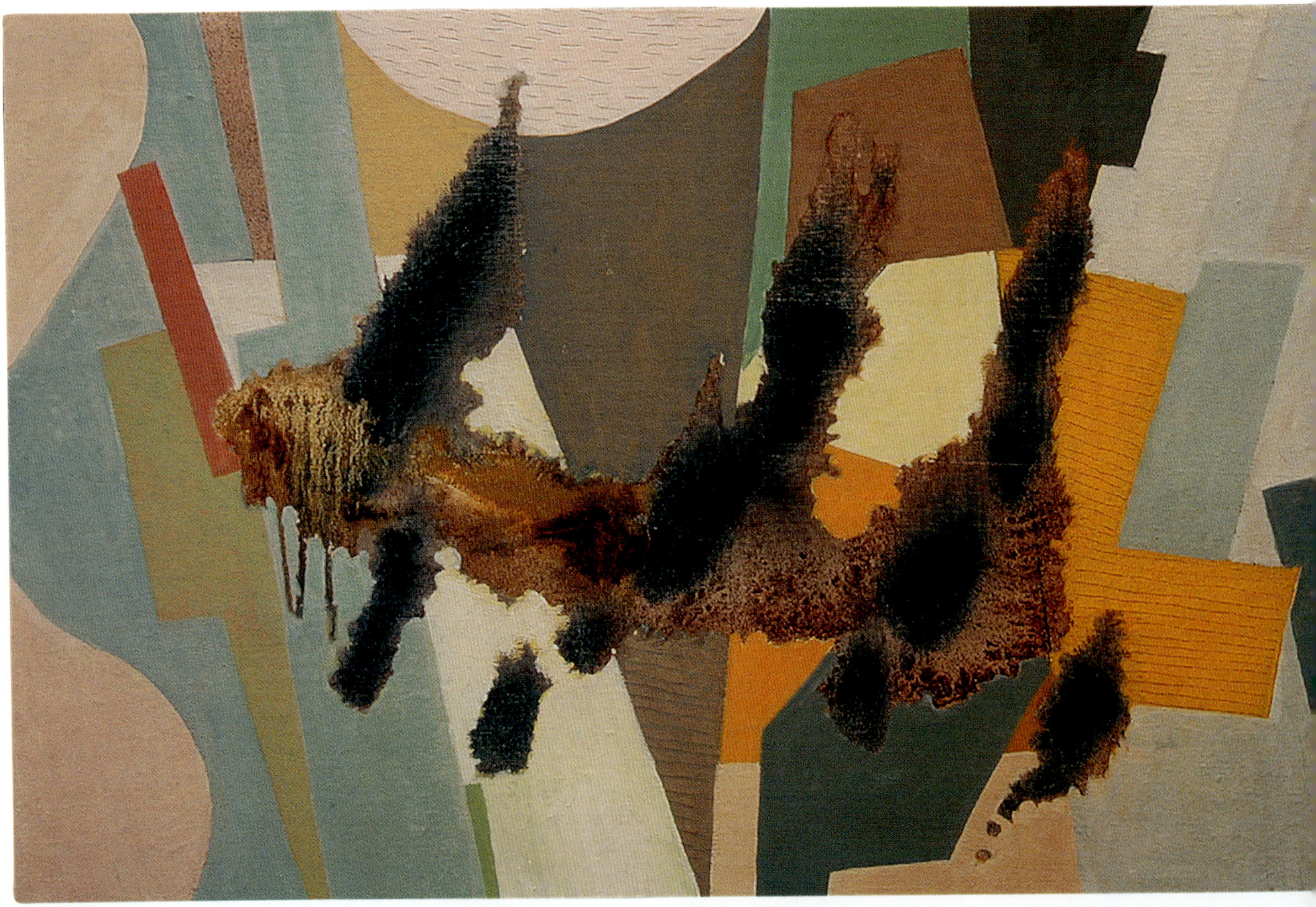

Locus, oil on linen, 17" x 25", 2004. *Courtesy of Lohin-Geduld Gallery.*

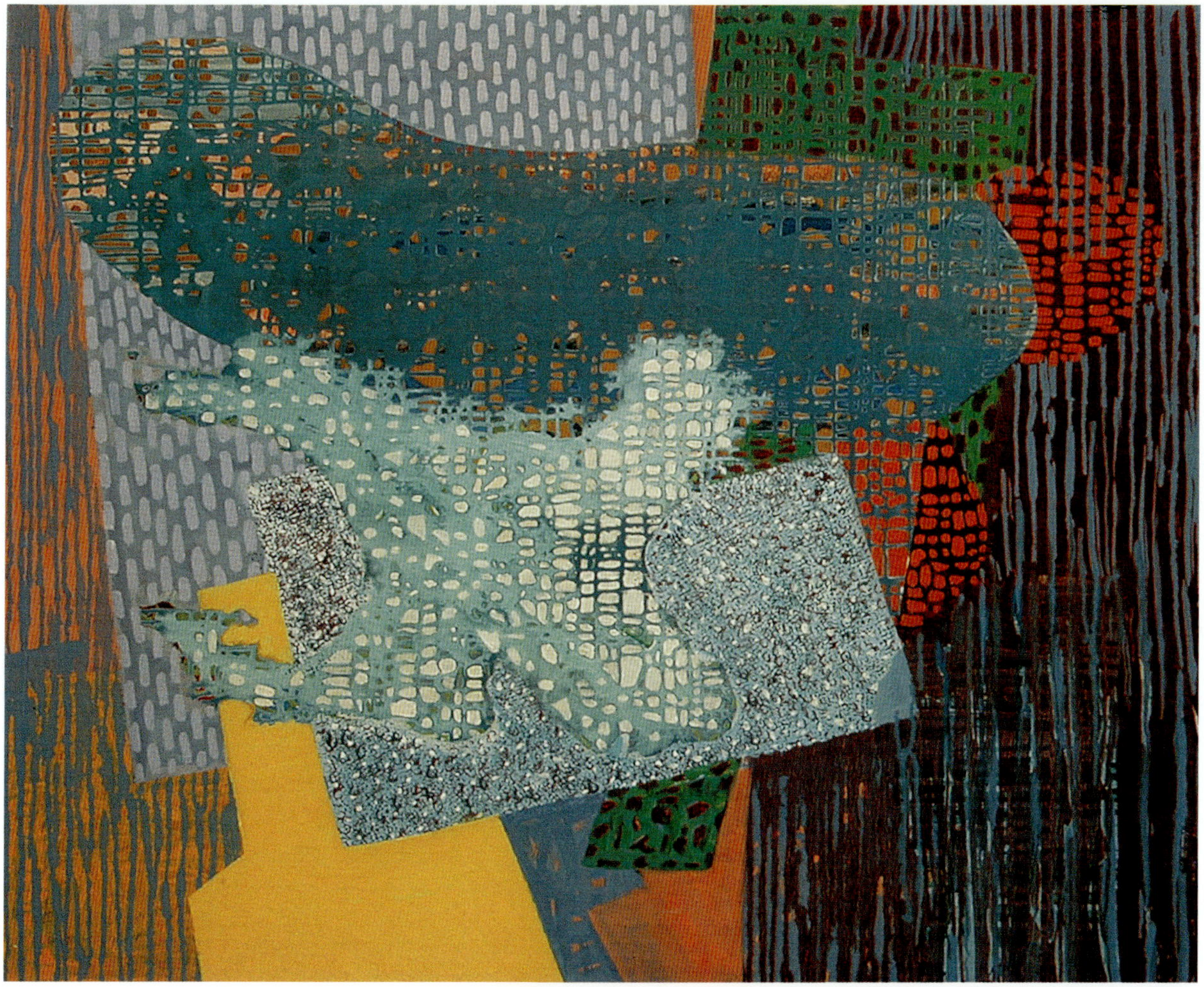

Nestle, oil on linen, 31" x 37", 2005. *Courtesy of Lohin-Geduld Gallery.*

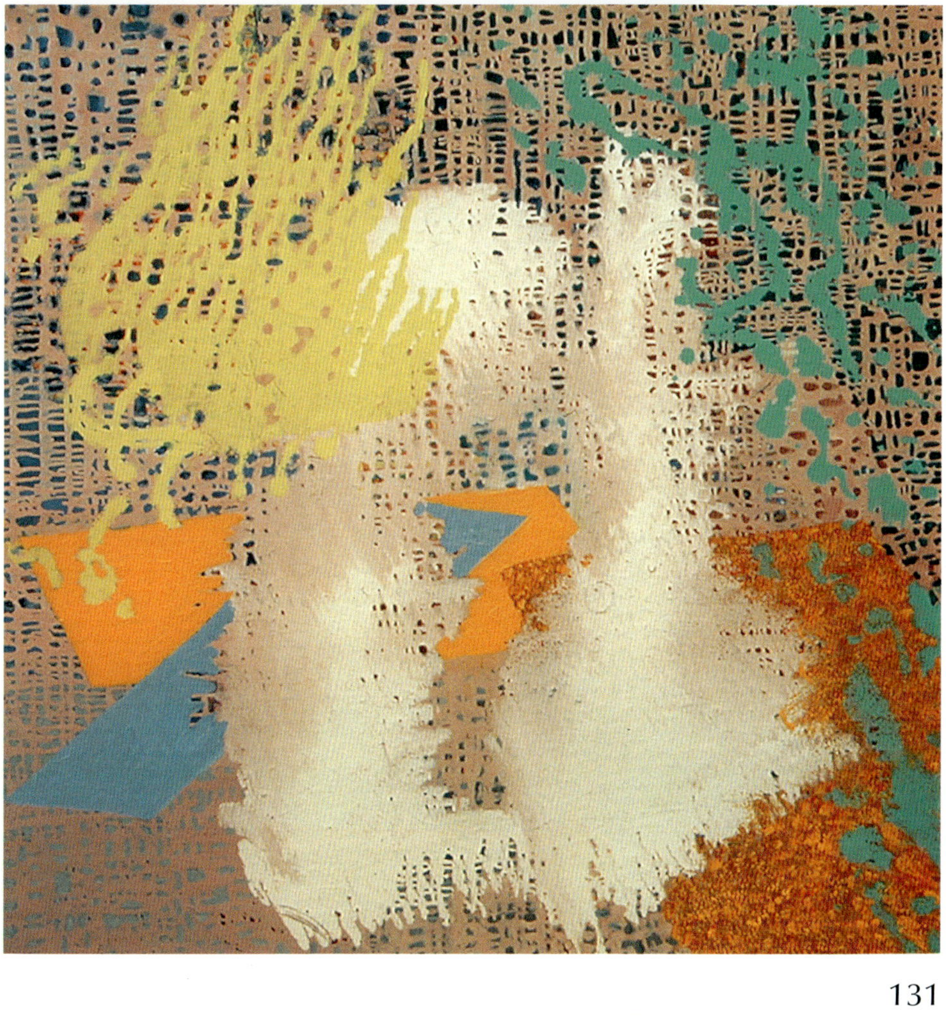

Good Pair, oil on linen, 31" x 31", 2005. *Courtesy of Lohin-Geduld Gallery.*

Wolf Kahn

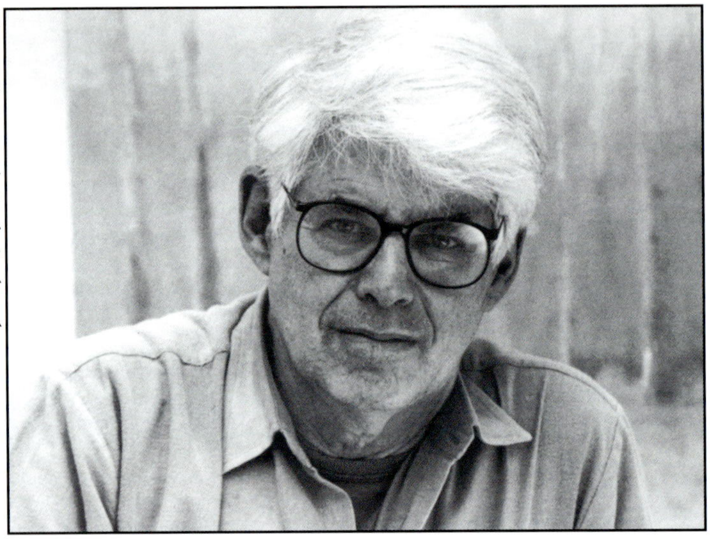

Photograph © 1994 by Linda Southworth.

Wolf Kahn, whose father was a celebrated German orchestra conductor, lived with his grandmother before the family moved to the United States, where he joined them after years at school in England during World War II. Kahn attended New York's High School of Music and Art, later studying with Stuart Davis at the New School for Social Research, and at Hans Hofmann's School. He earned a BA at the University of Chicago, then returned to New York, where he continued to develop life-long friendships with many distinguished artists.

Winning a John Simon Guggenheim Memorial Fellowship, he had several one-man exhibitions at New York's Borgenicht Gallery and has exhibited work at the National Academy of Design, where he was elected a member.

Accorded many other honors in his long career, Kahn has received an art award from the American Academy and Institute of Arts and Letters in New York, and later was elected to membership. He has long been on the Advisory Committee of the Vermont Studio Center, the National Board of the College Art Association, and received the Vermont Council on the Arts' Lifetime Achievement Award. Kahn's travels have taken him to paint in Europe, Egypt, Mexico, Hawaii, and Kenya, and he has conducted workshops in painting and pastel in many locations.

Kahn's luminous, color-filled paintings and pastels capture the clear light and softness of his many landscape

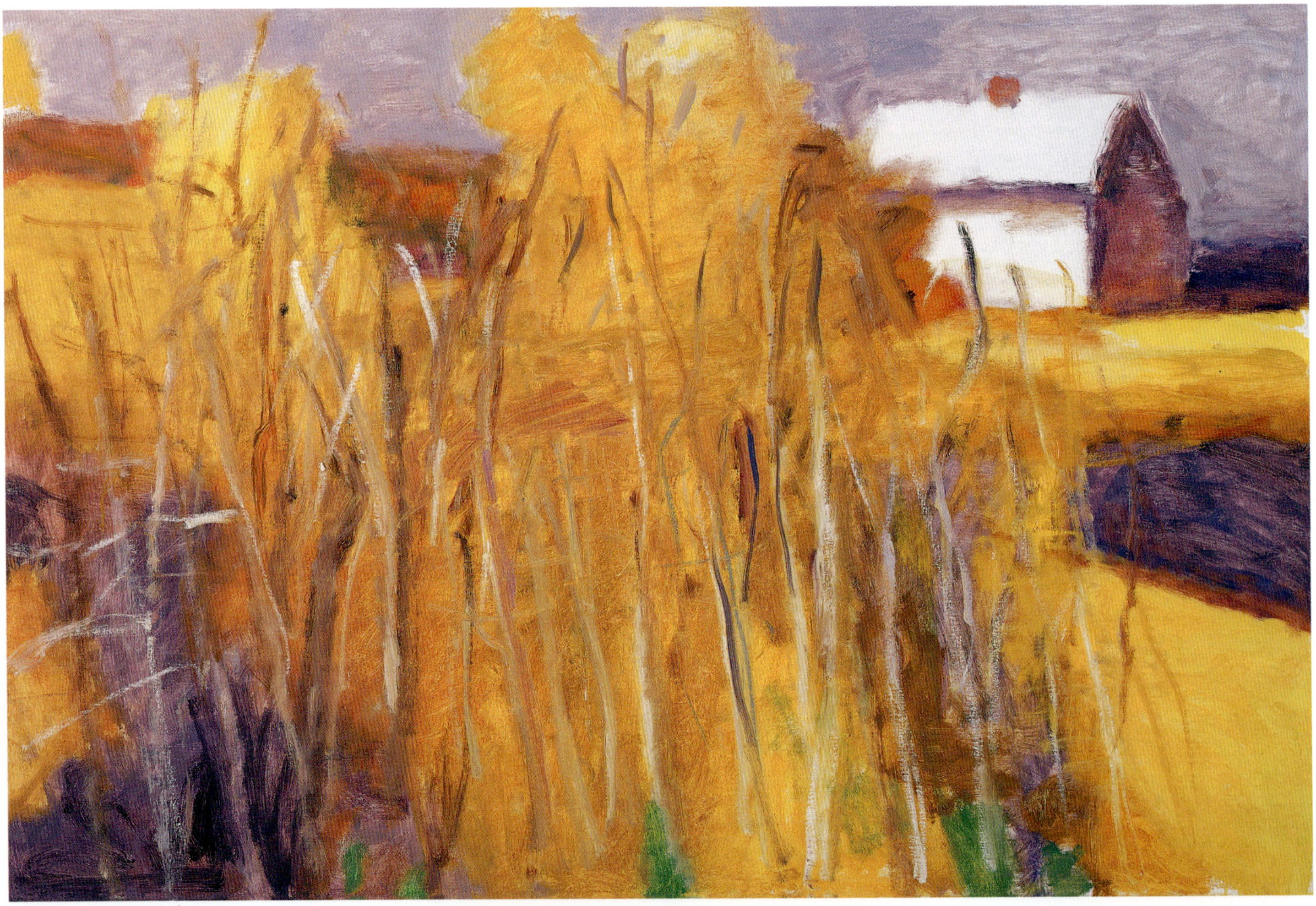

House on a Hill II, oil on canvas, 36" x 52", 2003. *Courtesy of the artist and Ameringer & Yohe Fine Art. All art © Wolf Kahn/Licensed by VAGA, New York, NY.*

subjects, often revealing a simple structure such as a barn or a stand of trees against a field of unexpected hues. His works are to be seen in virtually every major museum, university, and public collection.

He is represented by the Ameringer & Yohe Gallery in New York.

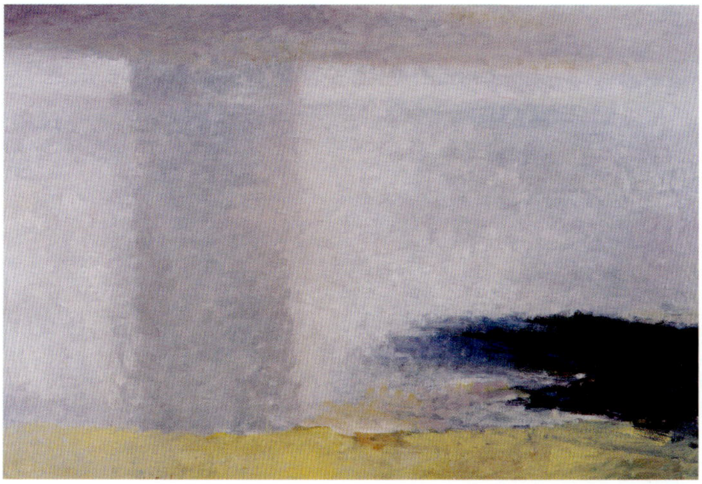

The Rain in Maine, oil on canvas, 52" x 72", 2003. *Courtesy of the artist and Ameringer & Yohe Fine Art.*

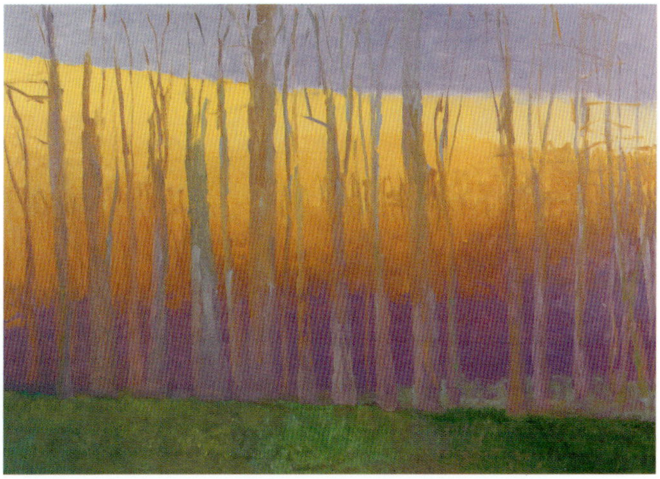

Large Tree Line, oil on canvas, 52" x 72", 2005. *Courtesy of the artist and Ameringer & Yohe Fine Art.*

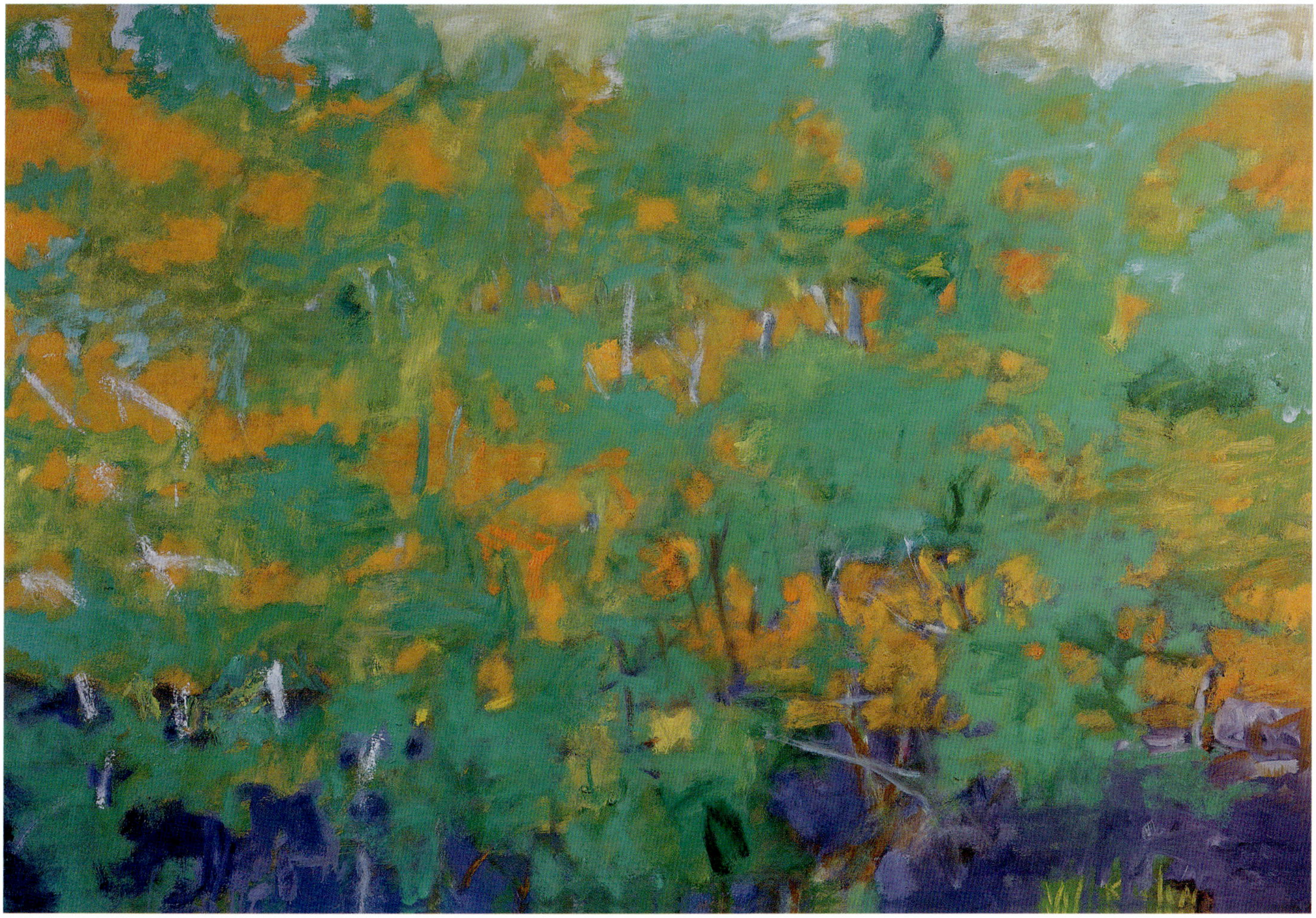

Foliage in an Orange Setting, oil on canvas, 36" x 52", 2004. *Courtesy of the artist and Ameringer & Yohe Fine Art.*

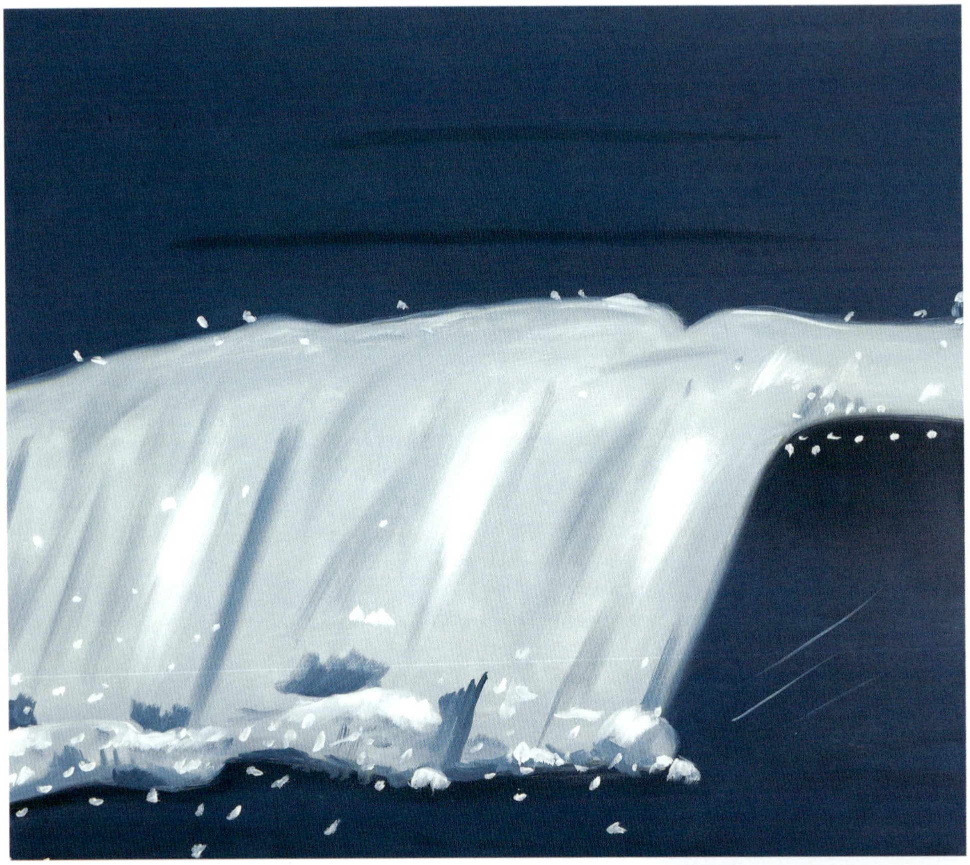

Blue Wave, oil on linen, 96" x 108", 2001. *Courtesy of Alex Katz Studio.*

Alex Katz, who, in the early 1960s, "played a major role in the emergence of a new perceptual realism in painting," according to one of his biographers, Irving Sandler, is widely known for large, flat, planar portraits in a manner Sandler calls, "hard edge realism."[112] Defying categorization, however, Katz has experimented with ideas encountered during and following his years of study at The Cooper Union ("provincial modernism")[113] and the Skowhegan School of Painting and Sculpture in Maine ("provincial regionalism, to meld street savviness, fashion consciousness, and the energies and rhythms of jazz, dance and modern poetry").[114]

Katz has said, "... If you get the surfaces right, you get everything else right. I want style, the manner of

Purple Wind, oil on canvas, 90" x 66", 1995. *Courtesy of Alex Katz Studio.*

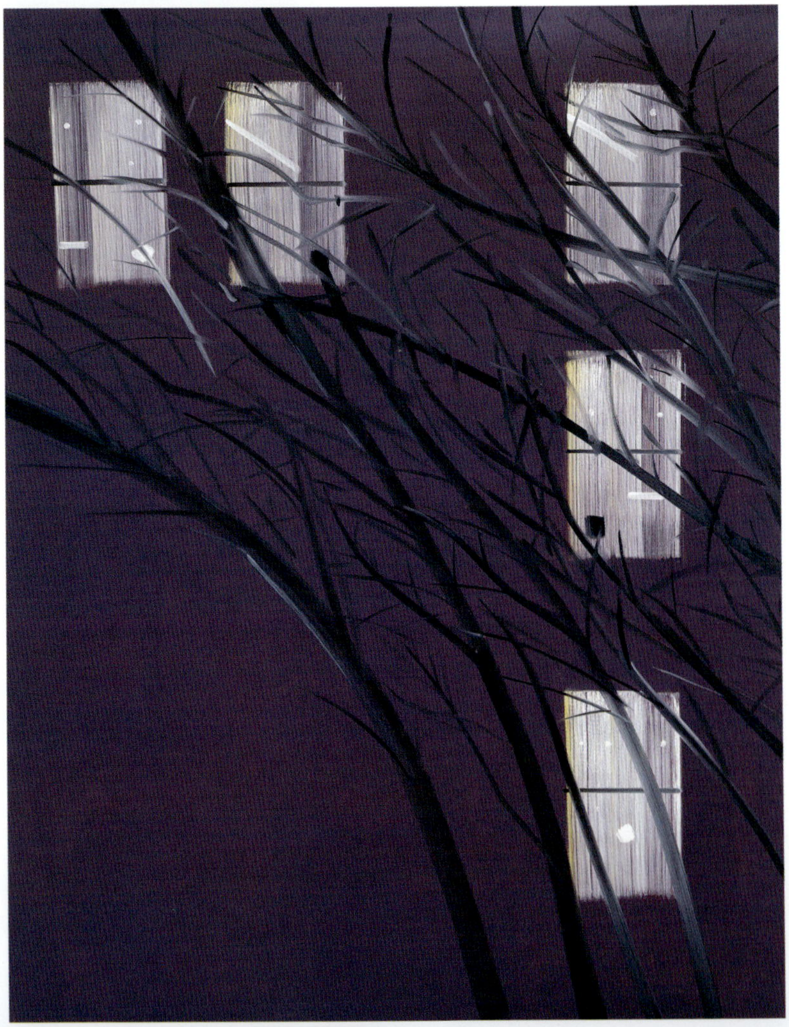

Alex Katz

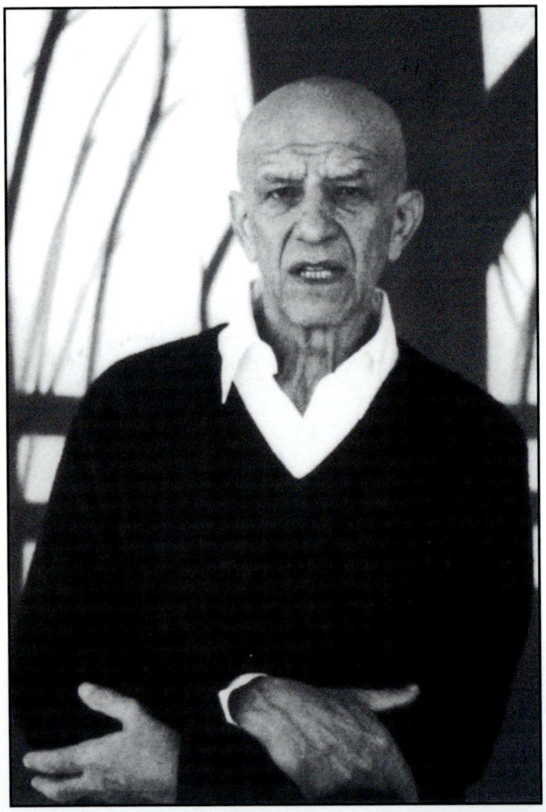

Photograph by Vivien Bittencourt. Courtesy Alex Katz Studio.

painting, to be the dominant function ... part of the thing of elegance, the look that New York painting has... big, not small or fussy. Pizzazz. ..."[115] He works from life but says (about those who use photographs), "The thing is to make an interesting painting. How you make it doesn't matter much."[116]

Accorded honors too numerous to list, Katz's works have been the subject of major exhibitions at the Marlborough, Robert Miller, and PaceWildenstein galleries in New York, the Whitney Museum of American Art, the Carnegie Museum of Art, Pittsburgh, the Baltimore Museum of Art, the Saatchi Collection, London, and the Addison Gallery of American Art at the Phillips Academy, Andover, Massachusetts, as well as many in Germany, Italy, Austria, and Spain.

Among his many honors and awards are his elected membership to the National Academy of Design and the establishment of the Alex Katz Visiting Chair in Painting at The Cooper Union Art School. Katz, who has taught at Pratt, Yale, and the New York Studio School, is represented by PaceWildenstein in New York.

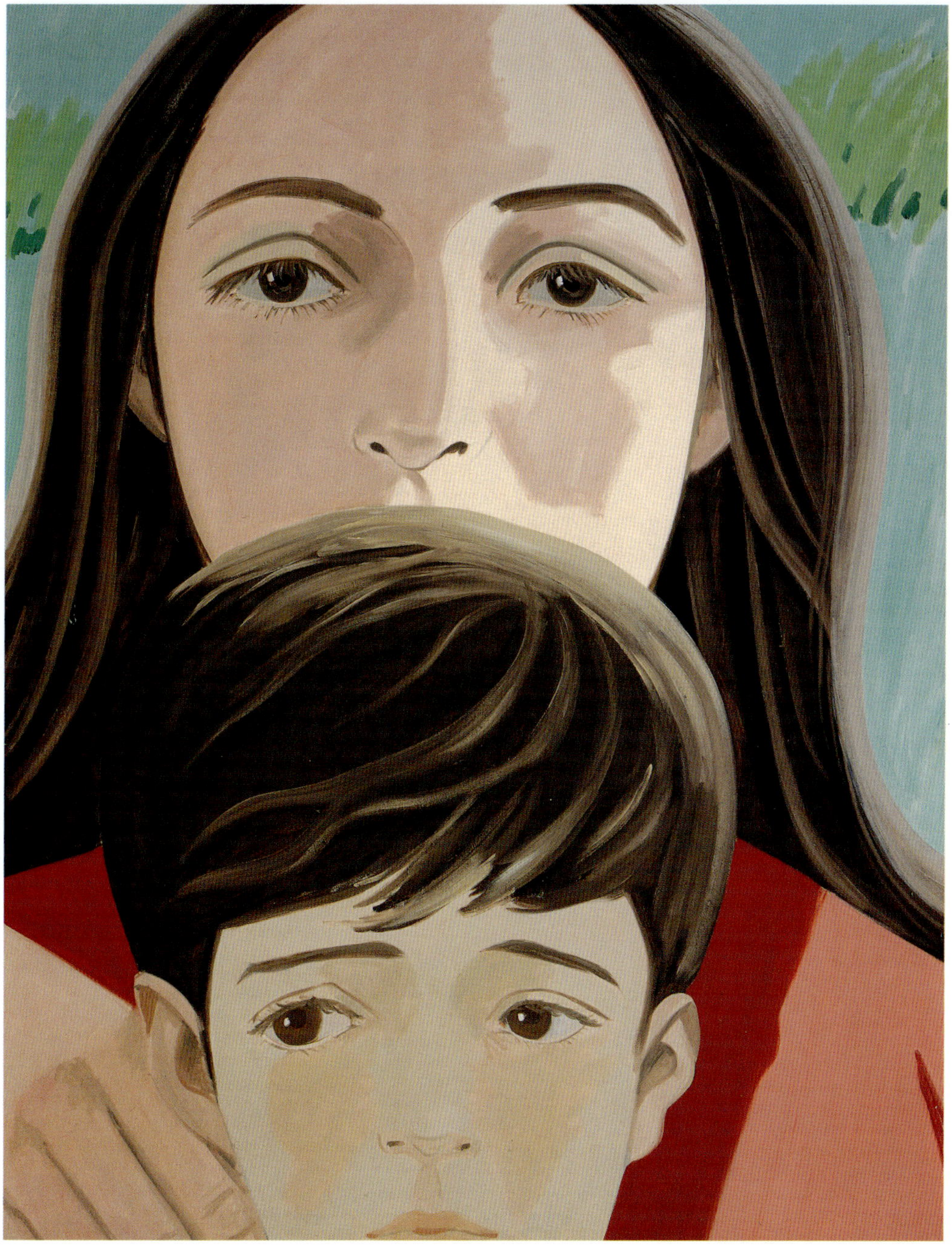

Ada and Vincent, oil on linen, 95" x 71", 1967. *Courtesy of Alex Katz Studio. All photographs by Oren Slor. All art © Alex Katz/Licensed by VAGA, New York, NY.*

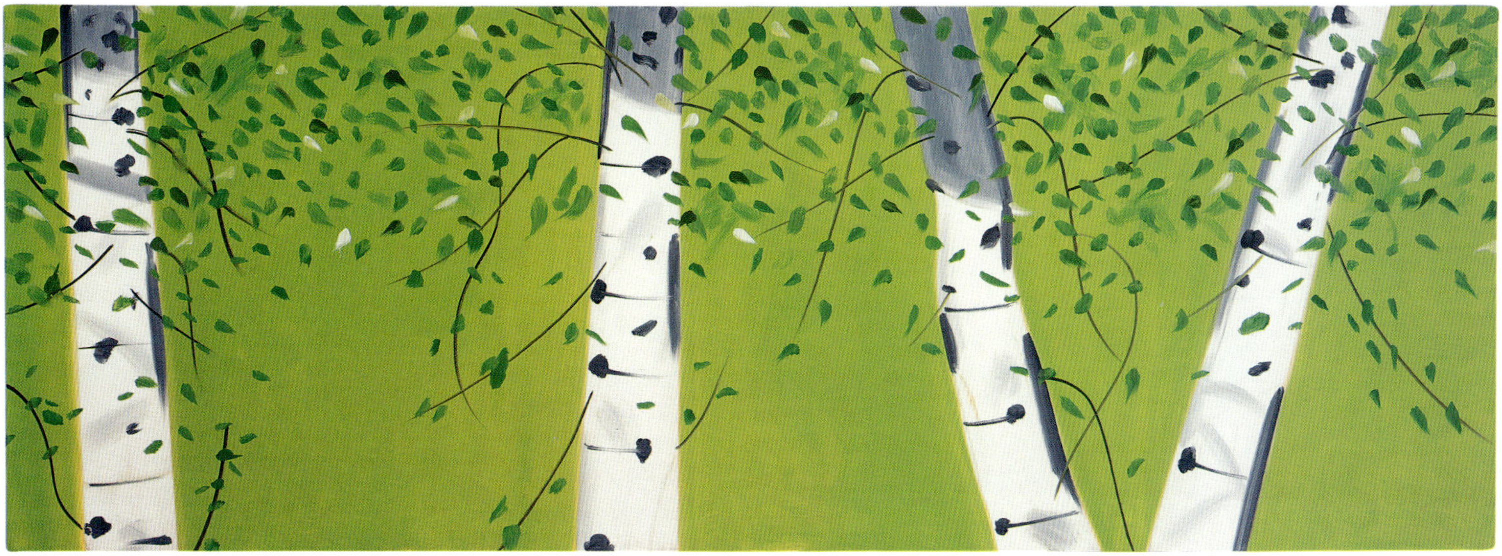

Four Birches, oil on linen, 60" x 180", 2004. *Courtesy of Alex Katz Studio.*

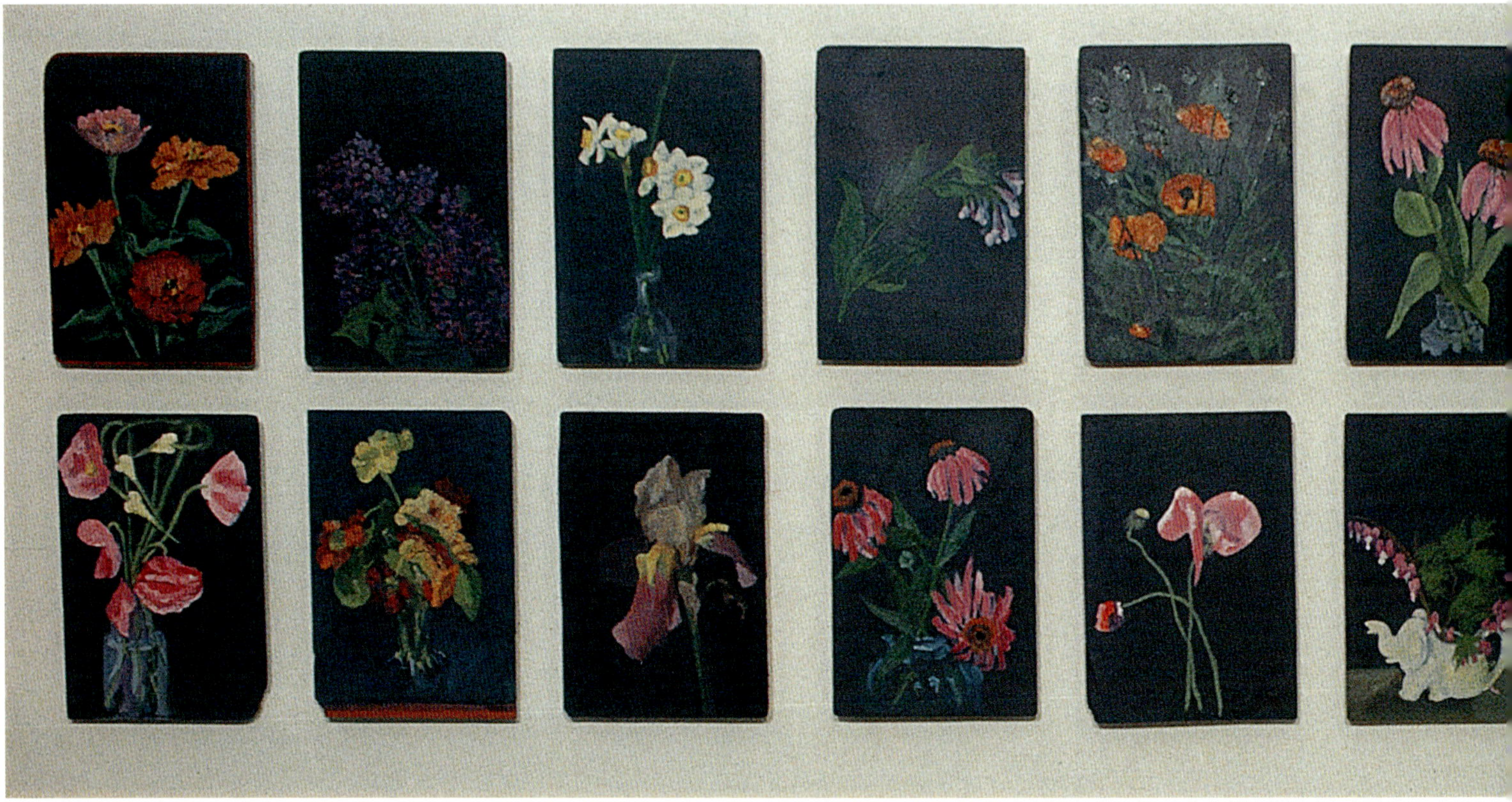

Flowers, eighteen oil on slate panels, each 12" x 8", c.2001-02. *Photograph by Sara English.*

Barbara Kulicke

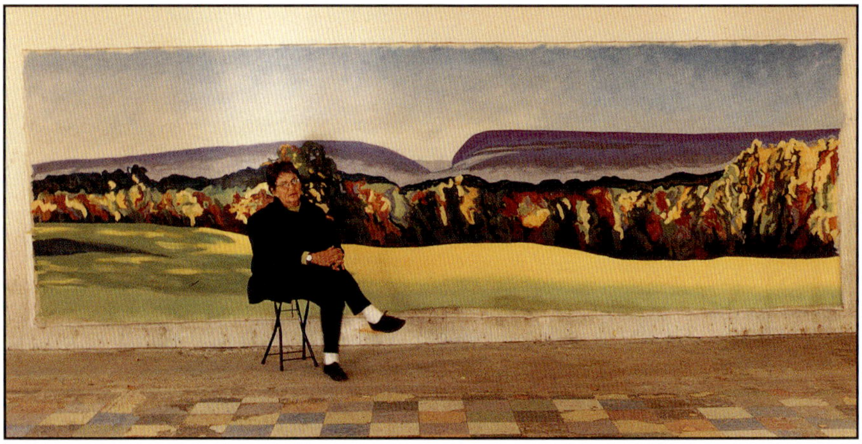

The artist and *Fall Gap* in gallery, oil on canvas, 6' x 18', 2001. *Photograph by Sara English.*

Barbara Kulicke, widely known as the co-founder of New York's Kulicke Framing Company, where she was able to study and work with images by such luminaries as Motherwell, de Kooning, and Franz Kline ("I framed them all"),[117] has spent many years painting multiple serial variations of several landscape views seen near her idyllic, country studio which "overlooks a small lake with a modest hill. . . ."[118]

Often painting on a panoramic scale, with minimal detail and broad, brushy, color-filled areas, Kulicke is as comfortable with small, individual units of landscape or flowers, painted in oils on panels of slate. She personally cultivates a wide variety of flowers, as a response to the Chinese saying, "To plant a garden is to believe in the future."[119]

Kulicke studied at the Tyler School of Fine Arts, Temple University, Philadelphia, as well as at Colorado College and Connecticut College. She has been the recipient of a New Jersey State Council of Arts Fellowship Award for Artistic Excellence and was commissioned by Bristol-Myers Squib to paint a thirteen-foot mural on slate. Her works have been seen in many one-person and group exhibitions, and are in numerous private collections, including those of Anita Shapolsky, George Braziller, Lois Dodd, and Andre Emmerich.

She is represented by the artist-run Prince Street Gallery in the Chelsea area of New York, which gives her "a great deal of freedom in my painting and selection of what to exhibit. . . ."[120]

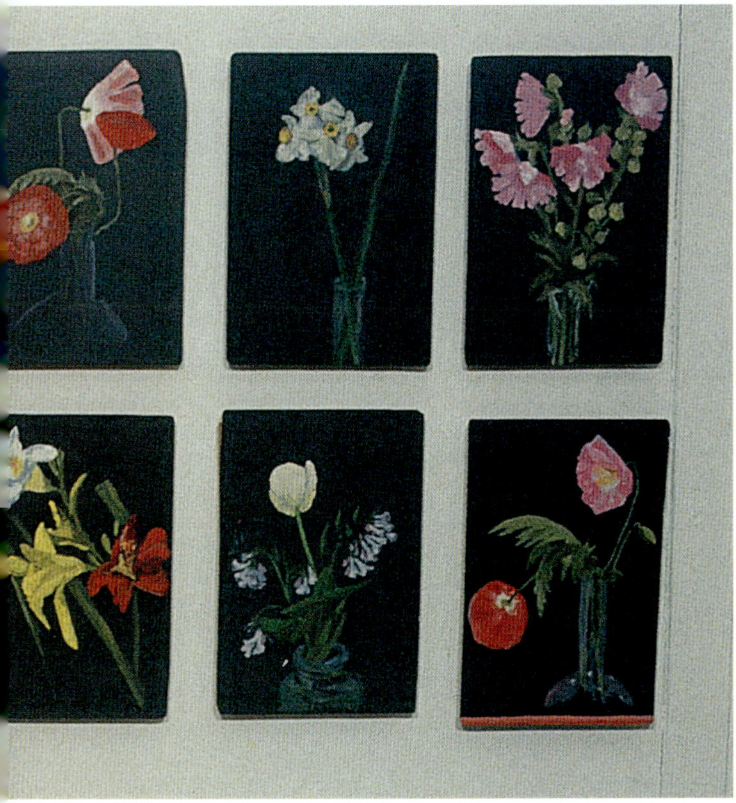

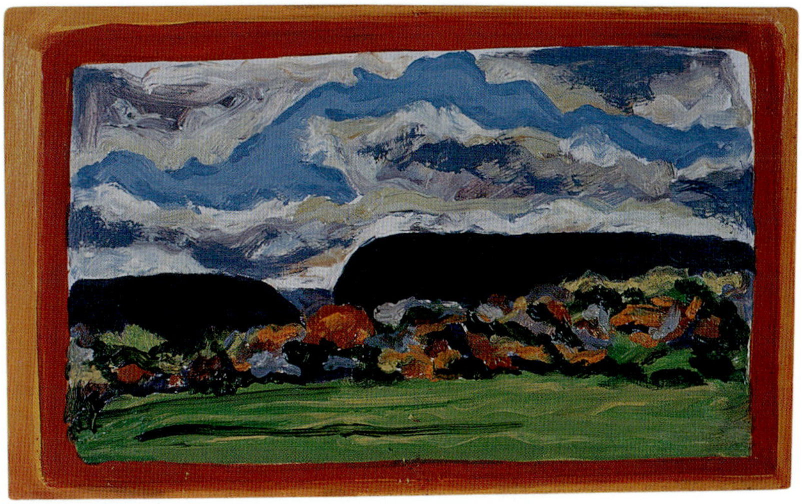

Fall Painting, oil on canvas, 9" x 18", 2003. *Photograph by Sara English.*

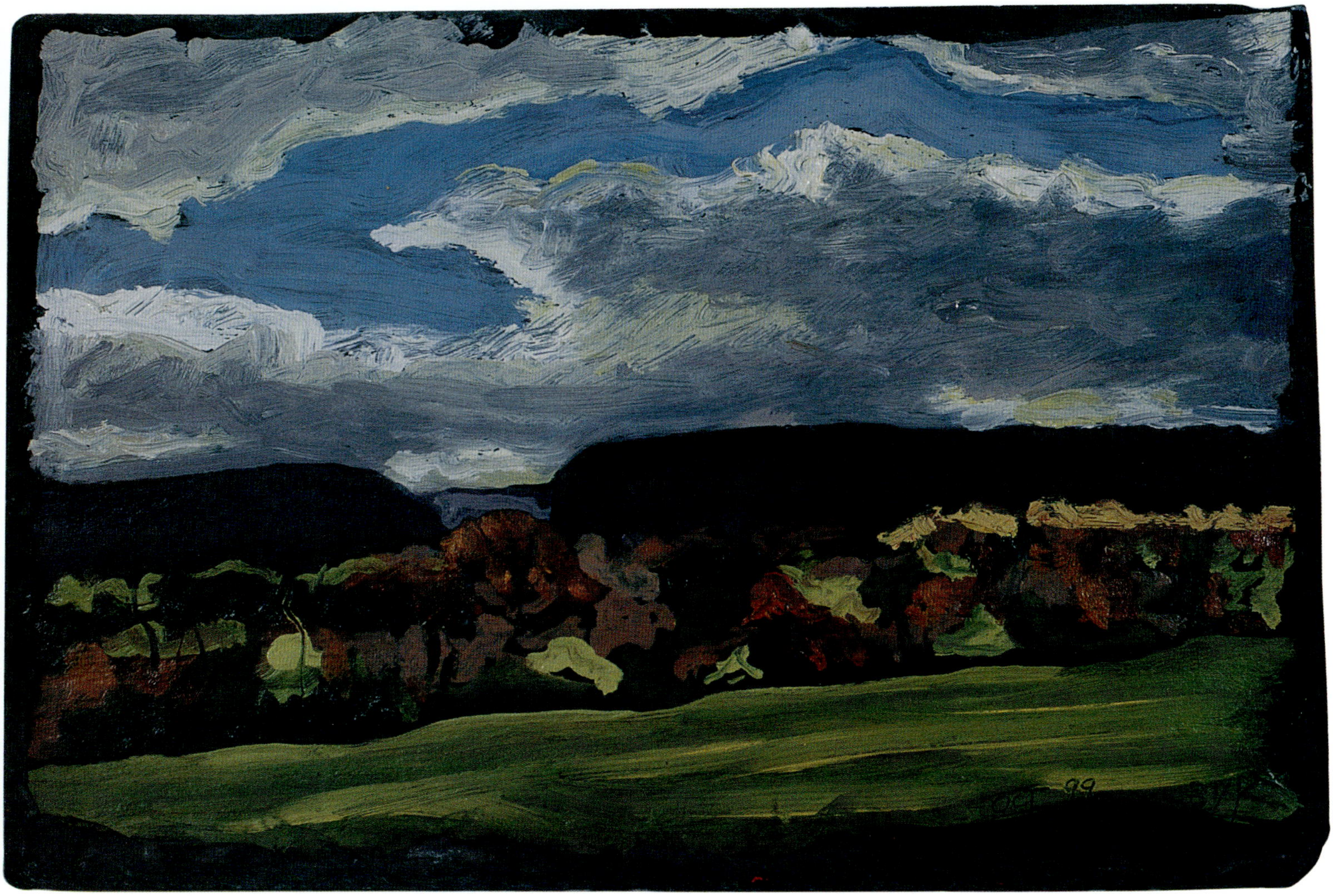

Fall Gap, oil on slate, 8" x 12", 2003. *Photograph by Sara English.*

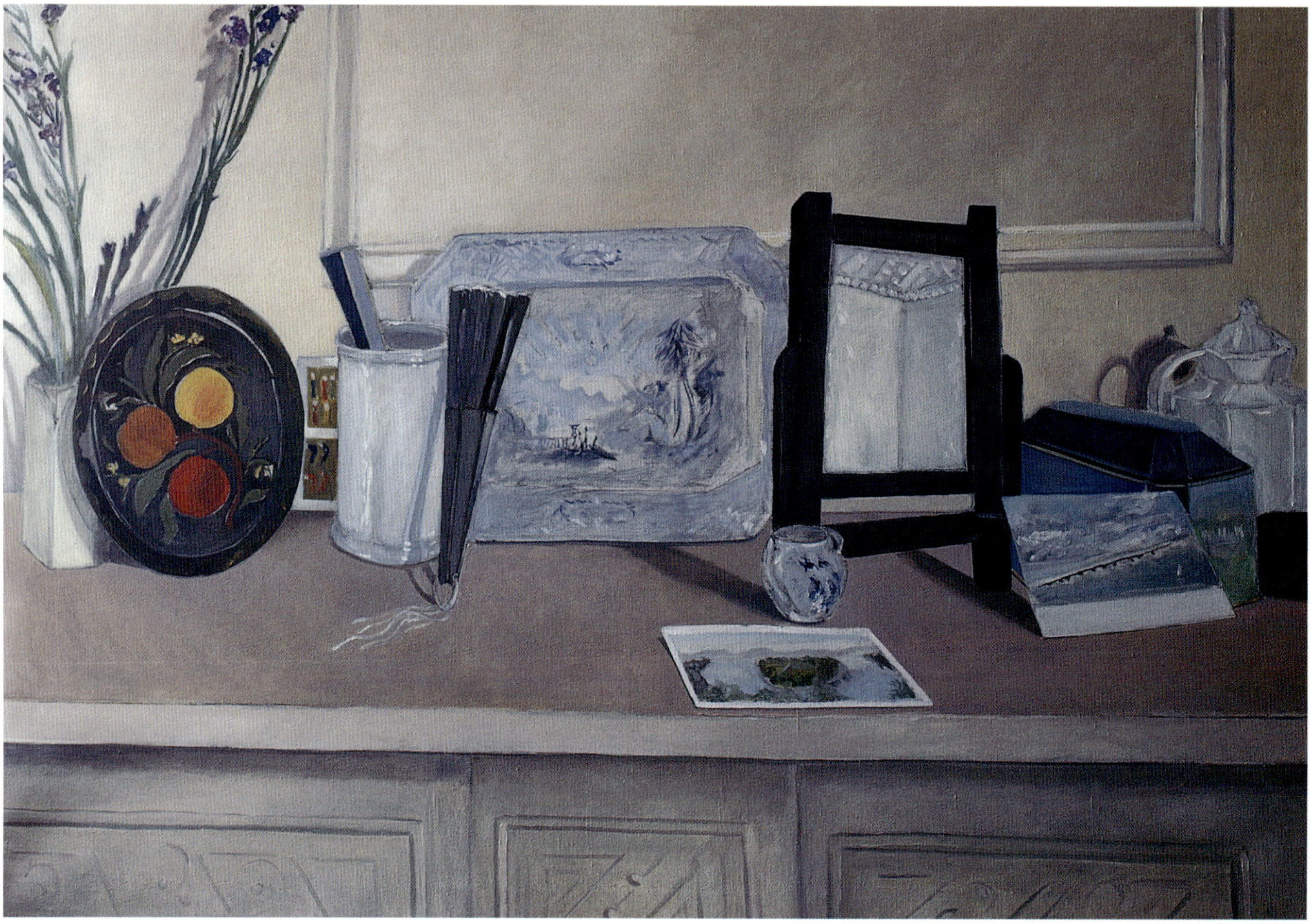

Still Life on Mantel, oil on canvas, 44" x 60", 1987.

Marion Lerner-Levine

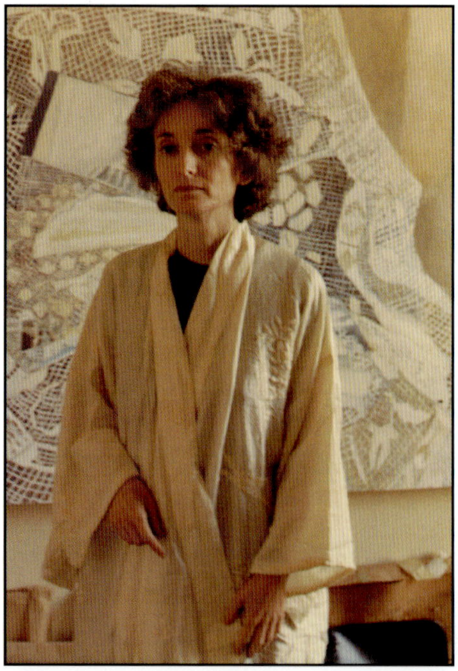

Photograph by Frances Siegal.

Marion Lerner-Levine, who paints "in the Realist tradition,"[121] began with landscapes and yardscapes but "soon developed a love of still-life, in which I try to convey a sense of the magic and mystery of objects."[122]

Lerner-Levine, born in London, graduated with honors from the School of the Art Institute of Chicago, where she studied painting and printmaking, and has since been awarded fellowships from the Yaddo Foundation, the Adolph and Esther Gottlieb Foundation, a CAPS Fellowship from the New York Foundation for the Arts, and a Painting Fellowship from the National Endowment for the Arts.

She has taught in the Brooklyn College Adult Education Program, the School of General Studies at U.C.L.A., and has been a visiting artist at the School of the Art Institute of Chicago. Her works have been exhibited in many New York galleries, and she is affiliated with Chelsea's artist-run Prince Street Gallery.

In her meticulously detailed "tablescapes,"[123] Lerner-Levine often uses an upended perspective and unconventional subjects from her many personal collections, frequently incorporating objects with type or printed pictures. Committed to painterly values, she says, " ... these are not actually 'trompe l'oeil,' as they are not tightly rendered ... and fail at illusionism, yet they suggest it.... I work toward an individual interpretation of still life space ... a profound re-vision of traditional visual ideals ... using objects as symbols of visual impressions and emotions. ... I paint from direct observation, but allow surreal elements into my work ... trying to transform still life into a poetic whole, turning description into interpretation."[124]

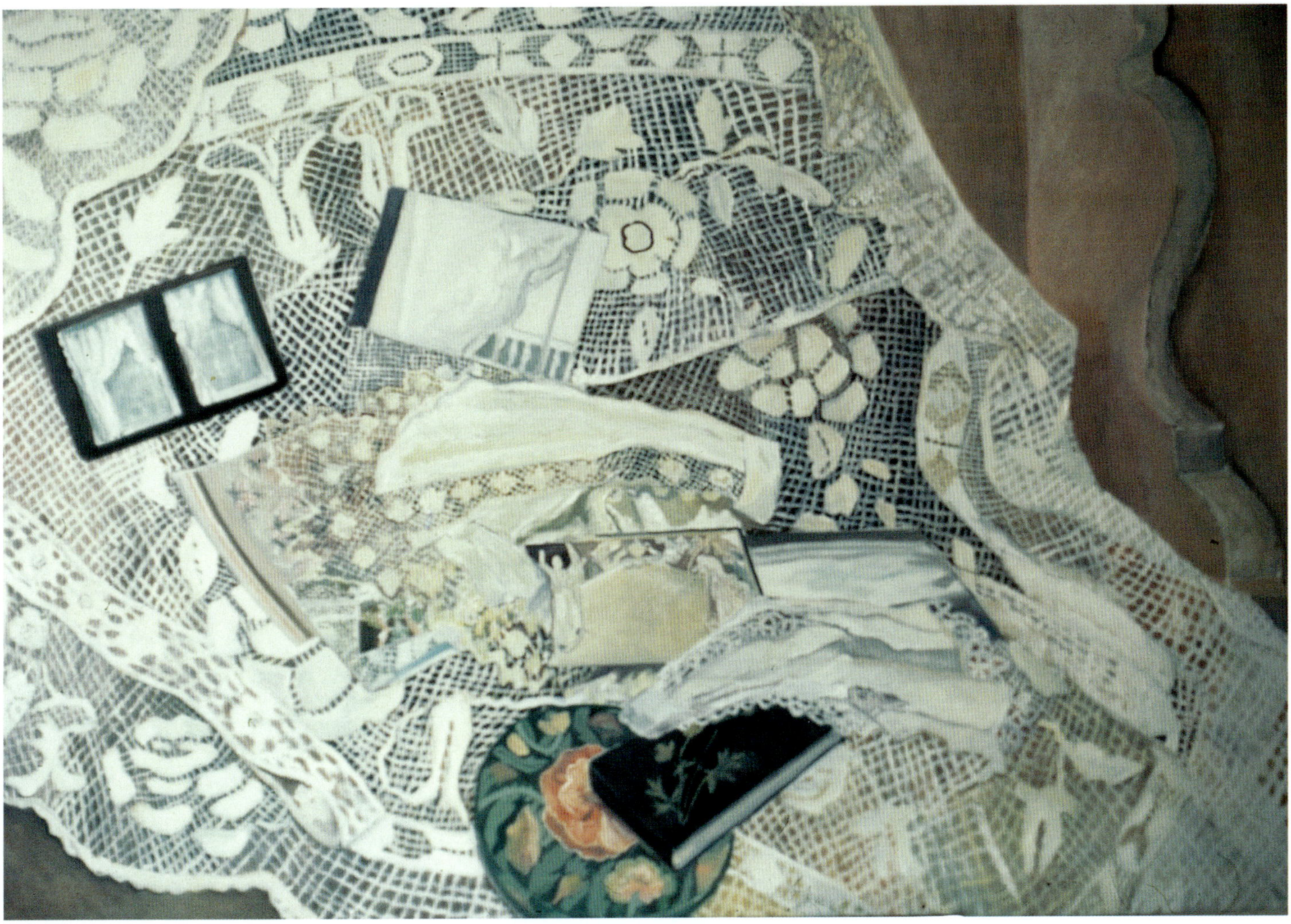

Lace on Lace, oil on canvas,
42" x 60", 1987.

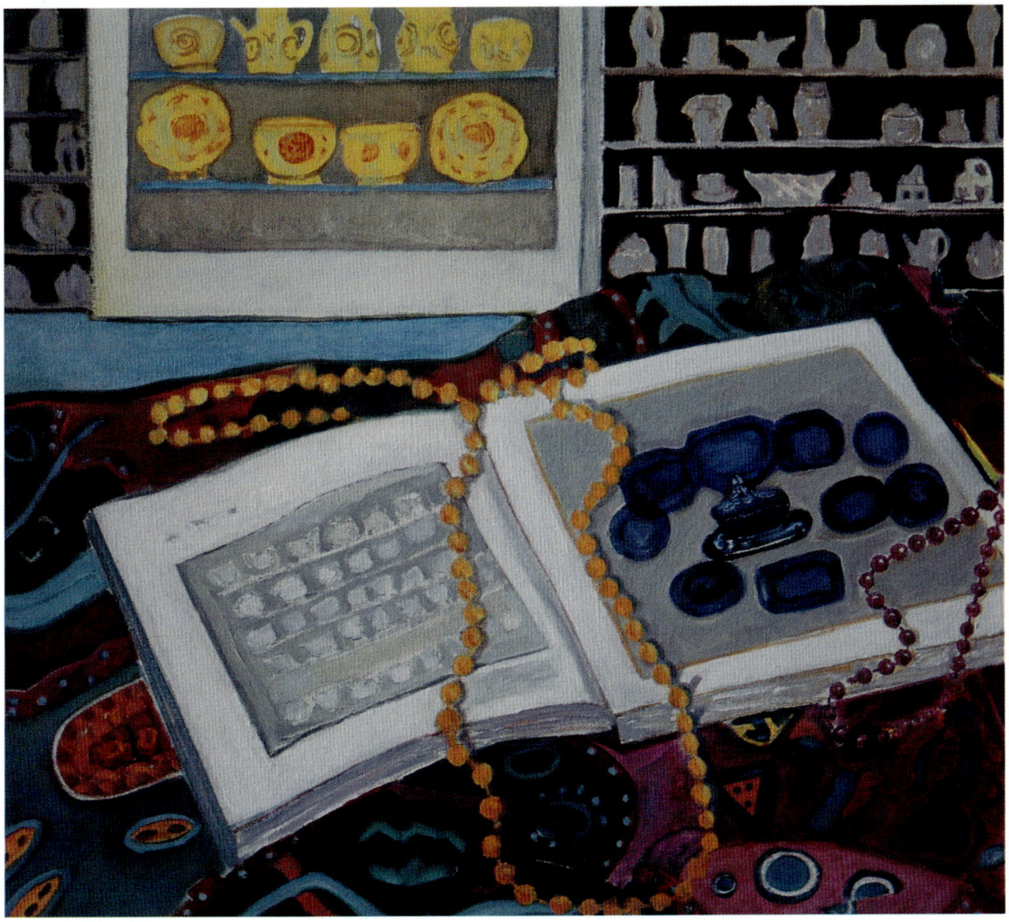

Beads, oil on canvas,
22" x 24", c. 2000-01.

Jack Levine

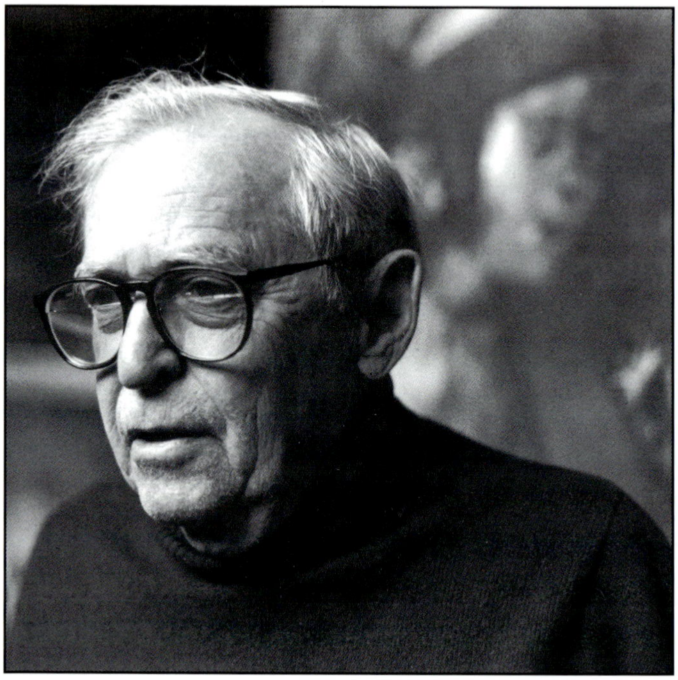

Courtesy of D C Moore Gallery.

Jack Levine, called America's foremost Social Realist painter, says his works are:

> ...an accumulation of improvisations. I add things until it is spoiled, cover everything and start over. ... Art with a social message, de rigueur in the 30s ... was considered passé by the 60s, but I ... had a commitment to sustain it ... with topics ... I needed to do. ... In the 70s it seemed as if that political motivation—that desire to satirize, to tweak the noses of the powers that be—had died in me ... but I [now] realize I was doing as much of that as I had ever done. ... I still believe I have some mission in life to say what I think about the world. And let the avant-garde go hang.[125]

A student of Dr. Denman Ross at Harvard, Levine was encouraged and supported in his early efforts; his first exhibition at Harvard's Fogg Art Museum was held when he was seventeen. Levine went on to work for the WPA, his paintings soon acquired by the Museum of Modern Art and the Metropolitan Museum of Art.

Levine's work has been seen in many solo and retrospective exhibitions at the Institute of Contemporary Art in Boston, the Phillips Collection, and the Whitney Museum of American Art, as well as New York's Jewish Museum. His paintings are in many major museums and private collections. He is an elected National Academy member and has been President of the American Academy of Arts and Letters.

Printmaking is also explored richly by Levine as a means to add his sophisticated commentary on our collective social, political, and spiritual lives. "I am primarily concerned with the condition of man," he says. " ...The satirical direction I have chosen is an indication of my disappointment in man. ... I have high expectations for the human race."[126]

Levine is represented by the D C Moore Gallery on Fifth Avenue in New York.

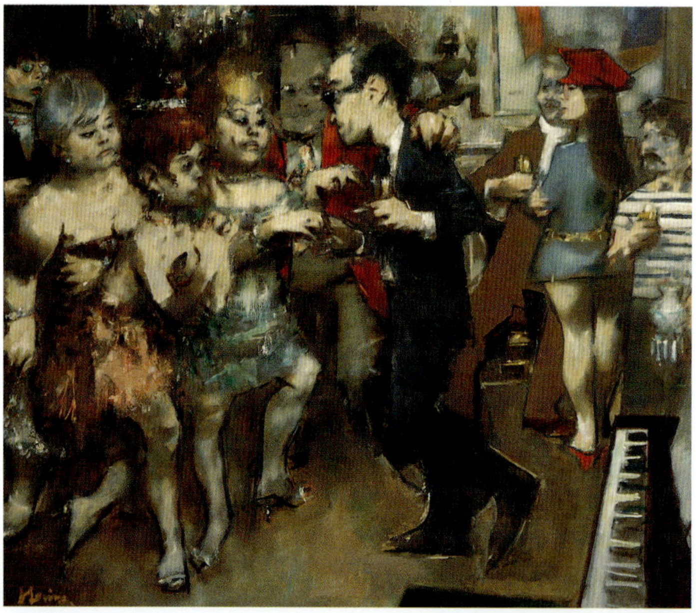

Self Portrait at Westchester Party, oil on canvas, 41" x 47", 1971. *Courtesy of D C Moore Gallery.*

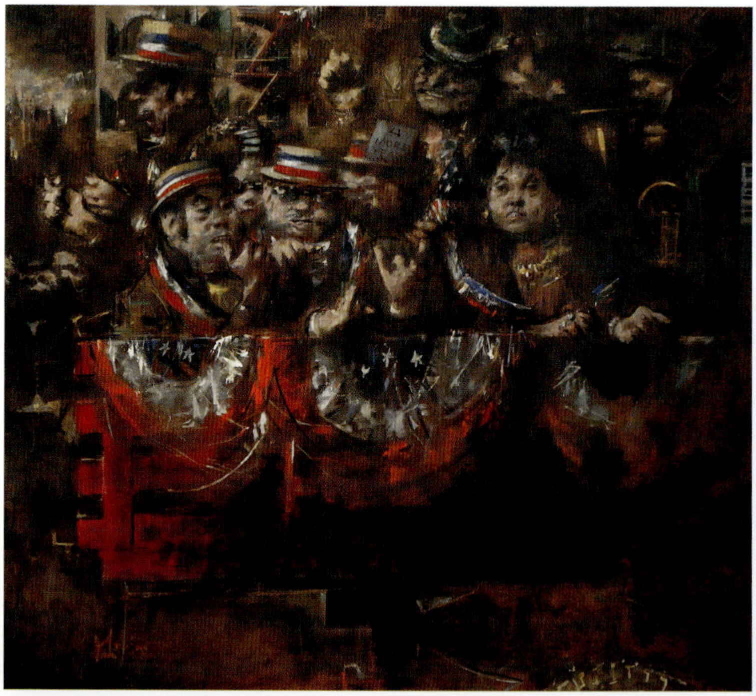

Bandwagon (Four More Years), oil on canvas, 84" x 90", 1973. *Courtesy of D C Moore Gallery.*

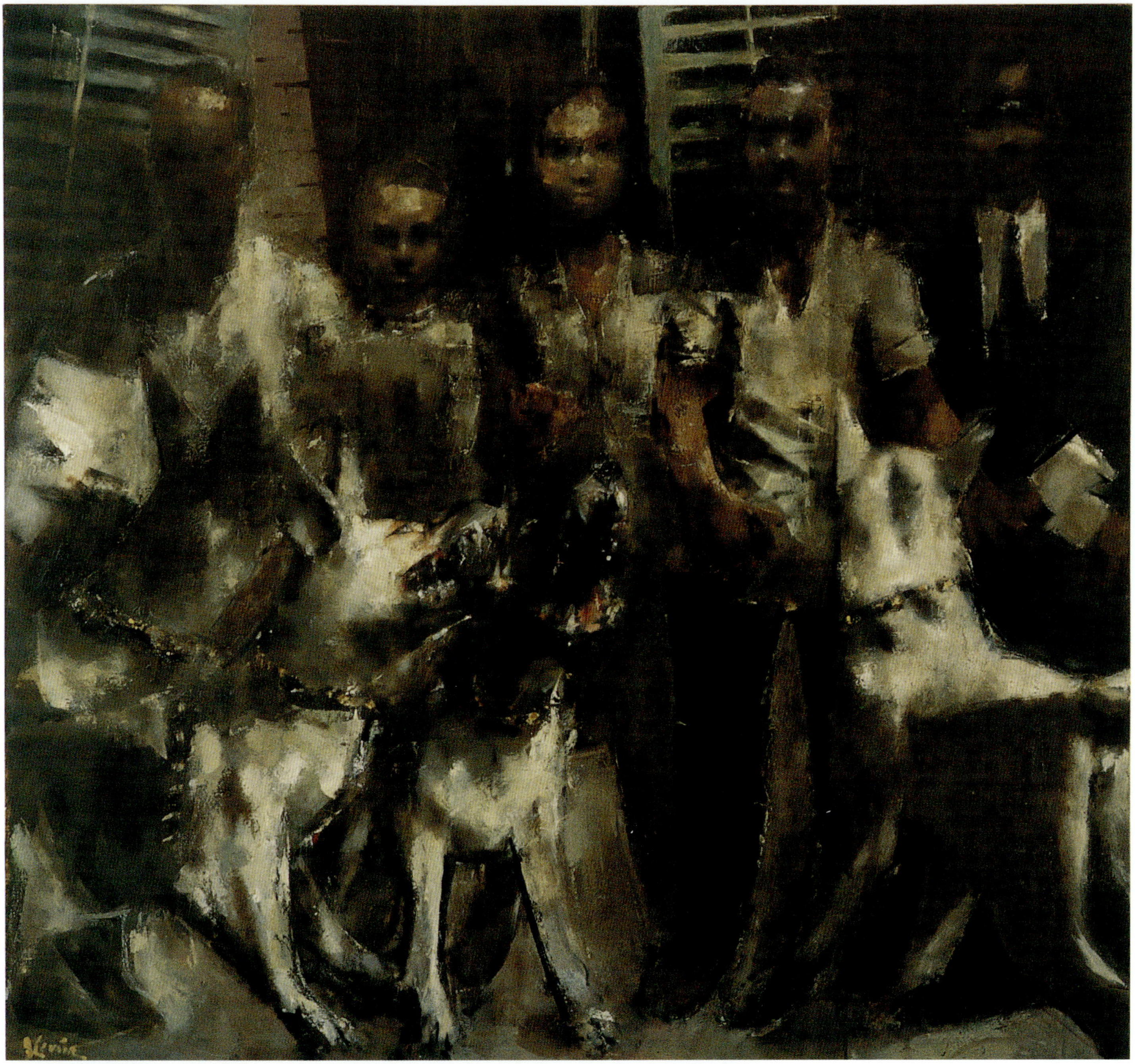

Birmingham, oil on canvas, 71" x 75.5", 1963. *Courtesy of D C Moore Gallery. All art © Jack Levine/Licensed by VAGA, New York, NY.*

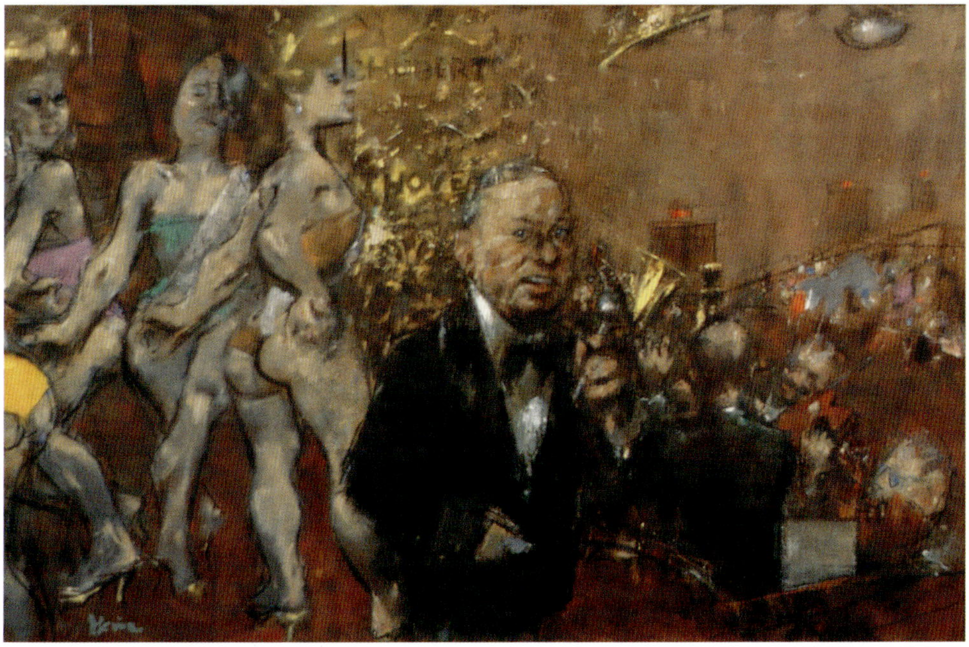

Orpheus in Vegas, oil on canvas, 40" x 60", 1984. *Courtesy of D C Moore Gallery.*

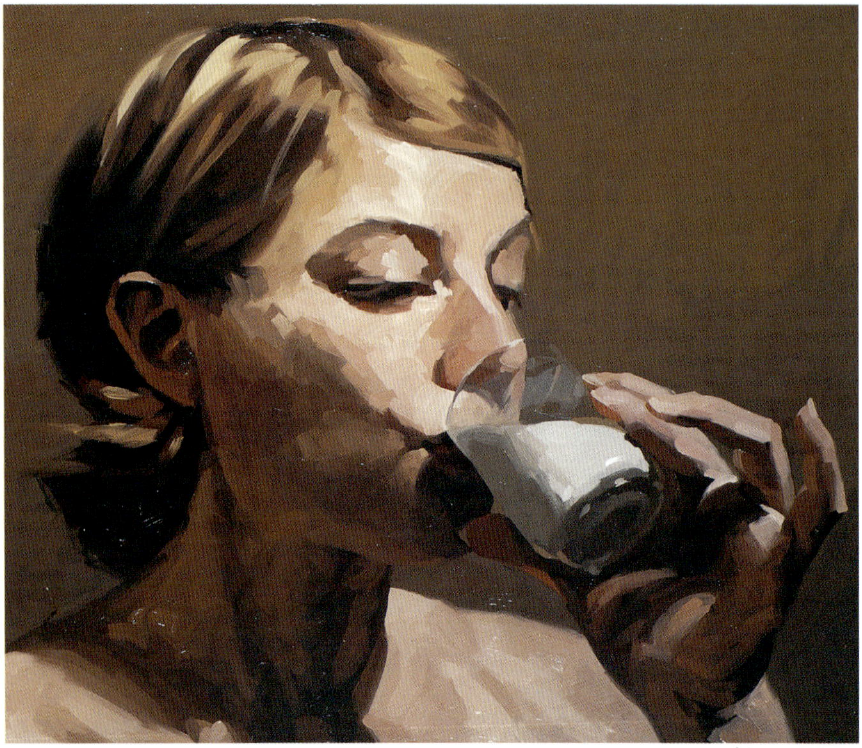

Lindsay Drinking Milk, oil on panel, 35" x 40", 2004. *Courtesy of Allen Sheppard Gallery*.

Dik Liu

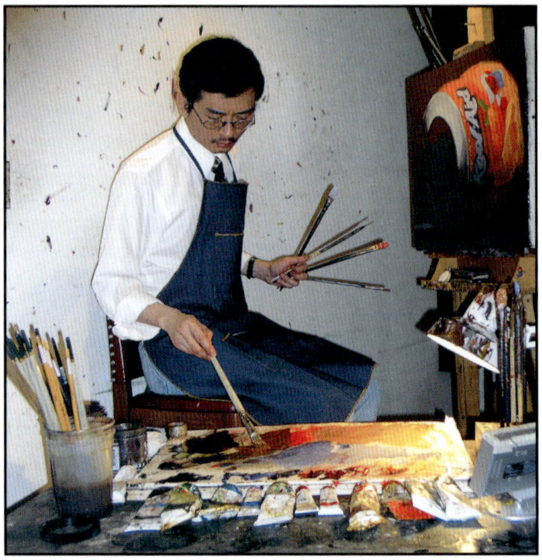

Courtesy of the artist.

Dik Liu, an MFA graduate of Yale University's School of Art and a BFA recipient from Boston's Massachusetts College of Art, has devoted much of his time to teaching painting and color at the Brooklyn Campus of Long Island University, the Parsons School of Design, the Fashion Institute of Technology, Fairleigh Dickinson University, Hofstra University, The Cooper Union's School of Extended

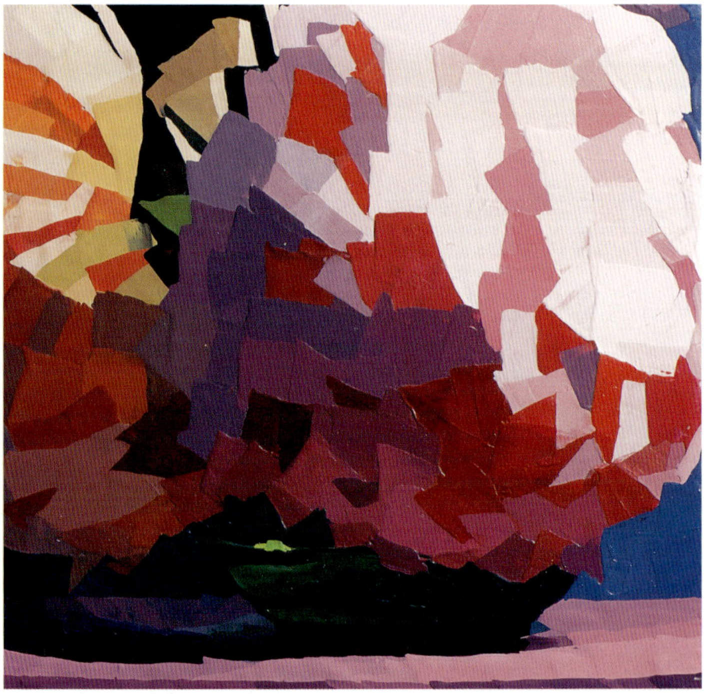

Flower Covering Vase, oil on panel, 12" x 12", 2002. *Private collection*.

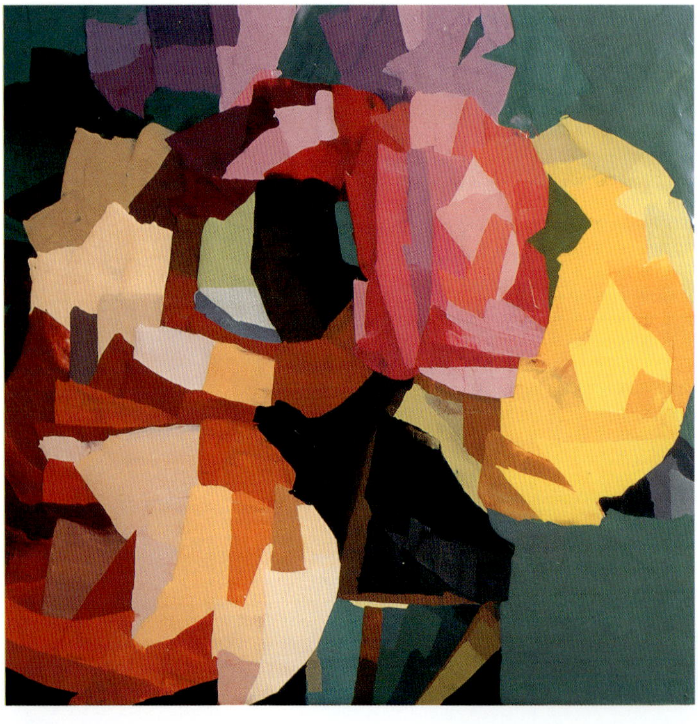

Three Flowers on a Green Ground, oil on panel, 12" x 12", 2002. *Private collection*.

Studies, and, while at Yale, as a teaching assistant to Bernard Chaet.

His many exhibitions include regular showings at the Allen Sheppard Gallery and several annual exhibitions of the National Academy of Design.

Liu loves seeing, and paints to depict the sensation of seeing different colors and textures: flowers, fruits, glass, metal. Heeding the words of the poet, Ezra Pound, he says, "I paint to make it new ... to reinvent realistic painting anew, by seeing the world fresh. I use slabs of color not to depict the world but [its] imprints on my retinal wall ... I paint

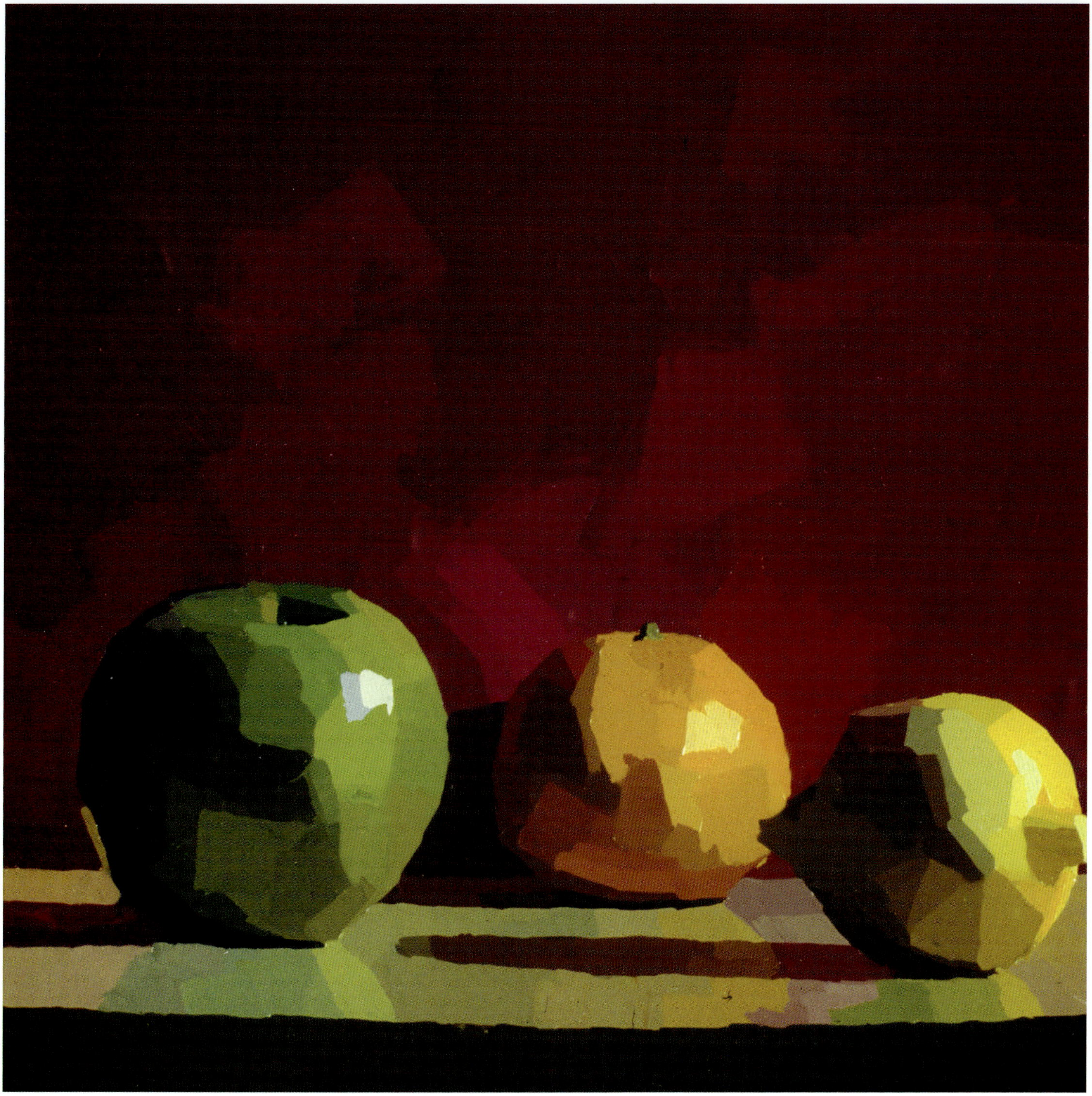

Three Fruits on a Burgundy Ground, oil on panel, 12" x 12", 2000. *Private collection.*

realistically by … mimicking … retinal sensations to make realism anew and to renew with it our expectation of seeing, itself." Liu adds, "I replicate retinal excitements by pumping the hues to a Technicolor intensity, [to] match the saturated light I see. … Then, I place slabs of these hues onto my paintings, condensing the objects to a few palette knife strokes. I abridge the realism of light and space to its marrow."[127]

More recently, Liu has expanded to include other subject matter in his repertoire, such as models in the act of eating and still life compositions of junk food, in his never-ending search for new visual sensation.

Vincent Longo

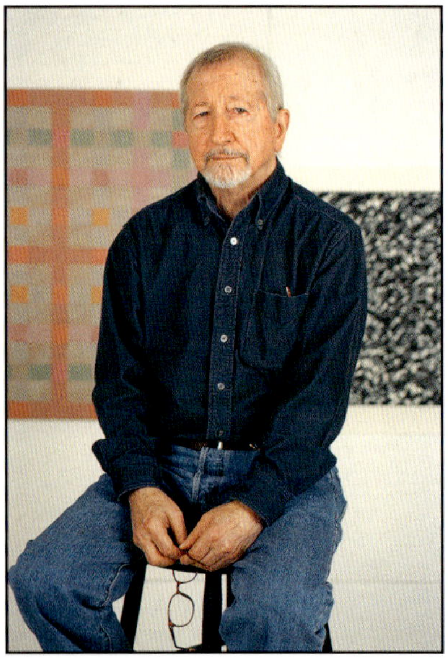

Photograph by Jean Vong.

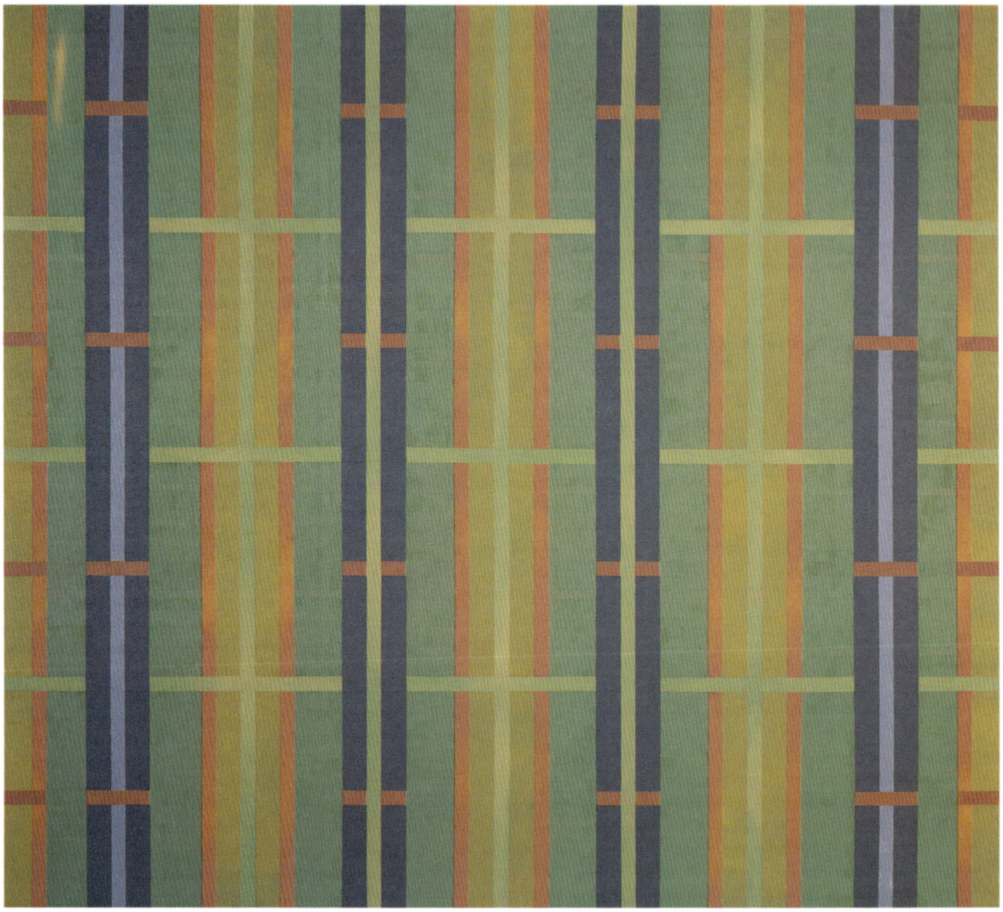

Lattice: 3 x 4, acrylic on canvas, 60" x 66", 1999. *Courtesy of the artist.*

Vincent Longo creates paintings that "balance the geometry of the grid and ... the lyrical structures of color, ... achieve perfection, yet startle at the same time. The eye is dazzled ... yet there is no ... trickery. The craftsmanship is flawless, but it is the gift for chromatic grace that moves us,"[128] says Hilton Kramer in *The New York Times*.

Longo, a retired professor at Hunter College, has been called one of the last of the great abstract painter/printmakers who emerged during the late 1940s and 1950s. A native New Yorker, he was graduated from The Cooper Union, and later studied at the Brooklyn Museum Art School with Max Beckmann and Ben Shahn. He taught at the Brooklyn Museum Art School and Bennington College, then at Hunter College for almost thirty-five years.

Recipient of many awards, notably a John Simon Guggenheim Memorial Fellowship and an NEA Grant, Longo is an elected member of the National Academy of Design and a member of the American Abstract Artists.

Longo's work has been exhibited widely and may be found in many major art museums, such as the Metropolitan Museum of Art, the Solomon R. Guggenheim Museum, the Brooklyn Museum, and the Museum of Modern Art in New York, the Yale University Art Gallery in New Haven, and the Victoria and Albert Museum in London.

In New York, his work is to be seen at the Wooster Arts Space in the Soho area, and in Amagansett at Butler's Fine Art.

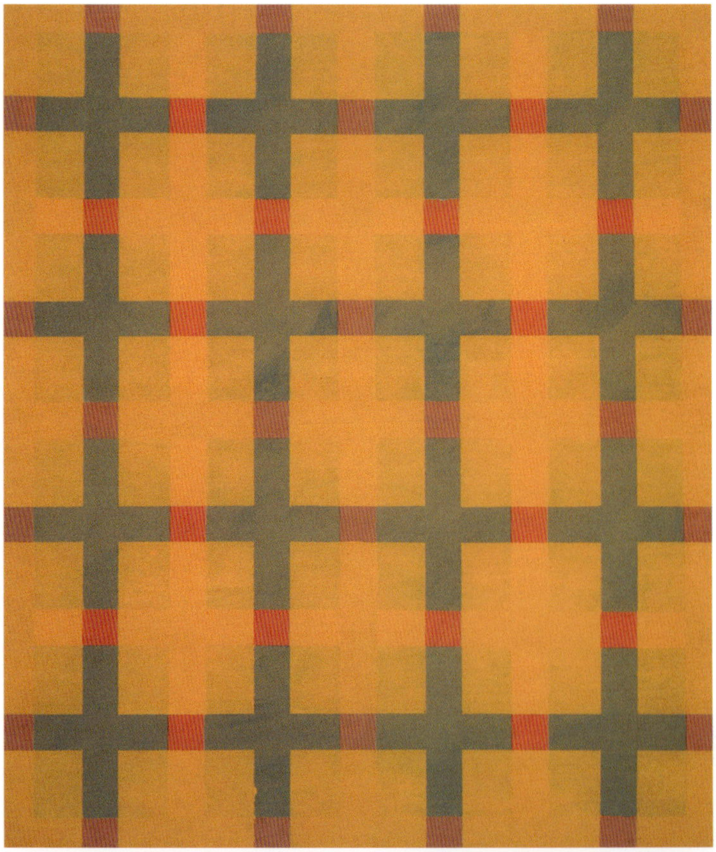

Red Check Yellow, acrylic on wood, 24" x 20", 2003. *Courtesy of the artist.*

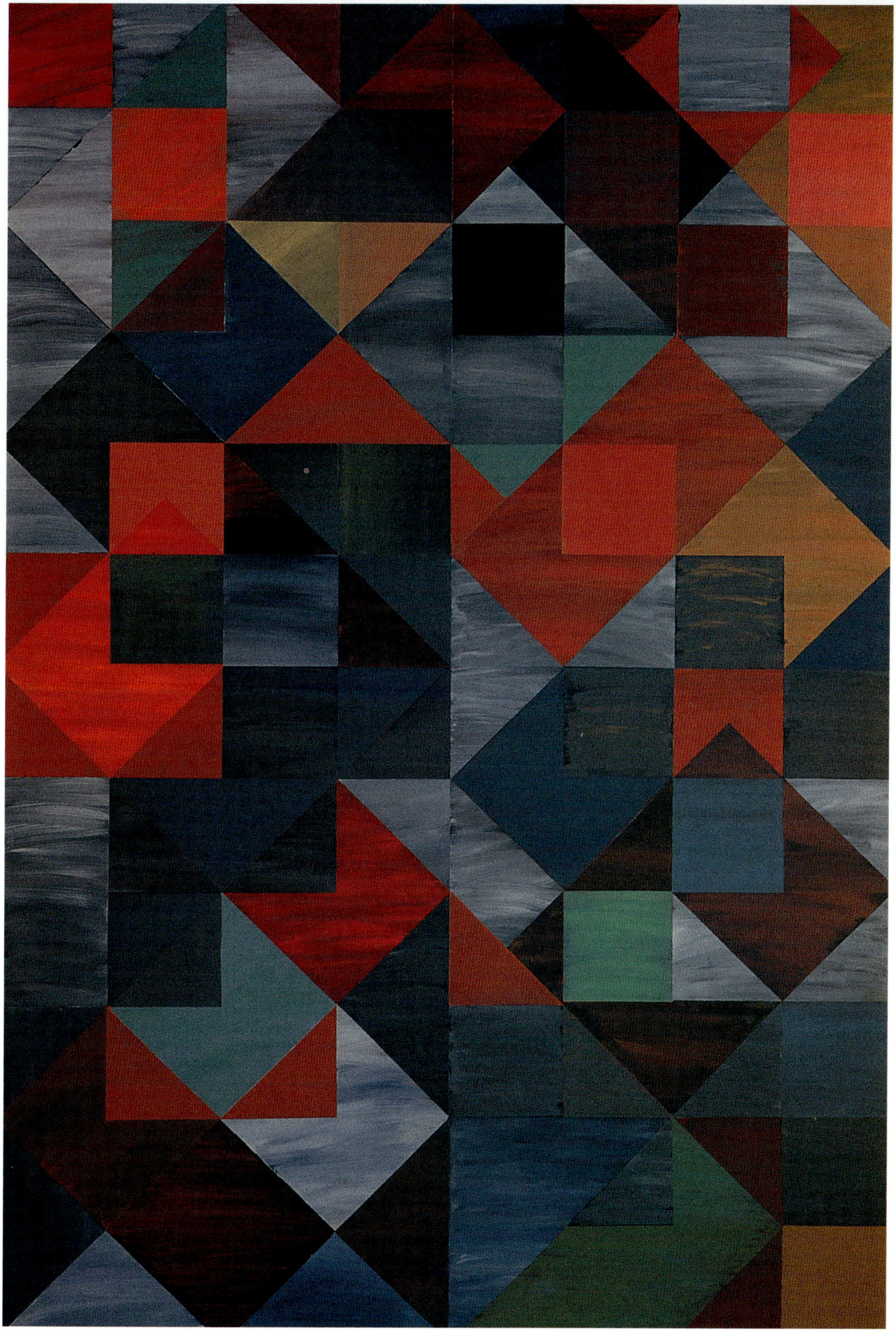

Through the Lattice, acrylic on wood, two panels: 72" x 48", 1988. *Courtesy of the artist.*

Robert Mangold

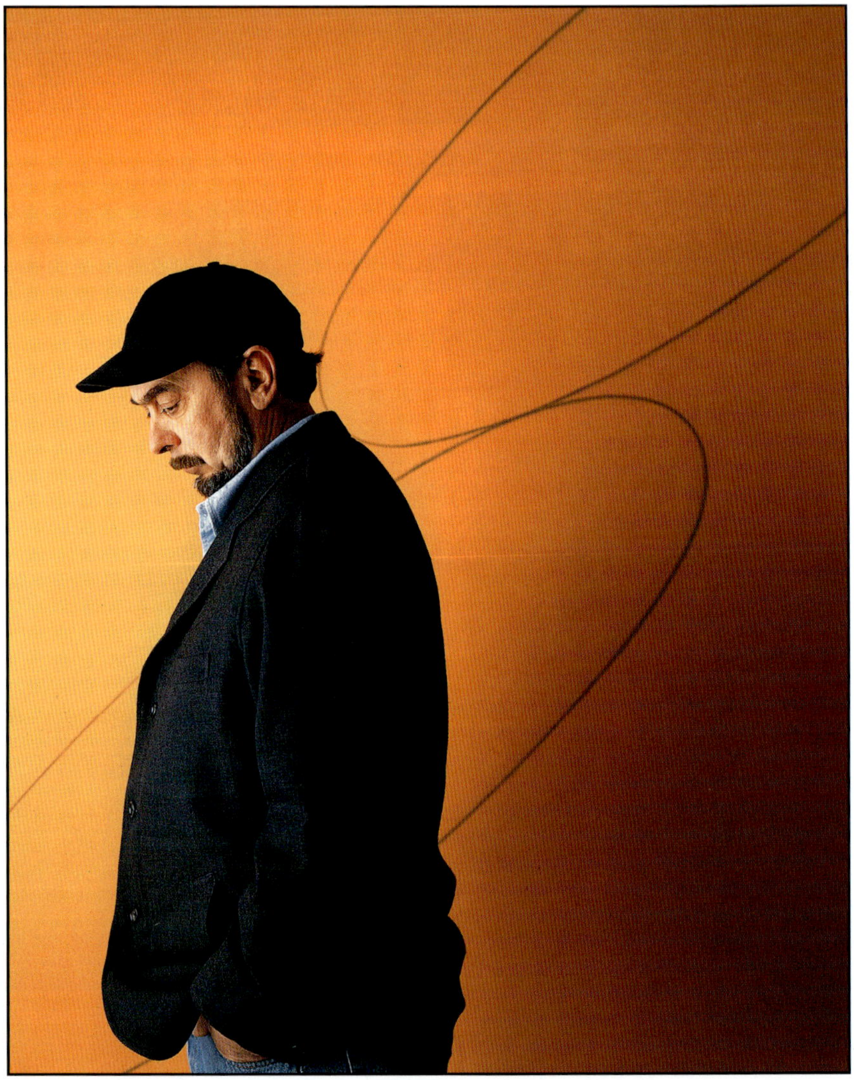

Photograph by Todd Eberle. Courtesy of PaceWildenstein.

Robert Mangold began working in his distinctive Minimalist style in the mid 1960s, just after he received his second degree, an MFA, from the Yale University School of Art and Architecture. His large, often shaped canvases (called "eccentric geometries"[129] in a BBC world service program) have been the subject of major museum exhibitions and retrospectives.

His exploration of the relationship between color and shape focuses on a painting's boundary, color, and linear elements. He has said that most art, which questions the nature of its medium, is really about communication, and has the power to transcend culture.[130]

Mangold has taught at the School of Visual Arts, and received a John Simon Guggenheim Memorial Fellowship award, among others.

Among his numerous museum exhibitions are the first major exhibition of Minimalist paintings at the Jewish Museum, plus exhibitions at the Solomon R. Guggenheim Museum in New York, the Museum of Contemporary Art in San Diego, and the Stedelijk Museum in Amsterdam.

Mangold has had paintings included in a Whitney Museum of American Art Biennial, a Venice Biennale, and over 125 American and European exhibitions, and has been the subject of a catalogue raisonné. His works in painting and printmaking are in major museum collections around the world.

Married to a Yale classmate, the painter Sylvia Plimack, he is a trustee of Yale University and a member of the American Academy of Arts and Letters. He is represented by PaceWildenstein.

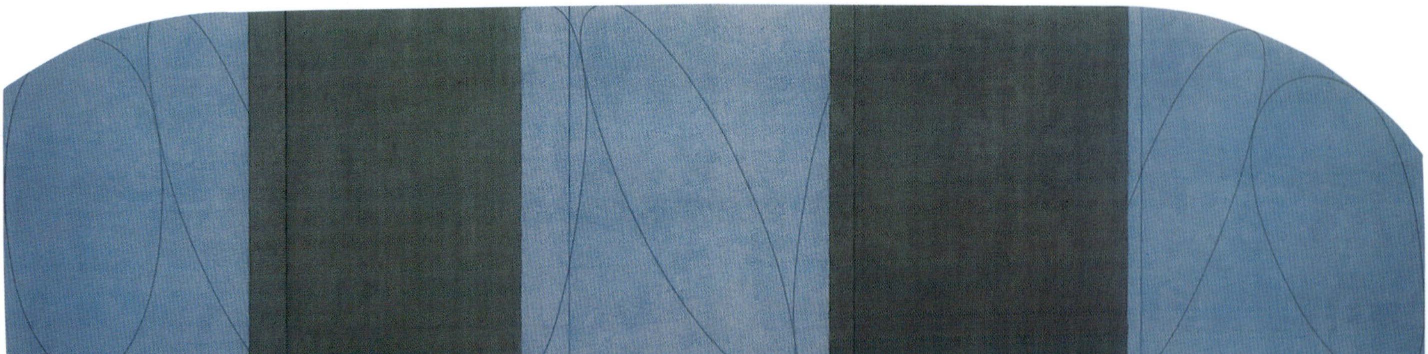

Blue/Black Five Panel Zone Painting, acrylic and black pencil on canvas, 90" x 27' 6", 1998.
All art © Robert Mangold and ARS, New York. Courtesy of PaceWildenstein.

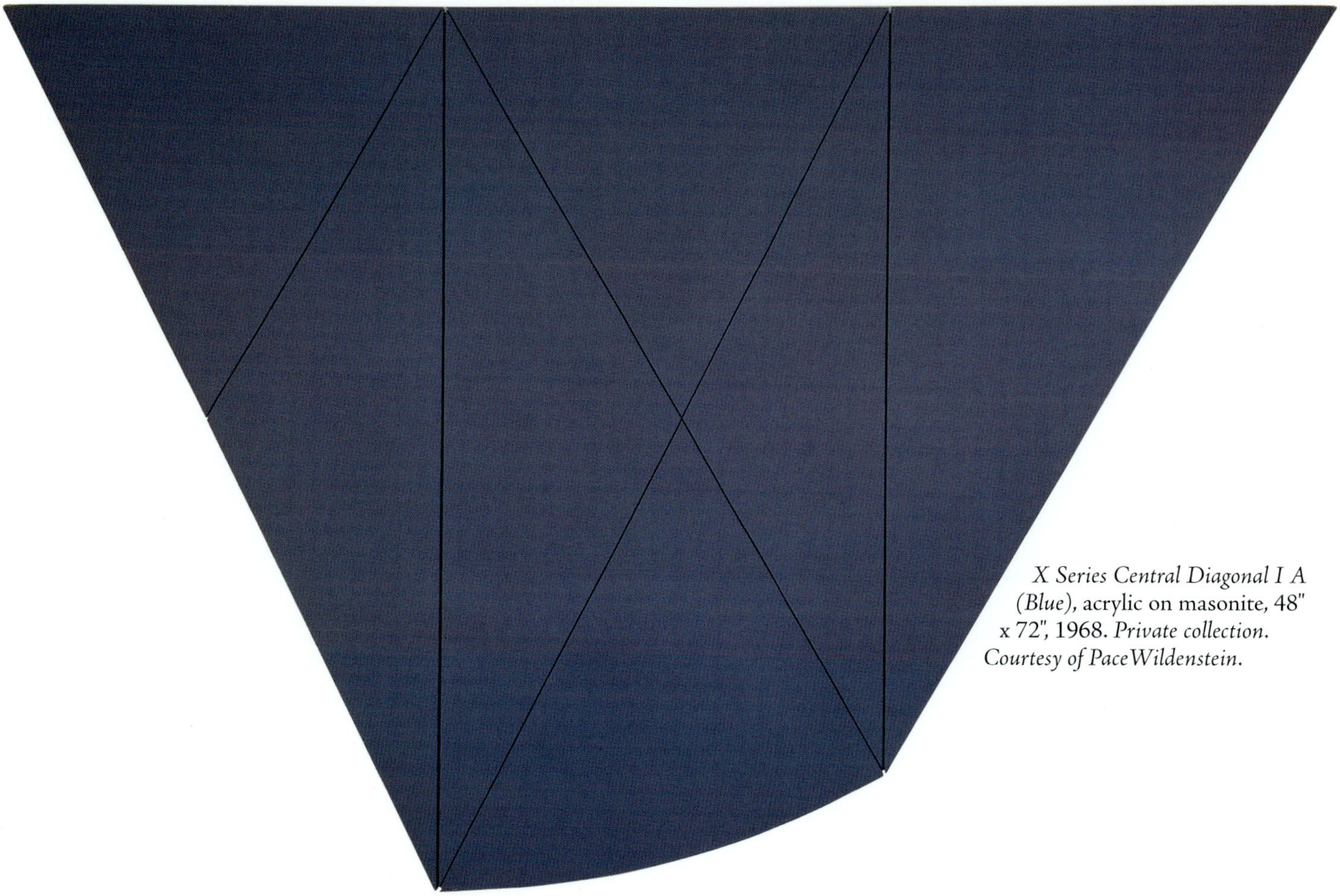

X Series Central Diagonal I A (Blue), acrylic on masonite, 48" x 72", 1968. *Private collection. Courtesy of PaceWildenstein.*

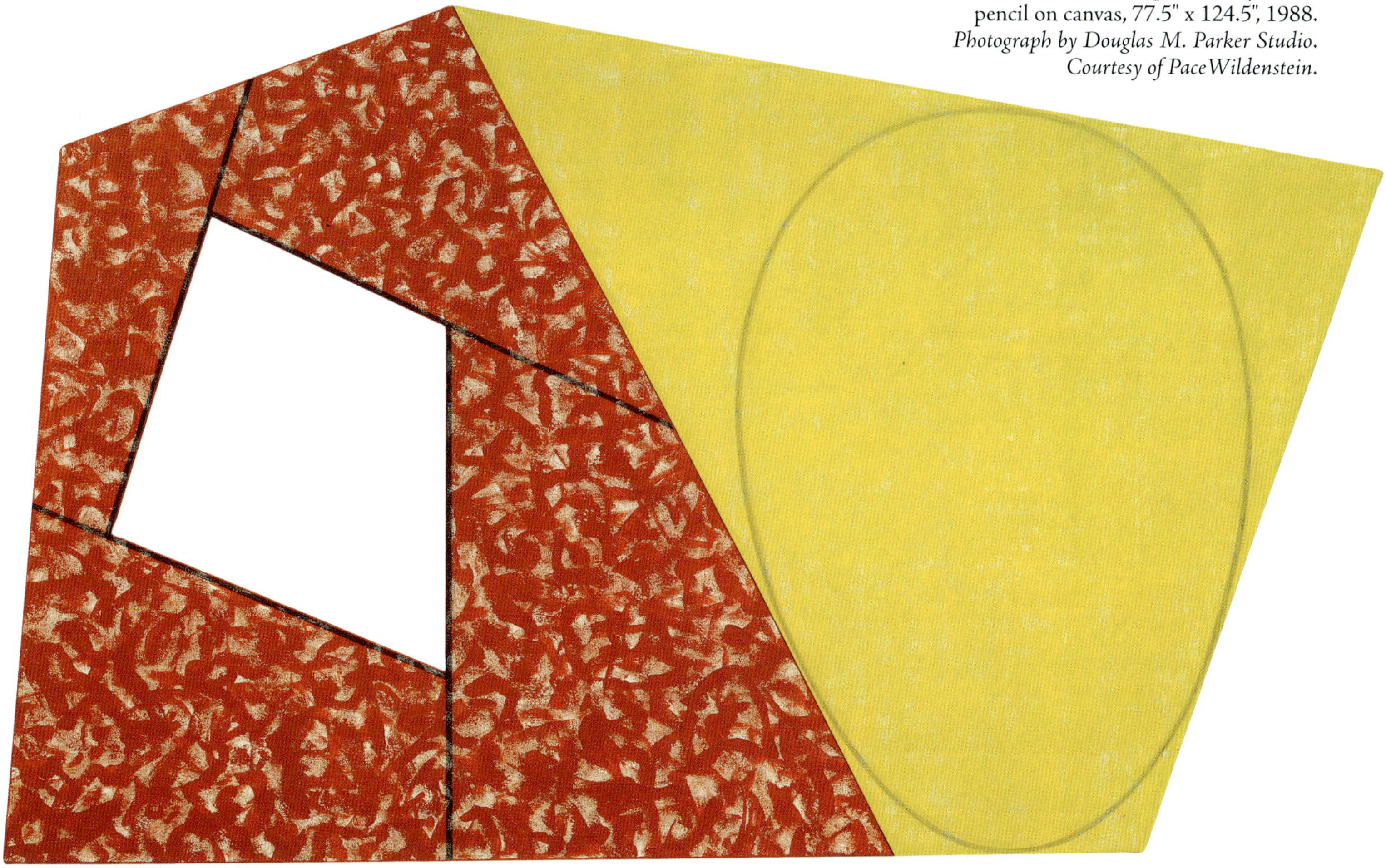

Red Frame / Yellow Ellipse #2, acrylic and pencil on canvas, 77.5" x 124.5", 1988. *Photograph by Douglas M. Parker Studio. Courtesy of PaceWildenstein.*

Helene K. Manzo

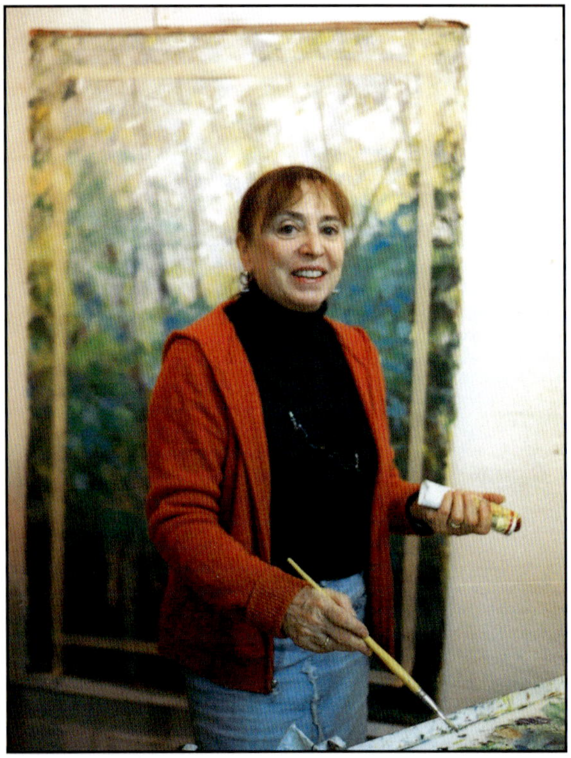

Photograph © Cynthia Dantzic

Helene K. Manzo, recipient of two residencies at the Vermont Studio Center, says all her work "starts with an observed landscape. The concentration required in looking ... and questioning the appearance of objects, along with history, literature, intuition and emotion, helps me interpret my experience and feelings visually. Mark-making and color set the ... mood. Through the palette ... the subtlety and power of a simple hue. ... the paintings evolve from a totally observed landscape to one of feelings, dreams ... memory."[131]

A graduate of New York University and Pratt Institute, Manzo also studied at the Art Students League and the Brooklyn Museum Art School. She has an extensive teaching career including appointments as Artist in Residence at Long Island University and PS 193 in Brooklyn, and has been an adjunct faculty member at St. John's University, Suffolk Community College, Marymount College, Teachers College of Columbia University's Visual Arts Program for the Girl Scout Council of New York, and Long Island University.

Manzo was commissioned to create a mosaic mural and tile wall project at PS 224 under the Sites Program, Public Art for Public Schools, in Brooklyn. She conducts after-school art programs at Temple Beth Elohim, and in her own Park Slope studio in Brooklyn.

Equally known for her work in monotype printmaking, Manzo has been included in numerous group exhibitions throughout the East Coast, and is represented by the artist-run Blue Mountain Gallery in Chelsea, where she often has solo exhibitions. She is a regular participant at Minerva Durham's celebrated Crosby Painting Studio in Manhattan.

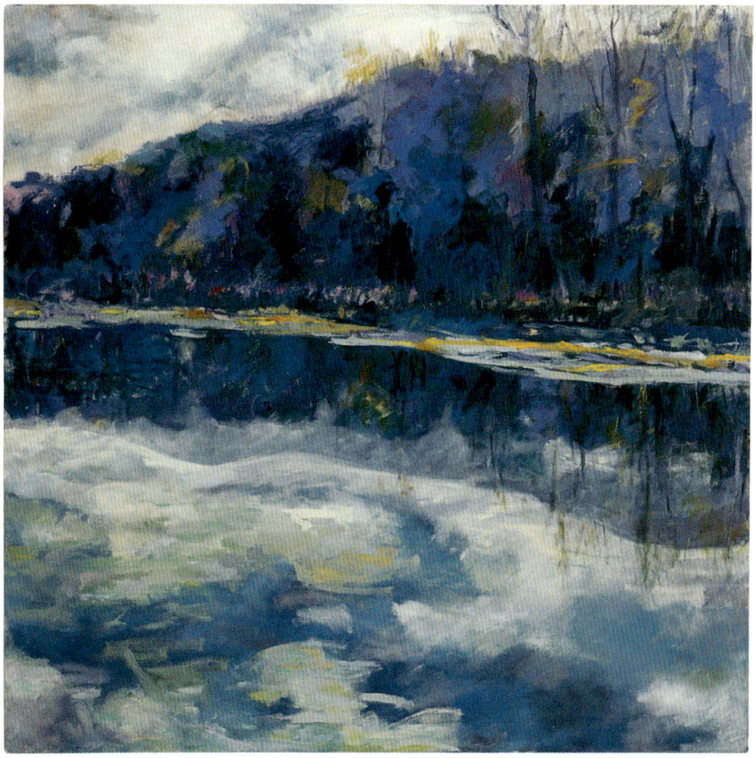

Roxbury Water, oil on canvas, 40" x 40", 1999.

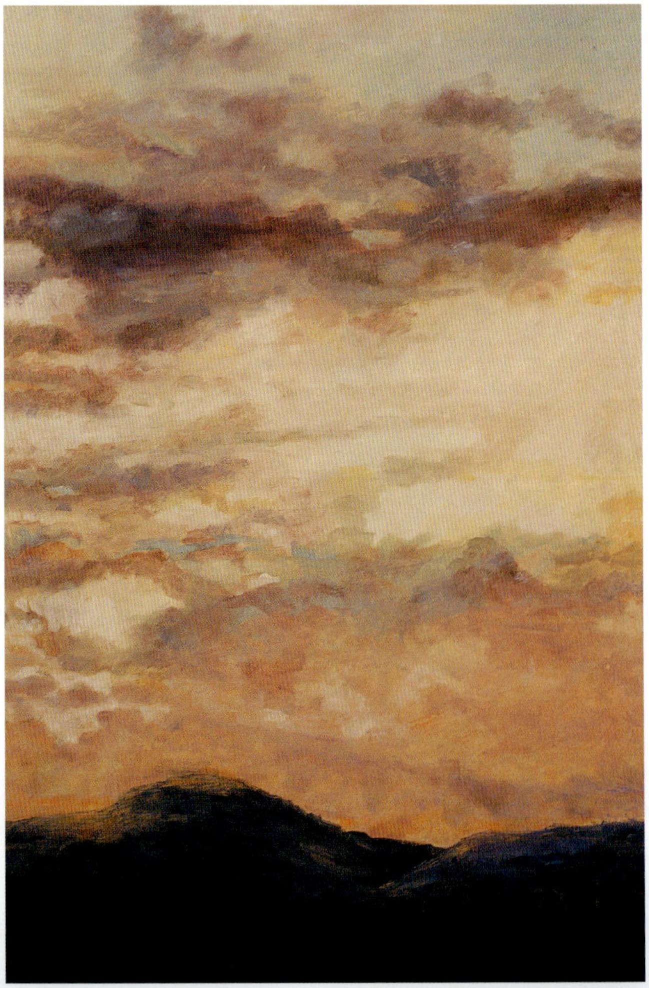

Park City Sky, oil on canvas, 30" x 20", 2002.

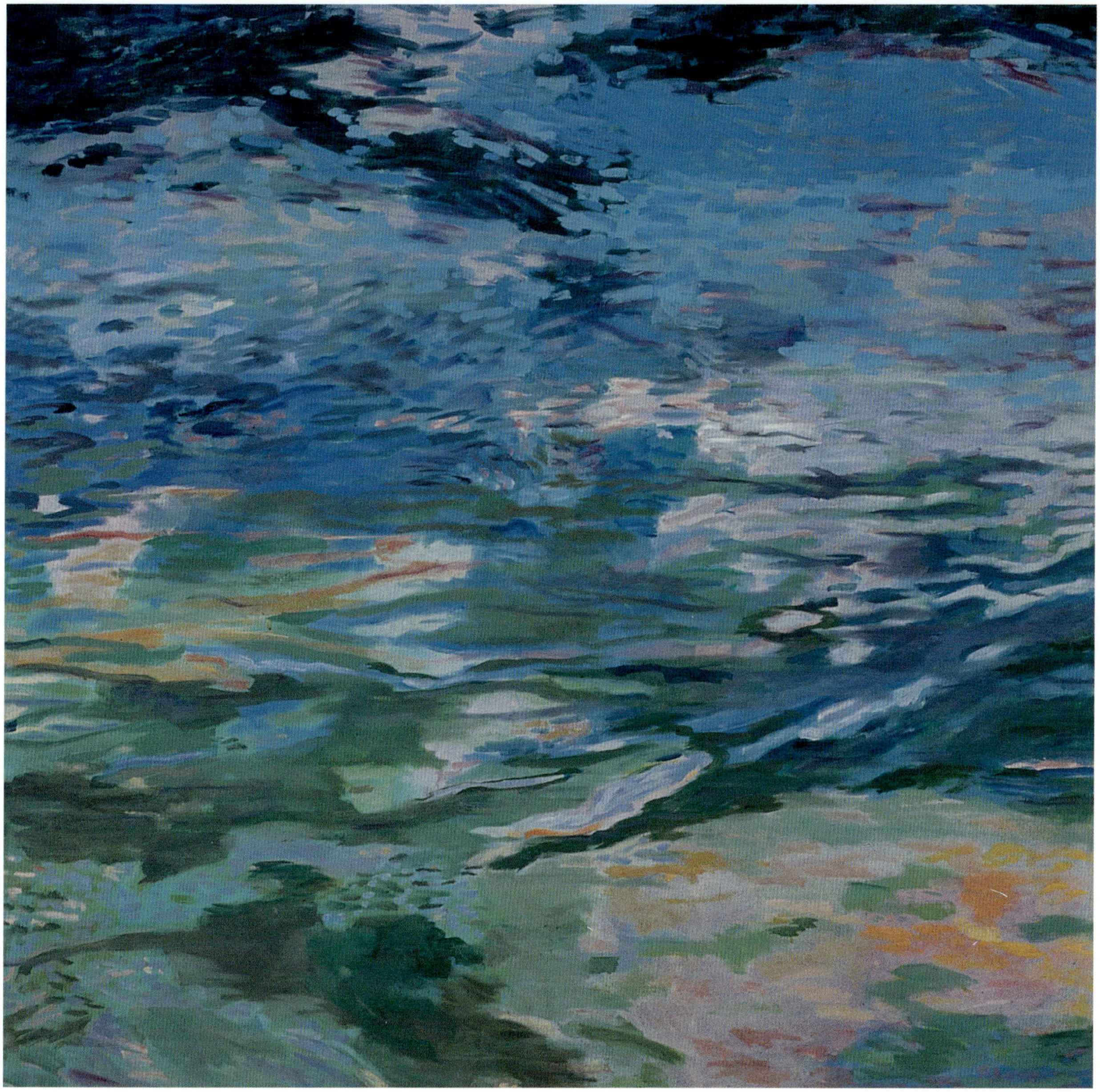

Botanic Gardens Water, oil on canvas, 60" x 60", 1986.

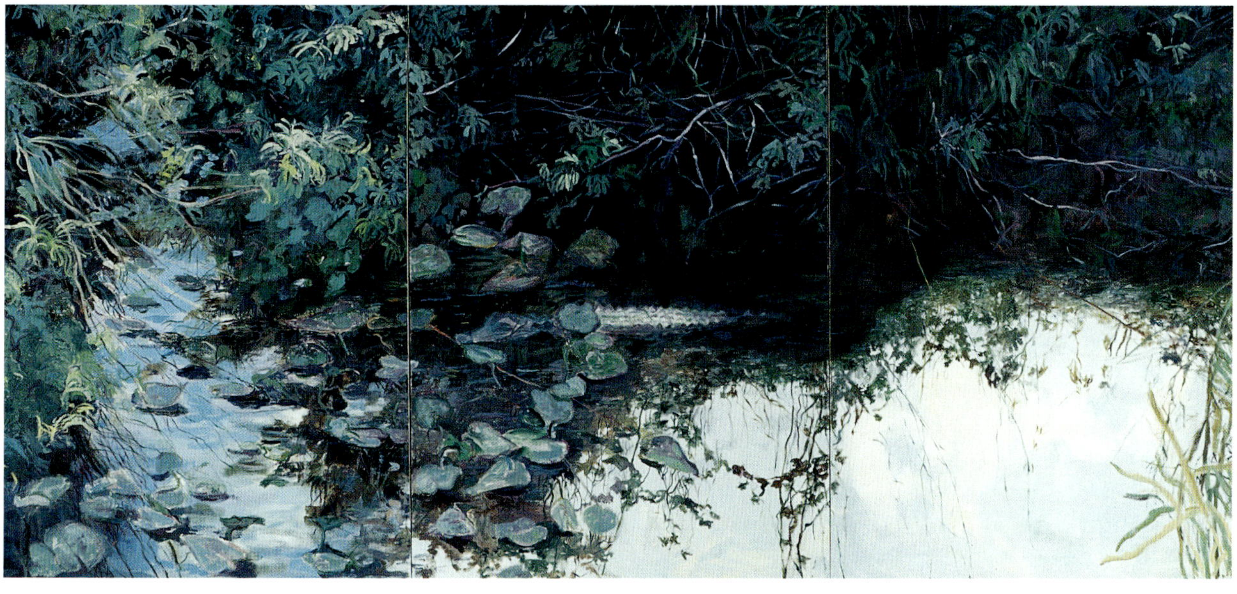

Everglades (Florida Series), oil on canvas, three panels, each 60" x 40", 1994.

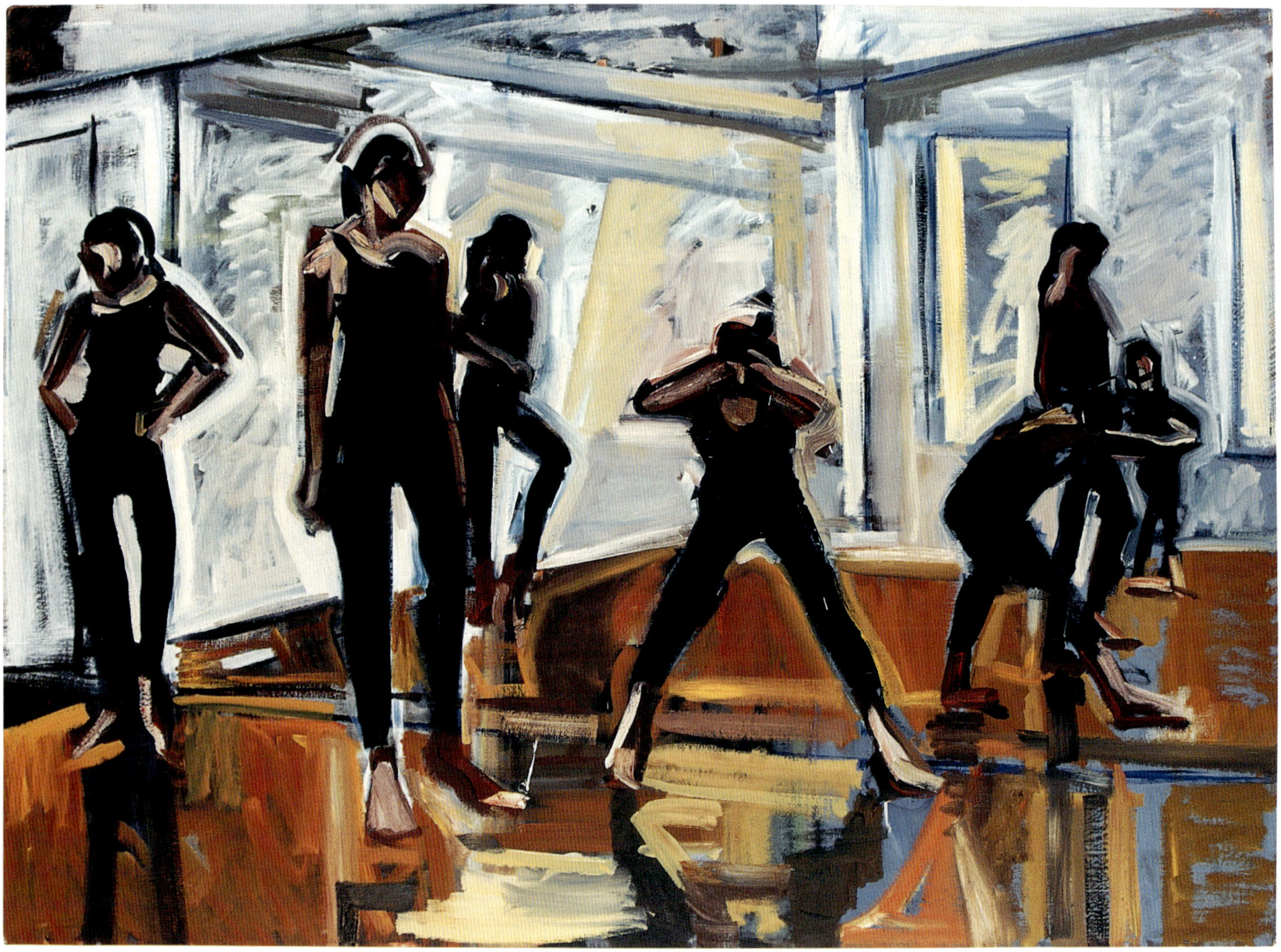

Young Dancers, oil on linen, 65" x 87", 2002.

Anthony Martino

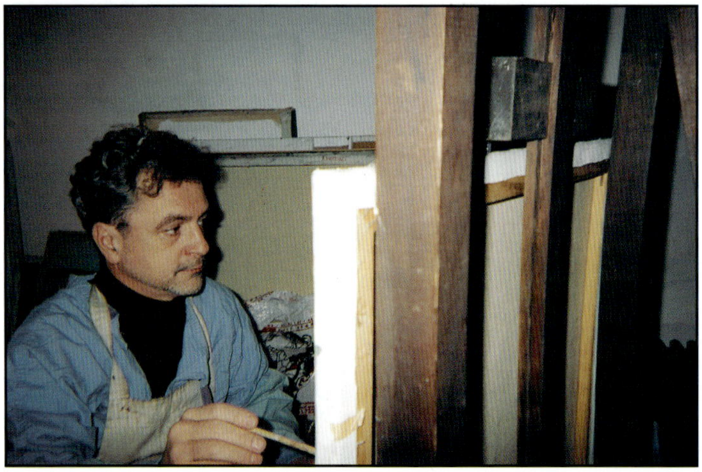

Courtesy of the artist.

Anthony Martino, member of the National Society of Painters in Casein and Acrylic, works equally in both mediums. Winner of a Purchase Award at the National Academy of Design, he has taught at the National Academy as well as the Brooklyn Campus of Long Island University, the Fashion Institute of Technology, the New York Academy of Art, the New York Studio School, Queens College of the City University of New York's Continuing Education Program, and the Ramaz School in New York.

Martino holds degrees in painting from the Maryland Institute College of Art and the Parsons School of Design. He has won scholarships and fellowships from the Skowhegan School of Painting and Sculpture, the Maryland Institute College of Art, Johns Hopkins University, Artists for Environment Foundation of Columbia, New Jersey, and the Parsons School of Design.

His solo exhibitions include the College of William and Mary, Williamsburg, Virginia, the Contemporary Realists Gallery, San Francisco, and the Bowery Gallery in New York.

Of his numerous group exhibitions, these titles give a good overview of Martino's painterly concerns: "Dancers Offstage,"[132] "Contemporary Nudes,"[133] "About Faces: A Celebration of the Portrait,"[134] "Signs of the Flesh,"[135] and "Grand Traditions."[136] He exhibits regularly with the Zeuxis Association of Still Life Painters, and at Westbeth's Gallery, where he resides and shares studio space with his wife, the painter Judy Cuttler.

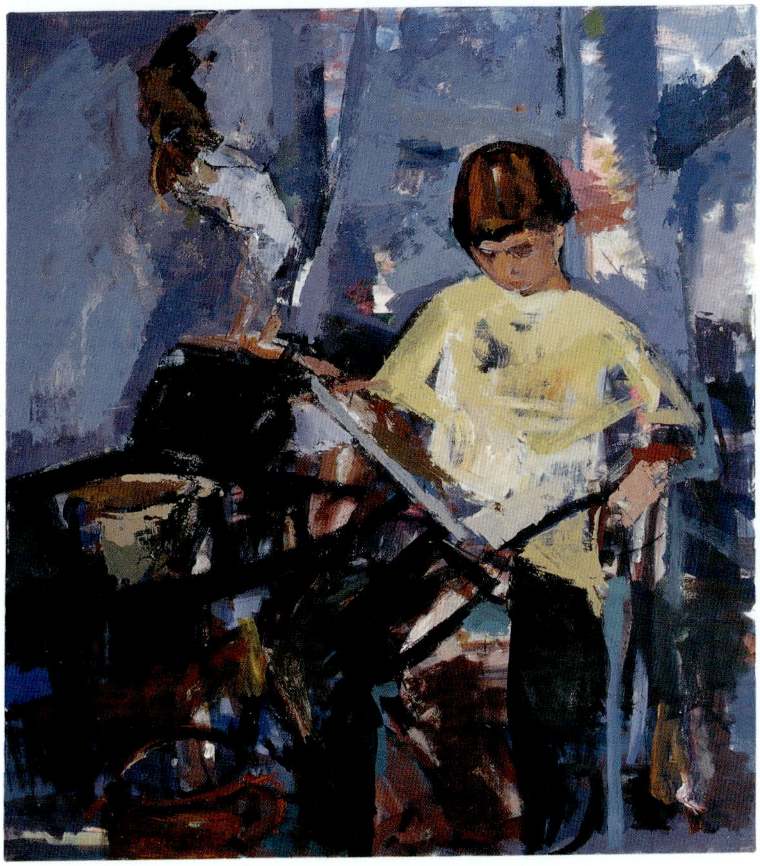

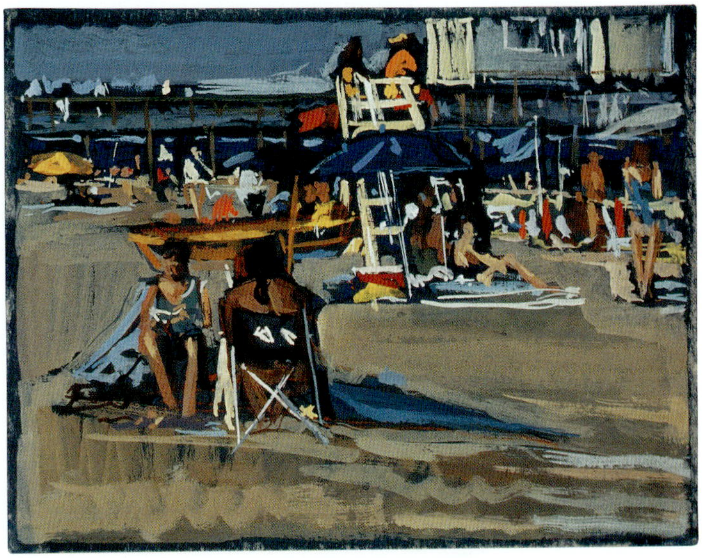

Surfer's Beach, casein on panel, 11" x 15", 2003. *Prize, National Society of Painters in Casein and Acrylic.*

Portrait of Nicholas, oil on canvas, 48" x 32", 2002.

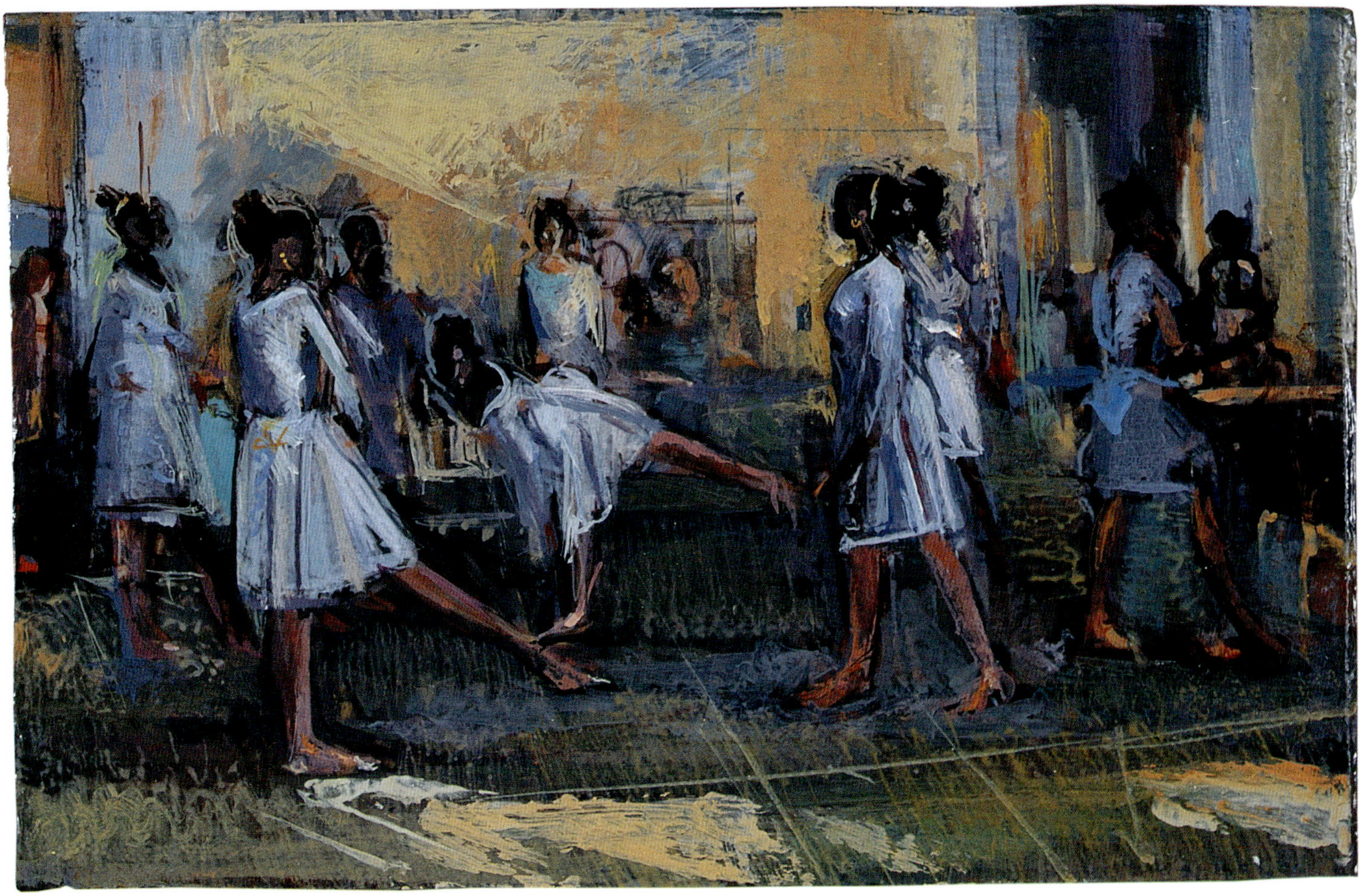

Dancers Offstage, oil on panel, 8" x 12", 2005.

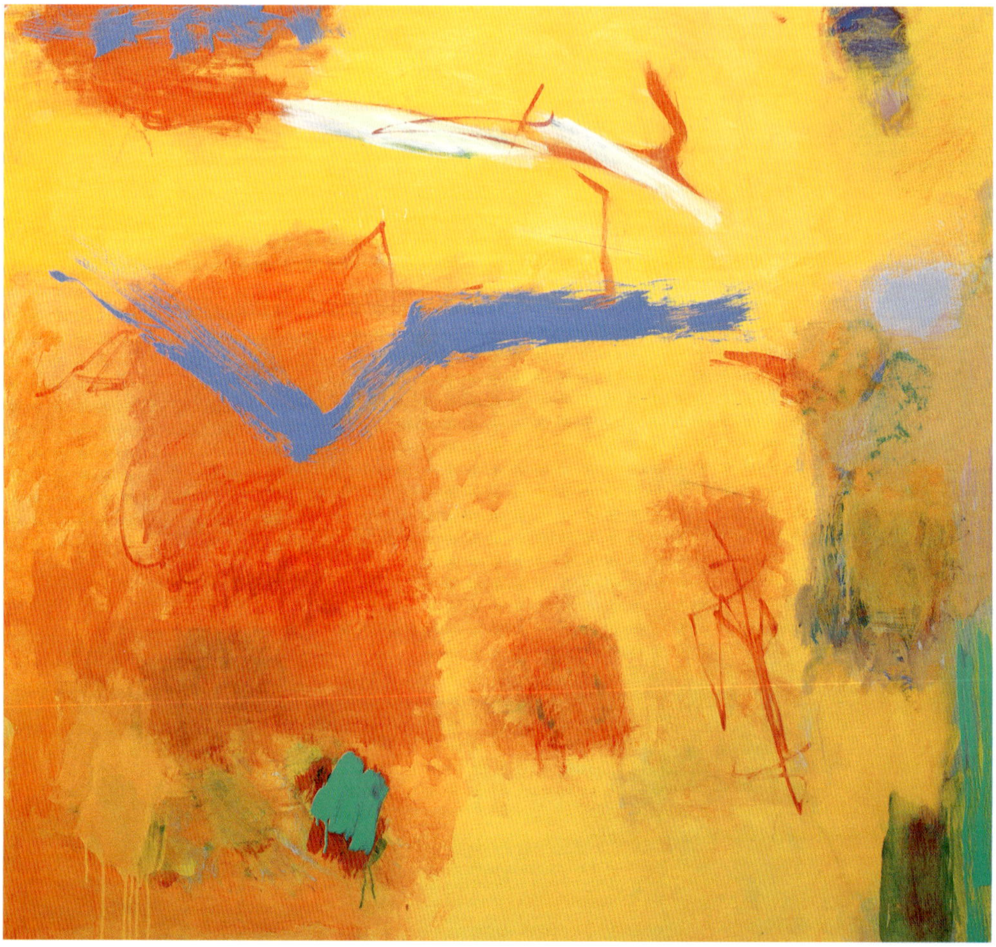

Until Just Then, oil on canvas, 50" x 52", 1999. *Courtesy of the artist and David Findlay Jr Fine Art. All art © Emily Mason/ Licensed by VAGA, New York, NY.*

Emily Mason

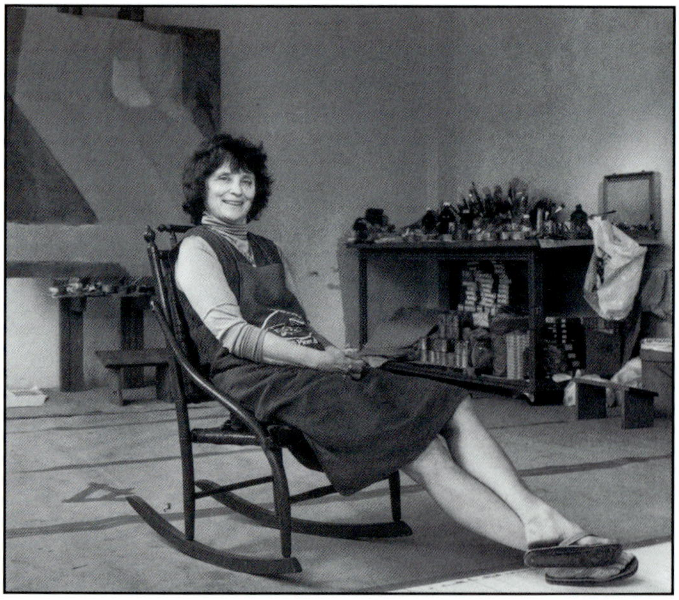

Photograph © Tommy Naess.

Emily Mason, the third generation painter of a four-generation tradition that includes her grandmother, Ann Train Trumbull, and her mother, Alice Trumbull Mason (a founder of the America Abstract Artists), is the mother of the painter Cecily Kahn and wife of the painter Wolf Kahn.

She studied at Bennington and at The Cooper Union. A faculty member at Hunter College for over twenty-five years, Mason has received a Fulbright grant and a Yale-Norfolk Summer Art School grant, among other honors. She is an elected member of the National Academy of Design. Her numerous solo exhibitions include the Grace Borgenicht and Associated American Artists galleries in New York, Marlboro College in Vermont, the Pacific Northwest College of Art in Portland, Oregon, and the Brattleboro Museum of Art in Vermont.

Group exhibitions include many family-related showings with such titles as, "...Two Generations of Abstract Art,"[137] "A Family in Art,"[138] "Couples Show,"[139] "Among Family,"[140] and "American Women Artists – The Twentieth Century."[141]

Mason's paintings are founded in Abstract Expressionism, where the painterly movement of oil on canvas is of primary importance. Like the process of her mother, she often works the canvas, placed on the floor, from all sides. She considers her painting "intuitive, ... when you over-plan, you get too tight and ... lose the freedom ... essential for successful painting."[142] Her often large, boldly colored, yet jewel-like paintings are "saturated with layers of opaque and transparent pigments, creating a ... sense of depth, space and movement."[143] She is represented by David Findlay Jr Fine Art.

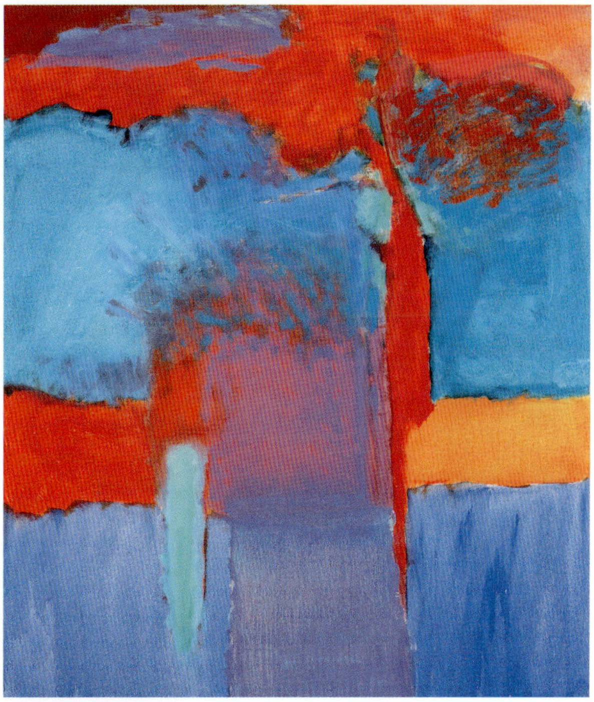

Hot Spring, oil on canvas, 48" x 40", 2002. *Courtesy of the artist and David Findlay Jr Fine Art.*

Juice, oil on canvas, 72" x 60", 2004. *Courtesy of the artist and David Findlay Jr Fine Art.*

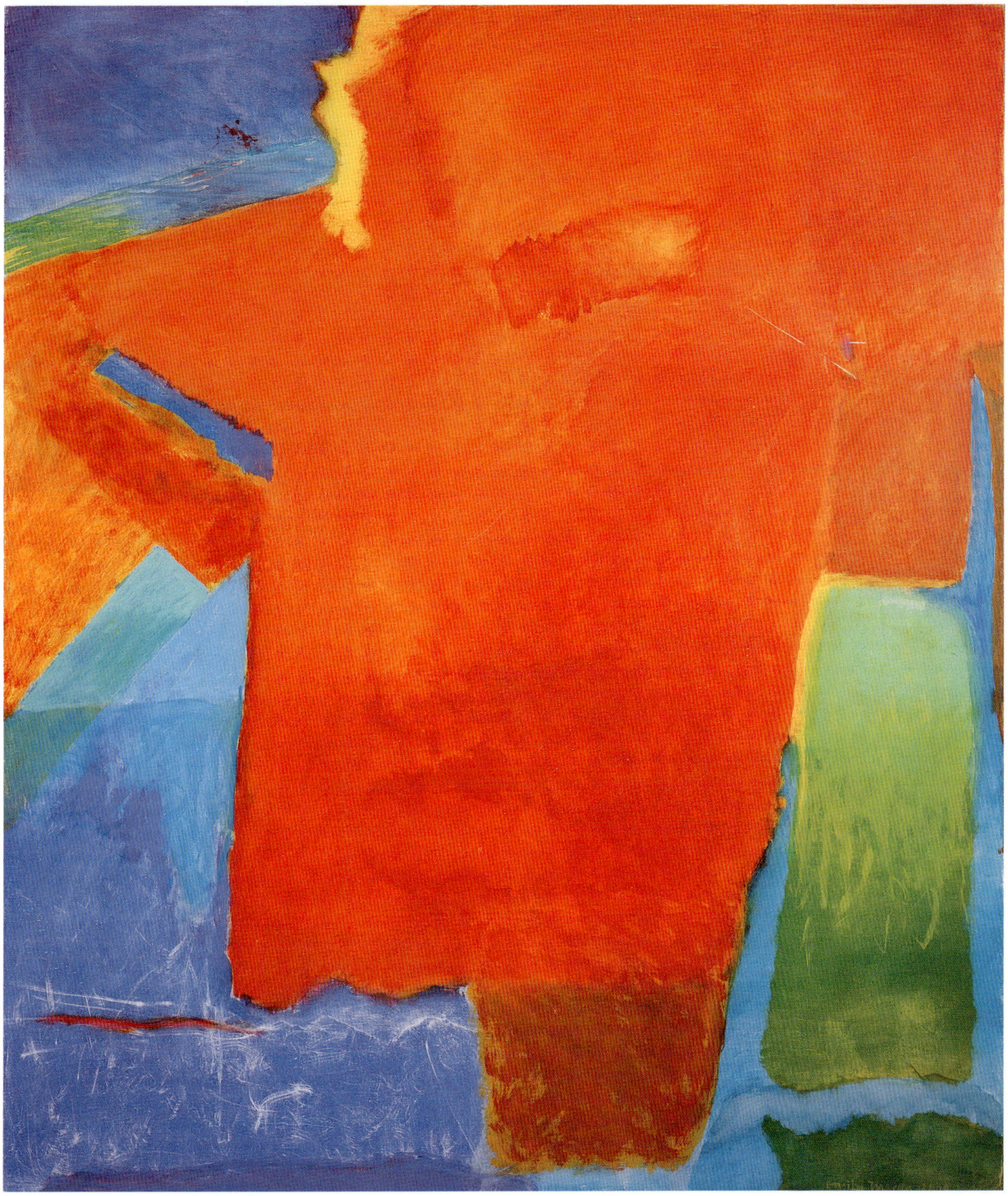

Richard Mayhew

Courtesy of ACA Gallery

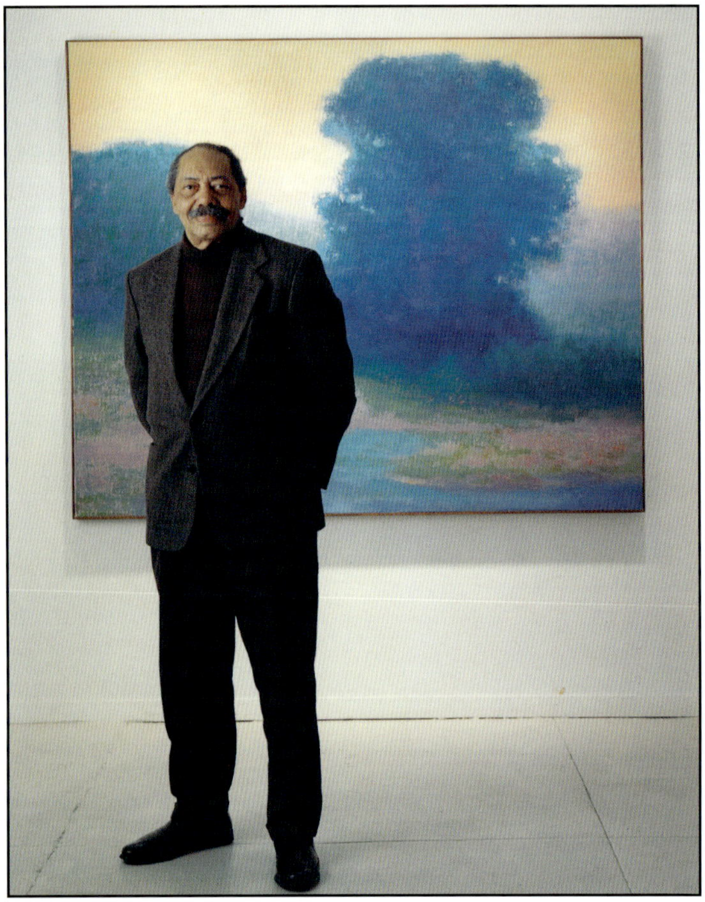

Richard Mayhew, whose evocative, strikingly color-filled free-form abstractions suggest but do not represent specific landscapes, is involved with "the spiritual feeling of space … a universal space with the illusion of time."[144] A boyhood apprenticeship to James Wilson Peale, whom he met during summers near Long Island Sound, led to studies at the Brooklyn Museum Art School, the Art Students League, Columbia University, and the Hans Hofmann School of Fine Arts. After years of European study, Mayhew began to exhibit in New York. John Canaday has referred to "the strength … certainty and sheer handsomeness"[145] of his early landscapes.

A lengthy career in academe has included faculty appointments at the Brooklyn Museum Art School, Hunter College, Smith College, and fourteen years at Pennsylvania State University.

Mayhew was a central member of Spiral, a group of distinguished black New York-based artists and writers who exhibited together, and met to discuss social issues in relation to their work and their dedication to the cause of achieving civil rights in the art world.

A descendant of both Shinnecock Indian and African-American families, Mayhew acknowledges his grandmother's reverence for the earth and sea and her belief in his unlimited potential. Romare Bearden wrote, "… he represents a bridge between the older black artists who developed through the WPA, and those who, after … matured during the turbulent civil rights movement and the use of abstract expressionism."[146]

In addition to several exhibitions with Spiral, Mayhew's work has been included in many group and over thirty solo showings, and was the subject of a retrospective at the Studio Museum in Harlem. Until its closing, the Midtown Payson Gallery represented Mayhew. He is affiliated with ACA Gallery, is an elected member of the National Academy of Design, and his works are to be seen in the permanent collection of most major museums.

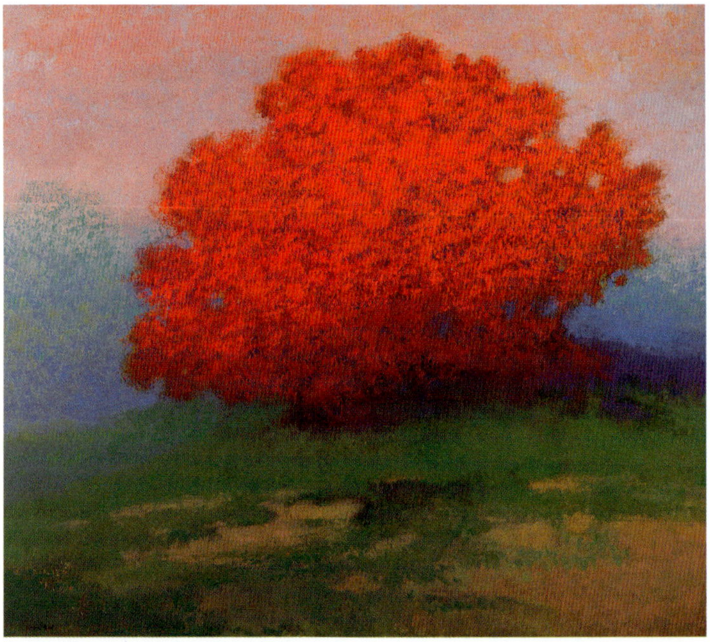

Love Bush, oil on canvas, 47" x 51", 2000. *Courtesy of ACA Gallery.*

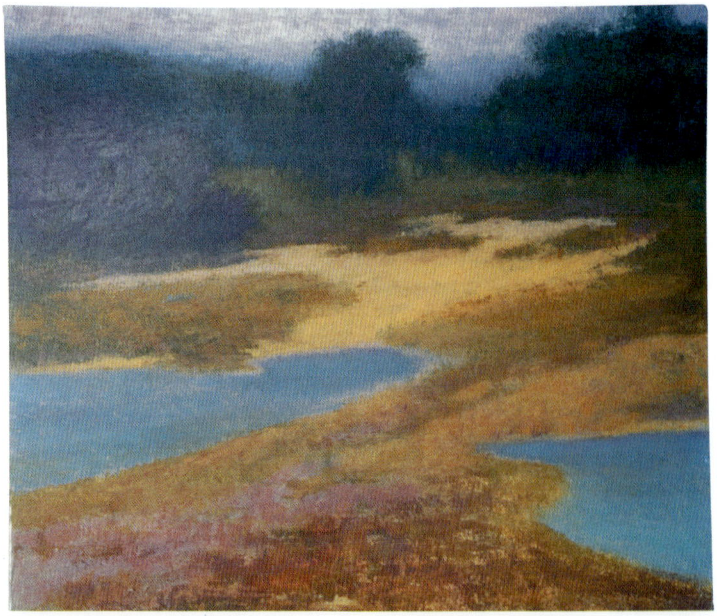

Spiritual Space, Series #20, oil on canvas, 40" x 52", c.1975. *Courtesy of the artist.*

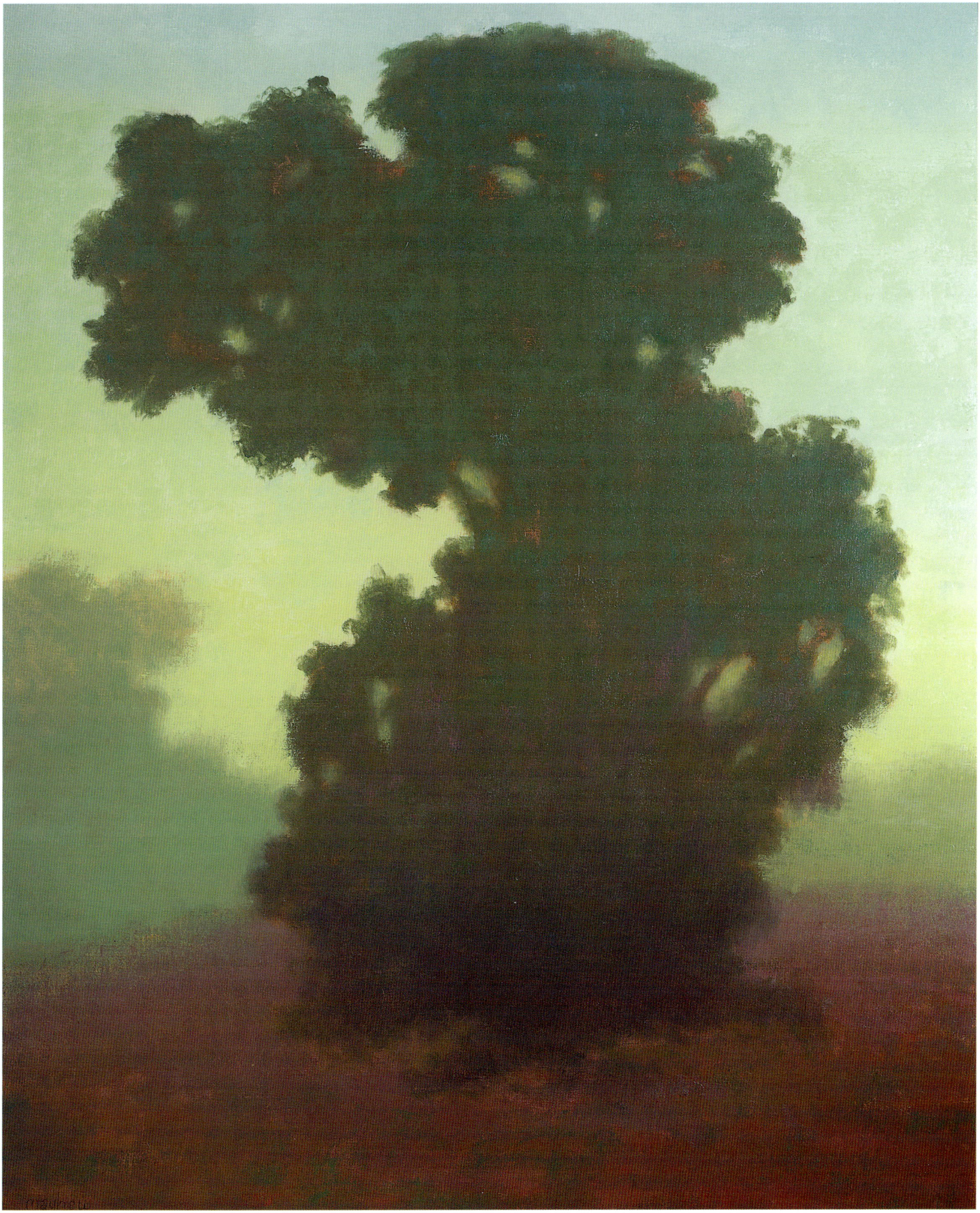

Cello Solo, oil on canvas, 60" x 48", 2002. *Courtesy of ACA Gallery.*

Mary Beth McKenzie

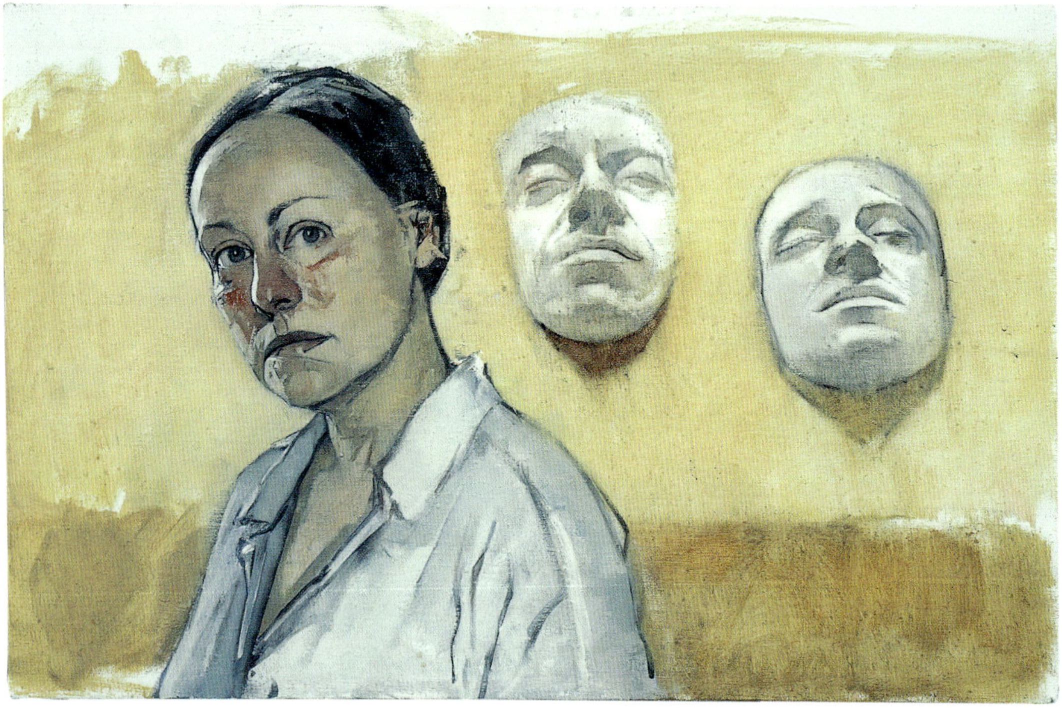

Self Portrait (Life Masks), oil on canvas, 20" x 26", 1999.

Mary Beth McKenzie, who frequently uses herself as a model, always works directly from life, enjoying both the human interaction and her direct response to shape and color. She says, "... [since] painting is about relationships ... I judge each area by its relationship to surrounding areas. ... Leaving some ... less finished ... or more out of focus ... allows the imagination to finish them and gives more importance to the detailed parts."[147] She points to Rembrandt, Van Gogh, Kollwitz, and Schiele as artists who left a number of revealing self-portraits (which are) "extremely personal ... very hard to paint ... [since] you see yourself differently from the way

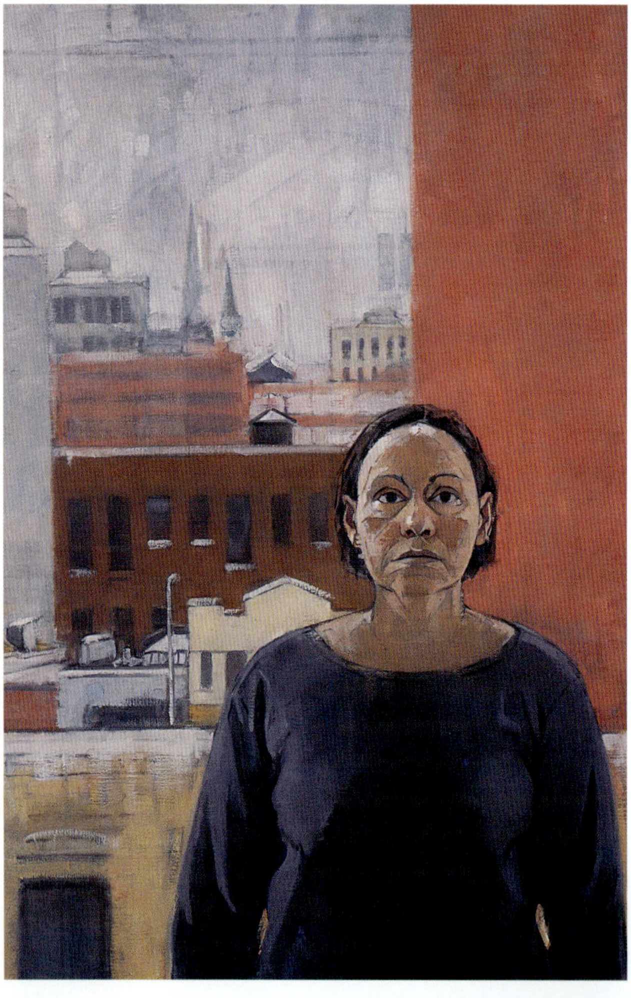

Self Portrait (Front Window), oil on canvas, 46" x 30", 2001.

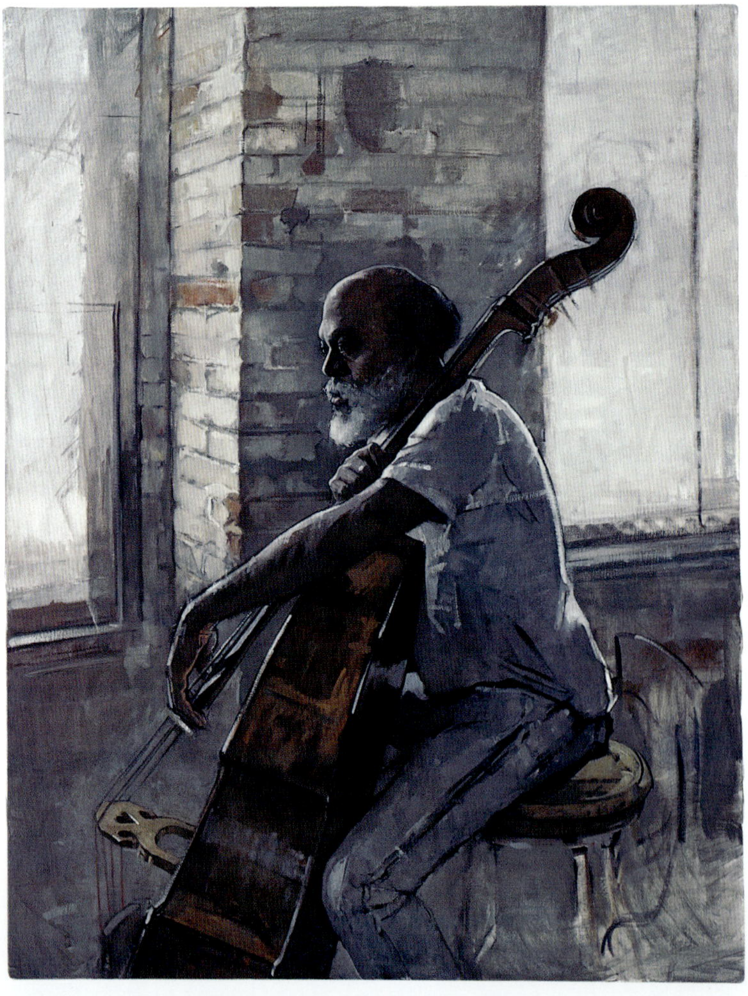

Bass Player at Rest, oil on canvas, 64" x 48", 1989.

anyone else does. ... Objectivity is a ... problem [but] you allow yourself to take chances more freely ... the model [is] always available."[147]

McKenzie, an elected member of the National Academy of Design, where she has taught for twenty-five years, studied at Boston's Museum of Fine Arts, Cleveland's Cooper School of Art, the Art Students League, and the National Academy of Design in New York.

She has had several solo exhibitions in New York and has been included in many group exhibitions, including "Looking at You, Self Portraits," at the Metropolitan Museum of Art, and "Challenging Tradition: Women of the Academy 1826-2003," at the National Academy of Design Museum, New York.

McKenzie's works are in the collections of the Metropolitan Museum of Art, the Smithsonian Institution's National American Museum, the National Museum of Women in the Arts, the Museum of the City of New York, and the Brooklyn Museum, to name a few.

Winner of numerous awards, she has received Medals of Honor from Audubon Artists, Allied Artists, and several prizes from the National Academy of Design. She is represented by the Spanierman Gallery in New York.

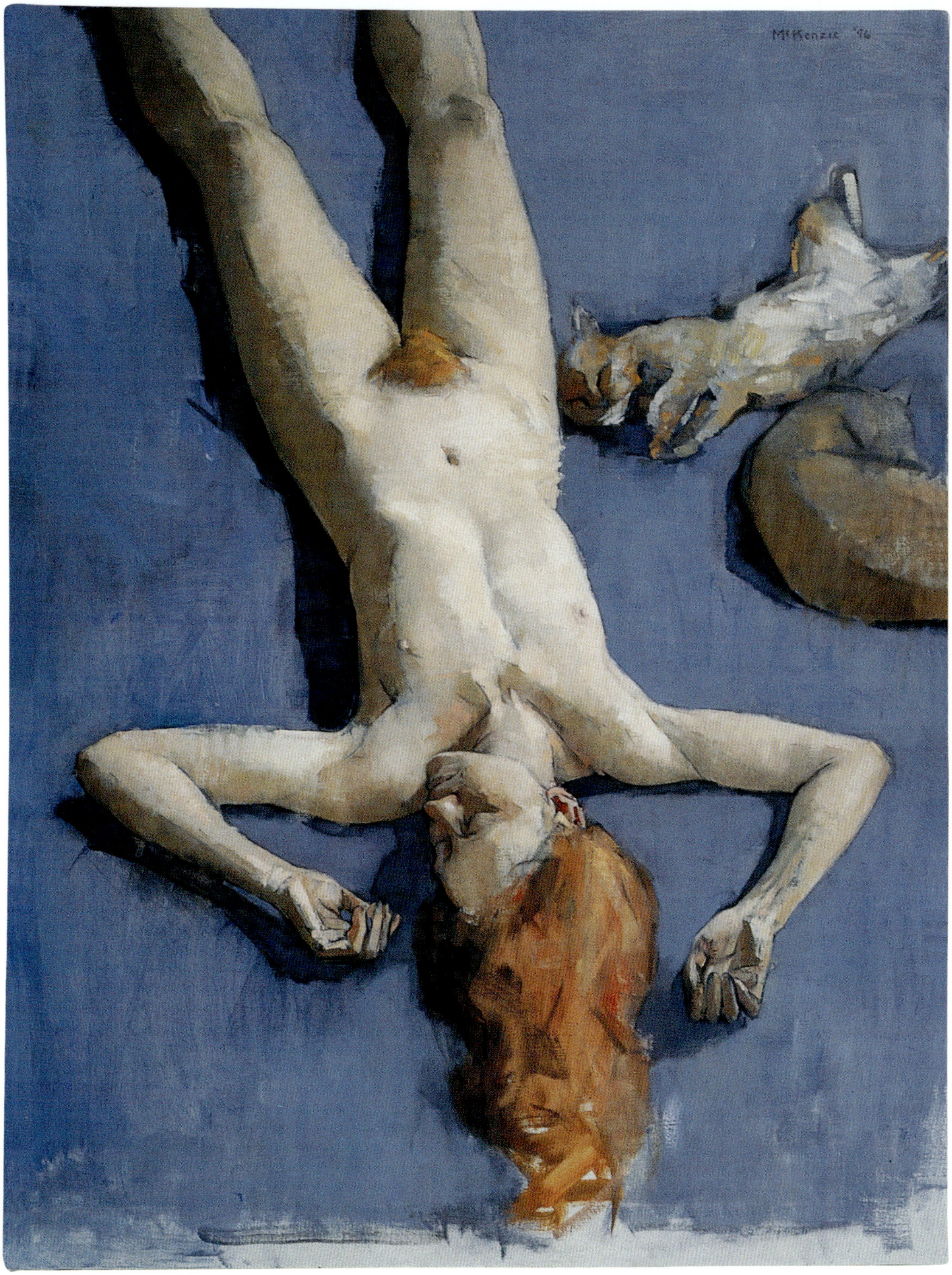

Inverted Figure, oil on canvas, 50" x 36", 2000.

Lee Anne Miller

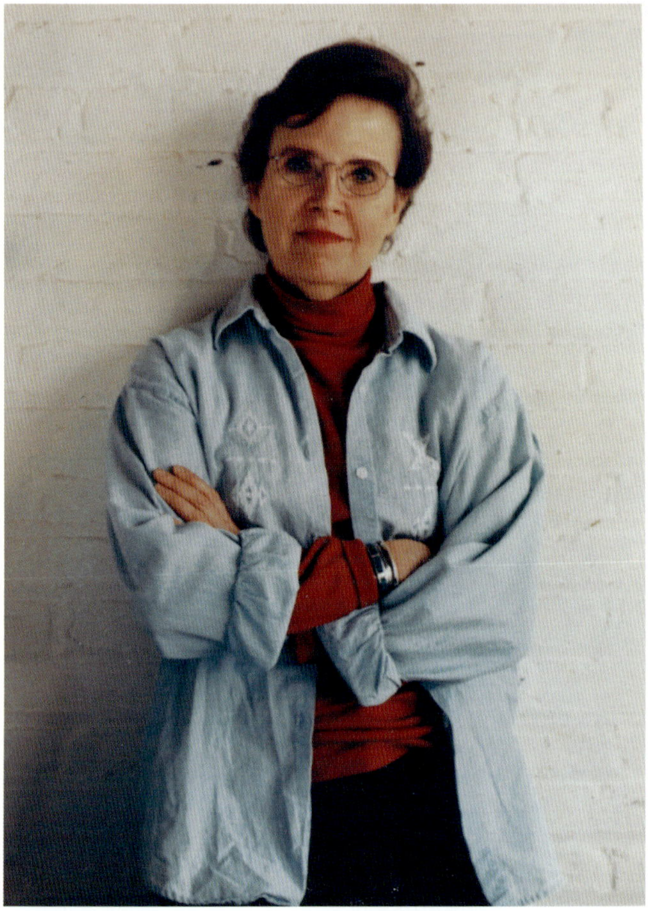

Photograph by Dennis Hall.

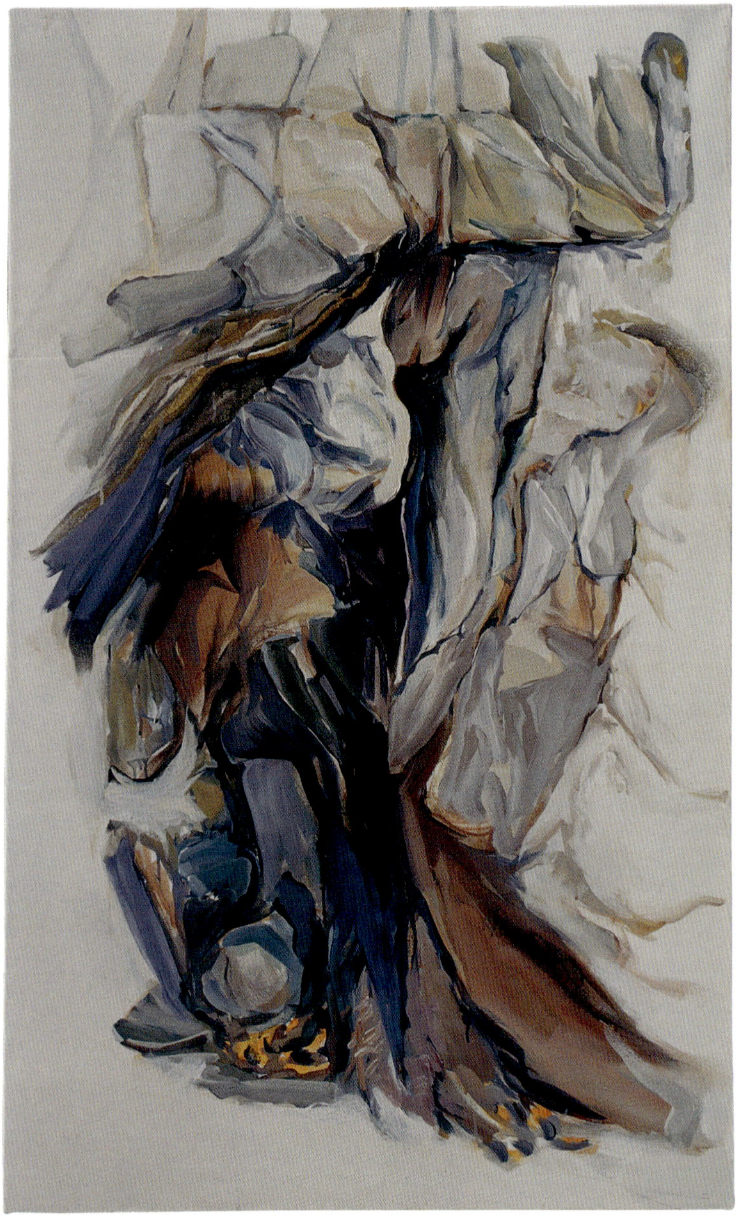

Hideaway, acrylic on canvas, 60" x 36", 2004-05.

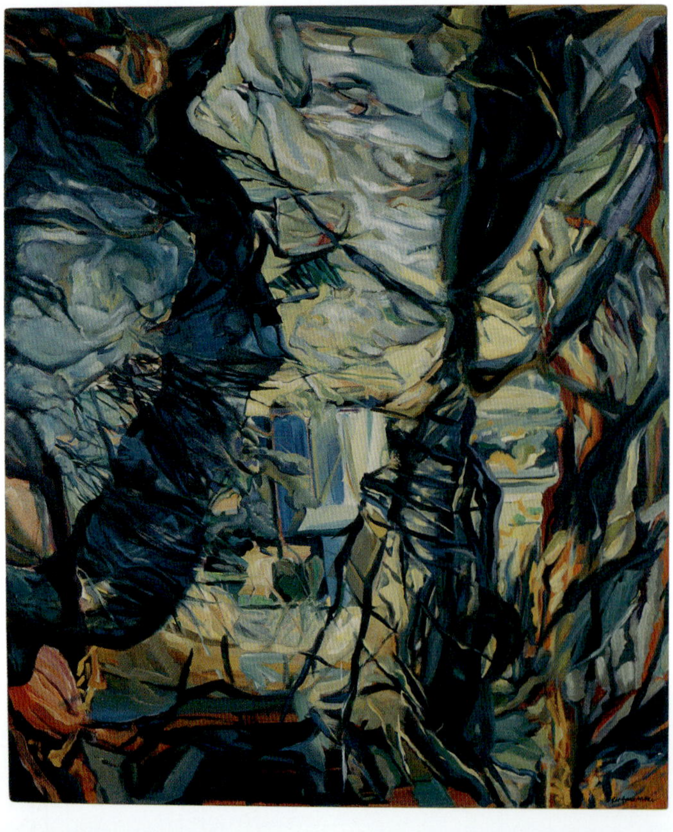

Shadow Vision (Refuge Series), oil on linen, 76" x 62", 1995.

Lee Anne Miller, longtime professor of Art at The Cooper Union School of Art, served as its Dean for ten years. She won a Fulbright Fellowship, and has received several grants in Art from the University of Missouri – Kansas City, and the Tamarind Institute in New Mexico. After studies at Utah State University, she earned an MFA at the Cranbrook Academy of Art, then studied at New York's Pratt Graphics Art Center. She has also taught at the Cleveland Institute of Art, East Texas State University, the University of Missouri – Kansas City, and Wayne State University in Detroit.

Miller says her large, nature-inspired paintings respond to a life-long fascination with its forms and forces. Her sense of color, atmosphere, and form was strongly influenced by the natural environment of the West, which gave her a "rich exposure to a dramatic, varied landscape, an early framework for a visual language. Always retaining something of the mysterious, her art never seems definable or repeatable."[148] As she says, "The language of paint presents interpretation and metamorphosis ... combining the simulation of the real with the ambiguity of the abstract."[149]

Miller generally works in series, focusing on "a theme, location or idea ... enhancing personal experience through observations, imagination and memory."[150] "Nature Transformed," an extensive exhibition of her paintings, elicited such comments as, "a consummate modernist ...,"[151] "unabashed love of the medium of paint and the physical act of painting,"[152] and "superb ability to retain both spontaneity and tremendous control."[153] Miller's series include landscapes in Southern France, Hawaii, Utah, and New York's Central Park, as well as areas in the American Southwest.

Her works are included in many museum and corporate collections, and she has served on the Board of Directors of the Greater New York Chapter of the Fulbright Association and of the College Art Association, has been President of the Women's Caucus for Art, and received Utah State University's outstanding Alumna Award during its Centennial year.

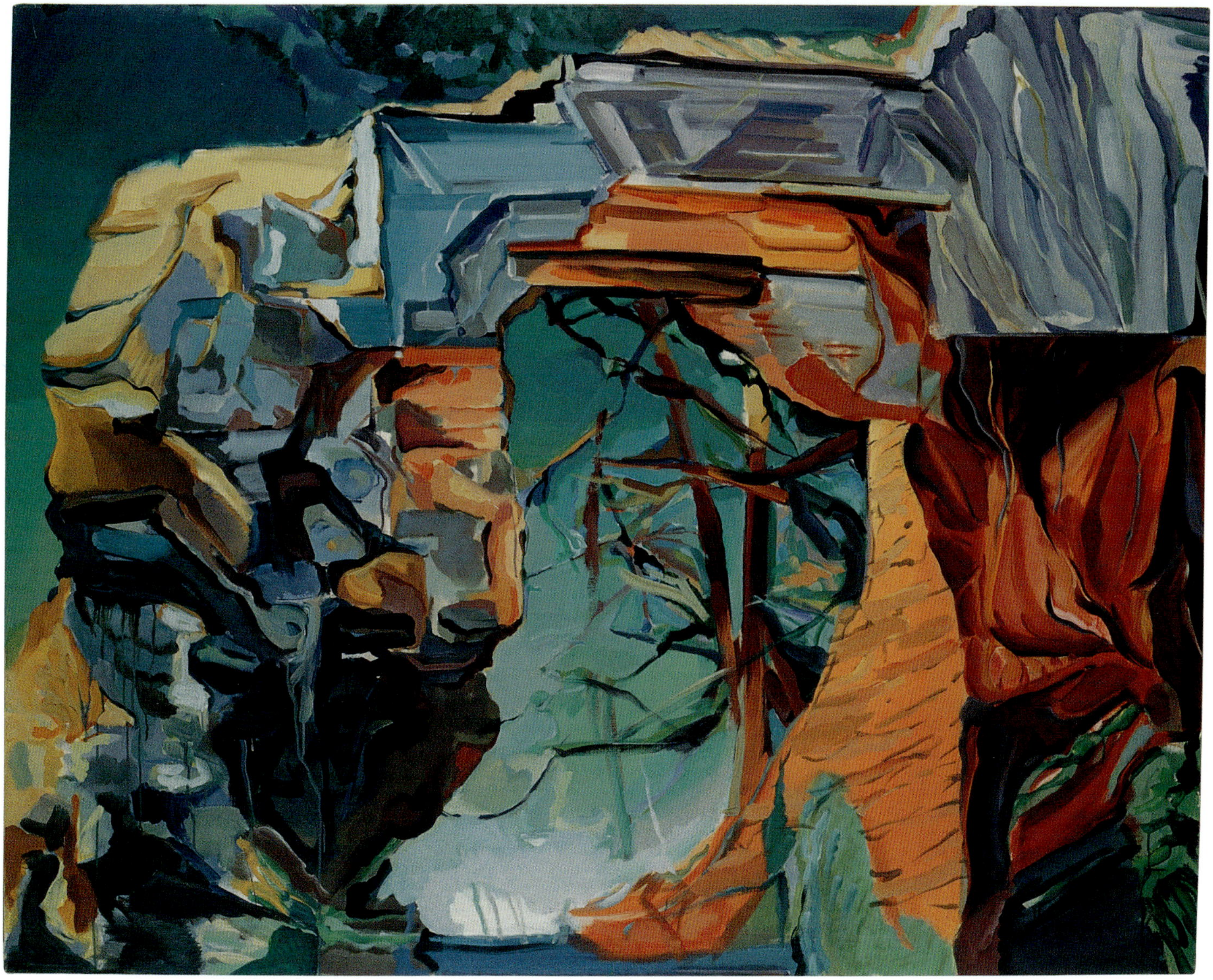

La Citadelle IV (Vestiges Series), acrylic on linen, 76" x 62", 1993.

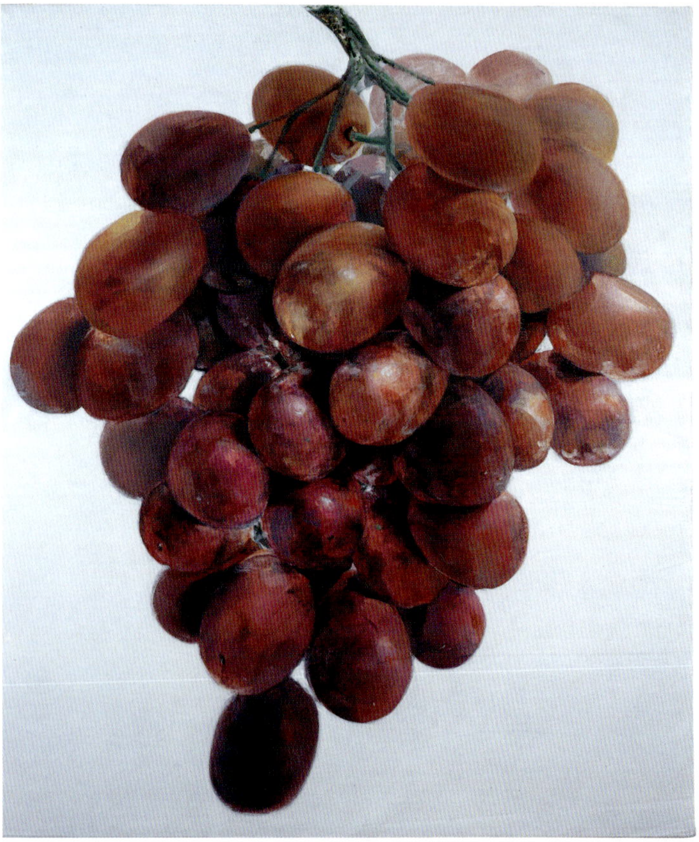

Red Grapes, acrylic on canvas, 59" x 50", 1966. *Courtesy of Babcock Galleries.*

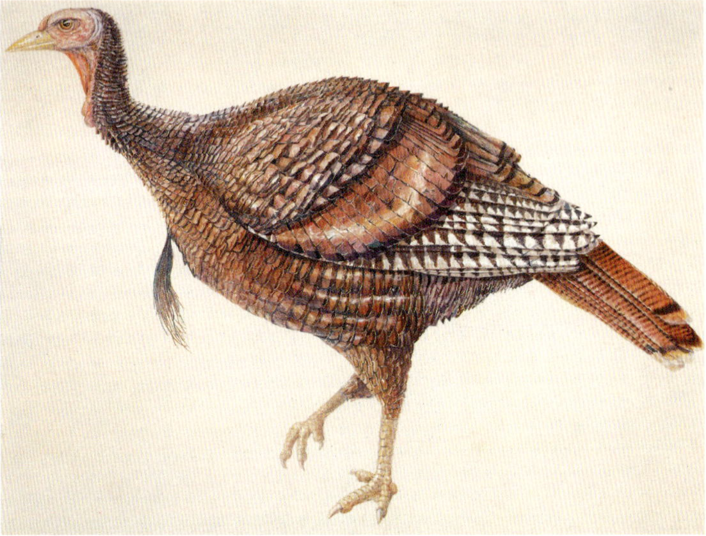

Wild Turkey, acrylic on canvas, 57" x 74", 1974. *Courtesy of Babcock Galleries.*

Don Nice

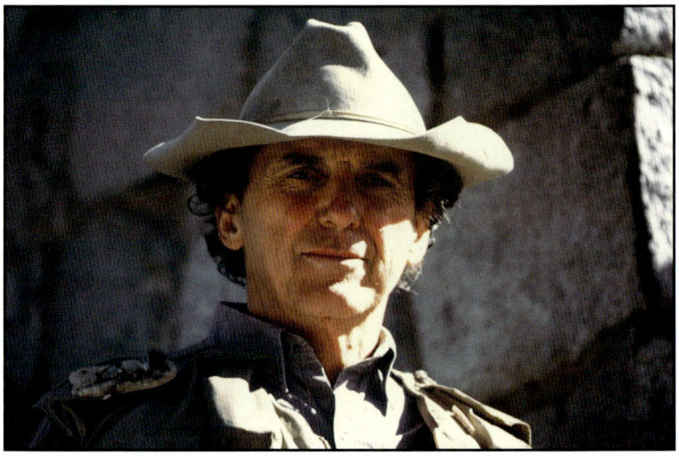

Photograph by Gregory Kondos.

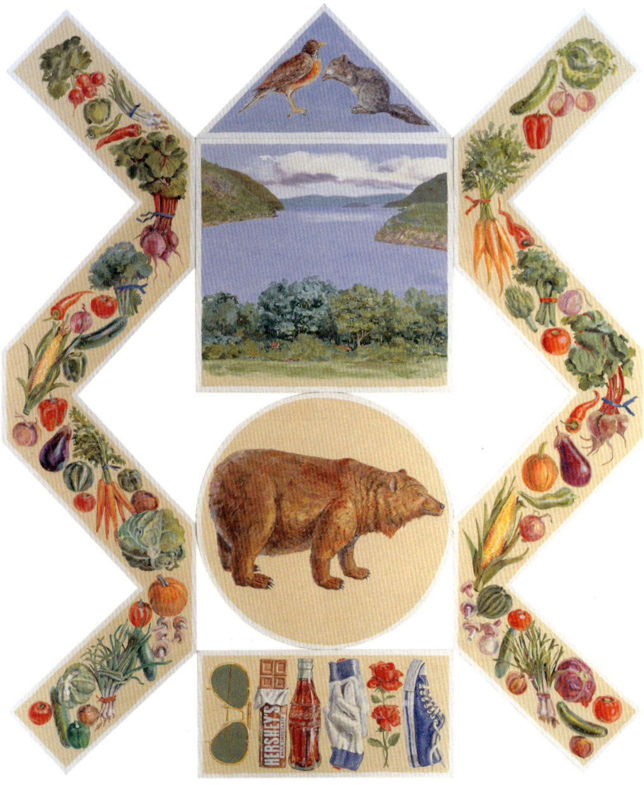

American Totem: Zigzag Cornucopia, oil on canvas, 108" x 92", 1981. *Private collection. Courtesy of Babcock Galleries.*

Don Nice, called a "Realist with an edge"[154] by Gail Scott, "paints recognizable objects in new and startling ways, translating them into icons, engaging in esthetic concerns such as figure-ground relationships, compositional structure and the search for avenues to preconscious sources of creative energy."[155]

Constantly drawing, making studies in color, he prepares a rich resource of material for his paintings. Early works incorporated popular culture subjects, but he kept himself apart from the Pop Art mainstream, later reinforcing content to encase often-outsized objects within highly structured frameworks. Nice seeks to bring the viewer "to a new understanding of the relationship of specific American content to our world, its spaces and its inhabitants."[156]

Nice has used the Renaissance predella panel format—small images surrounding a main altarpiece—to present a single large-scale subject such as an animal or commonplace object amidst related images on individual canvases. Experimenting with materials and formats, he constantly renews his vision and has introduced the horizonless "spinner" to be viewed from all directions equally.

His childhood on the range in the West, and early athletic success, were followed by military and teaching experiences, then by studies in Italy on the GI Bill. There, he met Oskar Kokoschka, who opened his eyes to light, color, forms, and spaces, and was "the biggest influence"[157] in his life. After studies at Yale School of Art, Nice taught at New York's School of Visual Arts for twenty-four years. His work has been seen in over sixty solo exhibitions around the world and is in over seventy major museum collections.

An elected member of the National Academy of Design, Nice is represented by the Babcock Galleries in New York.

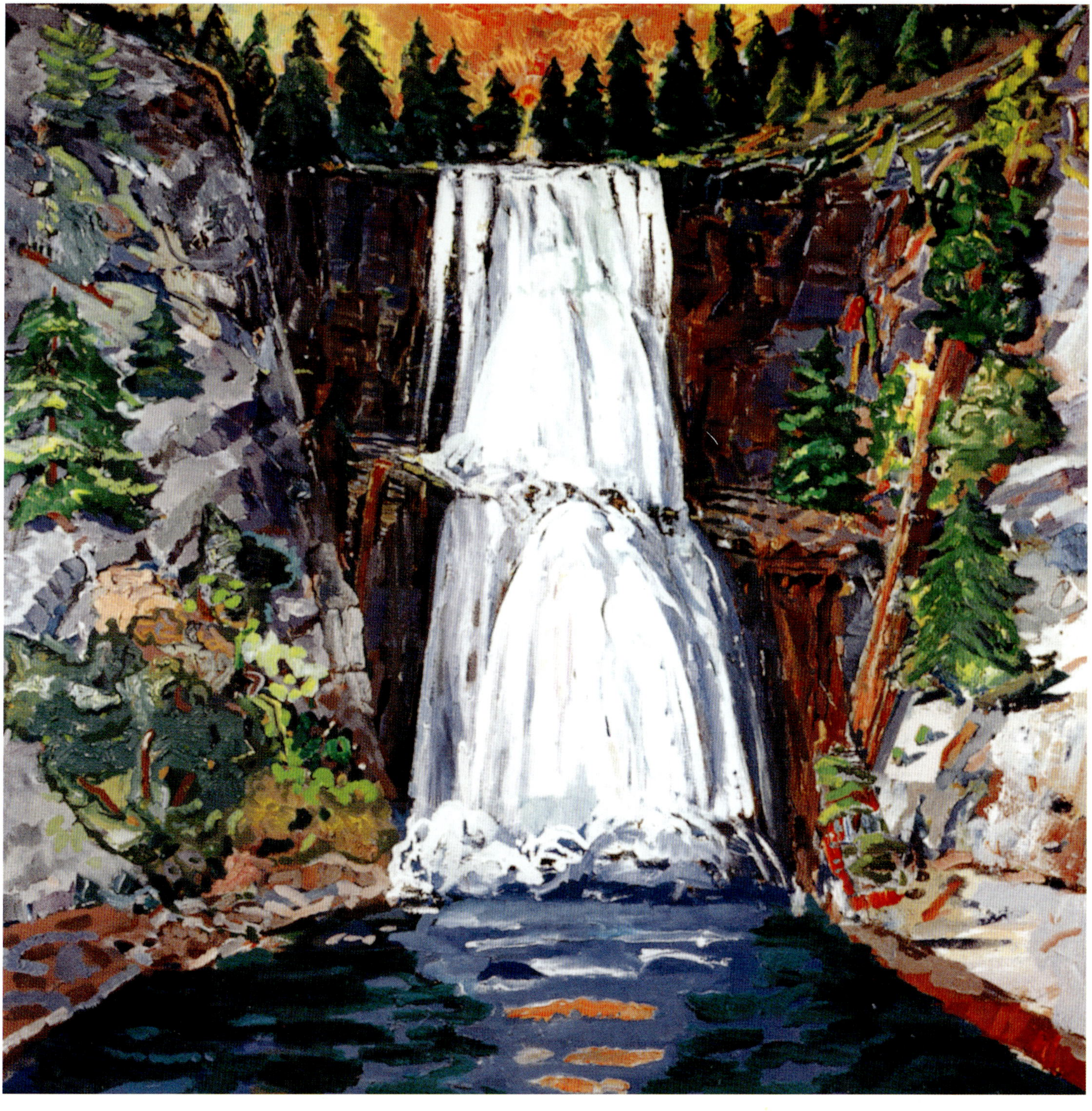

Indian Brook Falls, oil on canvas, 60" x 60", 1993. *Private collection. Courtesy of Babcock Galleries.*

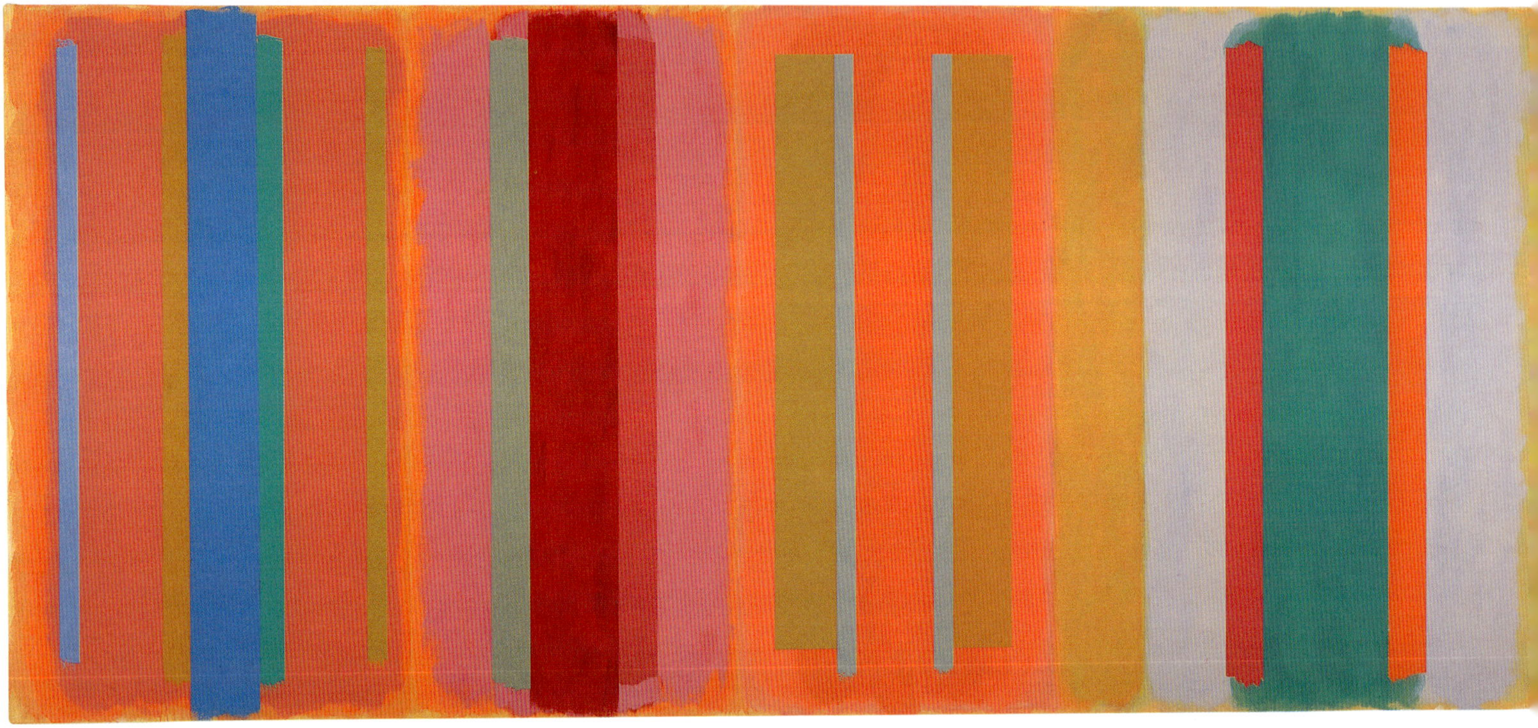

Contra Bass, acrylic on canvas, 60" x 156", 2001.

Doug Ohlson

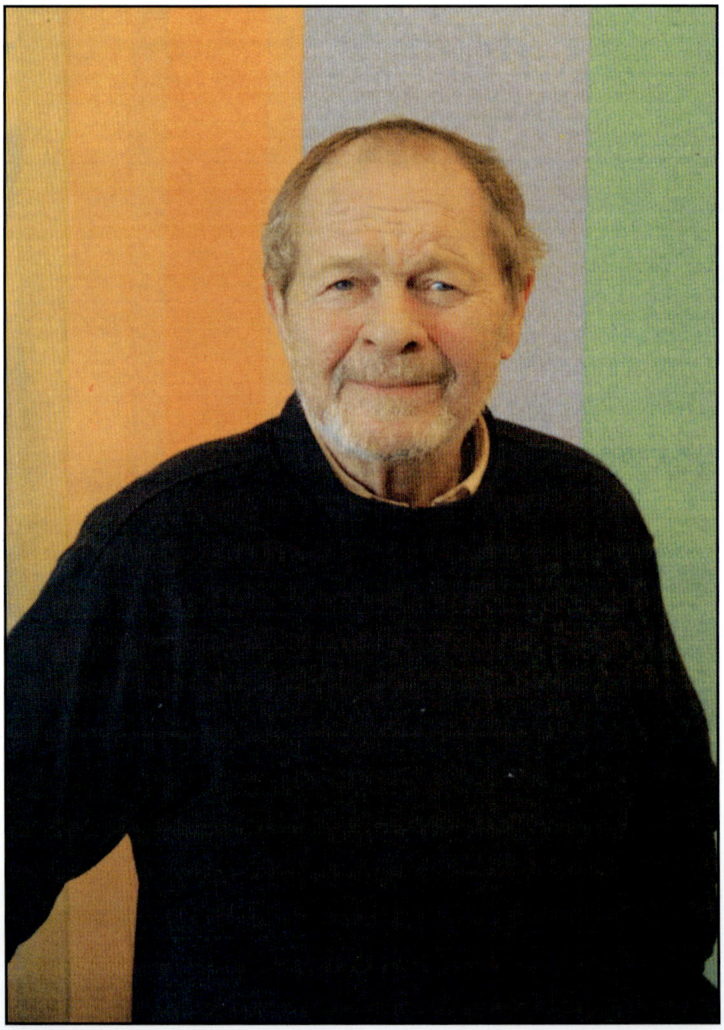

Photograph by Bryan Canniff Design.

Doug Ohlson's early placement of simple rectangular and square shapes within the canvas field, echoing the perimeter, brought a special sense of color to "resound in unison ... throughout the ambivalent space in which they reside. [Later] softer, sometimes melted-edge same-value color harmonies reaffirmed the more vigorous aspects of his paintings' structure, seeking to use the edge without framing the center, to keep it alive. ... His control of color is arrived at by intuition rather than scientific theory,"[158] says E. C. Goossen. Richard Waller adds, "His explorations of color provide a compelling tension and harmony beyond the immediate delights of his color interactions ... exploring the interplay of color as his primary impetus."[159]

Winner of a John Simon Guggenheim Memorial Foundation Fellowship, Ohlson has a record of solo and group exhibitions numbering in the dozens, notably many showings at the Fischbach, Andre Zarre, and Susan Caldwell galleries in New York, and at the Museum of Modern Art, the Whitney Museum of America Art, and the Corcoran Gallery of Art in Washington, D.C., to name a few.

A graduate of the University of Minnesota, Ohlson is a retired Professor of Art at Hunter College, where he taught for thirty-five years. He is represented in New York by the Andre Zarre Gallery.

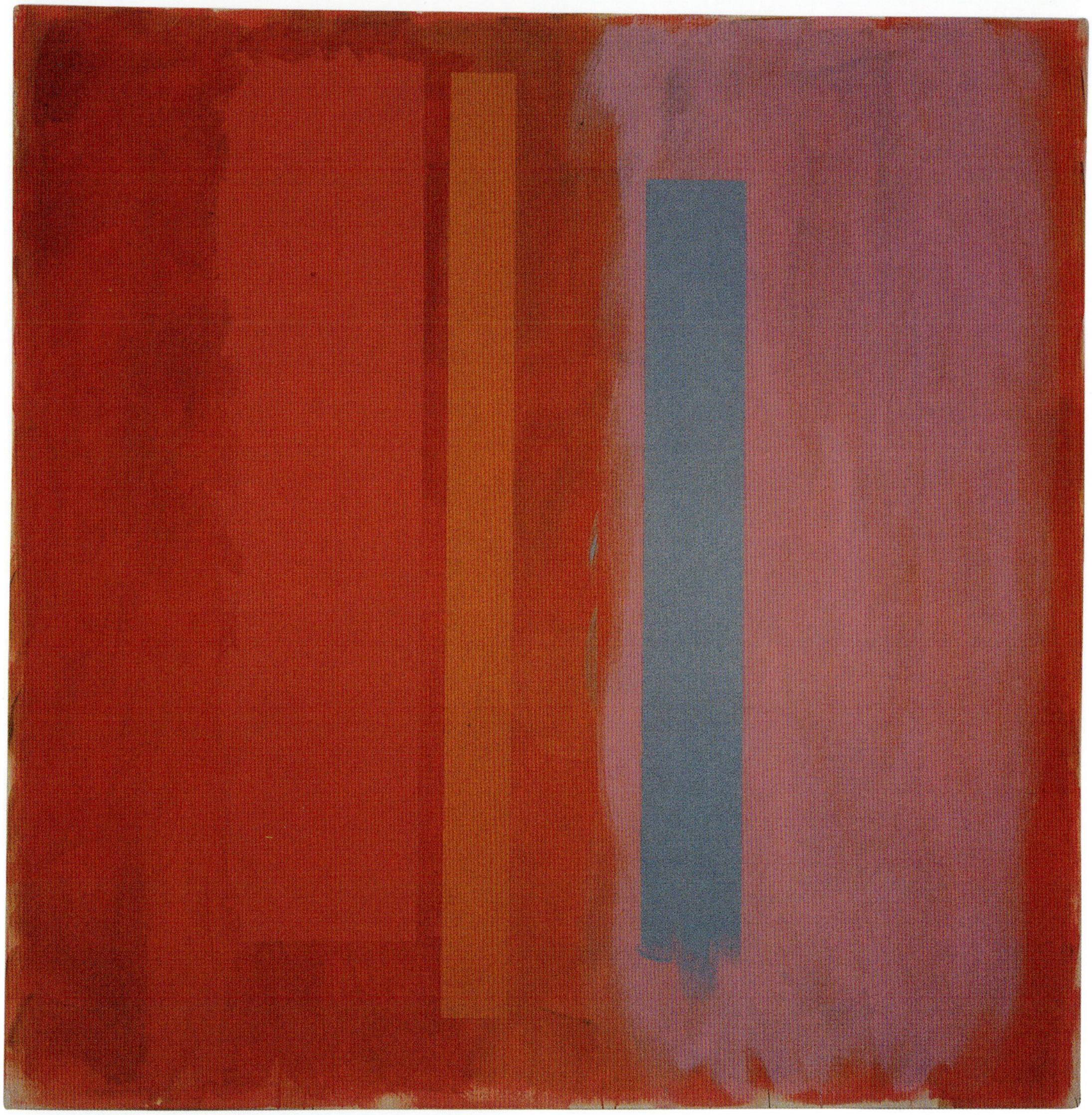

Ghost, acrylic on canvas, 78" x 76", 1991. *Collection of Marie Tanner and Guiseppe D'Arcangelo.*

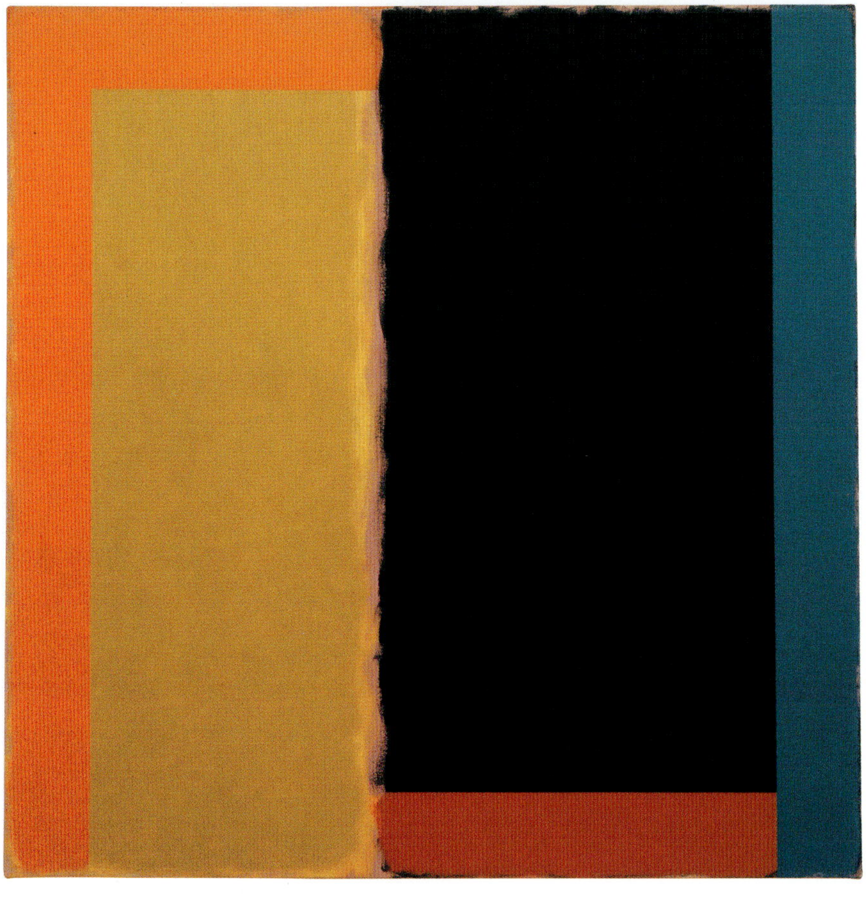

Gilt, acrylic on canvas, 62" x 60", 1984. *Collection of Rochelle and Larry Sullivan.*

Philip Pearlstein

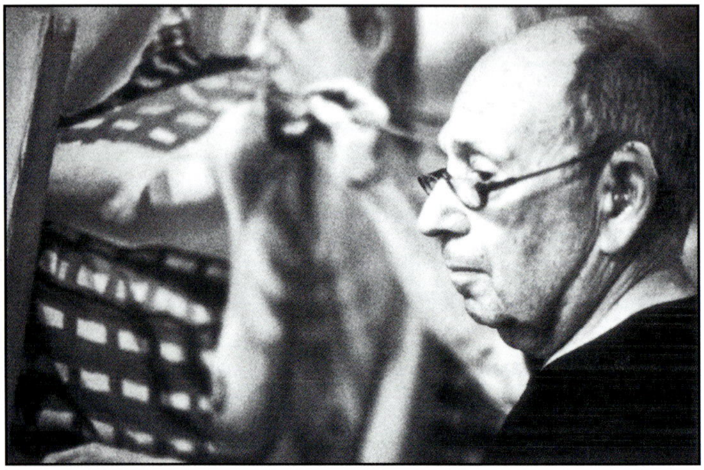

Photograph © Brian Rigney Hubbard.

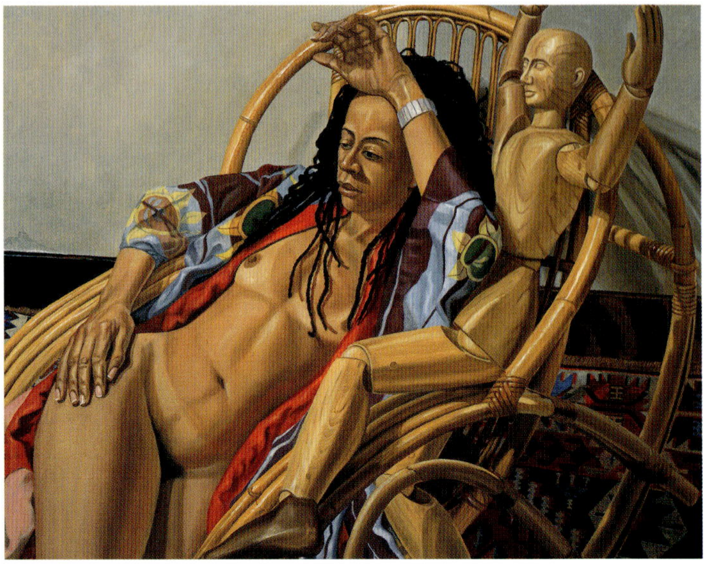

Model on Bamboo Lounge with Artist Mannequin, oil on canvas, 48" x 60", 2005. *Photograph by Oren Slor. © Philip Pearlstein. Courtesy of Betty Cuningham Gallery.*

Philip Pearlstein, President of the American Academy of Arts and Letters, and an elected member of the National Academy of Design, paints people and landscapes from direct observation, where he says the intensity of working from living models forces him to confront the technical challenges of capturing the play of light over forms and the specifics of color his eye sees. In refutation of the claim by abstractionists that the camera has made realist painting obsolete, Pearlstein has said he wants to make the *camera* obsolete, and aims to break the flatness of the picture plane, to capture the spatial relationships seen, without artistic editing. What is painted between the outlines is critical in creating meaningful art for him, and the honesty of attempting to recreate forms visually is the hallmark of his realist painting.[160]

Focusing on the formal elements—pattern, composition, color, light, and highly finished detail—Pearlstein crops his large nudes tightly, leaving to the viewer's imagination completion of the image beyond the edge of the canvas.

A student of art historian Irwin Panofsky at New York University's Institute of Fine Arts, where he received his master's degree, Pearlstein also attended the Carnegie Institute of Technology, received a Fulbright Fellowship, and began an extensive series of solo and group exhibitions of his paintings, drawings, and prints, now seen around the world in most major museum and other public collections. Retrospectives of his work include those held at the Milwaukee Art Museum, the Carnegie Museum of Art, and the Hirshhorn in Washington, D.C.

His lengthy academic career includes teaching at Pratt Institute in Brooklyn, then twenty-five years with the Art Department at Brooklyn College, where he served as distinguished professor before his retirement.

Pearlstein is represented by the Betty Cuningham Gallery in New York.

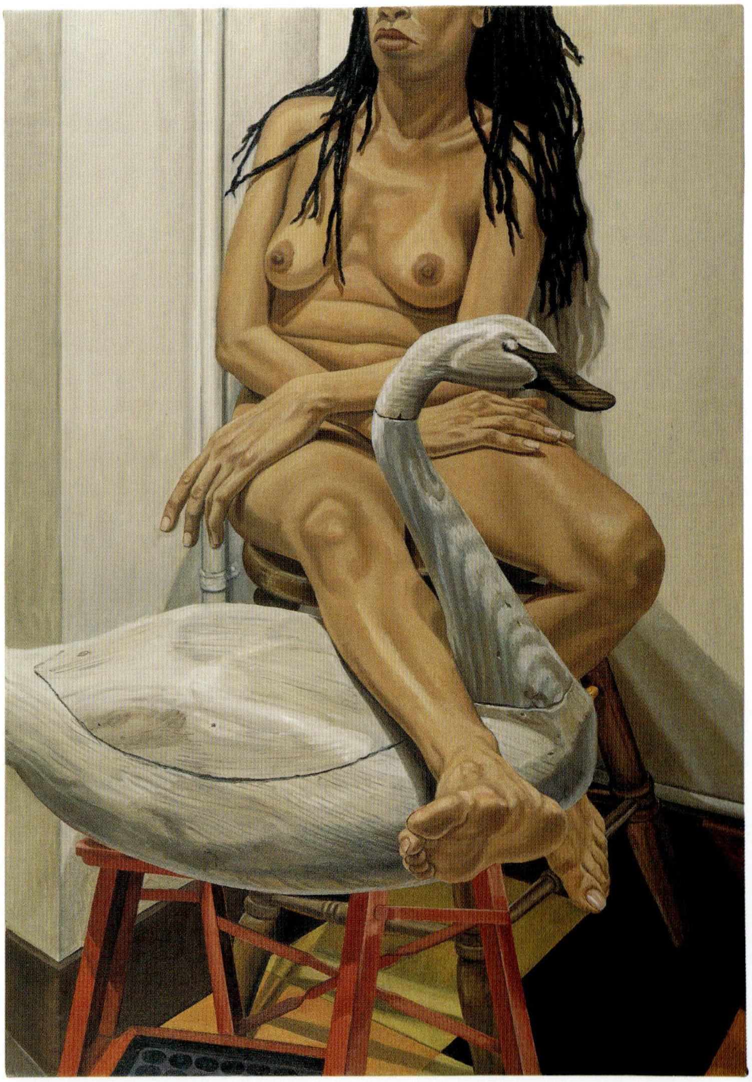

Model with Swan Decoy on Ladder, oil on canvas, 50" x 34", 2002. *Photograph by Oren Slor. © Philip Pearlstein. Courtesy of Betty Cuningham Gallery.*

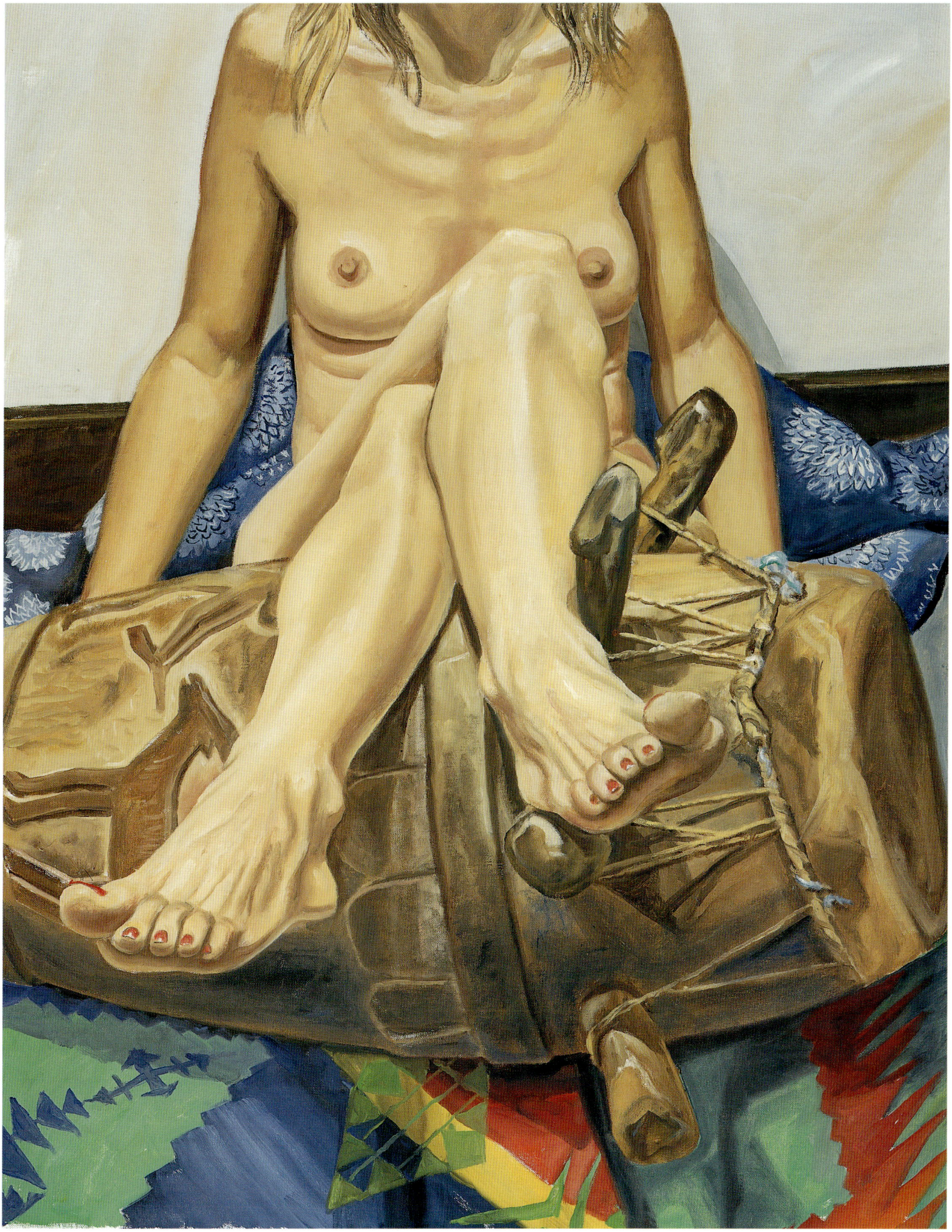

Model with Legs Crossed over African Drum, oil on canvas, 34" x 26", 2005.
Photograph by Oren Slor. © Philip Pearlstein. Courtesy of Betty Cuningham Gallery.

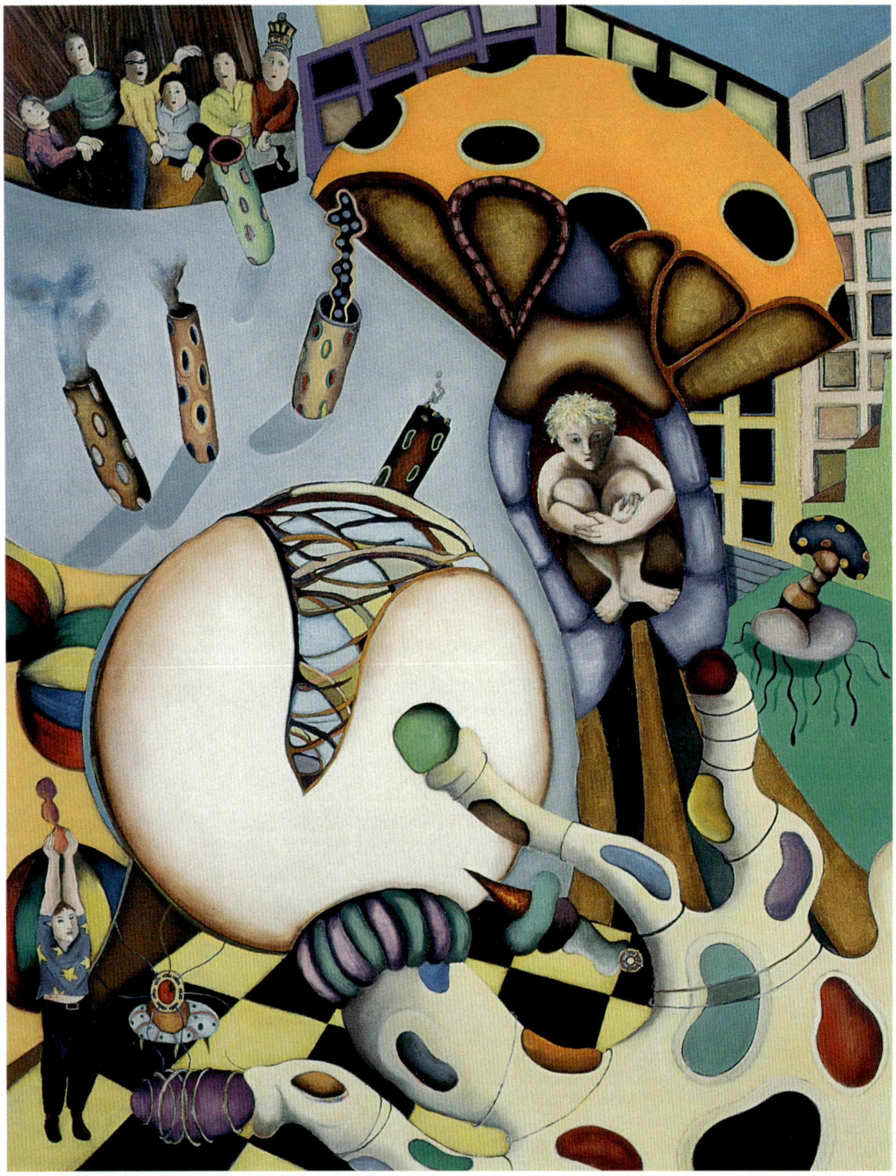

Magical Thinking / Paranoid Thoughts, oil on panel, 35" x 27", 2004.

Tracy Phillips

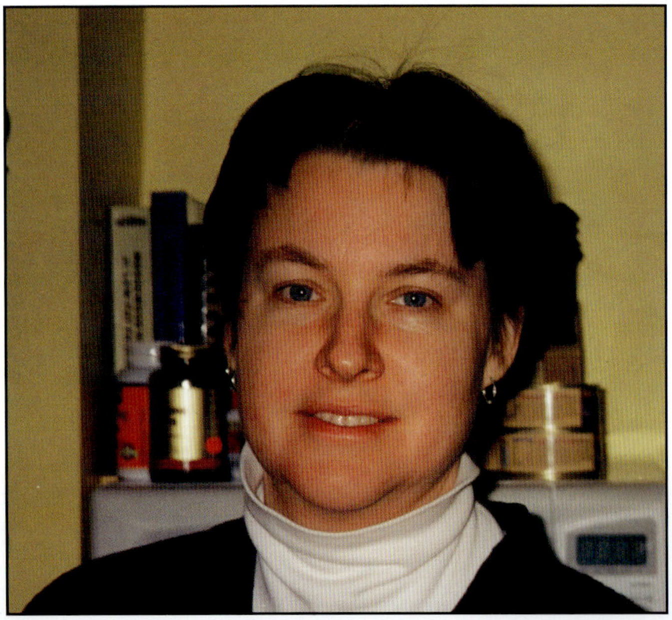

Courtesy of the artist.

Tracy Phillips, who does not work from models, draws upon memory and imagination, using an intuitive process to create her "psychologically layered,"[161] formally complex paintings filled with recurrent themes of "(dis)connection, (dis)location, contradiction, irreverence, fragmentation, (dis)association, and whimsy."[162]

In their ambiguity, her paintings "seek to evoke interpretation, drawing the viewer in to discover meaning."[163]

Phillips, who received her BFA from the Parsons School of Design, also holds degrees from Pratt Institute and Fordham University.

Recipient of awards from the National Association of Women Artists, she is a member of the Brooklyn Waterfront Artists Coalition and the Brooklyn Arts Council.

Phillips' paintings have been exhibited in solo and group exhibitions throughout the United States, including the Williamsburg Art and Historical Center and the Diane Boisvert Gallery in Brooklyn, the Islip Museum on Long Island, New York, and the Detroit Museum of New Art.

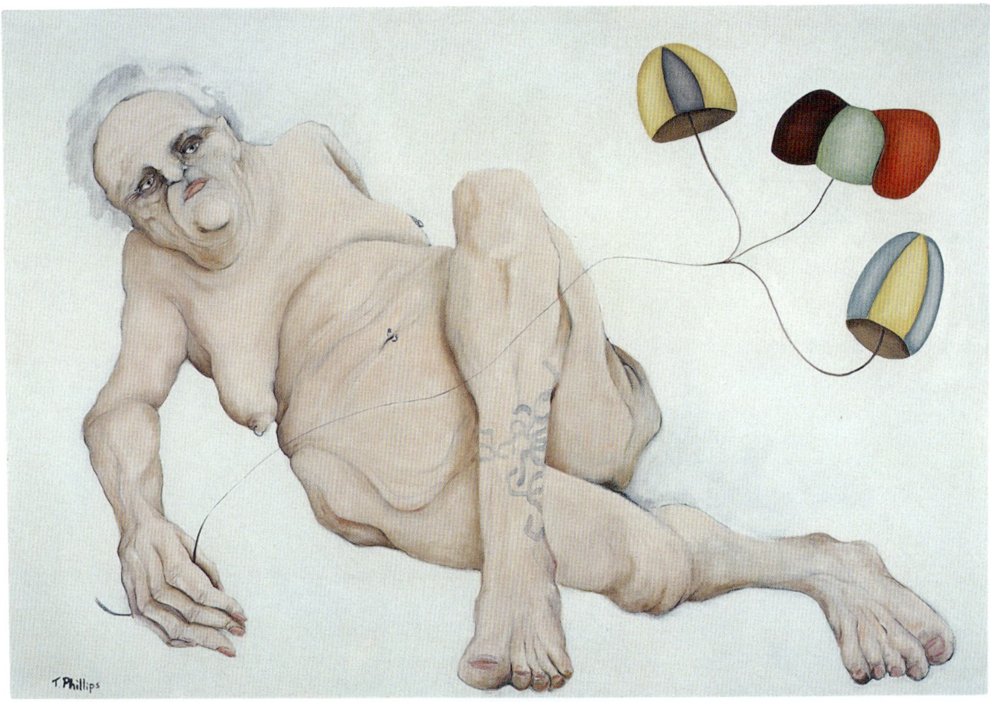

The Moment Before She Willed Her Balloons into Cerberus, oil on linen, 38" x 54", 2005.

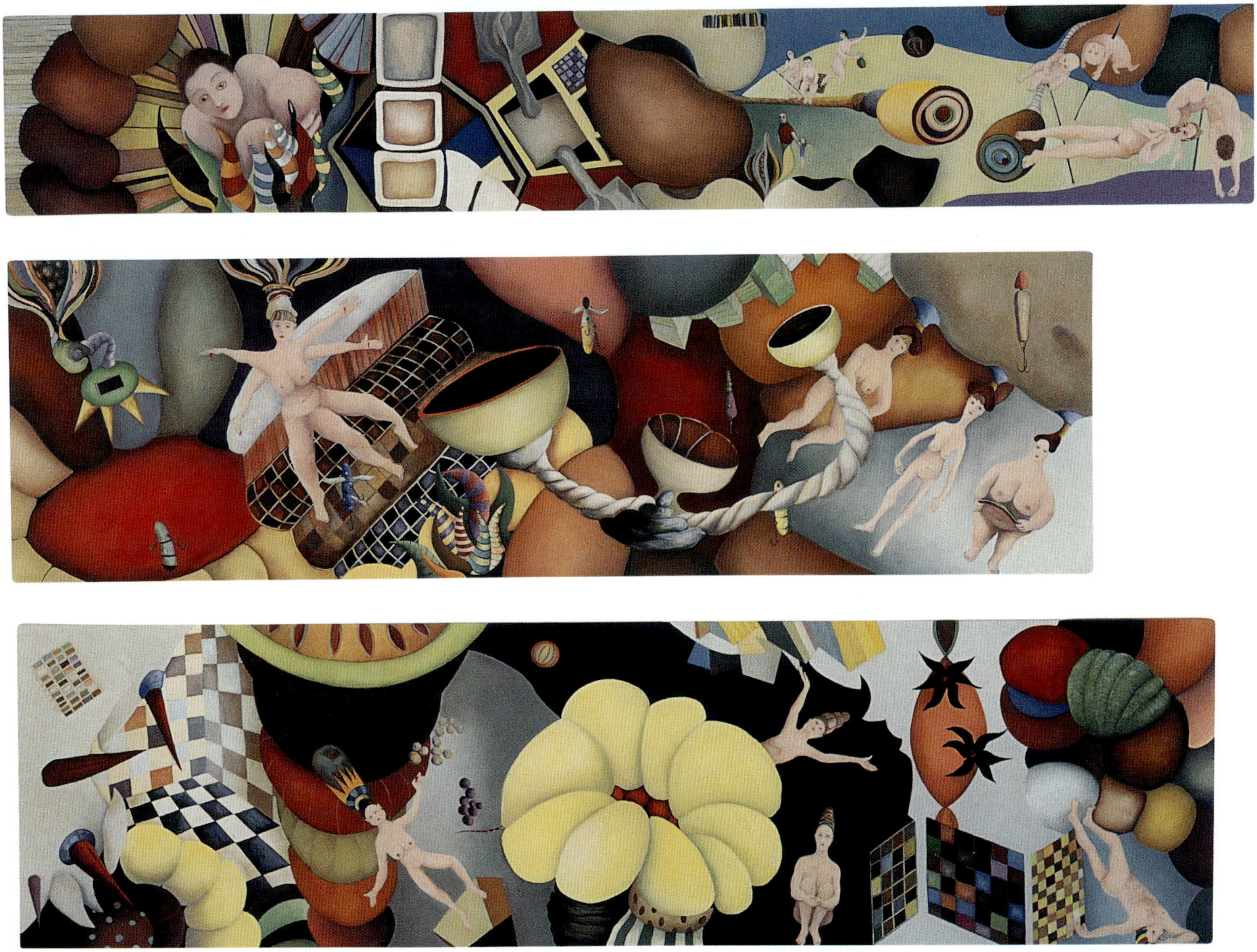

Non-sense-less, oil on panels, 30" x 49", 2003.

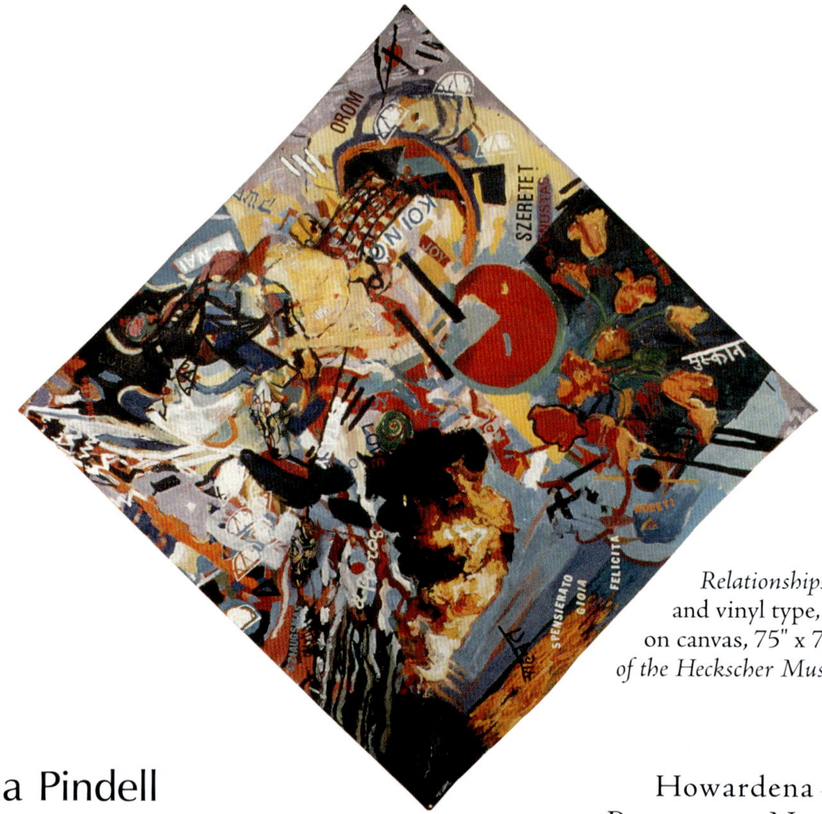

Relationships (Kandinsky #1), acrylic and vinyl type, nails, plexiglas, mirror, on canvas, 75" x 75", 1995-96. *Collection of the Heckscher Museum, Huntington, NY.*

Howardena Pindell

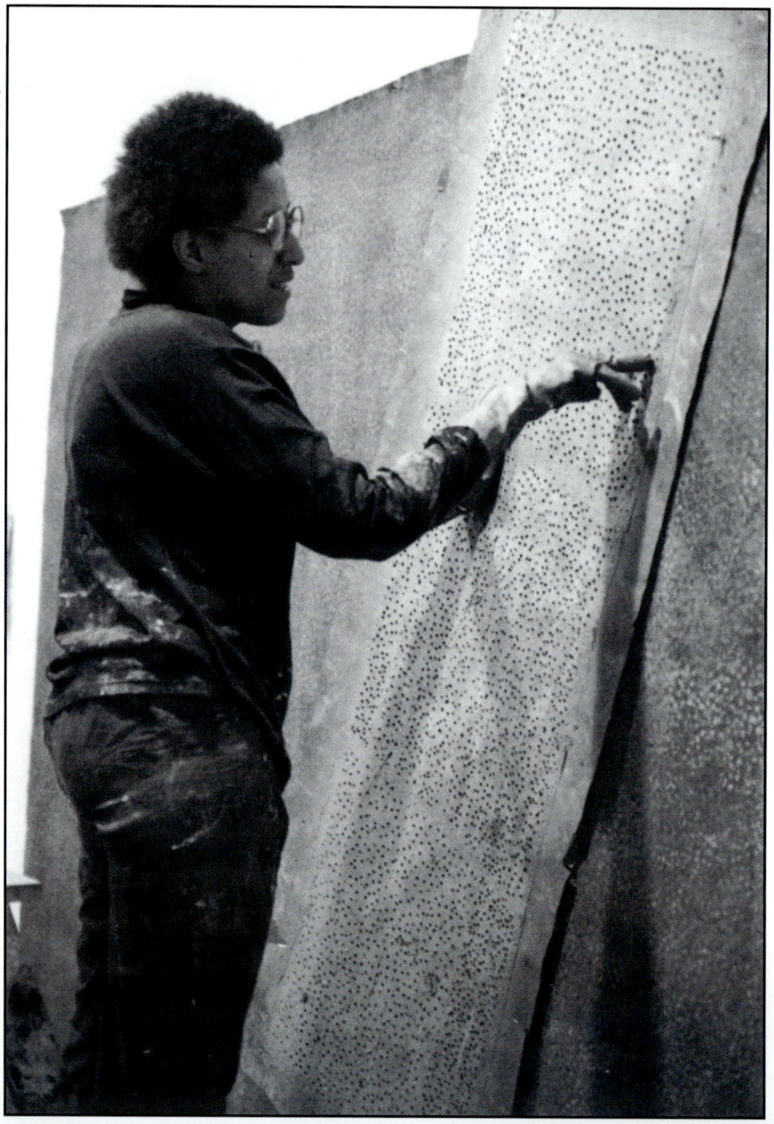

Courtesy of the artist.

Howardena Pindell is Director of MFA Programs at New York's State University at Stony Brook, where she has taught for over twenty-five years in a widely ranging academic career. She is driven by a passionate response to political and societal issues, which emerge as the major imagery in her complex, multi-media works. Her subjects range from an exploration of feelings about self and family to the historical past, including slavery, civil injustice, and human rights. She has developed a series of works incorporating split-color photographs from her extensive travels, in strips surrounded by painted areas, as a counterpoint to her large emotionally charged canvases, "as a resting place."[164]

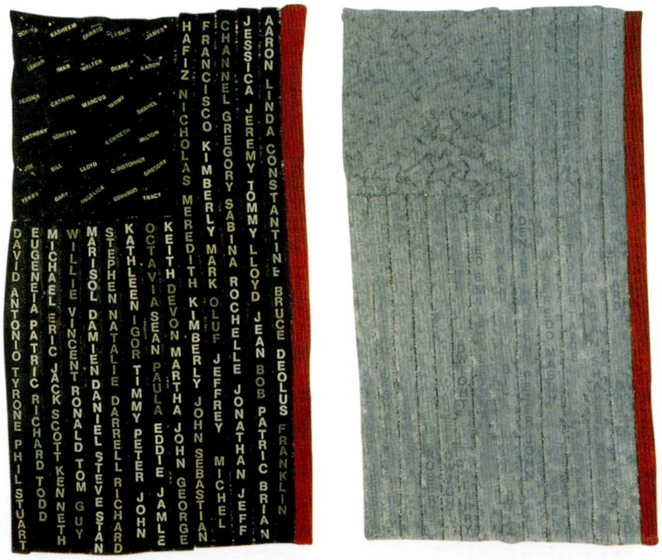

Separate but Equal: Genocide: AIDS, acrylic, oil stick, vinyl type, on sewn canvas, two panels, each 72" x 48", c.1990-92.

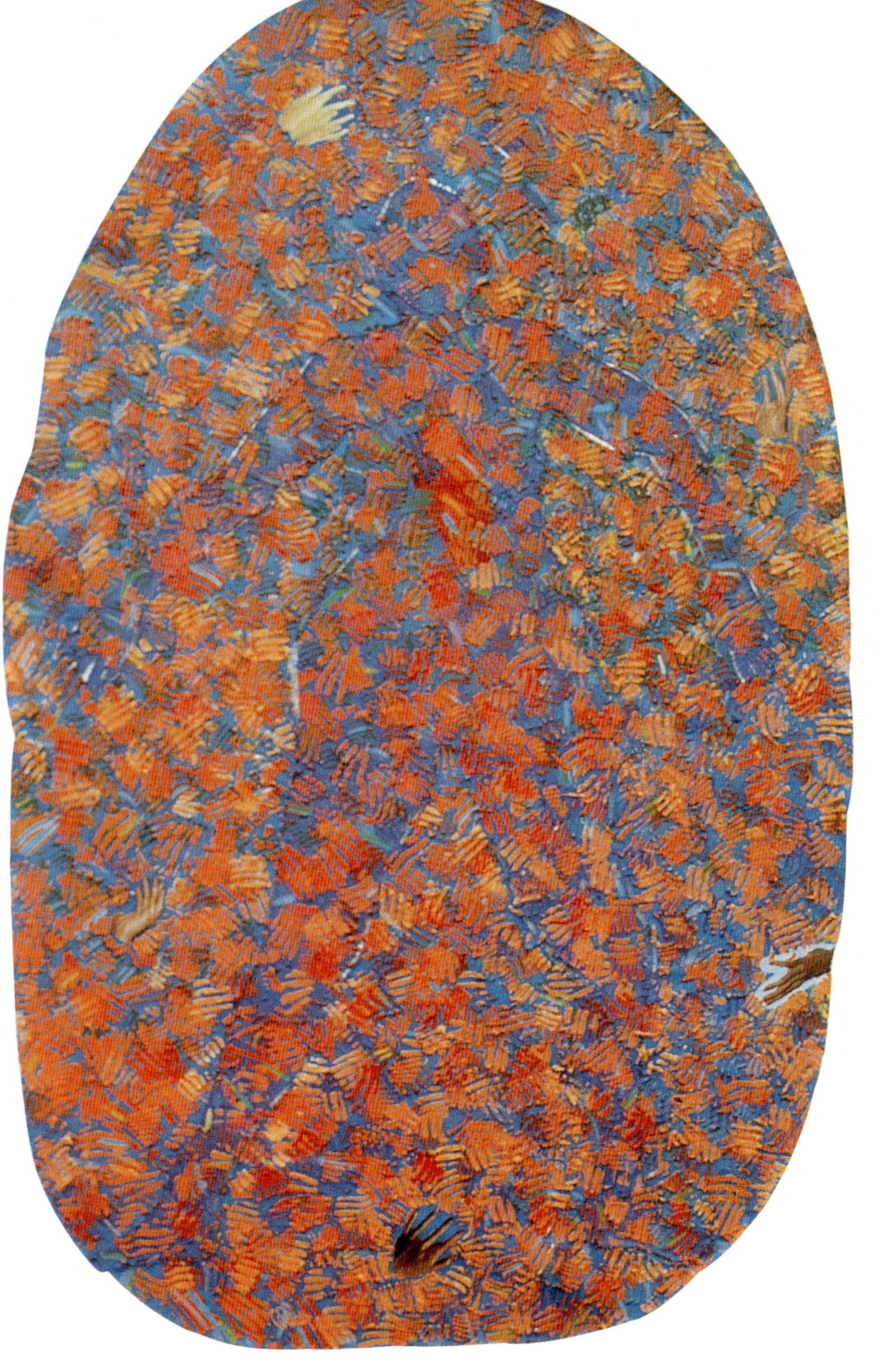

Autobiography: Fire: Suttee, acrylic, paper, polymer, photo-transfer on canvas, 90" x 56", c.1986-87. *Collection of Peter Huber, Norfolk, Virginia.*

Pindell, who holds a BFA from Boston University and a Yale MFA, where she studied with Nicolas Carone, is ever mindful of her special identity as "a black female artist in a white-dominated art world,"[165] and her own unique poly-cultural European/Jewish/Native American/African/French-Canadian/Jamaican heritage.

Carla Maria Verdino-Sullwold writes of Pindell's "skillful, imaginative, and tempestuous transformation of the material into the spiritual."[166] Pindell has won numerous grants and awards, including a John Simon Guggenheim Fellowship and a National Endowment for the Arts Fellowship. She has been awarded Honorary Doctorates of Fine Arts by Massachusetts College of Art in Boston and Parsons School of Design in New York.

Her works are to be seen in most major museums, including New York's Metropolitan Museum of Art and Harvard's Fogg Art Museum, and have been the subject of numerous major solo and group exhibitions. Pindell is represented by the N'Namdi Gallery and the Ellen Sragow Gallery in New York.

Stephanie Rauschenbusch

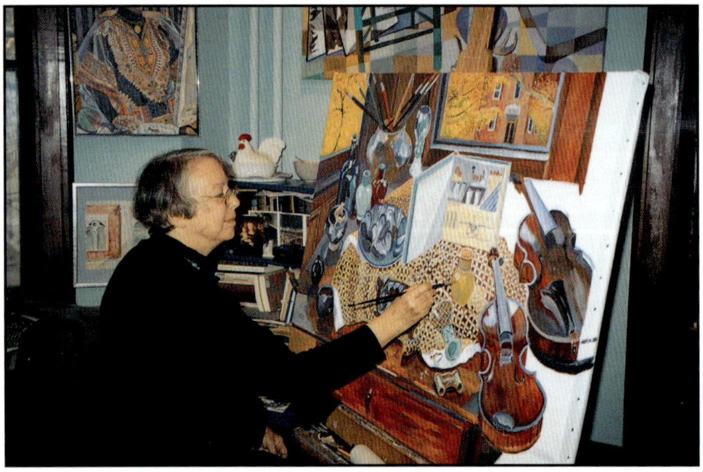

Courtesy of the artist.

Stephanie Rauschenbusch, whose work has been the subject of over a dozen solo exhibitions at the Noho Gallery, often uses the grid as a compositional device in her landscape paintings, which reflect her frequent European travels as well as the American West and many New York locations. "The point of the grid is modern—pushing toward abstraction ... and making colors central and essential. Color changes ... as objects ... pass through [it]. At my studio, as I looked out the windows at the Brooklyn and Manhattan bridges, the panes became a grid. ... It may also be seen as a quilt or tile pattern; I see it as a sort of play."[167]

Rauschenbusch is an honors graduate of Columbia University and Radcliffe College. As a doctoral candidate, she received a Danforth Foundation Kent Fellowship, a Woodrow Wilson Fellowship, and Phi Beta Kappa membership. Study at the New York Academy of Art and the Art Students League are highlights of her extensive education. She also completed an Artist's Residency at Cape Cornwall in England.

Rauschenbusch's works have been shown in many group and one-person exhibitions, including "Color Harmonious and Discordant" for the Women's Caucus for Art at Marymount Manhattan College, "American Women Artists at Cape Cornwall ..." at The Painting Center, New York City, and "Art and the Law," which traveled to Brandeis University's Rose Art Museum and the University of Virginia Museum. Her still life paintings have evoked such responses as John Russell's, "in a quiet way, ... a distinguished show,"[168] and Kate Millet's, "... these paintings are an essay on the still life: conscious/erudite, full of references and jokes and bits of this or that master. A lifetime of seeing ... intensified to a crush of understanding."[169]

Her works may be seen in many private and corporate collections. She is represented by the Noho Gallery in New York.

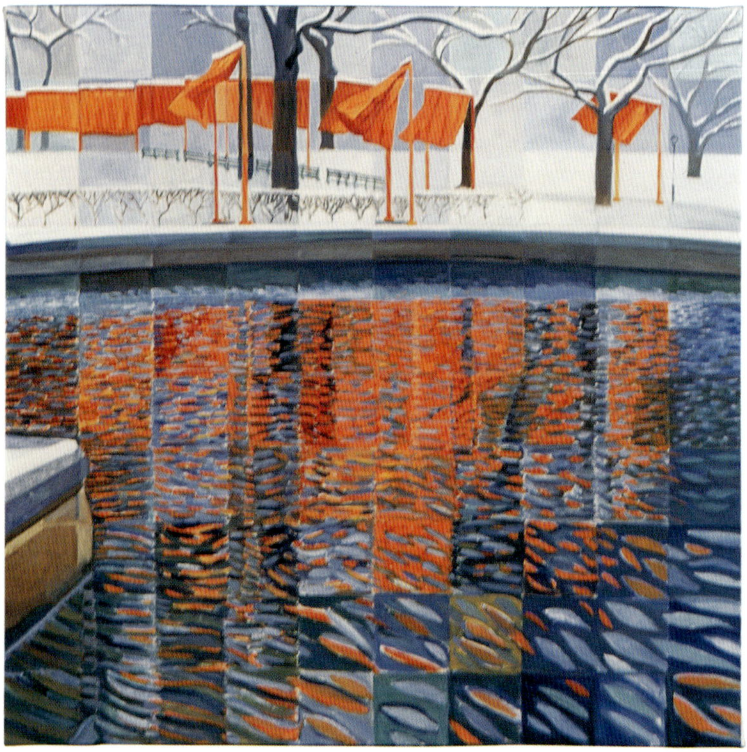

Christo's Gates Reflected in the Conservatory Water #1, oil on canvas, 40" x 40", 2005.

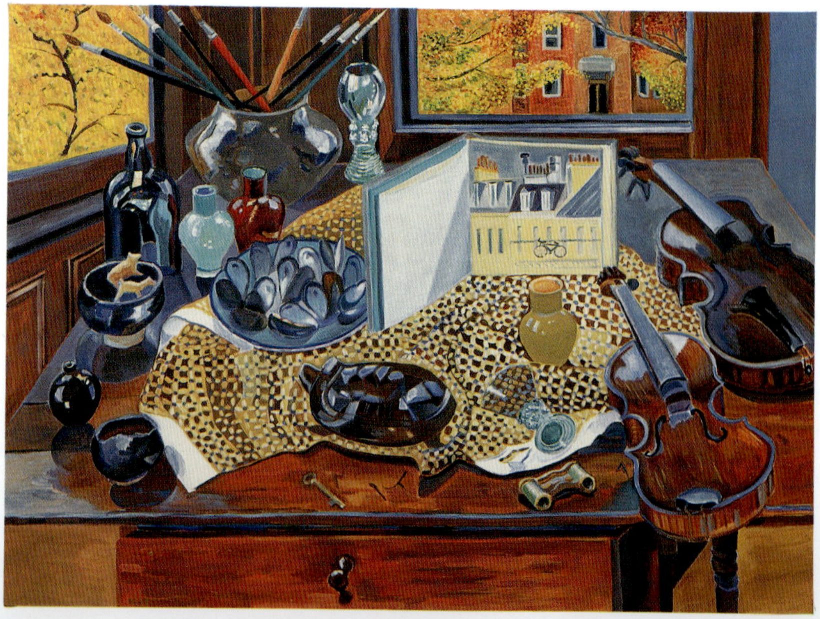

After Pieter Claesz's Still Life with Turtle, oil on linen, 36" x 48", 2005.

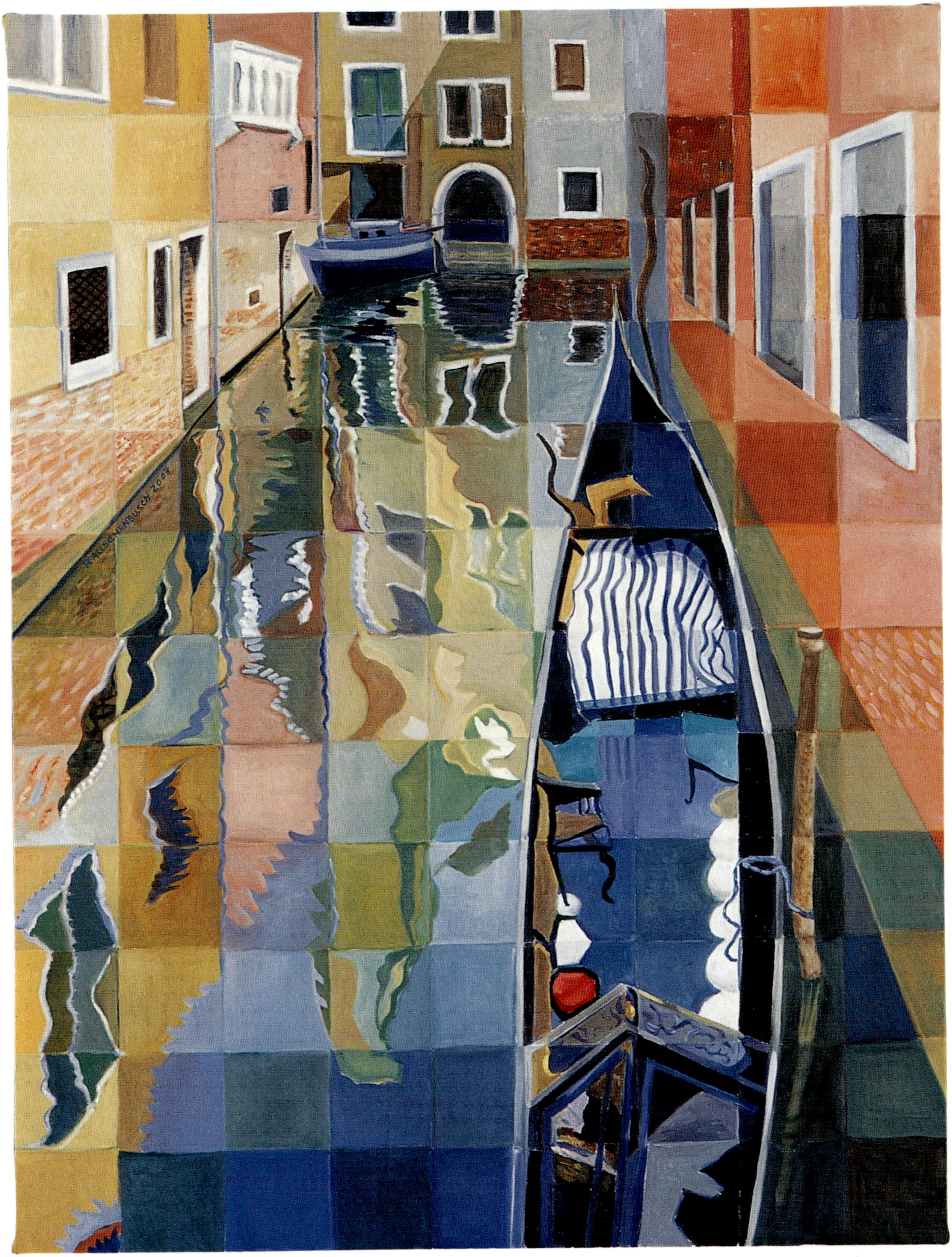

From a Venetian Bridge, oil on canvas, 48" x 36", 2003. *Collection of Hyo Sang Lee.*

Catherine Redmond

Catherine Redmond, for whom New York City has long been "a beacon ...,"[170] says, "Place matters. My work has always focused on it ... and my search to find something true within it!"[171] Through the orchestration of "strips, bands and spreads of pattern ... insisting on the flatness of the picture plane ... [she creates] quasi illusionistic still-life set-ups, [where] rectangular windows suddenly open into a perspectival space. ... Quite a ride ...with a supple shifting between representation and abstraction, Redmond ... [creates] a seamless weave of the two ..."[172] according to David Tannous.

Redmond, who studied at the Art Students League with Robert Beverly Hale, Lennart Anderson, and Vaclav Vytlacil, credits Larry Campbell with a special generosity, and many specific observations that she still remembers, though she is sustained by those who went before ... Hartley, Cézanne, Fra Angelico, notably.

A graduate of Harpur College, SUNY, Binghamton, New York, and a student at Cornell, she has received grants from Pratt Institute, The Cleveland Institute of Art, and the Art Students League.

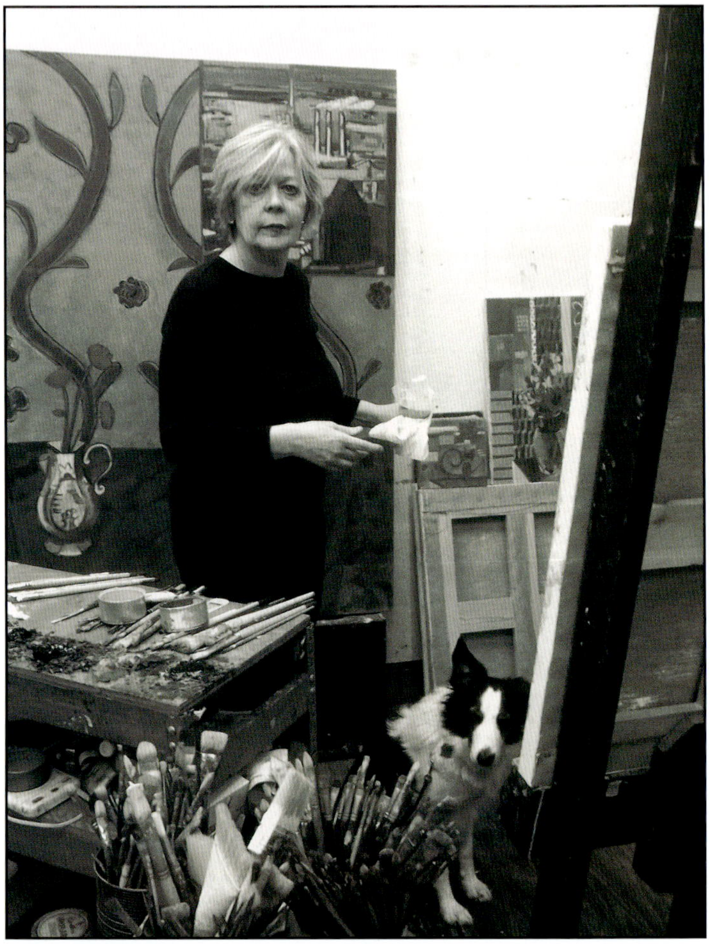

Catherine Redmond in the studio with Molly. *Photograph by Mireille Miller.*

Redmond's teaching career includes appointments at Pratt Institute, the Art Students League, The Cleveland Institute of Art, and the Vermont Council on the Arts.

Her many group exhibitions throughout the United States and in Korea include such titles as "New York Day and Night,"[173] "New York Perspectives,"[174] and "Rediscovering the Landscape of the Americas."[175] Her solo exhibitions have been seen at the Butler Institute of American Art in Youngstown, Ohio, M. D. Modern and Blue Mountain Galleries, and David Findlay Jr Fine Art in New York, which represents her work.

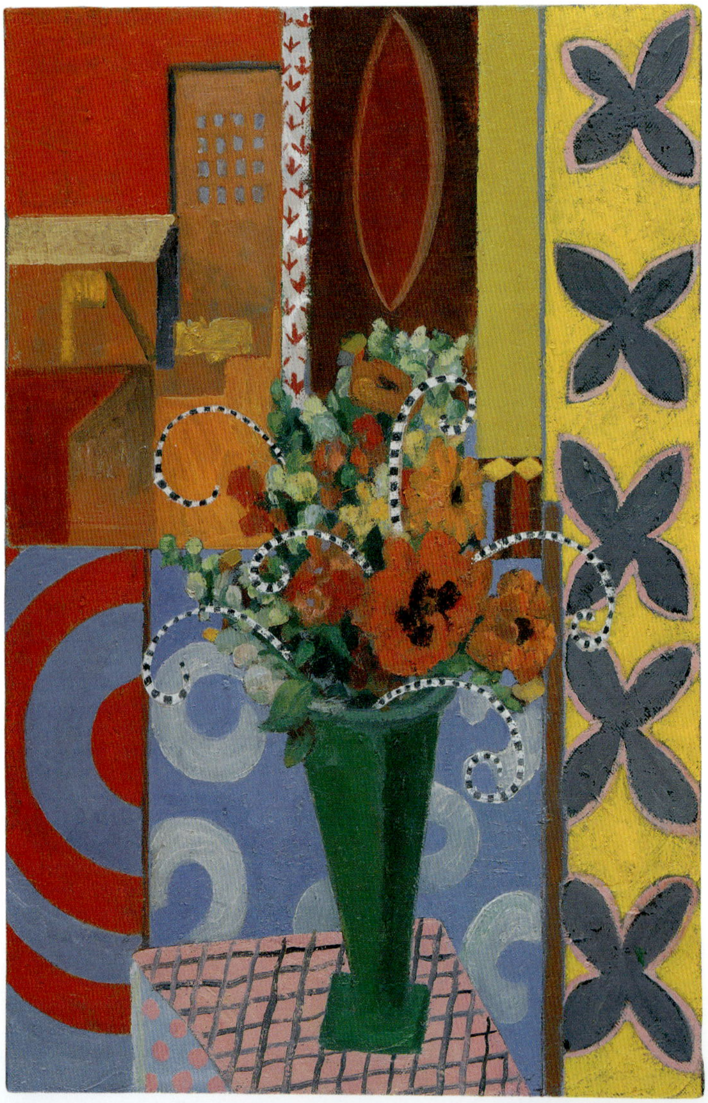

Fortuna, Fortuna, oil on linen, 22" x 14", 2005. *Private collection. Courtesy of David Findlay Jr Fine Art.*

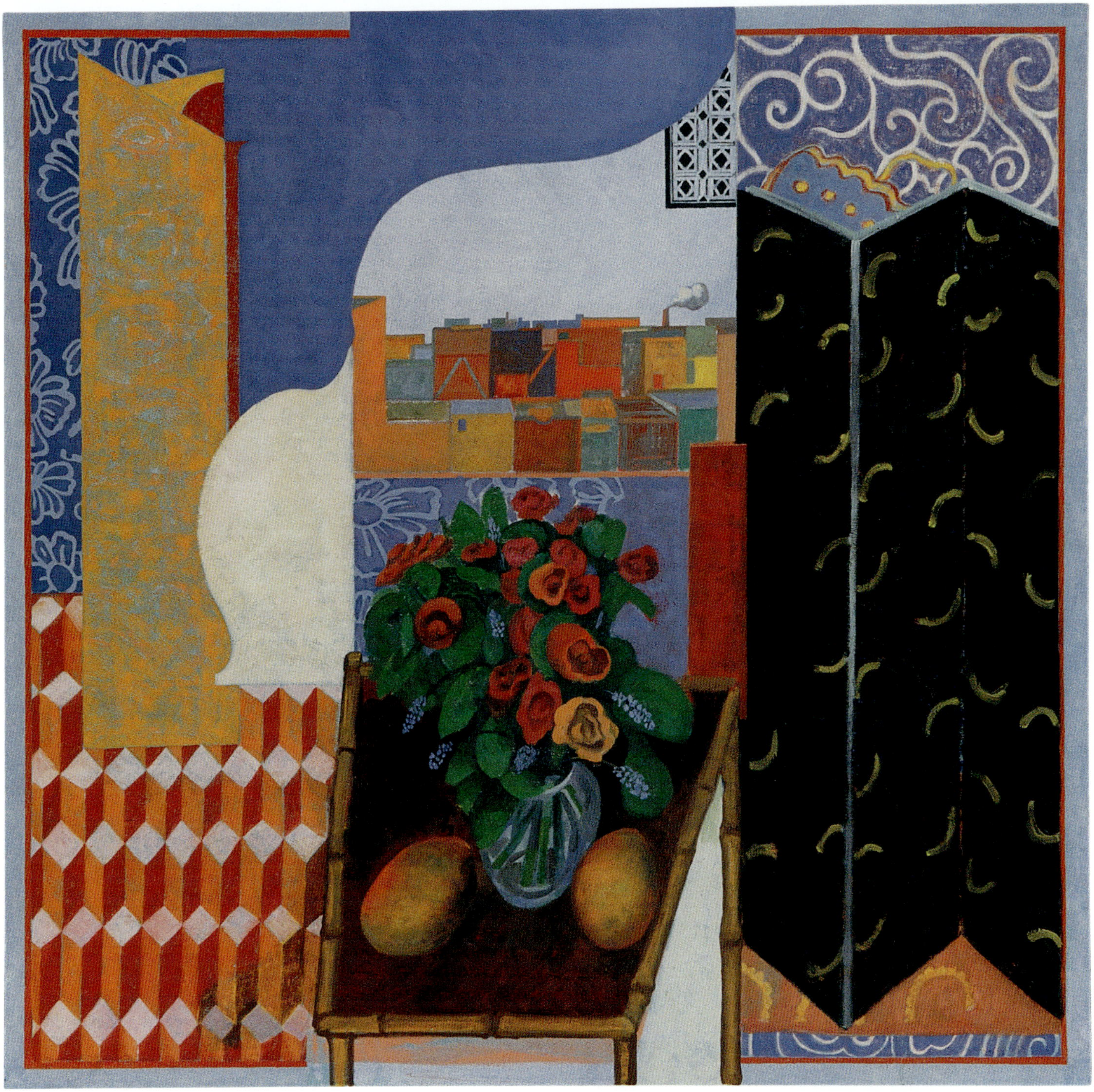

The Orientalist's Room, oil on canvas, 50" x 50", 2003. *Courtesy of David Findlay Jr Fine Art.*

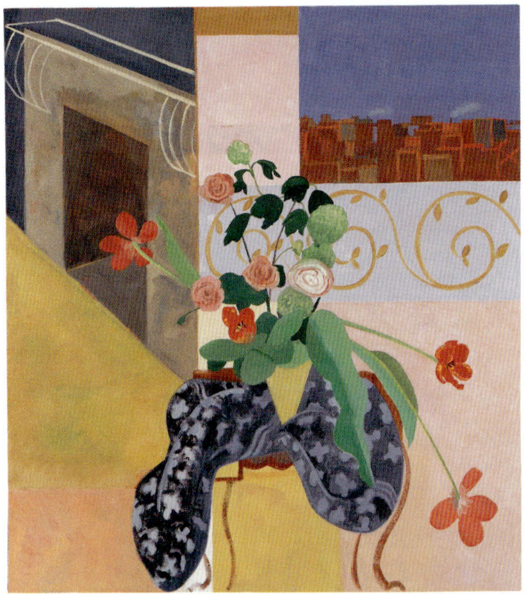

Remembering Magritte, oil on canvas, 60" x 60", 2003. *Courtesy of David Findlay Jr Fine Art.*

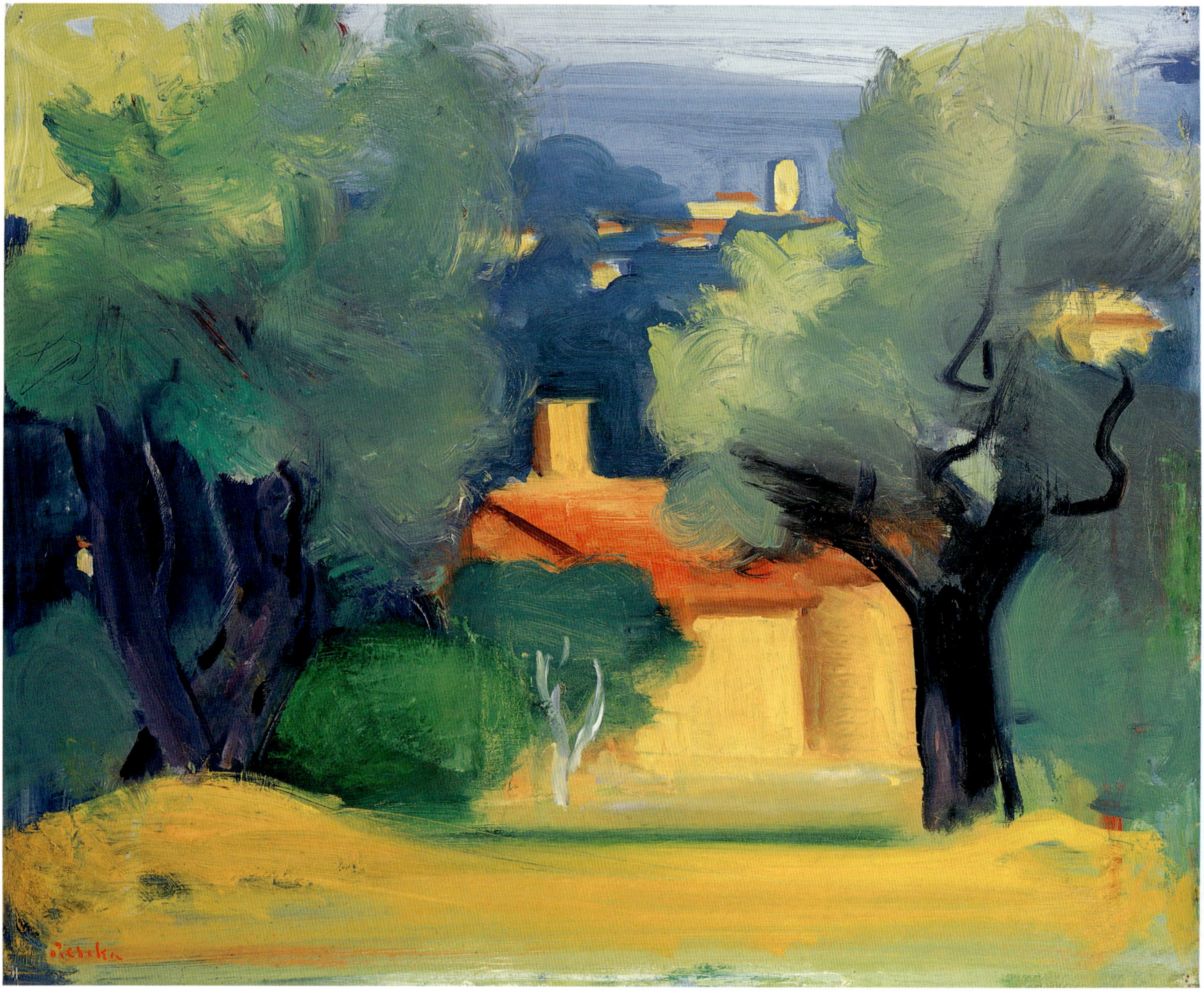

Fayence Through the Trees, oil on canvas, 21.25" x 25.5", 1997. *Courtesy of Salander-O'Reilly Galleries.*

Paul Resika, whose early exhibitions include "Painters from Cold Water Flats" at the historic Jacques Seligmann & Company Gallery, studied at the Hans Hofmann School of Fine Arts after several years with Sol Wilson in New York. Following travels in Europe and study in Rome and Venice, he began to concentrate on landscapes and marine subjects. His works have been described by Peter Gallo as "updated, symbolist … painting, modest in scale, and … highly efficient, … his daring color has lifted his work above … naturalism. Broad, flat planes of color in constructivist fashion, shallow space, sparse use of gestural line, all recall the style of his teacher, [Hofmann]."[176]

Resika, elected to the National Academy of Design, has had dozens of solo exhibitions throughout the United States, notably at the George Dix, Peridot, Graham Modern, and the Salander-O'Reilly Gallery, which represents his work.

His many group exhibitions have been seen at the National Academy of Design, The American Academy of Arts and Letters, the Metropolitan Museum of Art, and Parsons School of Design, among others in the United States, at several exhibitions of "American Painters in Venice,"[177] Italy, and at other European locations. Resika's works are in many major museum and public collections such as the Metropolitan Museum of Art and the National Academy of Design, the Chase Manhattan Bank, and the Society of Memorial Sloan-Kettering Cancer Center in New York.

Paul Resika

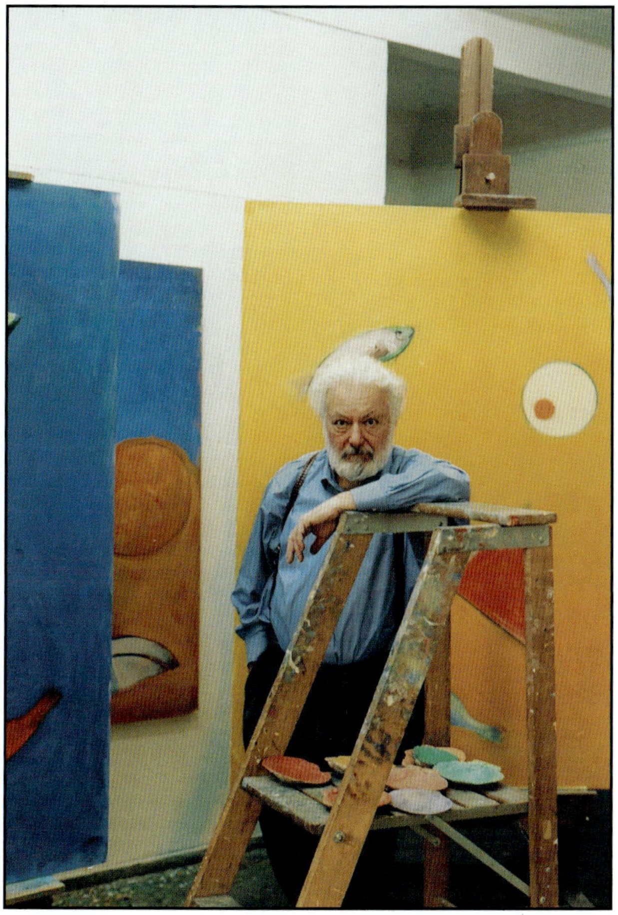

Photograph by Blair Resika.

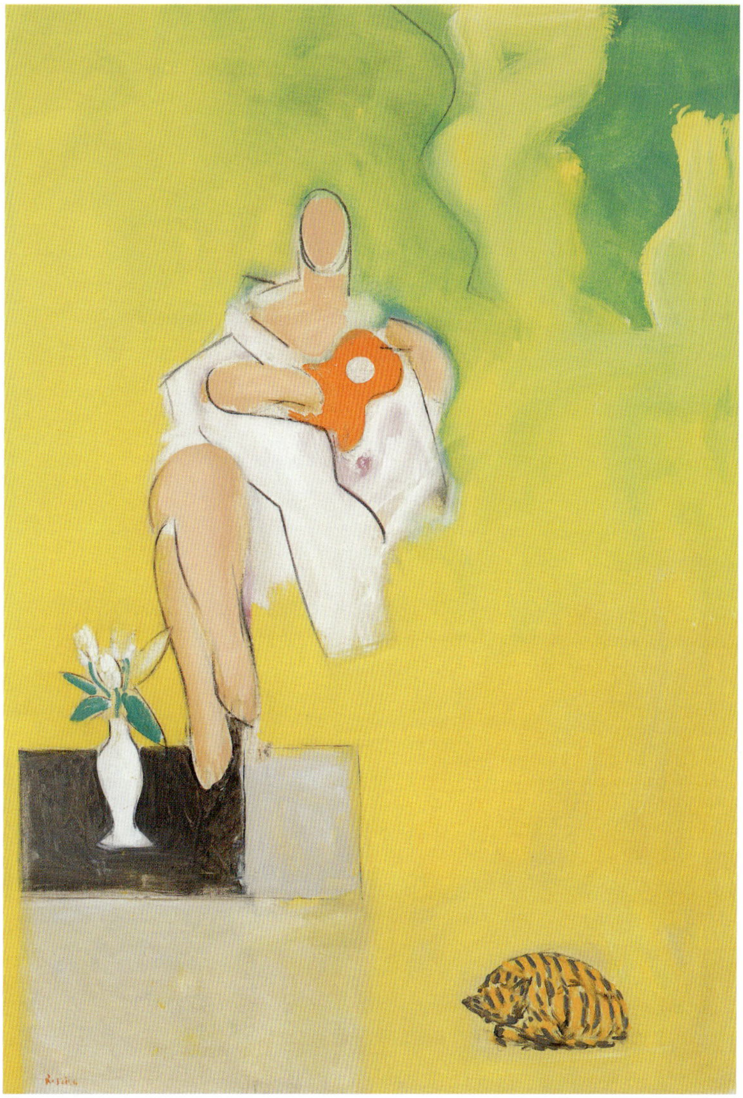

Striped Cat, oil on canvas, 76" x 51", 2003. *Courtesy of Salander-O'Reilly Galleries.*

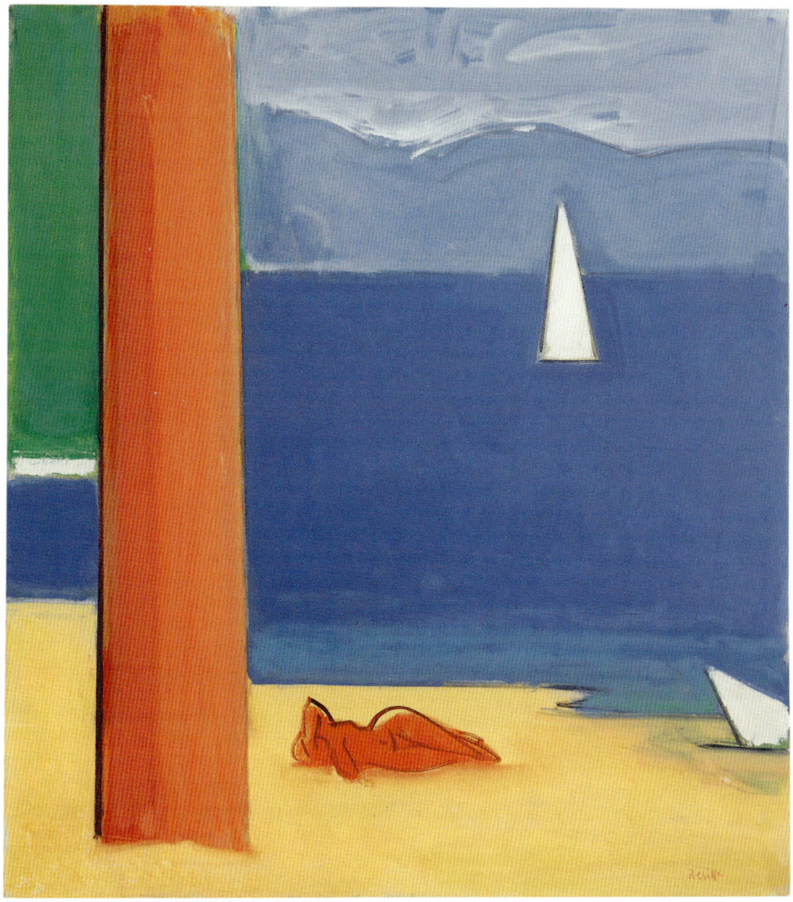

Noon, oil on canvas, 60" x 52", 2004. *Courtesy of Salander-O'Reilly Galleries.*

Robert Richenburg

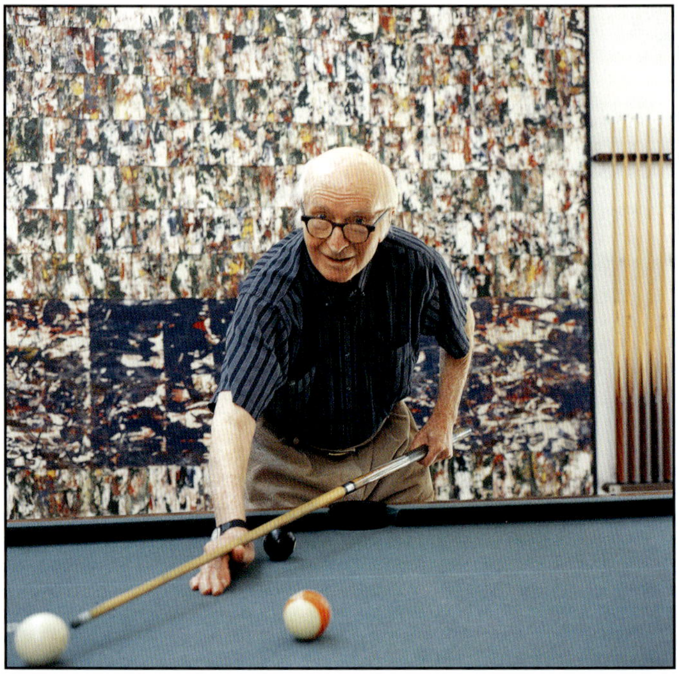

Photograph by Regina Cherry.

Robert Richenburg, a student of Hans Hofmann, Amedée Ozenfant, Reginald Marsh, and George Grosz, was a participant in the historic Ninth Street Show of early abstract expressionists, a member of the legendary Artist's Club, and a regular at the Cedar Tavern. He taught at Pratt during this time, and through all these activities got to know many major figures in the New York Art world. Irving Sandler called him, "one of the most forceful painters on the New York Art scene."[178]

His works, now in most important public and many corporate collections, were first seen in group exhibitions at the Artist's Gallery at the New School for Social Research and the Stable Gallery Annuals, and later included in major New York art museum exhibitions.

A career change, to teach at Cornell in Ithaca, New York, introduced a period of experimentation with many new mediums, techniques, and ideas. Wartime experiences during World War II encouraged receptiveness to incorporating found objects in his work, which increasingly presented a dark, tragic view of life. Applying black over sections of vividly colored canvases, then scraping away selectively with a palette knife, Richenburg achieved a new direction, later refined by layering and scraping grid-like black and color surfaces. "The result was a tremendous, explosive energy,"[179] says Bonnie L. Grad of Brandeis University's Rose Art Museum, which held a retrospective of the artist's works.

Of the black paintings, Richenburg has said, "I try to find the inner structure of the light beneath ... a long, desperate encounter between the light, the darkness and myself ... to find the real beauty of order ... within the process of its decay."[180]

He is represented by David Findlay Jr Fine Art in New York.

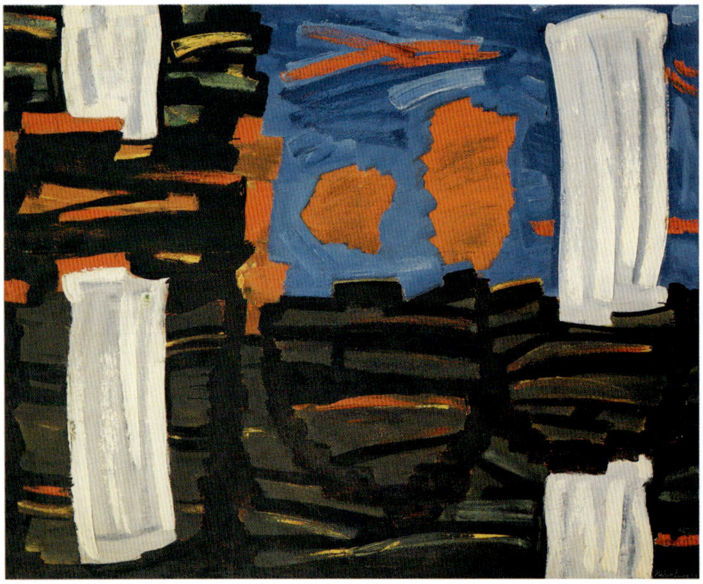

Redeem, oil on canvas, 50" x 60", 1953. *Courtesy of David Findlay Jr Fine Art.*

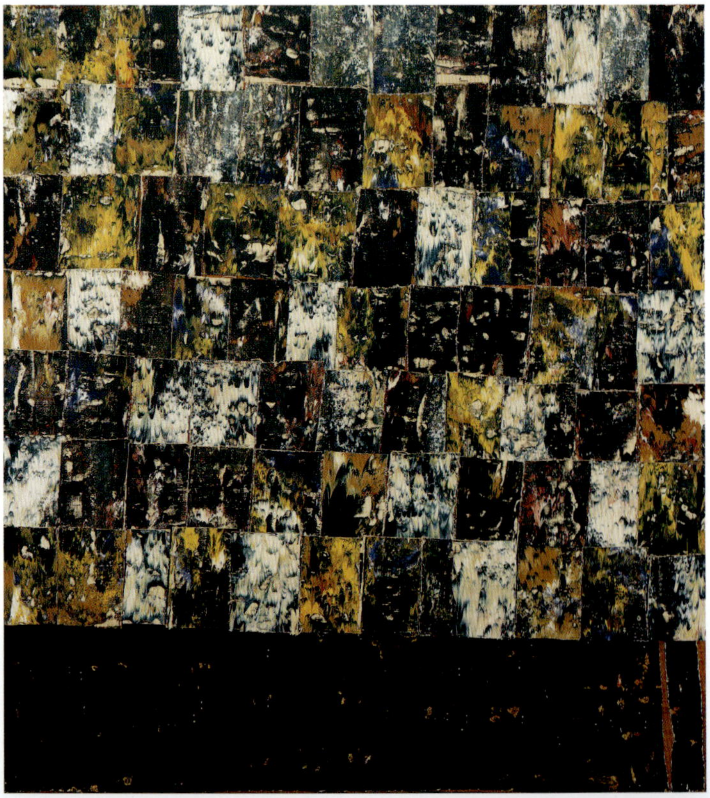

Dark Below, oil shingle on plywood, 47" x 42", 1962. *Courtesy of David Findlay Jr Fine Art.*

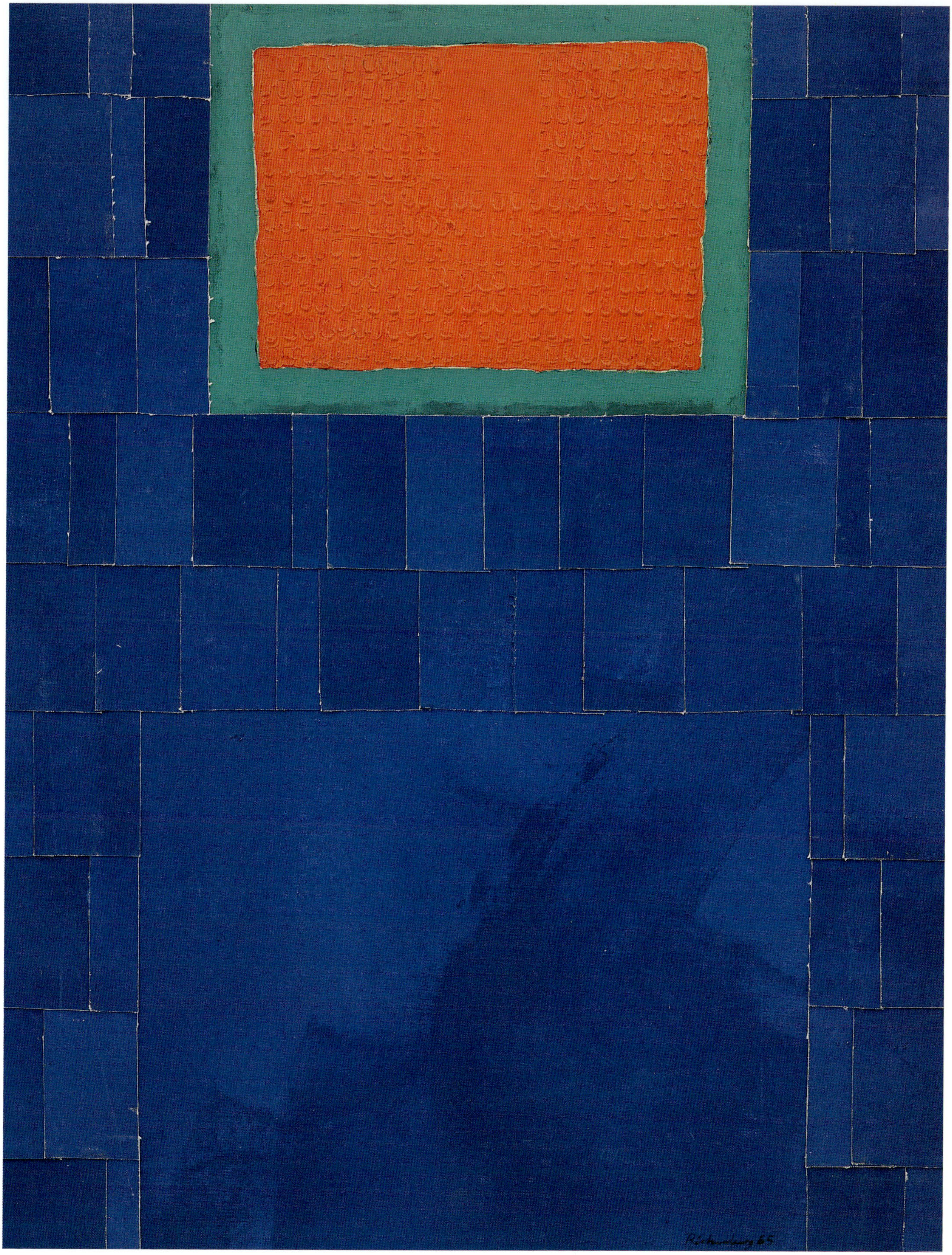

Red Top, acrylic on canvas collage on wood, 48" x 36", 1965. *Courtesy of David Findlay Jr Fine Art.*

Faith Ringgold

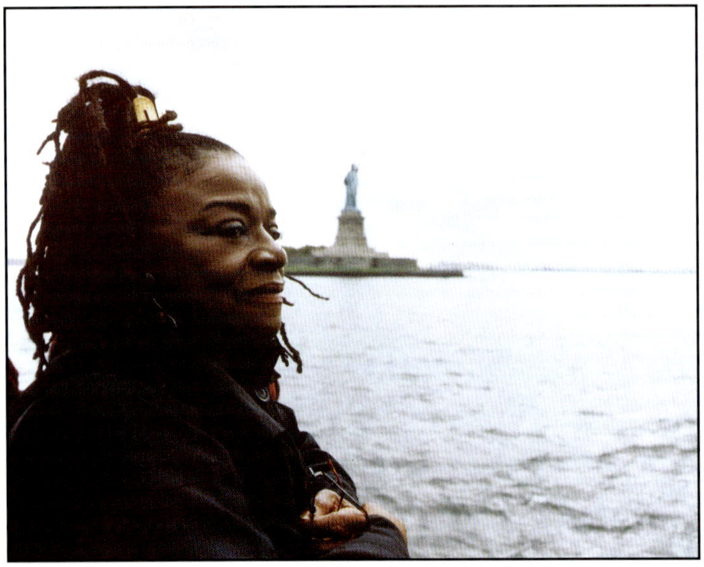

Courtesy of Faith Ringgold Studios.

Faith Ringgold's daughter, Michelle Wallace, identifies her as "an Afro-American artist contending with the selective amnesia of the Euro-American establishment, haunted by vestiges of psychological slavery, [who aims to achieve] a transition ... to a condition of spiritual freedom and full psychic citizenship."[181]

In her series paintings, "The French Collection," "American Collection," "American People Series," "Black Light Series," and others, Ringgold has imagined or re-created specific events in the history of the African-American experience in Europe and in the United States.

Born in Harlem, Ringgold learned to make quilts (a family tradition), went on to study at City College, and taught in the public schools before earning an MA and traveling to Europe.

Deeply involved in civil rights and feminist activities, incorporating fabric and "folk art"[182] materials in her work, and expressing narrative content, she has long focused on issues of slavery, racism, and sexism, often utilizing a grid format in "painted story quilts,"[183] recalling and giving new life to the quiltmaker's modules.

A Professor Emerita of Art at the University of California, San Diego, Ringgold resides on both coasts. She has won numerous major awards, including a John Simon Guggenheim Memorial Fellowship and two National Endowment for the Arts awards, and her work is included in the permanent collection of many museums worldwide. She has a lengthy record of solo and group exhibitions, has received seventeen honorary doctorates, and has written and illustrated over a dozen children's books. She is President of the Anyone Can Fly Foundation, providing grants for the study of the visual culture of the African Diaspora.

Ringgold is represented by the ACA Gallery in New York.

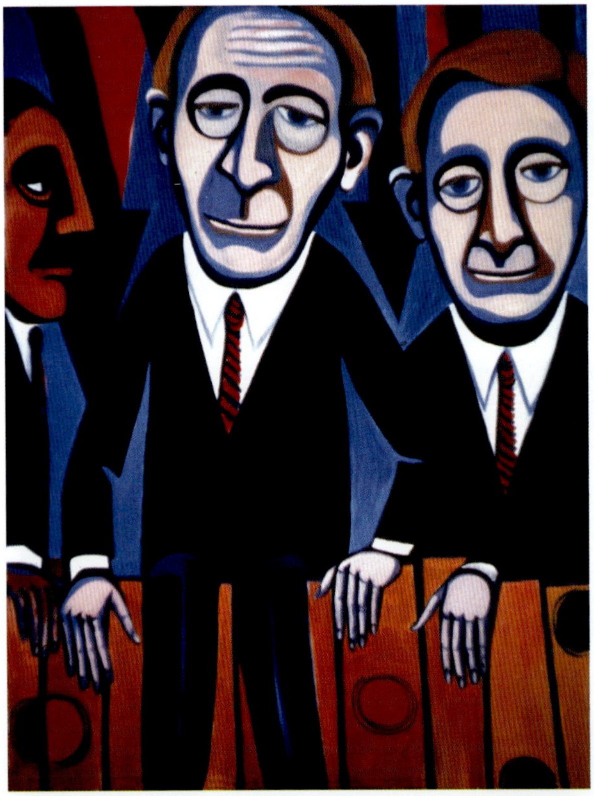

Three Men on a Fence (American People Series), oil on canvas, 40" x 30", 1964. *Courtesy of Faith Ringgold Studios.*

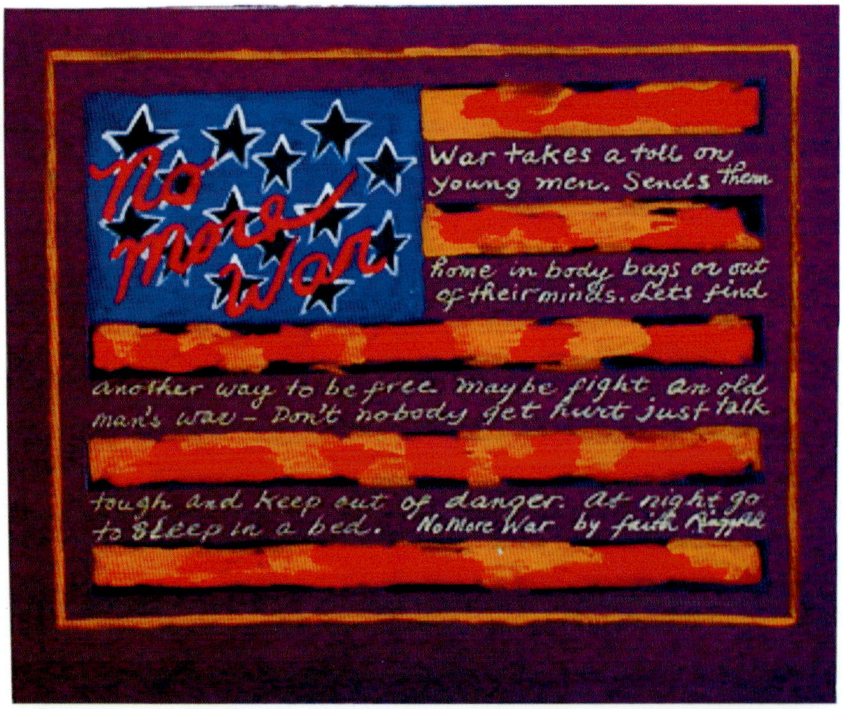

Freedom Flag #5: No More War, acrylic on paper, 8.5" x 11", 2002. *Courtesy of Faith Ringgold Studios.*

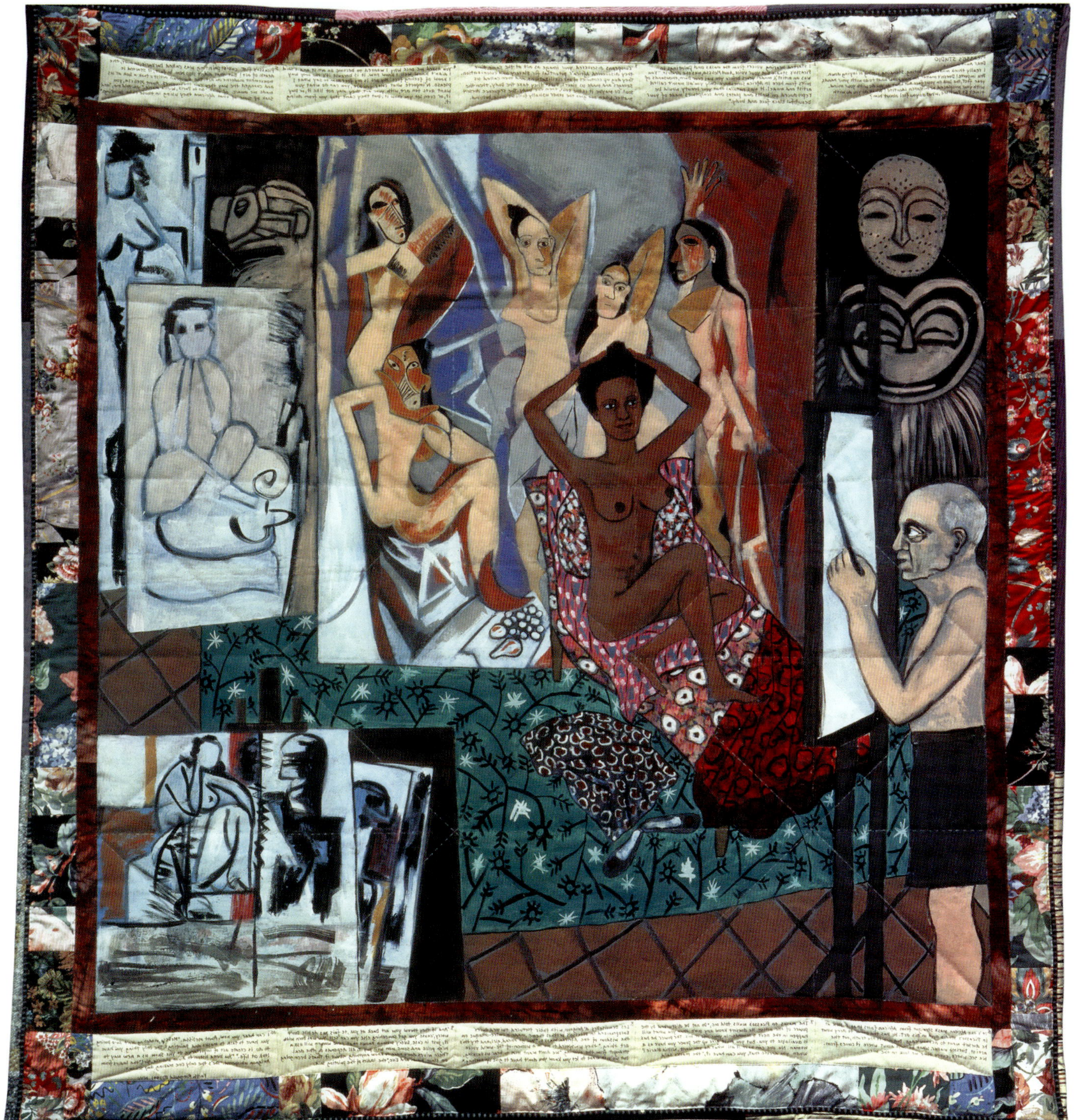

Picasso's Studio (The French Connection Series #7), acrylic on canvas with pieced fabric border, 73" x 68", 1991.
Courtesy of Faith Ringgold Studios.

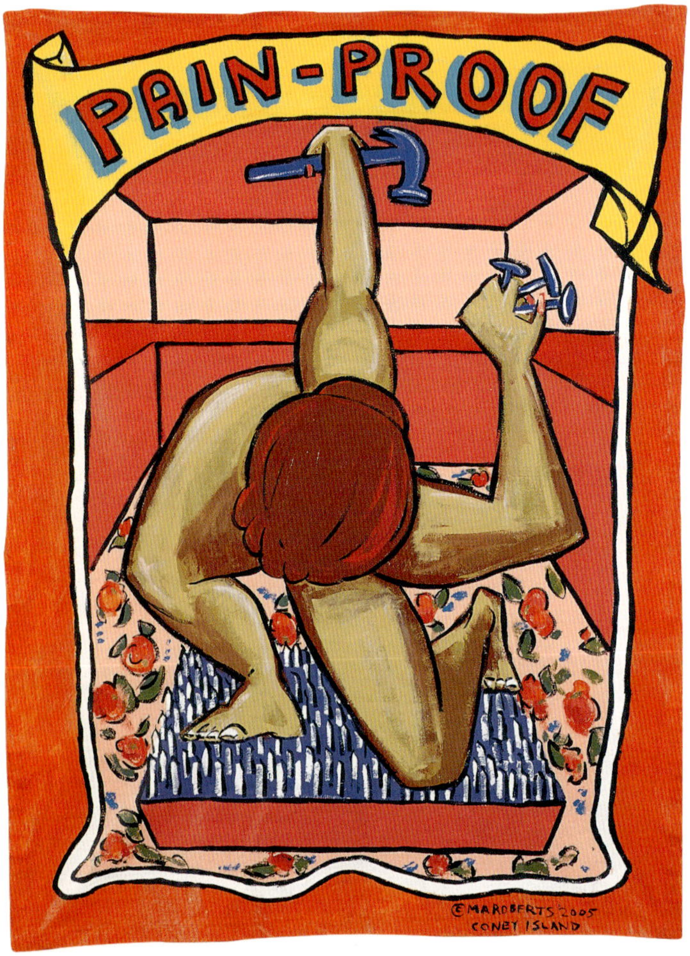

Marie Roberts

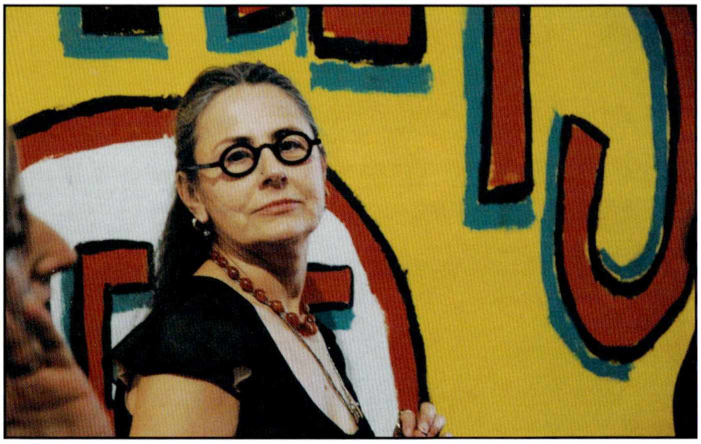
Photograph © Morgan Taylor.

Pain Proof Back, acrylic on canvas, 7' x 5', 2005.

Circus Sideshow, acrylic on canvas, 4' x 6', 2003.

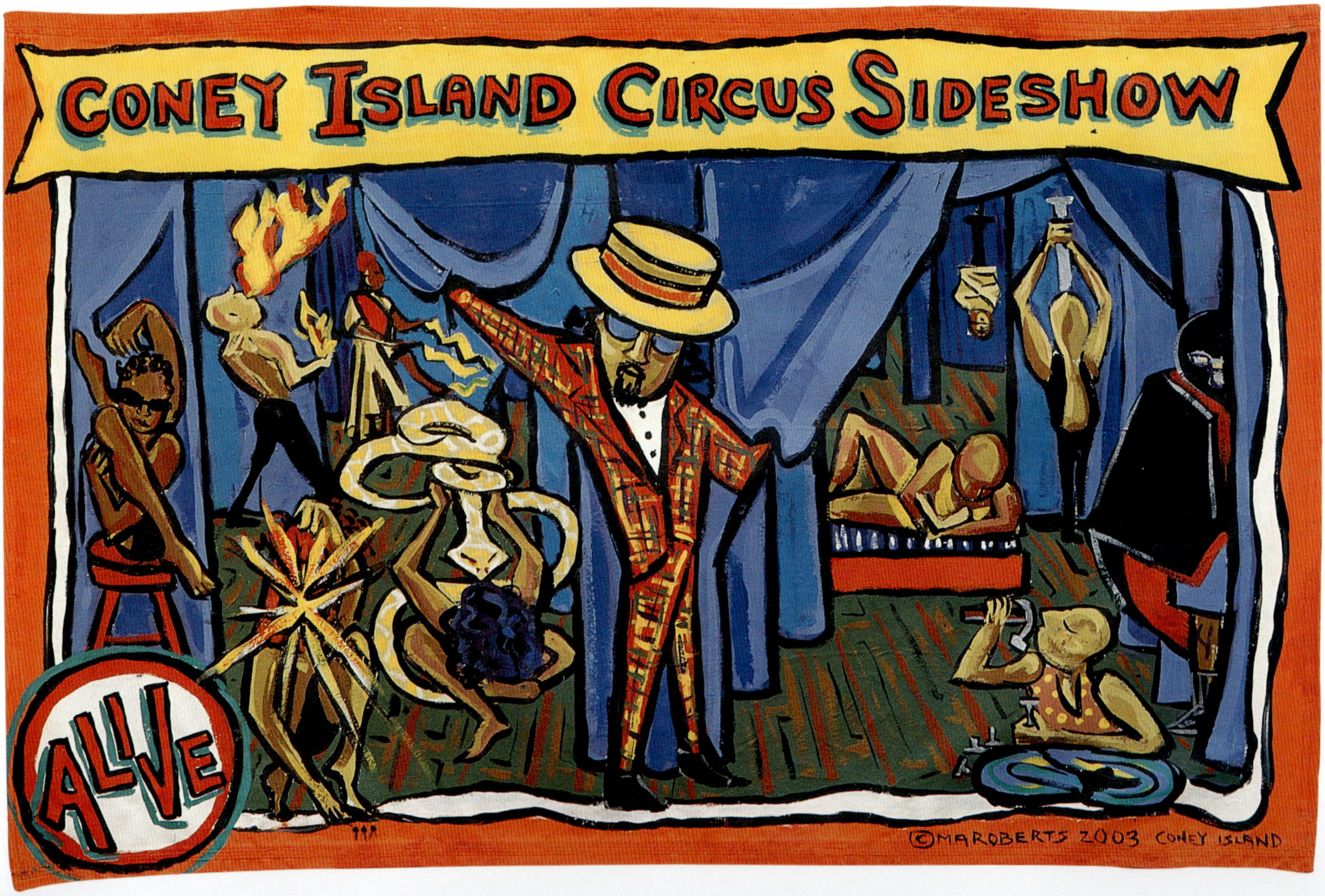

Marie Roberts, who still lives in her childhood home in Coney Island, recalls her Uncle Lester, and other family members' amusement park memories. (He actually sold his own snake oil!) Roberts says her banners and paintings of sideshow characters and performers "bring to the genre ... years as a practicing, educated painter."[184] A student at the Brooklyn Museum Art School, Brooklyn College, the Art Students League, and other local art schools, she received her BA in Art from Brooklyn College and her MFA from Queens College of the City University of New York. A Professor of Art at Fairleigh Dickinson University, she has also taught at Parsons School of Design and the School of Visual Arts.

Roberts' many solo and group exhibitions, including installations of her banners, have been held at the Bowery Gallery, P.S. 1, Brooklyn's Long Island University's Salena Gallery, Rotunda Gallery, Waterfront Art Coalition (BWAC), the Brooklyn Museum, and The NAWA (National Association of Women Artists) Feminist Expo in New York City and Baltimore.

Recipient of a Gold Medal Grumbacher Award, a Margaret O'Brien Painting Prize, and others, she has works in the collections of the New York Metropolitan Transit Authority, Bryn Mawr College, the Williamsburg Art and Historical Society, and Merck Corporation, among others.

She has been commissioned to paint many banners, often as backdrops, for the Knitting Factory, the Siren Music Festival in Coney Island, and the Merck Corporation, and is the Artist-in-Residence at Coney Island USA in Brooklyn, New York.

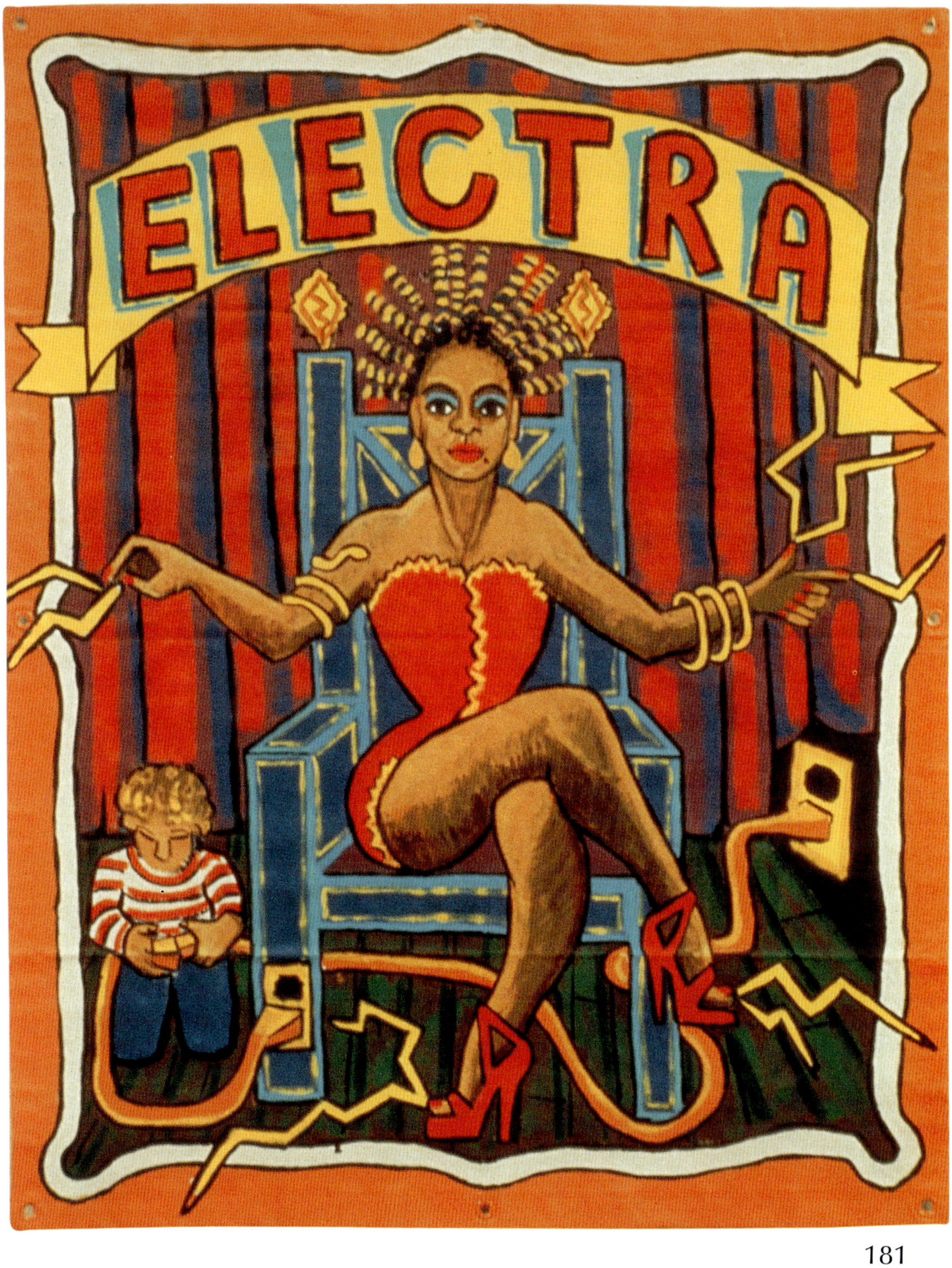

Electra, acrylic on canvas, 60" x 48", 1997.

Dorothea Rockburne

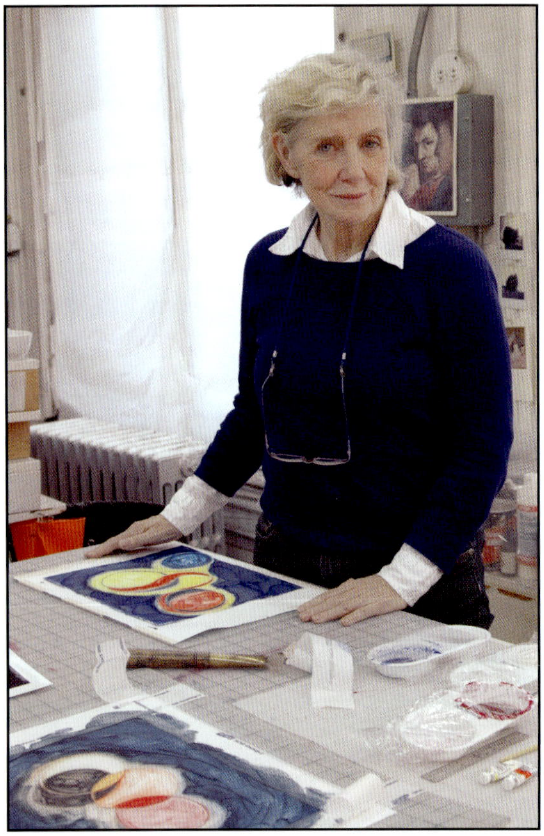

Courtesy of the artist.

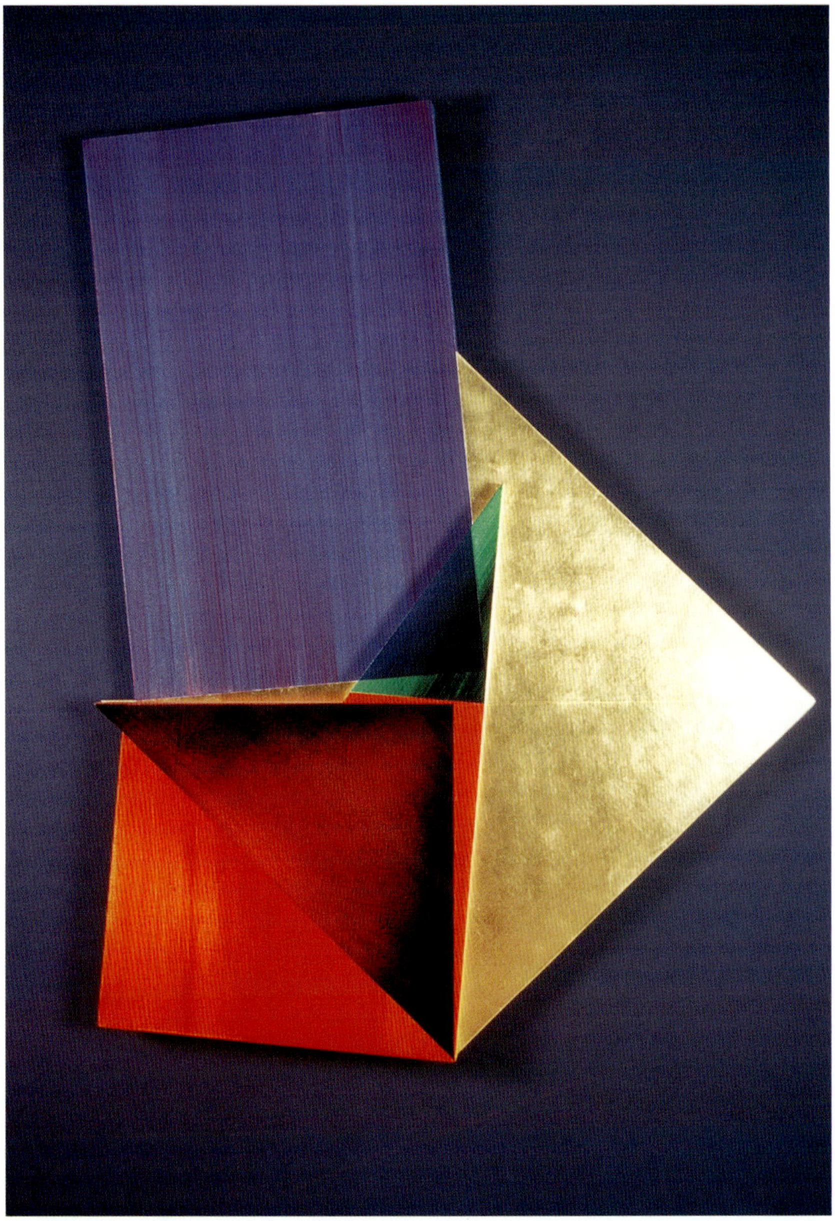

Pascal State of Grace, oil and goldleaf on gessoed linen, 75.5" x 57.5", c.1986-87. *Courtesy of Greenberg Van Doren Gallery, New York.*

Dorothea Rockburne, whose paintings often refer to such historic figures as Blaise Pascal and Mozart, believes "the inner workings of nature can be described through certain forms of mathematics. By employing these forms as structure, I work from nature."[185]

Born in Canada and educated first at Montreal's Ecole des Beaux Arts, Rockburne studied painting with Franz Kline, Philip Guston, Jack Tworkov, and Esteban Vicente, music with John Cage, dance with Merce Cunningham, and mathematics with Max Dehn at the historic Black Mountain College in North Carolina.

Her many solo exhibitions have been held at such locations as the Museum of Modern Art, the Rose Art Museum of Brandeis University, the Andre Emmerich Gallery, and the Portland Museum of Art. Rockburne's works may be seen in the collections of many museums, including the Metropolitan Museum of Art, the Whitney Museum of American Art, the Solomon R. Guggenheim Museum, the Brooklyn Museum, the Albright-Knox Art Gallery, the Corcoran Gallery of Art, and the National Gallery of Art in Washington, D.C. Elected to the National Academy of Design, Rockburne has won many honors, such as the Jimmy Ernst Lifetime Achievement Award in Art from the American Academy of Arts and Letters, a John Simon Guggenheim Memorial Fellowship Award, the Milton and Sally Avery Distinguished Professorship at Bard College, and an honorary Doctorate of Fine Arts from the College for Creative Studies.

A series of her works, combining innovative materials and techniques such as cut and folded paper and canvas, and created according to the rules of topology and the Golden Section, has been seen in numerous American and European exhibitions. Later series include works based on Egyptian, angelic, mythological, spatial and astronomical themes.

Rockburne is represented by the Greenberg Van Doren Gallery in New York.

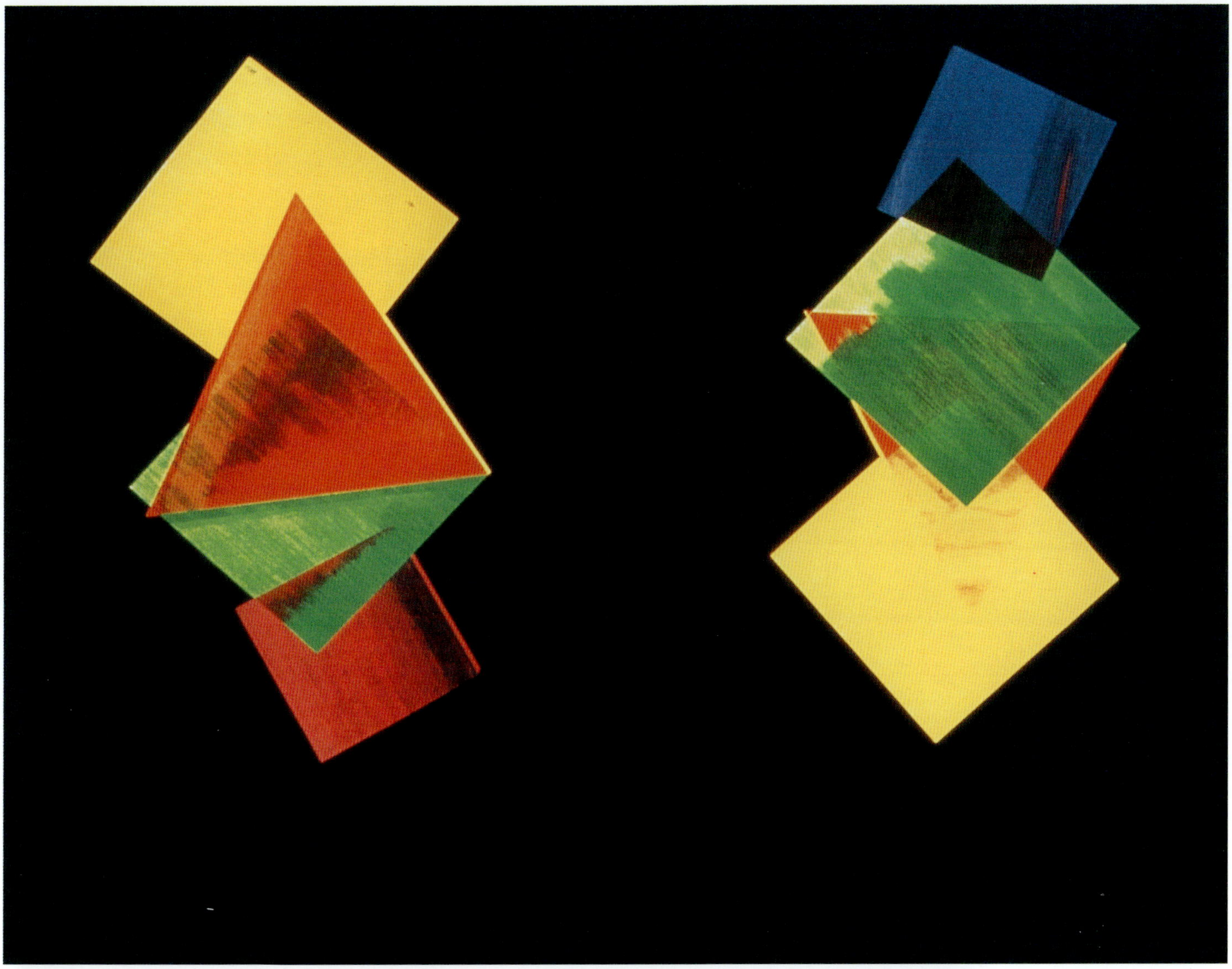

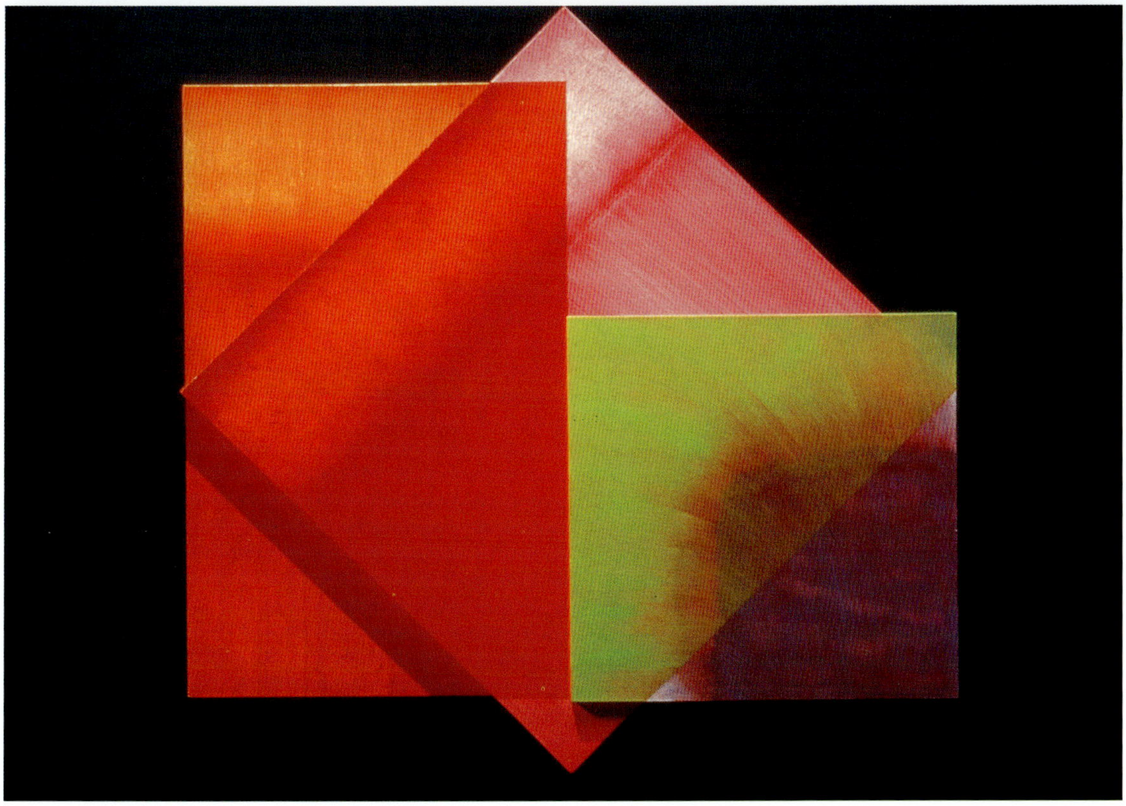

Mozart and Mozart Upside Down and Backward, oil on shaped canvas, 89" x 46", c.1985-86. *All art © ARS, New York. Courtesy of Greenberg Van Doren Gallery, New York.*

Pascal's Provincial Letters, oil paint on gessoed linen, three panels, 67" x 67" x 8", 1987. *Courtesy of Greenberg Van Doren Gallery, New York.*

Shunji Sakuyama

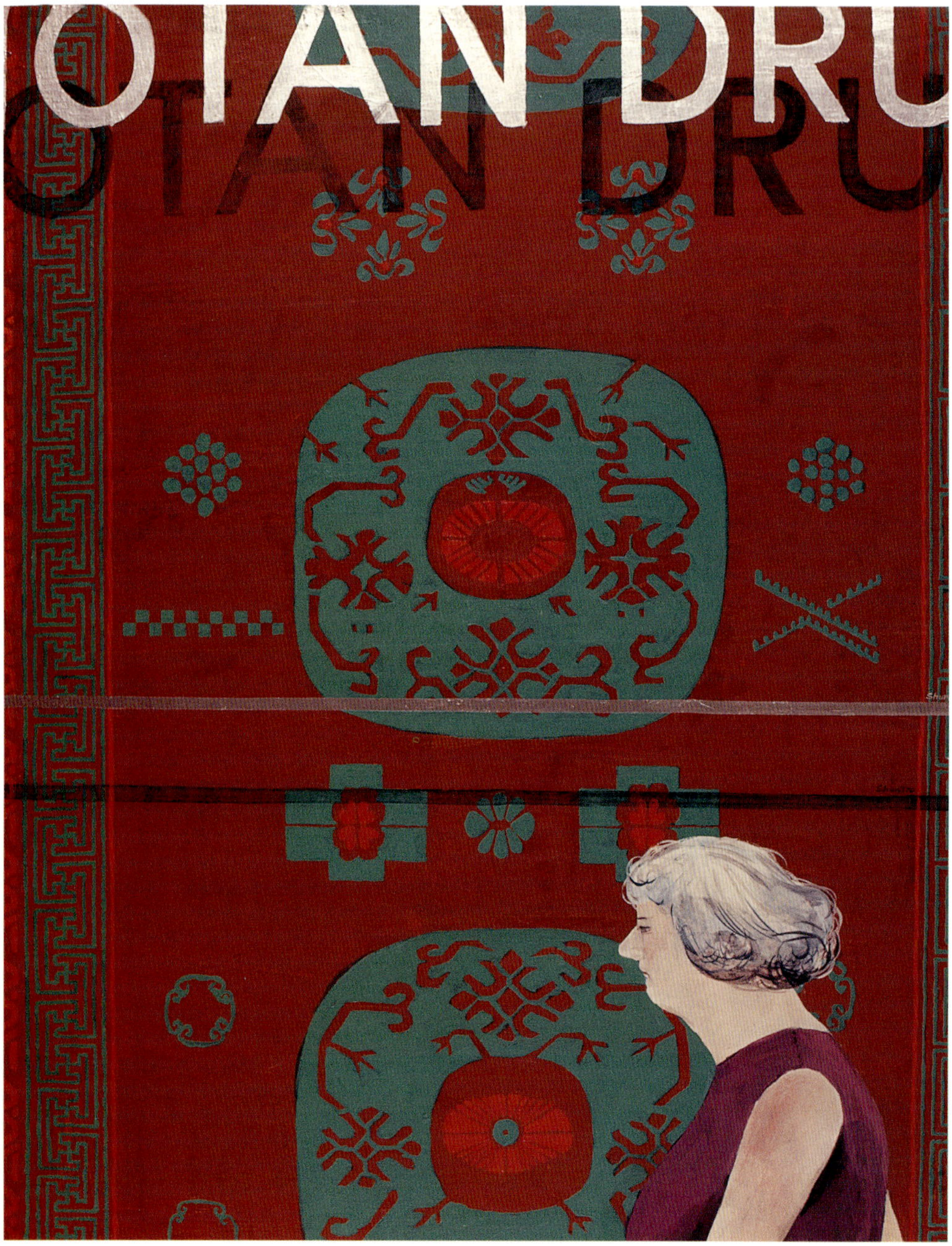

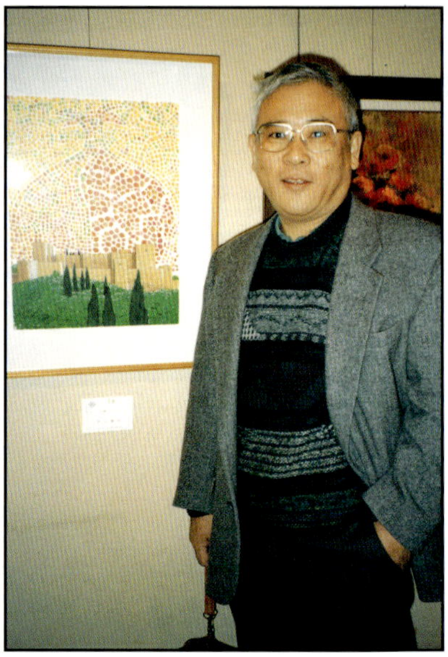

Courtesy of the artist.

Drug Store, oil on canvas, 52" x 36", 1972.

Shunji Sakuyama, born in Japan and a graduate of Tokyo's Gakugei College, received his MFA from Brooklyn College. He also studied at the Brooklyn Museum Art School and at the Pratt Graphics Center.

A long-time resident of Park Slope in Brooklyn, he has conducted painting classes for Japanese artists at the Brooklyn Museum Art School, and has been a teacher of English to Japanese-speaking students for many years.

Sakuyama's series of storefront windows, often seen from inside with lettering reversed, has provided him with an interesting method of introducing Western viewers to the Asian way of reading the picture plane—from right to left, in contrast to the Western left-to-right "orientation."

His many solo exhibitions have been held in Tokyo and Osaka in Japan, in London, and in the United States, where locations have included Connecticut as well as the Chino, Western Press, and Long Island University Galleries in New York. Group exhibitions including Sakuyama's prints and paintings have been seen at the Elaine Benson Gallery in Bridgehampton, New York, Suffolk County Community College, the Brooklyn Museum, the Museum of the City of New York, and galleries in Stamford, Connecticut and Chicago, Illinois, as well as in Taipei, Taiwan.

Winner of awards at the New England Art Exhibition and the Berkshire Art Exhibition, Sakuyama has works in the collections of the Brooklyn Museum, the Museum of the City of New York, the New York Historical Society, the Berkshire Museum, and many private collections.

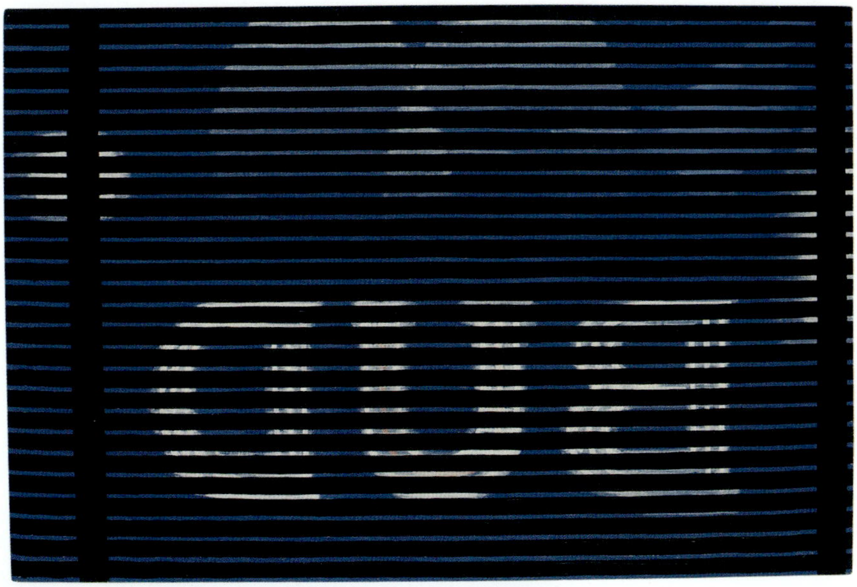

Sundown, oil on canvas, 34" x 50", 1984.

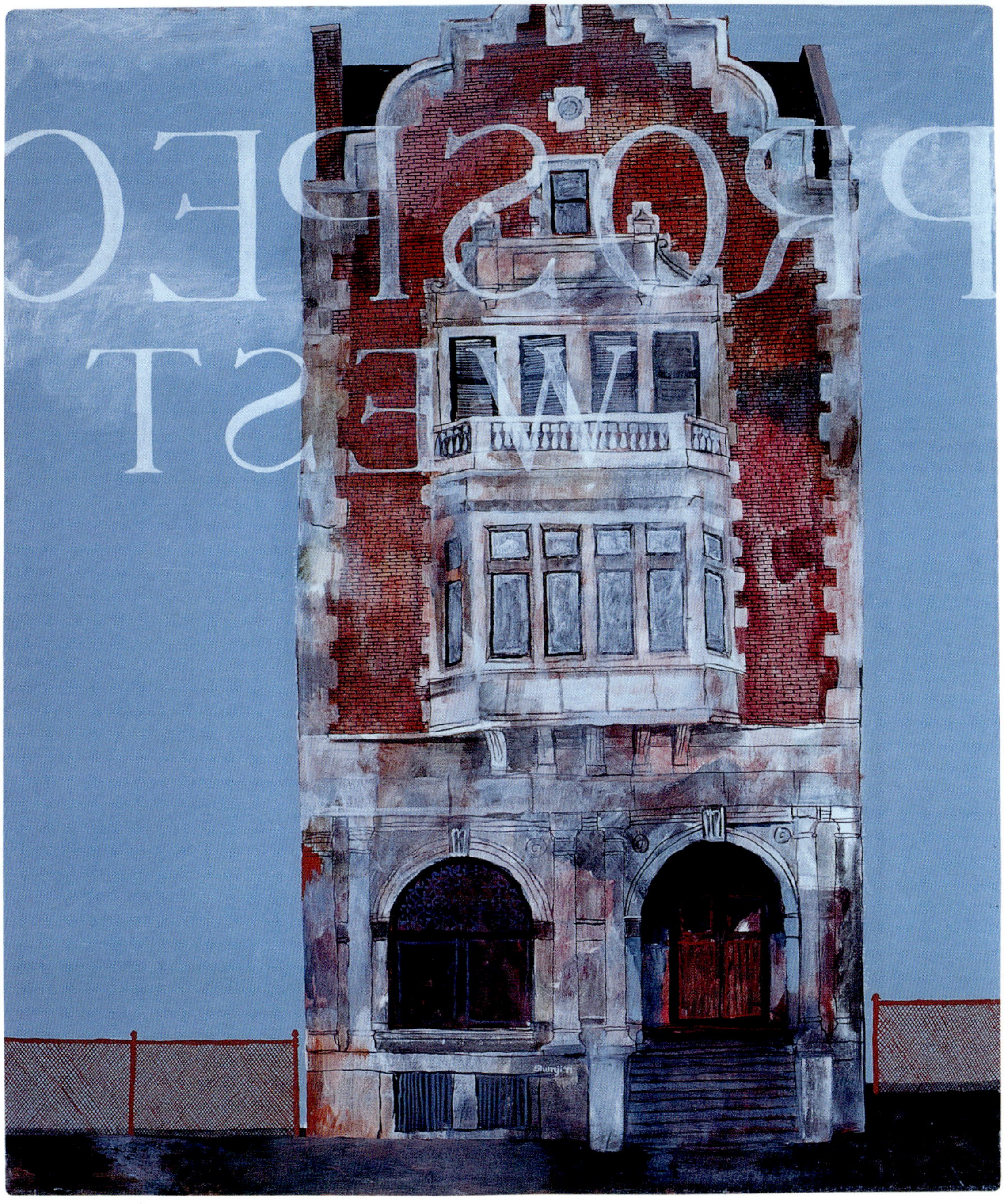

Prospect Park West, oil on canvas, 68" x 40", 1971.

William Scharf

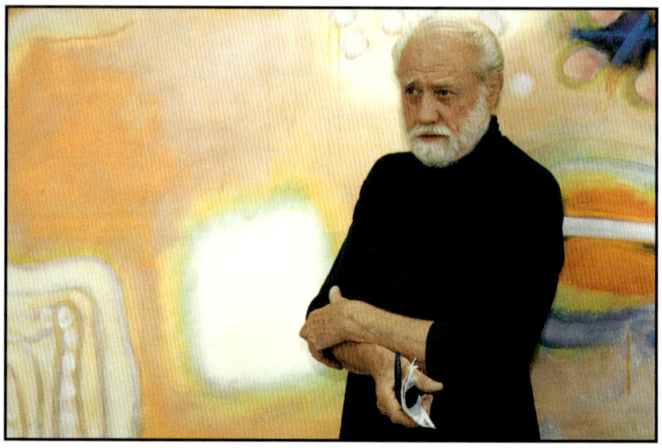

Courtesy of the artist.

William Scharf is an elected National Academician, whose "drips, broad strokes and spatters align him to the New York School, and have … roots in the abstract expressionist tradition, resisting easy classification,"[186] according to Meredith Ward. "His enigmatic titles, mysterious iconography and rich, dense colors suggest a kinship with [the] visionary. … [His] formal discipline, honed over five decades … mediates between emotive content and visual experience."[187]

Scharf, a graduate of the Pennsylvania Academy of Fine Arts and a student at the University of Pennsylvania, the Barnes Foundation, and the Academie de la Grand Chaumiere in Paris, also studied and traveled throughout much of Europe and served as a studio assistant to Arshile Gorky and Mark Rothko. He has taught at the Art Students League, the School of Visual Arts, and the Art Center of the Museum of Modern Art in New York, and at the San Francisco Institute of Fine Arts in California.

Scharf's numerous solo exhibitions have been held at the Meredith Ward, Richard York, Lerner-Heller, and David Herbert galleries in New York, the Phillips Collection in Washington, D.C., the Mississippi Museum of Art, the High Museum in Atlanta, and the San Francisco Art Institute, among others. Group exhibitions include those at the National Academy of Design, the Anita Shapolsky, Denise Bibro, Hirschl-Adler and Martha Jackson galleries in New York, the Smithsonian's National Museum of American Art, and the Phillips Collection in Washington, D.C.

His work is in the collections of the Brooklyn Museum, the Chase Manhattan Bank, the Museum of Modern Art, the Solomon R. Guggenheim Museum, the Yale University Art Gallery, and many others. He is represented by Meredith Ward Fine Art in New York.

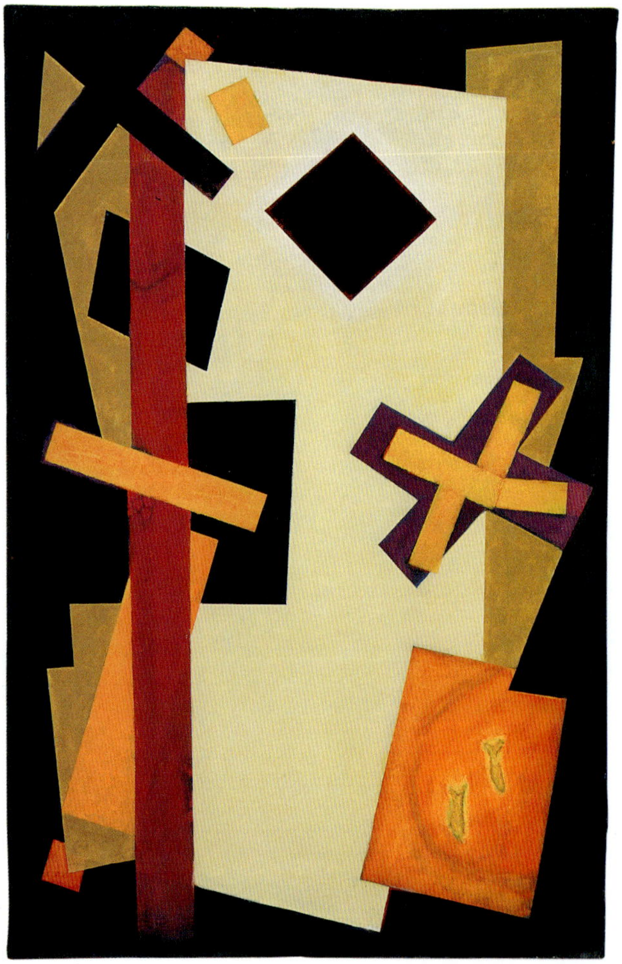

Solstice Eclipse, acrylic on canvas, 74" x 45.5", 2003. *Courtesy of Meredith Ward Fine Arts.*

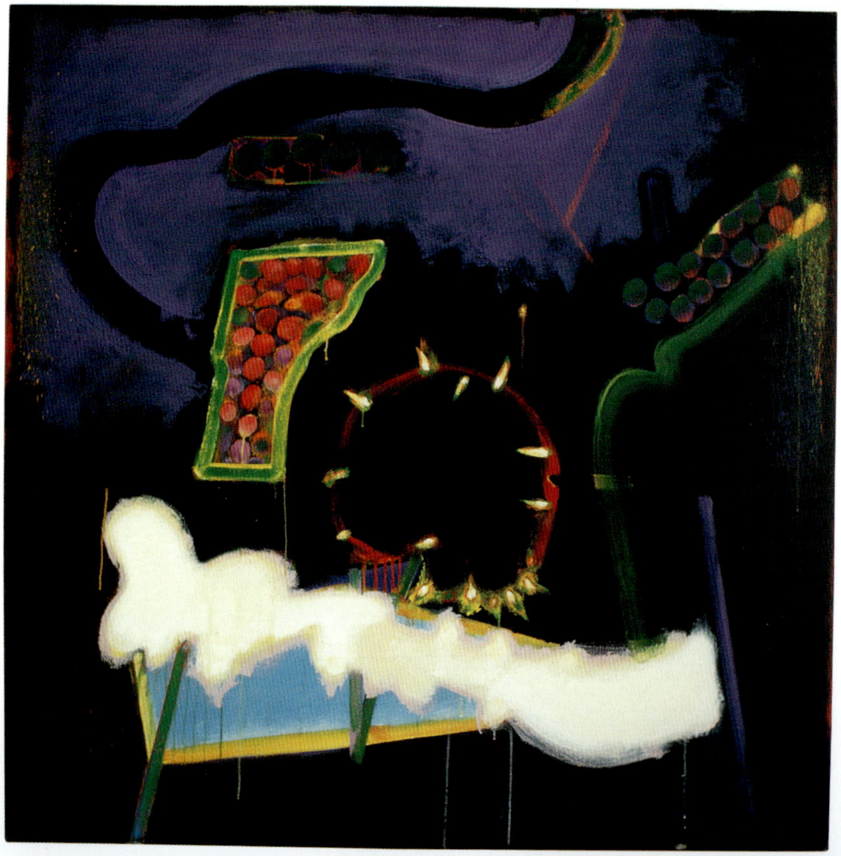

Of Martyred Fruit, acrylic on canvas, 5' 6" x 5' 6", c.1980s. *Courtesy of Meredith Ward Fine Arts.*

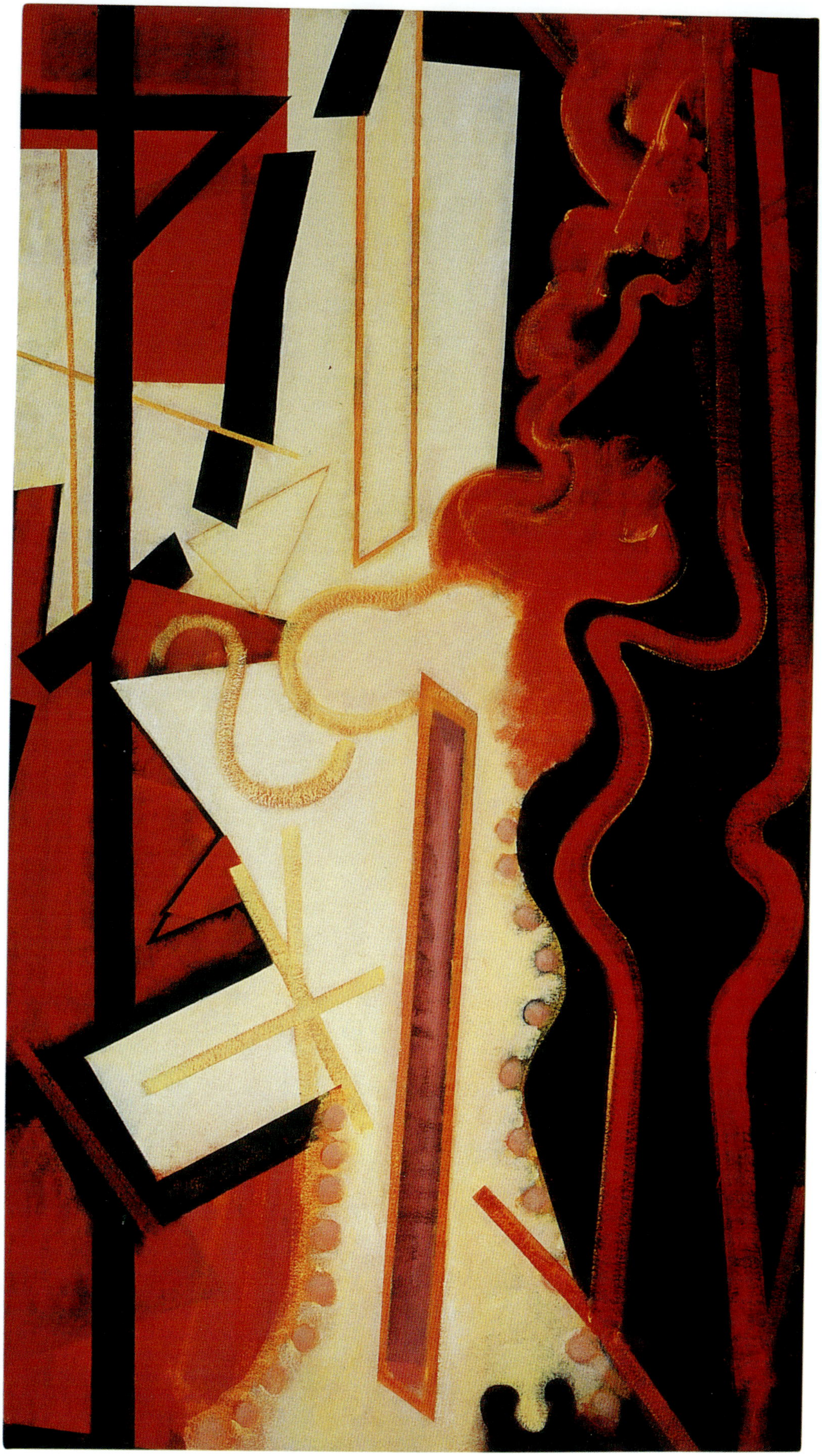

A Bride to Fire, acrylic on canvas, 68" x 39", 1997. *Collection of Kate Rothko Prizel.*

Laura Schiavina

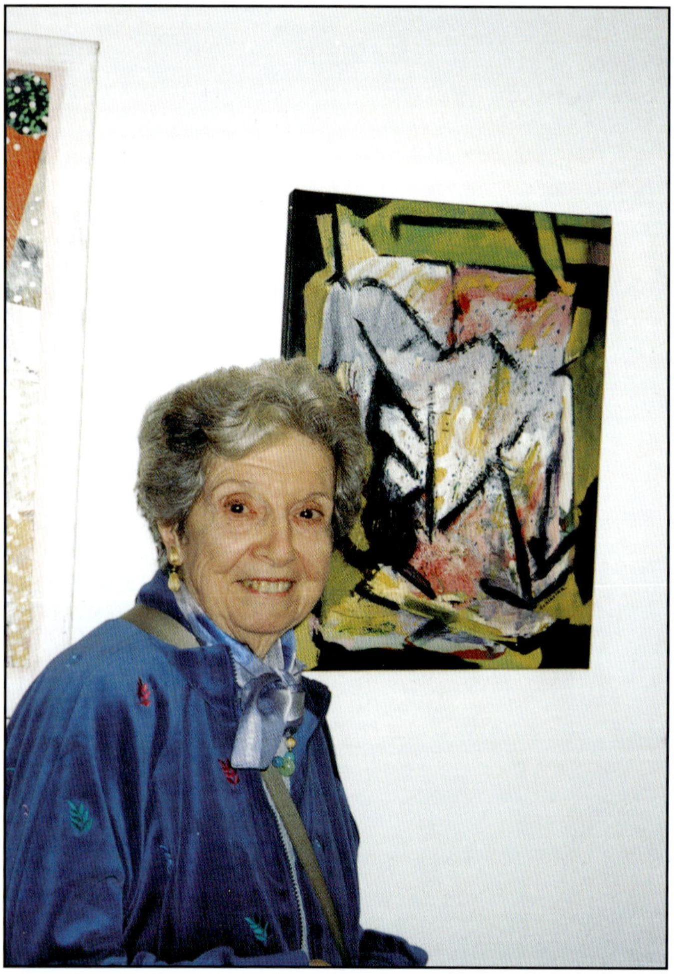

The artist with *Enlightenment*, 1998. *Courtesy of the artist.*

Laura Schiavina singles out her study with Will Barnet, "who made me feel like an artist," though each of her teachers was "just right at that point ... I thank them all."[188] She pursued a non-art-related business career for many years, while studying at the Traphagen School of Fashion and participating in many summer art workshops. She studied monotype printmaking at the Blackburn Studio.

A member of some dozen art organizations, Schiavina belongs to the NAWA (National Association of Women Artists), Audubon Artists, and the National Collage Society. She was among the first women accepted by the Salmagundi Club.

A winner of several prizes at the Salmagundi Club and the NAWA, as well as the National Arts League and the National League of American Pen Women, Schiavina has participated in many group exhibitions held at the Venezuela General Consulate and the National Arts Club, among others, with such titles as "Celebrating 25 Years of Women at the Salmagundi Club,"[189] "Colors,"[190] "Women by Women,"[191] "Catholic Artists ...,"[192] and "Inner/Outer World."[193]

Schiavina has developed a technique of applying dried skins of acrylic paint to her canvases and other innovative collaged elements, originally inspired by natural forms and landscapes; she works freely and abstractly, juxtaposing colors and shapes, resulting in works called by Lisa Collado, "gems of Mozartean design. Her aim is to provide visual delight."[194]

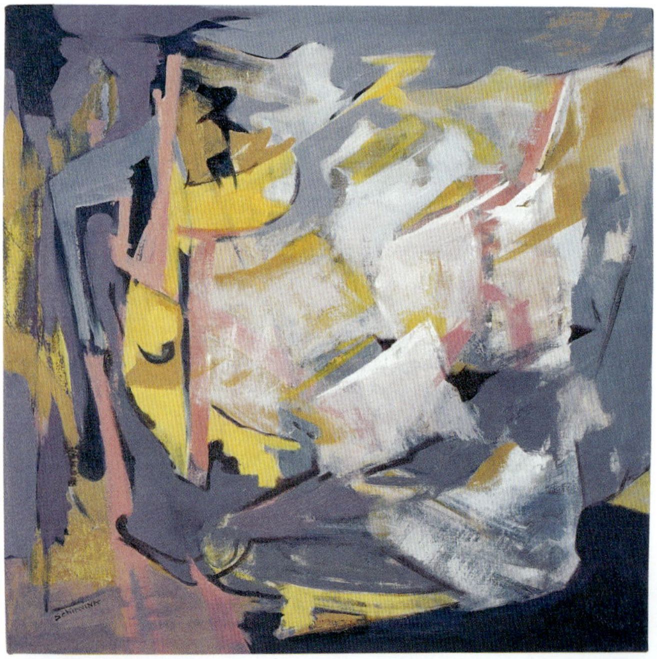

Snow Squares, acrylic on canvas, 30" x 30", 1990.

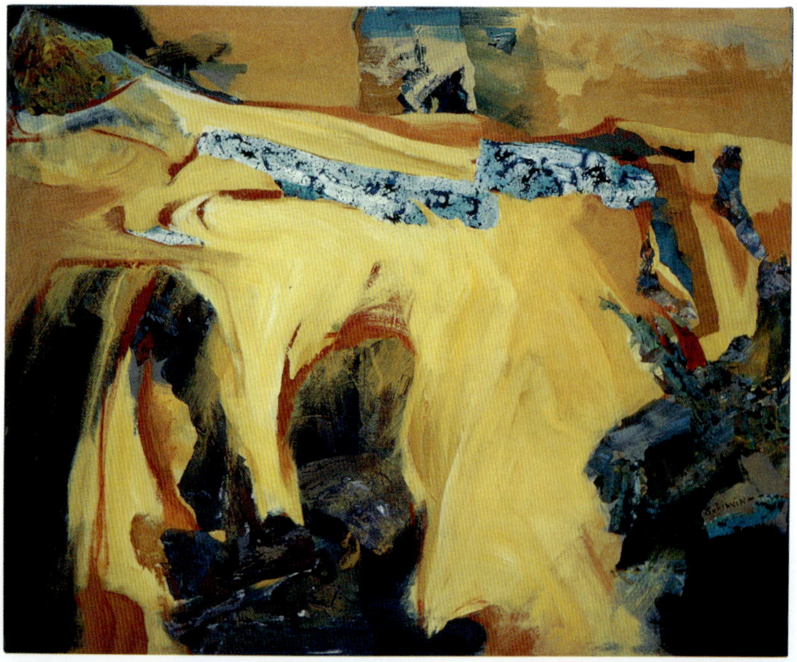

Golden Moment, acrylic and collage on canvas, 30" x 36", 1993.

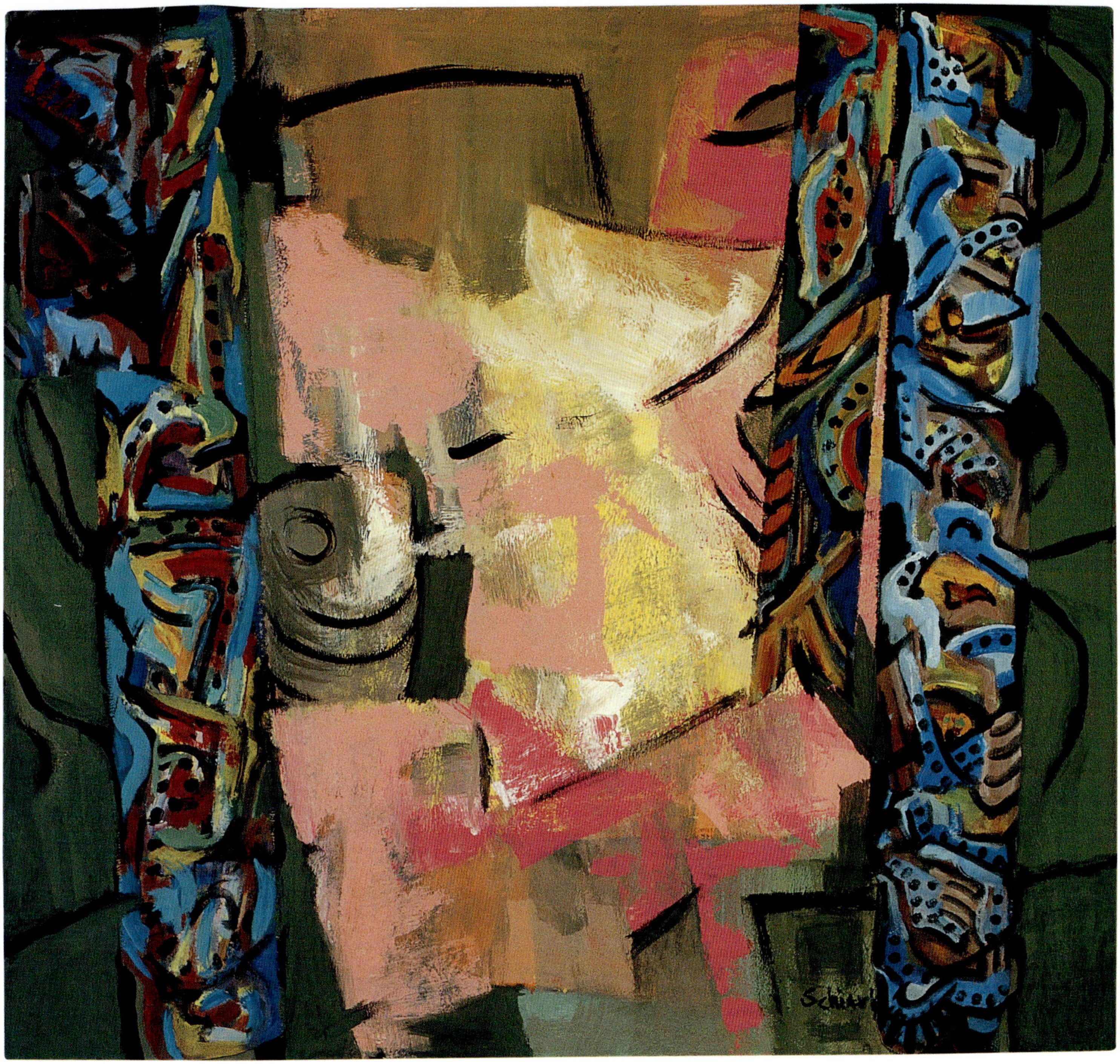

Hear the Beat, acrylic and collage on canvas, 38" x 40", 2000.

Johan Sellenraad, who moved from the Netherlands to Chicago before settling in Soho, New York (and a country location in rural Pennsylvania shared with his wife, the painter Ellen Cibula), has completed many public commissions in ceramic tile, concrete, and other materials, as well as pursuing his lifelong focus, painting.

Winner of a National Endowment for the Arts Fellowship in Painting, Sellenraad has taught at the Brooklyn Campus of Long Island University for almost forty years, and has also been on the faculty of the Parsons School of Design. Recipient of a BFA from Chicago's School of the Art Institute and an MFA from the University of Chicago, he has had numerous solo exhibitions, notably, "Brooklyn Bridge. City Hall to Water Street," at the Whitney Museum of American Art, "Flint Sit-Down Strike Labor Monument" at Wayne State University, Detroit, and "Utah Paintings" at David Findlay Jr Fine Art. His many group exhibitions include "Three New York Artists" at the Galerie GEE in the Netherlands, "Myths and Gods," "Public Art, WPA to the Present," "The Great East River Bridge" at the Brooklyn Museum, "Large Scale Painting" at The Cooper Union, and "America '76," sponsored by the U.S. Department of the Interior.

Sellenraad's main interest is "not the subject matter itself,"[195] often a disparate arrangement of specific domestic, rural, and other objects in a contained interior space, but in his and the viewer's "response to these images and the visual and physical sensations they create," according to Marcia Tucker, of the Whitney. She says, "he focuses our attention on spaces, how we move in them, how we perceive forms and understand ourselves kinesthetically in relation to them (so that) … changing light and color (are) more important …"[196]

Johan Sellenraad

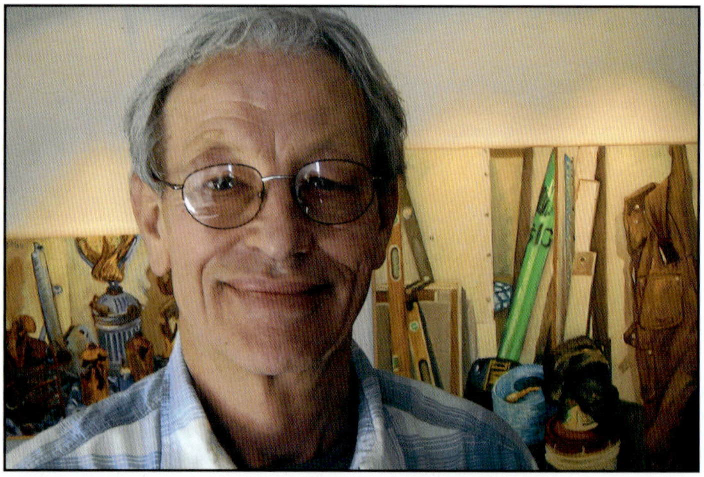

Courtesy of the artist.

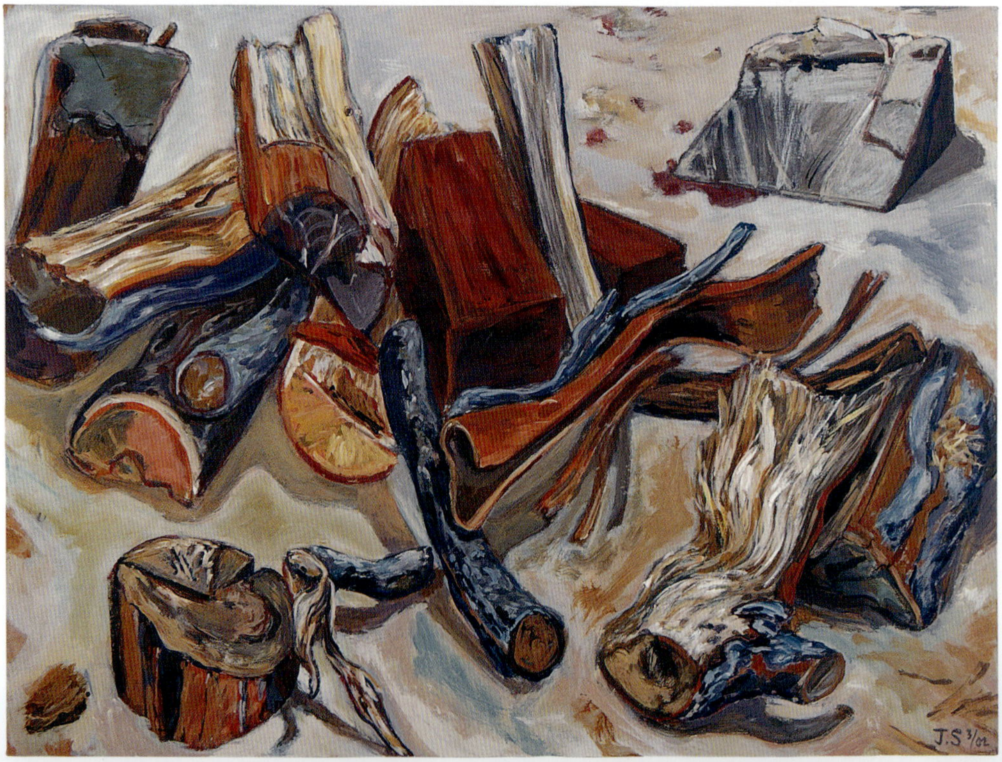

Assorted Woodpile, acrylic on canvas, 41" x 54", March, 2002.

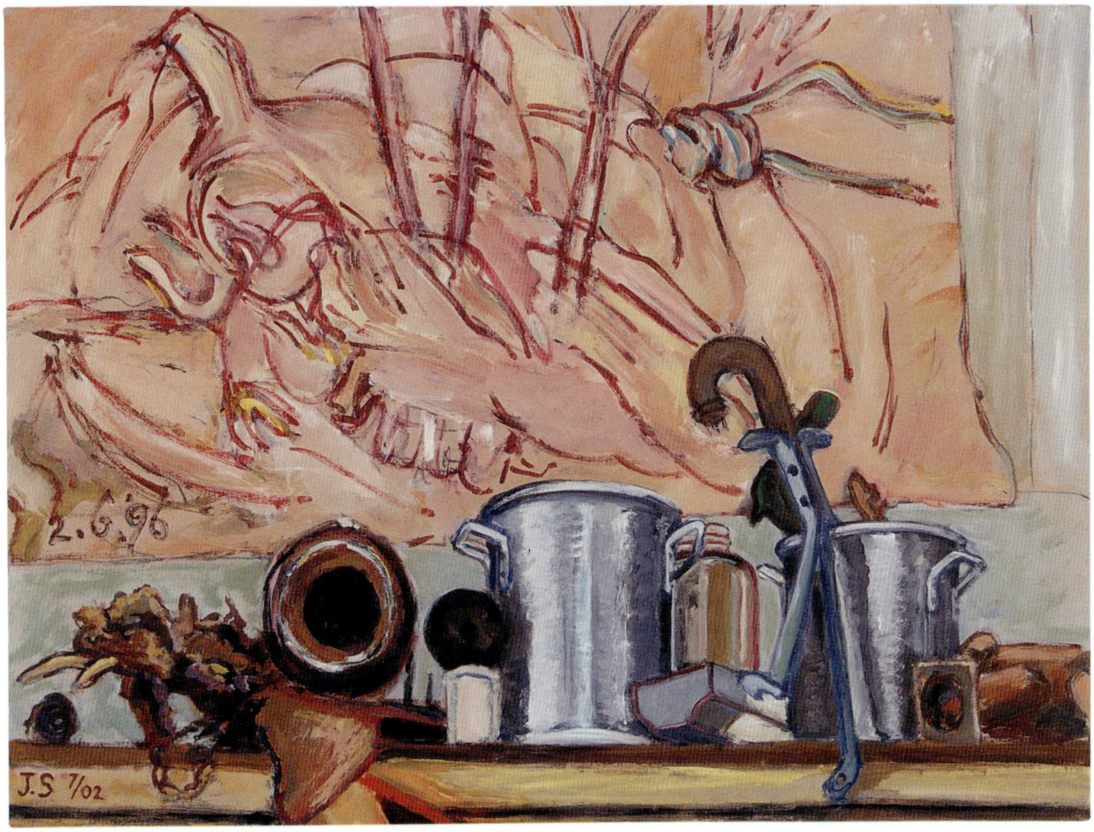

Studio: High Shelf, acrylic on canvas, 41" x 54", July, 2002.

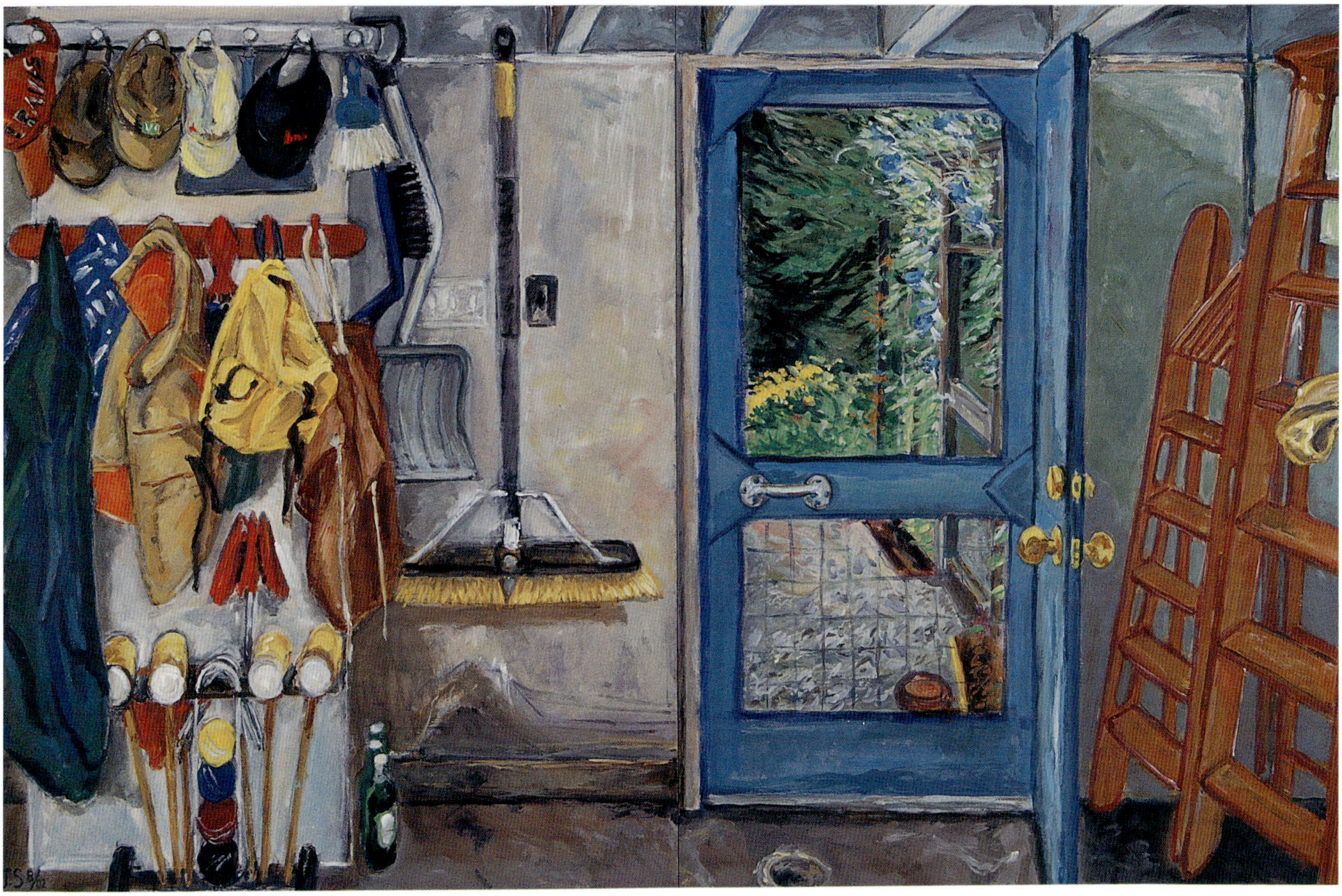

Summer, acrylic on canvas, 54" x 82", August, 2002.

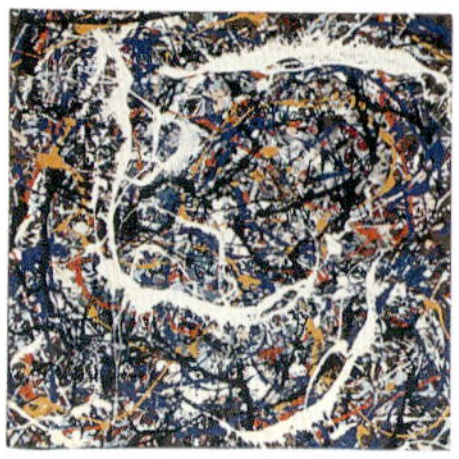

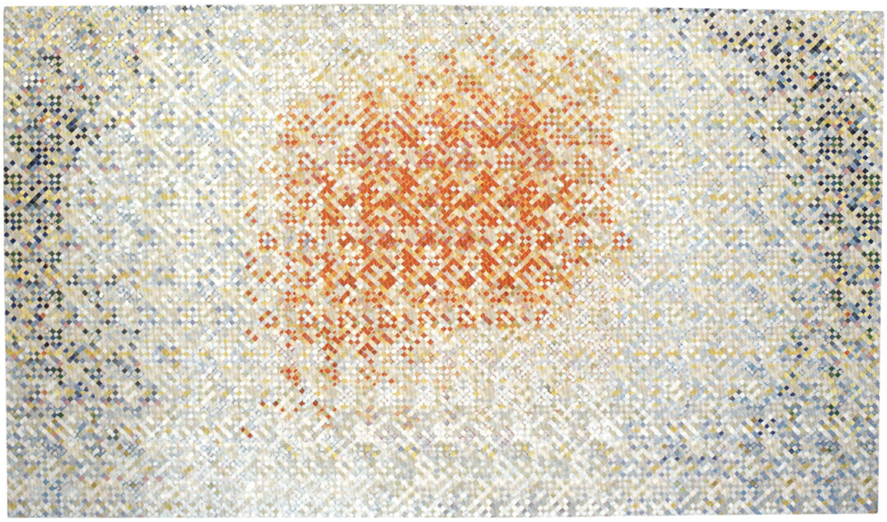

Let There Be Light!, acrylic, flashe, mirrors on canvas, two panels 64" x 96", c.1988-2000.

Kendall Shaw, whose most important influences were his father, who was "a fine New Orleans pianist, and black marching Jazz bands, for their abstract content,"[197] also credits his many teachers and friends: "Rothko, Davis, Crawford, Guglielmi, Kohlmeyer and the pattern and decoration artists such as Schapiro ... also Stravinsky!"[198]

A graduate of Tulane University who has received its Distinguished Alumnus Award, he earned a degree in Chemistry as well as an MFA in Painting, before teaching at Tulane, Columbia University, Hunter and Lehman Colleges of the City University of New York, the Brooklyn Museum Art School, and Parsons School of Design.

A prolific writer, Shaw says, "my perception begins with the certainty that everything is in motion ... all is energy. ... The grid ... is rhythmic, considered, rational ... The thrown

Kendall Shaw

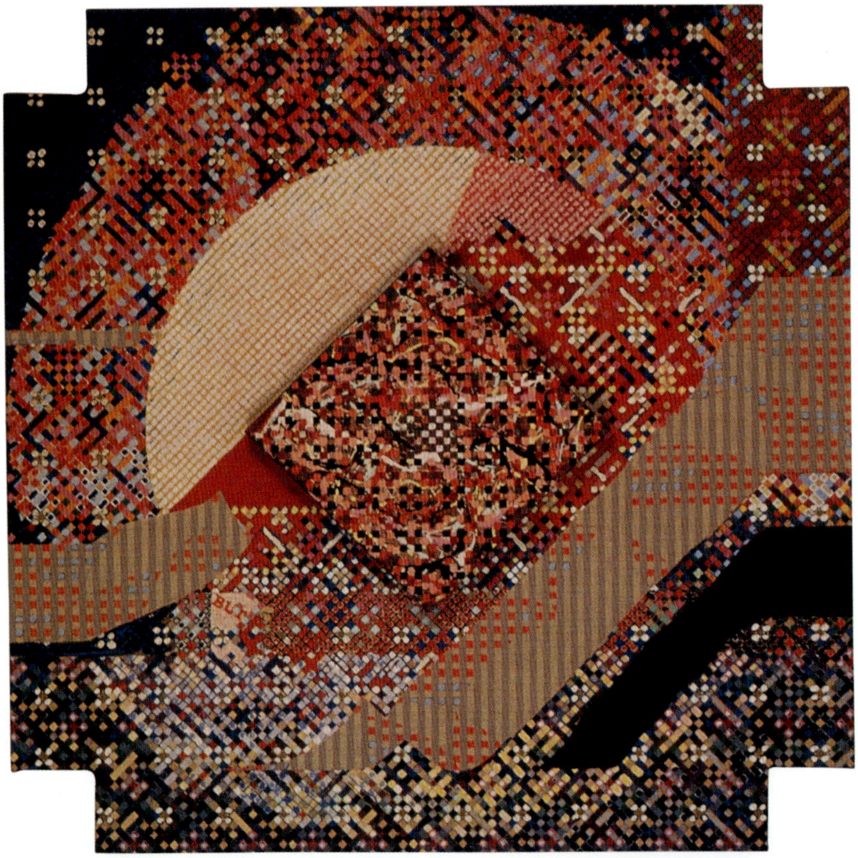

But, acrylic, vinyl, mirrors on canvas, two panels 60" x 60", c.1985-2001.

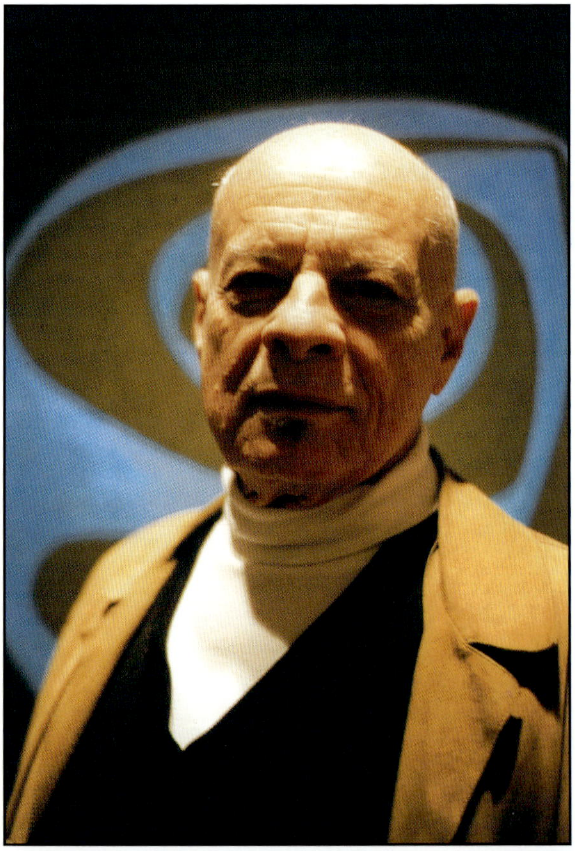

The artist at Will Barnet reception.
Photograph © Cynthia Dantzic.

marks, linear, melodic, spontaneous ... The two are combined. ... The mirrors ... confuse ... color-space; squares become stars. My works [like] the Abstract Expressionists' ... are tragic and timeless ... always having more to reveal ... they are passionate, not sad or happy. As a former chemist, I seek not purity, but reality ... from appearance [of things] out of the imperceptible to its disappearance into the imperceptible ..."[199]

Shaw's earlier paintings often reflected an appreciation of his socially active, early feminist grandmother, Emma Lottie. Later works reveal personal fantasies; as he says, "the erotic is the center of our lives."[200]

Shaw's numerous solo exhibitions, largely in New York and New Orleans, also include a major retrospective at the University of Virginia's Marsh Art Gallery. Group exhibitions across the United States, in Japan, and Europe have been held at many major galleries and museums, such as the Smithsonian, the Brooklyn Museum, the Lerner-Heller, Anita Shapolsky, and Aaron Berman galleries. His works are in many public collections.

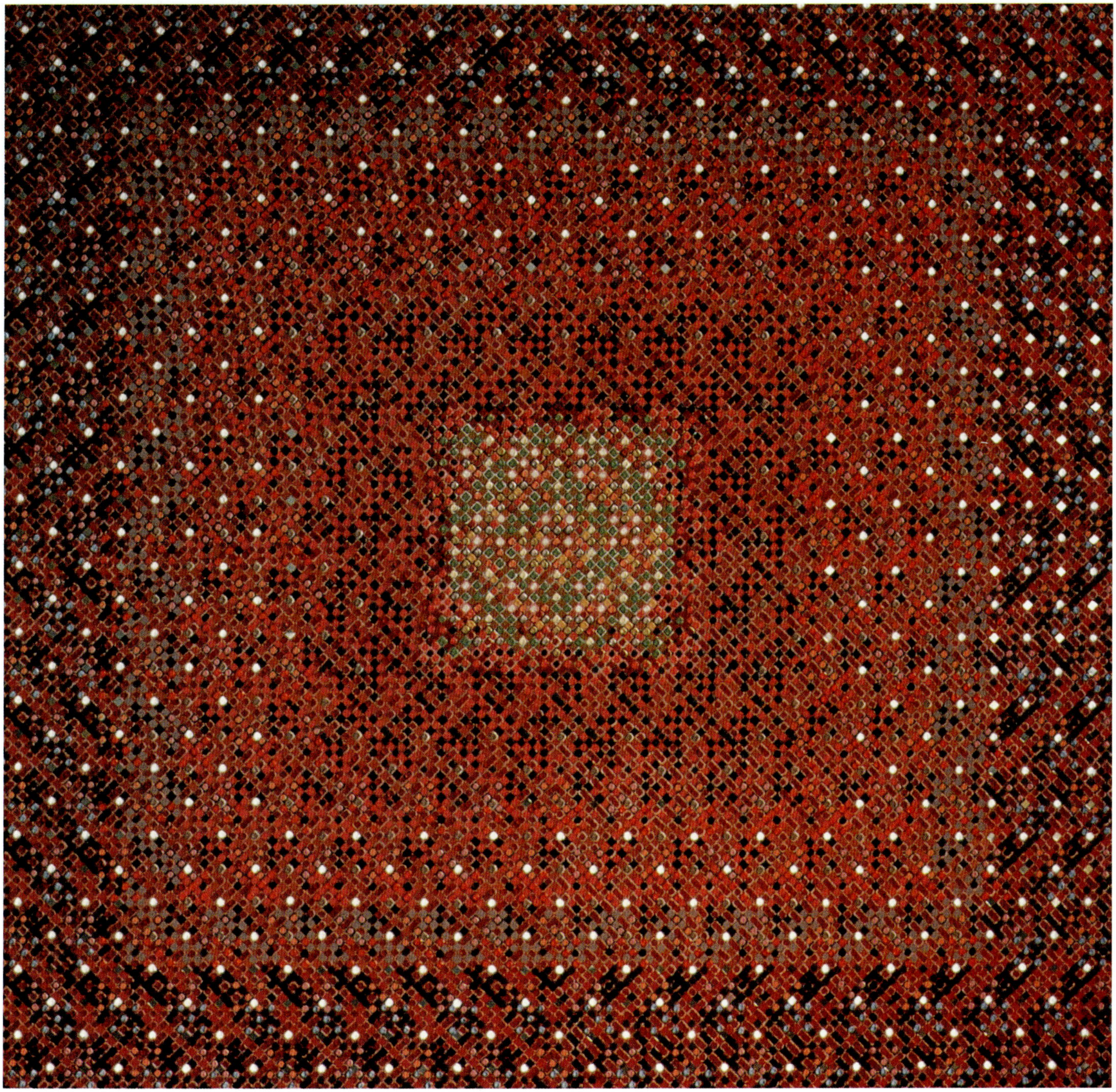

NAZCA, acrylic and mirrors on canvas, 72" x 72", 1980. *Collection of Norma and William Roth. All art © Kendall Shaw/Licensed by VAGA, New York, NY.*

Susan Sills

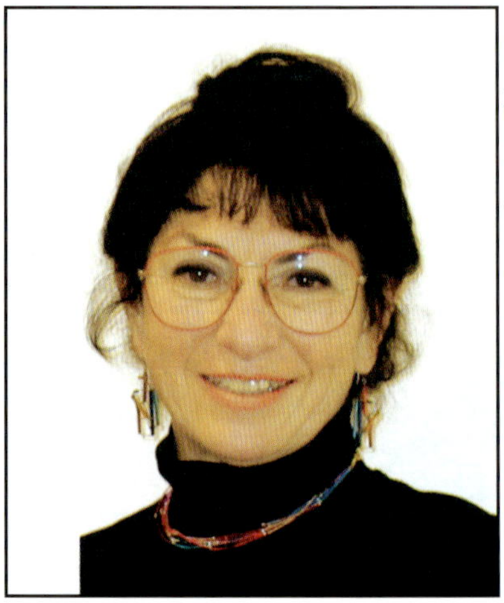

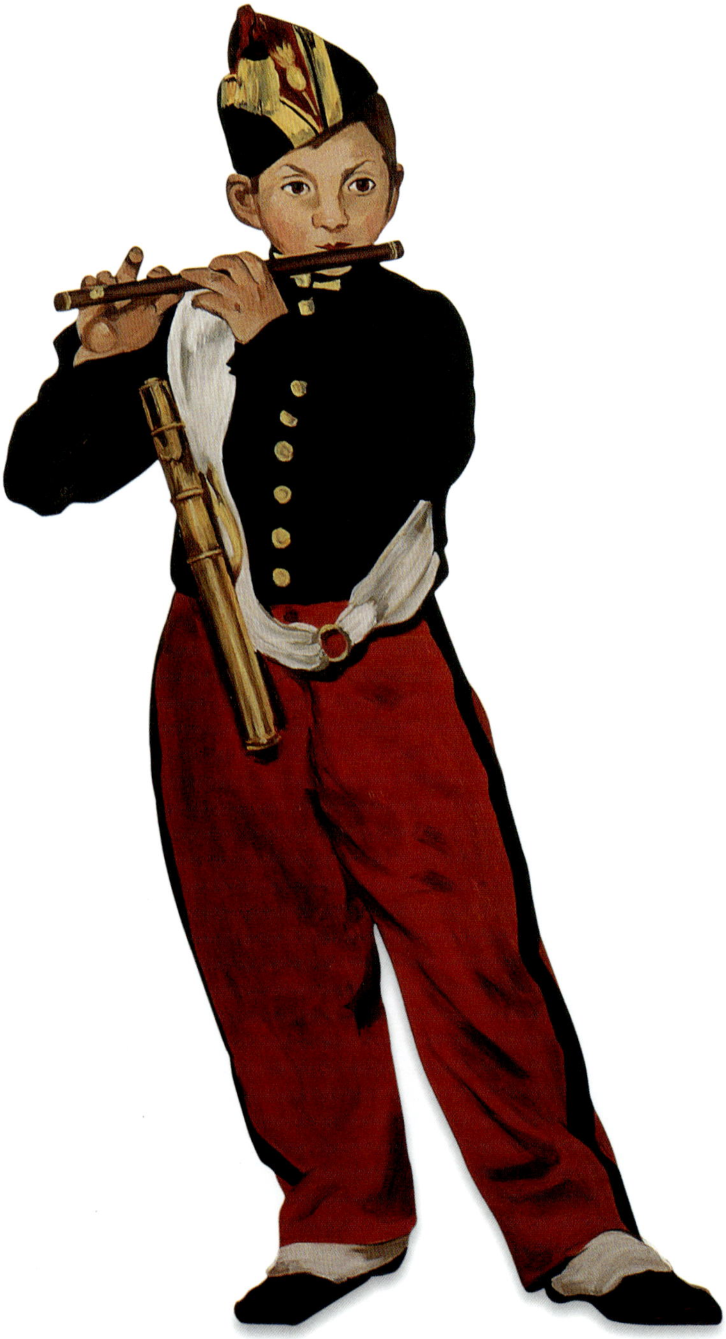

Manet's Mazurka, oil on birch shaped panel, 51" x 26", 1994.

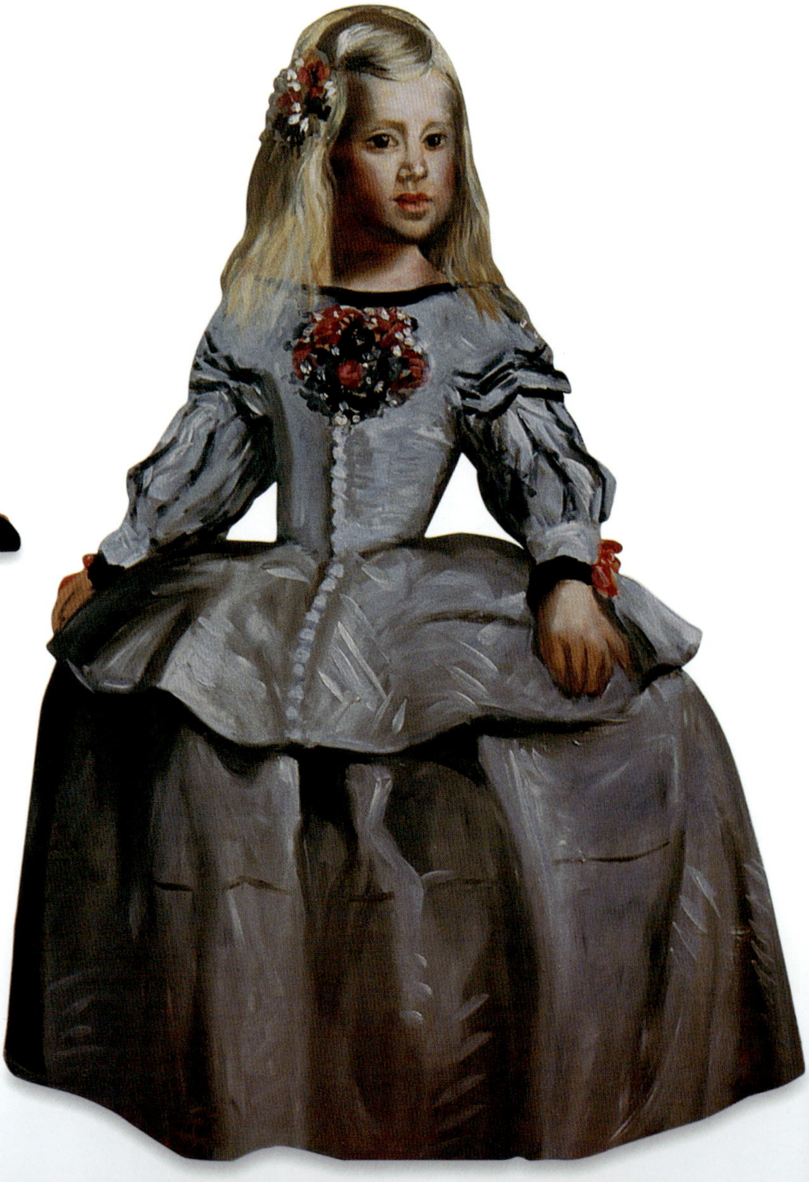

Diego's Darling, oil on birch shaped panel, 43" x 30", 1994.

Susan Sills, whose idea of painted life-size cutouts from the old Masters was given the Whitney Museum's imprimatur in its "Contemporary Cutouts" exhibition, often combines these paintings with real-life found objects, to "bring exalted subjects down to earth ... taking us on a journey through art history with wit and humor."[201]

Sills' "painterly skills ... imbue her hybrid art form with a compositional and narrative logic all their own. She has an uncanny ability to duplicate any Old Master's style down to the most minute brushstroke. [She] owns the art of the cutout,"[202] says Ed McCormack. Often placing these figures in new settings and configurations, Sills' groupings "provide fresh insights ... and gently challenge our established beliefs about art history."[203]

Sills' works have been shown in five solo shows in Tokyo, as well as throughout the United States—at the Pensacola Museum of Art and at the Viridian Artists Gallery, among others.

She has been included in many group exhibitions in the United States and in Japan, and is represented by the Viridian Gallery.

A student of Joan Semmel and Joyce Kozloff at the Brooklyn Museum Art School, Sills is a graduate of Queens College of the City University of New York. She is represented by Viridian Artists.

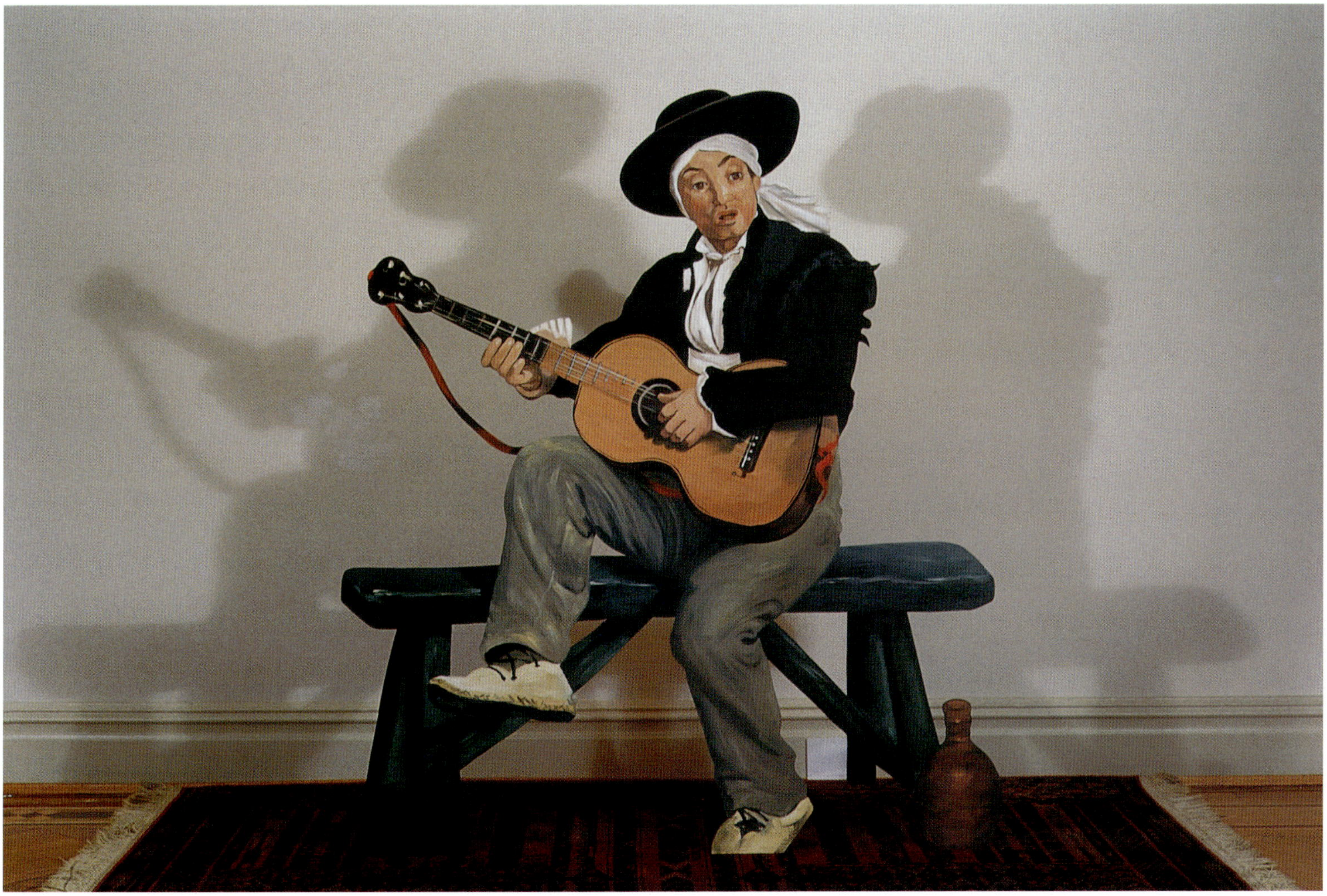

Manet's Guitarist, oil on birch shaped panel, 48" x 48", 2003.

Pat Steir

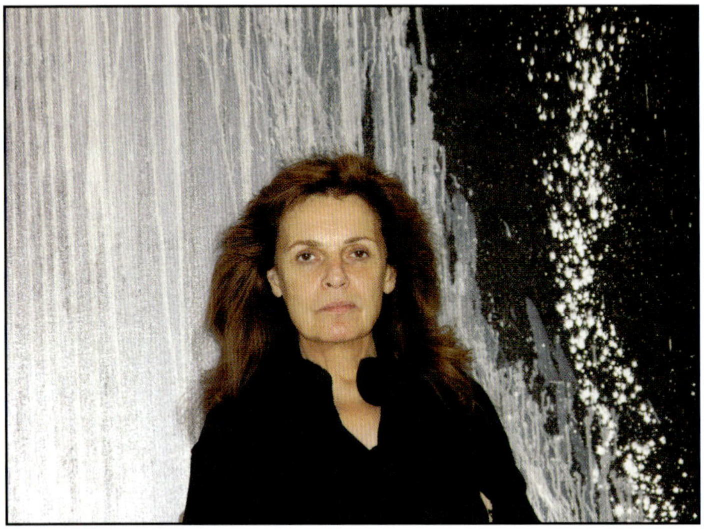

Courtesy of Cheim & Read.

Pat Steir, a founding member of "Printed Matter" bookshop and *Heresies* magazine, is on the editorial board of Semiotext and has been an art director at Harper and Row. She has received an honorary Doctorate of Fine Arts from her alma mater, Pratt Institute, and has been named an Alumni Honoree by Pratt and Boston University.

Her dozens of major solo exhibitions throughout the United States and Europe bear such titles as, "The Rhythm of Silence,"[204] "Waterfall of Dreams,"[205] "Red Yellow Blue I Love You,"[206] "Distant Horizon,"[207] "Moon Mountain Ghost Water,"[208] "Wind Water Stone,"[209] and "The Moon and the Wave."[210]

Steir's works have been included in numerous group exhibitions, from the High Museum of Art in Atlanta to the Museum of Modern Art, the Corcoran Gallery of Art in Washington, D.C., the Whitney Museum of American Art, the Max Protech Gallery, and the Brooklyn Museum, among many dozens of others across the United States and Europe. "Quietly Non-Violent,"[211] "... Speak(s) an Intimate Language,"[212] "Beauties and Beasts ...,"[213] "Arbitrary Order,"[214] and "Myths of Sensibility,"[215] some of the titles of reviews of her work, give a sense of Steir's subtle, "magic power"[216] (this last from *LeFigaro* in France).

Winner of a John Simon Guggenheim Memorial Fellowship and several grants from the National Endowment for the Arts, among others, Steir has works in most major United States museum collections and many corporate collections.

She is represented in New York by Cheim & Read.

Blue River, oil on canvas, 150" x 624", 2005. *Courtesy of Cheim & Read.*

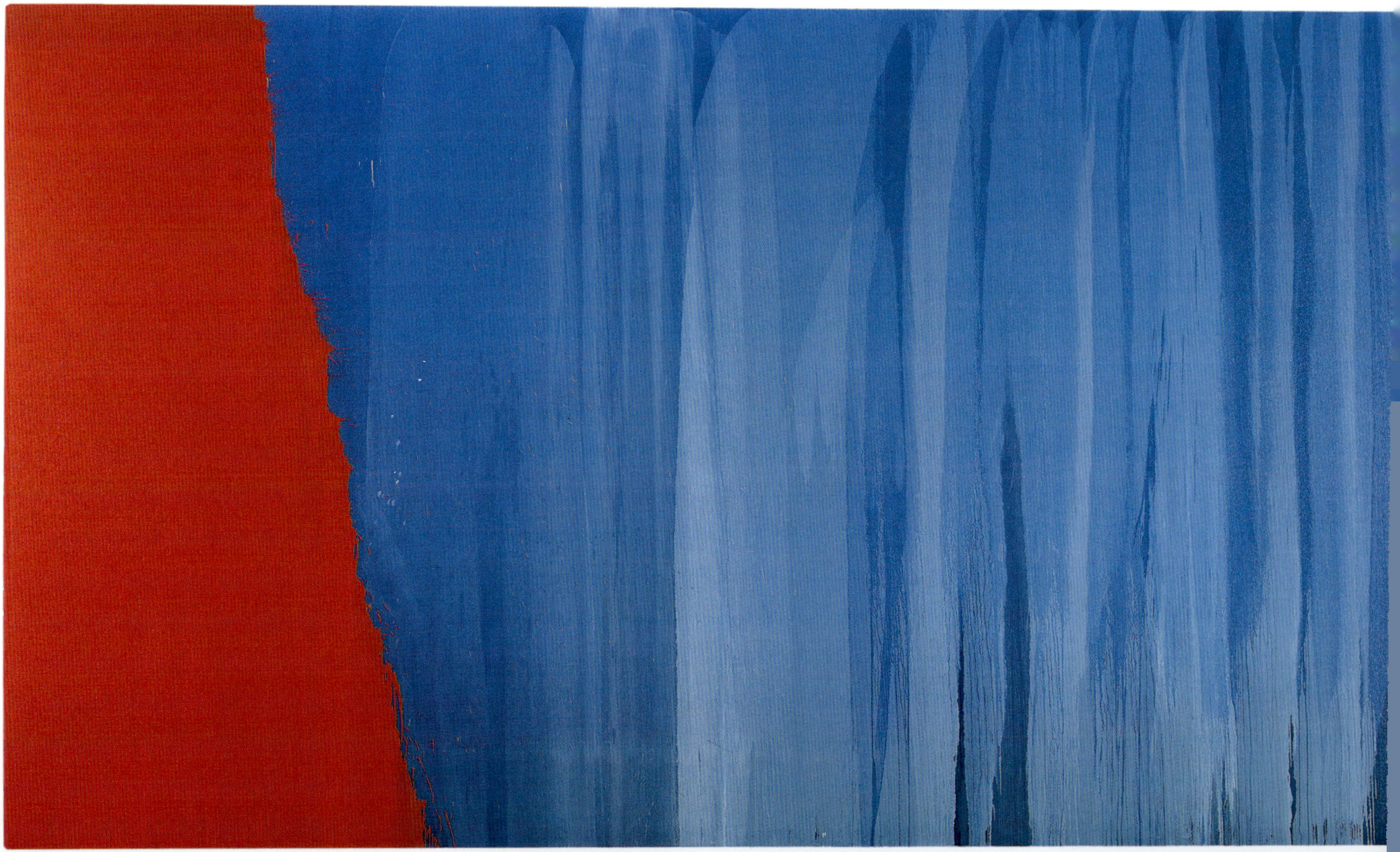

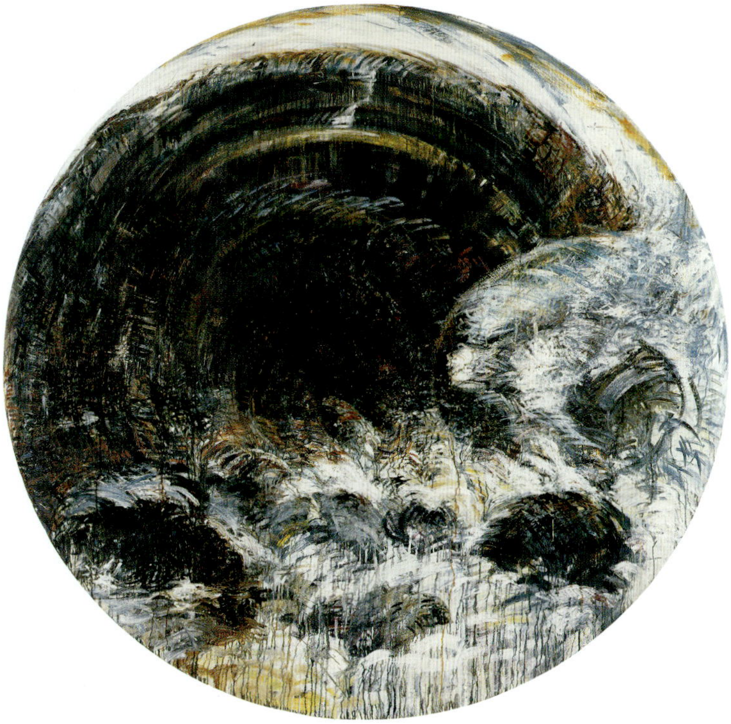

The Moon and the Wave: Courbet's Moon, oil on canvas, 7' diameter, c.1986-87. *Courtesy of Cheim & Read.*

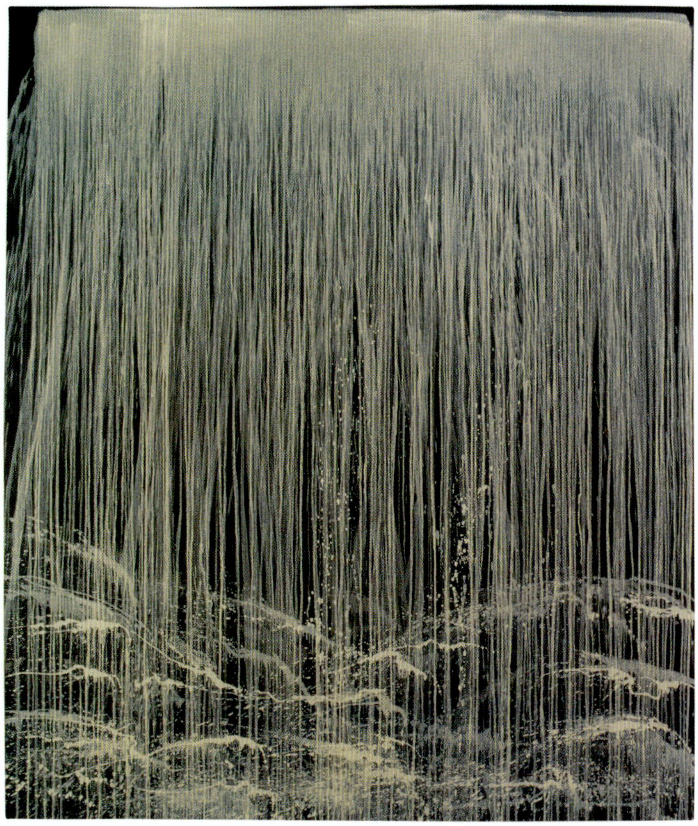

Curtain Waterfall, oil on canvas, 138.5" x 116.5", 1991. *Courtesy of Cheim & Read. Collection of National Gallery of Art, Washington, D.C.*

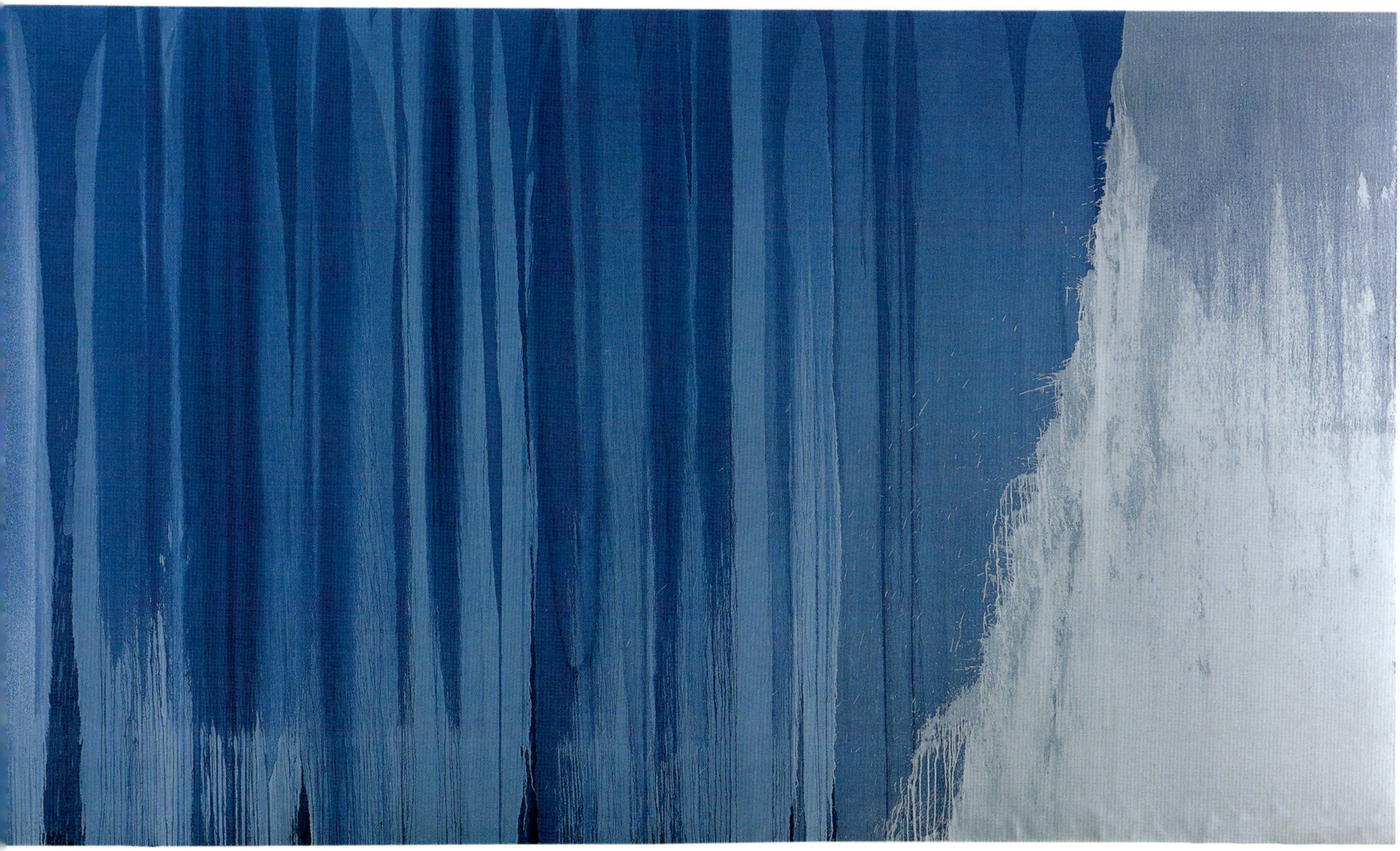

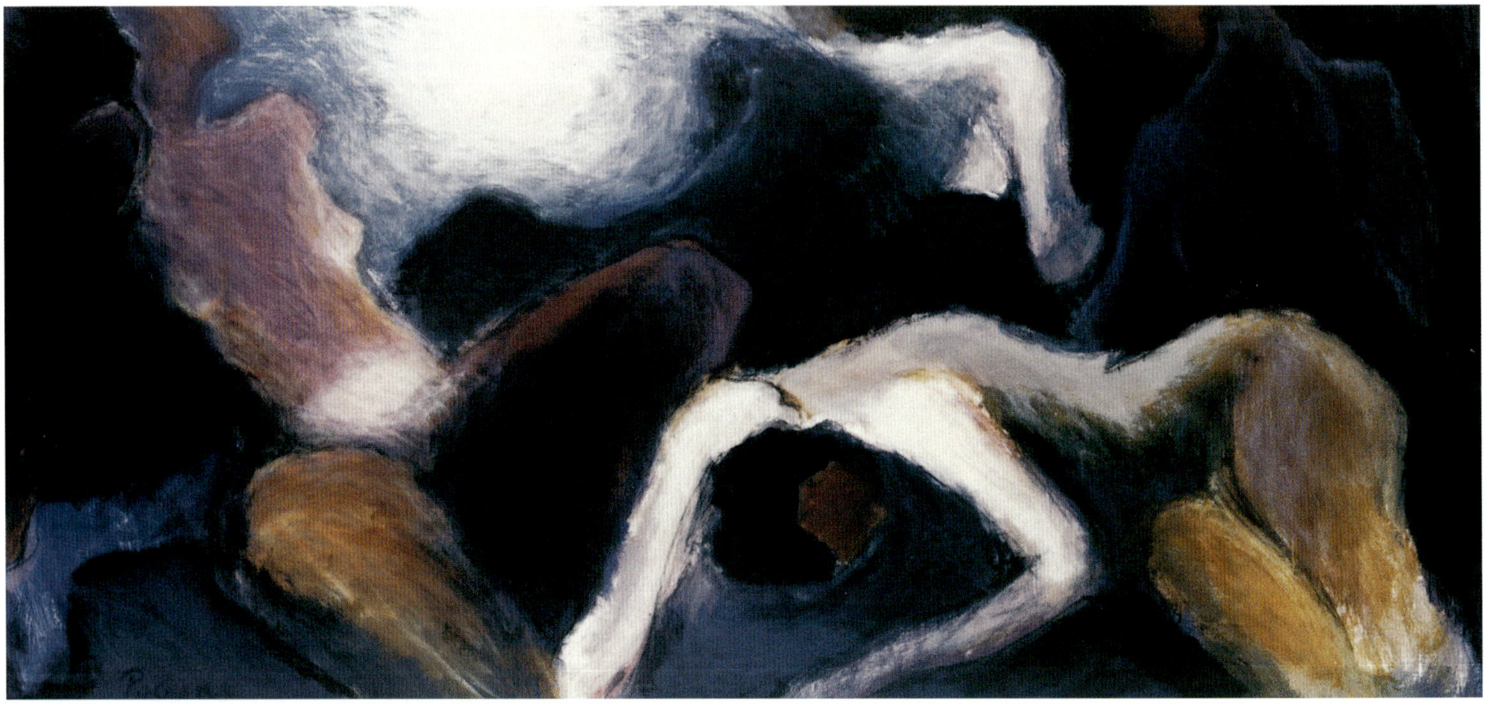

Moon Light, acrylic on linen, 46" x 92", 1991. *Courtesy of June Kelly Gallery. Collection of Mr. and Mrs. Chumpik Kim.*

Posoon Park Sung

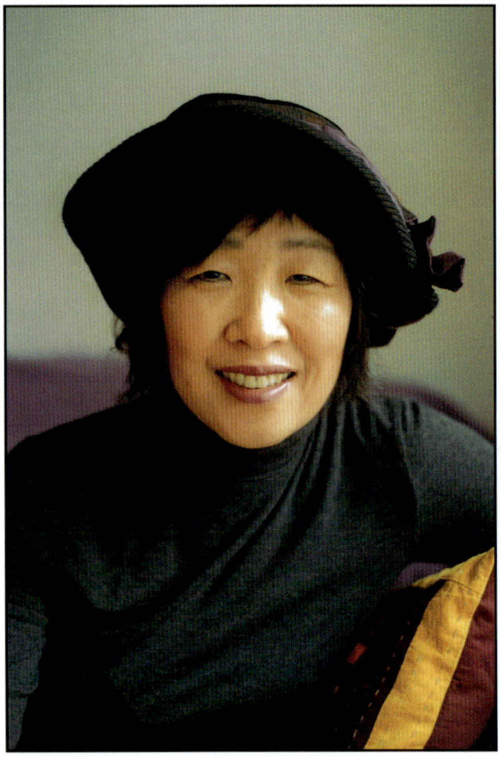

Photograph © Cynthia Dantzic.

Posoon Park Sung, in a subtle, quiet amalgam of Eastern and Western traditions, creates "sensitive, haunting canvases in a magical realist style,"[217] often reflecting a particular autobiographic experience or reverie. Speaking of "Anam Cara," the title of her exhibition at the June Kelly Gallery, Sung says, "it is Celtic for 'soul friend.' Everyone has a body and a soul ... alone but not alone, the soul connects us, and always to God. Religion within us ... helps feed our soul in our daily life; it is our connection to the human soul ... not visible, but of the spirit. ..."[218]

Schooled first in her native Korea at Hong-Ik University, Sung studied for her MFA at Pennsylvania State University with Richard Mayhew and George Zoretich, joined the faculty of Pennsylvania State, and later taught at Harrisburg Area Community College (where she is Professor Emerita), and then at the University of Tampa.

With all her travels and relocations, Sung continues to maintain a residence and studio in New York. Despite severe, life-threatening illness, she has kept up a full exhibition schedule, culminating in a major solo show at the June Kelly Gallery in New York. Her exhibitions have been seen at museums and galleries in many states, from the Doshi Center for Contemporary Art in Harrisburg, Pennsylvania, to the Lebo Robbins Gallery in Aspen, the N'Namdi Gallery in Detroit, and the University of Hawaii, in Hilo. Sung's paintings have also been shown at the Ueno Tokyo Metropolitan Museum of Art in Japan and the Simon Gallery in Seoul, Korea.

A major work created for the Big Apple Fest in New York, sponsored by the Avon Foundation, is now on permanent display at the Sloan-Kettering Memorial Hospital Center in New York.

Sung is represented by the June Kelly Gallery.

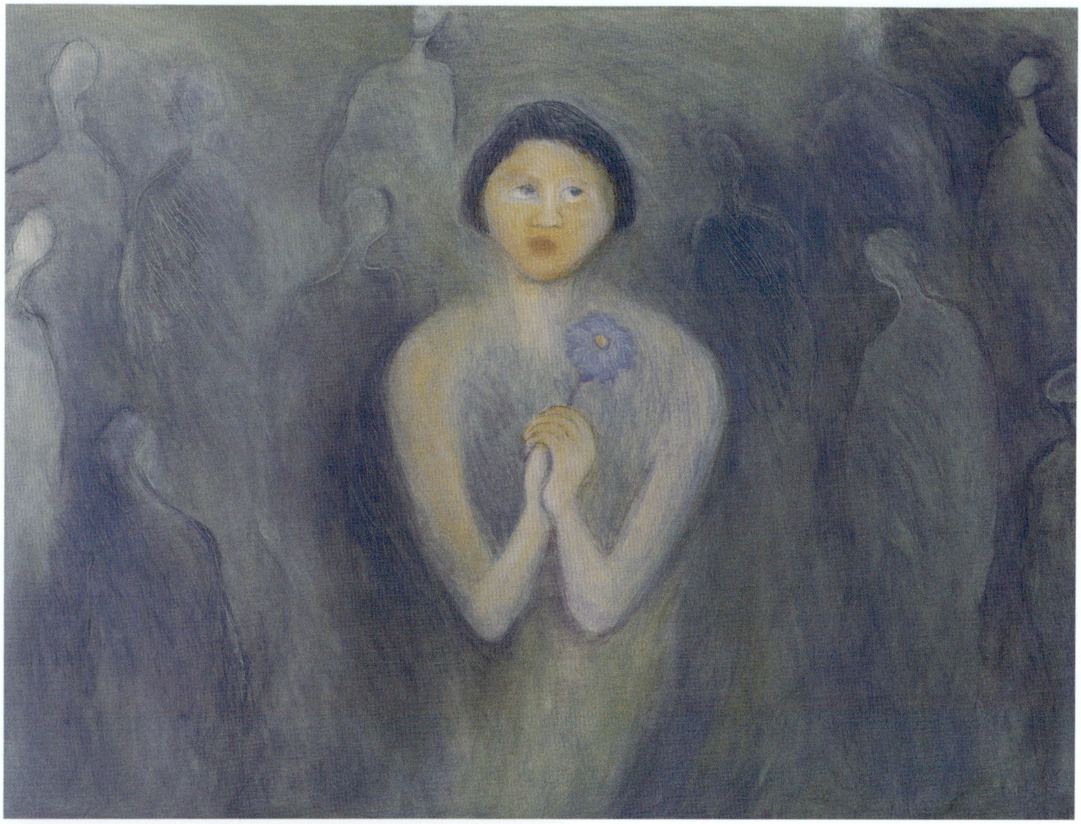

Choice of Mind, acrylic on canvas, 36" x 48", 2005. *Courtesy of June Kelly Gallery. Photograph by Becket Logan.*

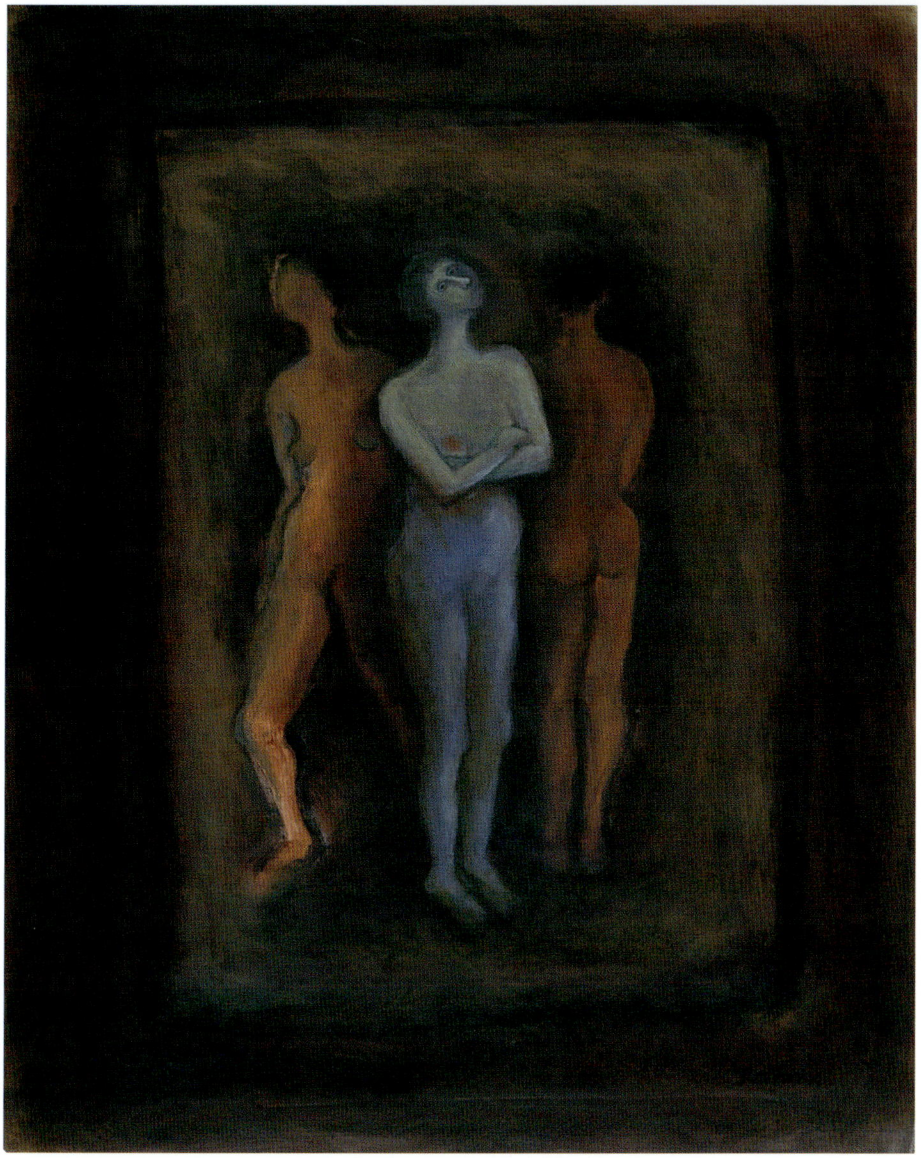

Anticipation I, acrylic on canvas, 40" x 31", 1997. *Courtesy of June Kelly Gallery.*

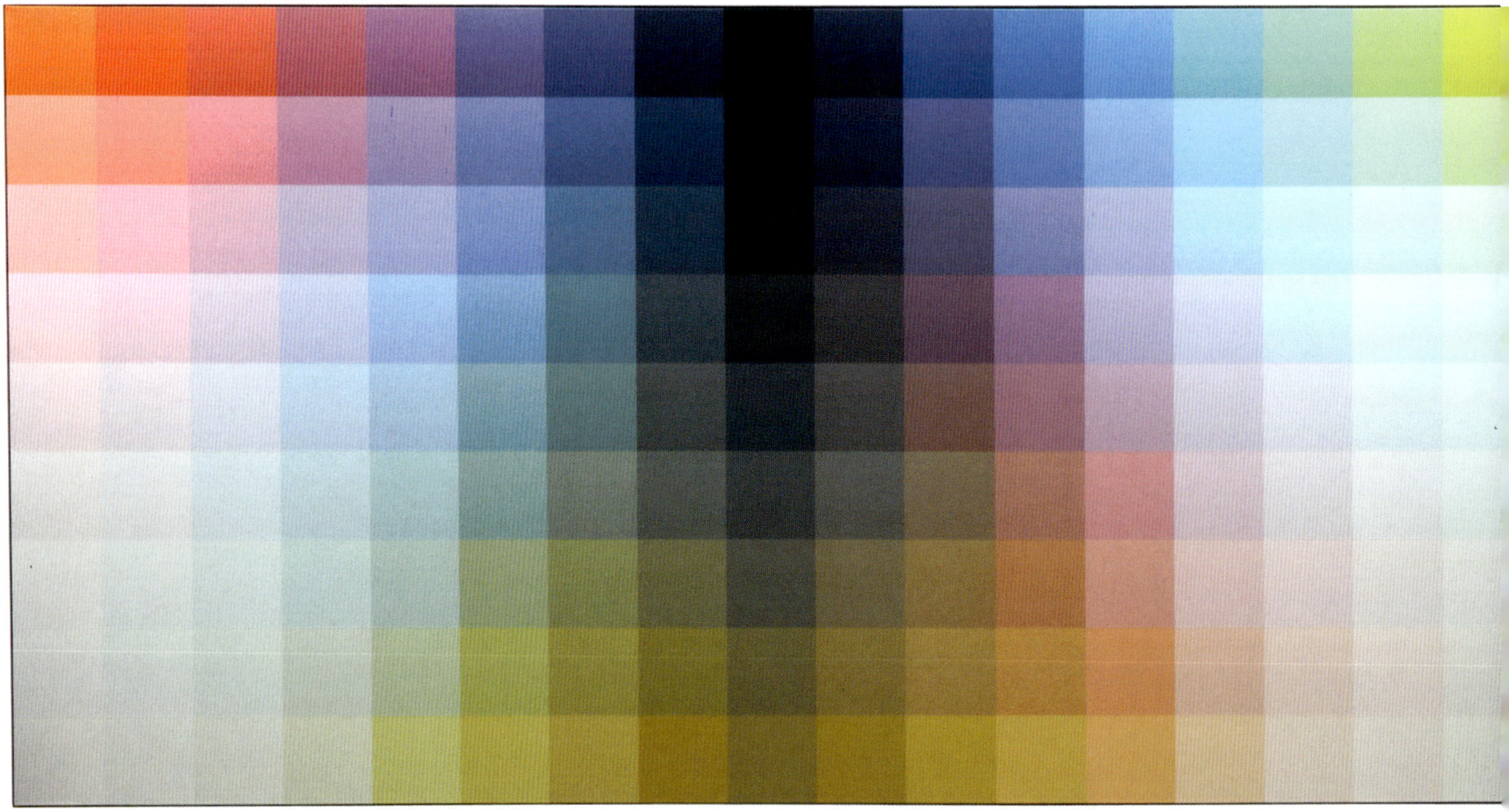

Untitled, acrylic on canvas, 9' x 17', 1983. *Collection of Johnson and Johnson.*

Robert Swain

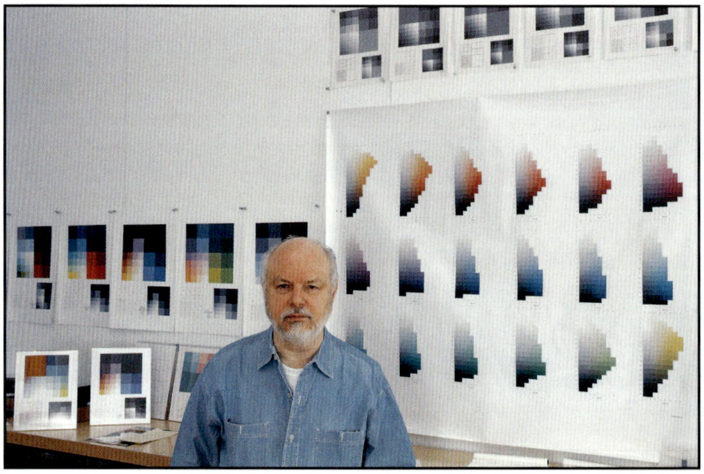

Photograph by Pierre Obando.

Robert Swain, for whom color is content in painting, believes color transmits feelings when freed from cultural restraints, through the perception of energy (wavelengths) from the electromagnetic spectrum, which varies greatly as particular colors generate distinct energies. His often grid-based, subtly graduated color compositions reveal carefully studied geometric structure and harmonies. A series of paintings of simple squares, within a larger square or rectangle, reveals the classic geometry of the Golden Section.

A Professor of Fine Arts at Hunter College for close to forty years, Swain has had fourteen one-artist exhibitions, including two major museum shows, at the Everson Art Museum in Syracuse, New York, and the Columbus Gallery of Fine Arts in Columbus, Ohio.

Included in over sixty group shows, his works have been seen at the Museum of Modern Art, the Whitney Museum of American Art, the Albright-Knox Art Gallery, the Metropolitan Museum of Art, and twice at The Corcoran Gallery of Art.

Highlights of his many awards and grants include a John Simon Guggenheim Memorial Fellowship, two grants from the National Endowment for the Arts, and the College Art Association's Distinguished Teaching of Art Award. Swain has completed some dozen commissions and architectural installations, notably those for Skidmore, Owens and Merrill, Johnson & Johnson, the University of Buffalo, and the Schering Laboratories. He is represented in many private and public collections, including the Metropolitan Museum of Art, the Detroit Institute of Art, and the Corcoran Gallery in Washington, D.C.

Swain, a graduate of the American University in Washington, D.C., has studied and traveled extensively in Central America and Europe.

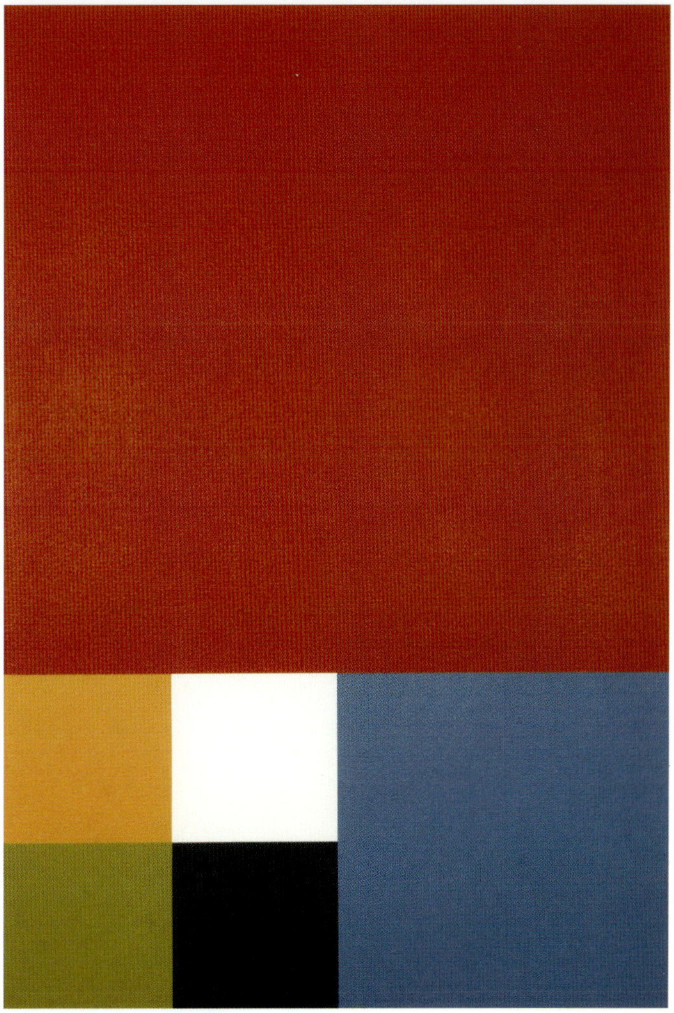

Untitled, acrylic on canvas, 6' x 4', 1988. *Collection of Albright-Knox Gallery*.

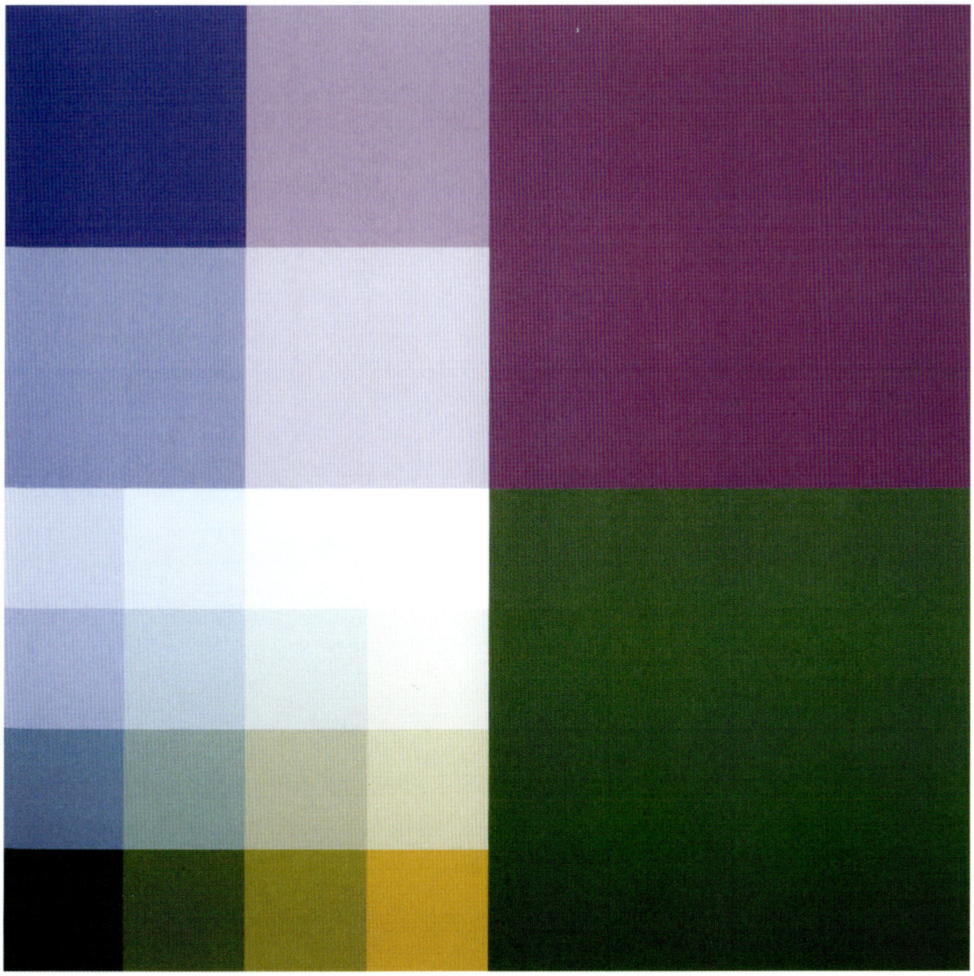

8x8–5A 4A 117B/117B X-4A, acrylic on canvas, 8' x 8', c.1999-2001.

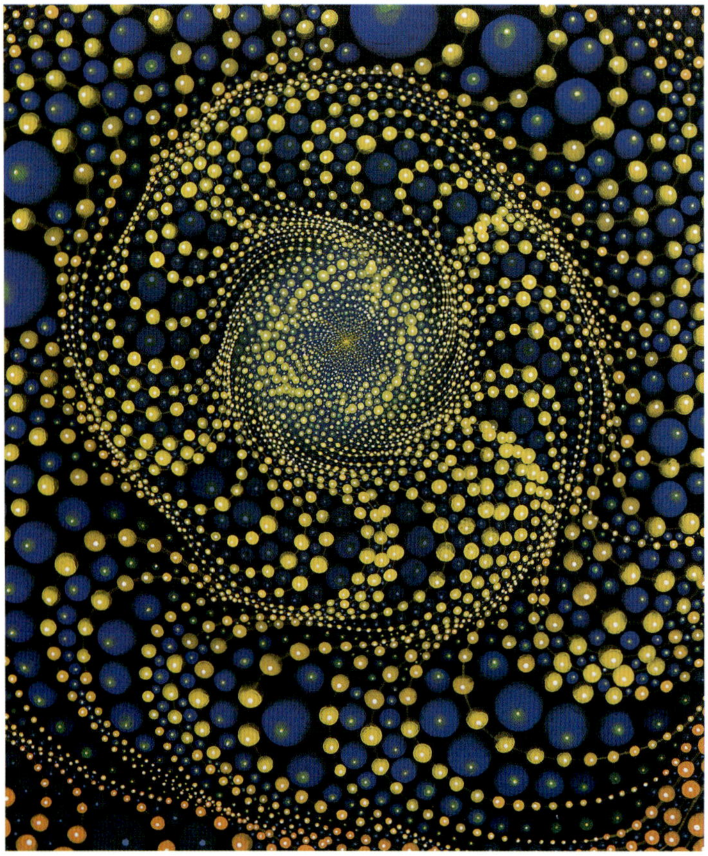

Shaker (blue), acrylic on wood, 24" x 20", 2004. *Private collection.*

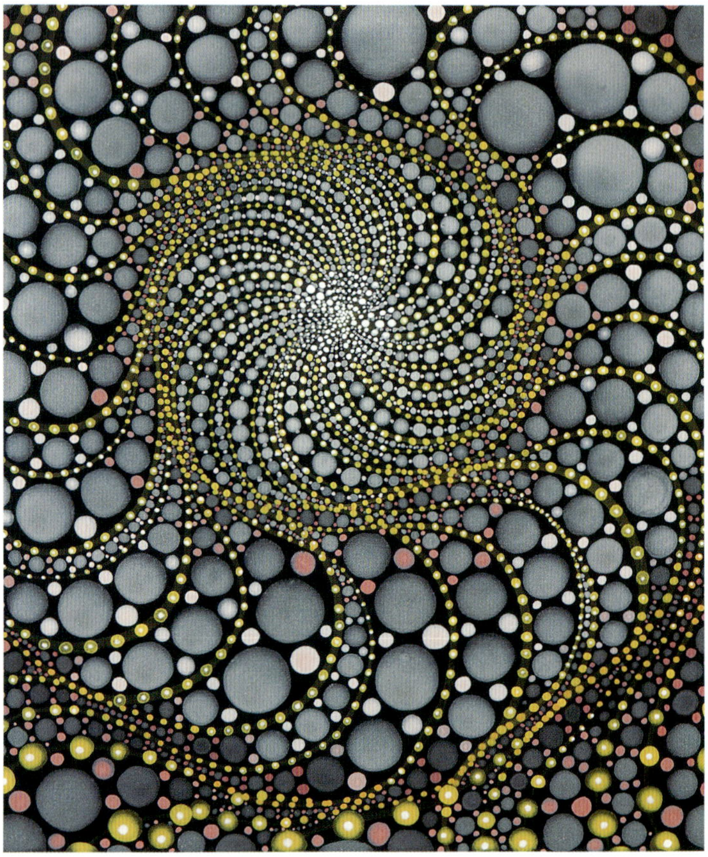

Silver Wheel, acrylic on wood, 12" x 10", 2004. *Private collection.*

Barbara Takenaga

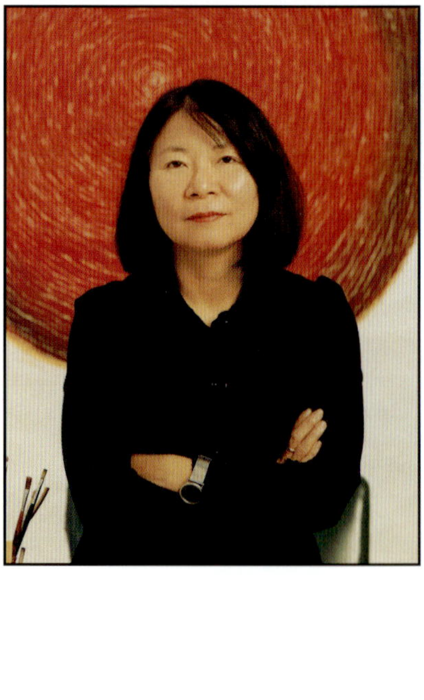

Courtesy of the artist.

Barbara Takenaga, equally at home in her New York and Williamstown, Massachusetts studios, has participated in such group exhibitions as, "Good Vibrations,"[219] "From Natural to Techno Universes ...,"[220] "Mindscape,"[221] "Radial Gradient,"[222] "Obsessive Pleasures,"[223] "Accumulations,"[224] "Cascade of Scales,"[225] and "Eye Tattoos."[226]

Robert Kushner says, "breaking all ... expectations, this new body of paintings, offers sublime pleasure, dizzying exhilaration [... and] leaves me breathless. ... They are wild, ecstatic, yet often preternaturally serene."[227]

"Although her works show a strong affinity with the Op Art movement in investigating pulsations of color and form, Takenaga employs a layering of dots, splashes, and pinwheels to create imperfect, off-center vortices, somehow more resonant with the forms of nature ... to create an array of vibrating optics that offer delight, awe, humor and pleasure," adds Lisa Tamiris Becker.[228]

Takenaga, who received her BFA and MFA from the University of Colorado at Boulder, has had over a dozen solo exhibitions and is Professor of Art at Williams College, in Williamstown.

She has received a Purchase Award from the American Academy of Arts and Letters, and her works are in many public collections, including those of The News Corporation, Fidelity Investments, and Citigroup, in New York, the University of Colorado Museum, the DeCordova Museum and Sculpture Park, Lincoln, Massachusetts, the Hallmark Fine Arts Program in Kansas City, and the Museum of Nebraska Art, in Lincoln.

Takenaga is represented by McKenzie Fine Arts in New York.

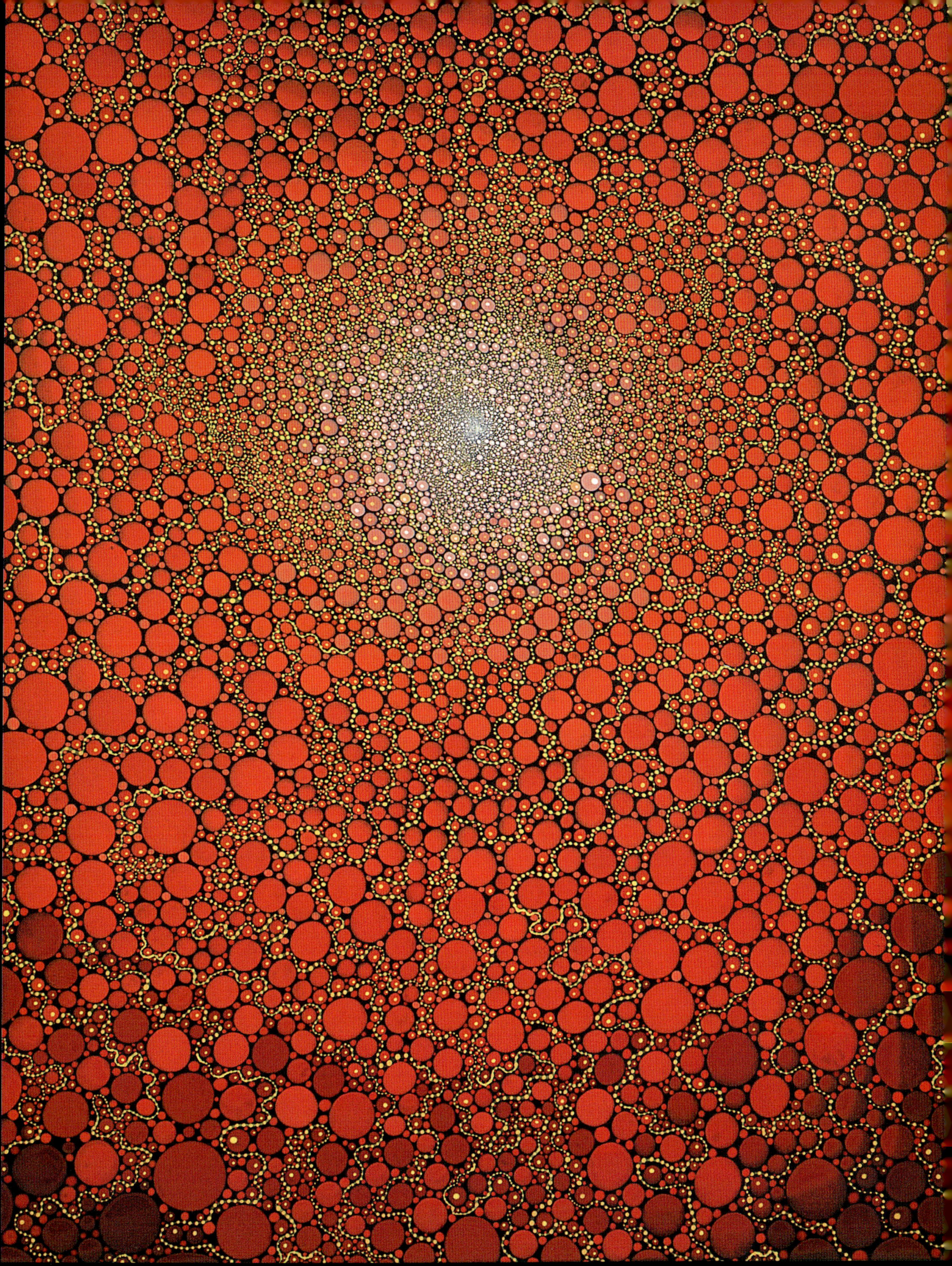

Tremolo #4, acrylic on canvas, 60" x 45", 2005. *Collection of DeCordova Museum.*

Bob Tomlinson, a scholar of French literature and aesthetics, as well as a painter, often draws on biblical and other literary themes for inspiration. Combining layers of oils and collaged papers on canvas, he "employs classical anatomy as a vehicle for gestural abstraction," says Laurence Downes.[229]

A graduate of Pratt Institute and the City University of New York's Graduate Center, where he has been a Director of African Studies, he has lectured, published, and exhibited widely in Europe and throughout the United States. His solo exhibitions have taken place at Pratt Institute and New York Community College, and also in Paris and London. Group shows include, "Atlantan African-American Artists,"[230] "5e Biennale de Paris,"[231] and exhibitions at the John Whibley Gallery, London, Contemporary Christian Art Gallery, Cross Cultural Group, and Contemporary Black Artists in America in New York as well as at the Viridian Artists Gallery, which represents his work.

Bob Tomlinson

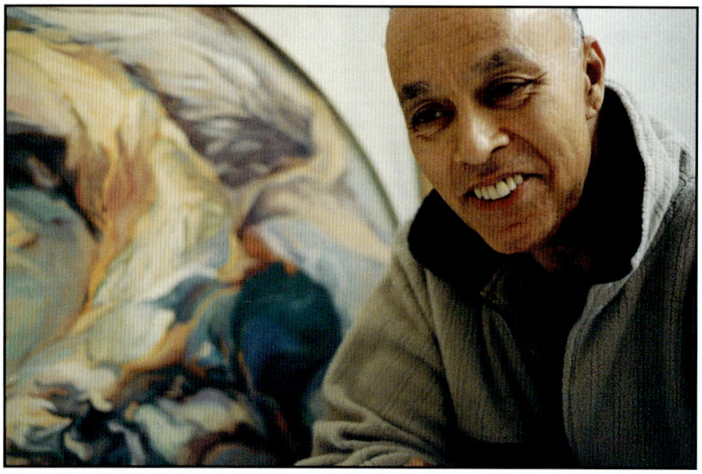

Photograph by Blaise Giuliani.

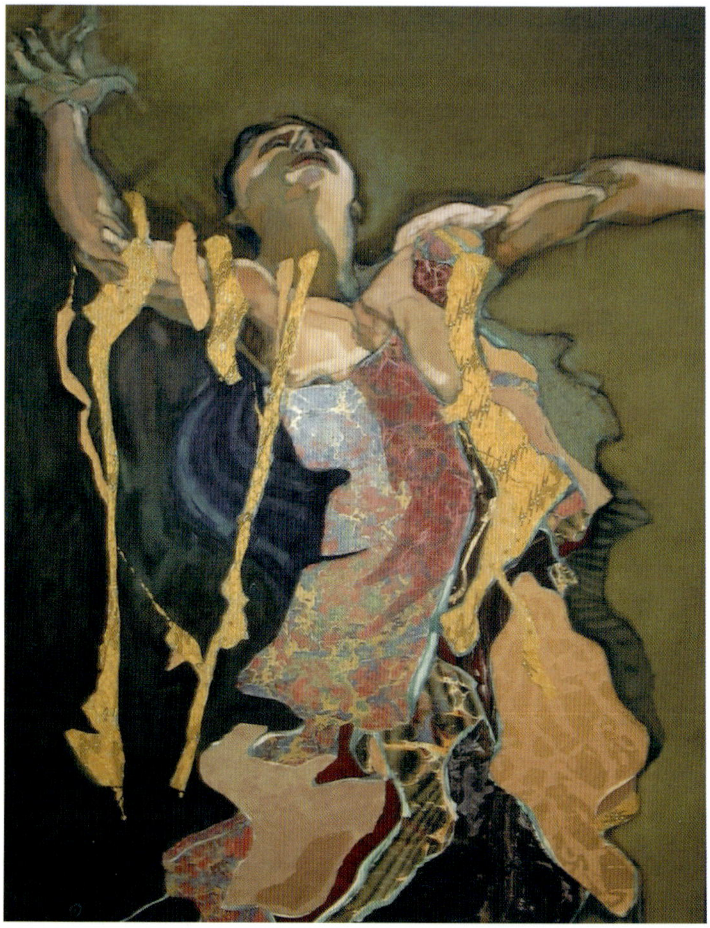

Dance II: The Gaze of Death, oil and collage on canvas, 40" x 30", 2005.

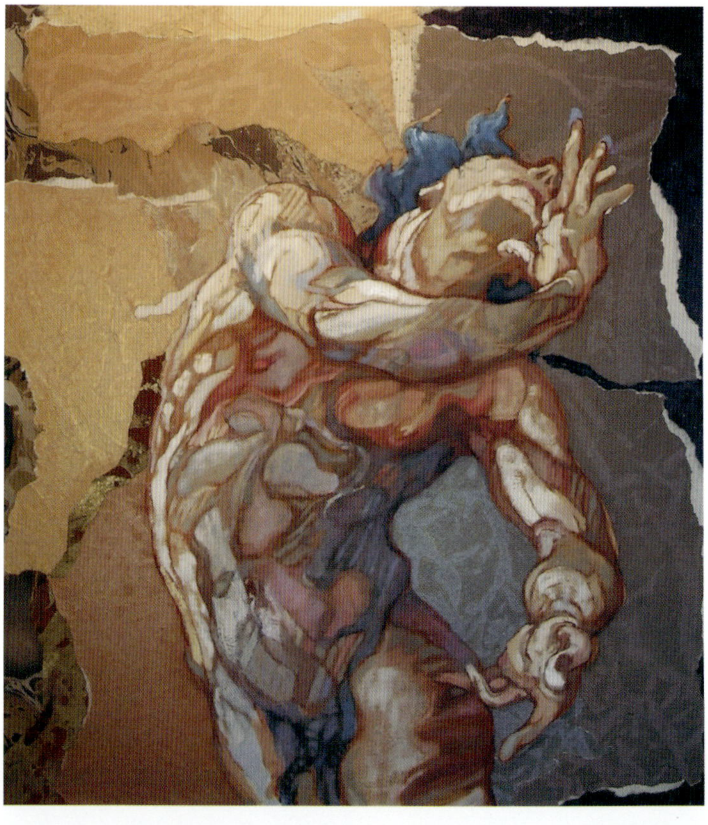

IOKANAAN III: The Averted Gaze, oil and collage on canvas, 40" x 32", 2005. *Collection of Ms. Gabriella E. Morris.*

A winner of many awards, including two travel grants from the President's Commission on the Status of Minorities at Emory University and a Ford Foundation Advanced Study Fellowship, Tomlinson has a long history in academe, having taught French and English at Emory University in Atlanta, Georgia, where he is Professor Emeritus, and at several schools in Paris, as well as at Hunter College in New York.

Tomlinson says he has been "inspired particularly by Antoine Watteau, on whom I have done much academic work. His elusive feelings, swirling arabesques and vague melancholy can ... be sensed in my own work ... and Richard Lindner, who ... taught artistic integrity; we should ignore praise and blame for the truth ... if only we had the strength and courage to descend into the depths and bring it to the surface."[232]

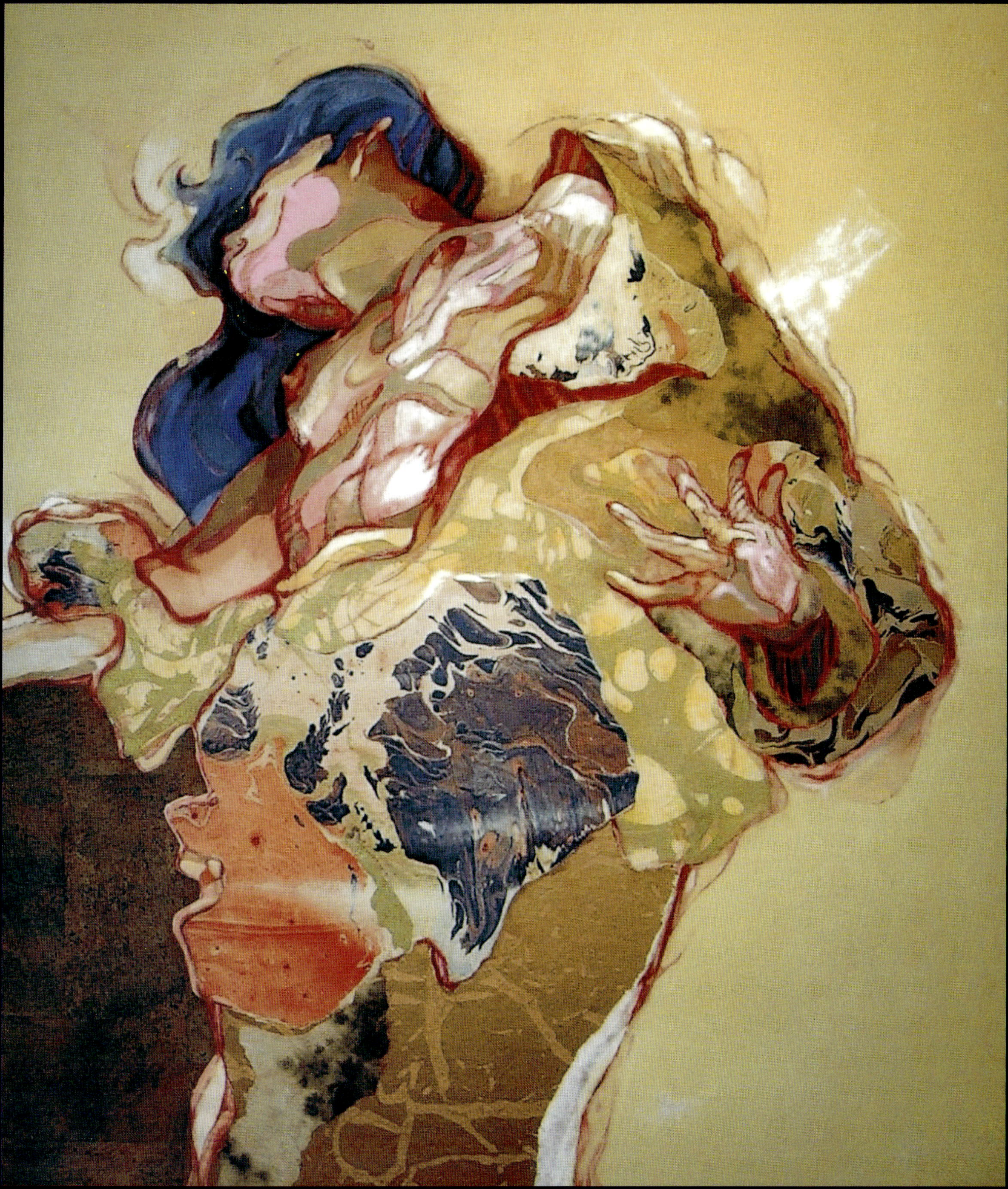

Dance I: The Alternation, oil and collage on canvas, 40" x 32", 2004.

George Tooker

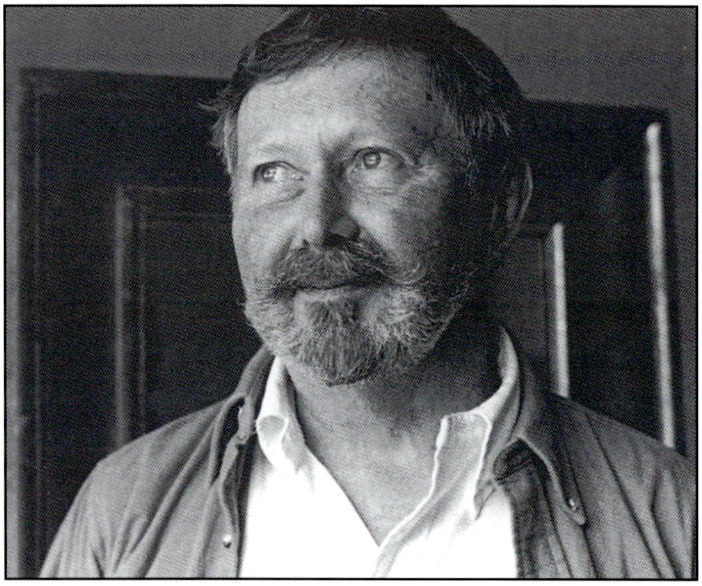

Courtesy of D C Moore Gallery.

George Tooker, the long-celebrated Brooklyn-born figurative painter whose style is often described as "magic realism," studied at the Art Students League with Reginald Marsh after attending Harvard University. At the League, where Tooker also taught for several years, Paul Cadmus encouraged him to work with classic egg tempera, his medium of choice ever since.

Elected to the National Academy of Design, a member of the American Academy of Arts and Letters, and recipient of many other honors, Tooker has his papers on deposit at the Smithsonian's Archives of American Art in Washington D.C.

Early political involvement with socially conscious groups following his familiarity with textile communities near his boyhood prep school in Andover, Massachusetts, contributed to Tooker's choice to be "more of a reporter or observer of society than an interpreter."[233] His numerous solo and group exhibitions bear such titles as, "Reality and Dream ...,"[234] "50 Years of Painting and Study Drawings,"[235] "Surrealism, USA,"[236] "Everyday Mysteries ...,"[237] "Boundless/Silence, States of Infinity,"[238] "Magic Vision,"[239] "Magic Realism: America's Response to Surrealism,"[240] "Human Concern, Personal Torment,"[241] "Symbolic Realism,"[242] and "Paintings from the Museum of Modern Art"[243] (at the National Gallery of Art, Washington, D.C.).

Tooker's works are in most major public collections, notably the Metropolitan Museum of Art, the Brooklyn Museum, the National Academy of Design, the New York Historical Society, and the Whitney Museum of American Art in New York, and the Smithsonian Institution's National Museum of American Art and Hirshhorn museums in Washington, D.C.

He is represented in New York by the D C Moore Gallery.

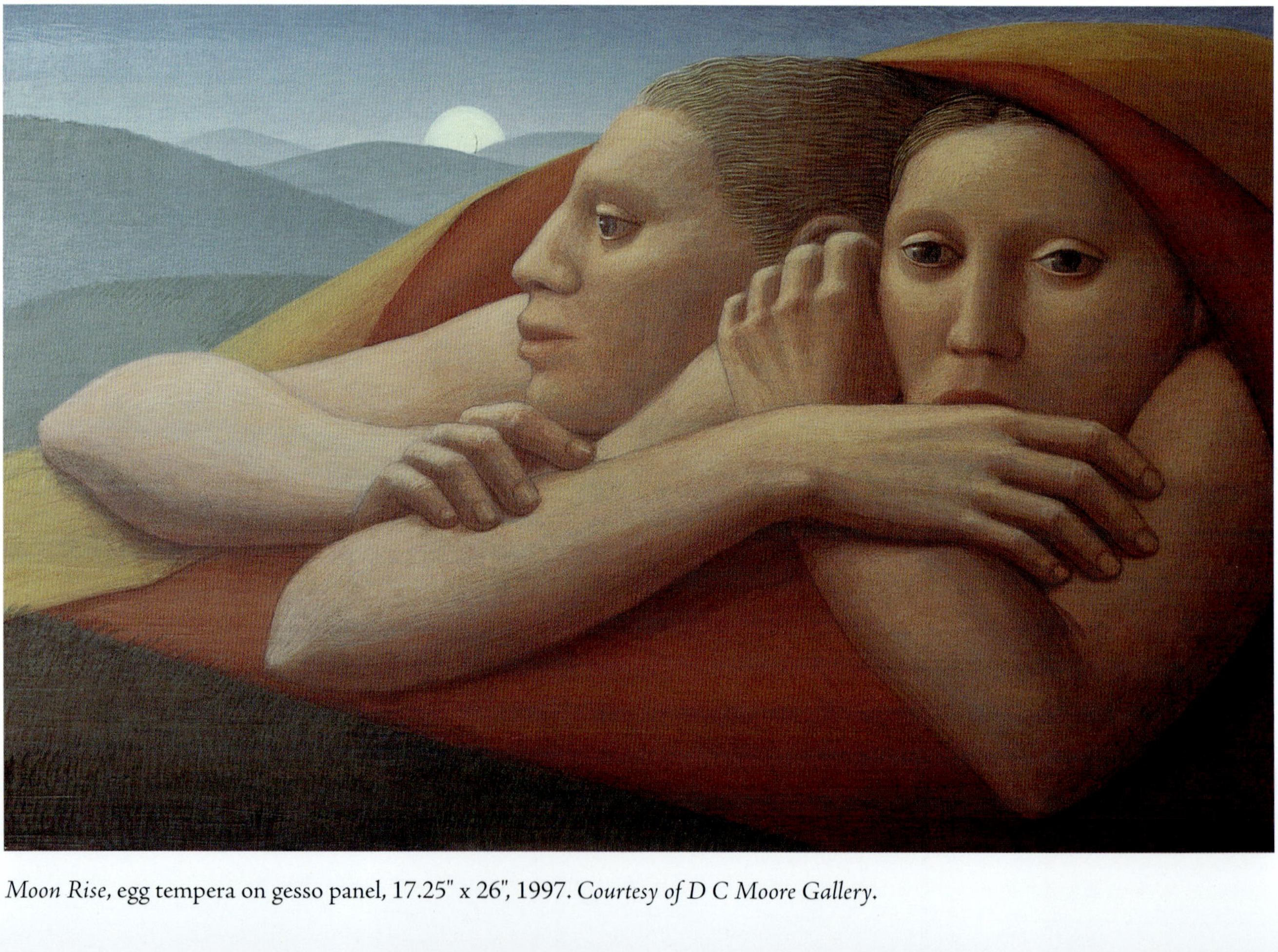

Moon Rise, egg tempera on gesso panel, 17.25" x 26", 1997. *Courtesy of D C Moore Gallery.*

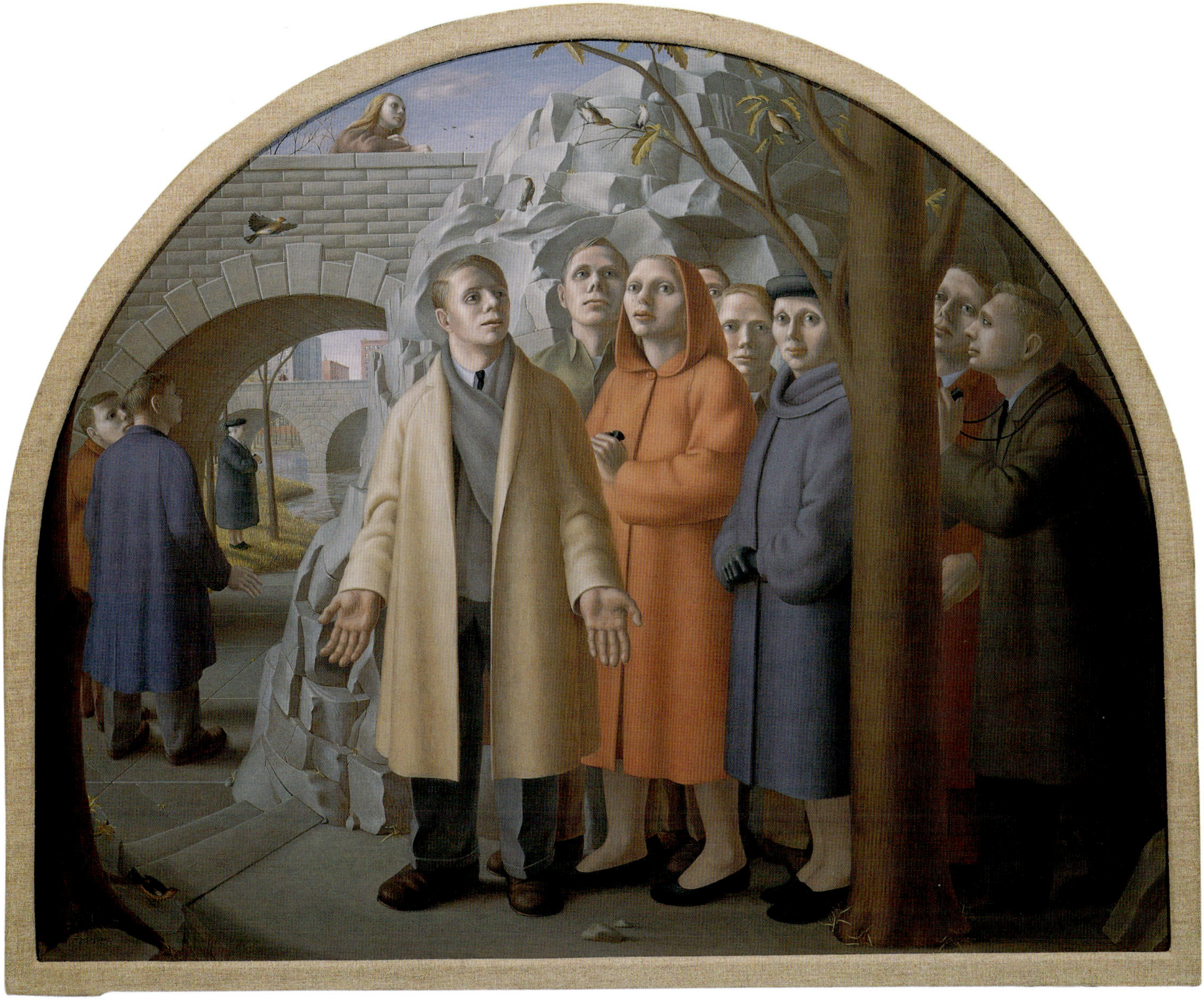

Bird Watchers, egg tempera on gesso board, 28.75" x 34.75", 1948. *Collection of New Britain Museum of American Art, Gift of Olga H. Knoepke.*

The Subway, egg tempera on composition board, 18" x 36", 1950. *Collection of the Whitney Museum of American Art, New York; Purchase, with funds from the Juliana Force Purchase Award, Photograph by Geoffrey Clements, New York.*

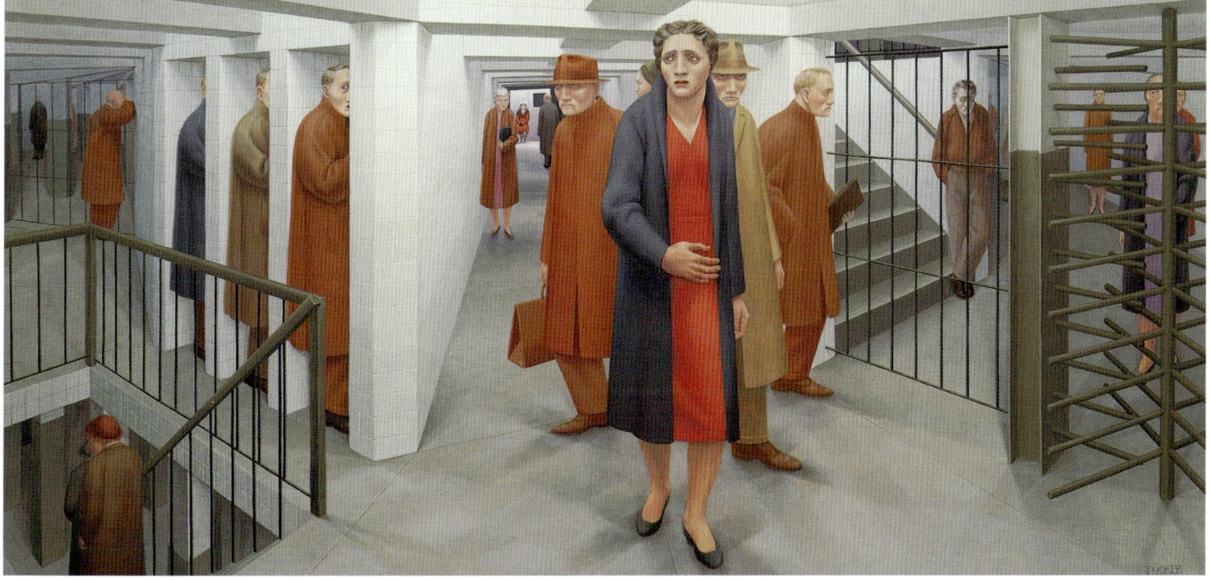

Vivian Tsao

Vivian Tsao, whose "pulsating interiors recall a cross between Gwen John and Bonnard in their almost-mystical sense of expansiveness"[244] (David Cohen), feels an affinity with the nuanced, subliminal work of Antonio López García. After receiving a BA in Fine Arts from Taiwan's Normal University, she left her native China to study for an MFA at Carnegie Mellon University in Pittsburgh, then lived in the Middle East, where she painted daily, studying the subtle effects of light and space, which, she says turned her "away from the expressionistic" and channeled her "into the intimate."[245]

Tsao has traveled widely throughout Europe as well, and has a long record of writing on art in the Chinese language, including many reviews, essays, and interviews with such artists as Philip Pearlstein and Antonio López García, and the critic Hilton Kramer.

A recipient of grants from the New York State Council on the Arts and Carnegie Mellon University, Tsao has taught at the National Teachers College in Taipei and has been on the faculty of New York's Pace University for over fifteen years.

Her more than sixty solo and group exhibitions of oils and pastels include those at the American Academy of Arts and Letters, the Brooklyn Museum, Taiwan Province Museum, Taipei Fine Arts Museum, the National Gallery, Taiwan, and several at New York's Ceres Gallery, which represents her work.

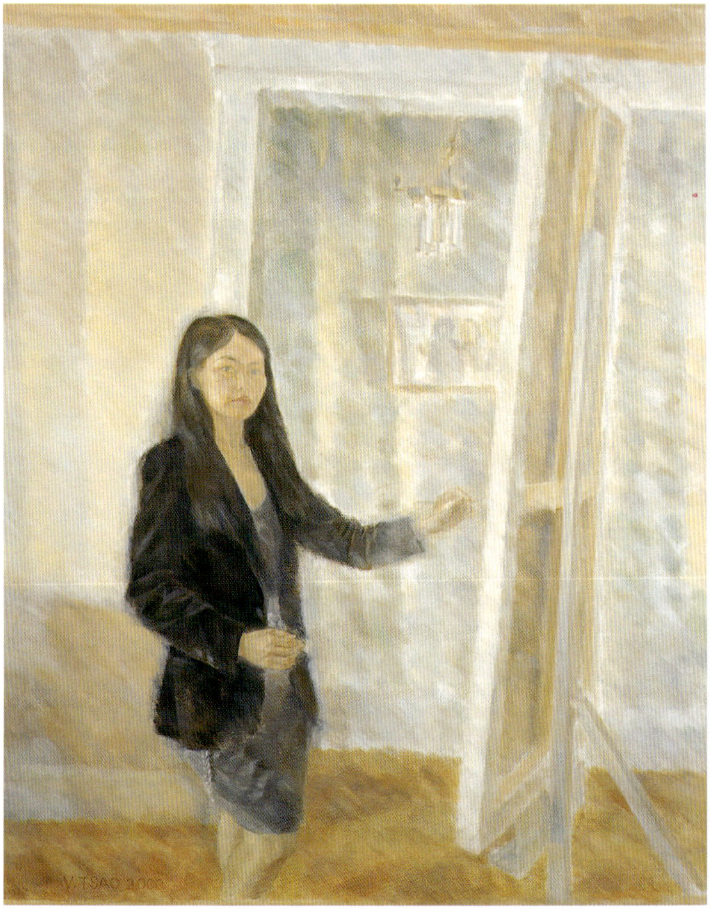

Mirrored Afternoon (self portrait), oil on canvas, 48" x 38", c.1997-2000. *Photograph by D. James Dee. Courtesy of the artist.*

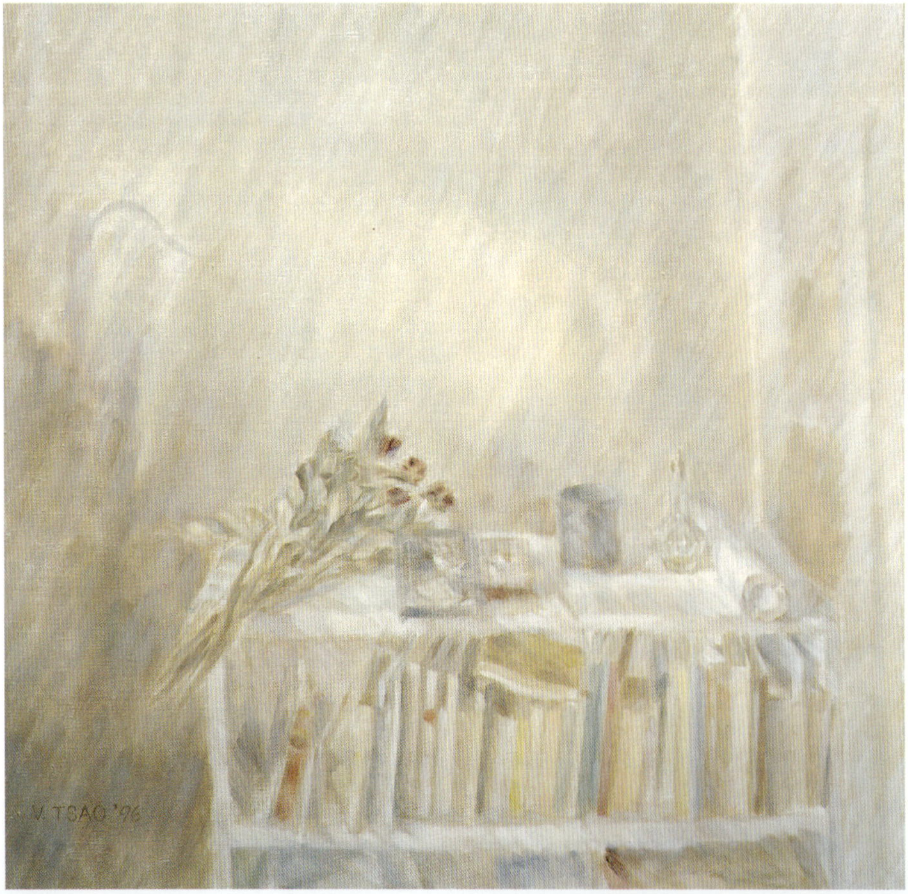

A Chinese Bookcase, oil on canvas, 36" x 36", 1996.

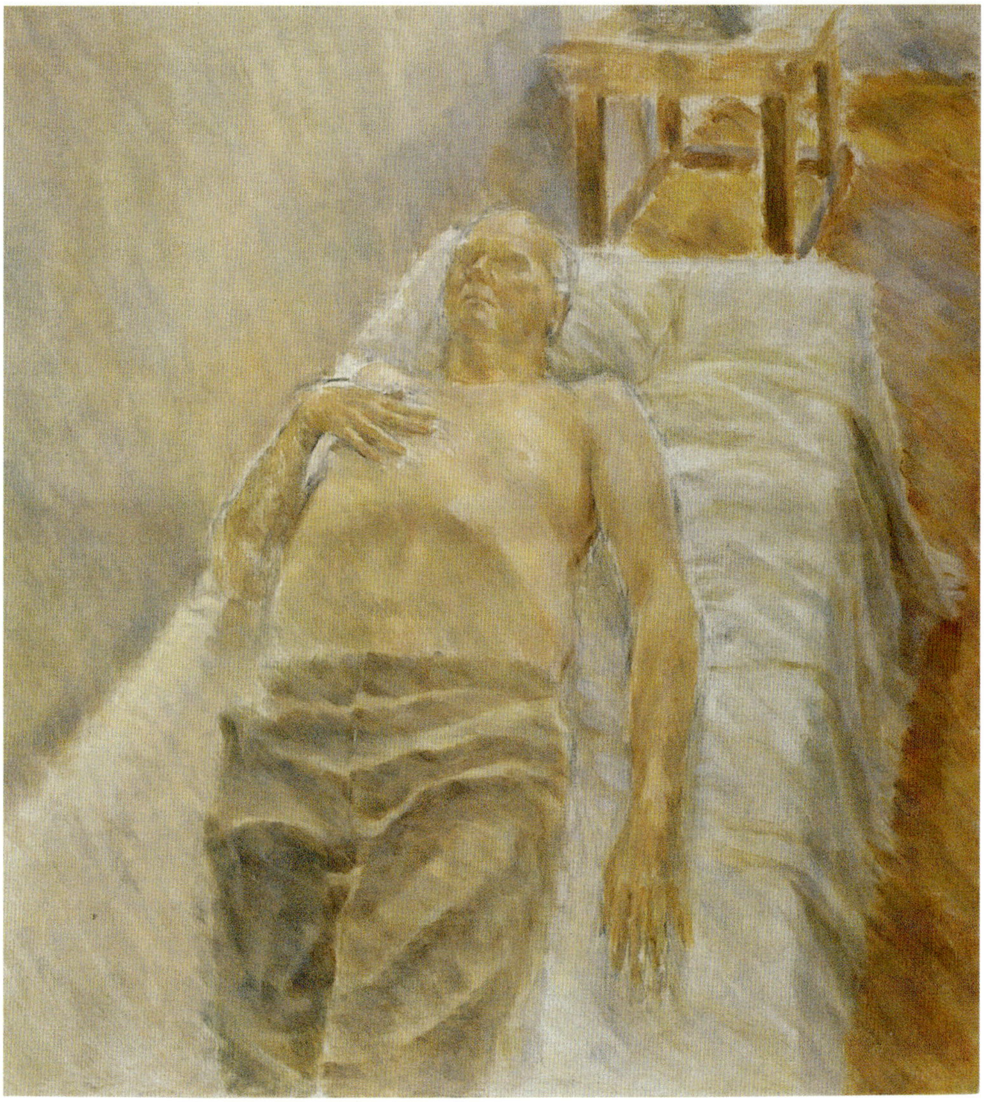

September. oil on canvas, 36" x 32", c.1995-96.

Maple Leaf and Rice Paper, oil on canvas, 24" x 36", c.1999-2002. *Photograph by D. James Dee.*

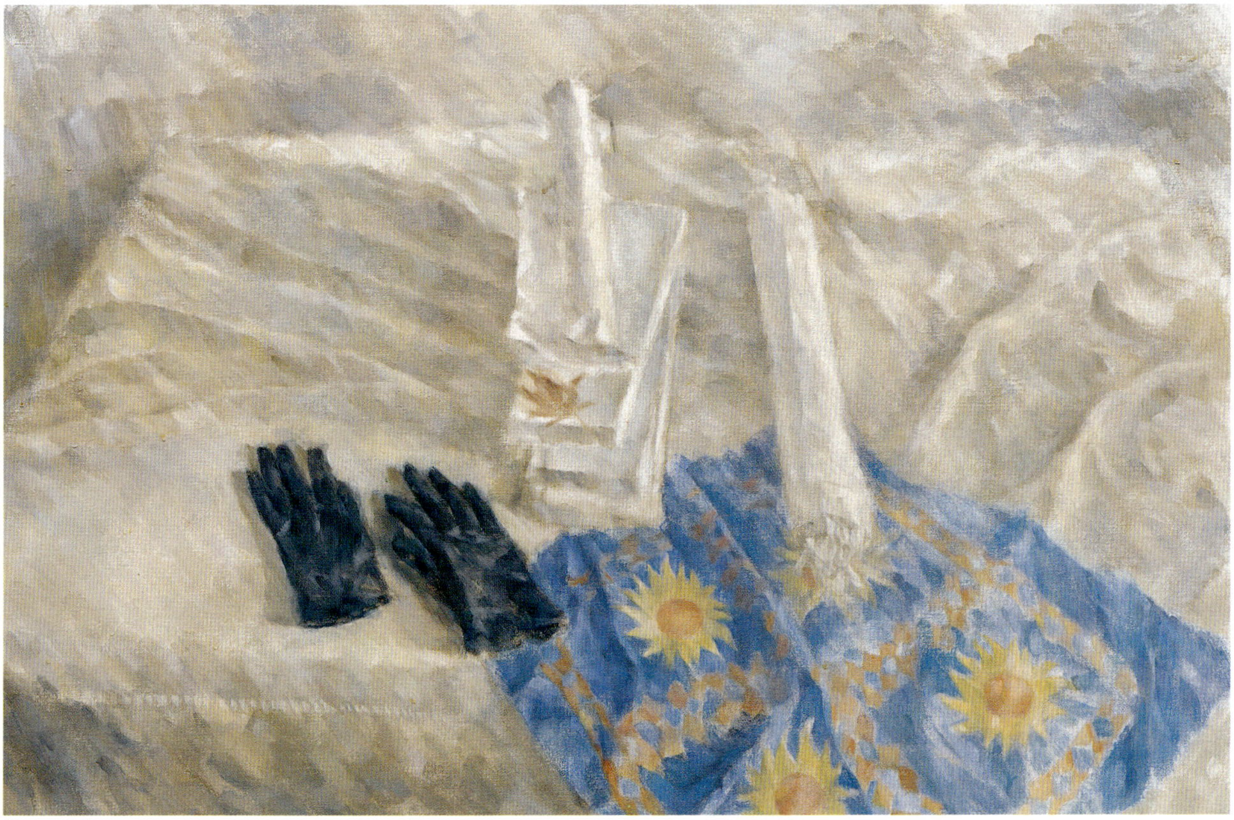

Audrey Ushenko

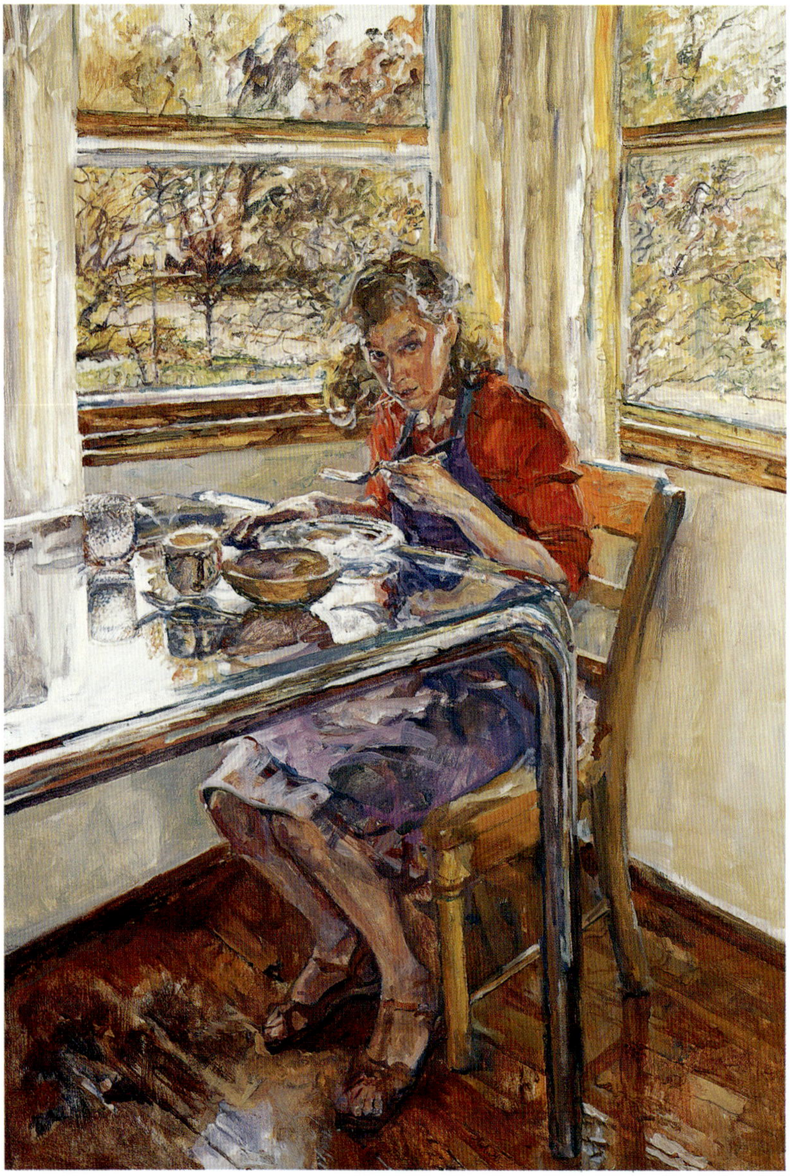

The Bean Eater (self portrait), oil on canvas, 36" x 24", 1995. *Courtesy of Denise Bibro Fine Art.*

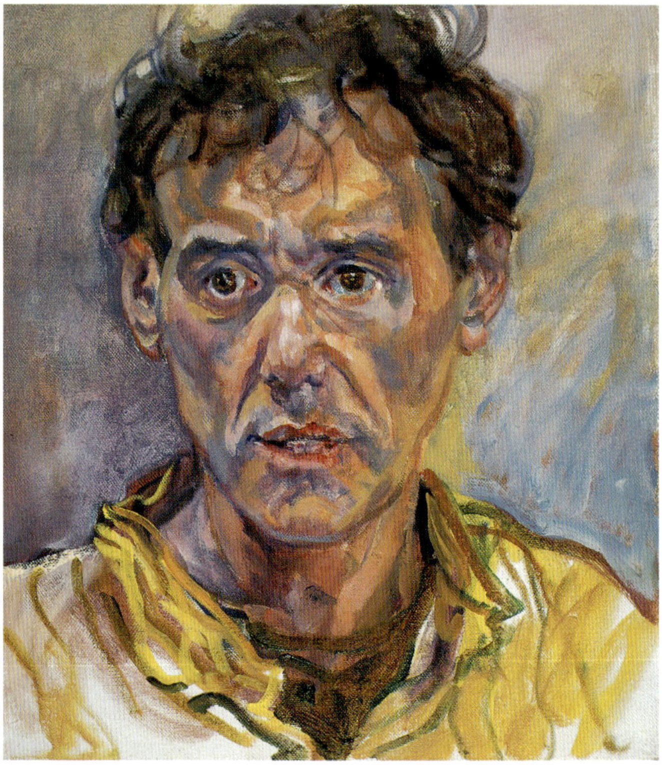

Study for Doubting Sunday (Don Perlis), oil on canvas, 14" x 12", 2000. *Courtesy of Denise Bibro Fine Art.*

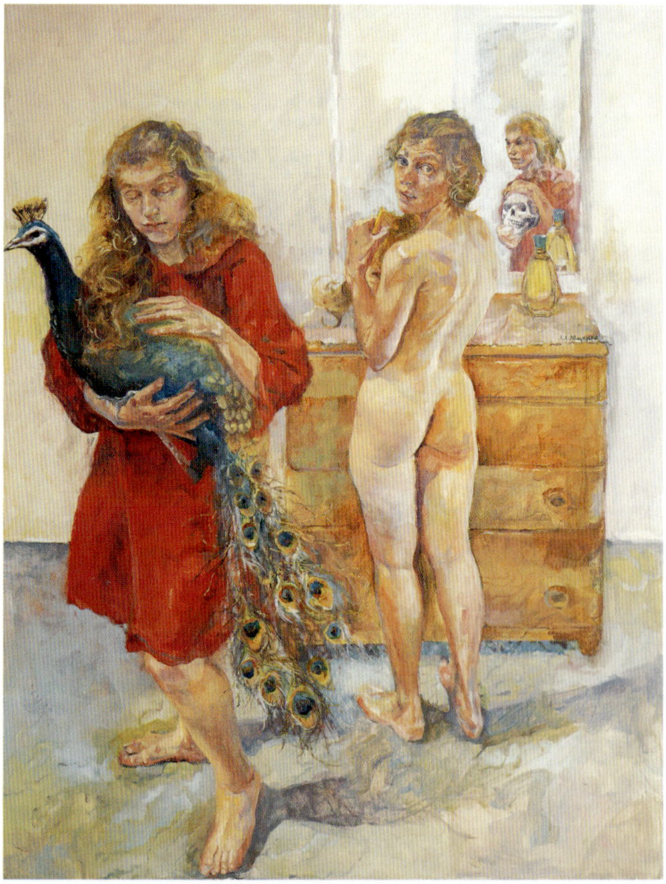

Vanitas IV, oil on linen, 48" x 36", 1979. *Courtesy of Denise Bibro Fine Art.*

Audrey Ushenko, daughter of a philosopher colleague of Einstein at Princeton, was raised in an academic environment. Equally at home in the roles of painter, art historian, and art educator (as well as a classically trained pianist), she is an elected member of New York's National Academy of Design, where she has also taught. In addition, she has been on the faculties of Indiana University, the University of Illinois, Northwestern University, and Valparaiso University in Indiana, and has been an Artist in Residence and Visiting Artist at the Maryland Institute of Art, Saint Louis University Museum of Art, and Adrian College, in Mississippi, among others. Her PhD in Art History and MA in Painting from Northwestern University followed study at Indiana University and the Art Institute of Chicago.

Winner of several awards at the National Academy of Design, Ushenko has had dozens of solo and group exhibitions throughout the United States, and her work is in many public collections including the National Academy of Design, the Everson Museum of Art, and the Polish Museum of America in Chicago.

Represented by the Denise Bibro Gallery in New York, where she has had numerous exhibitions and sometimes sets up her easel to paint, Ushenko has been called "a big-hearted romantic satirist ... who gives us a new form of salon painting, both magnificent and discreet."[246] Her many museum projects consist of narrative paintings, each set and executed in its space.

Ushenko creates these and other highly stylized dramatic, serial tableaux, "typically staged in contemporary settings, often including herself, friends and colleagues, but representing universal signifiers. She uses myth to make a narrative drama about life experiences without being too specific. ..."[247] Laurence Alloway has classified Ushenko "among the image-makers rather than realists ... whose strength lies not in what is seen ... but in the belief system associated with shared images."[248]

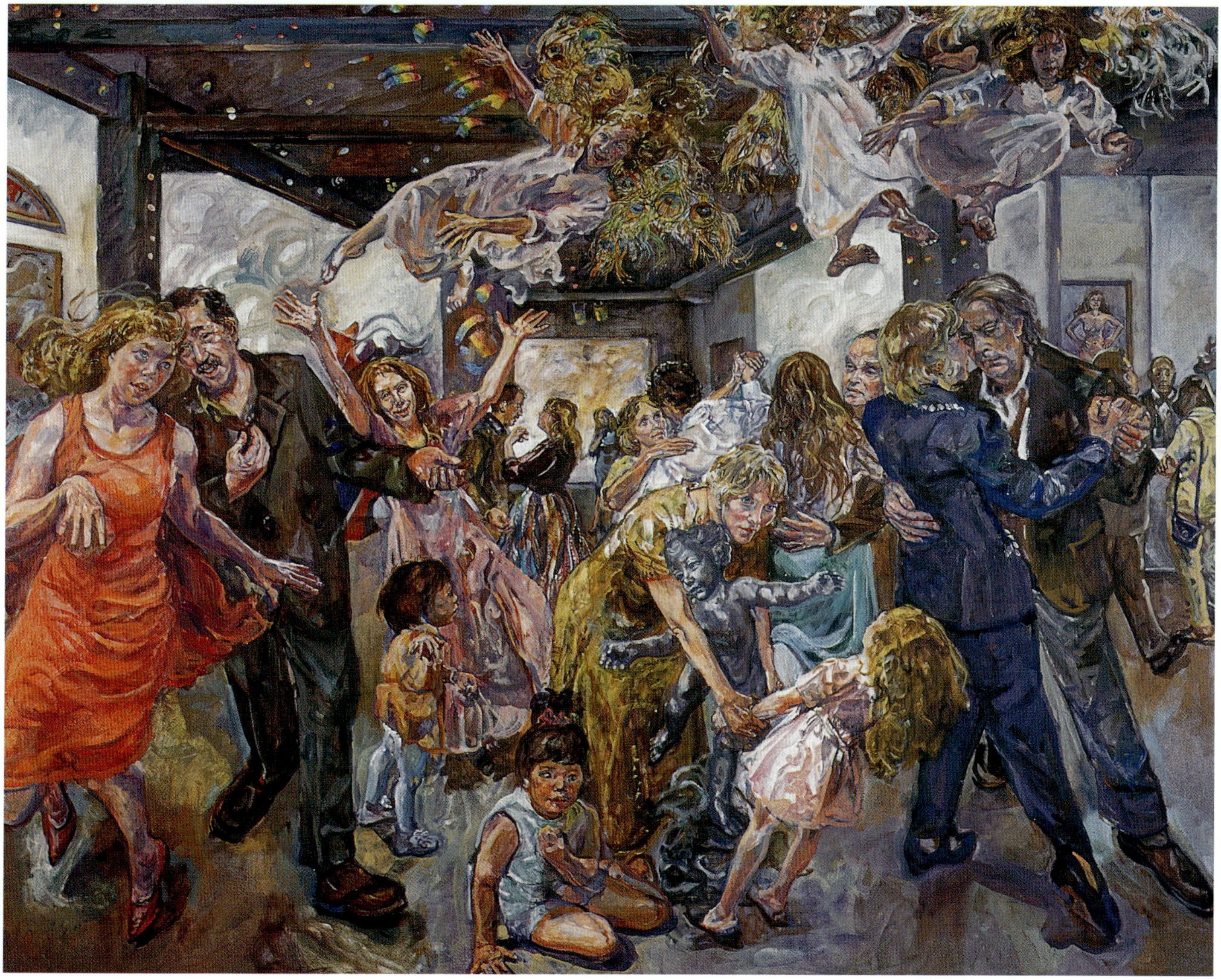

Many Years, oil on linen, 48" x 60", 2001. *Courtesy of Denise Bibro Fine Art.*

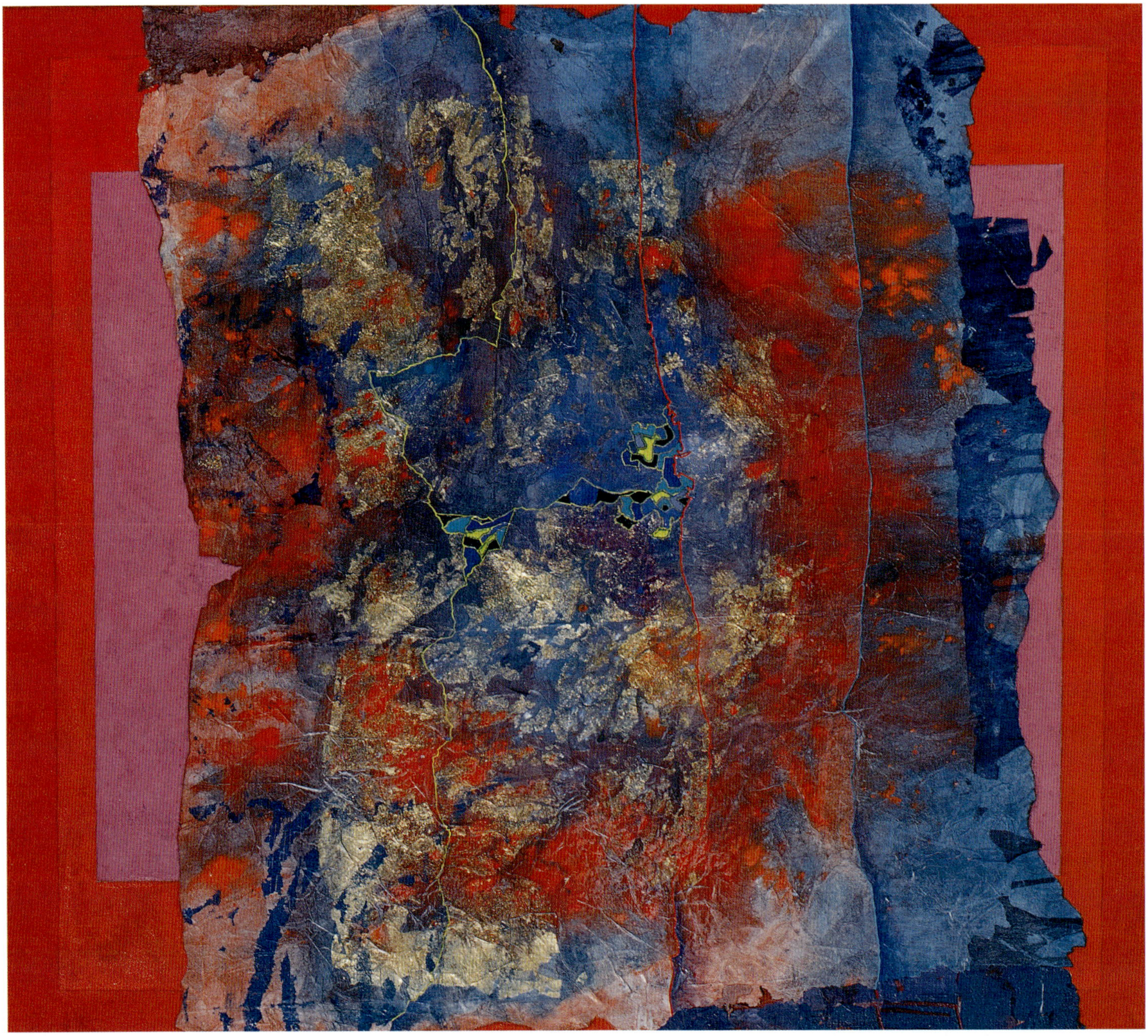

Resounding Echoes Deeper Layer, mixed media on canvas, 42" x 46", 2000.

Gian Berto Vanni

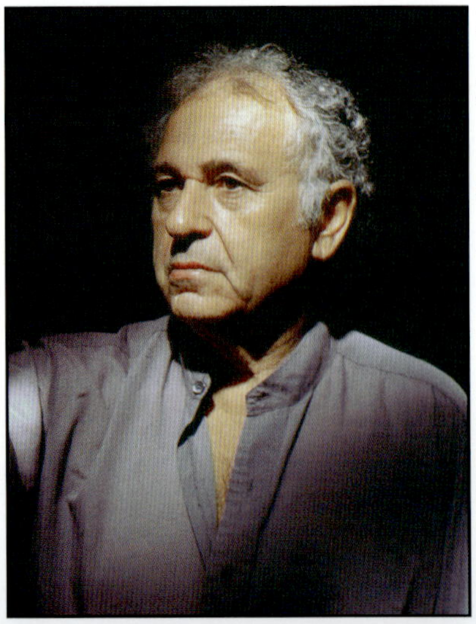

Courtesy of the artist.

Gian Berto Vanni, who was born in Rome, attended the School of Art and Architecture in Rome; thereafter, he studied on a scholarship in Holland, then came to the United States to study with Josef Albers at Yale, on a Fulbright Grant. Here, he began to appreciate the idea of employing "a coexistence of multiple styles within one canvas, so long as a formal coherence is carried throughout the work ...,"[249] which has since become his leitmotif.

After Yale, Vanni spent years in Europe and New York developing "paintings of fragmentations in space ... gradually replacing geometric fragments by the organic, eventually recovering shapes, and experimenting, among other ideas, with partitioned canvases, silkscreen printing and bas reliefs."[250]

After exhibiting widely in Europe, Vanni felt the need to return to New York, where his primary residence has remained ever since. Vanni, who works on his canvases at first from all sides, flat on the ground, has traveled the globe to see and study art from the "four corners of the world,"[251] and is convinced that "harmonies unforeseen from these ancient creators are the representation of life itself, and our possibility to believe in something, and its opposite, to realize life cannot be conceived under a single unifying banner."[252]

A faculty member at The Cooper Union for many years, Vanni has had many solo and group shows throughout Europe and the United States. His works are in public collections in Italy, Germany, and Holland, and at the Seattle Museum of Art in Washington.

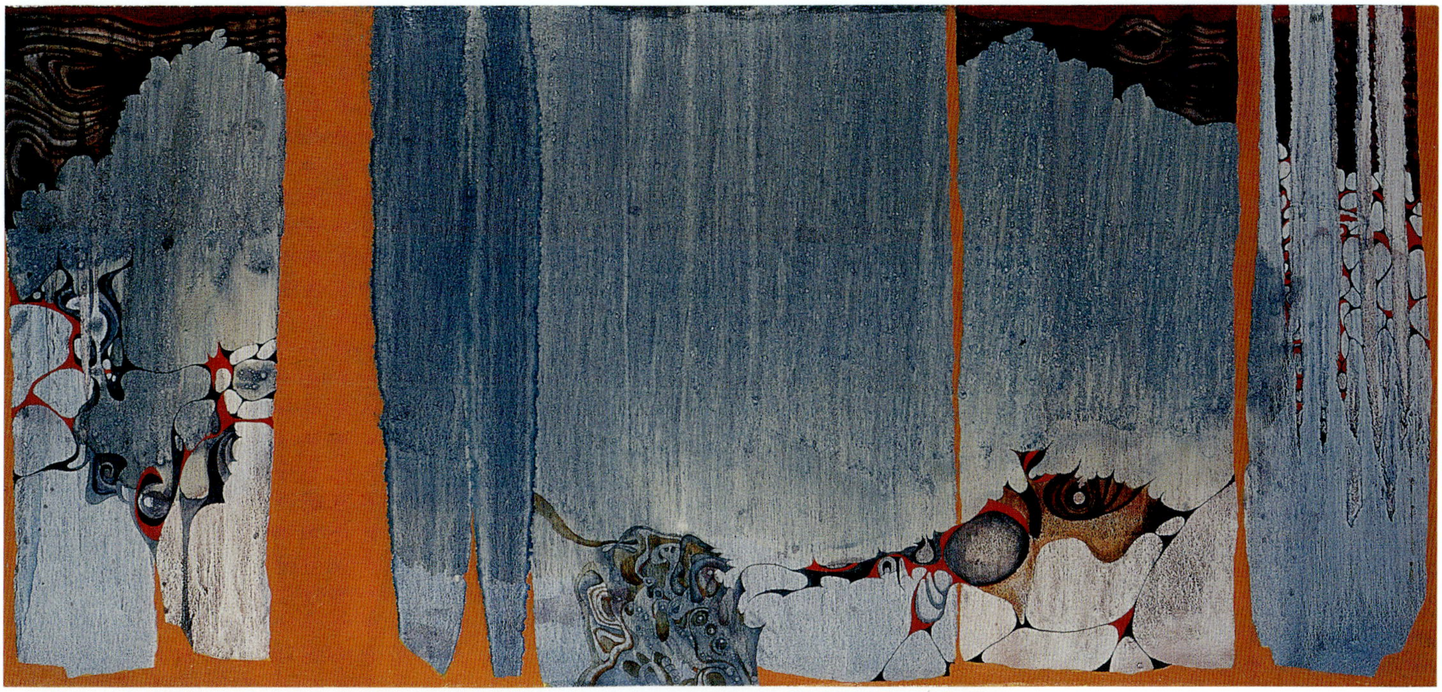

Prehistoric Dream, oil on canvas, 22" x 47", 2005.

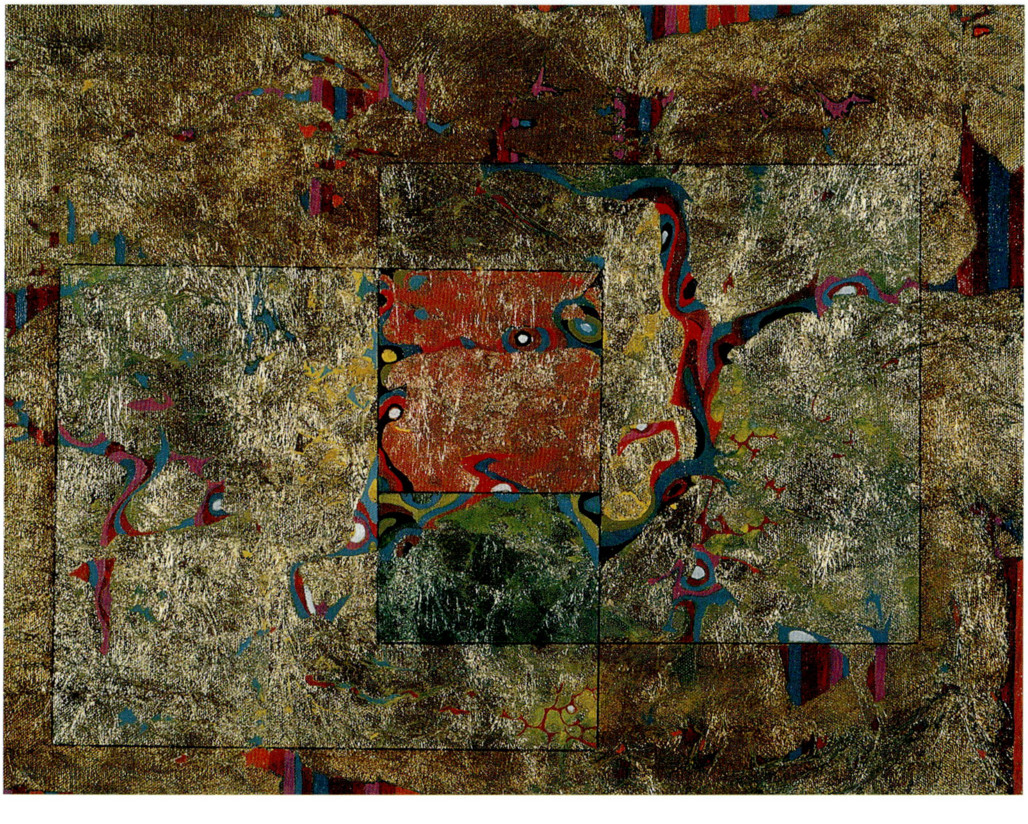

Gold in Squares, oil, gold on canvas, 14" x 18", 2004.

Ella Yang

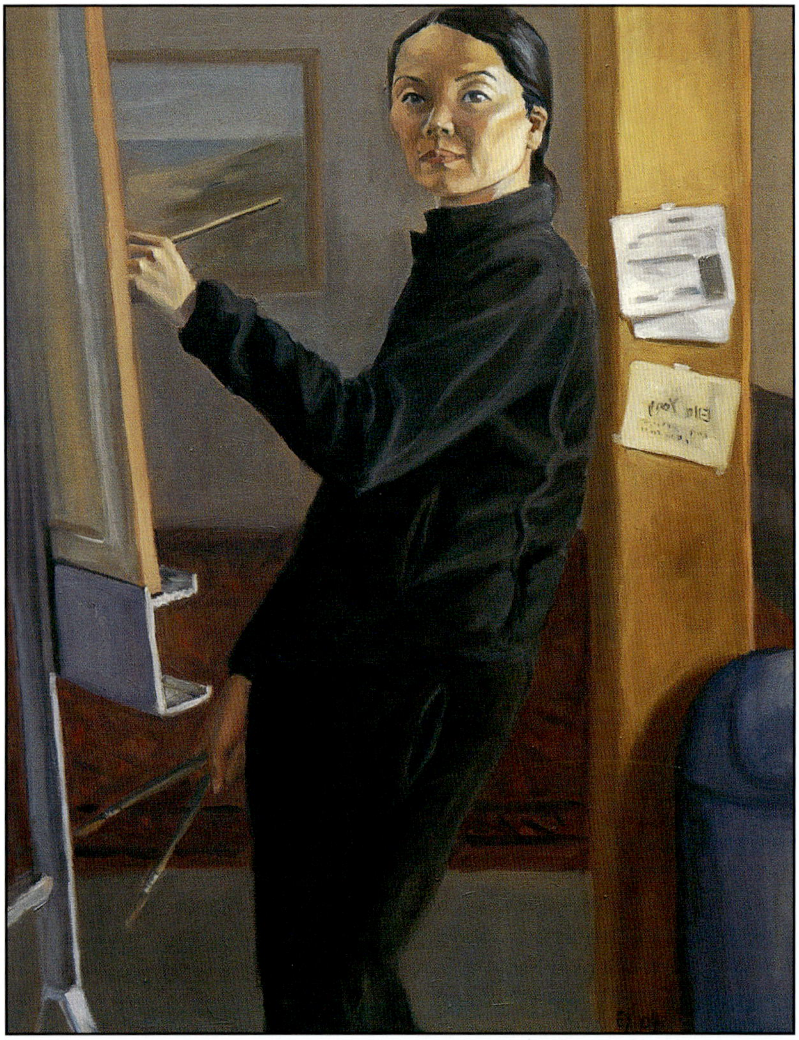

Self Portrait (in fleece), oil on canvas, 26" x 20", 2004. *Courtesy of the artist.*

Ella Yang returned to painting full time after earning her BA in Architecture at Yale and an MBA at Columbia University, then devoting almost twenty years to the corporate world. She attended the International School of Art in Todi, Italy for a summer, which convinced her to make the courageous decision. "I paint mostly in Brooklyn, New York, where I enjoy the street life, rooftops, industrial neighborhoods, and Prospect Park. Sometimes, I venture into Manhattan, too," she says, "Oil painting from nature, … having an enjoyable outdoor experience, is a large part of the reason I select scenes to paint. … I work on site, directly, and use a limited palette … my goal: to find a simple way to capture the spirit of a place … [or figure], not being judgmental, an important part of the process. … Each subject has a unique vivacity … [which] if captured on canvas might reveal some of nature's ingenuity."[253]

Yang has participated in many local "open studio" and other exhibitions sponsored by the Gowanus Artists, and at several galleries in Brooklyn, Chappaqua, New York, and Greenwich, Connecticut. Her group exhibitions include: "Crossing Brooklyn Bridge," at the Williamsburg Art and Historical Society, "Talking Hands," at the AIR Gallery, and a "Small Works Invitational" at the Blue Mountain Gallery, in New York.

Yang is a regular at the Spring Studio, one of two celebrated studios that provide professional models for artists, organized and run for many years by Minerva Durham in the Soho area of Manhattan. She also paints during her travels to Italy and the American West.

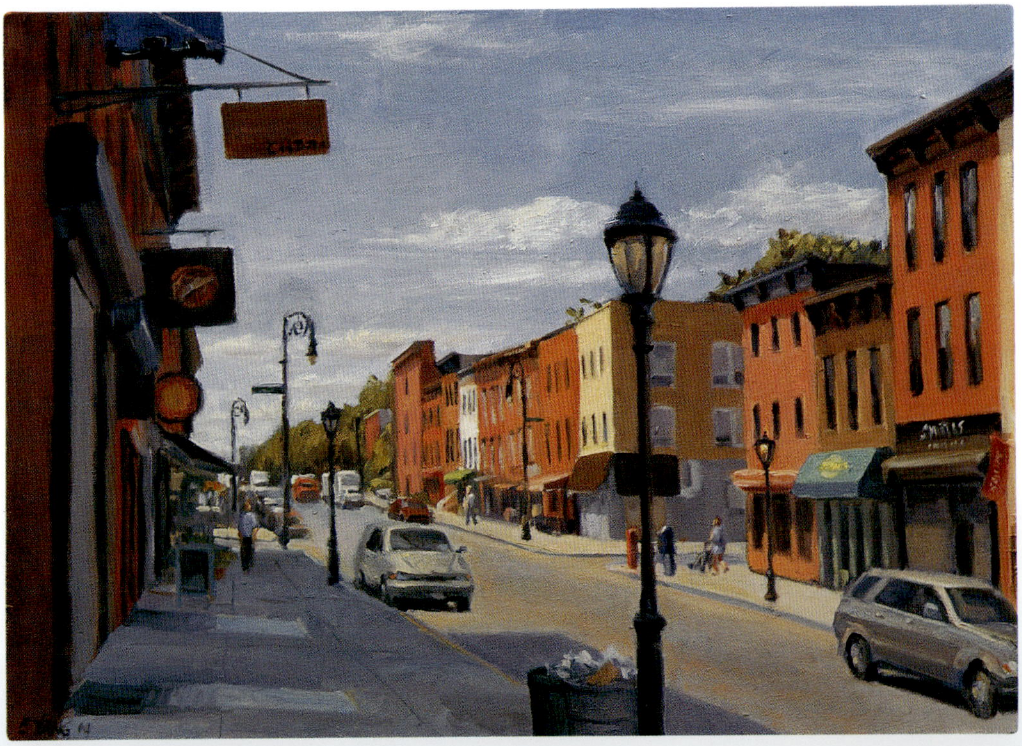

Summer Morning on Smith Street, oil on canvas, 16" x 22", 2004. *Courtesy of the artist.*

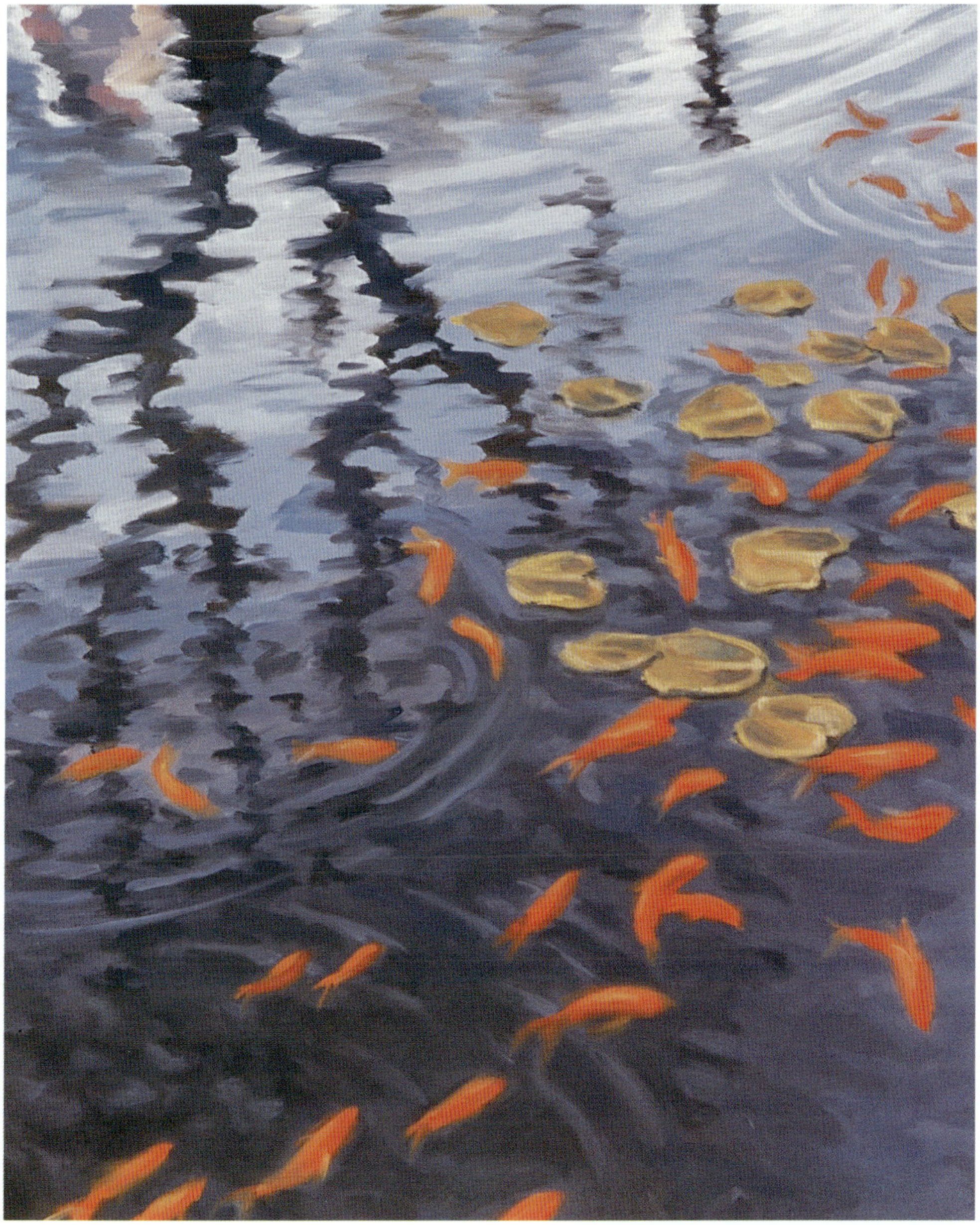

Fish Pond Reflections, oil on canvas, 20" x 16", 2003. *Courtesy of the artist.*

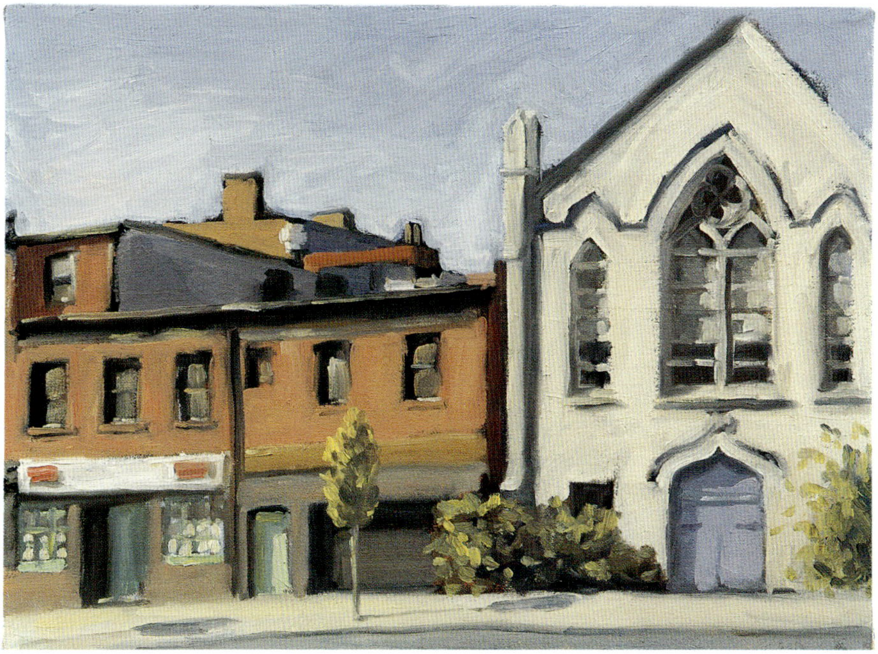

Bodega and Church in Cobble Hill, oil on canvas, 12" x 16", 2005. *Courtesy of the artist.*

Darryl Zudeck

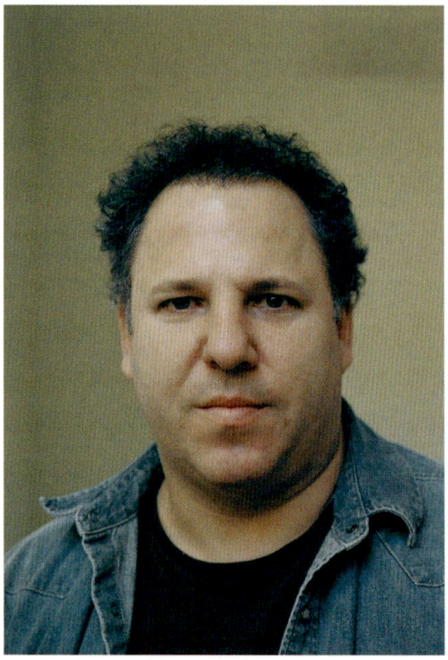
Photograph by Mary Engel.

Darryl Zudeck, whose "magic is that he makes us see,"[254] shows us that, "existence ... is precious because it is ephemeral."[255] "... [His subjects] are given an intensity of presence so that they appear to transcend our ordinary experience ... are given *more* than life ... presenting a hyper-reality we seldom ... can know in reality,"[256] comments Raymond J. Steiner.

Zudeck says, though based on traditional realism, his modern contemporary paintings, rendered to a high degree of finish, use realism as a vehicle to make the viewer look at his people and objects with a heightened sensibility.[257]

He names Claudio Bravo, Chuck Close, Antonio López García, William Bailey, Harvey Dinnerstein, Steve Assael, and Max Ginsburg as major influences.

Zudeck attended the High School of Art and Design, the Art Students League, the Brooklyn Museum Art School, the School of Visual Arts, and the Pels School of Art in New York, before embarking first on a career as an illustrator and winning several awards in that field. As an illustrator, his clients included *The New York Times*, Harper's, Doubleday, McGraw Hill, Simon and Schuster, CBS Records, the Chase Manhattan Bank, and Motown Records.

Winner of an Audubon Artists' Grumbacher Gold Medal, among others, Zudeck's paintings have been seen in solo and group exhibitions at the Gallery Henoch, which represents his work, as well as such locations as the Salmagundi Club, Allied Artists, the Art Directors Club, and galleries in Nantucket, Massachusetts, and Tokyo, Japan.

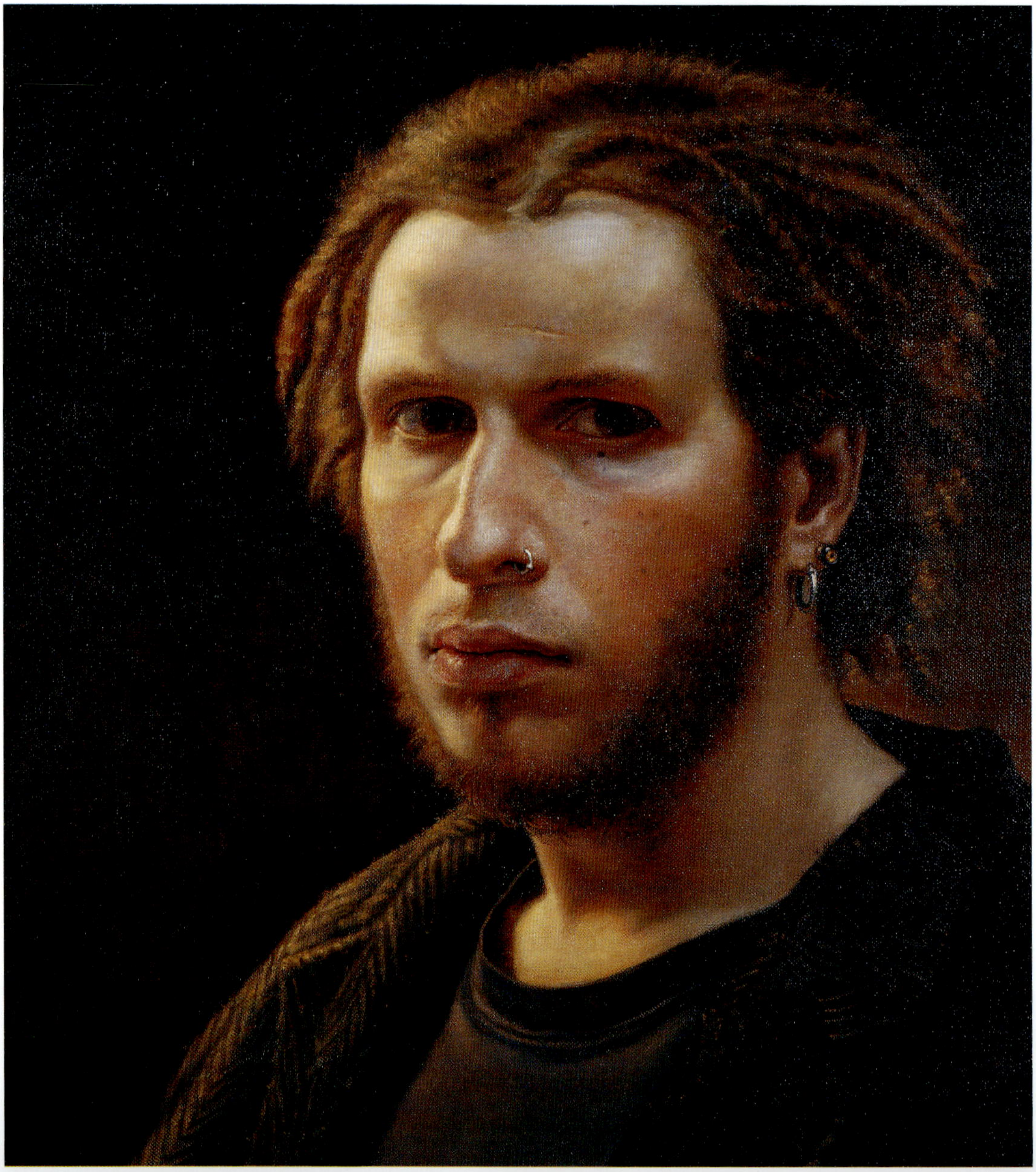

George, oil on linen, 18.5" x 16.5", 2002. *Courtesy of Gallery Henoch.*

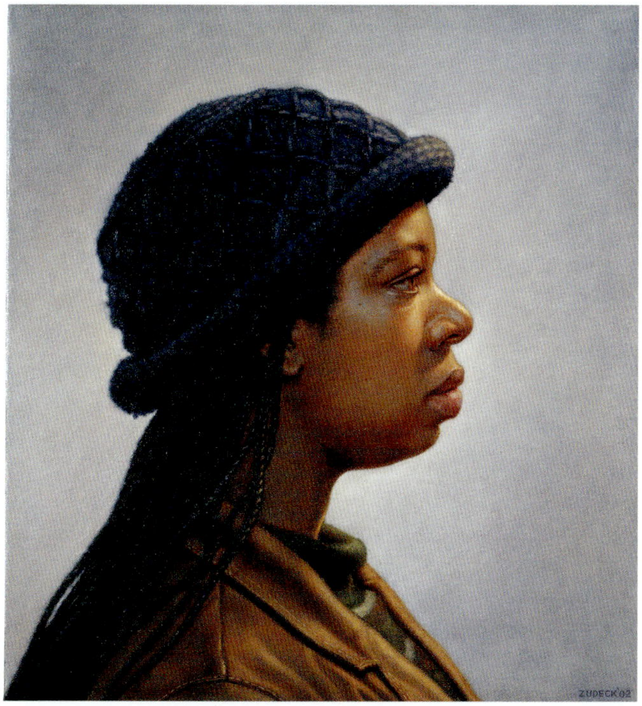

Diane II, oil on linen, 18" x 16.25", 2002. *Courtesy of Gallery Henoch.*

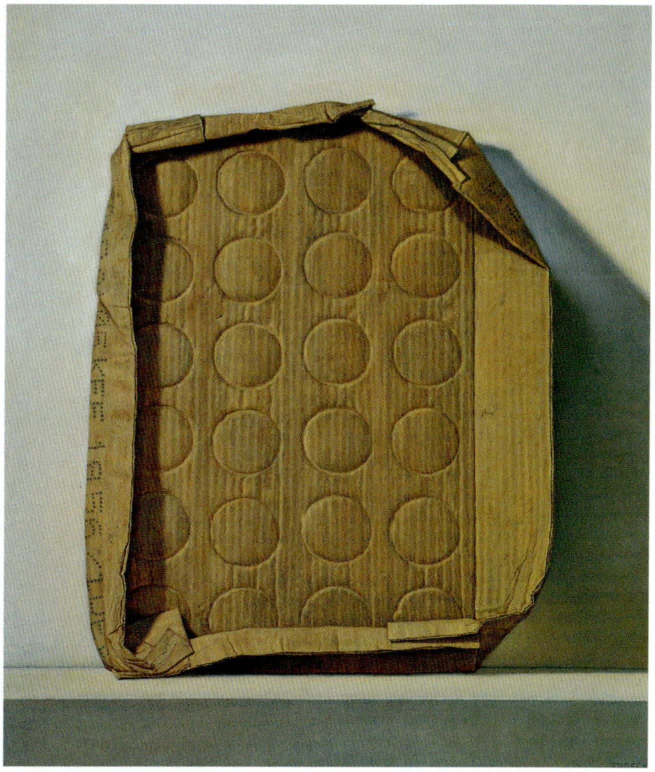

Circles, Flattened Box, oil on linen, 24" x 20", 2005. *Courtesy of Gallery Henoch.*

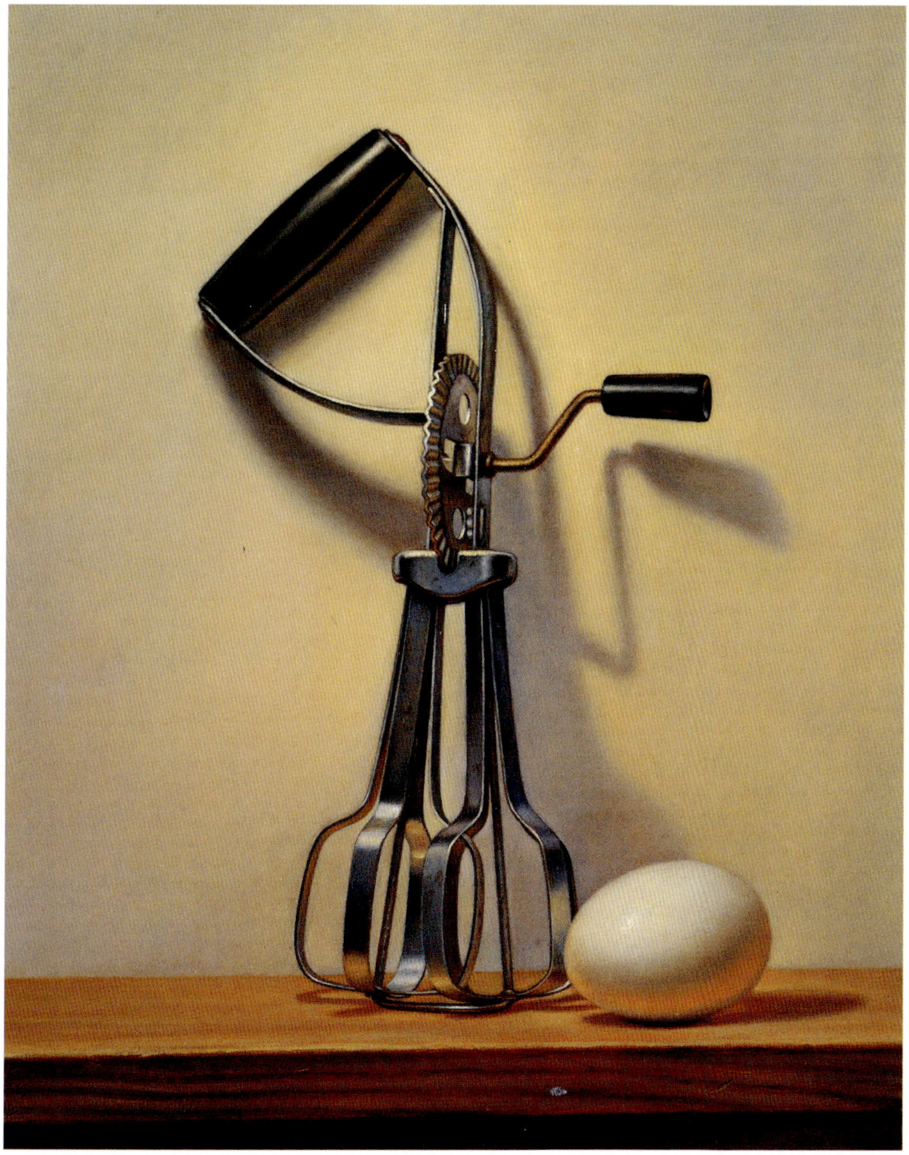

George, oil on linen, 18.5" x 16.5", 2002. *Courtesy of Gallery Henoch.*

Notes

1. Alder, Kelynn Z., from statement sent to the author, October 17, 2005.
2. Alder, Kelynn Z., "In the Land of the Aborigines," AD NEWS, Vol. 9, issue 16, September, 1990.
3. Alder, op. cit., October 17, 2005.
4. Anderson, Arthur, from statement sent to the author, October, 2004.
5. Mullarkey, Maureen, "Lennart Anderson at Salander-O'Reilly Galleries," Studio Matters © 2002.
6. Andrews, Benny, quoted in "Making Faces, Art that Champions the Individual," by Ariella Budick, *Newsday*, January 12, 2001, Section B, p. 31.
7. Kramer, Hilton, "Baker, A First-Rate Realist Adds a Few Drips, Just in Case," *The New York Observer*, May 30, 2005, p. 20.
8. "Will Barnet in his Own Words," from statement sent to the author by Babcock Galleries, Fall, 2005.
9. Marsi, Rick, "Artist Jack Beal: His Brushes Catch the Beauty of Life," *Press & Sun Bulletin*, Binghamton, NY, November 15, 1987, pp.1c, 7c. illus.
10. Beal, Jack, from statement sent to the author, July 28, 2005.
11. Beerman, Miriam, from statement sent to author, Fall, 2005.
12. Ibid.
13. Raynor, Vivien, "Redemption Through Pain, Solitary or Shared," *The New York Times*, July 21, 1996.
14. Behnke, Leigh, quoted by Gerrit Henry, in catalogue essay for exhibition at Fischback Gallery, New York, NY, February, 1991.
15. Berg, Siri, from statement sent to the author, July 14, 2005.
16. Birmelin, Robert, from statement sent to the author, March 12, 2005.
17. Ibid.
18. Bolmeier, Jane, from statement sent to the author, Fall, 2005.
19. Bolmeier, Jane, "Views of Provincetown Bay at the Red Inn," Summer, 2004.
20. Ibid.
21. Ibid.
22. Press Release for "Richmond Burton: New Paintings," Cheim & Read, New York, NY, September 8, 2004.
23. Nahas, Dominique, "A Few Remarks on Richmond Burton's 1 AM Paintings," from Press Release, Cheim & Read, NY, April 25, 2001.
24. Sandler, Irving, catalogue essay for exhibition, "Charles Cajori, a Survey," David Findlay Jr Fine Art, New York, NY, May 7-28, 2005.
25. Ibid.
26. Forge, Andrew, "Cajori, Paintings 1952-92," catalogue essay, Central Connecticut State University, New Britain, CT, November-December, 1992.
27. Ibid, catalog statement.
28. Cantarella, Virginia, from statement sent to the author, Fall, 2005.
29. Press Release for "Nicholas Carone: A Selection of Works on Paper," Lohin-Geduld Gallery, New York, NY, October 15 – November 19, 2005.
30. Ibid.
31. Chaet, Bernard, "Face to Face," David Findlay Jr Fine Art, New York, NY, December, 2004.
32. Cibula, Ellen, "Universe, Paintings by Ellen Cibula," Delaware Arts Center Gallery, Narrowsburg, NY, September-October, 2003.
33. Clark, Edward, "Un Musée Pour Harlem," Paris, *L'Art Vivant*, November, 1968, published by Galerie Maeght.
34. Cavaliere, Barbara & George N'Namdi, Editors, "Ed Clark: For the Sake of the Search," Belleville Lake Press, 1997.
35. Clark, Marcia, from statement sent to the author, Fall, 2005.
36. Ibid.
37. Wye, Deborah & Robert Storr, Biographic writings on Chuck Close, The Museum of Modern Art, New York, NY, 1998, and *Wikipedia*, the free encyclopedia.
38. Collado, Lisa, from statement sent to the author, November 8, 2005.
39. Coppedge, Arthur, from conversation with the author, November, 2005.
40. Cuttler, Judy, from statement sent to the author, July 15, 2005.
41. Blaine, Nell, letter re: Judy Cuttler, May, 1982.
42. Rubenstein, Betty, "Nothing So-So about SoHo Show," *Tallahassee Democrat*, December 1, 1989.
43. Cuttler, Judy, from statement sent to the author, July 15, 2005.
44. Goodman, Jonathan, "Lisa Corinne Davis at June Kelly," *Art in America*, July, 2003.
45. Deon, Dorothy, preface to catalogue, Seoul Theological University, 2004.
46. Bruner, Miriam, "Doro," self-published, 1994.
47. Dinnerstein, Harvey, *International Artist Magazine*, December-January, 2005.
48. Ibid.
49. Ibid.
50. Dinnerstein, Simon, from statement sent to the author, November 13, 2005.
51. Ibid.
52. Dintenfass, Marylyn, from statement sent to the author, Fall, 2005.
53. Ibid.
54. Weisgall, Deborah, 'Knowing a Place,' for "Lois Dodd: Small Paintings," Alexandre Gallery, New York, NY, December, 2003-January, 2004.
55. Ibid.
56. Ibid.
57. Erlebacher, Martha Mayer, "Project Title: The Cycle of Life," from artistic statement sent to the author, Fall, 2005.

58. Fishko, Robert, "Martha Mayer Erlebacher: Paintings," Forum Gallery, New York, NY, November-December, 2003.

59. Peterson, Gregory J., "A Dialogue Between Gregory J. Peterson and Richard Estes," *www.artcritical.com*, an online periodical, David Cohen, Editor, 2002.

60. Fabozzi, Paul, "New York Series: 2003-Present," from artistic statement sent to the author, Fall, 2005.

61. Fabozzi, Paul, "Rome: The Layers of Memory, 1999-2002," from Artistic Statement sent to the author, Fall, 2005.

62. Ferrando, David, from statement sent to the author, Fall, 2005.

63. Ibid.

64. Hughes, Robert, "Nothing if Not Critical," Harvill Press, London, 2004.

65. Ibid; and statement from Mary Boone Gallery, New York, NY, Fall, 2005.

66. Berlind, Robert, Interview for "Janet Fish," D C Moore Gallery, February 1-March 5, 2005.

67. Ibid.

68. Ibid.

69. Ibid.

70. Ibid, p.18.

71. Ibid, p.36, 1991; and "Janet Fish: Real and Surreal," Stephen Bennett Philips, in book "Janet Fish," cited above.

72. Donohue, Marlena, "Louise Fishman," April-June, 2002, Manny Silverman Gallery, West Hollywood, CA.

73. Ibid.

74. From statement sent to the author, Fall, 2005.

75. From commencement address, Pennsylvania Academy of the Fine Arts, May, 1984.

76. Grove Dictionary of Art, Macmillan Publishers, Limited, 2000.

77. Godfrey, Robert, "Master Paintings from the Butler Institute of American Art," Harry N. Abrams, New York, NY, 1994, p.334.

78. Cummings, Paul, Ed., "Drawing: The International Review," The Drawing Society, New York, NY, November-December, 1983.

79. From statement by the artist, quoted in University of Michigan Museum of Art exhibition catalogue, July-September, 1990.

80. "American Views: Memory, Nostalgia and the Idea of Place," the Parrish Art Museum, Southampton, NY, 2002.

81. "Surroundings: Responses to the American Landscape, Selections from the Permanent Collection of the Whitney Museum of American Art," San Jose Museum of Art, San Jose, CA, 1999.

82. "Abstraction/Realism: The Great Debate," Susquehanna Art Museum, Harrisburg, PA, 1999.

83. "Women's Work: A Century of Achievement in American Art," the Columbus Art Museum, Columbus, GA, 1995.

84. "New Approaches to the Still Life," Tower Fine Arts Gallery, SUNY College at Brockport, NY, 1003.

85. "Color as a Subject," the 167th Annual Exhibition, National Academy of Design, New York, NY, 1992.

86. "The Painterly Landscape," C. Grimaldis Gallery, Baltimore, MD, 1986.

87. "American Women Artists, Part One: Pioneers," Sidney Janis Gallery, New York, NY, 1984.

88. "Students of Hans Hofmann," The Museum of Modern Art, New York, NY, 1963.

89. Fallon, Michael, "The Column: The Doomed Artist, part 1," www.mnartists.org, June 19, 2004.

90. Goodnough, Bob, quoted in Press Advisory for Art Committee for the New Castle County Courthouse Exhibition, New Castle, DE, October 11, 2005.

91. Greenberg, Clement, essay in Martin Bush's "Goodnough," Abbeville Press, New York, NY, 1982.

92. Goodnough, Miko, quoted by Chris Serico, in *Trader Country*, N. Salem, NY, June 17, 2004.

93. Andrews, Benny, from statement sent to the author, July 27, 2005.

94. Zimmer, William, catalogue, "Mary Hambleton," Pamela Auchincloss Gallery, New York, NY, April-May, 1991.

95. Hambleton, Mary, in conversation with Ron Janovich, *The Brooklyn Rail*, March, 2004.

96. Zimmer, op. cit.

97. Janovich, op. cit.

98. Hansen, Glen, Lehigh University Art Galleries, published statement, July 13, 2005.

99. Interview between Glen Hansen and Exhibition Curator, Ricardo Viera.

100. Hyneman, Esther, from statement sent to the author, Fall, 2005.

101. Hyneman, Esther, "Artist's Statement: Confessions of a Realist," *Feminist Studies 23*, No. 3, Feminist Studies, Inc., © 1997.

102. Koster, Anna, "National Retrospective of Yvonne Jacquette," Press Release, Stanford University's Cantor Arts Center, Stanford, CA, September 10, 2001.

103. Ibid.

104. "Yvonne Jacquette: Vantage on High," D C Moore Gallery, New York, NY, 1997.

105. Berlind, Robert, "Eye in the Sky," *Art in America*, February, 2004.

106. Cohen, David, "A Cocktail of Perception and Invention: The Vast, Dark and Dramatic Paintings of Yvonne Jacquette," *The New York Sun*, September 4, 2003.

107. "The LAPD Project: The Legacy of Pattern and Decoration," Shoshana Wayne Gallery, Santa Monica, CA, 2003.

108. "Pattern: Between Object and Arabesque," Porin Taidenmuseo, Pori, Finland, 2002.

109. "Geometric Abstraction, 1937-1997," Snyder Fine Art, New York, NY, 1997.

110. "Five Contemporary Masters," Paris – New York – Kent Gallery, Kent, CT, 1996.

111. Kahn, Cecily, Artist's Statement, undated.

112. Cohen, David, *The Art Journal*, December, 22, 1998, on Irving Sandler's, "Alex Katz," Harry N. Abrams, New York, NY, 1998.

113. Ibid.

114. Ibid.

115. Katz, Alex, in "Artist and Art," www.theartists.org.

116. Cohen, David, "A Chat with the Painter," a conversation with Alex Katz, *The New York Sun*, September 9, 2004.

117. Kulicke, Barbara, statement in essay by Vivian Raynor for exhibition at Prince Street Gallery, New York, NY, 1999.

118. From statement, July 13, 2005.

119. Chinese proverb in Press Release for "Flowers," Prince Street Gallery, New York, NY, 2002.

120. Kulicke, op. cit.

121. Levine, Marion Lerner, from statement sent to the author, 2005.

122. Ibid.

123. Ibid.

124. Ibid.

125. Levine, Jack, from statement sent to the author, 2005.

126. Levine, Jack, in American Art of the 20th Century, George Krevsky Gallery, New York, NY, 1997.

127. Liu, Dik, from statement sent to the author, Winter, 2002.

128. Kramer, Hilton, *The New York Times*, October 8, 1976.
129. "Eccentric Geometries: Robert Mangold," BBC World Service: Meridian – The World of Ideas, December, 2005.
130. Ibid.
131. Manzo, Helene K., from statement sent to the author, 2005.
132. "Dancers Offstage," Gibson Gallery, SUNY Potsdam, Potsdam, NY, 2003.
133. "Contemporary Nudes," One Penn Plaza, New York, NY, 1988-9.
134. "About Faces: A Celebration of the Portrait," Civic Arts Gallery, Walnut Creek, CA, 1987.
135. "Signs of the Flesh," Salena Gallery, Long Island University, Brooklyn, NY, 2004.
136. "Grand Traditions," Mississippi Museum of Art, Jackson, MS, 1996.
137. "...Two Generations of Abstract Art," Newcomb College, Tulane University, New Orleans, LA, Washburn Gallery, New York, NY, Skidmore College, Saratoga Springs, NY, 1982.
138. "A Family in Art," Kornbluth Gallery, Fairlawn, NJ, 1983.
139. "Couples Show," Kornbluth Gallery, Fairlawn, NJ, 1991.
140. "Among Family," Associated American Artists, New York, NY, 1992.
141. "American Women Artists – The Twentieth Century," Knoxville Museum of Art, Knoxville, TN and Queensborough Community College, Bayside, NY, 1989.
142. Mason, Emily, quoted in "The Art of Emily Mason," by Michael Culver, Curator, The Ogunquit Museum of American Art, Ogunquit, ME, 2005.
143. Ibid.
144. Mayhew, Richard, from statement for the Parish Gallery, Georgetown, WA, 2005.
145. Canaday, John, reviewing Richard Mayhew at the Midtown Payson Galleries, *The New York Times*, 1969.
146. Bearden, Romare, quoted in statement, www.richardmayhew.com, December 23, 2005.
147. McKenzie, Mary Beth, from The Resource of Art Quotations: painter, December 23, 2005, Robert Genn, Editor.
148. Miller, Lee Anne, from statement sent to the author, 2005.
149. Ibid.
150. Ibid.
151. Gibbs, Linda Jones, Museum of Art at Brigham Young University, 1996.
152. Ibid.
153. Ibid.
154. Scott, Gail, "Don Nice: Earth Totems," Babcock Galleries, New York, NY, 1998.
155. Ibid.
156. Ibid.
157. Nice, Don, quoted by Tammis K. Groft, Chief Curator, Albany Institute of History & Art, Albany, NY, 2005.
158. Goossen, E.C., "Doug Ohlson, 20 Years of Painting: 1982-2002," Hunter College, New York, NY, 2002.
159. Waller, Richard, Director, Marsh Gallery, Modlin Fine Arts Center, Richmond, VA, 1992.
160. Pearlstein, Philip, Art & Optics: statement, 2005.
161. Press Release for Tracy Phillips, "Inverted Realities," Williamsburg Art & Historical Center, Williamsburg, Brooklyn, NY, 2005.
162. Ibid.
163. From Artist's Statement, 2005.
164. Pindell, Howardena, postcard from Brazil to Lowery Stokes Simms, 1977.
165. Hill, Shawn, Howard Yezerski Gallery, 1991, Bay Window, Boston, MA, January 17, 1991, and Bob Derden, "Howardena Pindell," Georgia State University, Atlanta, GA, 1992.
166. Verdino-Sullwold, Carla Maria, "Howardena Pindell: Volcanic View of the Self," *Crisis*, January, 1990.
167. Rauschenbusch, Stephanie, from statement sent to the author, 2005.
168. Russell, John, *The New York Times*, December 23, 1983.
169. Millet, Kate, "A.D.," Norton and Company, 1995.
170. Redmond, Catherine, from statement sent to the author, 2005.
171. Ibid.
172. Tannous, David, Catalogue essay for "Twelve, Catherine Redmond," David Findlay Jr Fine Art, New York, NY, 2003.
173. "New York Day and Night," David Findlay Jr Fine Art, New York, NY, 2001.
174. "New York Perspectives," M B Modern, New York, NY, 1998.
175. "Rediscovering the Landscape of the Americas," Gerald Peters Gallery, Santa Fe, NM, 1996.
176. Gallo, Peter, "Paul Resika at Salander-O'Reilly" Art in America, November, 2001.
177. Grosser, Maurice, "American Painters in Venice," catalogue, Ca'Giustinian, Venice, Italy, 1952.
178. Sandler, Irving, Art International, April 1961.
179. Grad, Bonnie L., "Robert Richenburg: Abstract Expressionist," Catalogue essay, Brandeis University, Waltham, MA, 1993.
180. Richenburg, Robert, statement: "About the Black Paintings," 1959.
181. Wallace, Michelle, "The Mona Lisa Interview," Art in Context Center for Communications, 1997-2002.
182. Ibid.
183. Ibid.
184. Roberts, Marie, from statement sent to the author, 2005.
185. Rockburne, Dorothea, from statement sent to the author, 2005.
186. Ward, Meredith, essay for "William Scharf, Recent Paintings," Richard York Gallery, New York, NY, 2004.
187. Ibid.
188. Schiavina, Laura, from statement sent to the author, June, 2005.
189. "Celebrating 25 years of Women at the Salmagundi Club," 1999.
190. "Colors," of Hunters Point Artists Community, New York, NY, 1991, at International Design Center of New York, 1991.
191. "Women by Women," Port Washington Public Library, Port Washington, NY, 1991.
192. "Catholic Artists," Lowenstein Library Gallery, Fordham University at Lincoln Center, New York, NY, 1984.
193. "Inner/Outer World," a Women's Studio Center Exhibit at Queens Theater in the Park, Flushing, Queens, NY, 2002.
194. Collado, Lisa, "Laura Schiavina," statement for proposed book project, 1999.
195. Tucker, Marcia, Whitney Museum of American Art, New York, NY, 1974.
196. Ibid.
197. Shaw, Kendall, from statement sent to the author, 2005.
198. Ibid.
199. Shaw, Kendall, "Referential Paintings," statement, November 1, 1988.
200. Shaw, Kendall, "Tape and Eros," statement, December, 1994.
201. McCormack, Ed, "Susan Sills and Her Band of Art Historical All-Stars," Art & Studio, April, 2002.

202. Ibid.
203. Nemec, Vernita, Viridian Artists, "Susan Sills," Press Release, April, 2005.
204. "...The Rhythm of Silence," Locks Gallery, Philadelphia, PA, 2003.
205. "Waterfall of Dreams," Piece Unique, Paris, France, 2001.
206. "Red Yellow Blue I Love You," Madison Art Center, Madison, WI, 2001.
207. "Distant Horizon," Galleria Bonomo, Bari, Italy, 2001.
208. "Moon Mountain Ghost Water," Marlborough Chelsea, NY, 1999.
209. "Wind Water Stone," Robert Miller Gallery, New York, NY, 1997.
210. "The Moon and the Wave," M. Knoedler & Co., Inc., New York, NY, 1987.
211. Howell, George, "...Quietly Non-Violent," *The Buffalo News*, Buffalo, NY, October 18, 1984.
212. Muchnic, Susan, "...Speak(s) an Intimate Language," *Los Angeles Times*, April 11, 1983.
213. "Beauties and Beasts," Pratt Manhattan Center Gallery, New York, NY, 1984.
214. "Arbitrary Order," Contemporary Arts Museum, Houston, TX, 1983.
215. Hughes, Robert, "Myths of Sensibility," *TIME*, March 20, 1972.
216. Nuridsany, Michel, "une puissance magique," *Le Figaro*, Paris, November 16, 1979.
217. Goodman, Jonathan, catalogue essay for "Anam Cara," June Kelly Gallery, New York, NY, January, 2006.
218. Sung, Posoon Park, catalogue statement for "Anam Cara," June Kelly Gallery, New York, NY, 2006.
219. "Good Vibrations," McKenzie Fine Art, New York, NY, 2005.
220. "From Natural to Techno Universes...," Dorsky Gallery Curatorial Program, New York, NY, 2005.
221. "Mindscape," Pavel Zoubok Gallery, New York, NY, 2004.
222. "Radial Gradient," Gregory Lind Gallery, San Francisco, CA, 2004.
223. "Obsessive Pleasures," Pavel Zoubok Gallery, New York, NY, 2003.
224. "Accumulations," Islip Art Museum, New York, NY, 2002.
225. "Cascades of Scales," James Graham & Sons, New York, NY, 2002.
226. "Eye Tattoos," Quint Contemporary Art, LaJolla, CA, 2005.
227. Kushner, Robert, "Barbara Takenaga," catalogue essay, McKenzie Fine Art, Inc., New York, NY, 2005.
228. Becker, Tamiris, Director, Colorado University Art Museum, Boulder, CO, 2005.
229. Downes, Laurence, "Bob Tomlinson's 'Salome' Paintings: Anatomy in the Abstract," Gallery Studio, April-May, 2005.
230. "Atlantan African-American Artists," Alma Simmons Memorial Gallery, Atlanta, GA, 1985.
231. "5e Biennale de Paris," Galerie Lambert, Paris, 1967.
232. Tomlinson, Bob, from statement sent to the author, 2005.
233. "George Tooker," © 2006, www.RoGallery.com.
234. "Reality and Dream, The Art of George Tooker," Ogunquit Museum of American Art, Ogunquit, ME, 1996.
235. "50 Years of Painting and Study Drawings," Addison Gallery of American Art, Andover, MA, 1994.
236. "Surrealism, USA," National Academy Museum, New York, NY, 2005.
237. "Everyday Mysteries...," D C Moore Gallery, New York, NY, 2004.
238. "Boundless/Silence, States of Infinity," D C Moore Gallery, New York, NY, 2002.
239. "Magic Vision," Arkansas Arts Center, Little Rock, AR, 2001.
240. "Magic Realism: America's Response to Surrealism," Southern Alleghenies Museum of Art, Loretto, PA, 1999.
241. "Human Concern, Personal Torment: the Grotesque in American Art," Whitney Museum of American Art, New York, NY, 1969.
242. "Symbolic Realism," Edwin Hewitt Galley, New York, NY, 1950.
243. "Paintings from the Museum of Modern Art," the National Gallery of Art, Washington, D.C., 1963.
244. Cohen, David, Arts and Letters, *The New York Sun*, March 11, 2004.
245. Tsao, Vivian, "Painting and Me," article in her book, *The Mark of Time: Dialogues with Vivian Tsao on Art in New York*, written in Chinese, translated by the author into English, National History Museum, Taiwan, 2003.
246. Henry, Gerrit, "Audrey Ushenko at Denise Bibro," *Art In America*, March, 2003.
247. Ground, Stanley I., "Audrey Ushenko, Allegories and Myths," catalogue essay, University Museum, Southeast Missouri State University, Cape Girardeau, MO, 2001.
248. Alloway, Lawrence, Catalogue: "The Critics Choice," October, 1983.
249. Vanni, Gian Berto, "Fifty Years of Painting," self-published, 1949-1953.
250. Ibid.
251. Ibid.
252. Ibid.
253. Yang, Ella, from statement sent to the author, 2005.
254. Steiner, Raymond J., "Critique – Darryl Zudeck at Gallery Henoch," *Art Times*, January-February, 2003.
255. Ibid.
256. Ibid.
257. Zudeck, Darryl, from statement sent to the author, August, 2005.

Suggested Reading (Selected)

Anuszkiewicz, Richard. *Anuszkiewicz*. New York: Harry N. Abrams, Inc., 1977.

Arnheim, Rudolph. *Simon Dinnerstein, Paintings and Drawings*. New York: Hudson Hills Press, 1999.

Arthur, John. *Realists at Work*. New York: Watson-Guptill, 1983.

Ashton, Dore, Ed. *Twentieth Century Artists on Art*. New York: Pantheon Books, 1985.

Berlind, Robert, & Stephen Bennet Phillips. *Janet Fish*. New York: D C Moore Gallery, 2005.

Cavaliere, Barbara & George N'Namdi, Eds. *Ed Clark: For the Sake of the Search*. Belleville Lake Press, 1997.

Dinnerstein, Harvey. *Harvey Dinnerstein: Artist at Work*. New York: Watson Guptill, 1978.

Doty, Robert. *Will Barnet*. New York: Harry N. Abrams, Inc., 1984.

Driscoll, John. *Don Nice: The Nature of Art*. Petaluna, California: Pomegranate Communications, 2004.

Ebony, David. *Emily Mason, The Fifth Element*. New York: George Braziller, 2006.

Elderfield, John. *Helen Frankenthaler*. New York: Harry N. Abrams, Inc., 1989.

Farrington, Lisa E. *Faith Ringgold, (David C. Driskell Series of African American Art #3)*. Petaluma, California: Pomegranate Communications, 2004.

Flack, Audrey. *On Painting*. New York: Harry N. Abrams, Inc., 1981.

Friedman, Martin. *Close Reading: Chuck Close and the Artist Portrait*. New York: Harry N. Abrams, Inc., 2005.

Garver, Thomas H. *George Tooker*. Petaluna, California: Pomegranate Communications, 2002.

Gerdts, William. *The Great American Nude*. New York: Traeger, 1974.

Glueck, Grace. *New York-The Painted City*. Salt Lake City: Peregrine Smith Books, 1992.

Goodnough, Bob. *Bob Goodnough: Paintings and Sculpture*. Newberger Museum of Art, SUNY, Purchase, New York, 1999.

Gruber, J. Richard. *American Icons: From Madison to Manhattan, The Art of Benny Andrews, 1948-1997*. University Press of Mississippi, 2005.

Heller, Jules & Nancy G. *North American Women Artists of the Twentieth Century: A Biographical Dictionary*. New York: Abbeville, 1987.

Herskovic, Marika, Ed. *New York School Abstract Expressionists: Artist's Choice by Artists*. New York School Press, 2000.

Kertess, Klaus. *Jane Freilicher*. New York: Harry N. Abrams, Inc., 2004.

Lewis, Samella. *African-American Art and Artists*. University of California Press, Berkeley revised edition, 2003.

Pindell, Howardena. *The Heart of the Question*. New York: Midmarch Arts Press, 1997.

Protter, Eric, Ed. *Painters on Painting*. New York: Courier Dover Publications, 1997. (Re-publication of revised edition, published by Grosset & Dunlap, New York, 1971.)

Sandler, Irving. *From Avant-Garde to Pluralism, An On-The-Spot History*. Lenox, Massachusetts: Hard Press Editions, 2006.

Sandler, Irving. *Alex Katz*. New York: Harry N. Abrams, Inc., 1998.

Spring, Justin. *Wolf Kahn*. New York: Harry N. Abrams, Inc., 1996.

Storr, Robert. *Philip Pearlstein: Since 1983*. New York: Harry N. Abrams, Inc., 2002.

Strand, Mark, Ed. *Art of the Real: Nine American Figurative Painters*. New York: Clarkson N. Potter, 1983.

Index

Note: In this abbreviated index, you will find a selection of those artists, art educators, art schools and universities, art galleries, museums and other institutions, organizations, awards, and references most likely to be of use to readers of this book.

Aaron Berman Gallery, 186
ACA Gallery, 3, 26, 84, 154, 178
Adolph and Esther Gottlieb Foundation, 68, 113, 138
AIR Gallery, 214
Albers, Josef, 12, 22, 28, 64, 100, 104, 212
Albright-Knox Art Gallery, 182, 200
Alder, Kelynn Zatarain, 4, 17, 18
Alexandre Gallery, 3, 88
Aljira Center, 3
Allen Sheppard Gallery, 142
Allied Artists, 157, 216
Alloway, Laurence, 211
Alston, Charles, 20
American Abstract Artists, 44, 130, 145
American Academy and Institute of Arts and Letters, 36, 88, 132
American Academy of Arts and Letters, 84, 111, 127, 140, 146, 164, 174, 182, 202, 206, 208
Ameringer & Yohe Gallery, 3, 107, 133
Amos, Emma, back cover, 20
Anderson, Arthur, 22
Anderson, Lennart, cover, 24, 172
Andre Emmerich Gallery, 136, 182
Andre Zarre Gallery, 162
Andrews, Benny, 4, 26, 120
Anita Shapolsky Gallery, 3, 136, 186, 193
Anuszkiewicz, Richard, 7, 28
ARS (Artists Rights Society), 32, 146, 182
Art Directors Club, 216
Art Institute of Chicago, 38, 60, 62, 102, 109, 138, 211
Art Students League, 24, 36, 40, 56, 78, 80, 82, 116, 125, 148, 154, 170, 172, 181, 186, 206, 216
Artists Gallery, 204
Ashton, Dore, 4, 118
Assael, Steven, 30
Associated American Artists, 152
Atlantic Gallery, 22
Audubon Artists, 157, 188, 216
Babcock Galleries, 3, 36, 161
Baechler, Donald, 32
Bailey, William, 216
Baker, Richard, 34
Bard College, 182
Barnes Foundation, 186
Barnet, Will, 9, 36, 188
Bartlett, Jennifer, 74
Baskin, Leonard, 100
Beal, Jack, cover, 38, 108
Bearden, Romare, 20, 154
Beckmann, Max, 145
Beerman, Miriam, 40
Behnke, Leigh, back cover, 42
Bell, Leland, 72
Bennington College, 120, 145
Berg, Siri, 44
Betty Cuningham Gallery, 3, 164
Birmelin, Robert, 46, endsheets
Black Mountain College, 182
Blaine, Nell, 72
Blue Mountain Gallery, 3, 64, 148, 214
Bob Blackburn Printmaking Studio, 20, 76, 188
Bolmeier, Jane, 48
Boston Museum School, 54
Bowery Gallery, 3, 72, 150, 181
Brandeis University, 170, 176, 182
Brata Gallery, 62
Brooklyn Academy of Music, 76
Brooklyn Arts and Cultural Association (BACA), 116
Brooklyn Arts Council (BAC), 166
Brooklyn College (CUNY), 70, 88, 111, 138, 164, 181, 184
Brooklyn Museum, 24, 40, 54, 59, 70, 76, 82, 84, 116, 125, 127, 145, 148, 154, 157, 181, 182, 184, 186, 190, 192, 193, 195, 196, 206, 208, 216
Brooklyn Museum Art School, 70, 84, 125, 145, 148, 154, 181, 184, 192, 195, 216
Brooklyn Waterfront Artists Coalition (BWAC), 166
Burton, Richmond, 50
Butler's Fine Art, 145
Cadmus, Paul, 206
Cajori, Charles, 13, 52
Canaday, John, 154
Cantarella, Virginia Hoyt, 54
CAPS Grant, 129, 138
Carone, Nicolas, back cover, 56, 169
Ceres Gallery, 208
Chaet, Bernard, 58, 64
Cheim & Read Gallery, 3, 32, 50, 196
Cibula, Ellen, 60, 190
City College of New York (CUNY), 84, 178
Clark, Ed, 7, 12, 62
Clark, Marcia, 3, 64
Close, Chuck, cover, 8, 66, 216
Cole, Thomas, 64
Collado, Lisa, 68, 188
College Art Association, 132, 159, 200
Columbia University, 52, 111, 118, 125, 148, 154, 170, 192, 214
Cooperstown Annual Exhibition, 54
Coppedge, Arthur, back cover, 14, 70
Corcoran Gallery of Art, 70, 111, 162, 182, 196, 200
Crawford, Ralston, 192
Crosby Painting Studio, 148
Cuttler, Judy, title page, 13, 72, 150
D C Moore Gallery, 3, 100, 127, 140, 206
Danforth Foundation, 170
David Findlay Jr Fine Art, 3, 28, 52, 56, 59, 152, 172, 176, 190
Davis, Lisa Corinne, 74
Davis, Stuart, 36, 132, 192
Deceus, Francks Francois, 76
deNiro, Robert, 72
Denise Bibro Gallery, 3, 211
Deon, Dorothy, 78
Diane Boisvert Gallery, 166
Dickinson, Edwin, 24
Dinnerstein, Harvey, 80, 82, 216
Dinnerstein, Rachel, cover, 82
Dinnerstein, Simon, back cover, 84
Dintenfass, Marylyn, 86
Dodd, Lois, 88, 136
Durham, Minerva, 148, 214
Eakins, Thomas, 80
East Hampton Gallery, 4
Elaine Benson Gallery, 184
Ellen Sragow Gallery, 169
Empire State Building, 7
Empire State College (SUNY), 68
Erlebacher, Martha Mayer, 90
Estes, Richard, 92
Ethical Culture Society, 82
Ettinger Gallery, 3
Fabozzi, Paul F., 94
Fairleigh Dickinson University, 142, 181
Fashion Institute of Technology (SUNY), 78, 142, 150
Feeney, Paul, 107
Ferrando, David, 97
Ferren, John, 86
Fischbach Gallery, 3, 42
Fischl, Eric, 98
Fish, Janet, 100
Fishko, Robert, 3, 90
Fishman, Louise, 102
Flack, Audrey, 8, 104
Flomenhaft Gallery, 3, 20
Ford Foundation, 204
Fordham University, 166
Forge, Andrew, 4, 52
Forum Gallery, 3, 30, 90
Franklin Riehlman Fine Art, 86
Frankenthaler, Helen, 4, 107
Freckelton, Sondra, 10, 108
Freilicher, Jane, 110
Frey-Norris Gallery, 80
Frick Collection, 118
Fulbright Fellowship, 56, 66, 84, 152, 159, 164, 212
Fuller Building, 9, 46, 59, 88
Gallery Henoch, 3, 216
Gechtoff, Sonia, 113
George Adams Gallery, 38
Ginsberg, Max, 216
Goodnough, Bob, 114
Goossen, E. C., 162
Gorky, Arshile, 186
Gowanus Artists, 214
G. R. N'Namdi Gallery, 62, 169, 198
Grace Borgenicht Gallery, 132
Grebenak, Louis 70, 84
Greenberg, Clement, 114
Greenberg Van Doren Gallery, 3, 107, 182
Gross, Cheryl, 116
Grosz, George, 176
Gruenebaum Gallery, 113
Gussow, Sue Ferguson, cover, 118
Hale, Robert Beverly, 172
Hambleton, Mary, 120
Hans Hofmann (and School of Fine Arts), 12, 48, 56, 107, 110, 111, 114, 132, 154, 174, 176
Hansen, Glen, 16, 122
Harvard University, 206
High Museum, 70, 186, 196
Hirschl-Adler Gallery, 186
Hofstra University, 142
Holly Solomon Gallery, 128

Howard University, 102
Hunter College (CUNY), 4, 74, 116, 129, 130, 145, 152, 154, 162, 200, 204
Hyneman, Esther, 125
Islip Museum, 166
Jacques Seligmann & Company Gallery, 174
Jacquette, Yvonne, cover, 127
Jaudon, Valerie, 15, 128
Jewish Museum, 40, 102, 140, 146
Jim Kempner Fine Art, 107
John Simon Guggenheim Memorial Fellowship, 52, 114, 132, 145, 146, 178, 182, 196, 200
June Kelly Gallery, 3, 74, 198
Kahn, Cecily, 130, 152
Kahn, Wolf, back cover, 130, 132, 152
Karp, Ivan, 92
Katz, Alex, 64, 100, 134, 135
Kenkeleba Gallery, 3, 76
Kline, Franz, 136, 182
Knoedler & Company, 3
Kokoschka, Oskar, 161
Kollwitz, Käthe, 80, 156
Kozloff, Joyce, 195
Kramer, Hilton, 4, 34, 145, 208
Kraushaar Gallery, 113
Kroll, Leon, 56
Kulicke, Barbara, 136
Kuniyoshi, Yasuo, 40, 80
Kushner, Robert, 4, 202
Lehman College (CUNY), 192
Leo Castelli Gallery, 92
Lerner-Levine, Marion, 138
Lesbian Herstory Archives, 125
Levine, David, 70, 84
Levine, Jack, 140
Levy, Julian, 80
Liu, Dik, cover, 10, 142
Lohin-Geduld Gallery, 3, 52, 56, 130
Long Island University (LIU), 54, 70, 76, 125, 142, 148, 150, 181, 184, 190
Longo, Vincent, back cover, 145
Louis K. Meisel Gallery, 104
M. D. Modern Gallery, 172
MacDowell Colony for the Arts Fellowship, 86, 125
Mangold, Robert, 146
Manzo, Helene K., 148
Marlborough Gallery, 3, 92
Marsh, Reginald, 176, 206
Martha Jackson Gallery, 186
Martino, Anthony, 72, 150
Mary Boone Gallery, 3, 98
Maryland Institute College of Art, 32, 34, 74, 150
Marymount College, 148
Mason, Alice Trumbull, 130, 152
Mason, Emily, back cover, 130, 152
Mason Gross School of the Arts at Rutgers University, 20
Max Protech Gallery, 196
Mayhew, Richard, cover, 4, 9, 20, 84, 154, 198
McGee Gallery, 3
McKenzie, Mary Beth, cover, 156
Medgar Evers College (CUNY), 76
Meredith Ward Fine Art, 3, 186
Metropolitan Museum of Art, 30, 59, 80, 86, 97, 100, 104, 122, 127, 140, 145, 157, 169, 174, 182, 198, 200, 206
Miller, Lee Anne, 159
Millet, Kate, 170
Mississippi Institute of Arts and Letters, 129
Moore College of Art, 127
Murray, Elizabeth, 74
Museum of Modern Art, 20, 28, 66, 92, 98, 107, 111, 113, 118, 127, 140, 145, 162, 182, 186, 196, 200, 206
Museum of the City of New York, 116, 157, 184
National Academy (NA), 10, 24, 28, 36, 38, 46, 52, 56, 58, 70, 80, 82, 88, 92, 98, 100, 102, 107, 109, 111, 113, 114, 127, 132, 134, 140, 142, 145, 150, 152, 154, 157, 161, 164, 174, 182, 186, 206, 211
National Arts Club (NAC), 36, 188
National Association of Women Artists (NAWA), 68, 125, 166, 181, 188
National Civil Rights Museum, 76
National Endowment for the Arts, 24, 26, 86, 90, 138, 169, 178, 190, 196, 200
National Museum of Women in the Arts, 102, 104, 129, 157
National Society of Painters in Casein and Acrylic, 150
New Britain Museum of American Art, 4
New School for Social Research, 36, 40, 84, 132, 176
New York Academy of Art, 90, 98, 125, 150, 170
New York Artists Equity, 48
New York Foundation for the Arts, 86, 138
New York Historical Society, 184, 206
New York Studio School, 56, 72, 82, 135, 150
New York University, 20, 42, 44, 68, 104, 107, 113, 114, 118, 129, 148, 164
Nice, Don, 160, 161
Ninth Street Show, 56, 176
Noho Gallery, 3, 170
Ohlson, Doug, 162
Ozenfant, Amedée, 176
Pace University, 208
PaceWildenstein, 3, 66, 135, 146
Pamela Auchincloss Gallery, 120
Panofsky, Irwin, 164
Parsons School of Design, 18, 44, 60, 74, 84, 86, 102, 118, 120, 127, 142, 150, 166, 169, 174, 181, 190
Pascal, Blaise, 182
Peale, James Wilson, 154
Pearlstein, Philip, 9, 100, 164, 208
Peck, Augustus, 72
Pels School of Art, 216
Pennsylvania Academy of Fine Arts, 4
Peter Findlay Gallery, 46
Phillips, Tracy, 166
Phoenix Gallery, 3, 78
Pindell, Howardena, 168
Plimack, Sylvia, 146
Poindexter Gallery, 113
Pollock, Jackson, 56, 114
Pollock-Krasner Foundation, 68, 113
Pratt Graphics Art Center, 159, 184,
Pratt Institute, 30, 74, 90, 102, 104, 116, 148, 164, 166, 172, 196, 204
Prince Street Gallery, 3, 136, 138
Queens College (CUNY), 26, 46, 86, 113, 150, 181, 195
Rauschenbusch, Stephanie, 170
Redmond, Catherine, 172
Resika, Paul, 174
Rhode Island School of Design (RISD), 40, 120, 127, 130
Richenburg, Robert, 4, 176
Ringgold, Faith, cover, 178
Robert Miller Gallery, 3, 135
Robert Schoelkopf Gallery, 109
Roberts, Marie, 181
Rockburne, Dorothea, 11, 182
Rome Prize, 84
Rose Art Museum (Brandeis University), 170, 176, 182
Rose, Barbara, 86
Rothko, Mark, 86, 186, 192
Rotunda Gallery, 181
Russell, John, 170
Sakuyama, Shunji, 184
Salander-O'Reilly Gallery, 3, 174
Salmagundi Club, 188, 216
Sandler, Irving, 4, 52, 134, 176
Schapiro, Miriam, 68, 192
Scharf, William, 186
Schiavina, Laura, 188
Schomburg Center for Cultural Research, 76
School of Visual Arts, 18, 30, 42, 80, 116, 122, 129, 146, 161, 181, 186, 216
Sellenraad, Johan, 60, 190
Semmel, Joan, 195
Shahn, Ben, 145
Shaw, Kendall 192
Sidney Janis Gallery, 128
Sills, Susan, 11, 195
Silvermine Annual Exhibition, 54
Skowhegan School of Painting and Sculpture, 134
Slutzky, Robert, 104
Smith, Tony, 114
Smithsonian Institution
National Museum of American Art, 186, 206
Hirshhorn Museum, 206
Society of Memorial Sloan Kettering Cancer Center, 174
Solomon R. Guggenheim Museum, 92, 145, 146, 182
Soyer, Isaac, 70
Soyer, Moses, 80
Spanierman Gallery, 157
Spiral, 20, 154
Spring Studio, 214
St. John's University, 94, 148
Stable Gallery, 59, 176
State University of New York (SUNY)
New Paltz Campus, 64
Stony Brook Campus, 168
Steir, Pat, 196
Stone, Allan, 92
Suffolk County Community College (SUNY), 148, 184
Sung, Posoon Park, 198
Susan Caldwell Gallery, 162
Swain, Robert, 200
Takenaga, Barbara, 202
Tam, Reuben, 70
Tamayo, Rufino, 107
Tanager Gallery, 52, 88
The Cooper Union, 56, 72, 88, 102, 104, 109, 118, 134, 135, 142, 145, 152, 159, 190, 213
The Painting Center, 130, 170
The Responsive Eye, 28
Tibor de Nagy Gallery, 3, 34, 110
Tomlinson, Bob, 204
Tooker, George, back cover, 17, 206
Traphagen School of Fashion, 188
Trumbull, Ann Train, 152
Tsao, Vivian, spine, 208
Tucker, Marcia, 190
Tworkov, Jack, 74, 182
UFA Gallery, 76
University of Rochester, Memorial Art Gallery, 4
Ushenko, Audrey, 211
VAGA (Visual Artists & Galleries Association), 20, 28, 36, 44, 88, 100, 102, 128, 132, 134, 141, 152, 192
Vanni, Gian Berto, 212
Venice Biennale, 98, 114, 146
Viridian Gallery, 3, 195
Von Lintel Gallery, 3, 128
Vytlacil, Vaclav, 172
Waller, Richard, 162
Welliver, Neil, 64, 100
Westbeth (and Gallery), 48, 72, 113, 150
Whitney Museum of American Art, 3, 24, 40, 80, 92, 98, 100, 107, 114, 135, 140, 146, 182, 190, 196, 200, 206
Williamsburg Art and Historical Center, 166, 181, 214
Women's Caucus for Art, 125, 159, 170
Women's Studio Center, 3
Woodrow Wilson Fellowship, 170
Woodruff, Hale, 20, 114
Wooster Arts Space, 145
Works Progress Administration (WPA), 36, 140, 154, 190
Yaddo Foundation, 90, 138
Yale University School of Art and Design, 64, 74, 129, 142, 145, 146, 186
Yang, Ella, cover, 14, 214
York College (CUNY), 22
Zeuxis Association of Still Life Painters, 150
Zudeck, Darryl, 216

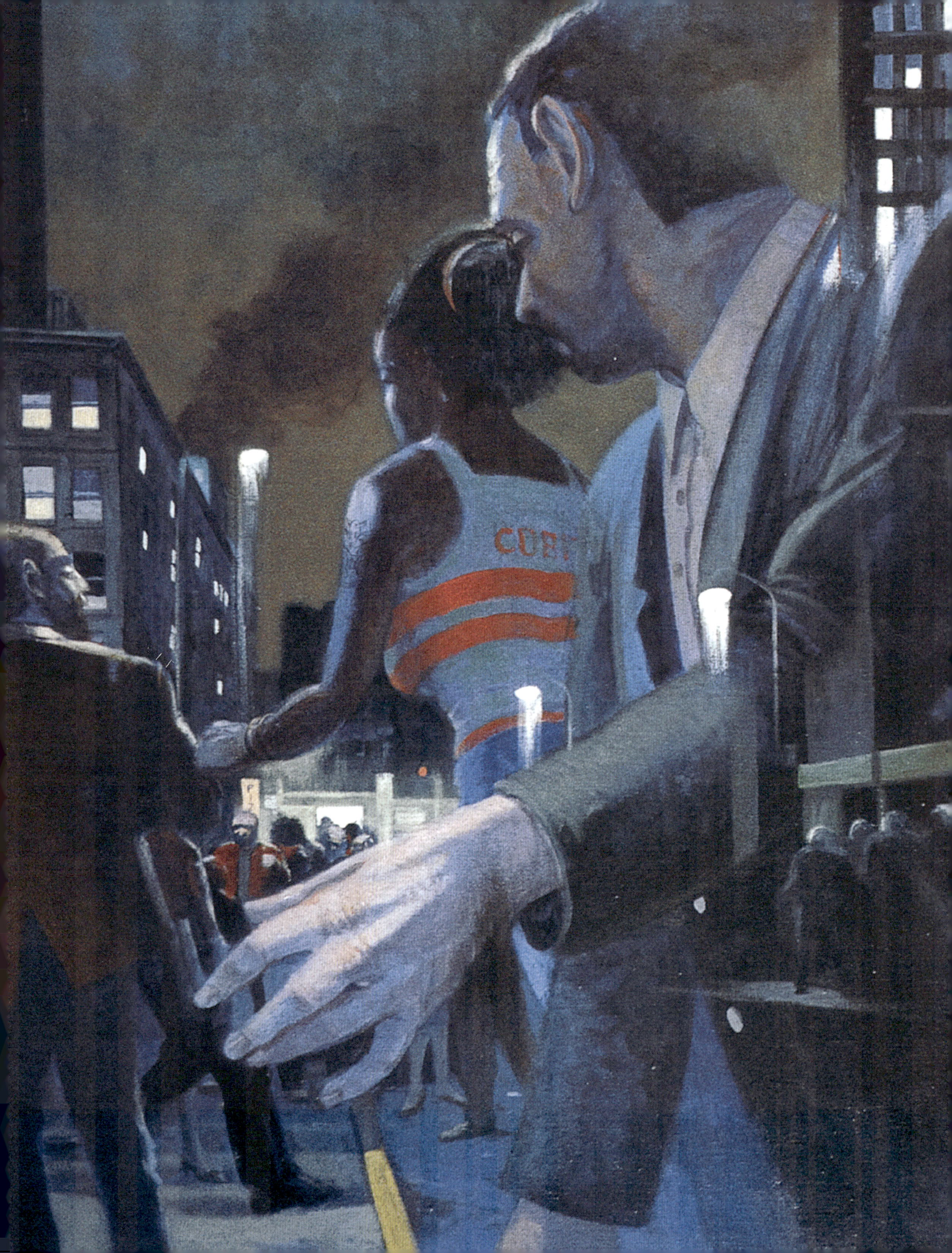
CUB